PRINCE
ALL THE SONGS

PRINCE
ALL THE SONGS
THE STORY BEHIND EVERY TRACK

BENOÎT CLERC

MITCHELL
BEAZLEY

CONTENTS

THE GOLD EXPERIENCE

CHAOS AND DISORDER

EMANCIPATION

CRYSTAL BALL

THE TRUTH

THE NEW POWER GENERATION
NEWPOWER SOUL

PRINCE
THE VAULT... OLD FRIENDS 4 SALE

RAVE UN2 THE JOY FANTASTIC

PRINCE
THE RAINBOW CHILDREN

PRINCE
MUSICOLOGY

PRINCE
3121

PRINCE
PLANET EARTH

PRINCE
LOTUSFLOW3R / MPLSOUND

PRINCE
20TEN

PRINCE & 3RDEYEGIRL
PLECTRUMELECTRUM

PRINCE
ART OFFICIAL AGE

PRINCE
HITNRUN PHASE ONE

PRINCE
HITNRUN PHASE TWO

PRINCE
WELCOME 2 AMERICA

His Royal Badness, the Kid from Minneapolis, or The Artist… his nicknames don't really matter—it is Prince who has made fans' hearts race for more than 40 years.

FOREWORD

It's a blessing to be a Prince fan.

Singing along to *Kiss* as a child, being a teenager falling in love for the first time to *Diamonds and Pearls*, learning your first guitar chords to *Endorphinmachine*, dancing the summer away to *Push It Up*, growing into adulthood with *Musicology*, and, finally, crying your eyes out listening to *Baltimore*… to be accompanied by Prince's songs throughout your life is a blessing. When the possibility of *Prince All the Songs* was first raised, we had to find a sensible way to pay tribute to this incomparable artist, without neglecting any of his abundant output. Besides his 39 official albums, Prince's discography extends like tentacles in all directions. Prince spent his adult life relentlessly recording, committing countless tracks to tape day and night, most completed within a few hours and stored in The Vault in Paisley Park, the place where he lived and worked in the suburbs of Minneapolis. Faced with what is rumored to be an infinite production, a compromise had to be found. In the end, the choice was made quickly: the selection would include all the songs officially released by Prince and subsequently by The Prince Estate, which has managed his musical legacy since his death in 2016.

Prince: All the Songs is a chronological portrait of a man whose whole life was devoted to his work. The secrets of Prince's most popular and his least known songs are hidden in his private life, in his successes and failures, in his personal tragedies, and in the happiest moments of his life. Through anecdotes and hitherto unpublished technical details, this book sheds new light on the 684 tracks that make up Prince's official discography and takes us on a journey into the life of this much-loved artist who will remain forever immortal.

Notice:

This book only covers songs performed by Prince.

Unless otherwise stated, remixes are not considered songs in their own right and are therefore not included here.

Credits for songwriters and composers follow the official information on the albums, although, in most cases, Prince has sole ownership of the rights.

Unless otherwise stated, the recording dates in the technical notes do not include the editing and mixing dates of the songs.

A young Prince Rogers Nelson, photographed by Robert Whitman in 1977.

THE KID FROM MINNEAPOLIS PLAYS HIS FIRST NOTES

In the late 1950s, the streets of Minneapolis resembled a picture postcard, in common with much of America in the boom years of the post-war period. The architecture in this city in northeast Minnesota was varied, with Tudor-style residences still standing alongside modern high-rise buildings for a time, until the 1961 urban renewal plan wiped out nearly half of the city's historic buildings. Neon signs lit up the stores, but behind this scenery typical of the American dream lurked a more complex reality.

Minneapolis at that time suffered from major inequalities between the black and white communities, and certain minorities were frequently targeted by the police.

There were few jazz clubs where African-American musicians could perform, and you had to go to the Uptown community centers if you wanted to dance to the swing of John Lewis Nelson's Prince Rogers Trio, for example. Nelson was a talented pianist who married Vivian Howard in 1938, and the couple had four children: Sharon, Lorna, Norrine, and John R. But in 1956, John Nelson suddenly upped and left the marital home, preferring to spend his time playing music, which he alternated with a job as a plastics molder at Honeywell, a heating control systems company. It was at a concert given by his band at the Phyllis Wheatley House, a social center for African-American families in north Minneapolis, that John met Mattie Della Shaw, herself recently divorced from her first husband, Alfred Jackson Sr. The beautiful Della Shaw, who would occasionally sing in the band, also had a child, Alfred Jackson Jr. What started out as a friendly and professional relationship between the two artists soon morphed into a romance and, on 31August 1957, the pianist and the singer were married.

Skipper enters the scene

On 7 June 1958, the couple's first child was born. He was called Prince Rogers Nelson after his father's stage name: Prince Rogers. The couple soon nicknamed the boy Skipper to differentiate him from his father. Prince grew up in the family home on 915 Logan Avenue in Minneapolis with his sister Tyka, born in 1960, and his sunny, cheerful mother who was devoted to her children. John, on the contrary, was more standoffish, a man of few words and more absent father than role model to his son. When John abandoned his wife and their two children in 1965, Prince took refuge in music, composing his first song on the piano his father had left behind in the living room. The song was called *Funk Machine*. When his father was still around, Prince had been forbidden to touch the piano, so he used to wait for him to go out every day before sitting down to teach himself the theme tunes from his favorite television series: *The Man From U.N.C.L.E* and *Batman*. With his father gone, Prince, who loved sports and music, became the man of the house and took care of his sister, to whom he remained very close for the rest of his life. When Mattie married her third husband Hayward Baker a few years later, relations within the household became strained. "I disliked him immediately [...]," Prince would admit several years later. "He would bring us a lot of presents all the time, rather than sit down and talk with us and give us companionship. I got real bitter because of that, and I would say all the things that I disliked about him, rather than tell him what I really needed. Which was a mistake, and it kind of hurt our relationship."[1]

A view over Minneapolis in the 1950s. In the center of the picture is the Andrus Building, which was renamed Renaissance Square in 1983 after renovation work by the firm of architects Miller, Hanson, Westerbeck & Bell.

From basketball to guitar

When he was 12 years old, Prince decided to move in with his father, with whom he shared a love of music which began at a Prince Rogers Trio concert he attended as a small boy. "It was great, I couldn't believe it, people were screaming. From then on, I think I wanted to be a musician."[2] After a brief spell at Lincoln Junior High School, which was situated near their house, Prince settled into Bryant Junior High School. There he met André Anderson, and the two soon became inseparable. They didn't know it at the time, but they had something in common: Fred Anderson, André's father, had once been a bass player in the Prince Rogers Trio. "It was the first day [...]," said the man, later known as André Cymone, "and I saw this one kid who looked odd. And I remember thinking: 'He reminds me of me. I was always the outcast and the weirdo [...]'"[3] Back then, Prince was also close to his cousin Charles Smith—with whom he shared a love of music—as well as his half-brother Duane. Duane was Vivian's child from an extramarital affair she had just before her husband left home, and John had taken him in after his mother's death. He and Prince became inseparable during their school years, through their shared passion for basketball. While Duane Nelson quickly made his mark with his sporting prowess, when the three friends were together, they were more interested in music and formed their first band when they were just 13 years old. The band was called Phoenix. Prince played guitar, André was on bass, and Charles on drums. At the time, the teenagers were discovering Sly and the Family Stone, Stevie Wonder, and the catchy pop/funk of The Jackson 5, with whom they could easily identify because the lead singer, Michael, was the same age as Prince and André. The Jackson 5's 1969 hit, *I Want You Back*, was on every turntable and soon became part of the trio's list of covers.

It was when Prince went to Central High School to finish his education that things began to get serious for him. He dropped basketball for music, choosing to spend his time working relentlessly on various instruments. Life with his father became increasingly stormy, and John ended up kicking his son out of the house after catching him in flagrante with a girl. Prince lived for a while with his Aunt Olivia on the south side of town but, once again, his desire for freedom was too great. So, he found a place of refuge at his friend André's house at 1244 Russell Avenue North. André's mother, Bernadette Anderson, was well-liked by everyone. She was known as "Queen Bernie," a nickname

The guitarist Carlos Santana and his bass player David Brown performing onstage at the Woodstock music festival on 16 August 1969.

that reflected her love for her six children and the affection she showed to those around her. When Prince came knocking on her door, he was welcomed with open arms. In return, he was told he had to finish his studies and pass his exams.

André Anderson's basement

Prince shared André's room for a while before deciding to retreat to the solitude of the basement. Bernadette was patient with him and put up with the endless music sessions that often disturbed her sleep: "Sometimes it'd drive me crazy. I'd be in bed, and everyone's supposed to be sleeping, and all of a sudden I'd hear this guitar in the basement, and Prince was playing Minnie Ripperton, and singing it [...] Then above my head was André doing the same thing."[4] The boys rehearsed in the house's cramped basement, and the band, which now included André's sister Linda on Farfisa organ and a neighbor, Terry Jackson, on percussion, began working on a quality set list: Bobby Womack's *Woman's Gotta Have It* and *Across 110th Street*, and Santana's *Black Magic Woman*. The band, renamed Grand Central, also covered Graham Central Station's *The Jam*, which Prince would use onstage in the mid-1990s to introduce his musicians. The band's only original composition was a song called *Do You Feel Like Dancing?*. The musicians worked flat out and competed fiercely against the other bands on the local scene in Minneapolis: Flyte Tyme (featuring at various times Cynthia Johnson on vocals, James "Jimmy Jam" Harris and Monte Moir on keyboards, Jellybean Johnson on drums, and Terry Lewis on bass); Mind & Matter; and the most important of all, The Family, led by the virtuoso bass player Sonny Thompson, who would go on to join The New Power Generation in 1991.

FOR PRINCE ADDICTS

As penniless teenagers, Prince and André Cymone loved to wander the aisles of Knut Koupee, one of Minneapolis' music stores, but were regularly kicked out by the owner as they couldn't afford to buy anything. After signing his first contract, Prince returned to the store and bought his Hohner Madcat guitar, which he would play until his death in 2016.

The members of Grand Central, all set to conquer Minneapolis. From left: Linda Anderson, André "Cymone" Anderson, Morris Day, Terry Jackson, Prince, and William Doughty.

The boys in Grand Central were highly motivated and, encouraged by the friendly rivalry between the city's bands, they took up residence at Terry Jackson's house, which gave them a more comfortable rehearsal space. Finally, a second percussionist, William Doughty, joined the band. "We devoted everything to it," Doughty recalled later. "That's all we did. Half the time we didn't even stay in school. Half the day in school, half the day in the basement."[5] Despite their combative spirit, the musicians alas fell victim to the segregation that was still widespread in the city, where the doors of most clubs remained closed to them. Nevertheless, they were welcomed by some, including The Riverview, The Cozy Bar, and The Peacock Alley.

Meeting Morris Day

In 1974, Charles Smith's involvement with the local football team meant he could no longer perform his duties as Grand Central's drummer. A few missed rehearsals were enough for the others to decide to part company with him. Meanwhile, one of the band's fervent admirers had been itching to take up the drumsticks for the group: his name was Morris Day. Morris was a close friend of André Anderson's, and one day he invited Anderson to his house where he gave an unofficial audition. He executed a whole range of rhythmic patterns borrowed from Tower of Power, performing the feverish *What Is Hip?* and *Soul Vaccination* to perfection, thus convincing André of his talent. A week later, Day was invited to come to a Grand Central rehearsal with his own drums, and he impressed the team with his knowledge of the various tunes sung by Prince, by now the leader of the band. Sly and the Family Stone's *Dance To The Music*, Santana's *Evil Ways*, Funkadelic's *Free Your Mind and Your Ass Will Follow*, and James Brown's *Get On The Good Foot* all succumbed to Morris Day's powerful yet subtle playing, and within days his flamboyant performance led to him replacing Charles Smith in the band. This was the beginning of a friendship between Prince and the future singer of The Time (see page 64) that would endure for over 40 years.

The first professional contacts

Shortly after Morris Day joined the band, his mother Lavonne Daugherty offered to manage Grand Central. Lavonne was incredibly energetic and very enthusiastic about the idea of getting involved in her son's musical endeavors and she renamed the band Grand Central Corporation. "Mom was [...] always upbeat and encouraging, assuring us that it was only a matter of time before we'd get our big-time break,"[6] Morris Day would say in 2019. She contacted Linster "Pepé" Willie, the new husband of Prince's cousin Shauntel Manderville. Willie was the nephew of Clarence Collins, the baritone singer with Little Anthony and The Imperials, a doo-wop group who had had a hit with the 1958 song *Tears On My Pillow*. After having worked for a time as his uncle's assistant, Willie had built up quite a few connections in the record industry and responded to Lavonne's call. He met the band and followed them for several months, offering advice and tips to help them progress. In particular, he urged Grand Central Corporation to move on from cover versions and concentrate on writing original songs: "I showed them how to construct a song. I talked about intros and outros, verses, the hook, the chorus, the bridge, and everything in between. I was impressed with how well they took direction. It didn't take but another rehearsal or two to see them get the hang of it [...]"[7]

Delighted by what he had seen, a few months later, Pepé asked Dale Menten from the Cookhouse Studio in

Tito, Jackie, Michael, Marlon, and Jermaine (aka The Jackson 5) in 1971 when the young Prince still identified with the leading performer in *I Want You Back*.

Although the members of Grand Central were impressed by The Jackson 5's hits, they quickly distanced themselves from this influence. "We were amazed that when we went to see them, that their equipment wasn't plugged up, and that Jermaine really couldn't play the bass and sing,"[4] says Charles Smith.

Minneapolis to have the musicians in for a work session. This enabled the boys to familiarize themselves with a professional work environment, but it was also an opportunity for Prince to prove his talents to Pepé Willie, who happily called on him a year later to join some sessions with his band, 94 East.

From Grand Central to Champagne

In early 1976, Grand Central Corporation went to the ASI Studios in Minneapolis to record their first demo. Lavonne paid for the sessions out of her own pocket, and six tracks were immortalized on vinyl: *39th St Party*, *Lady Pleasure*, *Machine*, *You're Such A Fox*, *Grand Central*, and *Whenever*. Only Prince, Morris, and André played on these tracks, with David Rivkin operating the console. Rivkin and Prince would soon cross paths again. In February of that year, Prince gave his first ever interview to the *Central High Pioneer*, a student newspaper, in which he confided his inability to read music: "I've had about two lessons, but they didn't help much. I think you'll always be able to do what your ear tells you, so just think how great you'd be with lessons also."[8] To signal the definitive departure of Charles Smith, who had come up with the name Grand Central, the band renamed itself Champagne (sometimes spelled Shampayne) and carried on doing the rounds of the studios. For their next recording sessions, the band headed to Moon Sound Studios. The owner, Chris Moon, a lover of funk and rhythm and blues (R&B) music, was on the lookout for the next soul stars in a Minneapolis where he felt rock 'n' roll bands were taking up too much space. During these sessions, Moon, who wrote lyrics and composed in his spare time, fell under Prince's spell, and he proposed a collaboration that would benefit both parties: "I pulled Prince aside, told him I'd like to chat with him for a few seconds, 'I've got an idea for you. I'm looking to put together some music that I have written. I'm also looking to find an artist, package an artist up, to provide him with studio time for free, to get a package together, collaborate on some material, and get the music out there. It's a very simple thing, I don't want any contracts, no paperwork, just a handshake, and the beautiful part is the only person that has anything to lose is me.'"[9] Prince accepted the deal. He was 17 years old when he left Champagne and locked himself away in Chris Moon's basement for months. It was there that the first compositions of a genius in the making took shape.

The Prince Rogers Trio, with Prince's father at the piano.

A close collaboration with Chris Moon

In the months that followed his meeting with Chris Moon, Prince worked continuously to master his instruments and the recording equipment. He wrote, composed, and developed his musical technique every evening after school, playing guitar, bass, drums, and keyboards. David Rivkin's brother, a session drummer called Bobby "Z." Rivkin, offered his services, but the young prodigy preferred to wield the drumsticks himself. The two men remained friends, however, and Bobby Z. became a prominent member of The Revolution a few years later.

After a few months of Prince exclusively occupying his studios, Moon decided it was time to make his collaboration with him pay off. He sought professional partners for him, cowrote the song *Soft and Wet* with him, and suggested he shorten his stage name to Prince. For his part, Prince felt it was time to start recording some proper demos. Fourteen songs were produced, including *Love Is Forever, Aces, Baby, I'm Yours, Diamond Eyes, Don't Forget*, and *Don't Hold Back*. In the autumn of 1976, Prince decided to try his luck in New York and moved in with his half-sister Sharon Nelson, bringing with him copies of a four-track demo featuring *Baby, Soft and Wet, Love Is Forever*, and *Aces*. Prince quickly attracted the attention of a French producer called Danielle Mauroy, who despite all the goodwill she showed toward him, did not seem to grasp the full extent of the young man's ambitions: "She was only looking at me as a singer. The kind that opts for the silk capes, high-heeled shoes, and white Cadillacs [...] I tried to explain that even though I didn't have the key to the recording industry, that I knew myself and that I knew for sure what I would and wouldn't do for that Key. I told her I never considered myself a singer. I saw myself as an instrumentalist who started singing out of necessity [...] My voice is just like one of the instruments I play. It's just one thing I do."[10] The collaboration was short-lived and the artist's journey to try his luck in the city seemed to have led nowhere.

Owen Husney, the young Prince's mentor

While Prince's trip to New York had ended in failure, Chris Moon had moved on to more promising territory. He had arranged to meet Owen Husney, the founder of The Ad Agency in Minneapolis, which specialized in promoting music artists. The 28-year-old Husney also ran a small artists' support agency and promoted concerts at the Art Deco Marigold Ballroom on Nicollet Avenue. Husney was used to being approached by a variety of people, and within days of Moon's request, agreed to see him: "Chris pressed play and messed with the volume while I shuffled through the papers on my desk [...] As Chris' cassette rolled on, I was compelled to hear more. It was that feeling when you bite into something so great you immediately take two more bites before swallowing the first one."[11] When Moon told him that Prince was the only musician playing on the demo, Husney couldn't believe his ears. They immediately called Prince in New York, who answered in a soft, discreet voice. The young

The Nelson clan, including Lorna, Prince's half-sister (front left), and their father, John (center), in the early 1970s.

singer was planning to leave the Big Apple and return to Minneapolis the following week, and so a meeting was arranged at Owen Husney's house, since Prince preferred the privacy of someone's home to an office full of employees.

Launching the Prince satellite into orbit

Once Prince and Owen were introduced to one another, the serious business could begin. In December 1976, Husney founded the American Artists, Inc. agency with his friend Gary Levinson and officially became Prince's manager. Lee Phillips, a well-known Los Angeles lawyer, was hired to represent the young artist. Husney provided accommodation for Prince in a small studio apartment at 2012 Aldrich Avenue South, in south Minneapolis, and gave him the keys to his Loring Park offices. Every night, Prince and his friends would take over the space: Prince on guitar and keyboards, Bobby Z. on drums, Bobby's cousin Robbie Paster would play bass some evenings, and the ever-present André Cymone would alternate between 4- and 6-string bass. Every day at sundown, the band moved the furniture out of the way and launched into their jam sessions, which sometimes carried on into the early hours of the morning. The desks would then be put back again before the agency's staff arrived for work. Some recordings that attest to the young musicians' virtuosity are well known to fans and are now circulating unofficially as the "Loring Park Sessions."

After a few weeks, Owen Husney organized an initial recording session for Prince at Sound 80 Studios, the same place where Bob Dylan had recorded some of the tracks from the album *Blood On The Tracks* in 1974: *Tangled Up In Blue*, *You're A Big Girl Now*, *Idiot Wind*, *Lily, Rosemary and The Jack of Hearts*, and *If You See Her, Say Hello*. David Rivkin, the brother of Bobby Z., was now the regular recording engineer at Sound 80, and was the obvious choice for the session. Early 1977 was spent producing these new demos, comprising the tracks *Baby*, *Soft and Wet*, and *Make It Through The Storm*. For his part, Owen Husney started putting together promotional tools to accompany his young protégé's demo in the making. Assisted by Jeff Farmakes, the art director at The Ad Agency, Husney produced 15 luxurious press kits featuring photos of Prince with the artist's name above the images. While some of the photos were taken by Larry Falk at the Moon Sound Studios, the most notable emerged from three shoots with Husney's photographer friend Robert Whitman at Husney's home, in front of the Schmitt Music store in Minneapolis, and at Whitman's studio in the city's Kemps Ice Cream Building. Using his Nikon 35mm camera, the photographer captured the first images of a future international star on Kodak Tri-X film.

Welcome to Warner Bros. Records

In spring 1977, Owen Husney sent out demos and press kits to several record companies, including Warner Bros. Records, CBS, A&M, RSO, and ABC/Dunhill, and flew to Los Angeles with his protégé to reach for the moon. On 19 May, RSO sent a rejection letter to Husney, who then

During this legendary photo shoot at the home of Owen Husney, the latter deliberately placed a portrait of his mother on the piano so that she would be preserved for posterity.

FOR PRINCE ADDICTS

After signing his contract with Warner Bros. in June 1977, Prince recorded a song called *I Hope We Work It Out*, a thank-you song with a frenzied disco beat in which he unashamedly declared how keen he was to work with his new allies: "We can work it out, making music naturally, me and W.B." It remains unreleased to this day.

decided to contact Russ Thyret of Warner Bros. Records, with whom he had worked on the publicity campaigns for Randy Newman's *Good Old Boys* and Little Feat's *Feats Don't Fail Me Now* in 1974. Husney was equally uncompromising in his plans for his young artist, whether his discussions were with Thyret or the CBS executives, with whom he established a solid contact from the outset. Prince had to be signed for three albums, and he would record alone without a backing band. To convince CBS that this was even feasible, Husney booked The Village Studios, in Los Angeles, and invited the label's executives to attend a recording session for *Just As Long As We're Together*. Prince duly delivered, switching from one instrument to another without discrediting himself. This unprecedented performance convinced the men in suits, but they nevertheless stipulated that the first album be produced by Verdine White, the bassist from Earth, Wind & Fire. Prince categorically refused, leaving the field open for Warner Bros. Records, who offered the artist a contract he could not refuse. Three albums to be recorded in the space of 27 months, the first within six months. Prince was to be coproducer of the first album, but he would be assisted by a producer appointed by the label, and $60,000 was allocated for the recording of each of the three albums. On 24 June 1977, the record company issued a cheque for $80,000 as a downpayment, payable to "Prince Rogers Nelson and American Artists," and on 25 June, Prince signed his first artist's contract with Warner Bros. It was the beginning of a long love/hate relationship between the artist and his record company.

PRINCE

FOR YOU

For You · In Love · Soft and Wet · Crazy You · Just As Long As We're Together
Baby · My Love Is Forever · So Blue · I'm Yours

Released in the USA by Warner Bros. Records:
7 April 1978 (LP ref.: BSK 3150)
Released in the UK and Europe by Warner Bros. Records:
1984 (LP ref.: WB K 56 989)
Best chart ranking in the USA: 138
Best chart ranking in the UK: did not make the charts

Posing for Darlene Pfister Prois of the *Minneapolis Tribune* on 18 April 1978.

A SENSUAL, ELEGANT DEBUT ALBUM

Once the collaboration between Prince and Warner Bros. Records had been made official, a new studio session was arranged, with the aim of demonstrating to the label's management that Prince was able to play all the instruments on his first album. As he had done before with CBS, the musician excelled during this demonstration. Nonetheless, Mo Ostin and Russ Thyret felt that despite his technical mastery the young artist was not experienced enough to produce a hit record. This time, the name of Maurice White, cofounder and producer of most of Earth, Wind & Fire's records, was put forward. Faced with a categorical refusal on the part of Prince—who preferred David Rivkin, sadly also too inexperienced in the label's view—Owen Husney considered working with the recording engineer Tommy Vicari, whose work on the original soundtrack of Brian de Palma's movie *Phantom of the Paradise* (1974) had been a success. Moreover, at the age of just 29, Vicari had worked with one of Prince's idols, Carlos Santana, on the album *Moonflower*, made by his group in 1977. This persuaded the artist, who now seemed more open to compromise. Vicari would be coproducer on the record—or rather, more accurately, executive producer, which meant he would bring into play his technical and artistic expertise, so taking charge of the recording.

Under the Sausalito sun

The first recording sessions took place in the autumn of 1977 at the Sound 80 Studios in Minneapolis. Following problems with the new and recently installed console, Vicari decided it was impossible for him to work there. He suggested to Husney that they transfer production of the album to Los Angeles, a setting to which he was accustomed. Husney was against the idea because he was anxious to shield his protégé from all distractions, and instead opted for the Record Plant studios in Sausalito, California, to provide a more tranquil setting that would be more conducive to the work awaiting the young artist. Prince, Owen, and Britt, the manager's wife, moved into a house on Corte Madera Avenue, Mill Valley, and work sessions began on 1 October. Each night, the team were on the job. Although relations between Prince and Vicari seemed friendly at the outset, they quickly deteriorated, and the singer developed a profound hostility toward the technician. Apart from David Rivkin, who was brought in for the voice takes to provide technical support and offer some advice to Prince, no one found favor in the eyes of the young man, who was determined to be the only one in charge. André Cymone, who was privileged to attend a fair number of sessions, was also in his friend's good books. After three months of recording, a few overdubbing sessions were held at the Sound Labs studios, in Hollywood, whereupon the team declared the record complete. Some of the recorded songs were removed from the album's final tracklist, including *Make It Through The Storm*, *Bump This*, *Shine Your Light*, *E-Pluribus Funk*, *Waiting for You*, and *Life Is So Neat*.

A hit—up to a point

When it was released on 7 April 1978, *For You* stood out more for the quality of its arrangements than for the quality of the songwriting. Although the single *Soft and Wet* reached No.12 in the Billboard Hot Soul Singles chart, critics more often emphasized the multi-instrumentalist's performance on the

In 1977 Owen Husney organized a meeting between Prince and one of his idols, Carlos Santana. Having been invited to the latter's house, the singer and his manager were asked to remove their shoes. "I don't remove my shoes for anybody,"[11] Prince declared, leaving it to Husney—on all fours and in his stockinged feet—to clean up the muddy footprints from the white carpet in the hallway.

In order to shoot the famous portrait of Prince, naked with a Gibson Hummingbird guitar on his knees, the photographer Joe Giannetti photographed the singer from three different angles in Husney's house, then went to the Macy's store in San Francisco, where he took several shots of a queen-sized bed in front of an arched window. The superimposition of these four images produced the legendary photograph that appeared in the booklet accompanying the album *For You.*

album than his qualities as a songwriter. Husney arranged a series of meetings with fans in several US cities, including Chicago, San Francisco, Houston, Charlotte, and, of course, Minneapolis, which gave Prince a hero's welcome on his return from California. "It was weird. It was mostly kids from 11 to 20. They were relating to me being so young. There's been ads in the teen magazines and my age has really come up. The kids would ask me if my real name is Prince, what 'Soft and Wet' means, and did I really play all those instruments myself."[12] Although Prince was enthusiastic about the passion shown by his admirers, the artist seemed disappointed by the marketing of his first piece of work, as sales did not take off. In the summer of 1978, he moved into a house at 5215 France Avenue South, in Edina, on the outskirts of Minneapolis, and started work on new songs using a TEAC 4-track tape recorder. It was during this period that he embarked, for the first time, on writing songs for other people; for a while he worked with the singer Sue Ann Carwell, though he quickly ended this partnership due to lack of time.

Cavallo, Ruffalo, and Fargnoli: new masters come on board

From the release of his first album, Prince's aim was to perform his music onstage; for that, he needed to find some musicians. Despite his hesitation regarding this project, which he considered premature, Owen Husney supported his protégé and engaged the services of the famous William Morris Agency, which would help him set up a tour for the artist. For his first backing band, Prince wanted a heterogeneous group. He chose Bobby Z. as drummer and his faithful friend André Cymone on bass, and auditioned a guitarist from Twin Cities—Dez Dickerson, who had replied to an advertisement in the *Twin Cities Reader.* "Dez was a very strong rock, black guy and he didn't listen to black music at all," Bobby Z. said..."He was a Zeppelin freak."[13] Two keyboard players were also taken on: Matt Fink, a friend of Bobby Z., and Gayle Chapman, a friend of Charles Smith, who was Prince's cousin.

Rehearsals began and were held at a frantic pace in a hall in Del's Tire Mart building, until the band's equipment was stolen. They then relocated to the home of "Pepé" Willie, who was always there to support Prince. During this time, and despite the effort he was investing in his artist, Husney was well aware that relations with him were deteriorating. Prince, who was unhappy with his first album's lack of success, now rejected his mentor and deliberately kept his distance, to the point of provoking an irreparable break. "Prince didn't have enough experience to know that this is a really slow process," Owen Husney explained. "I think by that point he had been told so much that he was fantastic so much that he believed that he was really going to be successful on the first album. And when he wasn't, he was really disappointed."[14] Very soon, Prince parted company with his manager, who was quickly replaced by Bob Cavallo and Joe Ruffalo, two prominent managers who specialized in representing artists and already had groups such as Weather Report and Earth, Wind & Fire in their portfolio. A third person, Steve Fargnoli—hired by them to work more closely with Prince—later completed this high-powered trio.

A guitar duel between Prince and his guitarist Dez Dickerson onstage at the Capri Theater on 5 January 1979.

The Capri Theater fiasco

Prince's first official performance took place on 5 January 1979 at the Capri Theater in Minneapolis. To support the venue's owner, who wanted to convert his movie theater into a concert hall, Prince planned three live performances in a row, which would also act a springboard for his planned tour. The first evening, the audience was sparse—only his friends, family, and a few fans showed up. As for the set on 6 January, it was aimed at convincing the managers from Warner Bros. Records, who had made a trip from Los Angeles, of Prince's potential as a live performer. Alas, a catalog of technical problems, as well as the artist's lack of self-confidence, meant that he struggled to convince the audience of businessmen, who dismissed the idea of a tour out of hand. Following the fiasco of the first two evenings, the 7 January concert was simply cancelled. Unable to perform *For You* onstage, Prince concentrated on writing his second album. On 19 January 1979, he told the *Twin Cities Reader*: "I've written 20 songs for the next album [...] I didn't have any particular thing I was trying to accomplish on the first record—I was just putting down what I heard in my head. I wouldn't say the second one will be like the first, but it'll sound like me."[15]

FOR YOU

Prince / 1'06

Musician: Prince: vocals, backing vocals / **Recording: The Record Plant, Sausalito, California:** 1 October 1977 to 22 December 1977 / **Sound Labs, Hollywood:** January to February 1978 (overdubs) / **Technical team: Producers:** Prince, Tommy Vicari / **Recording engineer:** Tommy Vicari / **Assistant recording engineers:** Steve Fontano, David "Dave" Roeder

Prince had already worked on four different versions of this *a cappella* introduction during the preliminary recordings of 1976, which were made in André "Cymone" Anderson's basement. The introduction was effective and inspired the singer in a subsequent session a year later, during which he again experimented with multiple voice parts—jazzy and gospel scats—on the demo of the unreleased *Down a Long Lonely Road*.

IN LOVE

Prince / 3'38

Musician: Prince: vocals, electric guitar, bass, drums, synthesizers, Pollard Syndrum, backing vocals / **Recording: The Record Plant, Sausalito, California:** 1 October 1977 to 22 December 1978 / **Sound Labs, Hollywood:** January to February 1978 (overdubs) / **Technical team: Producers:** Prince, Tommy Vicari / **Recording engineer:** Tommy Vicari / **Assistant recording engineers:** Steve Fontano, David "Dave" Roeder

At the height of the disco era, the young artist regaled his audience with an irresistible piece, which could have given him his first hit if he had decided to release it as a single to promote the album. Instead, the song appeared on the B-side of the album's second single, *Just As Long As We're Together*, on its US release in November 1978, and deprived the public of its ultra-dancing, swaying rhythm. The sound of the Moog Polymoog 203a synthesizer, much appreciated by the artist, is ever-present, bringing the album a modernity reminiscent of the productions of Giorgio Moroder, whose albums *Knights in White Satin* (1976) and *From Here to Eternity* (1977) Prince may have heard.

HEADPHONES AT THE READY

In the song *In Love*, at 2'10, fans will recognize a short, humming melody that Prince would reuse for some choruses in *Sex Shooter*, a hit by Apollonia 6 (see page 91) in 1984.

Single

SOFT AND WET

Prince, Chris Moon / 3'01

Musician: Prince: vocals, electric guitar, bass, drums, synthesizers, Hohner Clavinet, slapstick, backing vocals / **Recording: The Record Plant, Sausalito, California:** 1 October 1977 to 22 December 1978 / **Sound Labs, Hollywood:** January to February 1978 (overdubs) / **Technical team: Producers:** Prince, Tommy Vicari / **Recording engineer:** Tommy Vicari / **Assistant recording engineers:** Steve Fontano, David "Dave" Roeder
Single: A-side: ***Soft and Wet***/3'01 / **B-side:** ***So Blue***/4'26 / **Released in the USA by Warner Bros. Records:** 7 June 1978 (single ref.: WBS 8619) / **Best chart ranking in the USA:** 92

Although it had been cowritten with Chris Moon, *Soft and Wet* underwent a few modifications when it was recorded. The original lyrics "Angora fur, the Aegean Sea, it's a soft, wet love that you have for me" were replaced by words that displayed, in his very first single, the singer's most salacious side: "Hey, lover, I got a sugarcane/That I want to lose in you/ Baby, can you stand the pain?" It had been Moon's idea to aim at a young audience in search of strong sensations, and

The rapper MC Hammer used a sample from *Soft and Wet* for his song *She's Soft and Wet* on his hit album *Please Hammer Don't Hurt 'Em*, released in 1990.

he steered his protégé in that direction during their first sessions at Moon Sound Studios. "Who's gonna buy his music? Teenage Girls because they're going to think that Prince is sexy. What are they thinking about? Girls are a little more mature than boys [...] He sat in front of the piano and I noticed that we were on the same track on this one."[2]

In 1978, however, the singer did not seem ready to project the controversial image that appeared a few years later and would cling to him for the rest of his life: "It doesn't seem like me [...] Mainly because where I live is kind of isolated from the musical scene in itself. I can only tell what's going on from reading magazines. When I hear *Soft and Wet* on the radio, it seems like someone else is singing."[16] In March 2018, Chris Moon put his rights to the song on eBay, leaving open the possibility of a potential buyer acquiring the asset via a "direct offer" of €414,000. "I'm nearing retirement age, so I'm selling off some of my assets [...] Anyone who buys this probably shouldn't be doing it for financial purposes. It's more about owning one of the most unique collectibles ever related to Prince."[17] Moon eventually withdrew the offer for sale after a few days, and continued to receive royalties from *Soft and Wet*, as well as from the cover, *She's Soft and Wet*, recorded by the rapper MC Hammer in 1990.

FOR PRINCE ADDICTS

Soft and Wet initially had the title *Soft When Wet*. This was quickly changed to avoid any confusion with *Slippery When Wet* by The Commodores, which was released in 1975 on their album *Caught in the Act*.

CRAZY YOU

Prince / 2'17

Musician: Prince: vocals, electric guitar, acoustic guitar, percussion, backing vocals / **Recording: The Record Plant, Sausalito, California:** 1 October 1977 to 22 December 1978 / **Sound Labs, Hollywood:** January to February 1978 (overdubs) / **Technical team: Producers:** Prince, Tommy Vicari / **Recording engineer:** Tommy Vicari / **Assistant recording engineers:** Steve Fontano, David "Dave" Roeder

Anxious to find out how the recording of its new artist's first album was progressing, in the autumn of 1977 Warner Bros. Records sent its representatives to Sausalito to observe a work session by Prince at the Record Plant studios. Once comfortably ensconced in the control room alongside Tommy Vicari, the men in suits could admire the musician laying down the tracks of his new song, *Crazy You*, a gentle ballad accompanied by an acoustic guitar. Then, one of them made the blunder of paying the artist a tactless compliment: "Unbelievable. This song will be great once a bass guitar is added."[11] Turning to his guests, Prince shot back: "There is no bass on this song, that's the way I planned it! Now get out of my studio. Get out!"[11]

Single

JUST AS LONG AS WE'RE TOGETHER

Prince / 6'24

Musician: Prince: vocals, electric guitar, bass, drums synthesizers, Hohner Clavinet, percussion, claps, finger snapping, backing vocals / **Recording: The Record Plant, Sausalito, California:** 1 October 1977 to 22 December 1978 / **Sound Labs, Hollywood:** January to February 1978 (overdubs) / **Technical team: Producers:** Prince, Tommy Vicari / **Recording engineer:** Tommy Vicari / **Assistant recording engineers:** Steve Fontano, David "Dave" Roeder

Single: A-side: *Just As Long As We're Together* (Edit)/3'25 / **B-side:** *In Love*/3'38 / **Released in the USA by Warner Bros. Records:** 21 November 1978 (single ref.: WBS 8713) / **Best chart ranking in the USA:** did not make the charts

With this irresistible disco track, Owen Husney convinced first CBS, and then Warner Bros. Records, that Prince didn't need a backing band—revealing, twice, the behind-the-scenes workings of a recording session. Apart from providing a demonstration of unparalleled virtuosity, the session revealed a faultless song perfect for the dance floor, just as the soundtracks of *Saturday Night Fever* and *Grease* were vying for No.1 position in the US charts and being played in countless clubs worldwide. The song consists of two distinct parts: the first contains verses and choruses, the second an instrumental section, which had already been recorded at Moon Sound Studios in 1976 and given the title *Jelly Jam*. Despite its qualities, the song failed to satisfy fans and did not make the Billboard Hot 100 chart when it was released as a single in November 1978, an injustice that can be rectified today by dancing to the song. It is perfect in every way and also foreshadowed Prince's attraction to quality disco music, confirmed the following year with *Sexy Dancer*.

Owen Husney, Prince's first manager, photographed by David Brewster of the *Minneapolis Tribune*.

BABY

Prince / 3'09

Musicians: Prince: vocals, electric guitar, acoustic guitar, bass, drums, piano, synthesizers, Fender Rhodes piano, bells, backing vocals / **Patrice Rushen:** synthesizers / **Recording: The Record Plant, Sausalito, California:** 1 October 1977 to 22 December 1978 / **Sound Labs, Hollywood:** January to February 1978 (overdubs) / **Technical team: Producers:** Prince, Tommy Vicari / **Recording engineer:** Tommy Vicari / **Assistant recording engineers:** Steve Fontano, David "Dave" Roeder / **Arrangements:** Patrice Rushen, Charles Veal

A soul ballad similar in style to Diana Ross's first solo songs for Motown (think *I Wouldn't Change the Man He Is* or *Where There Was Darkness*, in 1970), *Baby* tackles the painful theme of a couple of young lovers who have an unwanted pregnancy and are determined to overcome this ordeal. Prince wrote *Baby* during his trip to New York in 1976. "I wrote like I was rich, like I had been everywhere and seen everything and been with every woman in the world. But I liked that," explained the singer, who, it is too easily assumed, is the young man who figures in the story. "I always liked fantasy and fiction—I used to write stories when I was younger. Like *Baby* from the first album [...]"[18] Working on an earlier version of the song, Owen Husney had offered Prince the option of a string orchestra, bringing in the official ensemble of the WAYL radio station, which specialized in classical music. The resulting takes were not retained for the final version, but instead replaced by strings played on a synthesizer. It should be pointed out, however, that the sound resembles an orchestra of real musicians so closely as to be indistinguishable. The synthetic string arrangements were made with the help of the pianist Patrice Rushen, the only outsider who plays on *For You*, although she is not credited. Rushen, a friend of Tommy Vicari, had met Prince during the recording of the album, and took part in a session during which she worked on the arrangements for *Baby* with her boyfriend, Charles Veal. She plays the synthesizer in the song.

MY LOVE IS FOREVER

Prince / 4'09

Musician: Prince: vocals, electric guitar, bass, drums, synthesizers, Fender Rhodes piano, percussion, backing vocals / **Recording: The Record Plant, Sausalito, California:** 1 October 1977 to 22 December 1978 / **Sound Labs, Hollywood:** January to February 1978 (overdubs) / **Technical team: Producers:** Prince, Tommy Vicari / **Recording engineer:** Tommy Vicari / **Assistant recording engineers:** Steve Fontano, David "Dave" Roeder

More than any other song on the album, *My Love Is Forever* makes clear Prince's desire to replace certain acoustic instrument with modern keyboards, such as Moog, Oberheim, and ARP synthesizers. "We originally planned to use horns, but it's really hard to sound different if you use the same instruments. By not using horns on this record, I could make an album that would sound different right away. So I created a different kind of horn section by multi-tracking a synthesizer and some guitar lines."[19] The song, which was still entitled *Love Is Forever* when Prince and Chris Moon wrote it together in 1976, is a new foray into the disco style, which Prince would abandon with his third album in 1980.

SO BLUE

Prince / 4'26

Musician: Prince: vocals, electric guitar, acoustic guitar, bass, drums (played with brushes), percussion / **Recording: The Record Plant, Sausalito, California:** 1 October 1977 to 22 December 1978 / **Sound Labs, Hollywood:** January to February 1978 (overdubs) / **Technical team: Producers:** Prince, Tommy Vicari / **Recording engineer:** Tommy Vicari / **Assistant recording engineers:** Steve Fontano, David "Dave" Roeder

In the same musical vein as *Crazy You*, *So Blue* is a languorous ballad, which Prince was inspired to write after listening intensively to *Blue Motel Room*, a song by Joni Mitchell that featured on her eighth album, *Hejira*, which was released in 1976. The day of Matt Fink's audition, Prince asked him, in a peremptory tone, whether he had learned the score of *So Blue*. Mindful of the fact that, if it went well, this meeting could take him a long way, Fink was wrong-footed by the question, even though he had learned the singer's whole repertoire in preparation for this rite of passage. "I said, no, I didn't. Oh God! Then he laughed and said, 'Don't worry about it. There's no keyboard on that one.' So he played a joke on me, just to break the ice. Then we started jamming on stuff."[2] He would go on to become Doctor Fink, in the band The Revolution.

I'M YOURS

Prince / 5'01

Musician: Prince: vocals, electric guitar, acoustic guitar, bass, drums, Pollard Syndrum, Hohner Clavinet, backing vocals / **Recording: The Record Plant, Sausalito, California:** 1 October 1977 to 22 December 1978 / **Sound Labs, Hollywood:** January to February 1978 (overdubs) / **Technical team: Producers:** Prince, Tommy Vicari / **Recording engineer:** Tommy Vicari / **Assistant recording engineers:** Steve Fontano, David "Dave" Roeder

In *For You*'s last song, Prince abandons disco temporarily to flaunt his guitar virtuosity. Initially this is on the bass guitar, as suggested by his friend André Cymone (according to Charles Smith, who had been present at a few jam sessions between the two). It mixes whip-like slapping with discreet harmonics, over a diabolical drum pattern. The intro is followed by the electric guitar, to which Prince finally pays homage, regaling us with an impetuous riff. The critics were right: Prince was an ace on the 6-string guitar, as testified by Tim Carr in the *Minneapolis Tribune*, in April 1978: "Prince shows that his guitar playing need not cower beneath his synthesizers."[19] The song is a real demonstration of the multi-instrumentalist's skill. As Prince explained, "[...] you have to pretend each time that this is going to be your only track and that you're the only guy who's going to play that instrument. So every time you go into the recording booth, you have to play like it's your only shot. If you do that, what you end up with is a whole band that is playing with the same intensity."[19]

FOR PRINCE ADDICTS

So, what is this instrument called the "Orr bass" mentioned in the credits on *For You*? It is not a new kind of bass guitar, but simply one made by the Minneapolis luthier Chuck Orr and used by Prince at the time. He plays the instrument in the clip of *I Wanna Be Your Lover*, 1979.

Even though he was firmly opposed to Tommy Vicari during the recording of *For You*, Prince was unaware that the recording engineer had worked closely with the pianist Mike Melvoin on the original soundtrack of the musical horror-comedy *Phantom of the Paradise*, which was released ion 1974. As well as being a distinguished musician, Melvoin was also the father of Wendy Melvoin, a future guitarist for Prince in the band The Revolution.

PRINCE

I Wanna Be Your Lover · Why You Wanna Treat Me So Bad?
Sexy Dancer · When We're Dancing Close And Slow · With You · Bambi
Still Waiting · I Feel For You · It's Gonna Be Lonely

Released in the USA by Warner Bros. Records:
19 October 1979 (LP ref.: BSK 3366)
Released in the UK by Warner Bros. Records:
19 October 1979 (LP ref.: K 56772 – BSK 3366)
Best chart ranking in the USA: 22
Best chart ranking in the UK: did not make the charts

Portrait of Prince by the photographer Rick Malkin who was also the drum tech for the famous session drummer Eddie Bayers.

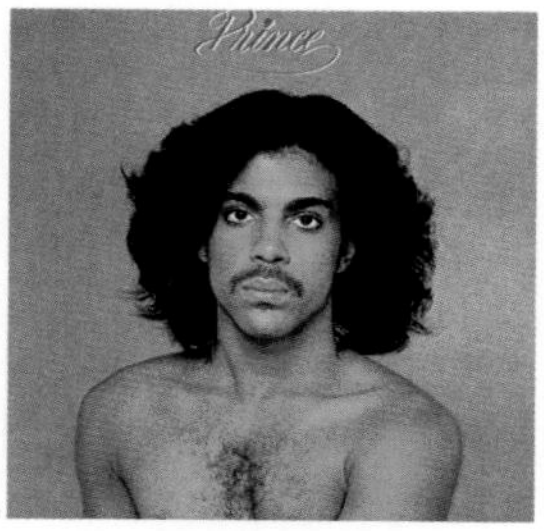

THE SWANSONG OF THE DISCO ERA

After the debacle of the concerts at the Capri Theater in January 1979 (see page 23), Prince needed more than ever to reassure the management of Warner Bros. Records, with whom the cost of the album *For You* still rankled. Indeed, the contract between Prince and the record label, which was signed in June 1977, stipulated that a budget of $180,000 would be allocated to produce his first three records. However, the bill from the Record Plant studios alone came to $170,509. Acutely aware that he needed to regain the confidence of his partners, Prince embarked on writing his second album with a precise goal: to produce as many hits as possible, and thus ensure a secure future within the Warner stable. "I spent too much money in the studio for the first album, so they looked at me, like, here's a child in here trying to do a man's job. So I tried to do the best the second time around and make a hit and do it for the least amount of money."[20] Mission accomplished—for Prince's second album cost Warner only $35,000.

Return to California

The recording sessions for *Prince* began at the end of April. The singer gathered together the demos he had worked on with André Cymone and Bobby Z., in the basement of his house in Edina, since he dropped plans for a tour and settled in at Alpha Studios, Burbank, in Los Angeles County. The facility belonged to the recording engineer Gary Brandt, a friend of Bob Cavallo, who had installed a professional studio in his basement. On the advice of Cavallo, Brandt would be the record's recording engineer, and no executive producer would be hired to help Prince during recording sessions. The sessions took place in perfect harmony between Prince and his technician over the seven weeks of recording, with Brandt dispensing pieces of precious technical advice to his client who seemed, for once, prepared to listen to someone else's opinion. Nevertheless, this was Prince's album and, despite the regular presence of André Cymone and Bobby Z., the singer remained the only one in the driving seat. "He already had everything in his head," Gary Brandt recalled. "He knew where the parts were going so it was just basically getting it onto tape [...] As long as my suggestions didn't infringe too much on his musical direction, he was reasonably open-minded."[2]

Once the backing tracks had been recorded in Burbank, Prince needed to find somewhere else to put his flight cases because Gary Brandt, who was engaged in two other artistic projects, could not take care of the rest of the production, which involved numerous overdubs and the mixing of the album. This task fell to Bob Mockler, of Hollywood Sound Recorders studios, who completed the sessions by mid-June 1979. The newly completed record revealed many new aspects of its creator to listeners. The disco spirit, which was everywhere in the previous album, alternated here with the FM rock of tracks such as *Bambi* and *Why You Wanna Treat Me So Bad?* The ballads *It's Gonna Be Lonely* and *Still Waiting* softened the ever-present energy, while the tracks *I Wanna Be Your Lover*, *Sexy Dancer*, and *I Feel For You* were surely tailor-made for American radio stations. In less than two months, Prince had pulled off a masterstroke: to produce, on his own, an album of the highest caliber, which elevated him to legendary status. At the same time, he succeeded in reassuring Warner Bros. Records, which would soon give him the green light to embark on his first US tour.

The concert at The Roxy Theatre, on 26 November 1979, got off to a bad start, as Matt Fink related: "The managers had hired a guitar tech who mis-tuned all the guitars. We hit the first chord of the first song, and the guitars and the bass were a good three or four steps out of tune with the keyboard [...]"[24] After a few attempts at adjusting their instruments, the musicians stopped playing and only resumed the set after they had been tuned correctly.

The Rebels—a digression

Once the album had been sent for pressing, Prince started concentrating on a new project. He took advantage of the summer of 1979 to gather his musicians at Mountain Ears Studio in Boulder, Colorado, from 10 to 22 July. His idea was to form a group in which each member could blossom and suggest songs of their own. Being well aware of Dez Dickerson and André Cymone's desire for freedom, Prince offered them a platform in the shape of The Rebels, a group that included Prince, Dez, and André, but also Bobby Z., Matt Fink, and Gayle Chapman. "Prince wanted to do something different [...] It was done quickly [...] Songs were written in the studio, the day of recording."[21] Two instrumental pieces and seven songs were recorded in total: *You*, *The Loser*, *If I Love You Tonight*, *Disco Away*, *Thrill You or Kill You*, *Hard to Get*, and *Too Long*. Prince stayed in the background, mostly leaving it to Chapman, Dickerson, or Cymone to perform the songs. "We stayed at this great hotel where you could have all the shrimp you wanted 24 hours a day," Dez Dickerson recalled. "We were still kids, so hanging out in the mountains and eating shrimp all day didn't suck."[22] Although the mention of seafood emphasizes how well the group were getting along at that time, a few months later, when Prince was preparing to take his band on the road, The Rebels' record sadly never saw the light of day. "Prince presented the idea to Warner Brothers," Fink explained. "The second Prince album wasn't even out yet, so they thought a release under another name would confuse people."[21] Besides cementing the group's cohesion, the episode of The Rebels allowed Prince to venture into new musical territory, which he would soon expand on with his third album.

First US tour

At the end of the summer of 1979, buoyed up by his backing band's team spirit, Prince organized a private concert in Los Angeles that left the management of Warner Bros. Records stunned. Sweeping away the bad memories of the Capri Theater show, Prince shone with self-confidence and a mesmerizing stage performance, showing his partners that he had at last found his direction. The single *I Wanna Be Your Lover* was a clear hit with the public from its initial release on 24 August 1979 and would go on to sell more than one million copies in the space of a few months. When *Prince*—the singer's second eponymous album—was released, it met with an extraordinary reception. The press and the fans were unanimous: a star had been born. However, now the singer was busy preparing his future concerts and conducting rehearsals with his band at a frenzied pace, given that the first date, at The Roxy Theatre in Los Angeles, was 26 November. When the big evening arrived, the band put on a convincing show, reeling off the tracks from the singer's two albums. Subsequent concerts were more sparsely attended—for example, in Cincinnati and Dallas, where the group played to audiences of only around 20 people. Finally, after a concert at Ole Man River's in Avondale, Los Angeles, the tour came to an end when Prince became ill with pneumonia. It was following these lackluster dates that Steve Fargnoli came on the scene as the singer's new manager. He took matters in hand and decided that his protégé deserved better than a series of dates in small clubs without an audience. He hired a personal assistant—Jamie Shoop—for Prince, and threw his artist in at the deep end, getting him nationwide exposure with appearances on *American Bandstand*, on 16 December 1979, and *The Midnight Special* on 8 January 1980. Dick Clark, the host of *American Bandstand*, would never forget Prince's appearance on his show. The artist did not speak to him and remained silent in response to his questions throughout the program. "The night before he told us that he wasn't going to talk to Dick Clark, and that none of us should talk to Dick Clark," Bobby Z. revealed. "No matter what happens, that's just the way it's going to be."[13] For his part, the presenter remembered the occasion with amusement. "I've always said that was one of the most difficult interviews I've ever conducted, and I've done 10,000 musician interviews."[23]

The singer and bass player Rick James, seen here at the peak of his career in 1981, would soon be ousted by the person who once performed the first parts of his shows.

On the road with Rick James

Once the promotion of the album was put in place and the singer had recovered from pneumonia, the second segment of the Prince Tour could begin. On 9 February 1980, a concert at the Orpheum Theatre in Minneapolis set the tone for the tour. The stage outfits were devilishly sexy. Gayle Chapman, dressed in a satin babydoll nightgown, regularly left her keyboard to strike provocative poses at the front of the stage, and even rewarded Prince with a classic French kiss before a dumbfounded audience. That evening, a new song was presented to the audience: *Head*. The title was an allusion to fellatio and gave those present a foretaste of the new Prince, soon to be revealed to the whole world. Very quickly, the singer and his musicians joined the tour of Rick James, a funk singer whose styles of clothing and music were largely borrowed from Bootsy Collins, and who had been propelled to the top of the charts in 1978 by his album *Come Get It!*. Prince took advantage of this opportunity to display his talent, and on every leg of Tour '80 (while promoting *Fire It Up*, the new album by the dreadlocked funkateer), it was the singer from Minneapolis who had audiences at his feet. Wearing black briefs and thigh boots, with his Fender Telecaster slung over his shoulder (his famous Hohner Madcat would appear only later in the tour), and flaunting a wavy hairstyle in place of his Afro cut, Prince conquered the hearts of the audiences, even if it meant eclipsing the headline act, Rick James. "We started to kick his butt. We would play for 40 minutes, and we were young and hungry, up-and-coming, and he played for like two hours and put people to sleep."[13]

On 3 May 1980, Tour '80 came to an end at the Capital Centre in Landover, Maryland. After this last set, Prince returned to Minneapolis and set about writing his third album: the subversive, electrifying *Dirty Mind*.

FOR PRINCE ADDICTS

Having decided to play the keyboard dressed in a black-and-white-striped prison uniform, Matt Fink was surprised to see Rick James come onstage in an outfit very similar to his. Prince asked Fink whether he had some other idea. Fink suggested he dress up as a doctor. "[...] they sent out the wardrobe people to a uniform shop," the keyboard player recalled. "And that night, I became Doctor Fink."[25]

The musician Patrice Rushen brought a personal touch to the recording of *Baby* in 1979.

Single

I WANNA BE YOUR LOVER

Prince / 5'47

Musician

Prince: vocals, electric guitar, acoustic guitar, bass, drums, synthesizers, Hohner Clavinet, backing vocals

Recording

Alpha Studios, Burbank, Los Angeles County: end April to 13 June 1979

Hollywood Sound Recorders, Los Angeles: May to June 1979

Technical team

Producer: Prince

Recording engineer: Gary Brandt (Alpha Studios), Bob Mockler (Hollywood Sound Recorders)

Assistant recording engineer: Mark Ettel (Alpha Studios)

SINGLE

A-side: ***I Wanna Be Your Lover***/2'57

B-side: ***My Love Is Forever***/4'08 (USA); ***Just As Long As We're Together***/6'24 (UK)

Released in the USA by Warner Bros. Records: 24 August 1979 (single ref.: WBS 49050)

Released in the UK by Warner Bros. Records: 24 August 1979 (single ref.: K 17537)

Best chart ranking in the USA: 11

Best chart ranking in the UK: 41

Genesis

Patrice Rushen met Prince during the recording of *For You*. Their relationship was a strictly professional one, especially as the singer's boyfriend was present and even took part in the arrangements for *Baby*, in which his partner played the synthesizer. Soon afterward, having just completed the demos for his second album, Prince suggested two songs to Rushen, *I Wanna Be Your Lover* and *I Feel For You*, while she was in the middle of writing her own new album, *Pizzazz*. Rushen declined, with the result that neither of the two songs appeared on the album, which was released in October 1979, and so Prince recorded them for his eponymous album. Although the singer denied having had a romantic involvement with Patrice Rushen, in *Right On!* magazine in December 1979, a future associate of the singer, Alan Leeds, described the feelings Prince had for this beautiful woman: "One of the songs Prince wrote in 1979 was actually inspired by and intended as a demo for Patrice Rushen. Despite a serious crush on the singer/keyboardist he didn't get the song on her album. But he did gain a friend and his first Gold record."[26] Two clips were made to promote the single. The first, featuring the group, was quietly shelved by Warner Bros. The second—on which Prince played all the instruments—proved to be a record-breaker.

Production

The album version of *I Wanna Be Your Lover* was cut by 2'50 for its release as a single. The song's second section is a formidable instrumental passage, enough to make the most anti-disco listener wiggle their hips. The synth pads—which are considerably more discreet than on the preceding album—combine with muted funk plucking on the guitar and notes on the Hohner Clavinet, hammered out in the manner of Stevie Wonder on *Superstition* (1972). Bob Mockler applied all his skill to the mixing of this song and working with the young Prince made a real impression on him: "It says on the album, 'Remixed by Bob Mockler and Prince.' That's probably the last time he ever put anybody's name before his. That's my proudest achievement as a recording engineer."[2]

1979

Prince, Bobby Z., and Dez Dickerson onstage at the Ritz, New York, on 22 March 1981.

Single

WHY YOU WANNA TREAT ME SO BAD?

Prince / 3'49

Musicians: Prince: vocals, electric guitar, bass, drums, synthesizers, Hohner Clavinet, backing vocals / **André Cymone:** backing vocals / **Recording: Alpha Studios, Burbank, Los Angeles County:** end April to 13 June 1979 / **Hollywood Sound Recorders, Los Angeles:** May to June 1979 / **Technical team: Producer:** Prince / **Recording engineers:** Gary Brandt (Alpha Studios), Bob Mockler (Hollywood Sound Recorders) / **Assistant recording engineer:** Mark Ettel (Alpha Studios)
Single: A-side: *Why You Wanna Treat Me So Bad?*/3'49 / **B-side:** *Baby*/3'09 / **Released in the USA by Warner Bros. Records:** 23 January 1980 (single ref.: WBS 49178) / **Best chart ranking in the USA:** did not make the charts

1979

Having first touched on it with *I'm Yours*, Prince attempted a fusion of disco with FM rock sounds in *Why You Wanna Treat Me So Bad?* He succeeded in blending two musical styles regarded as contradictory with panache, producing a high-quality song that was released as a single in the US and New Zealand. The only breach of the singer's self-imposed rule was that André Cymone appeared in discreet backing vocals in the choruses. The bass player, a childhood friend of Prince's, had wanted to break free of the artistic dictatorship imposed by the young star for some time. The omission of his name from the record's credits caused an inevitable split between them. "He sang a small harmony part that you really couldn't hear," Prince explained. "There was a typo on the record, and André didn't get any credit. That's how the whole thing started. I tried to explain that to him, but when you're on the way up, there's no explaining too much of anything. People will think what they want to."[27]

Single

SEXY DANCER

Prince / 4'18

Musician: **Prince:** vocals, electric guitar, bass, drums, synthesizers, piano, claps, backing vocals / **Recording:** **Alpha Studios, Burbank, Los Angeles County:** end April to 13 June 1979 / **Hollywood Sound Recorders, Los Angeles:** May to June 1979 / **Technical team:** **Producer:** Prince / **Recording engineers:** Gary Brandt (Alpha Studios), Bob Mockler (Hollywood Sound Recorders) / **Assistant recording engineer:** Mark Ettel (Alpha Studios)
Single: A-side: *Sexy Dancer*/4'18 / **B-side:** *Bambi*/4'21 / **Released in the UK by Warner Bros. Records:** 11 April 1980 (single ref.: K 17590) / **Best chart ranking in the UK:** did not make the charts

It took some nerve in 1980 to release a single without a single verse of lyrics; the choruses alone are sufficient in this disco anthem, whose rhythm is driven by the singer's clapping hands. Although the song's high point is the piano passage at 3'29, the story of *Sexy Dancer* could have been very different. Prince recorded many different solos during the sessions—a bass guitar solo to begin with, combining slapping with single notes with a slightly saturated sound, followed by a freestyle electric guitar solo with prominent feedback and, finally, a flurry of muted funk plucking on the guitar at 6'58—all of which might have been used for the song. An uncut 8'50 version, tailor-made for the dance floor, was released as a maxi-single in April 1980 in the UK.

WHEN WE'RE DANCING CLOSE AND SLOW

Prince / 5'18

Musician: **Prince:** vocals, acoustic guitar, bass, drums, synthesizers, piano, backing vocals / **Recording:** **Alpha Studios, Burbank, Los Angeles County:** end April to 13 June 1979 / **Hollywood Sound Recorders, Los Angeles:** May to June 1979 / **Technical team:** **Producer:** Prince / **Recording engineers:** Gary Brandt (Alpha Studios), Bob Mockler (Hollywood Sound Recorders) / **Assistant recording engineer:** Mark Ettel (Alpha Studios)

Behind this innocent ballad there lurk some bawdy lyrics in which Prince sings to his lover, without false modesty: "I want to come inside of you/I want to hold you when we're through." The singer seems torn between sensuality and sentimentalism in this song, which is far removed from the romanticism of his first album. However, he returns to a romantic tone in other songs on the album, such as *With You* and *Still Waiting*. As for the recording, when doing the mixing Bob Mockler was given a rhythmic base that was too powerful to give the song the languor that fitted its subject. Since, in 1979, digital sequencers had not yet replaced consoles in the recording studio, Mockler decided to create the fade-out of each bass guitar note manually, making it disappear after four beats, thus allowing the drums and acoustic guitar to benefit from the space they needed every two bars in the song.

WITH YOU

Prince / 3'59

Musician: **Prince:** vocals, electric guitar, bass, drums, Fender Rhodes piano, piano, synthesizers / **Recording:** **Alpha Studios, Burbank, Los Angeles County:** end April to 13 June 1979 / **Hollywood Sound Recorders, Los Angeles:** May to June 1979 / **Technical team:** **Producer:** Prince / **Recording engineers:** Gary Brandt (Alpha Studios), Bob Mockler (Hollywood Sound Recorders) / **Assistant recording engineer:** Mark Ettel (Alpha Studios)

Here, Prince plunges deep into the heart of his love of soul to create a song of unquestionable melancholy. The singer, who unleashes his finest head voice, had shortly beforehand justified using his vocal cords in this way to *Minneapolis Star Tribune* journalist, Jon Bream, who had asked why he used falsetto so often: "Because when my voice changed it went down, and I couldn't get any power out of it [...] The energy to I couldn't get it from that voice. With the higher voice, it was easier to hit the higher notes [...] And it also hurts in my lower voice to sing, when I sing too hard. It doesn't hurt in my falsetto."[12] In the summer of 1986 David Rivkin produced the first album by Jill Jones, the new protégée of Prince and his newly founded label Paisley Park Records. She was also a coproducer on the album and made a cover of *With You*, recorded at Electric Lady Studios in New York during the summer, which notably featured the renowned drummer, Steve Gadd, and Steve Stevens, Billy Idol's guitarist. "I got all the players," Rivkin said. "Steve Stevens was a friend of Jill's and he was terrific."[28]

With *Still Waiting*, Prince followed in the footsteps of The Five Satins, unforgettable performers of *I'll Remember (In the Still of the Nite)* in 1956.

BAMBI

Prince / 4'22

Musician: Prince: vocals, electric guitar, bass, drums, percussion / **Recording: Alpha Studios, Burbank, Los Angeles County:** end April to 13 June 1979 / **Hollywood Sound Recorders, Los Angeles:** May to June 1979 / **Technical team: Producer:** Prince / **Recording engineers:** Gary Brandt (Alpha Studios), Bob Mockler (Hollywood Sound Recorders) / **Assistant recording engineer:** Mark Ettel (Alpha Studios)

Did the overly explicit lyrics force Prince to omit the words at the end of *Bambi* from the booklet of the album's American version? For although the lines "Bambi, I know what you need/Bambi, maybe you need to bleed" seem innocent when taken out of context, they merely serve to emphasize the indelicate character of the song, in which Prince tries to persuade a young woman that she will discover *real* carnal pleasure in his arms, rather than in the company of another woman. "Come on, baby, and take me by the hand/I'm gonna show what it's like to be loved by a man," he assures the young beauty. The song almost never made it onto the album, as Prince felt it contrasted too much with the overall tone. But Bob Mockler, who loved the song, managed to persuade the singer to add it to the tracklist of his second LP. *Bambi* was only released as a single in Belgium and the Netherlands, and was covered by the rapper T C Ellis on his 1991 album *True Confessions*, produced by Paisley Park Records.

Single

STILL WAITING

Prince / 4'24

Musician: Prince: vocals, acoustic guitar, bass, drums, synthesizers, piano, backing vocals / **Recording: Alpha Studios, Burbank, Los Angeles County:** end April to 13 June 1979 / **Hollywood Sound Recorders, Los Angeles:** May to June 1979 / **Technical team: Producer:** Prince / **Recording engineers:** Gary Brandt (Alpha Studios), Bob Mockler (Hollywood Sound Recorders) / **Assistant recording engineer:** Mark Ettel (Alpha Studios)
Single: A-side: *Still Waiting* (Edit)/3'48 / **B-side:** *Bambi*/4'21 / **Released in the USA by Warner Bros. Records:** 25 March 1980 (single ref.: WBS 49226) / **Best chart ranking in the USA:** did not make the charts

By using the conventions of doo-wop music—triplets and the plaintive singing of a spurned lover—in *Still Waiting*, the second US single from the album, Prince pays homage to the genre's hits, such as *The Great Pretender* by The Platters and *I'll Remember (In the Still of the Nite)* by The Five Satins, released in 1955 and 1956, respectively. Rumor has it that this bluette was written for Kim Upsher, a high-school friend with whom Prince had a romantic relationship some time before recording the album. The singer himself offered a clue to journalist Cynthia Horner in an interview for the December 1979 edition of the magazine *Right On!* when she asked whether he had a girlfriend. He answered: "I had one but she left me. I wrote some songs about it on the album."[29]

The eccentric funk diva Chaka Khan achieved international success in 1984 with her cover of *I Feel For You* by Prince, who was one of her greatest admirers.

In 1978, determined to meet his idol Chaka Khan, Prince used his talent as a mimic, telephoning the singer at her hotel and pretending to be Sly Stone, who was then close to the star, and suggesting she come to meet him at Electric Lady Studios. "I found this short little guy in this one studio with a guitar. I asked, 'Where's Sly?' He said, 'That was me.' [...] I wanted to strangle him. I said, 'Okay, nice meeting you,' and I left.'"[30]

I FEEL FOR YOU

Prince / 3'24

Musician: Prince: vocals, electric guitar, bass, drums, synthesizers, Hohner Clavinet, claps, backing vocals / **Recording: Alpha Studios, Burbank, Los Angeles County:** end April to 13 June 1979 / **Hollywood Sound Recorders, Los Angeles:** May to June 1979 / **Technical team: Producer:** Prince / **Recording engineers:** Gary Brandt (Alpha Studios), Bob Mockler (Hollywood Sound Recorders) / **Assistant recording engineer:** Mark Ettel (Alpha Studios)

Initially offered to Patrice Rushen for her album *Pizzazz* (she politely declined), *I Feel For You* was finally recorded by Prince for his own album. The Pointer Sisters produced their own version in 1982 for their album *So Excited!*, as did Rebbie Jackson for *Centipede* in 1984. But the most famous cover of *I Feel For You* is undoubtedly that recorded by Chaka Khan in 1984, with Stevie Wonder on harmonica, which incidentally was her greatest hit. Without false modesty, she said: "[...] when I heard that song *I Feel For You* I felt that we could not let this song go unheard or unmessed-with. I gotta bring it back!"[31] On 18 October 2019, an acoustic preliminary version of the song, recorded by Prince during the preparation of this second album, was offered for download by NPG Records to mark the 40th anniversary of the release of the *Prince* album.

IT'S GONNA BE LONELY

Prince / 5'26

Musician: Prince: vocals, electric guitar, bass, drums, synthesizers, Fender Rhodes piano, piano, backing vocals / **Recording: Alpha Studios, Burbank, Los Angeles County:** end April to 13 June 1979 / **Hollywood Sound Recorders, Los Angeles:** May to June 1979 / **Technical team: Producer:** Prince / **Recording engineers:** Gary Brandt (Alpha Studios), Bob Mockler (Hollywood Sound Recorders) / **Assistant recording engineer:** Mark Ettel (Alpha Studios)

In this most classical of ballads, Prince sings of the sadness of the rejected lover, a subject he would often tackle with all his characteristic modesty. In 1985, when he was at the peak of his fame, he confided in the journalist Neal Karlen about his loneliness: "[...] if people want to come by, it will be fine. Sometimes it gets lonely here. To be perfectly honest, I wish more of my friends would come by [...] A lot of the time they think I don't want to be bothered."[27]

PRINCE

DIRTY MIND

Dirty Mind · When You Were Mine · Do It All Night · Gotta Broken Heart Again
Uptown · Head · Sister · Partyup

Released in the USA by Warner Bros. Records:
8 October 1980 (LP ref.: BSK 3478)
Released in the UK by Warner Bros. Records:
8 October 1980 (LP ref.: K 56862–BSK 3478)
Best chart ranking in the USA: 45
Best chart ranking in the UK: did not make the charts

Without asking the photographer's permission, Andy Warhol used this shot by Lynn Goldsmith for one of his colour silk screen prints in 1984.

FOR PRINCE ADDICTS

When Warner Bros. Records sent radio stations a copy of *Dirty Mind* in 1980, the label was well aware of the provocative nature of Prince's songs. Accordingly, it placed a black sticker on the sleeve that read: "Programmers: Please Audition prior to Airing."[36]

AT THE PEAK OF SYNTHPOP

In the summer of 1980, Prince moved from Edina to Orono, a small town on the shores of Lake Minnetonka, west of Minneapolis, taking a house at 680 North Arm Drive. He set up the bedrooms and kitchen of his new quarters as a home studio, which he called "Uptown" on the album sleeve. There, he recorded many preliminary versions of pieces that would become the songs on his third album, *Dirty Mind*. Some of these (such as *Plastic Love Affair*, *Eros*, *Rough*, and *When the Shit Comes Down*) found their way into the singer's archives; others he worked on in more depth, before passing them to his managers. Although Prince was self-sufficient when putting together these songs, he quickly came up against an insoluble problem. He could not do without a recording engineer. On the advice of his assistant, Jamie Shoop, the artist sought the services of Don Batts, an expert in the use of electronic instruments and a highly qualified recording engineer. Quickly hired by Prince to help him make his new album, Batts became a vital partner. "I walked into the rehearsal. About three minutes later, someone broke a keyboard. So I walked over and unscrewed and fixed that [...] Two or three hours later, I was hired."[2] Setting to work on producing his new album, Prince put the finishing touches to his songs, which he recorded in a spontaneous fashion, without trying to reproduce arrangements written during previous sessions, as he had done for his first two records. "On the other albums, I used to sit down and say, 'What's gonna sound best?' I'd make sure it was in a relative key and things like that. I tried to do it from an intellectual point of view, and I don't think that was so wise. Now I tend not to analyze my own stuff. I just do it!"[32] On listening to his new songs, Prince's managers felt that, despite their indisputable qualities, they needed more thorough mixing, so they could be played by radio stations. This task was entrusted to Mick Guzauski who, under the singer's guidance, carried out his assignment at the Hollywood Sound Recorders studios in Los Angeles. Bob Mockler, who had already worked on *Prince*, was brought in to work on the mixing of two songs: *Head* and *Do It All Night*.

In Allen Beaulieu's viewfinder

When *Dirty Mind* was released, on 8 October 1980, its songs, with lyrics that were provocative to say the least, elicited much press comment. *Head* enthused about fellatio, *Sister* told the story of an incestuous relationship between Prince and his sister, while *Do It All Night* described the singer's fantasies. As he once said: "Sex is always the most interesting thing to write about. It's the one subject people can't talk about without losing their cool [...] My family, my father and my mother, life and death are far more personal to me than sex."[33] Although it was warmly received by the critics, the album enjoyed only critical success, reaching no higher than No.45 in the US charts. The sleeve also conveyed the outrageous and bawdy new direction taken by the artist, illustrated with photographs which were the result of collaboration with the photographer Allen Beaulieu, whose work Prince had discovered while he was still living at André Cymone's. André's mother, Bernadette, had put a poster on the wall for the 1978 edition of the African-American fashion show "Shades of Blackness Fashion Extravaganza." Shot by Beaulieu, it featured Ron Edwards and J D Steeles . "For that poster I shot black people on a black background with black clothes. I literally shot what it said: shades of blackness. And that's what caught Prince's eye."[34]

When staying in New York, the day before their first concert at The Ritz, Prince and his musicians were woken during the evening of 8 December 1980 by the wail of police sirens. John Lennon had been murdered a few streets away from their hotel, in front of the Dakota Building. "New York was a pretty scary [...] experience to us," said Don Batts, the technician on the tour.

In 1980, when putting the finishing touches to his third album, the singer contacted Beaulieu and hired him for a three-day stint. In the end, there were several sessions. During the first, the singer was photographed in red shorts and white braces, in front of a curtain peppered with small holes through which light shone, giving the illusion that a cascade of stars was unfolding behind him. A second session produced the album sleeve. For the occasion, Beaulieu picked up a mattress at a yard sale for $25, which he brought to his studio. Prince stood in front of the springs dressed in briefs, a bandana, and a studded trench coat designed by André Cymone's sister. A week later, satisfied with this work, Prince invited his musicians to be photographed in turn. He then held a further session at the home of his ex-girlfriend Kim Upsher for the back of the sleeve, where the song titles would be spray-painted on the wall in the background. Finally, more promotional photographs were shot at the singer's home.

The "Dirty Mind Tour"

A new musician, Lisa Coleman, made her appearance in the pictures for the album. Gayle Chapman was a member of The Way International, a religious organization based in Ohio, and no longer played the role of sex symbol onstage, much less indulged in long kisses with Prince at every concert. She decided to quit, and was replaced as keyboard player by Lisa Coleman, a 19-year-old from California who was prepared to let rip in front of Prince's audiences. "He picked me up at Minneapolis Airport. We were both so quiet, so shy, it almost didn't work out. He got a bad vibe of me, thought I was a big hippy girl. But then I started playing piano, and he grabbed his guitar and joined me."[35]

On 4 December 1980, Prince and his band gave the first concert of the Dirty Mind Tour in Buffalo, New York state. From the first performance, the show combined provocation with explicitly sexual postures. Matt Fink (better known as Doctor Fink) was on keyboard, hiding behind his surgeon's mask, while Prince wore the outfit shown on the album's sleeve—which at the time allowed him to maintain a certain ambiguity regarding his sexuality. "People ask us about the way we dress, why do we dress so outrageously, why does it look like we're gay? One girl asked me about our costumes and I pulled her close and asked her if she'd be more comfortable in just her underwear. She giggled and said she would. For me to be standing onstage in a polyester suit would be kind of constricting."[37] During another interview, Prince added: "If it wasn't against the law, I wouldn't wear anything."[38] After 12 dates on the USA's East Coast, the tour ended in Detroit on 20 December, and did not resume until the following March. During this second series of concerts, one in particular was to change Prince's image in the eyes of the public. Although he was supported by the African-American community, which gave him good rankings in the Billboard Hot Soul Singles chart, the singer needed to appeal to a wider audience if he was to fill concert venues more easily, feature on radio stations, and attain the status of a universally recognized star to which he laid claim. The reviews in the New York press, which were full of praise after his concert at The Ritz on 11 March 1981, brought him the visibility he so badly wanted and acted as an ideal launchpad for showing the world his revolutionary music. In the UK, where the Prince explosion had also been felt, the prestigious *New Musical Express* (*NME*) accorded the singer his first British front-page coverage, with the headline: "Prince: Strutting with the new Soul Monarch."[39] As Bobby Z. said, "That was like the turning point. That was our audience. It was industry-posers, hip black people, hip white people, people that saw this as something new."[13]

From then on, Prince benefited from an extraordinary word-of-mouth reputation in the US. His stage performances were on everyone's lips, and most of the time received more attention than the insolent lyrics of his songs. Benefiting from a good press in America, a short tour was organized in Europe. Prince and his musicians appeared at the Paradiso, in Amsterdam, on 29 May 1981; the Lyceum Theatre, in London, on 2 June; and, finally, the Palace, in Paris, on 4 June (initially planned for 3 June at 22:30, but the concert began four hours late). "After an interminable wait, I caught sight

Prince and his irreplaceable Hohner Madcat guitar, which he was to use until the end of his life.

of the new wonder of American funk standing in the third row," wrote the French journalist Philippe Manœuvre, who was present that evening. "The auditorium was full of disco fans who looked for all the world like the Village People [...] Whether he was singing about oral sex or making love to his sister, Prince's performance ultimately went down badly. The uproar in the hall irritated the star, who cut short his performance [...]"[40] After this painful first experience in the Old World, Prince returned to his native Minnesota and embarked on writing the next album after *Dirty Mind*.

Don Batts was not credited for his role as recording engineer on *Dirty Mind*, and was replaced on the sleeve notes by one Jamie Starr. This name was the first pseudonym created by Prince. He would soon use it to credit productions by his protégés The Time, Vanity 6, and Sheila E.

Acerbic pop with a punk attitude: the successful recipe that the American singer-songwriter Cyndi Lauper came up with in the early 1980s.

around on it, and Prince said, 'Why don't you come out to the house tonight and we'll do something with that.'"[41] Fink did as he suggested, and met up with Prince at his home studio, playing his keyboard melody while his host played the drums, before bringing the session to an end. "The next day, he showed up with a recording of the song, finished; vocal, lyric, melody, bass, guitar, edit, everything [...] He played it for the band and said, 'This is the title track of the next record.' That was *Dirty Mind*. That's how he worked."[41]

As well as being joint composer of the song, Doctor Fink was also credited as a musician on *Dirty Mind* for the synthesizer line that marked the song's introduction. When he went to Orono to play his part in making Prince's album, Fink had a choice of a multitude of keyboards—Prince possessed a Hohner Clavinet, a Fender Rhodes, an ARP Pro Soloist, and several Oberheims. He opted for an ARP Omni with an inimitable sound, and laid down the chords of the song, which were thus immortalized forever on the singer's 16-track Ampex MM1100 tape recorder. "It had a kind of funny, nasal quality to it," Lisa Coleman recalled. "But that's the *Dirty Mind* sound [...] If you play those chords on that keyboard, you'll swear you just put the album on."[42]

Single

DIRTY MIND

Prince, Doctor Fink / 4'11

Musicians: Prince: vocals, electric guitar, drums, bass, synthesizers, backing vocals / **Doctor Fink:** synthesizer / **Recording: North Arm Drive Home Studio, Orono, Minnesota:** May to June 1980 / **Hollywood Sound Recorders, Los Angeles:** June 1980 / **Technical team: Producer:** Prince / **Recording engineers:** Prince (Jamie Starr), Don Batts / **Mixing:** Prince, Mick Guzauski / **Assistant recording engineer (mixing):** Ron Garrett
Single: A-side: *Dirty Mind* (Edit)/3'54 / **B-side:** *When We're Dancing Close and Slow*/5'18 / **Released in the USA by Warner Bros. Records:** 26 November 1980 (single ref.: WBS 49638) / **Best chart ranking in the USA:** did not make the charts

1980

Determined to be master of his work, from the very beginning Prince appeared resistant to any outside intervention. The reality was more nuanced, as he also appreciated the talent of his associates and the ideas they could contribute. For the second time, the artist shared the credits for this song, which was the result of a rehearsal with his musicians. During this, a new song was created around a gimmick on the synthesizer, as Doctor Fink, the group's keyboard player, explained: "[...] the band started playing

WHEN YOU WERE MINE

Prince / 3'44

Musician: Prince: vocals, electric guitar, drums, bass, synthesizers, backing vocals / **Recording: North Arm Drive Home Studio, Orono, Minnesota:** May to June 1980 / **Hollywood Sound Recorders, Los Angeles:** June 1980 / **Technical team: Producer:** Prince / **Recording engineers:** Prince (Jamie Starr), Don Batts / **Mixing:** Prince, Mick Guzauski / **Assistant recording engineer (mixing):** Ron Garrett

Written in a hotel room in Birmingham, Alabama, on 17 April 1980, when Prince and his musicians were accompanying Rick James's Tour '80, *When You Were Mine* is one of the most pop songs the singer made. Built around a riff on the formidable Oberheim OB-SX synthesizer, it has an extremely effective chorus, which foreshadows the direction the artist would soon head in with songs such as *Little Red Corvette* and *When Doves Cry*, which were tailor-made for radio stations. Prince himself emphasized the influence of The Beatles on the writing of the song, admitting in July 1997 that he had written it after listening to John Lennon sing. He played it to his associate Doctor Fink during a stay in Orlando, Florida, when Prince gave his musicians a day off to visit the Walt Disney World amusement park. The song was covered in 1981 by Bette Bright and The Illuminations, making it the singer's first official cover version. "I like it a

Never afraid of being electrocuted, Prince knew how to delight audiences with his famous Hohner Madcat on the Dirty Mind Tour in 1981.

lot. It was really kind of thrilling to hear someone else do one of my songs for the first time,"[43] Prince said. The piece was covered again that same year by the group Hi-Fi, who then included it on their 1982 album *Moods for Mallards*. Cyndi Lauper later covered the song for her 1983 album *She's So Unusual*. "I didn't really know Prince when I first heard the song," she said. "He was just a skinny guy in a G-string and a jacket [...]"[44]

In a concert at The Bowery Electric, in New York, on 4 August 2017, André Cymone paid homage to his former associate by performing an effective cover of *When You Were Mine*. In the song's introduction, Cymone launched into an instrumental medley on his Fender Stratocaster of several songs by his friend: *When Doves Cry, Bambi, Why You Wanna Treat Me So Bad, Computer Blue*, and *Purple Rain*.

Single

DO IT ALL NIGHT

Prince / 3'42

Musician: **Prince:** vocals, electric guitar, drums, bass, synthesizers, vocals / **Recording:** **North Arm Drive Home Studio, Orono, Minnesota:** May to June 1980 / **Hollywood Sound Recorders, Los Angeles:** June 1980 / **Technical team:** **Producer:** Prince / **Recording engineers:** Prince (Jamie Starr), Don Batts / **Mixing:** Prince, Mick Guzauski, Bob Mockler / **Assistant recording engineer (mixing):** Ron Garrett
Single: **A-side:** *Do It All Night*/3'42 / **B-side:** *Head*/4'40 / **Released in the UK by Warner Bros. Records:** 6 March 1981 (single ref.: K 17768) / **Best chart ranking in the UK:** did not make the charts

In the highly explicit *Do It All Night*, Prince is remarkably precise in declaring his passion for his beloved, explaining what he plans to do: "I want to do it/Do it all night/I want to do it/Do it to you right." Prince explained: "I saw an analyst once because I was wondering why I was so sexual-minded [...] He asked me to talk about my childhood y'know, 'when you first experienced this and first experienced that?' I realized that, when I was young, I used to read my mother's dirty novels and I was more taken with them than anything—it was a lot better than comic books."[45] Bobby Z. was more pragmatic when he first heard this licentious song: "I was already used to *Head*, so if you're used to *Head*, then *Do It All Night* is not going to freak you out."[13]

GOTTA BROKEN HEART AGAIN

Prince / 2'13

Musician: **Prince:** vocals, electric guitar, drums, bass, piano, synthesizers, backing vocals / **Recording:** **North Arm Drive Home Studio, Orono, Minnesota:** May to June 1980 / **Hollywood Sound Recorders, Los Angeles:** June 1980 / **Technical team:** **Producer:** Prince / **Recording engineers:** Prince (Jamie Starr), Don Batts / **Mixing:** Prince, Mick Guzauski / **Assistant recording engineer (mixing):** Ron Garrett

In the midst of a flurry of high-quality pop-funk songs, Prince granted his listeners a moment of brief respite with this medium-tempo ballad which expresses the loneliness of the narrator, whose heart is broken once again. Nonetheless, as Prince confirmed, there was no room in *Dirty Mind* for loving feelings: "I guess I just wasn't in the mood for ballads. When I did the other records, I think I was in love, and I wasn't when I did this one."[46] The digression ended there. It was back to the dance floor with the next song.

Single

UPTOWN

Prince / 5'30

Musician: Prince: vocals, electric guitar, drums, bass, synthesizers, backing vocals / **Recording: North Arm Drive Home Studio, Orono, Minnesota:** May to June 1980 / **Hollywood Sound Recorders, Los Angeles:** June 1980 / **Technical team: Producer:** Prince / **Recording engineers:** Prince (Jamie Starr), Don Batts / **Mixing:** Prince, Mick Guzauski / **Assistant recording engineer (mixing):** Ron Garrett
Single: A-side: *Uptown* (Edit)/4'09 / **B-side:** *Crazy You*/2'15 / **Released in the USA by Warner Bros. Records:** 10 September 1980 (single ref.: WBS 49559) / **Best chart ranking in the USA:** did not make the charts

Uptown may not have made the US charts when it was released as a single on 10 September 1980, but it remains one of the high points of the album. The song is a disco explosion in which Prince tackles, without taboos and for the first time, the subject of homosexuality, while advocating openness to others as a way of life. "It's a song about a state of mind everyone has, but a lot of time people are afraid to show. An openness—being open to things you don't understand. The song takes the example of homosexuality and deals with the way I feel about life, that I'm open and do whatever I want."[46] In an interview with *Rolling Stone* magazine, he added: "Those who cannot deal with it have a problem within themselves."[47] This song, the bass line of which André Cymone claimed to have created, led to a disagreement between Prince and his childhood friend that was to bring their collaboration to an end. Cymone, who would not be credited on *Uptown*, was hurt by this deliberate exclusion on the part of the singer. The disagreement soon became a rift and caused Cymone to leave the band. In the summer of 1981, he quit and was replaced by Mark Brown, whom Prince soon gave the nickname "Brown Mark."

HEAD

Prince / 4'40

Musicians: Prince: vocals, electric guitar, drums, bass, synthesizers, claps, backing vocals / **Doctor Fink:** synthesizer / **Lisa Coleman:** spoken voice / **Recording: North Arm Drive Home Studio, Orono, Minnesota:** May to June 1980 / **Hollywood Sound Recorders, Los Angeles:** June 1980 / **Technical team: Producer:** Prince / **Recording engineers:** Prince (Jamie Starr), Don Batts / **Mixing:** Prince, Mick Guzauski, Bob Mockler / **Assistant recording engineer (mixing):** Ron Garrett

In September 1978, Prince had fallen under the spell of the young Darlene Marie during a stay in San Francisco. As the young woman was engaged, their romance ended abruptly and the singer offered his beloved, as a farewell gift, the song *Darling Marie*, which he recorded in May 1979 and subsequently locked away in one of his many storage places. When *Head*, one of the most provocative songs on *Dirty Mind*, was released, it was easy to see it as a nod to this short romance because the lyrics are so explicit, to say the least: "Remember when I met you, Baby/You were on your way to be wed." A little later in the song, the unfaithful woman, voiced by Lisa Coleman, is heard, determined to perform fellatio on him since she is preserving her virginity for her future husband... Written during the sessions with The Rebels, in Colorado, during July 1979, *Head* was performed many times during the tour with Rick James, including one unforgettable occasion when Gayle Chapman French-kissed Prince at the front of the stage. The song was released as a single in the Philippines in 1981. Aside from its irreverence and irresistible groove, the piece's undeniable high point is the ARP Omni-2 synthesizer solo recorded by Doctor Fink, captured after six completely improvised takes. A truly classic moment, proving that the singer already knew how to surround himself with the best musicians.

Head was pivotal because of the arrival of Lisa Coleman in the band. Prince asked her to speak in the song to test how far she was prepared to go. She rose to the challenge with flying colors. By contrast, Gayle Chapman, who was weary of her boss's unrestrained sexuality, left the band because of this very song: "I don't mind giving head," she explained. "But I just don't wanna sing about it."[14]

HEADPHONES AT THE READY
At 4'26 in *Head*, Prince's famous moaning can be heard for the first time. He was to push this further in the introductions to *Sexuality* (1981) and *D.M.S.R.* (1982), and it became a distinctive feature throughout his career.

SISTER

Prince / 1'33

Musician: Prince: vocals, electric guitar, drums, bass, backing vocals / **Recording: North Arm Drive Home Studio, Orono, Minnesota:** May to June 1980 / **Hollywood Sound Recorders, Los Angeles:** June 1980 / **Technical team: Producer:** Prince / **Recording engineers:** Prince (Jamie Starr), Don Batts / **Mixing:** Prince, Mick Guzauski / **Assistant recording engineer (mixing):** Ron Garrett

Prince revealed in a roundabout way that this song in defence of incest was inspired by his stay at the home of his half-sister Sharon Nelson in the autumn of 1976. It is an

HEADPHONES AT THE READY

The bass line of *Partyup*, written by Morris Day, was recycled for the first album by The Time and would become the synthesizer motif played by Prince on *Cool*, the band's second single.

The dandy Morris Day, vocalist with The Time and a close friend of Prince, seen here in 1983.

understatement to say that the artist liked to cover his tracks when offering some clarification of the story to Chris Salewicz of *New Musical Express*. More provocative than ever, he explained: "I write everything from experience."[48] When the journalist asked whether he had tried incest, the reply was: "How come you ask twice?"[48] In another interview, Prince confirmed: "It's part of life. It's something that's inside of all of us to some degree, whether we like it or not. We may think about it or encounter it in some form or other."[49]

PARTYUP

Prince / 4'24

Musician: Prince: vocals, electric guitar, drums, bass, piano, synthesizers, claps, backing vocals / **Recording: North Arm Drive Home Studio, Orono, Minnesota:** May to June 1980 / **Hollywood Sound Recorders, Los Angeles:** June 1980 / **Technical team: Producer:** Prince / **Recording engineers:** Prince (Jamie Starr), Don Batts / **Mixing:** Prince, Mick Guzauski / **Assistant recording engineer (mixing):** Ron Garrett

Morris Day, former drummer with Grand Central, decided to quit his job as a security guard in San José, where he lived with his mother and her cousin, to join Prince in Minneapolis. The reunion was a warm one. Prince, who was working on writing his third album, made his home studio available to Day, so he could work on his own demos. "The first thing that I started to cut was *Partyup*," Morris Day said. "It was a lot slower and funkier, but he liked it and he wanted it. It was just a bass and drum track at that point, but he wanted it."[50] Prince then made Day a proposal. In return for being allowed to use his new song, he offered him the choice of either $10,000 or a promise that he would help him secure a contract with a record label. The pragmatic Day chose the second option. Prince kept his promise, and the following year offered him a role as a vocalist with the group that he was going to set up and produce: The Time (see page 64). Regarding the lyrics, Prince's words championed partying as a way of life, as opposed to war, which was the specialty of politicians, whom he criticized for the first time in interviews. "That song is just about people who'd rather have a good time than go and shoot up one another. That's all—it's pretty basic. I just seem to read about a lot of politicians who're [...] starting a war that they don't have to go out and fight. I just think the people should have a little more to say in some of these foreign matters. I don't want to have to go out and die for their mistakes."[48]

Trench coat, wavy hair, and Madcat guitar slung over his shoulder: three distinctive trademarks of Prince—*Dirty Mind* version.

GOTTA STOP (MESSIN' ABOUT)

Prince / 2'54

Musician

Prince: vocals, electric guitar, drums, bass, synthesizers, claps, backing vocals

Recording

North Arm Drive Home Studio, Orono, Minnesota: May to June 1980

Hollywood Sound Recorders, Los Angeles: January 1981

Technical team

Producer: Prince

Recording engineers: Prince, Don Batts

Mixing: Prince, Mick Guzauski

SINGLE

A-side: *Gotta Stop (Messin' About)*/2'54

B-side: *Uptown* (Edit)/4'09

Released in the UK by Warner Bros. Records: 29 May 1981 (single ref.: K 17819)

Best chart ranking in the UK: did not make the charts

Genesis

The concert at The Ritz in New York, on 9 December 1980 (sometimes dated 10 December, because it started after midnight), attracted particular attention from critics. The singer, now firmly established in the Billboard Hot Soul Singles chart, had already won the hearts of the African-American community. Between the two series of concerts that made up the Dirty Mind Tour, Prince's managers were working to ensure the artist gained wider recognition through massive exposure on radio stations. The second concert at The Ritz, on 22 March 1981, helped achieve this goal. The press were unanimous: the singer was clearly a rock musician. Articles full of praise guaranteed Prince credibility on the US music scene. The UK also heard the message, which was quickly passed on in the prestigious *New Musical Express* (*NME*) by the journalist Chris Salewicz. It must be said that, a week before the *NME* came out, Warner Bros. Records had released, exclusively for the UK, a hitherto unreleased single: *Gotta Stop (Messin' About)*, a remnant from the sessions for *Dirty Mind* that had been rejected when the tracklist for the album was drawn up. The song was thus released only in the UK with, on the B-side, the danceable *Uptown*—replaced, for obscure reasons, by *I Wanna Be Your Lover* when the single was rereleased. The song did not gain a wide audience, but it brought Prince visibility in a country where he would perform his first concert on 2 June 1981, at the Lyceum Theatre, in London.

Production

Gotta Stop (Messin' About) is a song in the same vein as *When You Were Mine*—decidedly more rock than the disco song *Uptown* or the funky *Head* and *Partyup*. In it, the singer plays his power chords on the guitar. He explained this progressive change of direction in various interviews: "I think I matured in a sense. I reached puberty, I got new management, I got a new guitar which brought life into the sound of the album—most of the songs were written on guitar. The second album was written mostly on the piano."[43] It is worth noting the appearance of claps, marked by the effects of mixing, which would become one of the hallmarks of the "Prince sound" in recordings throughout his career. Although they are produced by hand in this song, later they would be created by the singer's successive drummers using MIDI drum pads.

CONT

PRINCE

CONTROVERSY

Controversy · Sexuality · Do Me, Baby · Private Joy · Ronnie, Talk to Russia
Let's Work · Annie Christian · Jack U Off

Released in the USA by Warner Bros. Records:
14 October 1981 (LP ref.: BSK 3601)
Released in the UK by Warner Bros. Records:
13 November 1981 (LP ref.: K 56950)
Best chart ranking in the USA: 21
Best chart ranking in the UK: did not make the charts

Sexy and provocative, Prince kept people guessing in 1981.

With the album complete, Prince allowed Allen Beaulieu just one day to create its visuals. His only request was a portrait of himself in front of some press cuttings. Rick, the photographer's brother, suggested the idea of *The Controversy Daily*, and Allen asked Prince to come up with a few ideas for front-page stories. "He wasn't prepared for the question, but right off the top of his head he says, 'Love Thy Neighbor, Do You Believe In God, Gun Control, Joni Mitchell,' all that."[34]

THE MINNEAPOLIS SOUND IS BORN

1981

The Dirty Mind Tour had barely finished, yet Prince was already firing on all cylinders. His first move was to leave the shores of Lake Minnetonka for a bigger home at 9401 Kiowa Trail, Chanhassen, near Lake Riley. As soon as he arrived, he had the house repainted in purple and asked Don Batts, his chief technician, to install a home studio worthy of the name. The basement was converted accordingly, as well as the singer's living room, which became home to a piano fitted with microphones that were connected to the console on the floor below. Although he was keen to record his fourth album, the insatiable artist first wanted to realize two musical projects that he had been secretly preparing for several months. Indeed, his encounter with the young Susan Moonsie, with whom he had been romantically involved for some time, led him to think of launching an all-female group like the Mary Jane Girls, formed by Rick James in 1979. He had the perfect, irreverent name for the group: The Hookers. Jamie Shoop, Prince's assistant, was asked to join the project, as was Brenda Bennett, the assistant costume designer on the Dirty Mind Tour. However, over the summer, although several songs had already been recorded, Prince changed his plans and finally decided to concentrate on The Time (see page 64), a project he had been working on even while giving his all to the tour of the winter of 1980–81. Rising from the ashes of Flyte Time, a Minneapolis band that Prince had come across performing in the city during the mid-1970s, The Time would bring together talented, experienced musicians. Prince recorded their first album in his new studio at Kiowa Trail in April and organized a contract with Warner Bros. Records, who released the record on 29 July 1981. Success was forthcoming: the album's production was the work of one Jamie Starr, a pseudonym created by Prince to produce *Dirty Mind* and other albums to come.

In the footsteps of Dirty Mind

Alongside this new adventure as a talent scout in Minneapolis, Prince embarked on the production of his own album. Between the spring and summer of 1981 he recorded five new songs at Kiowa Trail: *Controversy*, *Sexuality*, *Annie Christian*, *There's Something I Like About Being Your Fool*, and *Tick, Tick, Bang*. Although the last two songs were put aside, the others appeared on his fourth album. At the beginning of August, the singer flew to Los Angeles, where he spent some days at the Hollywood Sound Recorders studios in the company of the recording engineer Ross Pallone. This allowed him to record *Let's Work*, *Jack U Off*, *Do Me, Baby*, and *Ronnie, Talk to Russia*. Finally, he completed the album's production at the Sunset Sound studios, where he made the acquaintance of the recording engineer Peggy McCreary. She enabled him to finish his album under the best possible conditions and continued to be an invaluable associate until 1986. With her, Prince recorded the last piece on the forthcoming album: *Private Joy*. "The receptionist was really worried about me working with him because he wrote such dirty songs," McCreary recalled, "so my impression of who was going to walk into the studio and who actually did was totally different. He was very polite and quiet and well-mannered."[51]

BOP
CATS

The painful experience of Memorial Coliseum

On 5 October 1981, a few days prior to the release of *Controversy*, a performance was organized at Sam's, in Minneapolis, with the aim of presenting the singer's new songs to a handpicked audience (the club would soon be renamed First Avenue and become world-famous thanks to the scenes of *Purple Rain* shot there). That evening, which was nothing less than a warm-up concert for the tour, also provided an opportunity for the singer to introduce his new bass player, Mark Brown, who had replaced André Cymone. Brown, just 18 years old at the time, played bass with Fantasy, a band from the outskirts of Minneapolis that had earned its stripes at 7th St. Entry, a club in the city where Prince had been able to watch him and assess his playing many times. After a brief audition, the musician joined an adventure, the initiation of which turned out to be painful. Mick Jagger, who attended Prince's concert in New York the previous March, suggested he play the opening set of The Rolling Stones' two concerts in Los Angeles in October. Taking place a few days before the release of the artist's fourth album, it was an opportunity not to be missed. But when Prince and his musicians went onstage at the Memorial Coliseum on 9 October, the Stones' fans allowed only three songs to be performed before hurling missiles and loud boos at the

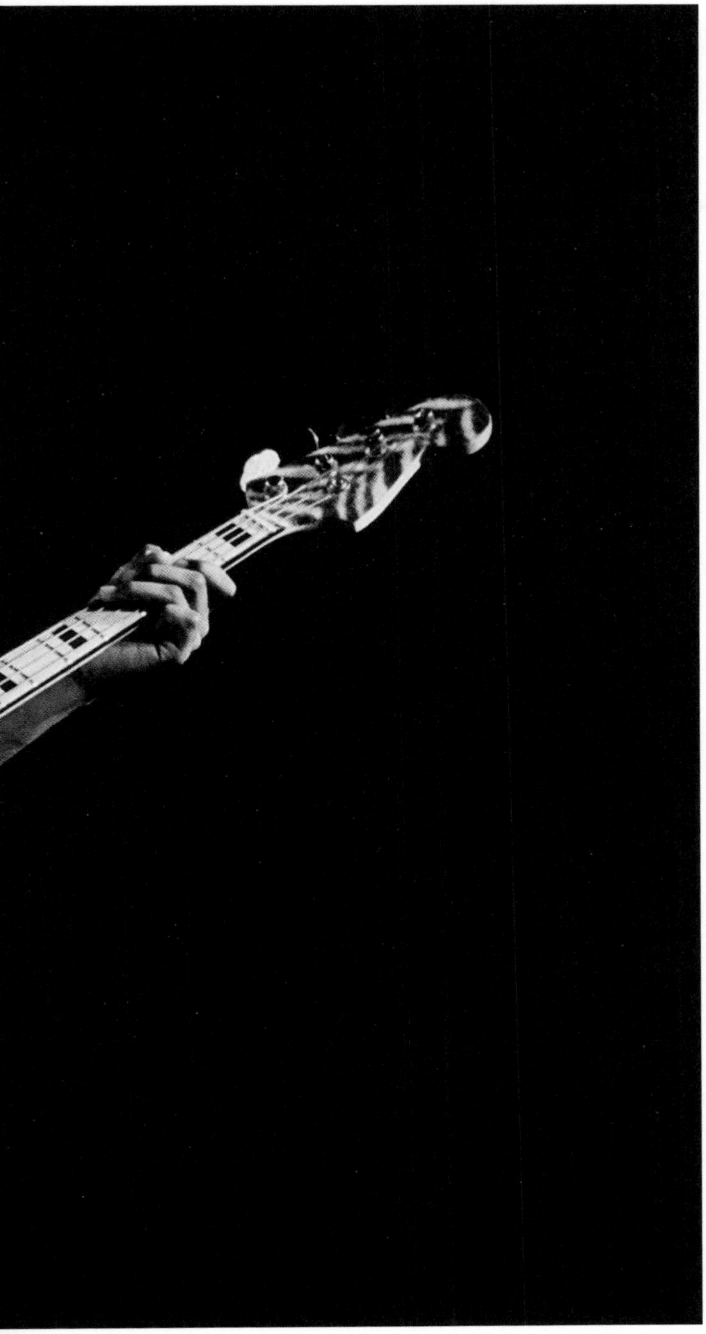

Side by side with the bass guitarist Brown Mark onstage at the Tower Theater in Upper Darby on 13 March 1982.

Now fully on board with the Prince adventure, Brown Mark would never forget the interminable days spent rehearsing with the band: "Prince loved to jam in B flat. Sometimes we'd go from 10am to 10 at night—I'd be rumbling [the bass] with one hand and making a sandwich with the other. As long as I didn't lose the pocket, he didn't care."[52]

musicians. After less than 15 minutes, Prince gave up and left the stage; he refused to keep his commitment to perform in the second concert, due two days later. However, persuaded by Jagger and Dez Dickerson, Prince eventually agreed to return to the stage on the Sunday. This time, the audience welcomed the artists with all kinds of flying objects: shoes, tomatoes, and bottles of Jack Daniel's. "It was catastrophic [...]," recalled Bobby Z. "The first note, of the first song, of the first show, an orange hit [Mark Brown's] bass. Knocked him out of tune [...] Then stuff came flying like you wouldn't believe."[13] This was too much for Prince, who left the stage after a few songs and quickly returned to Chanhassen.

The "Controversy Tour"

Despite the disastrous experience with The Rolling Stones, the reception to *Controversy* when it was released in the US on 14 October 1981 was unanimously positive. It reached No.21 in the Billboard chart and won general approval from the critics, who praised its artistic maturity and careful production. Prince still needed to prove himself in Europe, however, and would have to wait a year longer before he had the Old World at his feet.

The Controversy Tour began on 20 November 1981, at the Stanley Theatre in Pittsburgh, and continued until March 1982. The musicians received a warmer welcome this time, as testified by Mark Brown, who had by now been renamed "Brown Mark" by Prince. "I was blown away [...] There's 7,000 people there, they're all black, and they're screaming so loud I couldn't hear my own voice. I was like a deer in headlights, man. Women were passing out [...]"[35] The Time played the opening set throughout the tour; Charles Huntsberry, Prince's bodyguard, nicknamed "Big Chick" by the star, joined their ranks. After the final concert of the Controversy Tour, on 14 March 1982, Prince concentrated on producing a documentary telling the story of the tour, interspersed with sketches. The film, whose working title was *The Second Coming*, was shelved, but with Prince nothing went waste and everything was transformed: he revived the project in 1987 in the shape of the musical movie *Sign O' the Times*. From then on, the singer who never slept had only one obsession: to bring to fruition his project of an all-female group, which he had abandoned in favor of The Time the previous year. These three projects continued the work that had begun with *Dirty Mind*: to create the Minneapolis Sound, recognizable by its synthetic funk tones. Prince was to be its standard-bearer throughout his career.

Even though his guitar was not plugged in for this photo shoot, the guitarist Dez Dickerson was an integral part of Prince's live sound in 1981.

Single

CONTROVERSY

Prince / 7'14

Musicians

Prince: vocals, electric guitar, bass, drums, synthesizers, backing vocals
Lisa Coleman: backing vocals

Recording

Kiowa Trail Home Studio, Chanhassen, Minnesota: May to July 1981
Hollywood Sound Recorders, Los Angeles: August 1981 (overdubs)
Sunset Sound, Los Angeles: 14–23 August 1981 (overdubs, mixing)

Technical team

Producer: Prince
Recording engineers: Bob Mockler, Mick Guzauski, Ross Pallone, Peggy McCreary

Single

A-side: *Controversy*/3'39
B-side: *When You Were Mine*/3'44
Released in the USA by Warner Bros. Records: 2 September 1981 (single ref.: WBS49808)
Released in the UK by Warner Bros. Records: 9 October 1981 (single ref.: K 17866)
Best chart ranking in the USA: 70
Best chart ranking in the UK: did not make the charts

1981

FOR PRINCE ADDICTS

Two other versions of the single *Controversy* were made. Warner Bros. Records released the song on 29 November 1993 to promote the compilation *The Hits 2*, as well as the box set *The Hits/The B-Sides*, and NPG Records released a CD single of a live version of the song, recorded on 16 December 2003 at the Neal S. Blaisdell Center in Honolulu, which was included with the deluxe edition of the book of photographs *Prince in Hawaii: An Intimate Portrait of an Artist* (2004).

Genesis

According to André Cymone, who left Prince's band after the Dirty Mind Tour, weary of having to remind his boss of the authorship of certain songs, here was yet another track that was born of a jam session with him. Although the bass player made sure he was the cowriter of *Controversy*, he stepped back from any conflict regarding credits for songs, which Prince seemed to monopolize frequently. "At some point, he should probably give credit, because it's not like I can't write songs like that, still," Cymone said in 2018. "And thank goodness I've written other songs and had hits, so it's not like I'm some guy where that's the only song I ever wrote and it's so precious."[53] With the lyrics for *Controversy*, Prince defended his openness to the world, as he had in *Uptown* the previous year. "I just can't believe all the things people say/ Am I black or white, am I straight or gay?" he sang in astonishment, before concluding that controversy was the best way of conveying his ideas to the world around him.

Production

Prince's usual way of working was to write his songs at the piano, or on the guitar, bass guitar, or drums. He said he wrote *Controversy* with a pair of drumsticks in his hands (leaving aside the jam session episode described above). A straight rhythm accompanied by an extremely funky rhythm guitar—here was a formula that Prince would multiply infinitely, creating songs such as *Head*, *Partyup*, and *Let's Work*. The song's break, at 3'28, features an astonishing version of the Lord's Prayer, justified by the artist's faith, as confirmed by Dez Dickerson: "Prince feels like he has a special talent and God gave it to him. He told me we were sent to help people see [...] He had this sense that he was enlightened and we as a band were messengers who were there to bring this enlightenment to people who needed it. It was a musical mission. That's why he put the Lord's Prayer in the middle of *Controversy*."[54]

SEXUALITY

Prince / 4'20

Musician: Prince: vocals, electric guitar, bass, drums, synthesizers, backing vocals / **Recording: Kiowa Trail Home Studio, Chanhassen, Minnesota:** May to July 1981 / **Hollywood Sound Recorders, Los Angeles:** August 1981 (overdubs) / **Sunset Sound, Los Angeles:** 14–23 August 1981 (overdubs, mixing) / **Technical team: Producer:** Prince / **Recording engineers:** Bob Mockler, Mick Guzauski, Ross Pallone, Peggy McCreary

In this song, which was released as a single in West Germany, Japan, and Australia, Prince urges the listener to follow a very simple precept: "Sexuality is all you'll ever need/ Sexuality, let your body be free." It is an understatement to say the singer pursued his calling of sexual evangelization by releasing such songs, to the great pleasure of his fans. We can appreciate in passing the artist's moans in response to the whiplashes he suffers in the song's introduction—emphasizing, yet again, his irreverence.

Single

DO ME, BABY

Prince / 7'43

Musician: Prince: vocals, bass, drums, piano, synthesizers, backing vocals / **Recording: Hollywood Sound Recorders, Los Angeles:** August 1981 / **Sunset Sound, Los Angeles:** 14–23 August 1981 / **Technical team: Producer:** Prince / **Recording engineers:** Bob Mockler, Mick Guzauski, Ross Pallone, Peggy McCreary
Single: A-side: *Do Me, Baby* (Edit)/3'57 / **B-side:** *Private Joy*/4'25 / **Released in the USA by Warner Bros. Records:** 16 July 1982 (single ref.: 7-29942) / **Best chart ranking in the USA:** did not make the charts

When *Controversy* was released, in October 1981, André Cymone had already left the band. Imagine his surprise on discovering, when he heard the album, that it included one of the songs he had introduced to Prince during their sessions in New York a few years earlier. Having been asked by "Pepé" Willie to accompany the singer Tony Silvester—who wanted to record a few demos for the group The Imperials—in the studio, Prince and Cymone had taken advantage of a session at Music Farm Studios on 17 February 1979 to record a few new songs, including *Do Me, Baby*, which Cymone categorically claimed to have written. "It wasn't called *Do Me, Baby* but some of the lines were the same, and the music was the same. I'd written it for my girlfriend and it was called *Ooh Whatcha Do*, or something like that. She had a recording of it, and Pepé Willie had a recording of it, various people had a recording of it already. So that's why it became such a big deal."[53] Ill-gotten gains will be ill spent—the single *Do Me, Baby* was a flop and did not make the Billboard chart on its release in July 1982.

PRIVATE JOY

Prince / 4'37

Musician: Prince: vocals, electric guitar, bass, programming, synthesizers, backing vocals / **Recording: Sunset Sound, Los Angeles:** 14 August 1981 / **Technical team: Producer:** Prince / **Recording engineer:** Peggy McCreary

Private Joy is the only song to have been recorded entirely at the Sunset Sound studios, and also the first for which the Linn LM-1 Drum Computer was used—this was the first drum machine of its kind to offer acoustic prerecorded drum samples that could be modified at will, thanks to multiple functionalities. It was also programmable, which gave Prince great flexibility when creating the song's structure, as he could add breaks here or there and change the pattern. "That was the first moment that I knew things were going to change. When I heard *Private Joy*,"[13] said the drummer Bobby Z., who would soon have to add electronic percussion and MIDI drum pads to his drum kit. It was the last song to be recorded for *Controversy* and also marked the start of the collaboration between the singer and Peggy McCreary, a recording engineer at Sunset Sound, who would leave her mark on several of the artist's albums. La Toya Jackson included a cover of the song on her album *Heart Don't Lie* in 1984, which was released as a single in Japan but not in the US. "I loved the song and my record company loved it, but my father manages me and it was his decision to not release that cut."[55]

The US president Ronald Reagan and his Soviet counterpart Mikhail Gorbachev in the process of trying—perhaps—to reduce tensions between their two countries.

RONNIE, TALK TO RUSSIA

Prince / 1'51

Musicians: Prince: vocals, electric guitar, bass, drums, synthesizers, backing vocals / **Lisa Coleman:** backing vocals / **Recording: Hollywood Sound Recorders, Los Angeles:** August 1981 / **Sunset Sound, Los Angeles:** 14–23 August 1981 / **Technical team: Producer:** Prince / **Recording engineers:** Bob Mockler, Mick Guzauski, Ross Pallone, Peggy McCreary

"Thank God we got a better President now, with bigger balls than Carter. I think Reagan's a lot better,"[48] Prince declared in June 1981, referring to Ronald Reagan, who had been elected 40th president of the United States on 4 November 1980. The singer went so far as to create this very rock (possibly punk?) number entitled *Ronnie, Talk to Russia*, in which he encourages the president to use diplomacy at a time when the Cold War between the USSR and the US was at its height, and the North American continent feared a nuclear attack. Even though, with a certain clumsiness (and doubtless very little knowledge of the geopolitical situation at the time), Prince portrays the country led by Mikhail Gorbachev as solely responsible for the interminable conflict and fears for his own country's safety, the song remains irresistible for its pop lightness, which incidentally contrasts with its subject matter. One minute and 51 seconds of pure rock 'n' roll, to be listened to at full volume.

Single

LET'S WORK

Prince / 3'52

Musician: Prince: vocals, electric guitar, bass, drums, synthesizers, claps, backing vocals / **Recording: Hollywood Sound Recorders, Los Angeles:** August 1981 / **Sunset Sound, Los Angeles:** 14–23 August 1981 / **Technical team: Producer:** Prince / **Recording engineers:** Bob Mockler, Mick Guzauski, Ross Pallone, Peggy McCreary
Single: A-side: ***Let's Work*** (Edit)/2'56 / **B-side:** ***Ronnie, Talk to Russia***/1'48 / **Released in the USA by Warner Bros. Records:** 6 January 1982 (single ref.: WBS50002) / **Released in the UK by Warner Bros. Records:** 6 January 1982 (single ref.: K17922) / **Best chart ranking in the USA:** did not make the charts / **Best chart ranking in the UK:** did not make the charts

Although the song did not make the charts on its single release, *Let's Work* became a fan favorite, thanks to its numerous performances in concerts throughout the artist's career. Initially entitled *The Rock*, then *Let's Rock*, Prince thought of it when he saw a choreographed performance by young dancers in a club. Rewritten and reworked to be included on the *Controversy* album, just like *Head* and *Partyup*, the song contains all the ingredients of the Minneapolis Sound and is a tribute to the Africa-American community in the city. As Brown Mark said, "He played me *Let's Work*, and said, 'This one is for the brothers and sisters.'"[35] Definitely the most emblematic of the songs on *Controversy*, and one to be (re)discovered urgently.

ANNIE CHRISTIAN

Prince / 4'21

Musician: **Prince:** vocals, electric guitar, programming, synthesizers, backing vocals / **Recording:** **Kiowa Trail Home Studio, Chanhassen, Minnesota:** May to July 1981 / **Hollywood Sound Recorders, Los Angeles:** August 1981 (overdubs) / **Sunset Sound, Los Angeles:** 14–23 August 1981 (overdubs, mixing) / **Technical team:** **Producer:** Prince / **Recording engineers:** Bob Mockler, Mick Guzauski, Ross Pallone, Peggy McCreary

Fans like to speculate which drum machine was chosen to replace the drums in this song, which is a strange track, to say the least. Although the legendary Roland TR-808 and the Maestro Rhythm King MRK-2 (used by Sly Stone in 1971 on *There's a Riot Goin' On* and notably to provide the rhythm in the hit single *Family Affair*) have been suggested, it is impossible to be sure. The Roland CR-78 CompuRhythm, used by David Bowie in *African Night Flight* in 1979, had the same sound, which could also be found in the drum machines of all cheap organs at the time. It is thus a complete mystery, and all the more so since in subsequent years Prince used only one machine of this kind: the Linn LM-1 Drum Computer, which can be heard in *Private Joy*.

JACK U OFF

Prince / 3'08

Musicians: **Prince:** vocals, electric guitar, bass, backing vocals / **Bobby Z.:** drums / **Lisa Coleman:** synthesizers, backing vocals / **Doctor Fink:** synthesizers / **Recording:** **Hollywood Sound Recorders, Los Angeles:** August 1981 / **Technical team:** **Producer:** Prince / **Recording engineers:** Bob Mockler, Mick Guzauski, Ross Pallone

Performed during Prince's concerts in Europe at the end of the Dirty Mind Tour, *Jack U Off* is a pop number with salacious lyrics and a rockabilly feel, much loved by the Parisian gay community, which had flocked to Prince's concert at the Palace on 4 June 1981. "We didn't know how *Jack U Off* would be understood by the French audience," André Cymone recalled. "We sang: 'I'll Jack U Off' and the guys in the audience yelled '*Ouais! Jack Me Off! Branle-moi!*' [Yeah! Jack Me Off! Jack me off!]."[56] When Prince and his musicians performed the song at the Memorial Coliseum, in Los Angeles, on 9 October (see page 56), the reaction of The Rolling Stones' audience can only be imagined...

Recorded at the Hollywood Sound Recorders studios in August 1981, this song is the first recorded with his musicians, under live conditions, to have found its way onto one of the singer's albums. On an impulse, he invited Lisa Coleman, Doctor Fink, and Bobby Z. (relations between Dez Dickerson and Prince had worsened some time before, and the guitarist was not invited) to Los Angeles, and recorded the song during a night session lasting five hours. Ross Pallone, the recording engineer at the session, recalled: "Then when they left, Prince told me, 'I'm not going to use any of that. I just brought them out here to make you happy.'"[57] Eventually, and to his listeners' great pleasure, Prince kept this version to end his fourth album in the finest way possible, in the company of musicians who would soon go on to share his attainment of international renown.

The singer Robyn, a veritable star in Sweden thanks to her hits *Dancing On My Own* and *Call Your Girlfriend*, included a cover of *Jack U Off* as a bonus track on the UK reissue of her album *Robyn*, released in 2005.

Jack U Off is the first song in which Prince replaced the word "you" with the letter "U," a typographical signature that he would retain on all his records. He would soon adopt other signs to replace words, such as "B" for "be," "2" for "to," and "4" for "for."

No siesta for Prince, seen here playing while lying down onstage at the Paradiso, Amsterdam, on 29 May 1981.

FOR PRINCE ADDICTS

From 1982 to 1983, The Time were not content with only being a warm-up act for Prince on the 1999 Tour. The band's members also accompanied Vanity 6, the other warm-up act, hidden behind a curtain while the female singers performed their sexy set onstage.

THE TIME, AMBASSADORS OF THE MINNEAPOLIS SOUND

On 29 July 1981, The Time's first, eponymous album was released. The band from Minneapolis championed a brand of funk featuring irresistible synthetic sounds. Their single *Get It Up* was on every radio station, and even got to No.6 on the Billboard Hot Soul Singles chart a few months later. Produced by the singer Morris Day and one Jamie Starr, the record was a real success, flying the flag of the Minneapolis Sound, which was also championed by one... Prince. Even though the artist tried to hide the fact, fans of The Time quickly discovered that Jamie Starr was none other than Prince himself, hiding behind a pseudonym so as not to overshadow his protégés. "Let me clear up a few rumors while I have the chance. One, my name is Prince, it's not something I made up [...] Two, I'm not gay. And three, I'm not Jaime [sic] Starr."[58] The deception lasted only a short time, since the artist was quickly unmasked and would go on to win praise for multiple recordings he made in subsequent years.

The Time is born

It was by letting Prince have the song *Partyup*—of which he had just made a preliminary recording and played to the artist while he was working on *Dirty Mind*—that Morris Day hit the jackpot. Turning down the substantial sum of $10,000 offered by Prince, he opted instead for the promise of a helping hand with developing his future musical projects. With his return to the Dirty Mind Tour in April 1981, Prince embarked on recording the band's first album, which he wanted to make for his friend, the former drummer with Grand Central. Morris Day was with Prince during the recording at Kiowa Trail, and when the artist passed the songs to Warner Bros. Records, the delighted team signed up the project—even though the band did not yet exist. Two weeks before the record's release, the two associates recruited some former members of Flyte Time, a legendary band from the Twin Cities scene. Alexander O'Neal was to be on vocals, Terry Lewis on bass guitar, and James "Jimmy Jam" Harris on keyboards. Jesse Johnson, the guitarist of Enterprise (Day's band at the time), would be on guitar, with Morris on drums. Following the withdrawal of O'Neal, who had asked for too much money, Morris Day became, to his great surprise, The Time's vocalist.

Purple Rain and international recognition

Two albums (mostly written by Prince) and several hit singles later, The Time achieved international renown in 1984, thanks to their appearances in *Purple Rain*, which highlighted the rivalry between the Kid and the band. This rivalry was inspired by the war between the Mods and Rockers in *Quadrophenia*, the movie by Franc Roddam, which was released in 1979. Jerome Benton rejoined the team as an assistant to Morris Day, as did the keyboard players St Paul Peterson and Mark Cardenas. Despite the success of *Ice Cream Castle*, his band's third album, which featured the hits *Jungle Love* and *The Bird*, Morris Day left in 1985. "I did a lot with the early records [...] but I wanted to produce my own record. And write for myself."[59] When Prince refused to allow him to spread his wings, Morris Day quit, and recorded *Color of Success*, which did quite well in the US, reaching No.37 in the Billboard 200 chart on its release.

Swansong

The Time got back together onstage at the Roy Wilkins Auditorium, in Saint Paul, on 2 October 1987 for the Minnesota Black Musician Awards, and a fourth album was begun by Prince immediately afterward. Johnson, Lewis, and Jam were determined to get back to the band and to make a record; the unreleased album *Corporate World* was transformed into *Pandemonium*. Its release on 10 April 1990 was a resounding success, largely thanks to the single *Jerk Out*. As Morris Day explained: "I did this project so I could

Terry Lewis, Morris Day, and Jesse Johnson of The Time, performing onstage at the Palladium, New York, on 12 December 1981.

work with my buddies again [...] Everybody had a feeling that the band ended prematurely, that there were still some good years left in the band."[60]

The Time accompanied the singer Rihanna onstage in a classic performance of *Jungle Love* on the 50th anniversary of the Grammy Awards, on 10 February 2008, and the original lineup of the band released their fifth album, *Condensate*, under the name The Original 7ven in October 2011—Prince had control of the name The Time and refused to be involved in the band's reunion. Morris Day would publish his autobiography in 2019; the book was built around a fictitious conversation with the Kid of Minneapolis, his eternal friend.

Taking advantage of a break after a concert in New York, on 21 March 1983, Terry Lewis and Jimmy Jam went to MasterSound Studios in Atlanta, Georgia, to be producers, in the utmost secrecy, for the SOS Band. A snowstorm at Atlanta airport grounded the two of them, and they missed the concert on 24 March in San Antonio, Texas, where Prince played bass guitar offstage and Jerome Benton mimed onstage. A photograph of the sessions in Atlanta, published in the April issue of *Cash Box Magazine*, sealed their fate: Prince, having forbidden his musicians to be involved in any project other than The Time, expelled them from the band...

PRINCE

1999

1999 · Little Red Corvette · Delirious · Let's Pretend We're Married · D.M.S.R.
Automatic · Something In the Water (Does Not Compute) · Free · Lady Cab Driver
All The Critics Love U In New York · International Lover

Released in the USA by Warner Bros. Records:
27 October 1982 (LP ref.: 1-23720)
Released in the UK by WEA Records:
7 March 1983 (LP ref.: 92-3720-1)
Best chart ranking in the USA: 9
Best chart ranking in the UK: 28

Prince performing *1999* on the set of *Solid Gold* on 29 January 1983.

THE CONQUEST OF MTV

1982

The Controversy Tour launched on 14 March 1982 at the Riverfront Coliseum in Cincinnati, Ohio. As soon as Prince returned to Minneapolis, he set out to form The Hookers, the all-female band he'd been wanting to put together for more than a year. He immediately pulled out the songs he'd previously recorded for this project (*Wet Dreams, Drive Me Wild*, and *Make-Up*), then he recorded *Nasty Girl, Bite the Beat, He's So Dull*, and the formidable *If A Girl Answers (Don't Hang Up)*. The young Denise Katrina Matthews, nicknamed "Vanity" for the occasion, joined the project alongside Brenda Bennett and Susan Moonsie, thus completing the trio. The band, now named Vanity 6, released its eponymous album on 11 August 1982. While he was busy making this new ambition a reality, Prince launched into his new masterpiece, which he produced between his home studio at Kiowa Trail, in Chanhassen, Minnesota, and Sunset Sound studios in Los Angeles. He'd found a talented and trusted partner there: recording engineer Peggy McCreary, with whom he'd already worked on the *Controversy* album. Prince was never as prolific as he was in 1982. He was insatiable, constantly recording, and pulled no punches with Peggy McCreary. During those long and tiring recording sessions, Peggy never knew whether she was working on the second album by The Time, on Vanity 6's album, or on Prince's future record! By now, the Linn LM-1 Drum Computer had become ubiquitous and was the ideal device for Prince's needs. He no longer needed to relay information to a drummer, thereby saving time during sessions, or hold the drumsticks himself. Whether he was working at Kiowa Trail or Sunset Sound, Prince never let up: songs had to be finished in a single day, so he could quickly move on to the next idea.

As mainstream as possible

Of the many songs recorded during this time, only 11 made it onto *1999*. Of those, the singles *1999* and *Little Red Corvette* were particularly well suited to radio. They gave Prince a massive amount of airtime a few months later. "I think he was trying to become as mainstream as possible, without violating his own philosophy, without having to compromise any of his ideas," Matt Fink later said. "To some extent, he was trying to make the music sound nice, something that would be pleasing to the ear of the average person who listens to the radio."[62] Once the record was completed in August 1982, Prince demanded it be released as a double album. As he once said: "I didn't want to do a double album, but I just kept writing and I'm not one for editing."[58] Warner Bros. Records was somewhat resistant to this idea because the higher selling price would risk discouraging a young audience of meager means, but they eventually agreed. The record label could hear the album's potential on listening to the test pressing. While no one would dare say that Prince had calmed down at this point, it can, however, be noted that the themes he tackled had become more varied than in the past. Sex still occupied a prominent place in the lyrics (in *Lady Cab Driver* and *Automatic*, for example), but the women in them were often powerful, even dominant, like the singers of Vanity 6. Prince wouldn't have dreamed of treating them like objects, despite their revealing outfits.

The start of a revolution

When *1999* was released on 27 October 1982, it was an instant hit, thanks in part to the single of the same name that had come out a few weeks before. The design for the cover was

FOR PRINCE ADDICTS

It was thanks to Peggy McCreary that Prince started using a new method for recording his voice. Exhausted from the interminable sessions for *1999*, McCreary suggested Prince do his vocal takes alone in the control room, behind the console. This allowed him to arrange the inputs himself, a very delicate operation for McCreary after 11 hours of nonstop work. From then on, Prince never allowed anyone else in the studio while he was recording his voice.

1982

created from typography created by Prince himself. The type contained a strange message written in reverse in the "i" of Prince: "and the Revolution." Without much ado, the artist had introduced his future band to his fans, even if this was in a rather roundabout way. This band accompanied him until 1986. For the inner sleeve, Prince abandoned briefs and other provocative outfits in favor of a look inspired by the New Romantic movement, as epitomized by bands such as Duran Duran and Spandau Ballet. He first started using this style in 1982, and it came to represent his "Purple Rain" period. Purple dominated this album, as well as the façades of his house on Kiowa Trail, and it soon became an inherent part of Prince's visual universe. Thanks to the music channel MTV and its constant stream of music videos, the singles *1999*, *Little Red Corvette*, and *Delirious* brought the *1999* album to the top of the charts.

The "1999 Tour"

Due to the success of the album, the 1999 Tour, which started on 11 November 1982 in Chattanooga, Tennessee, paused in early January, then resumed from February to April 1983. During this time, a new recruit appeared onstage: Jill Jones, a young backing vocalist who had accompanied Teena Marie on the Dirty Mind Tour, where she opened for Prince. Jones, who did some vocals for *1999*, also appears in platinum blonde in the music video. Throughout the tour, Vanity 6 and The Time opened to an increasingly eclectic audience, to Prince's delight. The colossal success of *Little Red Corvette*, which reached No.6 in the Billboard Hot 100 chart on 21 May 1983, was helping him to achieve his aims. "The 1999 Tour audience was 90 percent black until *Little Red Corvette* came out," noted Monte Moir, the keyboardist for The Time. "All of a sudden it shifted drastically. It got to be half and half, if not 60-40 white. By the end of the tour, depending on what city, you could see that real cross-over was possible."[2] Aside from growing disagreements between The Time and Prince, and within Vanity 6, the tour was a success. It made more than $10m in revenue. When it ended at the UIC-Pavilion, in Chicago, on 10 April 1983, Prince had the United States at his feet. He was insatiable. Then he got back to work and started producing what would become the greatest record of the 1980s.

When Allen Beaulieu photographed Prince lying naked on a bed for one of the inner sleeves of *1999*, he set up the background according to the wishes of his client. Prince had asked him to take inspiration from Ridley Scott's movie *Blade Runner* (1982). "He said it was a lot of neon and a lot of smoke, so that's what I did. And he was running around naked in my little studio."[34]

When *1999* came out in March 1983 in the UK, Warner released it as a single album. *D.M.S.R.*, *Automatic*, *All The Critics Love U In New York*, and *International Lover* were left out. The wrong was righted on 9 November 1984, when the complete version of the album was released overseas.

Brown Mark, Prince, and Dez Dickerson onstage at the UIC Pavilion, Chicago, on 10 April 1983.

VANITY, PRINCE'S FIRST MUSE

On 25 January 1982, Prince attended the ninth American Music Awards at the Shrine Auditorium, in Los Angeles, where he met a 23-year-old Canadian actress named Denise Katrina Matthews. She wanted to get into music, but hadn't been able to persuade the prestigious William Morris Agency that she was talented enough as a vocalist. Her consolation prize had been two tickets for the music awards. When Prince made eye contact with Matthews backstage, it was love at first sight. He immediately tried to seduce her: "We tried on each other's jackets and realized that we fit each other's clothes," said Matthews. "I thought that was wonderful."[67] The first contact had been established. Their romantic relationship lasted for almost two years.

From The Hookers to Vanity 6

In addition to his emotional attachment, Prince had high professional ambitions for Denise Matthews. He decided to revive The Hookers, an all-female band he'd discarded in favor of The Time (see page 64) in 1981. Initially, the trio had been made up of Susan Moonsie, Prince's girlfriend at the time, Jamie Shoop, his personal assistant, and Brenda Bennett, wife of LeRoy Bennett, Prince's lighting and stage designer. Bennett had replaced Loreen, Susan's sister, who'd initially been slated to join the group. She'd also worked on video captions and costume design for the Dirty Mind Tour, and was the only real singer in the group. Jamie Shoop then stepped aside in favor of Denise Matthews, whom Prince nicknamed "Vagina," before changing it to a more sober "Vanity." Matthews once said, "You'll have to ask Prince, why Vanity?" before adding: "But I think the main reason is 'cause when he looks in the mirror, he sees me."[68] Once the group was formed, Prince named it Vanity 6, after its lead singer. According to some, the "6" referred to the breasts of the three members of the group.

A fleeting yet important adventure

Recorded between March and April 1982 (and adding to sessions for The Hookers from 1981), Vanity 6's first album (of the same name) came out on 11 August 1982. The album promotion was spearheaded by Richard Avedon's legendary photo showing Vanity sliding her hand under Prince's waistband on the cover of *Rolling Stone* magazine on 28 April 1983. But while the album met with critical success, the singles *He's So Dull* and *Nasty Girl* did not receive much airtime because of their rather licentious lyrics. Vanity 6 joined Prince on the Controversy Tour, where the musicians from The Time accompanied them each night, playing behind the scenes. But tensions in the group soon came to a head. Vanity could barely tolerate Prince's ambiguous relationship with Susan Moonsie and was even less thrilled that he'd given the leading role to Brenda Bennett, the only true artist in the band. In the spring of 1983, Prince began writing the trio's second album while also preparing for the movie *Purple Rain*. The three young women played an important role in the movie, but then Vanity quit the band,

Denise Matthews, aka Vanity, in 1983.

Richard Avedon shot the image for the iconic cover of *Rolling Stone* magazine's April 1983 issue.

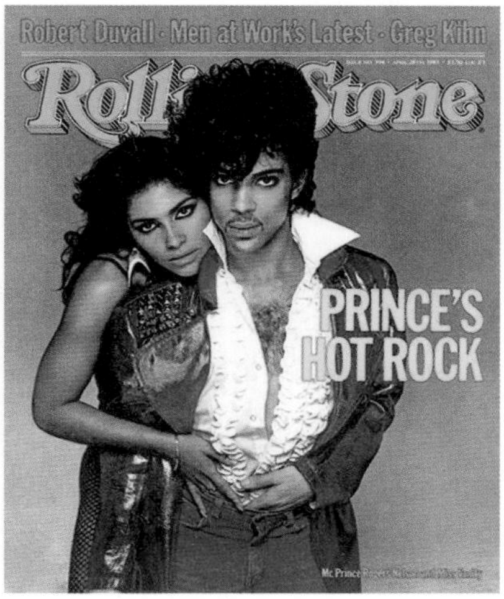

dead set on pursuing a solo career. Patricia "Apollonia" Kotero replaced her in the movie, so, of course, the band was renamed Apollonia 6 (see page 91).

Denise Matthews reborn

Vanity signed with Berry Gordy's prestigious label Motown and released two albums with them: *Wild Animal* (1984) and *Skin On Skin* (1986). Her two singles, *Pretty Mess* and *Under the Influence*, only met with mild success, so she slid into despair. Her life as a rock star was in ruins. In 1987, she got engaged to Nikki Sixx, the scandalous bassist for Mötley Crüe, and together they indulged their addictions to crack and cocaine. In 1994, Matthews came close to dying of kidney failure after an overdose. After three months of hospitalization, Vanity took back her birth name and converted to Christianity, a process she'd started two years before. "Vanity had to die so that I, Denise, could finally live on,"[68] she wrote in her autobiography in 1999. Denise Matthews became a born-again Evangelical and used her platform to spread a message of inner peace based on her experience. She died on 15 February 2016 at the hospital in Fremont, California, following the kidney failure she'd been battling for more than 20 years. Queen of the Prince universe, Denise "Vanity" Matthews will always hold a major role in Prince's history, and a special place in the hearts of her fans. On 16 February 2016, at his first concert for the Piano & A Microphone Tour, in Melbourne, Australia, Prince paid tribute to her onstage with a poignant interpretation of *Little Red Corvette*.

Susan Moonsie, Vanity, and Brenda Bennett, the three stars of Vanity 6.

IF A GIRL ANSWERS (DON'T HANG UP)

Vanity 6, Terry Lewis / 5'34

Musicians
Vanity: vocals, spoken word, backing vocals
Brenda Bennett: vocals, spoken word, backing vocals
Prince: spoken word, electric guitar, drums, percussion, claps, synthesizers
Terry Lewis: bass

Recording
Kiowa Trail Home Studio, Chanhassen, Minnesota: March to April 1982

Technical team
Producer: Prince (credited to "The Starr ★ Company and Vanity 6")
Recording engineer: Don Batts

Vanity 6 *Vanity 6* (album)
Released in the USA by Warner Bros. Records: 11 August 1982 (LP ref.: 9 23716-1)
Released in the UK by WEA International: 11 August 1982 (LP ref.: K 57 023)
Best chart ranking in the USA: 45
Best chart ranking in the UK: did not make the charts

Genesis

With few exceptions, Prince was the captain of the ship when it came to the trio's only album, since the songs credited to Vanity 6 (see page 72) were written by him. Dez Dickerson composed *He's So Dull*, while *Bite the Beat* was written in collaboration with Jesse Johnson, the guitarist from The Time. Terry Lewis, a virtuoso bass player, future producer, and another member of Morris Day's band, also contributed. Prince and Lewis worked together in the spring of 1982 on what turned out to be the album's most interesting piece: *If A Girl Answers (Don't Hang Up)*. It features an argument over the phone between Vanity and her rival, her boyfriend Jimmy's mistress. The song unfolds through a tense dialogue, which Vanity delivers flawlessly, beautifully setting her words to funky instrumentals. Jamie Starr—meaning Prince—of course plays the mistress, with a disarming humor that he had never shown before. (Jamie Star was the pseudonym used by Prince to produce other artists without giving away his identity.) Using his "Jamie Starr Voice," Prince surprises, again and again. He gave identical performances in *The Walk, Chili Sauce, Tricky*, and *Chocolate* by The Time. Jamie Starr also plays the role of an hilarious salesman in *Vibrator*—a song by Vanity 6 that never came out—in which Vanity goes to buy batteries for her vibrator and gets bullied by the grumpy shopkeeper.

Production

The song reveals Vanity's dexterity in delivering lyrics, even though her vocal abilities were very limited, at least according to photographer Allen Beaulieu. "Vanity was hard because she couldn't sing. I remember being there for a couple of her recording sessions, and Prince would get so mad at her: 'I gotta do one line at a time with her. It's push in, push out every song,' he'd yell."[34] It didn't much matter that Vanity didn't have the same talent as her producer. Prince made possible the impossible and gave life to this major song, in which Brenda Bennett doles out precious advice to her friend: "If a girl answers, hang up!"

Jesse Johnson, guitarist with The Time, was never far away when Prince was recording in his Kiowa Trail home studio.

Despite its bright colors, the photograph on the *1999* single was taken in black-and-white. Allen Beaulieu took it while shooting the video for *Little Red Corvette*. He then colorized the shot by hand. Prince loved the image and used it on several promotional materials.

Single

1999

Prince / 6'22

Musicians

Prince: vocals, electric guitar, bass, drums, synthesizers, programming, claps, electronic percussion, backing vocals
Bobby Z.: electronic percussion
Lisa Coleman: vocals, backing vocals
Jill Jones: vocals, backing vocals
Dez Dickerson: vocals, backing vocals
Jesse Johnson: backing vocals

Recording

Kiowa Trail Home Studio, Chanhassen, Minnesota: July 1982

Technical team

Producer: Prince
Recording engineer: Don Batts
Mixing: Peggy McCreary, David Leonard

1982

SINGLE

A-side: *1999* (Edit)/3'35
B-side: *How Come U Don't Call Me Anymore*/3'54
Released in the USA by Warner Bros. Records: 24 September 1982 (single ref.: 7-29896)
Released in the UK by WEA International: 7 January 1983 (single ref.: W 9896)
Best chart ranking in the USA: 12
Best chart ranking in the UK: 25

HEADPHONES AT THE READY

One of the most striking sounds in *1999* is the clapping, which Prince used throughout his career, and this can be heard from 0'35 into the album's title song. To produce this atypical sound, Prince used one of the snare buttons on a Linn LM-1 Drum Computer to simulate the noise created by beating the edge of a snare drum. He then lowered the tone of the sound and put it through several Boss guitar pedals, including the Distortion DS-1, which came out in 1978.

Genesis

In February 1982, as the Controversy Tour reached the southern United States, Prince and his musicians stayed in a hotel that offered free access to American TV network HBO. While Prince was in his room, his musicians took advantage of the offer and watched a documentary on Nostradamus called *The Man Who Saw Tomorrow* (1981), directed by Robert Guenette and narrated by Orson Welles. It is essentially based on Nostradamus' visions of the end of the world following a nuclear explosion, which he predicted for the year 1999. The next morning, everyone on the tour bus was talking about it, and when the musicians joined Prince for the sound check, he simply showed them the draft lyrics for *1999*. "Overnight, he turned this film into a song," Bobby Z. recalled. "He'd mixed this history of Nostradamus with a party theme, the end of the world with a massive party!"[63]

Production

In the summer of 1982, while his band was rehearsing, Prince worked on the last song for this album. One night, he played *1999* for his musicians, and together they fine-tuned the song in his studio at Kiowa Trail. Jesse Johnson, the guitarist for The Time, was also there. For the occasion, he lent Prince his Vox V846 Wah-Wah pedal, which features heavily throughout the song. Toward three in the morning, Prince woke up Jill Jones, who'd been staying with him since the end of the Dirty Mind Tour, and asked her to add her voice to the song. Dez Dickerson and Lisa Coleman were already in the studio, so the session could start. Dickerson was the first to record his voice for the entire song, followed by the two young women, and then they all sang the whole thing again in unison, at the same mic. The initial idea of keeping all the voices together was quickly abandoned, and Prince divided up the takes to highlight each of them in various parts of the song. The female voice in the first verse is a mix of Jones and Coleman. Prince, who'd recorded the introduction in high-pitched tones, asked Dez Dickerson to record *1999* using the same method to change the pitch and used his voice for the rest of the song. As usual, Prince recorded the whole song in one day.

Dez Dickerson achieved enduring fame thanks to his legendary solo on *Little Red Corvette.*

Single

LITTLE RED CORVETTE

Prince / 4'58

Musicians

Prince: vocals, electric guitar, bass, synthesizers, programming, backing vocals
Dez Dickerson: electric guitar, backing vocals
Lisa Coleman: backing vocals

Recording

Kiowa Trail Home Studio, Chanhassen, Minnesota: 20 May 1982

Technical team

Producer: Prince
Recording engineer: Don Batts
Mixing: Peggy McCreary, David Leonard

SINGLE

A-side: *Little Red Corvette*/3'08
B-side: *All The Critics Love U In New York*/3'15 (USA); *Lady Cab Driver*/5'05 (UK)
Released in the USA by Warner Bros. Records: 9 February 1983 (single ref.: 7-29746)
Released in the UK by WEA International: 4 April 1983 (single ref.: W 9688)
Best chart ranking in the USA: 6
Best chart ranking in the UK: 54

1982

On 8 February 1983, while she was putting the final touches to her song *Stand Back* in Los Angeles, which she said was inspired by *Little Red Corvette*, Stevie Nicks asked Prince for a few piano overdubs. He quickly agreed and recorded his part in less than 30 minutes. Nicks credited Prince in the song, which climbed to No.5 in the US charts.

Genesis

In early May 1982, Prince decided to invest in a brand new 24-track tape recorder for his studio at Kiowa Trail. Don Batts installed the machine and the many cables it needed to function. On 19 May, the renovation was finished, and the very next day, at 6am, Prince played his technicians and recording engineer the song he'd just finished on his new equipment: *Little Red Corvette*. It appears that Jamie Schoop, Prince's assistant, was one of the song's influences, as according to Don Batts, she owned this Chevrolet race car at the time. But Prince had actually written the lyrics while he and Vanity were sitting in the backseat of keyboardist Lisa Coleman's Ford Mercury Montclair 1964. "Prince was always borrowing my car because it was awesome," said the keyboardist. "He actually put a couple of dents in it, because it was so big."[64] The second single from *1999*, *Little Red Corvette*, allowed Prince to reach a wider audience, so he was no longer only associated with soul or funk music, but was also regarded as a real pop artist. When the video started airing widely on MTV, starting in February 1983, he found the fame he'd been searching for.

Production

The song was finished in record time (just like *1999*). It is one of the few songs not recorded by Peggy McCreary, although she did take care of the editing and mixing alongside her future husband, recording engineer David Leonard, another Sunset Sound employee. Dez Dickerson, the guitarist, was able to make his mark on the song by playing a powerful and melodic six-chord solo, in addition to some well-chosen backing vocals. "I must have played four or five different takes in a row, then we listened to them before cutting them into one," explained the guitarist. "So the solo you hear wasn't all played at once, it's an assembly of multiple musical phrases that I later had to relearn from A to Z to play it on stage."[65]

Quiffs, sinister looks, and leather boots…the Stray Cats' rockabilly style was all the rage in the early 1980s.

1982

Single

DELIRIOUS

Prince / 3'56

Musicians: **Prince:** vocals, electric guitar, bass, synthesizers, programming, backing vocals / **Lisa Coleman:** backing vocals / **Recording:** **Sunset Sound, Los Angeles:** 9 May 1982 / **Technical team:** **Producer:** Prince / **Recording engineers:** Peggy McCreary, David Leonard (mixing)
Single: A-side: *Delirious* (Edit)/2'36 / **B-side:** *Horny Toad*/2'13 / **Released in the USA by Warner Bros. Records:** 17 August 1983 (single ref.: 7-29503) / **Best chart ranking in the USA:** 8

Delirious was the third single from the album and Prince's third hit. Its rockabilly influences are similar to those found in *Jack U Off*, on the *Controversy* album. The style had been on the rise since the success of *Grease* (1978), Randall Kleiser's movie, and *Crazy Little Thing Called Love*, Queen's 1979 hit, which also paid tribute to the heyday of rock 'n' roll. But Prince and his musicians didn't have a real revelation until they arrived in London. On 30 May 1981, after a concert in Amsterdam the night before, Prince arrived in the English capital for a performance on 2 June. He and his musicians went to the Rainbow Theatre, where the Stray Cats were playing with the Lightning Raiders. Dez Dickerson told journalist Christophe Geudin how important that night was for Prince's writing. As he explained: "We knew they [the Stray Cats] were American, but we never listened to their music and we didn't know what to expect. The lights went out and these guys went onstage with their striped costumes and their incredible Pompadour-style haircuts. They hadn't played a single note yet but we were completely stunned! This evening marked Prince a lot and a few weeks after this concert, we started to wear the same kind of clothes and to adopt the same haircuts."[65]

HEADPHONES AT THE READY

The baby chirps at the very end of *Delirious* came from Sunset Sound's sound library, as did the heartbeats and footsteps in the introduction to *Free*.

There is no doubt that Prince was honored when his song was covered by the soul diva Tina Turner!

Single

LET'S PRETEND WE'RE MARRIED

Prince / 7'20

Musician: **Prince:** vocals, bass, synthesizers, programming, backing vocals / **Recording:** **Sunset Sound, Los Angeles:** 30 March 1982 / **Technical team:** **Producer:** Prince / **Recording engineers:** Peggy McCreary, David Leonard (mixing)
Single: **A-side:** *Let's Pretend We're Married*/3'40 / **B-side:** *Irresistible Bitch*/4'11 / **Released in the USA by Warner Bros. Records:** 23 November 1983 (single ref.: 7-29548) / **Best chart ranking in the USA:** 52

Those who say that Prince is modest had better behave! The singer returned to his old ways in the first verse of the last single to be released from the *1999* album, in which he catcalls his love interest, saying: "Excuse me but I need a mouth like yours/To help me forget the girl that just walked out my door." As Prince once explained: "Sex is something we can all understand. It's limitless. But I try to make the songs so they can be viewed in different ways."[58] Tina Turner's single *I Can't Stand the Rain*, released in March 1985, contained her version of the song on the B-side. It was recorded on 2 August 1984 in Chicago during her 1984 World Tour. Turner started each concert with this Prince cover.

The queen of aerobics and actress Jayne Kennedy made a fortune thanks to her exercise video *Love Your Body*, which was full of funk and disco hits.

In 1983, the queen of aerobics, Jayne Kennedy, included *D.M.S.R* in her home exercise video *Love Your Body*. In these sessions, her students got to perform all sorts of active moves to one of the grooviest beats around!

1982

D.M.S.R.

Prince / 8'15

Musicians: Prince: vocals, electric guitar, bass, synthesizers, programming, electronic percussion, claps, backing vocals / **Bobby Z.:** electronic percussion, cymbals / **Lisa Coleman:** claps, backing vocals / **Dez Dickerson:** claps, backing vocals / **Jamie Shoop:** claps, backing vocals / **Peggy McCreary:** claps, backing vocals / **Brown Mark:** claps, backing vocals / **Carol McGovney:** claps, backing vocals / **Poochie:** claps, backing vocals / **The Count:** claps, backing vocals / **Recording: Sunset Sound, Los Angeles:** 20 April 1982 / **Technical team: Producer:** Prince / **Recording engineers:** Peggy McCreary, David Leonard (mixing)

All fans know these four initials, which of course stand for "Dance, Music, Sex, and Romance," the four pillars of Prince's existence, which here takes the form of a relentless groove. The keyboards are biting and provide a backdrop to one of Prince's funkiest songs. "So to me the LinnDrum and the polyrhythm thing, along with the Oberheim—the OB8—the horns being simulated by a synth—that was the Minneapolis sound."[66] To embellish the song, which Prince considered an ode to the joy of living and sexual freedom, he asked his colleagues and friends to come to Sunset Sound studios and clap their hands and sing backing vocals with him in the choruses. As Peggy McCreary said: "We were all out there singing and he was giving us crap, jokingly saying that 'you white people ain't got no rhythm,' which I thought was funny because he had a white drummer."[2] Despite a notable appearance in Paul Brickman's movie *Risky Business* (1983), the song never came out as a single, but has nevertheless remained a favorite of fans.

HEADPHONES AT THE READY

Prince was determined to feed the rumor that he and Jamie Starr were two different people. He went so far as to insult his alter ego on *D.S.M.R.* at 6'33, exclaiming "Jamie Starr's a thief!" Jamie Starr was the one credited with producing the albums of Vanity 6 and The Time. The truth came out soon after.

"Real Drums At Your Fingertips" ran the slogan for the revolutionary Linn LM-1 Drum Computer drum machine when it was launched on the market in 1980.

AUTOMATIC

Prince / 9'27

Musicians: Prince: vocals, electric guitar, bass, synthesizers, programming, backing vocals / **Lisa Coleman:** backing vocals / **Jill Jones:** claps, backing vocals / **Recording: Sunset Sound, Los Angeles:** 2 May 1982 / **Technical team: Producer:** Prince / **Recording engineers:** Peggy McCreary, David Leonard (mixing)

With *Automatic*, a new alter ego was beginning to take shape in Prince's mind, although it didn't yet officially exist. Prince first used his female avatar, Camille (see page 142), in 1986, with *Shockadelica*, which came out as the B-side of *If I Was Your Girlfriend* in 1987—even though Camille had already appeared alongside Sheila E. in *Erotic City* in 1984, without being named. Nevertheless, this synthetic voice with its particularly high pitch, which Prince created by speeding up the track recorded at Sunset Sound, seems to have first appeared in 1982. You have to really listen to catch it, but Camille was essentially born at 4'37 into *Automatic*.

SOMETHING IN THE WATER (DOES NOT COMPUTE)

Prince / 4'00

Musician: Prince: vocals, synthesizers, programming, backing vocals / **Recording: Kiowa Trail Home Studio, Chanhassen, Minnesota:** April 1982 / **Technical team: Producer:** Prince / **Recording engineer:** Don Batts / **Mixing:** Peggy McCreary, David Leonard

Something In the Water (Does Not Compute) is played at a high speed, thanks to a modified Linn LM-1 Drum Computer pattern, slowed down, then reused in *I Would Die 4 U* in 1984. Here, Prince is suffering from unrequited love. He goes weak at the knees in front of the object of his desire, but she is indifferent to his charms. Prince compares human interactions to computer connections, which here he considers to be faulty. To make his point, he slips in some robotic sounds like the ones emitted by the droid R2-D2. Sound designer Ben Burtt had created these sounds for the movie *Star Wars* in 1977 using an ARP 2600 synthesizer.

FREE

Prince / 5'08

Musicians: Prince: vocals, electric guitar, bass, synthesizers, programming, piano, backing vocals / **Lisa Coleman:** vocals / **Jill Jones:** vocals / **Vanity:** vocals / **Wendy Melvoin:** vocals / **Recording: Sunset Sound, Los Angeles:** 25 April 1982 / **Technical team: Producer:** Prince / **Recording engineers:** Peggy McCreary, David Leonard (mixing)

Recorded with a Steinway piano in Studio 2 at Sunset Sound, *Free* was Prince's first pop ballad. Songs such as *Baby*, *Gotta Broken Heart Again*, and *Do Me, Baby*, on the other hand, followed the codes of soul music. "He was so amazing on any instrument he picked up, but the piano was something that was very pleasing," recalled Peggy McCreary. "And he loved my piano sound."[142] The song is flawless and forceful, supported by exceptional choruses. It's a precursor to melodic and melancholic songs like *Electric Intercourse* and *The Ladder*. Prince decidedly enters the category of languorous slows here—thousands of American teenagers danced to it in 1982—and by 1984, he was extending this style to the international stage with the hit of a generation: *Purple Rain*. Talented backing vocalists participated in the song: Lisa Coleman, Vanity, Jill Jones, and a new recruit, Wendy Melvoin, Coleman's girlfriend, who soon became one of Prince's most iconic guitarists. *Free* went largely unnoticed at the time, but it nevertheless deserves a place among Prince's most beautiful songs.

LADY CAB DRIVER

Prince / 8'25

Musicians: Prince: vocals, electric guitar, bass, drums, synthesizers, programming, backing vocals / **Jill Jones:** moans / **Recording: Sunset Sound, Los Angeles:** 7 July 1982 / **Technical team: Producer:** Prince / **Recording engineers:** Peggy McCreary, David Leonard (mixing)

There are so many funk ingredients scattered across *Lady Cab Driver* that one might think the song had been recorded for The Time. Jill Jones makes a remarkable appearance at 3'02, making all sorts of love moans. She is credited as the taxi driver on the album sleeve. One can speculate that Prince was using this song to fulfill a fantasy, imagining himself in pleasant company in the back of a cab.

ALL THE CRITICS LOVE U IN NEW YORK

Prince / 5'55

Musician: Prince: vocals, electric guitar, bass, synthesizers, programming, backing vocals / **Recording: Sunset Sound, Los Angeles:** 21 January 1982 / **Technical team: Producer:** Prince / **Recording engineers:** Peggy McCreary, David Leonard (mixing)

December 1980. While they were on the Dirty Mind Tour, Prince and his musicians became sure of one thing: the audience was mostly made up of soul and funk fans, who were members of the African-American community. Prince wanted to reach a wider audience and distance himself from the image of a soul singer, so he was trying to present himself as a rock singer. The two concerts he gave at The Ritz in New York (on 9 December 1980 and 22 March 1981) helped him reach this objective. New York City's rock press praised him, and from then on Prince enjoyed an unprecedented level of fame, which gradually anchored him to the world of American rock music. *All The Critics Love U In New York* is undeniably related to this key moment for Prince. It was the very first song he recorded with Peggy McCreary during the sessions for *1999* in January 1982 at Sunset Sound, during the break from the Controversy Tour.

INTERNATIONAL LOVER

Prince / 6'37

Musician: Prince: vocals, electric guitar, bass, drums, synthesizers, finger snapping, piano, backing vocals / **Recording: Sunset Sound, Los Angeles:** 14 January 1982 / **Technical team: Producer:** Prince / **Recording engineers:** Peggy McCreary, David Leonard (mixing)

International Lover was recorded in January 1982 for the second album of The Time, but in the end Prince decided to keep the song for his fifth album. He kept the song as it was, with the original voice narration recorded for Morris Day. At that time, while the Controversy Tour was on a break until the concert at the Richmond Coliseum, in Richmond, Virginia, on 28 January, Peggy McCreary was recording Prince at Sunset Sound, but she wouldn't have been able to tell you on which project she was working at any given time. "During that period he was also writing songs for Vanity 6 and he was writing songs for The Time. So we were doing those albums. I never knew what we were working on. I didn't know what was going on—the album that we were actually working on, until we assembled it."[142]

Prince dazzled by his microphone stand—which was soon to become an indispensable component of his stage act.

PRINCE AND THE REVOLUTION

PURPLE RAIN

Let's Go Crazy · Take Me With U · The Beautiful Ones · Computer Blue · Darling Nikki
When Doves Cry · I Would Die 4 U · Baby I'm A Star · Purple Rain

Released in the USA by Warner Bros. Records:
25 June 1984 (LP ref.: 1-25110; CD ref.: 9 25110-2)
Released in the UK by Warner Bros. Records:
13 July 1984 (LP ref.: 925 110-1; CD ref.: 9 25110-2)
Best chart ranking in the USA: 1
Best chart ranking in the UK: 7

Entertaining and sensual...
Prince onstage at the Joe
Louis Arena in Detroit on
11 November 1984.

On the subject of the shoes Prince wore during the Purple Rain Tour, he provocatively declared with a smile: "People say I'm wearing heels because I'm short. I wear heels because the women like 'em."[27]

1984

THE PURPLE RAIN WAVE COMES CRASHING IN

In 1982, Prince released *1999*, one of the most audacious albums of the early 1980s. He was on a roll that year, also masterminding the release of *What Time Is It?*, the second opus by The Time (see page 64)—who had already had a huge hit with the single *Cool* the previous year—then the first album by Vanity 6, a trio led by the feline Vanity (see page 72). In November 1982, Prince was on the road promoting *1999* across the United States, while at the same time writing down endless ideas every day in a closely guarded purple notebook. It contained all the elements of his new mammoth project: namely, to produce a full-length, partly autobiographical movie in which all the artists in the princely universe would participate, including the singer himself in the lead role. Although his managers, Bob Cavallo, Joe Ruffalo, and Steve Fargnoli, were initially reluctant when he presented the project to them, they ended up yielding to their young protégé's demands. Prince's contract with them was coming to an end, so they were practically compelled to help him to achieve his goal if they wanted to keep him in their stable. The trio started looking for a studio to finance the movie, the only selling point of which at the time was Prince himself, as no script had yet been written. After a series of rejections from the major Hollywood studios, Mo Ostin, Prince's loyal supporter at Warner Bros., decided to back the singer and his team in this crazy venture. In the spring of 1983, William Blinn, the executive producer of the *Fame* TV series, began writing an initial version of a script he called *Dreams*, which was based on Prince's notes, long discussions with the singer, and listening to songs for inspiration. "He wanted a picture that people would think of as 'weird' but couldn't get away from,"[2] Blinn said of his employer. Prince then asked his screenwriter to change the title of the movie to incorporate the word "Purple," a color he had been fond of for some time and used to paint his Kiowa Trail home. Albert Magnoli, a young filmmaker, fresh from collecting multiple awards for *Jazz* (1981), a short documentary about young musicians on the Los Angeles scene, was invited to join the venture as director. Production began in the summer of 1983 with a budget of $7 million dollars.

From Dreams to Purple Rain

Following the 1999 Tour, a number of changes were made to Prince's band. Guitarist Dez Dickerson left to pursue a solo career and was replaced by the 18-year-old novice Wendy Melvoin, Lisa Coleman's girlfriend. Her arrival marked the birth of The Revolution, Prince's most mythical backing band. Prince installed his musicians in premises known to fans as The Warehouse, in St Louis Park, close to Minneapolis. From May to December 1983, the members of The Revolution, The Time, and Vanity 6 rehearsed for their roles in the movie, in which they would be playing themselves. The script had been rewritten by Magnoli and given its definitive title: *Purple Rain*. Alan Leeds, tour manager for the 1999 Tour, was hired full-time to coordinate the work sessions at The Warehouse. The artists received acting lessons from the actor Don Amendolia, who later confided: "Jerome [Benton] was a hard worker. Morris [Day] wasn't as interested as some others, but he had natural abilities that others didn't have. Vanity was lazy. I think she didn't like to work hard. Prince was very, very good. He had the ability to be absolutely focused on what he was doing

The Kid, an emblematic character played by Prince in the movie *Purple Rain*.

"When he got the DX7 he used that thing to death,"[75] Susan Rogers said of the revolutionary Yamaha synthesizer Prince used during the *Purple Rain* sessions. Prince's recording engineer Shane T Keller bought the synthesizer from him in 1995, and it was auctioned on www.rrauction.com on 18 June 2020 and sold for the modest sum of $73,698.

with little trouble. He'd flip right out of his persona and be whatever character he had to be."[70] The Revolution rehearsed frantically, working through their leader's new songs to get everything right. As the band's bassist Brown Mark explained: "The more you rehearse, [...] the less you think about it, and then the more fun you have, and that was the key to The Revolution. We didn't think about it. He would throw up these cues, you know, and we knew every marker, we knew every cue, and we hit it [...] We danced, spin, split, jumping up risers..."[71] The musicians also took dance classes with John Command of the Minnesota Dance Theatre company to work on choreography and stage moves. At the same time, three costume designers were hired for the movie: Louis Wells, Vaughn Terry, and Marie France, a Frenchwoman. The three designers were asked to create a visual universe inspired by the New Romantics, Jimi Hendrix's stage outfits, and The Beatles in their *Sgt. Pepper's Lonely Hearts Club Band* period. Marie France gave Prince the idea of ruffles and lace, which she combined with pearls and colored, shiny fabrics. Prince would go on to adopt these ideas to create his new wardrobe.

The soundtrack of a generation

While preparing for his first movie, Prince was also busy recording his sixth album, which would be the soundtrack to *Purple Rain*. He had recently parted company with recording engineer Don Batts, who felt he had lost out financially, so in 1983 he hired a new engineer for his home studio: Susan Rogers. Her first assignment was to move Prince's studio from Kiowa Trail to St Louis Park, so the band could be recorded live playing the new songs for *Purple Rain*. Despite the appalling working conditions (interference, non-existent sound insulation, and so on), Rogers managed to lay down on tape the fabulous *Let's Go Crazy* and *Computer Blue* in these somewhat non-standard premises. "That's when I learned not to be afraid to try something just because it hasn't been done before. This was something that was unheard of in textbook engineering. You don't record a band live in a warehouse with no isolation between the musicians and the engineer. But I was learning the ways of Prince. Just hook it up and do it!"[70] In August 1983, Prince would continue production work on the album alongside Susan Rogers at Sunset Sound studios for five weeks, resulting in *Take Me With U*, *The Beautiful Ones*, and

After her departure from the group, Vanity was replaced by the no less talented Patricia Kotero, aka Apollonia (center). The female trio was then renamed Apollonia 6.

a host of tracks that remained unreleased until 2017, when the artist's estate released a valuable reissue of *Purple Rain*, complete with many rarities. These included *Possessed*, *Electric Intercourse*, and *We Can Fuck*. Prince returned to Sunset Sound in March 1984 for the final sessions, including the recording of *When Doves Cry*.

Birth of The Revolution

The group took on their iconic name when Wendy Melvoin joined, but one concert in particular marked the real emergence of The Revolution. On 3 August 1984, Prince and his troupe performed a benefit concert at First Avenue, in Minneapolis, in aid of the Minnesota Dance Theatre company, with whom the musicians had been working for several weeks. The concert raised over $20,000 for the dance theater company; it was also a warm-up for the upcoming tour and an opportunity for Wendy Melvoin to make her stage debut alongside her new colleagues. "I was 18 years old. I was scared to death but I loved it. It was my make or break evening. Prince's management were there to see if this new member was gonna work. All eyes were on the little girl just out of high school. But the extra pressure really made me go for it."[72] Even if every self-respecting fan deplores the fact that no official recording of the concert, which is considered one of Prince's most mythical, has yet been released, three of the songs played that night were used as backing tracks for *I Would Die 4 U*, *Baby I'm A Star*, and *Purple Rain*, and would feature on the album.

Apollonia Kotero makes her entry

In September 1983, pre-production for the *Purple Rain* movie got underway in Los Angeles. This was when Vanity decided to quit, slamming the door on her band Vanity 6 and relinquishing her role in the movie. The reason behind this decision may have been the end of her relationship with Prince, who appeared to flit from one woman to another, but she later claimed it was a choice she had to make at a decisive moment in her career when she was in the running for the role of Mary Magdalene in Martin Scorsese's *The Last Temptation of Christ* (1988). "If you're a very independent person, like I am, you don't base your career on what happens in your relationship with a man [...] As far as I'm concerned, your career is there for life; a man sometimes isn't."[73] Actress Patricia Kotero was selected from the seven

The guitar maker Dave Rusan proudly displays the first version of the legendary Cloud Guitar.

Prince sports lace and jewelry during the Purple Rain Tour in 1985.

FOR PRINCE ADDICTS

Prince and Dez Dickerson had separated on good terms at the end of the 1999 Tour and were back working together on the movie *Purple Rain*, in which Dickerson plays the leader of the group The Modernaires. The band appear in the movie at 25'10, performing the excellent song *(I Want 2 B A) Modernaire* onstage in First Avenue, in front of a crowd copying the band's choreographed dance routine. Alas, it wasn't until 8 September 2008 that the song was released as a single, in digital format.

hundred applicants to replace Vanity as the movie's female lead. Prince chose her stage name, Apollonia, and she quickly slotted into the team, partnering Prince to perfection. She also became the lead singer in the female trio—now, of course, renamed Apollonia 6.

The Cloud Guitar, a custom-built six-string

As preparation for the movie began, Prince contacted Jeff Hill, co-owner (with Karl Dedolph) of the Knut Koupee music store in Minneapolis. The singer wanted to have a guitar made to use in the movie. Hill referred him to the store's luthier, Dave Rusan, who immediately set about designing a prototype, based on a bass guitar designed by luthier Jeff Levin for Sardonyx Guitars in 1972. Rusan used an O'Hagan Shark guitar, which he resculpted, adding various pieces of wood. He made an identical copy of Levin's bass guitar and followed Prince's instructions: a guitar painted white with gold hardware. The Cloud Guitar soon emerged and became part of the movie's, and the artist's, visual imagery, as Prince subsequently used it for many years onstage and in the studio.

Purple Rain was shot from November to late December 1983 in Minneapolis, before the team relocated to Los Angeles the following January. The scenes shot in First Avenue are the most memorable, featuring six hundred extras on the set every day, none of whom could have known that they were attending a major event in rock history. At the same time, Prince, insatiable as ever, finished recording the Apollonia 6 album, The Time's third opus, made progress with his own record, and started planning production of the first LP by his new protégée: Sheila E.

The "Purple Rain Tour"

In summer 1984, Prince and The Revolution moved to the Flying Cloud Drive Warehouse, in Eden Prairie, Minnosota, a new location where they began rehearsing for the Purple Rain Tour, which was scheduled to begin in November. The singer inaugurated his production company, Paisley Park Records, with the debut album by Brown Mark's protégés Mazarati, and on 25 June, the album *Purple Rain* was released to the world. The album, which was preceded by the hugely successful single *When Doves Cry* (giving Prince his first No.1 hit on the Billboard chart), was an unprecedented triumph for the artist, selling over a million copies in a matter of days. The singles *Let's Go Crazy* and *Purple Rain* continued in the same vein and propelled Prince to the height of his fame. When the movie *Purple Rain* was released on 27 July 1984 and screened in over 900 theaters across America, it was also a hit despite its predictability. Prince and his managers followed it up with what was to become the singer's most epic concert tour. During the Purple Rain Tour, which ran from 4 November 1984 to 7 April 1985, the man now known as the Minneapolis Kid after his character in the movie performed 98 concerts in front of nearly two million people. It was a mythical tour performed exclusively in the United States, as Prince was already working on, and making good progress with, his next project, a more intimate album which was recorded during breaks between the months on the road. Exhausted by the pace of the Purple Rain Tour, Prince eschewed the idea of a European tour. "Purple Rain was a hundred shows, and around the seventy-fifth, I went crazy, and here's why. They didn't want to see anything but the movie. If you didn't play every song, you were in trouble. After seventy-five you don't know where you are

—somebody had to drag me to the stage."[74] Focused on his seventh album, Prince would go on to reinvent himself again in 1985, even if it meant destabilizing fans and critics around the world.

It was during the Purple Rain Tour that Prince introduced a way of communicating with his band that he would use for the rest of his life. Onstage, he informed his musicians of the number of hits they had to execute on the following bar. "'Hit me two times' is an easy instruction to follow," said Brown Mark. "But when he yells 'Hit me twenty-five times,' we have to do a percussive hit twenty-five times, and if we miss one, we are fined a hundred dollars."[76]

The virtuoso percussionist Sheila Escovedo was soon to become a member of Prince's inner circle.

SHORTBERRY STRAWCAKE

Jesse Johnson, Sheila E. / 4'44

Musicians: Prince: vocals, electric guitar, bass, drums, programming, synthesizers / **Sheila E.:** percussion / **Recording:** Sunset Sound, Los Angeles: 11 February, 1–4 April 1984 / **Technical team:** Producers: Sheila E., Prince (credited to Sheila E. and The Starr ★ Company) / **Recording engineer:** Prince (credited to The Starr ★ Company)
Sheila E. Sheila E. In The Glamorous Life (album) / Released in the USA by Warner Bros. Records: 4 June 1984 (LP ref.: 1-25107) / Released in the UK by WEA International: 4 June 1984 (LP ref.: 925 107-1) / Best chart ranking in the USA: 28 / Best chart ranking in the UK: did not make the charts

Prince and Sheila E. originally met in 1979 on one of the dates of the Prince Tour. She is the daughter of the percussionist Pete Escovedo who made a name for himself playing with Santana on *Moonflower* (1977) and *Inner Secrets* (1978). Sheila E. was already a renowned percussionist in her own right, having brilliantly accompanied George Duke, and she was about to join Marvin Gaye on his Midnight Love Tour. Prince took her under his wing, encouraging her to sing her own songs and taking her on the road with him as the opening act for the Purple Rain Tour. After persuading her to join him in recording *Erotic City*, which appears on the B-side of *Let's Go Crazy*, Prince produced his new protégée's first album, on which he sings (or rather mumbles) the track *Shortberry Strawcake*. The tune epitomizes the Minneapolis Sound, with Prince's blistering synthesizers replacing the horns of a very lively brass quartet. Although credited to Sheila E. and Jesse Johnson, *Shortberry Strawcake* was written by Prince himself, who was by now in the habit of being deliberately misleading in the sleeve notes of the albums he produced.

Morris Day and his majordomo Jerome (Benton), two key characters in the movie *Purple Rain*.

TRICKY

Morris Day / 3'12

Musicians: Prince: spoken voice, bass, synthesizers / **Morris Day:** spoken voice, drums / **Recording: Sunset Sound, Los Angeles:** 12 January 1984 / **Technical team: Producer:** Prince (credited to Morris Day, Jesse Johnson, and The Starr ★ Company) / **Recording engineer:** Prince / **Assistant recording engineer:** Bill Jackson / **The Time *Ice Cream Castles* (single)** / **Released in the USA by Warner Bros. Records:** 8 June 1984 (single ref.: 7-29247) / **Released in the UK by WEA International:** 8 June 1984 (single ref.: W 9247) / **Best chart ranking in the USA:** did not make the charts / **Best chart ranking in the UK:** did not make the charts

Although credited to his friend Morris Day, *Tricky* was, in fact, written by Prince himself and mainly featured Jamie Starr in hilarious form, spewing out a stream of insults. In truth, it was more a studio outtake than a real song and revealed the good-natured relationship between Day and Prince at the time. Note the presence of Morris Day on drums, introducing the track with a drum roll largely inspired by the one Prince used for the intro of *Irresistible Bitch*, an as yet unreleased track recorded between September 1982 and September 1983.

At 2'47 of *Tricky*, Prince starts scatting *Johnny's Theme* from *The Tonight Show*, a tune composed by Paul Anka and host Johnny Carson and based on an Anka song called *Toot Sweet (It's Really Love)*.

CHILI SAUCE

Morris Day / 5'45

Musicians: Prince: spoken voice, bass, programming, synthesizers, piano / **Morris Day:** spoken voice / **Sharon Hughes:** spoken voice / **Novi Novog:** violin / **Recording: Sunset Sound, Los Angeles:** 14–18 April 1983 / **Technical team: Producer:** Prince (credited to Morris Day and The Starr ★ Company) / **Recording engineers:** Peggy McCreary, Richard McKernan **The Time *Ice Cream Castle* (album)** / **Released in the USA by Warner Bros. Records:** 9 July 1984 (LP ref.: 9 25109-1) / **Released in the UK by WEA International:** 9 July 1984 (LP ref.: 925 109-1; CD ref.: W2 25109) / **Best chart ranking in the USA:** 24 / **Best chart ranking in the UK:** did not make the charts

Chili Sauce, whose working title was *Proposition 17*, explores the day-to-day life of dandy Morris Day, who instructs his butler (played by the irresistible Jerome Benton, a *Purple Rain* discovery) to ask the waiter to secure him the "sexiest" table in a fully booked restaurant. By turns a gentleman and a cad, Day chats to his girlfriend, played by actress Sharon Hughes, while the role of put-upon waiter is performed by Prince, or rather Jamie Starr, whose recognizable nasal voice and comedy acting are reminiscent of *Vibrator*, an unreleased Vanity 6 track well known to Prince fans.

The beautiful Apollonia, star of *Purple Rain* and backing vocalist for several songs on the movie's original soundtrack.

HEADPHONES AT THE READY

Six-string fans listen up! To get that guitar sound which packs a real punch at the end of *Let's Go Crazy*, Prince plugged his Hohner Madcat guitar into a Mesa/Boogie Mark IIB amp connected to two Bag End speakers.

Single

LET'S GO CRAZY

Prince and The Revolution / 4'39

Musicians: Prince: vocals, electric guitar, programming, backing vocals / **Wendy Melvoin:** electric guitar, backing vocals / **Brown Mark:** bass, backing vocals / **Bobby Z.:** drums, percussion, electronic percussion / **Lisa Coleman:** synthesizers, backing vocals / **Doctor Fink:** synthesizers, backing vocals / **Recording: The Warehouse, St Louis Park, Minnesota:** 7 August 1983 / **Technical team: Producer:** Prince / **Recording engineers:** Susan Rogers, David Leonard

Single: A-side: ***Let's Go Crazy***/3'46 (USA); ***Let's Go Crazy*** (Edit)/3'46 (UK) / **B-side:** ***Erotic City***/3'53 (USA); ***Take Me With U***/3'51 (UK) / **Released in the USA by Warner Bros. Records:** 18 July 1984 (single ref.: 7-29216) / **Released in the UK by WEA International:** 15 February 1985 (single ref.: W2000) / **Best chart ranking in the USA:** 1 / **Best chart ranking in the UK:** 7

Let's Go Crazy was Prince's second No.1 in the Billboard chart after *When Doves Cry*. It also features in the opening sequence to the movie *Purple Rain*. The version of the song we hear in the movie was recorded by Prince and The Revolution onstage at First Avenue on 3 August 1983. Four days after this legendary concert, Prince decided to record a new version of the song to be used on the album. Recording took place at The Warehouse, where the band were rehearsing. David Leonard came from Sunset Sound to help the singer's new recording engineer, Susan Rogers, and they recorded the band playing live, before adding the various overdubs, including the final guitar solo and the vocal tracks. "We just threw a nice piece of carpet on the floor and set the console in front of where the band rehearsed," Rogers later explained. "And I set up monitors on stands, wheeled over a tape machine, an outboard gear rack, got some snakes, and got everything wired up."[77] Prince wrote *Let's Go Crazy* in 1983 with the idea of making a single that could achieve airplay on the radio and appeal to the widest possible audience. With this in mind, he had to revise his initial text, as he explained in 1997: "My original draft of *Let's Go Crazy* was much different from the version that wound up being released. As I wrote it, *Let's Go Crazy* was about God and the de-elevation of sin. But the problem was that religion as a subject is taboo in pop music. People think that the records they release have got to be hip, but what I need to do is to tell the truth."[78]

Single

TAKE ME WITH U

Prince and The Revolution / 3'54

Musicians: Prince: vocals, acoustic guitar, bass, drums, electronic drums, tambourine, percussion, synthesizers, backing vocals / **Apollonia:** vocals, backing vocals / **Jill Jones:** vocals, backing vocals / **Lisa Coleman:** vocals, backing vocals / **David Coleman:** cello, finger cymbals / **Novi Novog:** violin / **Recording: Sunset Sound, Los Angeles:** 27–31 January 1984 / **Technical team: Producer:** Prince / **Recording engineers:** Peggy McCreary, David Leonard / **String arrangements:** Lisa Coleman, Prince

Single: A-side: ***Take Me With U***/3'52 / **B-side:** ***Baby I'm A Star***/2'55 / **Released in the USA by Warner Bros. Records:** 25 January 1985 (single ref.: 7-29079) / **Best chart ranking in the USA:** 25

Originally written and recorded for the first Apollonia 6 (see page 91) album, Prince retained *Take Me With U* for the soundtrack to *Purple Rain*. It was added at the last minute during the editing of the movie and required Albert Magnoli to add a sequence of images of the Kid on his motorbike with Apollonia. This was Prince's first official song as a duet, apart from his assorted appearances as Jamie Starr on tracks such as *If A Girl Answers (Don't Hang Up)* and *Vibrator* by Vanity 6. It was Patricia Kotero, aka Apollonia, who had the good fortune to share the mic with Prince in this pop song for which he recorded all the instrumental parts. Additional strings were played by David Coleman and Novi Novog (Suzie Katayama, present on *Baby I'm A Star* and *Purple Rain*, did not participate in the session on 30 January 1984, according to Coleman). Coleman's sister, keyboardist Lisa Coleman, did the string arrangements, supervised by Prince. When Apollonia recorded her vocal lines on 28 January 1984, Susan Rogers found herself in rather an awkward position, as the young woman's vocal performance left much to be desired. "She couldn't sing at all!" Rogers confided. "She was focused on acting and was not a strong singer. Prince came in and had the patience to coach her through line by line to get it."[75] The song would become the fifth single taken from *Purple Rain* and was released in the United States on 25 January 1985, just three months before the release of Prince's seventh opus *Around the World in a Day*.

It was on the initiative of Tipper Gore (second right) and in reaction to the explicit lyrics of *Darling Nikki* that the Parent Music Resource Center was created in 1985.

THE BEAUTIFUL ONES

Prince / 5'13

Musician: Prince: vocals, spoken voice, electric guitar, bass, drums, electronic drums, synthesizers, piano / **Recording: Sunset Sound, Los Angeles:** 20 September 1983 / **Technical team: Producer:** Prince / **Recording engineers:** Peggy McCreary, David Leonard

While working on *Purple Rain*, Prince fell madly in love with Susannah Melvoin, Wendy's twin sister. Susannah was in a relationship when she met Prince, so it was an impossible romance. Not one to give up easily, Prince had flowers delivered to Susannah's house every day for over a year until she finally succumbed to his charms. "It wasn't a day that went by where there wasn't a huge thing of flowers. Now it started to look like a funeral home because there was no way to keep up with the amount of flowers."[79] According to many sources close to the singer at the time, this budding love affair was at the heart of *The Beautiful Ones*, a song that was a last-minute substitute for *Electric Intercourse* in the movie and became one of the album's highlights. Vanity claimed she was the inspiration for the song, but was later contradicted by Prince, who insisted, somewhat virulently, that the text explicitly referred to the love triangle in *Purple Rain* between himself, Apollonia (see page 91), and Morris Day: "'Do you want him or do you want me,' that was written for that scene in *Purple Rain* specifically. Where Morris would be sitting with [Apollonia] [...] Vanity had just quit the movie. To then speculate, 'Well, he wrote that song about me?' [...] Why would you go around saying stuff like that?"[80]

COMPUTER BLUE

Prince, John L Nelson, Lisa Coleman, Wendy Melvoin / 3'59

Musicians: Prince: vocals, electric guitar, programming, synthesizers, backing vocals / **Wendy Melvoin:** electric guitar, spoken voice, backing vocals / **Brown Mark:** bass / **Bobby Z.:** drums, electronic drums, percussion / **Lisa Coleman:** synthesizers, spoken voice, backing vocals / **Doctor Fink:** synthesizers / **Recording: The Warehouse, St Louis Park, Minnesota:** 8 August 1983 / **Sunset Sound, Los Angeles:** 15–17 August 1983 (overdubs), 19, 20, 29, and 31 August 1983 (overdubs) / **Technical team: Producer:** Prince / **Recording engineers:** Susan Rogers (The Warehouse), David Leonard (Sunset Sound), Peggy McCreary (Sunset Sound)

On 7 August 1983, between takes during the recording of *Let's Go Crazy* at The Warehouse, Doctor Fink launched into a bass riff on the synthesizer that immediately caught Prince's attention. This kicked off a jam session based on the musical motif, and the whole thing was taped by David Leonard. The next day, Prince recorded *Computer Blue* using this riff and adding a break and a solo composed by his father, John L Nelson. Over the years, the jazzman passed on a few scores to his son and, in 1984, Prince decided to combine the melancholic *Father's Song* (which we hear, played on piano, at 57'45 in the movie) with his track *Computer Blue*, resulting in the most beautiful guitar solo on the album. On 18 August 1983, David Coleman, Novi Novog, and Suzie Katayama recorded some string parts, but instead Prince opted for pads played on the Oberheim synthesizer. That same day, Lisa Coleman and Wendy Melvoin left their mark on the track, with their now legendary introductory dialogue. The final song was 12 minutes long but was edited down twice to make room for the two tracks that were added at the last minute: *Take Me With U* and *When Doves Cry*. It wasn't until 2017 and the reissue of *Purple Rain* that we were able to enjoy the song, titled *Computer Blue (Hallway Speech Version)*, in its entirety.

DARLING NIKKI

Prince / 4'13

Musician: Prince: vocals, electric guitar, bass, drums, electronic drums, programming, synthesizers / **Recording: Kiowa Trail Home Studio, Chanhassen, Minnesota:** July 1983 / **Sunset Sound, Los Angeles:** 18–19 August 1983 / **Technical team: Producer:** Prince / **Recording engineers:** Don Batts (Kiowa Trail Home Studio—recording), Susan Rogers (Kiowa Trail Home Studio—mixing), Peggy McCreary (Sunset Sound—overdubs)

Darling Nikki was the last track recorded by Don Batts before he quit as Prince's recording engineer. Prince recorded it at Kiowa Trail and then gave the tape to Susan Rogers, the latest arrival in the artist's home. "The first song he had me put up was *Darling Nikki*. He had me put up a tape and said, 'Get a rough mix.'"[75] The song, which describes Prince's encounter with a woman masturbating in front of him, before she educates him in the ways of sex, was not to the liking of Tipper Gore, the then wife of senator and future vice-president Al Gore. She cofounded the American pressure group Parents Music Resource Center, which compiled a list of songs and called for advisory warnings based on specific criteria, such as "sex," "violence," or "occultism" to be attached to records to protect children from overly explicit content. *Darling Nikki* topped the list, closely followed by *Sugar Walls* by Sheena Easton (also written by Prince, using the pseudonym Alexander Nevermind), *Bastard* by Mötley Crüe, and *She Bop* by Cyndi Lauper. All these lucky artists got "Parental Advisory/Explicit Lyrics" stickers on their records, labels that are now well known to fans of hip-hop—a music genre that itself often uses choice lyrics-—around the world. In 1989, one of hip-hop's most famous representatives, the rapper Ice-T, "thanked" the movement in his song *Freedom of Speech*: "Hey PMRC, you stupid fuckin' assholes/The sticker on the record is what makes 'em sell gold."[81]

At 3'42 on *Darling Nikki*, Prince recites some lines, which when played backward feature the words: "'Hello, how are you?' 'Fine, fine; 'cause I know that the Lord is coming soon. Coming, coming soon. Fine, fine; 'cause I know that the Lord is coming soon. Coming, coming soon.'" As Susan Rogers who was responsible for this studio trick explained: "This is his way of asking for forgiveness for having lust in his heart, and doing it in a way that was artistic." She went on: "Great art comes from conflict, and he was conflicted, for sure."[75]

On 7 June 1984, Prince celebrated his birthday onstage at First Avenue in Minneapolis. For the very first time the group played the two-part track *Our Destiny/Roadhouse Garden* live, which featured on the *Purple Rain Deluxe Expanded Edition* in 2017.

Single

WHEN DOVES CRY

Prince / 5'52

Musician
Prince: vocals, electric guitar, electronic drums, programming, synthesizers, backing vocals

Recording
Sunset Sound, Los Angeles: 1–5 March 1984

Technical team
Producer: Prince
Recording engineers: Peggy McCreary, David Leonard

1984

SINGLE
A-side: *When Doves Cry*/3'49
B-side: *17 Days*/3'54
Released in the USA by Warner Bros. Records: 16 May 1984 (single ref.: 7-29286)
Released in the UK by WEA International: 22 June 1984 (single ref.: W 9286)
Best chart ranking in the USA: 1
Best chart ranking in the UK: 4

Genesis

Like *Take Me With U*, Prince recorded *When Doves Cry* while the movie *Purple Rain* was being edited. The song was written just after he broke up with Susan Moonsie (one of the Apollonia 6 singers, see page 91) and was undoubtedly inspired by this separation. It was so emotionally powerful that Prince insisted it be included in the movie, forcing the director to insert a sequence created from various rushes, interspersed with shots of the Kid on his motorbike. "This song was a surprise to me," said Lisa Coleman. "The simple instrumentation was refreshing, and I didn't think it would connect with people. I thought it was going to be an album track that only deep-track listeners would like for its honesty and raw vocal presence."[82] Defying all predictions, *When Doves Cry*, released as a single on 16 May 1984, was a huge success, giving Prince his first No.1 on the Billboard Hot 100 chart, a reaction that boded well for the planned release of the movie two months later!

Production

Prince and Susan Rogers had just spent over 30 hours solid on the track, but he was still not satisfied with the production. On the morning of Saturday, 3 March 1983, while searching for a formula that would turn his song into a masterpiece, Prince was about to make a decision that would change his life. He removed all unnecessary tracks from the song, transforming an overloaded production into a deliberately minimalist track, and then, encouraged by his friend and backing vocalist Jill Jones, who was sitting next to him, he suddenly decided to remove the bass track, which is what would make *When Doves Cry* really shine. All that remained was to add a synth line, played on the thirty-second note at a tempo of 116 BPM, which even for a virtuoso pianist like Prince was very difficult. Susan Rogers suggested that Prince slow down the tape recorder to a tempo of 58 BPM, allowing him to record his keyboard part at half the speed. Once the score was laid down, Rogers replayed the tape at its original speed, and the song then boasted two keyboard sequences played masterfully, at 4'57 and 5'46! "Prince always handed the football to me when we did *When Doves Cry* live," laughs Doctor Fink. "It was if he was saying, 'Here, you play it, dude.'"[83]

On 3 August 1983, Prince recorded three of his most famous songs onstage at First Avenue: *I Would Die 4 U*, *Baby I'm A Star*, and *Purple Rain*.

1984

Single

I WOULD DIE 4 U

Prince and The Revolution / 2'51

Musicians: **Prince:** vocals, electric guitar, synthesizers, backing vocals / **Wendy Melvoin:** electric guitar, backing vocals / **Brown Mark:** bass, backing vocals / **Bobby Z.:** drums, electronic drums, electronic percussion, backing vocals / **Lisa Coleman:** synthesizers, backing vocals / **Doctor Fink:** synthesizers, programming, backing vocals / **Recording:** **Record Plant Remote ("Black Truck"), First Avenue, Minneapolis:** 3 August 1983 / **Sunset Sound, Los Angeles:** 31 August to 3 September 1983 (vocals and overdubs) / **Technical team:** **Producer:** Prince / **Recording engineers:** David Leonard (First Avenue), David Rivkin (First Avenue), David Hewitt (First Avenue), Kooster McAllister (First Avenue), Peggy McCreary (Sunset Sound) **Single: A-side:** *I Would Die 4 U*/2'57 / **B-side:** *Another Lonely Christmas*/4'20 / **Released in the USA by Warner Bros. Records:** 28 November 1984 (single ref.: 7-29121) / **Released in the UK by WEA International:** 26 November 1984 (single ref.: W9121) / **Best chart ranking in the USA:** 8 / **Best chart ranking in the UK:** 58

During rehearsals in the summer of 1983, Prince introduced his musicians to *I Would Die 4 U* and *Baby I'm A Star*, two songs designed to segue into one another and conclude *Purple Rain* with a flourish. Once the band had got a handle on the songs, they were recorded live at the mythical First Avenue concert on 3 August 1983. *I Would Die 4 U* is the only song for which Doctor Fink programmed the Linn LM-1 Drum Computer. During the Purple Rain Tour, Bobby Z.'s acoustic drum kit was modified so he could reproduce the rhythmic sequences of the album. It was fitted with Simmons pads, so it could trigger all kinds of rhythmic patterns and sounds straight out of the LM-1, thanks to the MIDI drum pad technology. Doctor Fink synchronized his MemoryMoog synthesizer with Bobby Z.'s instrument and triggered the drum machine in perfect coordination with his synthesizer. The vocals and numerous overdubs were done at Sunset Sound in late August and early September.

In the autumn of 1984, while The Revolution and Sheila E. were at the Flying Cloud Drive Warehouse preparing for the Purple Rain Tour, a sneaky collaboration between the two bands took place, resulting in a full-length version of *I Would Die 4 U*, featuring Sheila E. on percussion and saxophonist Eddie "M" Mininfield, along with Miko Weaver, Prince's future guitarist. *I Would Die 4 U (Extended Version)* appeared on the maxi-single version.

BABY I'M A STAR

Prince and The Revolution / 4'20

Musicians: Prince: vocals, electric guitar, programming, synthesizers, claps, backing vocals / **Wendy Melvoin:** electric guitar, backing vocals / **Brown Mark:** bass / **Bobby Z.:** electronic drums, electronic percussion / **Lisa Coleman:** synthesizers, claps, backing vocals / **Doctor Fink:** synthesizers / **Jill Jones:** backing vocals / **David Coleman:** cello / **Novi Novog:** electric violin / **Suzie Katayama:** cello / **Recording: Record Plant Remote ("Black Truck"), First Avenue, Minneapolis:** 3 August 1983 / **Sunset Sound, Los Angeles:** 18 August 1983 (strings), 1–7 and 9–12 September 1983 (vocals and overdubs) / **Technical team: Producer:** Prince / **Recording engineers:** David Leonard (First Avenue), David Rivkin (First Avenue), David Hewitt (First Avenue), Kooster McAllister (First Avenue), Peggy McCreary (Sunset Sound) / **String arrangement:** Lisa Coleman, Prince

Although *Baby I'm A Star* was performed in a piano-vocal version to recording engineer Don Batts in 1981, its ultimate destiny was to conclude the movie *Purple Rain*, and to finally announce to the world the destiny that awaited Prince. The song was recorded during the concert at First Avenue, in Minneapolis, on 3 August 1983, to a largely subdued audience. "The concert was interesting because that was the first time that anybody had heard those songs, and nobody really applauded because they weren't familiar with that stuff,"[84] said recording engineer David Rivkin, who was manning the Record Plant's mobile studio, which had been rented for the occasion and was parked outside the venue. Rivkin therefore decided to add crowd applause recorded at a soccer game, which can be heard on this track and at the very end of *Purple Rain*.

On 18 August, Prince decided to add string parts to the three songs recorded at First Avenue. It was midnight in Los Angeles, and Susan Rogers was tasked with finding a string orchestra that could be there within an hour. She called on Suzie Katayama and Novi Novog, with whom she had recently worked. Lisa Coleman, who was in charge of the arrangements, also asked her brother, David, to come along to the session.

"I used my electric viola," Novog recalled. "I was just learning the song. I said 'Oh, let me do that part again.' He said, 'No, no, I like the feel.' He loved first takes."[85]

HEADPHONES AT THE READY

Lisa Coleman and Jill Jones were singing backing vocals on *Baby I'm A Star*. At one point, they burst into a giggling fit and Prince kicked them out of the studio. The difference is perceptible at the end of the song, as Prince was then left to record all the backing vocals on his own!

> **HEADPHONES AT THE READY**
> The scream heard at 2'42 of *Purple Rain* is not just another moan from Prince, but the scream of a happy audience member, immortalized forever on the recording!

Single

PURPLE RAIN

Prince and The Revolution / 8'41

1984

Musicians

Prince: vocals, electric guitar, synthesizers, backing vocals
Wendy Melvoin: electric guitar, backing vocals
Brown Mark: bass, backing vocals
Bobby Z.: drums, electronic drums, backing vocals
Lisa Coleman: synthesizers, backing vocals
Doctor Fink: synthesizers, backing vocals
David Coleman: cello
Novi Novog: violin, viola
Suzie Katayama: cello

Recording

Record Plant Remote ("Black Truck"), First Avenue, Minneapolis: 3 August 1983
Sunset Sound, Los Angeles: 15 August 1983 (overdubs), 18 August 1983 (strings and overdubs), 13–15 September 1983 (overdubs)

Technical team

Producer: Prince
Recording engineers: David Leonard (First Avenue), David Rivkin (First Avenue), David Hewitt (First Avenue), Kooster McAllister (First Avenue), Peggy McCreary (Sunset Sound)
String arrangement: Lisa Coleman, Prince

SINGLE

US version
"Other Side": *Purple Rain*/4'02
"This Side": *God*/3'59
UK version
A-side: *Purple Rain* (Short Version)/4'02
B-side: *God* (Vocal)/3'59
Released in the USA by Warner Bros. Records: 26 September 1984 (single ref.: 7-29174)
Released in the UK by WEA International: 10 September 1984 (single ref.: W9174)
Best chart ranking in the USA: 2
Best chart ranking in the UK: 8

Genesis

Prince always claimed that Joni Mitchell's music was one of his main influences. The album *Blue*, released by the Canadian singer in 1971, made a huge impression on him, and he paid homage to her by covering one of the best-known songs from the album: *A Case of You*. In the summer of 1983, while he was busy writing *Purple Rain*, Prince recorded a session accompanying himself on piano only, under the watchful eye of his recording engineer Don Batts. Among the tracks recorded that day was the first version of *Purple Rain*, which Prince followed up with *A Case of You*. Listening to the record, released in 2018 as *Piano & A Microphone 1983*, it's clear just how much Mitchell's influence is present in Prince's repertoire. Just by listening to *River* on *Blue*, for example, you can appreciate the extent to which the queen of folk inspired Prince in the writing of *Purple Rain*. As Prince progressed with the composition of the song, he was nevertheless troubled by his conscience, because the main chord grid and the piano arpeggios resembled another song: *Faithfully* by Journey, which had been released the previous April. He picked up the phone and called the Columbia offices in Los Angeles to talk to Jonathan Cain, the band's keyboardist and the writer of the song. "I want to play something for you, and I want you to check it out," Prince said to the musician when the phone call was finally arranged. "The chord changes are close to *Faithfully* and I don't want you to sue me."[86] As Cain said later: "I thought it was an amazing tune." He went on, explaining that he told Prince: "Man, I'm just super-flattered that you even called. It shows you're that classy of a guy. Good luck with the song. I know it's gonna be a hit."[86] *Purple Rain* would, of course, be a hit, although it would never reach the top spot on the Billboard Hot 100 chart, having to settle instead for No.2 in the week of 17 November 1984, behind Wham! and *Wake Me Up Before You Go-Go*.

Production

In 1983, after he and Stevie Nicks had worked together on *Stand Back*, Prince asked her to write the lyrics for a song he had just composed. "It was so overwhelming, that 10-minute track," the Fleetwood Mac singer said, "that I listened to it and I just got scared. I called him back and said, 'I can't do it. I wish I could. It's too much for me.' I'm so glad that I didn't,

Lace, jabot, and frock coat: three features of Prince's wardrobe during the *Purple Rain* era.

Overleaf: Prince, Wendy Melvoin (left), and Lisa Coleman (right) shared the Oscar for Best Original Song Score with *Purple Rain* on 25 March 1985, at the Dorothy Chandler Pavilion in Los Angeles.

because he wrote it, and it became *Purple Rain*."[87] Prince decided to present his new composition to his musicians, who rehearsed it to the point of exhaustion. Wendy Melvoin added her own personal touch: a reverse chord grid played on her purple Rickenbacker 330s, and suffused in a chorus effect that would become the signature intro. Despite his reputation as an autocratic tyrant, Prince liked to surround himself with musicians who brought their own experience and craft with them. "He saw each of us as like a band in our own right," Lisa Coleman explained. "Like, Mark was the funk band, Matt was the synth band, Wendy's the funky Joni Mitchell, I'm the girl thing...It was like he was in the studio with all his influences, and whether it was a girly song, a ballad, or some hot, funky, rock thing, he could deliver."[35] Once the song was finished, Prince recorded it onstage at First Avenue, in Minneapolis, on 3 August 1983 and added numerous overdubs during the sessions at Sunset Sound in Los Angeles. The song was edited down from 13 to eight minutes and 41 seconds, and notably stripped of its third verse. And the rest is history, *Purple Rain* remaining to this day Prince's most famous song, thanks to its polished composition and the chemistry with The Revolution.

On what would have been Prince's sixty-first birthday, Journey singer and guitarist Neal Schon paid a moving tribute to him by releasing a cover of *Purple Rain* in June 2019, which appeared on his album *Universe* the following year.

AROU

PRINCE AND THE REVOLUTION

AROUND THE WORLD IN A DAY

Around the World in a Day · Paisley Park · Condition of the Heart · Raspberry Beret
Tamborine · America · Pop Life · The Ladder · Temptation

Released in the USA by Paisley Park Records/Warner Bros. Records:
22 April 1985 (LP ref.: 1-25286; CD ref.: 9 25286-2)
Released in the UK release by Paisley Park Records/WEA International:
22 April 1985 (LP ref.: 925 286-1; CD ref.: 925 286-2)
Best chart ranking in the USA: 1
Best chart ranking in the UK: 5

Boa and lace…onstage at The Fabulous Forum, Inglewood, on 19 February 1985.

1985

INTROSPECTION AND EXPERIMENTATION AROUND THE WORLD

Tired of a never-ending tour and audiences that plainly only came to hear the songs from the movie, Prince brought the Purple Rain Tour to an abrupt end, without even venturing from American soil. By the time the tour finished in April 1985, Prince had already recorded his seventh album, and seemed ready to move on from the dazzling *Purple Rain* with work that took a more intimate turn than before. Between February 1983 and December 1984, Prince had laid down a series of pop tracks with dynamic choruses and lyrics that revealed an introspective side, far from the incendiary *Darling Nikki*, *The Beautiful Ones*, and *Baby I'm A Star*. Recorded partly at the Sunset Sound studios, in Los Angeles, and partly at the Flying Cloud Drive Warehouse in Eden Prairie, Minnesota, the tracks *Condition of the Heart* and *The Ladder* explored a singer's tormented soul, while *Pop Life*, *Raspberry Beret*, and *America* were clearly made for MTV and radio stations. Meanwhile, a track called *Paisley Park* heralded a new project to come: the construction of Prince's Neverland, which would only open in 1987.

Life and death of The Family

It's 1984. Ideas are coming thick and fast, and in June, with his producer hat on, Prince launched a new group built on the ashes of The Time (see page 64), from which the singer Morris Day appeared to want out. Day had left for Los Angeles before the release of the band's third album, *Ice Cream Castle*, evidently more interested in his solo career than in the band and leaving guitarist Jesse Johnson alone at the helm of a ghost ship. Prince soon took back control of the project, reshaping it to hatch his new creation: The Family. Considered one of Prince's most interesting side projects, the group was led by singer Susannah Melvoin, Wendy's twin sister and by then Prince's official girlfriend. Susannah shared the mic with The Time's keyboardist, St Paul Peterson; two other members of The Time, Jellybean Johnson and Jerome Benton, were invited to come along for the ride, and were joined in early July by saxophonist Eric Leeds, the brother of Alan Leeds, Prince's tour manager.

"Prince […] wanted something different," said David Rivkin, who coproduced The Family's album. "If people see a black person fronting the band, they think one thing. If they see a white person, some of those barriers are broken. Unfortunately, that's the way it is. Prince wanted a white guy so that people would listen. And he said, 'We've got to go after some of that Duran Duran money.'"[88] The group's first opus was recorded between July and October 1984, with titles such as *Nothing Compares 2 U*, *River Run Dry*, and *High Fashion*. Nearly a year went by before Prince decided to release the album *The Family*, on 19 August 1985. After several months of rehearsals, the group had given a single concert at First Avenue, in Minneapolis, on 13 August, before Prince abandoned the project once and for all, as by then he was already engrossed in the shooting of *Under the Cherry Moon* on the other side of the Atlantic.

1985

Prince with his bodyguard Charles "Big Chick" Huntsberry and his father, John L Nelson, in 1984.

FOR PRINCE ADDICTS

While the sleeve notes for *Around the World in a Day* suggest that some of the tracks were recorded at Paisley Park, this was not the case. In fact, Prince's fortress did not open for business until 1987, and the Paisley Park we are talking about here was actually the name Prince used for the Flying Cloud Drive Warehouse, where The Revolution rehearsed and recorded in the mid-1980s.

Prince's day trip

Around the World in a Day was released on 22 April 1985. Despite a disastrous listening session that left Warner executives hugely disappointed that they had not heard a *Purple Rain 2*, the record was well received by both the public and the media. It reached the top spot on the Billboard 200 chart, before being rapidly toppled, as it did not benefit from the major exposure that its predecessor had enjoyed. Notwithstanding the delicious single *Raspberry Beret* and other top-quality songs, the album was but a comet in Prince's discography, and unfairly considered one of his minor works. "He wanted to get as far away from *Purple Rain* [as possible],"[35] explained Bobby Z. "I sort of had a 'FU-attitude,'" Prince himself would say, "meaning that I was making something for myself and my fans and the people who've supported me thru [*sic*] the years, I wanted to give them something [...] Record sales and things like that, it really doesn't matter, you know."[89]

Although the Yamaha CP-80 electric piano was one of the key instruments of the *Purple Rain* period, it was replaced by an upright piano starting with the Parade Tour, so that Prince could jump and dance on it as he wished.

1985

AROUND THE WORLD IN A DAY

Prince, David Coleman, John L Nelson / 3'25

Musicians: Prince: vocals, programming, synthesizers, backing vocals / **Wendy Melvoin:** acoustic guitar / **Bobby Z.:** programming, backing vocals / **David Coleman:** cello, finger cymbals, darbuka, oud, backing vocals / **Doctor Fink:** backing vocals / **Lisa Coleman:** backing vocals / **Susannah Melvoin:** backing vocals / **Jonathan Melvoin:** tambourine, backing vocals / **Recording: Flying Cloud Drive Warehouse, Eden Prairie, Minnesota:** 16 August 1984 / **Technical team: Producer:** Prince / **Recording engineers:** Susan Rogers, David Leonard

In early June 1984, Lisa Coleman's brother, David, who had played cello on several songs for *Purple Rain*, took a call from Prince's managers. They told him that their client wanted to give him a birthday gift: a two-day unlimited access package to Sunset Sound Studios. Coleman took advantage of the opportunity to record a song called *Around the World in a Day* that he had written for an old high-school friend called Christine Maalouf. On quitting the studio, he played the song to Wendy Melvoin and Lisa, who immediately suggested that Prince give it a listen. With David's agreement, Prince then appropriated the song, altered the text of the verses, and, oddly, added his father's name to the song credits, although there was no apparent reason for him to do so. The Oriental sounds in the song inspired Prince in the writing of the album, which was all about being open to others and to the world in general.

Single

PAISLEY PARK

Prince and The Revolution / 4'41

Musicians: Prince: vocals, electric guitar, programming, finger cymbals, synthesizers, backing vocals / **Novi Novog:** violin / **Wendy Melvoin:** backing vocals / **Susannah Melvoin:** backing vocals / **Lisa Coleman:** backing vocals / **Recording: Flying Cloud Drive Warehouse, Eden Prairie, Minnesota:** September 1984 / **Technical team: Producer:** Prince / **Recording engineer:** Susan Rogers / **Single: "Other Side":** *Paisley Park*/4'38 / **"This Side":** *She's Always in My Hair*/3'27 / **Released in the UK by Paisley Park Records/WEA International:** 24 May 1985 (single ref.: W9052) / **Best chart ranking in the UK:** 18

Before Paisley Park became the place of sanctuary that Prince built in 1987, it existed in his mind as an imaginary place where everyone could become the person that they dreamed of being, and where the impossible was possible. He worked on and recorded the track *Paisley Park* in rehearsals with The Revolution (Susan Rogers later explained that the count-in at the start of both *Paisley Park* and *Raspberry Beret* were taken from the live recordings). He then completely reworked it at the Flying Cloud Drive Warehouse. A few flutes played on Yamaha DX7s, which were added at the end of *Paisley Park* along with some wonderful backing vocals from the Melvoin twins and Lisa Coleman, lend their weight to a polished production, resulting in a compelling pop track that would be released as a single in the UK in May 1985. "Paisley Park was a summary of what he intended to say," explained Susan Rogers. "It summed up his philosophy [...] He was getting away from the purple and glitter, and into something new."[2]

CONDITION OF THE HEART

Prince and The Revolution / 6'46

Musician: Prince: vocals, piano, acoustic guitar, finger cymbals, kettledrums, percussion, synthesizers, backing vocals. / **Recording: Sunset Sound, Los Angeles:** 9–10 October 1984 / **Technical team: Producer:** Prince / **Recording engineers:** Peggy McCreary, David Leonard

Recorded shortly before the start of the Purple Rain Tour, *Condition of the Heart* was one of Susan Rogers' "Sunday Songs." Although it was recorded during the week at Sunset Sound, Rogers explained that most of Prince's intimate ballads were recorded during Sunday sessions, when the members of The Revolution had a day off. In the lyrics, Prince refers to Wendy Melvoin, whom he frequently compares to the actress Clara Bow. He also implicitly sends a message to her sister, Susannah, with whom he has fallen madly in love. As proof, his heart beats for her at the end of the song, reproduced here on a set of kettledrums that Stephen Shelton, a Sunset Sound employee, was asked to find in record time to keep Prince satisfied.

Prince recorded the clip of *America* in the Théâtre de Verdure in Nice, France, on 27 October 1985.

FOR PRINCE ADDICTS

On 13 September 1997, Prince appeared on *The Muppet Show Tonight*, clearly enjoying his guest role chatting with America's most famous puppets. In a café, one of the animals bets him that he can't improvise a song about the desserts on the menu, at which point Prince launches into *Raspberry Sorbet*, a revamped version of *Raspberry Beret*.

1985

Single

RASPBERRY BERET

Prince and The Revolution / 3'31

Musicians: Prince: vocals, acoustic guitar, bass, programming, synthesizers, backing vocals / **Wendy Melvoin:** backing vocals / **Susannah Melvoin:** backing vocals / **Lisa Coleman:** backing vocals / **Novi Novog:** violin / **Suzie Katayama:** cello / **David Coleman:** cello / **Recording: Flying Cloud Drive Warehouse, Eden Prairie, Minnesota:** 12–13 September 1984 / **Technical team: Producer:** Prince / **Recording engineer:** Susan Rogers / **String arrangements:** Wendy Melvoin, Lisa Coleman
Single: US version / A-side: *Raspberry Beret*/3'31 / **B-side:** *She's Always in My Hair*/3'27 / **UK version / "Other Side":** *Raspberry Beret*/3'31 / **"This Side":** *Hello*/3'23 / **Released in the USA by Paisley Park Records/Warner Bros. Records:** 15 May 1985 (single ref.: 7-28972) / **Released in the UK by Paisley Park Records/Warner Bros. Records:** 15 May 1985 (single ref.: W8929) / **Best chart ranking in the USA:** 2 / **Best chart ranking in the UK:** 25

In April 1982, Prince recorded an initial version of *Raspberry Beret*—under a different name—at Sunset Sound. It bore a very synthpop signature, which was similar to the album *1999*. The joyfulness of the track made it an obvious choice for the album that followed *Purple Rain*, with its very pop flavor in which the defining characteristics were freshness and spontaneity. In the video, fans were treated to a version that was almost a minute longer, in which The Revolution perform in a colorful setting that epitomized the album. Fans tried to work out why Prince cleared his throat at the start of the video, something he spoke about to *Rolling Stone* magazine in September 1985: "I just did it to be sick, to do something no one else would do. I turned on MTV to see the premiere of *Raspberry Beret* and Mark Goodman [the host] was talking to the guy who discovered the backward message on *Darling Nikki*. They were trying to figure out what the cough meant too, and it was sort of funny. But I'm not getting down on him for trying. I like that. I've always had little hidden messages, and I always will."[27]

TAMBORINE

Prince and The Revolution / 2'46

Musician: Prince: vocals, bass, drums, tambourine, synthesizers, whistles, claps, finger cymbals, backing vocals / **Recording: Flying Cloud Drive Warehouse, Eden Prairie, Minnesota:** 27 September 1984 / **Saint Paul Civic Center (Record Plant Remote, "Black Truck"), Saint Paul, Minnesota:** 24 December 1984 / **Kiowa Trail Home Studio (Record Plant Remote, "Black Truck"), Chanhassen, Minnesota:** 24 December 1984 / **Technical team: Producer:** Prince / **Recording engineer:** Susan Rogers

Tamborine features a drum pattern played by Prince himself (replacing the usual Linn LM-1 Drum Computer) and an implicit reference to masturbation, picking up where *Darling Nikki* left off the year before. "Oh my God, there I go/Falling in love with the face in a magazine/All alone by myself/Me and I play my tambourine," sings the Kid from Minneapolis. This is clearly a nod to his detractors, including Tipper Gore, who put *Darling Nikki* at the top of the group's list of songs that needed to be censored.

Single

AMERICA

Prince and The Revolution / 3'40

Musicians: Prince: vocals, electric guitar, bass, programming, synthesizers, backing vocals / **Wendy Melvoin:** electric guitar / **Brown Mark:** bass / **Bobby Z.:** drums / **Doctor Fink:** synthesizers / **Lisa Coleman:** synthesizers / **Brad Marsh:** tambourine / **Recording: Flying Cloud Drive Warehouse, Eden Prairie, Minnesota:** 23 July 1984 / **Technical team: Producer:** Prince / **Recording engineer:** Susan Rogers
Single: A-side: *America*/3'40 / **B-side:** *Girl*/3'57 / **Released in the USA by Paisley Park Records/Warner Bros. Records:** 2 October 1985 (single ref.: 7-28999) / **Best chart ranking in the USA:** 46

On 23 July 1984, Prince and his musicians were rehearsing at the Flying Cloud Drive Warehouse. Susan Rogers, who recorded all the rehearsals, pressed play on the tape recorder, and captured a 21'46 version of a lengthy track the musicians had previously worked on. It was called *America*. "America is a very positive song, very patriotic," Prince explained. "A peaceful song. A plea to people in charge to remember what freedom is about. I've been to a lot of places in the world, but I haven't found any place quite like America."[90] Prince edited the track for the album, but the full version (which would have lasted even longer if the tape had been longer, according to Susan Rogers) appeared on the maxi-single version. On 27 October 1985, while in France filming *Under the Cherry Moon*, Prince offered lucky spectators at the Théâtre de Verdure, in Nice, a manic version of the song, performed in almost unbearable heat. Wendy Melvoin recounts, "There was no ventilation and it was over 100 degrees in the tent. And if you've watched the video, you can see we are full-on running around the stage. I remember both Prince and I had to have oxygen tanks brought to us because we almost passed out from heat exhaustion."[64] The version of *America* filmed that night became the official video for the single, which was released in the United States on 2 October 1985.

At 3'20 of *Pop Life*, Prince mixes *Barroom Brawl* and *Prize Fight, Large Arena*, two excerpts from *Authentic Sound Effects, Volume 4*, a record produced by Jac Holzman for Elektra Records in 1964. The idea was not new, as Queen had used *Carnival Midway* from *Authentic Sound Effects, Volume 1* in the intro to *Brighton Rock* in 1974!

FOR PRINCE ADDICTS

The Ladder and *Tamborine* were recorded on Christmas Eve 1984 in the mobile studio parked in front of Prince's home in Chanhassen, Minnesota, as he had sold his console to Jesse Johnson shortly before. Susan Rogers, who spent the holidays with Prince, said, "I was a Prince fan, what better place to be spending Christmas!"[85]

1985

Single

POP LIFE

Prince and The Revolution / 3'42

Musicians: Prince: vocals, bass, synthesizers, piano, backing vocals / **Drums:** Sheila E. / **Wendy Melvoin:** backing vocals / **Lisa Coleman:** backing vocals / **Recording: Sunset Sound, Los Angeles:** 19–20 February 1984 / **Technical team: Producer:** Prince / **Recording engineer:** Peggy McCreary / **String arrangements:** Lisa Coleman, Wendy Melvoin
Single: A-side: *Pop Life*/3'42 / **B-side:** *Hello*/3'24 (USA); *Girl*/3'51 (UK) / **Released in the USA by Paisley Park Records/Warner Bros. Records:** 10 July 1985 (single ref.: 7-28998) / **Released in the UK by Paisley Park Records/WEA International:** 14 October 1985 (single ref.: W8858) / **Best chart ranking in the USA:** 7 / **Best chart ranking in the UK:** 60

Pop Life was recorded on the same day as *Another Lonely Christmas*, the prestigious B-side of *I Would Die 4 U*, and is mainly known for being the first song that sees Prince entrust the drums to Sheila E., his new protégée. Sheila, who would soon replace Bobby Z. in the Prince universe, also played a part in editing the song when Prince was not in the studio. "Back then again, we were working with tape [...]," Sheila explained, "so cutting up tape and cutting up the pieces and taping them to the wall and marking them with what part it was, and so there was a wall full of cut parts of the song and we would tape it back together, and that's how I edited the song."[91] It was the first song recorded for the album, and set the tone for a vivid pop opus, which contrasted with the sparkly rock of *Purple Rain*.

THE LADDER

Prince, John L Nelson / 5'26

Musicians: Prince: vocals, synthesizers, piano, backing vocals / **Wendy Melvoin:** backing vocals / **Brown Mark:** bass, backing vocals / **Bobby Z.:** drums, percussion / **Lisa Coleman:** synthesizers, backing vocals / **Doctor Fink:** synthesizers / **Eddie Mininfield:** saxophone / **Susannah Melvoin:** backing vocals / **Taja Sevelle:** backing vocals / **David Coleman:** cello / **Suzie Katayama:** cello / **Sid Page:** violin / **Marcy Dicterow-Vaj:** violin / **Denyse Buffum:** viola / **Laury Woods:** viola / **Tim Barr:** double bass / **Annette Atkinson:** double bass / **Recording: Saint Paul Civic Center (Record Plant Remote, "Black Truck"), Saint Paul, Minnesota:** 31 October 1984 / **Flying Cloud Drive Warehouse, Eden Prairie, Minnesota:** November 1984 / **Kiowa Trail Home Studio (Record Plant Remote, "Black Truck"), Chanhassen, Minnesota:** 24 December 1984 / **Technical team: Producer:** Prince / **Recording engineers:** David Tickle (Saint Paul Civic Center), Robert "Cubby" Colby (Saint Paul Civic Center), Susan Rogers (Flying Cloud Drive Warehouse)

While The Revolution and Sheila E.'s Band were ready to hit the road for the start of the Purple Rain Tour, Prince took advantage of the last few days of rehearsals at the Saint Paul Civic Center to work on some new songs. Among them, *The Ladder*, a ballad with a chord progression written by Prince's father. "We have the same hands," the singer confided about John L Nelson. "We have the same dreams. We write the same lyrics, sometimes [...] With the music, we are a lot different [...] A lot of beautiful melodies are hidden beneath the complexity. That's why it takes me to pull all that out. That's why we work so well together [...] For example, *The Ladder*. He wrote the chords for that, but it had a little faster, a little bit more on the top hand. I just took the chords and gave it a simple melody on top."[90] The song was recorded during rehearsals on 31 October 1984 in a mobile recording studio connected to the hall, which is the reason why saxophonist Eddie Mininfield, a member of Sheila E.'s band, was invited to participate, although not everyone in the studio knew it would feature on Prince's next album.

Before joining Prince's group, the saxophonist Eddie Mininfield was in Sheila E.'s band.

TEMPTATION

Prince and The Revolution / 8'17

Musicians: Prince: vocals, spoken voice, electric guitar, bass, programming, synthesizers, piano, backing vocals / **Eddie Mininfield:** saxophone / **Recording: Capitol Studios, Los Angeles:** 7 December 1984 / **Kiowa Trail Home Studio (Record Plant Remote, "Black Truck"), Chanhassen, Minnesota:** 24 December 1984 / **Technical team: Producer:** Prince / **Recording engineers:** David Leonard (Capitol Studios), David Tickle (Kiowa Trail—Record Plant Remote), Robert "Cubby" Colby (Kiowa Trail—Record Plant Remote), Susan Rogers (Kiowa Trail—Record Plant Remote)

In early December 1984, Prince traveled to Los Angeles to attend one of the last concerts on The Jacksons' *Victory* tour at Dodger Stadium. Accompanied by Eddie Mininfield, the saxophonist in Sheila E.'s band, Prince took advantage of his visit to the City of Angels to go to Capitol Studios before the concert, where David Leonard was then working. He recorded the tortured *Temptation* there, closely watched by Mininfield, the only guest present at the session. "He had some really deep thoughts going on," Mininfield explained. "He had a serious concept in his brain and I think that is why he didn't want The Revolution to record it."[92] Prince would add his "conversation with God" (at 6'52 on the track) on Christmas Eve in the mobile studio at the Record Plant studios in New York City with Susan Rogers. "I think he intended to spend Christmas by himself," said Rogers. "I know he had some presents under the tree that people had given him but I don't think he was too interested in them. He was mainly interested in getting this record cut together."[2] Prince would confide in the pages of *Rolling Stone* magazine about the emotional loneliness he had apparently been feeling for some time: "Sometimes it gets lonely here. To be perfectly honest, I wish more of my friends would come by [...] Musicians, people I know. A lot of the time they think I don't want to be bothered."[27] *Around the World in a Day* was therefore completed in the early hours of 25 December 1984, in the parking lot of his home at Kiowa Trail, Chanhassen, with the ever-loyal Susan Rogers.

4 THE TEARS IN YOUR EYES

Prince and The Revolution / 2'45

Musicians: Prince: vocals, electric guitar, synthesizers, backing vocals / **Wendy Melvoin:** electric guitar, backing vocals / **Brown Mark:** bass / **Bobby Z.:** electronic drums / **Lisa Coleman:** synthesizers, backing vocals / **Doctor Fink:** synthesizers / **Recording:** Louisiana Superdome (Le Mobile Studios), New Orleans: 1–2 February 1985 / **Technical team:** Producer: Prince / **Recording engineer:** Susan Rogers
USA For Africa *We Are the World* (compilation) / **Released in the USA by Columbia:** 12 April 1985 (LP ref.: USA 40043; CD ref: 824 822-2) / **Released in the UK by Columbia/CBS:** 12 April 1985 (LP ref.: USAID F1) / **Best chart ranking in the USA:** 1 / **Best chart ranking in the UK:** 31

In 1985, Prince was invited to sing on *We Are the World* with Michael Jackson, but categorically refused. Although he was deeply moved by the idea of helping to raise money for famine relief in Africa (Ethiopia and Sudan, in particular), there was no way he would consider performing a song written by his rival (and Lionel Richie) and playing a secondary role, even for a such a deserving cause. Instead, Prince chose to donate a previously unreleased song for the *We Are the World* album that was released alongside the single. That was his way of contributing to the cause without having to appear anywhere near the King of Pop. On 31 January 1985, in the middle of the Purple Rain Tour, Prince composed a song in his hotel room—*4 the Tears in Your Eyes*—and the following day, he taught the song to his musicians from The Revolution during the sound check onstage at the Louisiana Superdome in New Orleans. Susan Rogers, working from Le Mobile Studios, a truck equipped to record the concert, captured the new song on tape. After the show, Prince and his recording engineer spent all night on the track, adding synthesizer overdubs and various vocal lines. On 4 June, Prince decided to produce a video to accompany it, and he donated an unreleased version of *4 the Tears in Your Eyes* to the USA for Africa endeavor. He, Lisa, and Wendy recorded a beautiful acoustic take, which later featured on the compilation *The Hits/The B-Sides* in 1993. The video was shown for the first time during the gigantic Live Aid charity concert on 13 July 1985 in Philadelphia.

Single

A LOVE BIZARRE

Sheila E. featuring Prince / 3'46

Musicians: Sheila E.: vocals, finger cymbals, shaker, percussion, backing vocals / **Prince:** vocals, electric guitar, bass, programming, synthesizers, backing vocals / **Eddie Mininfield:** saxophone / **Juan Escovedo:** percussion / **Stephan Birnbaum:** backing vocals / **Susie Davis:** backing vocals / **Jerome Benton:** backing vocals / **Recording:** Cheshire Sound Studios, Atlanta, Georgia: 8 and 20 January 1985 / **Technical team:** Producers: Sheila E., Prince / **Recording engineers:** Susan Rogers, Gary Platt
Single: A-side: *A Love Bizarre* (Edit)/3'46 / **B-side:** *A Love Bizarre (Part II)*/3'50 / **Released in the USA by Paisley Park Records/Warner Bros. Records:** October 1985 (single ref.: 9 28890-7) / **Released in the UK by Paisley Park Records/WEA International:** 20 January 1986 (single ref.: W8890) / **Best chart ranking in the USA:** 11 / **Best chart ranking in the UK:** 76

Buoyed by the success of the single *The Glamorous Life* and the warm reception she received as the opening act on the Purple Rain Tour, Sheila E. began recording her second solo album in January 1985. She took the opportunity to record new songs during every break between concerts, as she said in 2015: "If I had any time, if I had six hours, I would stop somewhere in a city, go and record, and then go right to soundcheck. That's how I got the second record done."[93] She was more involved than ever in the production, but Prince was never far away, and when he produced *A Love Bizarre*, an irresistible club track in which the two artists sing in unison, the opening seconds are unmistakeably the Kid's style. For Sheila E.'s second album, *Romance 1600*, she created a visual universe markedly inspired by Miloš Forman's film *Amadeus* (1984). The costume designer Marie France worked with her and her musicians, and people who bought the album were treated to a cover of a band clad in ruffles, lace, embroidery, and men with thin moustaches, a trend already adopted by Prince for his *Purple Rain* outfits.

Despite her virtuosic drumming skills, Sheila E. used the obligatory Linn LM-1 Drum Computer on the track, which she covered with a Boss flanger pedal effect, pushed to the extreme. Eddie Mininfield, the saxophonist in Sheila E.'s band, was invited to take part in the day's session. "I just remember walking in the studio and it just had to be one of the funkiest tracks and I was just happy to be a part of it."[92] Mininfield played the main melody line on the track, following the vocal line of the Prince/Sheila E. duet, and improvised a saxophone score throughout. Prince had recently developed a liking for the saxophone, and besides being a top-quality track in its own right, *A Love Bizarre* introduced this instrument into Prince's music. The saxophone would soon occupy a major place in his compositions, particularly in 1987, where it would play a significant role in the production of the album *Sign O' the Times*.

Sheila E. was soon to replace the drummer Bobby Z. in Prince's group.

YELLOW

Sheila E. / 2'11

Musicians: **Sheila E.:** vocals, percussion, drums / **Prince:** vocals, bass, programming, synthesizers / **John Liotine:** trumpet / **Steven Madaio:** trumpet / **Ron Jannelli:** trumpet, trombone / **Dick Hyde:** trombone / **Robert Martin:** saxophone / **Timothy Misica:** saxophone / **Recording:** **Sunset Sound, Los Angeles:** 8 February 1985 / **Technical team:** **Producer:** Prince (credited to Sheila E.) / **Recording engineers:** Susan Rogers, Peggy McCreary, David Tickle

Sheila E. *Romance 1600* (album) / **Released in the USA by Paisley Park Records/Warner Bros. Records:** 26 August 1985 (LP ref.: 9 25317-1; CD ref.: 9 25317-2) / **Released in Europe by Paisley Park Records/WEA International:** 26 August 1985 (LP ref.: 925 317-1; CD ref.: 9 25317-2) / **Best chart ranking in the USA:** 50 / **Best chart ranking in the UK:** did not make the charts

In addition to playing guitar and bass on *Toy Box* and providing backing vocals on *Dear Michaelangelo*, two tracks on *Romance 1600*, Prince performed a jazz duet on *Yellow*, which was recorded on 8 February 985 at Sunset Sound while the Purple Rain Tour took a few days break between concerts in Memphis and Tacoma. Prince and Sheila E. recorded the song in a few hours, before calling in a talented horn section, as Eddie Mininfield had gone home for a well-deserved rest.

PARA

PRINCE AND THE REVOLUTION

PARADE

Christopher Tracy's Parade · New Position · I Wonder U · Under the Cherry Moon
Girls & Boys · Life Can Be So Nice · Venus De Milo · Mountains · Do U Lie? · Kiss
Anotherloverholenyohead · Sometimes It Snows In April

Released in the USA by Paisley Park Records/Warner Bros. Records:
31 March 1986 (LP ref.: 1-25395; CD ref.: 9 25395-2)
Released in the UK by Paisley Park Records/WEA International:
1 April 1986 (LP ref.: 925 395-1 – WX 39; CD ref.: 925 395-2)
Best chart ranking in the USA: 3
Best chart ranking in the UK: 4

During the *Parade* period in 1986, Prince was reborn as an elegant, immaculately dressed dandy.

Clare Fischer and his son Brent created the score for *Under the Cherry Moon*. First, they transcribed Prince's songs, then Clare wrote the arrangements. To help in their task, they asked for a video showing the scenes that needed music, which they received when a chauffeur pulled up in a purple limo. "I think Prince was probably in the purple limo," said Brent Fischer. "But we never really knew for certain."[21]

1986

FUNK IN BLACK AND WHITE

The months that followed the release of *Purple Rain* were busy for Prince, who was more prolific than ever. *Around the World in a Day* had been recorded during the Purple Rain Tour, and by the time it came out, Prince was already back at Sunset Sound, ready to start making a new movie—*Under the Cherry Moon*—and its soundtrack, which would become his eighth album, *Parade*. So, on 15 April 1985, he launched into a five-week marathon, recording most of this next album as well as some other songs, which he filed away in his archives. During the first week of work alone, Prince recorded *Wendy's Parade*, *New Position*, *I Wonder U*, *Under the Cherry Moon*, *Life Can Be So Nice*, *Others Here With Us*, *Old Friends 4 Sale*, *Sometimes It Snows In April*, *Tibet*, and *Evolsidog*. In addition, he and Sheila E. recorded *Holly Rock*. This was released as a single by Sheila E. on 4 July 1986 in the US, having already featured on the original soundtrack for the 1985 movie *Krush Groove*, in which she starred. That was another busy week for Prince, who set up shop at Sunset Sound and practically never left. "We arranged to have a queen-sized bed in the studio, which we set up in the performance area in the middle of the room," explained Craig Hubler, the studio director. "I bought purple sheets and a purple bedspread [...] I made up his bed and the bed stayed there for some weeks, making him feel like home."[2] The rest of the recording took place in the summer of 1985 at The Revolution's new rehearsal studio, the Washington Avenue Warehouse, in Edina, Minnesota, where Prince recorded *Girls & Boys, Love or Money, Do U Lie?, Alexa de Paris,* and *Venus De Milo*, among many others songs that remained unreleased for a long time, including *Sexual Suicide* and *Empty Room*. Prince asked Clare Fischer, who'd already worked in 1984 on the eponymous album by The Family (released in August 1985), to write the orchestral arrangements for some of the songs on Parade, along with several instrumental parts that were only used in the movie. In an unusual move, Prince gave Fischer complete control over the arrangements. Even though the two men didn't get a chance to meet before producing the album, Prince was satisfied with the first results Fischer sent him. So, he decided to let Fischer do his own thing without interfering in his work. Fischer left his mark on dozens of Prince songs from then on, without ever meeting him in person.

Christopher Tracy on the French Riviera

A few months before, Prince had managed to persuade Warner Bros. to support his move to pursue a career in the movies. He was developing an idea for a romantic drama inspired by inter-war comedies and he was determined to make a feature-length movie in black-and-white. Faced with Warner's strong opposition, a compromise was reached. *Under the Cherry Moon* was filmed in color and released in black-and-white. All that was left to do was to write a script worthy of the movie's name. New York-based screenwriter Becky Johnson took on the challenge with a plot that follows the adventures of Christopher Tracy (played by Prince), a gigolo who moves to France to find a rich wife. His plan to seduce the young heiress Mary Sharon goes awry after he falls in love with her. Prince crossed the Atlantic on 18 June 1985 to film the movie. He visited Paris and the French Riviera, choosing the city of Nice and its Victorine studios as the filming location. Director Mary Lambert, who specialized in music videos, joined the adventure, as did

Fans hope to catch a glimpse of their idol at the première of *Under the Cherry Moon* in Sheridan on 3 July 1986.

British actress Kristin Scott Thomas, who gave a brilliant audition. She replaced Madonna, Prince's first choice for the role of Mary Sharon. Jerome Benton, a former musician with The Time (see page 64) and a close friend of Prince, played the role of Tricky, Christopher Tracy's accomplice. Mary Lambert, who was more conspicuous for her absence than for her investment in the project, was quickly sidelined and Prince stepped in as the movie's director, with moderately successful results.

The commercial failure of Under the Cherry Moon

Prince had a promising start to 1986. His single *Kiss* catapulted to the top of the Billboard Hot 100 chart on 2 February, paving the way for the album *Parade* to go platinum. On 3 June 1986, he received the platinum award for selling a million copies of a record from the Recording Industry Association of America. However, *Under the Cherry Moon* did not receive the same level of acclaim when it was released on 2 July. The critics were scathing and the box-office sales were hopeless: the movie was an artistic and commercial flop, which forced Prince to cancel his tours on American soil. A few scattered showings, including a pair of sold-out concerts at Madison Square Garden in New York, managed to satisfy Prince's most fervent fans, but he decided to reserve the Parade Tour for Europe, where he played between 12 and 31 August. He also held four concerts in Japan in early September.

The end of The Revolution

When Prince launched his European tour, he included some new musicians in the backing band. Saxophonist Eric Leeds and trumpet player Matthew "Atlanta Bliss" Blistan replaced some of the synthesizer parts normally played by Doctor Fink. Miko Weaver, Sheila E.'s guitarist, also stepped in, allowing Prince to set aside his 6-string guitar to focus on staging. Finally, Jerome Benton and two former security officers from the Purple Rain Tour, Wally Safford and Greg Brooks, formed a trio of dancers and backing vocalists, sometimes joined at the mic by Susannah Melvoin. But when Wendy Melvoin and Lisa Coleman complained about the changes, tensions started to rise, just as the group reached Japan on 5 September 1986.

Eric Leeds and a leaping Prince performing onstage at the Wembley Arena, London, in August 1986.

The guitarists of The Revolution, Wendy Melvoin and Miko Weaver, onstage at the Forest Vorst Nationa(a)l, in Brussels, on 27 August 1986.

On 6 September, Sheila E. replaced Bobby Z. for the entire sound check in Osaka, and two days later, onstage at the Yokohama Stadium, Prince was seized by a fit of rage and smashed his two iconic Cloud Guitars from the "Purple Rain" era. "I looked at Lisa, and I looked at Bobby," said Wendy Melvoin. "And he looked at me and said, 'That's it. It's over.'"[35] After returning from Japan, Prince left Wendy and Lisa to their own devices, and told Bobby Z. that Sheila E. would be taking his place at the drums. In the midst of this mess, Brown Mark decided to leave, followed by Jerome Benton. Doctor Fink kept his place in the band. On 17 October 1986, an official press release announced that Prince had disbanded The Revolution. "It was a fiercely busy time. I wish it could've gone on longer," explained Melvoin. "But [Prince] was like a hummingbird, going from one flower to the next, trying to get as much nectar as he could, and we were just a flower he was done with."[35]

FOR PRINCE ADDICTS

Between 26 December 1985 and 12 January 1986, Prince recorded an album at Sunset Sound with a new, short-lived group called The Flesh. He recorded some 20 songs with Lisa Coleman (synthesizers), Wendy Melvoin (guitar), Eric Leeds (saxophone), Jonathan Melvoin (percussion), Sheila E. (drums), and her guitarist Levi Seacer Jr. Sadly, the project was abandoned, and the album, although completed, was never released.

1986

CHRISTOPHER TRACY'S PARADE

Prince, John L Nelson / 2'09

Musicians: Prince: vocals, electric guitar, acoustic guitar, bass, drums, programming, synthesizers, finger snapping, backing vocals / **Lisa Coleman, Susannah Melvoin, Wendy Melvoin:** backing vocals / **Orchestra:** / **Mari Botnick, Oscar Chausow, Ron Clark, Isabelle Daskoff, Assa Drori, Henry Ferber, Pam Gates, Janice Gower, Endre Granat, Ed Green, Reginald Hill, Bill Hybel, William Hymanson, Pat Johnson, Karen Jones, Betty Moor, Irma Neumann, Donald Palmer, Sheldon Sanov, Joseph Schoenbrun, Terry Schoenbrun, Francine Walsh, Harold Wolf:** violin / **Myer Bello, Alan DeVeritch, Norman Forrest, Pamela Goldsmith, Allan Harshman, Margot MacLaine, Jorge Moraga, Carole Mukogawa, David Stock:** alto violin / **James Arkatov, Ray Kelley, Raphael Kramer, Frederick Seykora:** cello / **Chuck Domanico, Árni Egilsson:** upright bass / **Don Ashworth, Gene Cipriano, Jon Clarke, Dave Edwards, Gary Foster, Jim Kanter, Jack Nimitz, Dick Mitchell:** clarinet / **John Lowe, Joe Soldo, Bob Tricarico:** transverse flute / **Ray Brown, Rich Cooper, Bob Findley, Larry Ford, Bob O'Donnell, Allen Vizzutti:** trumpet / **Garnett Brown, Charles Loper, Morris Repass, Bill Watrous:** trombone / **David Duke, Marni Johnson, Joe Myer, Brian O'Connor, Calvin Smith, James Thatcher:** French horn / **Tommy Johnson:** tuba / **Brent Fischer:** timpani, percussion / **Recording: Sunset Sound, Los Angeles:** 17–19, 22–24 April, December 1985; January 1986 / **Monterey Sound Studios, Glendale, California:** summer of 1985 (orchestra) / **Technical team: Producer:** Prince / **Recording engineers:** Peggy McCreary, Susan Rogers / **Assistant recording engineers:** Mike Kloster / **Orchestra arrangements:** Clare Fischer

On 17 April 1985, Prince joined Susan Rogers and Peggy McCreary at the Sunset Sound studios in Los Angeles. They started the session with some drum takes, then Prince asked them to let the tape roll at the end of the first song, *Wendy's Parade* (Prince later changed the title to *Christopher Tracy's Parade*, using the name of his character from *Under the Cherry Moon*). In just one take, he followed it with three other songs that come one after the other on the album: *New Position*, *I Wonder U*, and *Under the Cherry Moon*. He then added his bass lines and the synthesizers. By the end of the day, he had almost finished four songs. Many overdubs were added in the following days, and Lisa Coleman and the Melvoin sisters added backing vocals in later sessions.

NEW POSITION

Prince and The Revolution / 2'21

Musicians: Prince: vocals, bass, drums, steel drums, programming, backing vocals / **Lisa Coleman, Wendy Melvoin:** backing vocals / **Recording: Sunset Sound, Los Angeles:** 17–19, 23 April 1985 / **Advision Studios, London:** November 1985 (overdubs) / **Technical team: Producers:** Prince, Lisa Coleman, Wendy Melvoin / **Recording engineers:** Peggy McCreary, Susan Rogers

By the time the Purple Rain Tour was over, most of *Around the World in a Day* had been recorded, and Prince was already writing *Parade*. So, Steve Fargnoli, his manager, suggested that Prince and his musicians go to Brazil for a few days to get some much-needed rest. They planned a ten-day stay at a hotel in Rio de Janeiro, with trips to the beach and all sorts of parties, but after three days, Prince went to see Alan Leeds, his tour manager. As Leeds explained: "Prince came to see me and said, 'Will you please check the flights, I want to go back. It's great, but I've seen enough. Let's go home.'"[94] Prince didn't retain many memories of this Brazilian experience, but it did foster in him a taste for steel drums, the melodic metal percussion instrument that can be heard in *New Position*, which Prince wrote in 1982 and rerecorded right after returning from South America. Clare Fischer added dazzling but cumbersome arrangements, which Prince did not retain. It was a good thing he didn't, as *New Position* shines for its striking funk simplicity.

I WONDER U

Prince and The Revolution / 1'40

Musicians: Prince: electric guitar, bass, drums, programming, synthesizers / **Wendy Melvoin:** vocals / **Lisa Coleman:** backing vocals / **Orchestra** (see ***Christopher Tracy's Parade***, left) / **Recording: Sunset Sound, Los Angeles:** 17–19, 22 April 1985 / **Monterey Sound Studios, Glendale, California:** 24 June 1985 (orchestra) / **Technical team: Producer:** Prince / **Recording engineers:** Peggy McCreary, Susan Rogers / **Orchestra arrangements:** Clare Fischer

Prince's inspiration for this interlude, sung by Wendy Melvoin, came from a conversation he had with a young woman in a club in Rio. She had said to him: "I...How do you say? I Wonder U...I Wonder U." It was her way of asking for sexual favors. The result was a curious and fleeting song, which Clare Fischer dotted with understated orchestral arrangements.

Prince as a dandy gigolo searching for conquests on the Côte d'Azur in the movie *Under the Cherry Moon*, in 1986.

UNDER THE CHERRY MOON

Prince, John L Nelson / 2'57

Musicians: Prince: vocals, bass, drums, programming, zills, synthesizers, piano / **Orchestra / Recording: Sunset Sound, Los Angeles:** 17–19, 24 April 1985 / **Monterey Sound Studios, Glendale, California:** 24 June 1985 (orchestra) / **Technical team: Producers:** Prince, Wendy Melvoin, Lisa Coleman / **Recording engineers:** Peggy McCreary, Susan Rogers, David Tickle / **Assistant recording engineers:** Mike Kloster / **Orchestral arrangements:** Clare Fischer

In June 1985, Prince was feeling overwhelmed with all his projects, including preparations for filming *Under the Cherry Moon*. In an unusual move for him, he entrusted Wendy and Lisa with the tapes he'd recorded for the *Parade* album and gave them free reign to add various arrangements. Since Sunset Sound was booked, they holed up at The Complex Studios in Los Angeles, where they added multiple overdubs to *Do U Lie?*, *Venus De Milo*, and *Under the Cherry Moon*. Prince did not keep the overdubs for *Under the Cherry Moon* on the album, the strings played by Novi Novog, Suzie Katayama, and David Coleman, or the upright bass lines Annette Atkinson and Richard Feves recorded on 24 April at Sunset Sound. In the end, he opted for a stripped-down version of the song, which set the tone for the upcoming movie—somewhere between burlesque and 1930s dark comedy. In fact, the working title of the movie was *Marx Brothers Project*, after the famous American comedians from the inter-war period.

Alexa Fiorini (left in the photo), the niece of Prince's manager, was given pride of place in the song *Alexa de Paris.*

Single

GIRLS & BOYS

1986

Prince and The Revolution / 5'30

Musicians

Prince: vocals, electric guitar, Roland G-707 Guitar-Synthesizer, zills, synthesizers, backing vocals
Wendy Melvoin: electric guitar, backing vocals
Brown Mark: bass, backing vocals
Bobby Z.: drums, electric drums
Lisa Coleman: synthesizers, backing vocals
Doctor Fink: synthesizers
Eric Leeds: saxophone, baritone saxophone
Susannah Melvoin, Sheila E.: backing vocals
Marie France: spoken word

Recording

Washington Avenue Warehouse, Edina, Minnesota: 8–9 July 1985

Technical team

Producer: Prince
Recording engineers: Susan Rogers, David Tickle

SINGLE

A-side: *Girls & Boys* (Edit)/3'27
B-side: *Under the Cherry Moon*/2'57
Released in the UK by Paisley Park Records/WEA International: 4 August 1986 (single ref.: W8586)
Best chart ranking in the UK: 11

Genesis

On 8 July 1985, when The Revolution moved into their new rehearsal space on Washington Avenue, they were feeling inspired, to say the least. "There was an energy in the house just because the grooves were so so good!"[95] It was a beautiful day and the atmosphere was relaxed. The musicians improvised on *Girls & Boys*, which had already been recorded. Prince played the song at high volume through the loudspeakers and asked his team to experiment with it while he issued all manner of instructions. This was how Prince's most French-sounding song came about: within the walls of the last room he rented before building Paisley Park, his fortress in Chanhassen, Minnesota. This space was also where he recorded most of *The Black Album* (1994), along with songs for several abandoned projects, including the albums *Dream Factory* and *Crystal Ball*. Seizing on the energy in the room, Prince and The Revolution recorded the future B-side of *Kiss, Love or Money*, as well as *Alexa de Paris*.

Production

By now, Eric Leeds was a fully fledged member of The Revolution. During the jam session for this song, he played a baritone saxophone line which Prince loved so much that he immediately grabbed his brand-new Roland G-707 synth guitar, which according to Bobby Z. "whines like a duck."[13] Prince then wanted to give the song a French touch, most likely inspired by the script from the movie that he was about to shoot. Night had already fallen by the time he sent for costume designer Marie France, with whom he'd collaborated since *Purple Rain*, and who was in Minneapolis at the time working on Prince's costumes. Without knowing the reason she had been summoned, Marie went to the Warehouse, where Prince handed her some lyrics to translate into French. Then he asked her to read the lyrics at the mic, without rehearsing them. She was surprised but obliging, and at Prince's signal, she went for it. "I read my little gibberish and I thought, 'Ok, the next take will be better.' Wendy and Lisa clapped and Prince said, 'That's good, it's a wrap.'"[96] Her participation was credited as "The French Seduction" on the album jacket.

HEADPHONES AT THE READY

Between 4'08 and 4'16 into *Girls & Boys*, Prince launches into his first rap, with great enthusiasm. While he later alternated between virulent criticism (*Dead On It*) and praise of rap (*Alphabet Street*), this short but significant interlude was delivered flawlessly.

LIFE CAN BE SO NICE

Prince and The Revolution / 3'12

Musicians: Prince: vocals, drums, electronic drums, programming, synthesizers, backing vocals / **Sheila E.:** bells / **Lisa Coleman, Wendy Melvoin:** backing vocals / **Recording: Sunset Sound, Los Angeles:** 17 and 22 April 1985 / **Technical team: Producer:** Prince / **Recording engineers:** Peggy McCreary, Susan Rogers

On the morning of 16 April 1985, Prince, Sheila E., Lisa Coleman, and Wendy Melvoin were at Sunset Sound, in Los Angeles, for what would become one of the longest jam sessions in the history of The Revolution. For almost 24 hours, the four musicians rehearsed *Life Can Be So Nice*, recorded it, and added overdubs. Wendy played the bass and an acoustic guitar line with a Brazilian feel inspired by the three days they had spent in Rio, while Sheila E. hammered on the bells. The next day, at around nine in the morning, as the musicians were getting ready to go home, Prince told them he wanted to record a whole new version of the song. They all complied, and the song was eventually finished. On 22 April, Wendy and Lisa added their backing vocals, after having rested for a while.

VENUS DE MILO

Prince and The Revolution / 1'54

Musicians: Prince: piano / **Sheila E.:** drums / **Orchestra:** (see ***Christopher Tracy's Parade***, page 128) / **Recording: Washington Avenue Warehouse, Edina, Minnesota:** 11 July 1985 / **Monterey Sound Studios, Glendale, California:** 13 August 1986 (orchestra) / **Technical team: Producers:** Prince, Lisa Coleman, Wendy Melvoin / **Recording engineers:** Susan Rogers, David Tickle / **Orchestral arrangements:** Clare Fischer

On 11 July 1985, Prince and Sheila E. attended a concert at the 7th St. Entry in Minneapolis, the club next to the famous First Avenue. Ring Theatre, a band from Texas, was playing. By now stars of Minneapolis, Prince and Sheila E. improvised two songs, *Girls & Boys* and *Holly Rock,* using the band's instruments. After their impromptu show, they returned to Edina for a recording session with recording engineers Susan Rogers and David Tickle. Sheila E. recalled: "He [Prince] said, 'I want to do something for the movie.'" As she then explained: "When we played it, it was so different for me, musically, so different from most anything we had done together."[61] This was how the instrumental piece *Venus De Milo* came to be. Clare Fischer's orchestrations were added in August 1986.

The legendary First Avenue and the club 7th St. Entry—two places that have been emblematic of Minneapolis ever since *Purple Rain*.

Single

MOUNTAINS

Prince and The Revolution / 3'58

Musicians: Prince: vocals, electric guitar, backing vocals / **Wendy Melvoin:** electric guitar, backing vocals / **Miko Weaver:** electric guitar / **Brown Mark:** bass, backing vocals / **Bobby Z.:** drums, electronic drums / **Lisa Coleman:** synthesizers, backing vocals / **Doctor Fink:** synthesizers / **Eric Leeds:** saxophone / **Atlanta Bliss:** trumpet / **Recording: Washington Avenue Warehouse, Edina, Minnesota:** 30 November, December 1985 / **Technical team: Producer:** Prince / **Recording engineer:** Susan Rogers **Single: A-side** ***Mountains***/3'58 / **B-side:** ***Alexa de Paris***/3'20 / **Released in the USA by Paisley Park Records/Warner Bros. Records:** 7 May 1986 (single ref.: 7-28711) / **Released in the UK by Paisley Park Records/WEA International:** 2 June 1986 (single ref.: W8711) / **Best chart ranking in the USA:** 23 / **Best chart ranking in the UK:** 45

In November 1985, as Prince was busy filming *Under the Cherry Moon* in Nice, he dispatched Lisa and Wendy to work on songs for the album at Advision Studios in London. They holed up there for a few days, during which time they made some changes to *New Position*, though these were not kept in the final mix. During their time in Britain, they composed *Mountains*, to which Prince later added his own lyrics. Once back together in Edina, The Revolution held a recording session which led to the version of the song that appears on the album. Miko Weaver, Sheila E.'s guitarist, participated in the session, as did Matthew Blistan (aka as Atlanta Bliss), Prince's new trumpet player. That same day, Prince and The Revolution recorded *Dream Factory*, which launched Prince's next musical venture.

DO U LIE?

Prince and The Revolution / 2'43

Musicians: Prince: vocals, electric guitar, bass, synthesizers, backing vocals / **Jonathan Melvoin:** drums / **Lisa Coleman, Wendy Melvoin:** backing vocals / **Sandra "Little Gipsy Girl" Francisco:** spoken word / **Orchestra:** (see ***Christopher Tracy's Parade***, page 128) / **Recording: Washington Avenue Warehouse, Edina, Minnesota:** July 1985 / **Monterey Sound Studios, Glendale, California:** August 1985 (orchestra) / **Technical team: Producer:** Prince / **Recording engineers:** Susan Rogers, David Tickle / **Orchestral arrangements:** Clare Fischer

What better day than Bastille Day to record a tribute to 1930s jazz, which included accordian lines simulated on the synthesizer? Prince wrote *Do U Lie?* on the French Riviera while waiting to shoot *Under the Cherry Moon* and recorded it in Edina, Minnesota, with drummer Jonathan Melvoin, who was Wendy's brother and a seasoned jazzman. "He [Jonathan Melvoin] was incredibly musical and he knew he had a great ear and was really subtle,"[95] confirmed Prince's guitarist, who was also at the sessions with Lisa Coleman. The voice in the introduction, which says, "*Les enfants qui mentent ne vont pas au paradis*" (Children who lie don't got to Heaven), belongs to Sandra Francisco (aka "Gipsy Girl" in the album's credits). Although the date and location of this voice recording remains unknown, it presumably took place in France, since at 0'03 in, we can hear a man say: "Ok, *merci*," which sounds like a recording engineer telling the girl that it was a wrap.

Single

KISS

1986

Prince / 3'38

Musicians

Prince: vocals, electric guitar, acoustic guitar, backing vocals
David Rivkin: programming, piano
Bruce "Tony Christian" DeShazer, Marvin "Marr Starr" Gunn: backing vocals

Recording

Sunset Sound, Los Angeles: 27–28 April 1985; 14–22 January 1986 (overdubs)

Technical team

Producer: Prince, David Rivkin
Recording engineers: David Rivkin, Peggy McCreary, Susan Rogers, Coke Johnson

SINGLE

A-side: *Kiss* (Single Version)/3'46
B-side: ❤ or $/3'57
Released in the USA by Paisley Park Records/Warner Bros. Records: 5 February 1986 (single ref.: 7-28751)
Released in the UK by Paisley Park Records/WEA International: 5 February 1986 (single ref.: W8751)
Best chart ranking in the USA: 1
Best chart ranking in the UK: 6

While putting together the final tracklisting for *Parade*, Prince asked Eric Leeds what he thought of the songs they'd recorded. "The first thing I took off the album was *Kiss*," said the saxophonist. "I didn't care for it then and I still don't do to this day [...] It shows what I know about pop music."[21]

Genesis

In April 1985, while Prince was recording in Studio 3 at Sunset Sound, his bass player, Brown Mark, was one studio over, producing the first album by Mazarati, the band he'd recently formed. Prince had written several songs to support his friend's project, including *100 MPH* and *Jerk Out*. The band accepted the first one, and turned it into a quality single, but they did not appreciate the second, with its dirtier lyrics, and refused to sing it. On 27 April, Mazarati asked Prince for a new song to replace *Jerk Out* (which later provided The Time with a hit single, after they reunited in 1990). So, Prince put his own session on hold and, in front of a stunned Susan Rogers, picked up an acoustic guitar and recorded a new song, *Kiss*, on the enormous green boom box he always had with him. He pulled out the tape, handed it to the band, and said, "Do what you want with this song." David Rivkin and Coke Johnson, Mazarati's producer and recording engineer, respectively, immediately started producing the song and finished it that same day. The next day, Prince listened to the tape while he played basketball in the courtyard of Sunset Sound. He then returned to the studio and told the band's frontman, Casey Terry: "It was too good for you, I take it back."[97] The bosses at Warner Bros. Records, who hated the song, were not pleased when Prince released it as a single on 5 February 1986, but *Kiss* soon became one of his biggest worldwide hits. In the United States, the song reached the top of the Billboard Hot 100 chart on 19 April that same year.

Production

As he got down to producing *Kiss*, David Rivkin used a pattern from the Linn 9000, the bone-chilling drum machine released in 1984, to which Brown Mark added a bass line. Prince's acoustic guitar was tuned to the Linn's hi-hat, on which Coke Johnson superimposed a gate pushed to its limit. He then embellished the song with a piano line. As Rivkin confessed: "The piano part I stole from a Bo Diddley song and the background vocals I stole from a Brenda Lee song called *Sweet Nothing*. So it's like a soup of everything!"[97] Casey Terry then added the main vocals and was quickly followed by his musicians and the backing vocalists, Tony Christian and Marvin Gunn. When Prince got *Kiss* back, he kept most of the arrangements, though it's impossible to credit the

FOR PRINCE ADDICTS

In 1991, Prince wrote *U* for Paula Abdul's second album, *Spellbound*. Perhaps Prince had appreciated the nod she'd given him in her song *State of Attraction* in 1988. The famous guitar gimmick from the *Kiss* chorus appears there at 1'57 in.

From left to right: Marvin "Marr Starr" Gunn, Aaron Paul Keith, Craig Powell, Sir Casey Terry, Tony Christian, Kevin Patrick, and Jerome Cox of the group Mazarati, photographed in 1986.

musicians with precision, since Rivkin and Johnson made extensive alterations to Mazarati's original recording. As he did with *When Doves Cry*, Prince removed the bass track, then added his famous guitar rhythm, which he borrowed from *Papa's Got A Brand New Bag* by James Brown (1965), before finally recording his own vocals. In this way, he transformed a folk ditty into a global hit.

Belgian photographer Rebecca Blake directed the famous music video for *Kiss*. She was already known for shooting the cover of *Romance 1600*, Sheila E.'s second solo album. Blake worked with Prince several times, directing the videos for the songs *Cream* and *Diamonds and Pearls*, in 1991.

For the 1986 Parade Tour, Prince adopted a peach color theme.

Single

ANOTHERLOVERHOLENYOHEAD

Prince and The Revolution / 3'58

Musicians: Prince: vocals, electric guitar, Roland G-707 Guitar-Synthesizer, bass, piano, programming, claps, backing vocals / **Susannah Melvoin:** backing vocals / **Orchestra:** (see ***Christopher Tracy's Parade***, page 128) / **Recording: Sunset Sound, Los Angeles:** 16–17 December 1985 / **Monterey Sound Studios, Glendale, California:** January 1986 (orchestra) / **Technical team: Producer:** Prince / **Recording engineers:** Susan Rogers, Coke Johnson / **Orchestral arrangements:** Clare Fischer
Single: A-side *Anotherloverholenyohead*/3'58 / **B-side:** *Girls & Boys*/5'30 (USA); ***I Wanna Be Your Lover*** (Edit)/2'56 (UK) / **Released in the USA by Paisley Park Records/Warner Bros. Records:** 2 July 1986 (single ref.: 7-28620) / **Released in the UK by Paisley Park Records/WEA International:** 20 October 1986 (single ref.: W8521) / **Best chart ranking in the USA:** 63 / **Best chart ranking in the UK:** 36 /

The single *Anotherloverholenyohead*—as in "Another lover/hole in your head"—was a commercial flop. Nevertheless, it remains a high-quality song. Prince recorded it on his own at Sunset Sound. Only Susannah Melvoin was invited to participate in the backing vocals, which were doubled and mixed with his. The irresistible slap bass line makes *Anotherloverholenyohead* one of the strongest moments of Prince's eighth album.

Lisa Coleman and Wendy Melvoin, cornerstones of The Revolution.

SOMETIMES IT SNOWS IN APRIL

Prince and The Revolution / 6'48

Musicians: Prince: vocals / **Wendy Melvoin:** acoustic guitar, backing vocals / **Lisa Coleman:** piano, backing vocals / **Recording: Sunset Sound, Los Angeles:** 21 April 1985 / **Advision Studios, London:** November 1985 / **Monterey Sound Studios, Glendale, California:** 27 July 1985 (orchestra) / **Technical team: Producer:** Prince / **Recording engineers:** Peggy McCreary, Susan Rogers / **Assistant recording engineer:** Coke Johnson

This was one of the greatest songs Prince ever recorded. He completed it in less than two hours with the help of his two most loyal musicians, Wendy Melvoin on the acoustic guitar and Lisa Coleman on the piano. Susan Rogers, who recorded this moment, remembers that: "He wanted to set a tone. He didn't normally do that. We lit candles, the lights were dimmed."[85] The lyrics to *Sometimes It Snows In April* make explicit reference to the tragic death of Christopher Tracy, the character in *Under the Cherry Moon*. On 21 April 1985, Prince sang, "sometimes I wish that life was never ending," a phrase with a particular resonance since Prince died 31 years after this session, on 21 April 2016. On that day, long ago in Los Angeles, the chemistry between Prince, Lisa, and Wendy had never been so palpable. Time seemed to stand still as they flowed to the rhythm of Lisa's guitar arpeggios. "*Sometimes It Snows In April* was really the pinnacle of our relationship together," said Lisa in 2009. "The three of us had kind of a love affair. And when we wrote that song [...] it was just the three of us sitting together in a room. I really loved it, and I had hoped we would follow that trail further, you know? Like make a whole record like that or something. But, that didn't happen."[98] This beautiful song is sure to induce chills in anyone who listens to it. It closes the *Parade* era in the most beautiful way.

FOR PRINCE ADDICTS

As recording began for *Sometimes It Snows In April*, Susan Rogers realized Wendy Melvoin's seat creaked and that the noise could be heard through the mics. She decided to change the chair, but Prince stopped her in her tracks. "No, leave it, I want it like that,"[85] he ordered, and he kept the creaks throughout the song.

♥ OR $

Prince and The Revolution / 3'57

Musicians: **Prince:** vocals, electric guitar, synthesizers / **Wendy Melvoin:** electric guitar, backing vocals / **Brown Mark:** bass / **Bobby Z.:** drums, electronic drums / **Lisa Coleman:** synthesizers, backing vocals / **Doctor Fink:** synthesizers / **Eric Leeds:** saxophone / **Orchestra:** **Mari Botnick, Oscar Chausow, Ron Clark, Isabelle Daskoff, Assa Drori, Henry Ferber, Pam Gates, Janice Gower, Endre Granat, Ed Green, Reginald Hill, Bill Hybel, William Hymanson, Pat Johnson, Karen Jones, Betty Moor, Irma Neumann, Donald Palmer, Sheldon Sanov, Joseph Schoenbrun, Terry Schoenbrun, Francine Walsh, Harold Wolf:** violin / **Myer Bello, Alan DeVeritch, Norman Forrest, Pamela Goldsmith, Allan Harshman, Margot MacLaine, Jorge Moraga, Carole Mukogawa, David Stock:** alto violin / **James Arkatov, Ray Kelley, Raphael Kramer, Frederick Seykora:** cello / **Chuck Domanico, Árni Egilsson:** upright bass / **Don Ashworth, Gene Cipriano, Jon Clarke, Dave Edwards, Gary Foster, Jim Kanter, Jack Nimitz, Dick Mitchell:** clarinet / **John Lowe, Joe Soldo, Bob Tricarico:** transverse flute / **Ray Brown, Rich Cooper, Bob Findley, Larry Ford, Bob O'Donnell, Allen Vizzutti:** trumpet / **Garnett Brown, Charles Loper, Morris Repass, Bill Watrous:** trombone / **David Duke, Marni Johnson, Joe Myer, Brian O'Connor, Calvin Smith, James Thatcher:** French horn / **Tommy Johnson:** tuba / **Brent Fischer:** timpani, percussion / **Recording:** **Washington Avenue Warehouse, Edina, Minnesota:** 8, 9, 13, and 18 July 1985 / **Monterey Sound Studios, Glendale, California:** January 1986 (orchestra) / **Technical team:** **Producer:** Prince / **Recording engineers:** Susan Rogers, David Tickle / **Orchestral arrangements:** Clare Fischer

Prince and The Revolution *Kiss* (single) / **Released in the USA by Paisley Park Records/Warner Bros. Records:** 5 February 1986 (single ref.: 7-28751) / **Released in the UK by Paisley Park Records/WEA International:** 5 February 1986 (single ref.: W8751) / **Best chart ranking in the USA:** 1 / **Best chart ranking in the UK:** 6

Prince recorded *Girls & Boys* with his full band at the Washington Avenue Warehouse, in Edina, Minnesota, on 8 July 1985. In a flash of creativity, they also recorded *Love or Money* and *Alexa de Paris*, two future B-sides that, for some reason, were left out of the 1993 compilation *The Hits/The B-Sides*. Prince sings *Love or Money* in a high-pitched voice, as in *Shockadelica*, *Feel U Up*, and *Rockhard in a Funky Place*, where Prince masquerades as his new female avatar, Camille (see page 142). The identity of the person being addressed in *Love or Money* remained a mystery until 17 November 1997, when it was revealed by Prince after one of his fans asked about this on his website love4oneanother.com. It was none other than Mary Sharon, Kristin Scott Thomas' character in *Under the Cherry Moon*. Another fan (and Prince expert), Willie Garrett, suggested in a 1994 letter in *NPG Magazine* that *Love or Money*, when played at 33rpm, was actually a tribute to Sly and The Family Stone. Prince responded that "If it were a tribute, [I'd] give props by saying names. The sound of the record is intentional."[99]

ALEXA DE PARIS

Prince and The Revolution / 3'20

Musicians: **Prince:** acoustic guitar / **Wendy Melvoin:** electric guitar / **Brown Mark:** bass / **Lisa Coleman:** synthesizers / **Doctor Fink:** synthesizers / **Sheila E.:** drums / **Orchestra:** **Mari Botnick, Oscar Chausow, Ron Clark, Isabelle Daskoff, Assa Drori, Henry Ferber, Pam Gates, Janice Gower, Endre Granat, Ed Green, Reginald Hill, Bill Hybel, William Hymanson, Pat Johnson, Karen Jones, Betty Moor, Irma Neumann, Donald Palmer, Sheldon Sanov, Joseph Schoenbrun, Terry Schoenbrun, Francine Walsh, Harold Wolf:** violin / **Myer Bello, Alan DeVeritch, Norman Forrest, Pamela Goldsmith, Allan Harshman, Margot MacLaine, Jorge Moraga, Carole Mukogawa, David Stock:** alto violin / **James Arkatov, Ray Kelley, Raphael Kramer, Frederick Seykora:** cello / **Chuck Domanico, Árni Egilsson:** upright bass / **Don Ashworth, Gene Cipriano, Jon Clarke, Dave Edwards, Gary Foster, Jim Kanter, Jack Nimitz, Dick Mitchell:** clarinet / **John Lowe, Joe Soldo, Bob Tricarico:** transverse flute / **Ray Brown, Rich Cooper, Bob Findley, Larry Ford, Bob O'Donnell, Allen Vizzutti:** trumpet / **Garnett Brown, Charles Loper, Morris Repass, Bill Watrous:** trombone / **David Duke, Marni Johnson, Joe Myer, Brian O'Connor, Calvin Smith, James Thatcher:** French horn / **Tommy Johnson:** tuba / **Brent Fischer:** timpani, percussion / **Recording:** **Washington Avenue Warehouse, Edina, Minnesota:** 8 July 1985 / **Monterey Sound Studios, Glendale, California:** 21 August 1986 (orchestra) / **Technical team:** **Producer:** Prince / **Recording engineers:** Susan Rogers, David Tickle / **Orchestral arrangements:** Clare Fischer

Prince and The Revolution *Mountains* (single) / **Released in the USA by Paisley Park Records/Warner Bros. Records:** 7 May 1986 (single ref.: 7-28711) / **Released in the UK by Paisley Park Records/WEA International:** 2 June 1986 (single ref.: W8711) / **Best chart ranking in the USA:** 23 / **Best chart ranking in the UK:** 45

Prince was inspired to write *Alexa de Paris* in the summer of 1985, while in France, after meeting the niece of his manager, Steve Fargnoli. Alexa Fiorini was a 15-year-old dancer who was taking ballet lessons at the Paris Opera. Prince asked to see her dance and Fargnoli organized a meeting at a private club in Paris. Prince composed this instrumental piece in her honor and gave her a small role in *Under the Cherry Moon* and another in the video for *Girls & Boys*, where she can be seen dancing in the crowd at 1'53 in. Recorded the same day as *Girls & Boys*, *Alexa de Paris* sounds more like Joe Satriani hard FM rock than anything from Prince's funk universe. The Revolution accompanies him throughout the song, while Sheila E. works the drumsticks with her usual virtuosity, embellishing the take with her incredible barrel fugues, a signature move she developed after becoming Prince's drummer in 1987. *Alexa de Paris* was released on the B-side of *Mountains* in May 1986.

Just this once...Prince abandons his Hohner Madcat and Cloud Guitar in favor of an Epiphone Emperor Thinline.

SIGN

PRINCE

SIGN O' THE TIMES

DISC 1

Sign O' the Times · Play in the Sunshine · Housequake · The Ballad of Dorothy Parker
It · Starfish and Coffee · Slow Love · Hot Thing · Forever In My Life

DISC 2

U Got the Look · If I Was Your Girlfriend · Strange Relationship
I Could Never Take the Place of Your Man · The Cross
It's Gonna Be A Beautiful Night · Adore

Released in the USA by Paisley Park Records/Warner Bros.Records:
30 March 1987 (LP ref.: 1-25577; CD ref.: 9 25577-2)
Released in the UK by Paisley Park Records/Warner Bros. Records:
31 March 1987 (LP ref.: 925 577-1 – WX 88; CD ref.: 925 577-2)
Best chart ranking in the USA: 6
Best chart ranking in the UK: 4

A new look for Prince, who frequently sported a pair of glasses during the promotion of *Sign O' the Times*.

There is a plasma lamp on the sleeve of *Sign O' the Times*. These lamps were very popular in 1987. Leroy Bennett, Prince's lighting and stage designer, had given it to him. So, Prince decided he wanted to build one for the stage, measuring 2.5m (8ft) in diameter, but that proved impossible because the electricity needed to power it would create too much interference during concerts. Even so, the lamp remained inseparable from the visual landscape of *Sign O' the Times*.

AN ALBUM MARKED BY ITS ERA

On 30 November 1985, the *Sign O' the Times* adventure began. That day, Prince and The Revolution were rehearsing at the Washington Avenue Warehouse, in Edina, Minnesota, where they were recording *Mountains*, which ended up on the *Parade* album. A few hours later, Prince and his fiancé Susannah Melvoin recorded *Dream Factory*. This song launched Prince's new project, even though *Under the Cherry Moon* and its original score hadn't been released yet. Prince and Susannah had just moved into their new home on Galpin Boulevard, in Chanhassen, and he was as happy as could be. To Susan Rogers' delight, he installed a brand-new studio with a soundproof booth for sound takes, and between November 1985 and April 1986, he started recording his ninth album, which was, of course, called the *Dream Factory*. The songs alternated between scathing funk and forceful pop. Prince put them together in the spring of 1986 to create a first draft of the album. "Dream Factory was the house," explained Susannah. "The house, and his easy access to his creative and imaginative place in that studio. He could access it in a second. Roll tape. He was editing tape, editing kick drums. He was just in there constantly, and it was just a fertile time."[100] By April 1986 the album's tracklisting already contained 11 songs: *Sexual Suicide*, *Strange Relationship*, *Visions*, *Dream Factory*, *Teacher, Teacher*, *It's A Wonderful Day*, *Big Tall Wall*, *And That Says What?*, *A Place In Heaven*, *Starfish and Coffee*, and *The Ballad of Dorothy Parker*. *It*, *In A Large Room With No Light*, *The Cross*, *Sign O' the Times*, and *I Could Never Take The Place of Your Man* soon completed the list, which led Prince to present *Dream Factory* as a double album. The summer of 1986 was already well on its way, but since the Parade Tour had ended in the dissolution of The Revolution, Prince had had to face the facts: this project was intended for a collective—so, it had lost its purpose. "It was going to be marketed as a group record, not a Prince record [...]," explained Alan Leeds, Prince's tour manager. "Whatever *Dream Factory* meant to him, it was inspired by the camaraderie of that group of people during that period of time."[2] The band broke up in October 1986 and Prince abandoned the *Dream Factory* project.

The birth of Camille

The day after The Revolution was officially pronounced dissolved, Prince set up shop in Sunset Sound and recorded *Housequake*. The high-pitched voice with which he chose to perform this song belonged to his new alter ego, Camille, who'd already performed *Shockadelica*, which was recorded the previous month. Camille was one of the names adopted by Adélaïde Herculine Barbin, who was declared female at birth in 1838 and later recognized as a hermaphrodite by the medical field. Prince played into this sexual ambiguity when he created Camille. He decided to gather new songs under this enigmatic identity and release an album in her name. So, the insatiable artist recorded the songs *Feel U Up*, *Rebirth of the Flesh*, *Rockhard in a Funky Place*, *Good Love*, and *If I Was Your Girlfriend*. He added *Shockadelica*, *Housequake*, and *Strange Relationship* to the selection and pitched the project to Warner Bros. Records, who scheduled a release date for January 1987. In the end, and without any official reason given, Prince abandoned the production of this record, which left him with a slew of unreleased songs. He considered releasing a triple album by adding new songs

1987

A poster for the movie *Sign O' the Times*, which was released in 1987.

Every day during the Sign O' the Times Tour 1987, Prince and Sheila E. held a cut-throat competition over their stage costumes. The loser had to pay the other $1,000. One night, sure she'd win with her new look, Sheila E. hid her legendary single pant leg outfit behind her drums, then unveiled them to her rival as she approached him in the foreground for a rap. "He looked and said, 'What is that you have on?' And I turned and smiled and said, 'Ahhh, I win!'"[101]

to the Camille project, including *Adore* and *Play in the Sunshine*. He called this priceless gold mine *Crystal Ball*.

From Crystal Ball to Sign O' the Times

When Prince pitched the idea to Warner Bros. Records, its managers brushed aside any plans for a triple album. They thought it would be impossible to sell such a product—they believed Prince's young audience would not have the means to buy the record, given the necessarily higher price tag. So, Prince fell back on a double album called *Sign O' the Times*, which he credited entirely to himself, combining several of the many songs recorded in the previous months, along with the last-minute addition of some new gems, including *Slow Love*, *Hot Thing*, and *Forever In My Life*. He hired photographer Jeff Katz to shoot the album cover. Dominated by a peachy color, this briefly eclipsed the purple of the *Purple Rain* period. "It was the 80s," recalled Susannah Melvoin. "All that horrible pastel was a thing. I wore peach. He wore peach. I had dresses in peach; we had peach pillows in our house."[54] But a dark record was hiding behind those warm colors. As its name suggested, it was heavily influenced by its time. Prince's breakup with Susannah Melvoin, the end of his friendship with Wendy, and the devastation of AIDS were all subjects covered in his lyrics, illustrating his concerns regarding the tragedies that defined this period. *Sign O' the Times* came out on 30 March 1987—for the sake of graphic consistency, the title of the record is commonly written without the peace sign and is pronounced "Sign of the Times." Preceded by a few weeks by the single of the same name, the album received a warm welcome in the United States and Europe. While it adheres to the synthetic funk line of some of the songs from *Parade*, it also stands out for its clean production, which regularly makes way for beautiful melodies and irresistible

Prince's Xanadu: Paisley Park where the singer lived and recorded until the end of his life.

rhythmic patterns. Around the same time that Prince was launching his label Paisley Park Records, with which he signed George Clinton, Jill Jones, and Mavis Staples, he and Eric Leeds also started the instrumental jazz rock project Madhouse. Meanwhile, the Sign O' the Times Tour 1987 took Europe by storm between 8 May and 29 June 1987. More than 350,000 spectators got to admire Prince's colorful staging, which American fans didn't see until the movie *Sign O' the Times* came out in American movie theaters the following October.

The launch of Paisley Park

Around the same time, Prince inaugurated his Paisley Park complex at Chanhassen. In 1984, he'd asked architect Bret Thoeny to build the colossal building, a fortress measuring more than 5,000 square metres (55,000 square feet). They worked on the design together and it was inaugurated on 11 September 1987. The complex included a concert hall, offices, storage rooms for musical equipment and instruments, two studios, and a control room in which Prince recorded some of his greatest albums between 1988 and 2016. Paisley Park had been a mystery for fans around the world. Now it became the place where the magic happened. To protect the countless tapes containing his unpublished songs, Prince asked Susan Rogers to create a secure place to store them and an archiving system to go along with it. He wanted a safe that could withstand natural disasters, fires, and floods. This is how The Vault was born, designed to protect the work of America's most prolific musician.

FOR PRINCE ADDICTS

Even though Prince had humiliated his rival Michael Jackson at a ping-pong match in Los Angeles some time before, the latter still contacted him to record a duo for his next single, *Bad*. When Prince heard the first line of the song, "Your butt is mine," he categorically refused to participate: "I'm saying, who's going to sing that to whom? Because you sure ain't singing it to me. And I sure ain't singing it to you. So right there we got a problem."[30]

It is indeed Cat Glover who is hiding behind this imposing, heart-shaped mirror!

When the *Sign O' the Times* single came out, rumors abounded. Who was hiding behind that huge, heart-shaped mirror on the front cover? Some said it was Prince, shaved and dressed as a woman, but it wasn't. It was Cat Glover, a new member of Prince's group. She took center stage in the following album, providing *Alphabet St* with an incredible rap section. She can also be seen on the back of the sleeve, wearing Prince's glasses and holding his Cloud Guitar. "Even my dad thought that was Prince," said Cat. "Prince's dad thought that was Prince!"[103]

Single

SIGN "O" THE TIMES

Prince / 5'02

Musician: **Prince:** vocals, electric guitar, programming, Fairlight SMI, tambourine / **Recording:** **Sunset Sound, Los Angeles:** 15 July 1986 / **Technical team:** **Producer:** Prince / **Recording engineers:** Susan Rogers, Coke Johnson
Single: A-side: *Sign O' the Times* (Edit)/3'44 / **B-side:** ***La, La, La, He, He, Hee*** (Edit)/3'20 / **Released in the USA by Paisley Park Records/ Warner Bros. Records:** 18 February 1987 (single ref.: 7-28399) / **Released in the UK by Paisley Park Records/WEA International:** 2 March 1987 (single ref.: W8399) / **Best chart ranking in the USA:** 3 / **Best chart ranking in the UK:** 10

On 24 June 1986, Prince read an article in the *Los Angeles Times* about the global spread of AIDS. Editor and MD Robert Steinbrook explained that the hope of a French vaccine had been dashed by the swift progression of the illness in the United States. Bad news kept coming, and the following 8 July, an earthquake shook North Palm Spring, followed by a tremor off the coast of San Diego. "He [Prince] didn't like that kind of stuff, you know," explained Susannah Melvoin, who shared his life at the time. "He liked to be in control. That was definitely being out of control."[102] During those same years, gang wars took over Los Angeles and America was still mourning the crew of the STS-51-L mission, who had been lost in the explosion of the *Challenger* space shuttle on 28 January 1986. These events had a significant impact on Prince. He was inspired to write an agonizing song, a reflection of his time, that stood in stark contrast to the hits of the day, including *I Wanna Dance With Somebody (Who Loves Me)* by Whitney Houston, *La Bamba* by Los Lobos, and *Open Your Heart* by Madonna, all of which were meant to be light and carefree. According to Prince, the only solution to the world disintegrating was to fall in love, get married, and have children. "We'll call him Nate (if it's a boy)," he sings at the end of the song, in which he describes all these terrible events. Thirty-five years after its release, *Sign O' the Times* alas remains more topical than ever, witness to an unhappy period that may never end.

Sign O' the Times was almost entirely recorded with the Fairlight CMI (Computer Musical Instrument), a revolutionary instrument. Half synthesizer, half sampler, the machine had a keyboard, a screen, and a microphone. It allowed the recording and processing of samples, which the user could modify and reinsert into compositions. Under Susan Rogers' watchful eye, Prince built the song at Sunset Sound, working in an almost "surgical" way. He put the song on tape and immediately listened to it on his car stereo. He returned shortly thereafter with the lyrics, which he recorded after embellishing the song with biting guitar rhythms.

PLAY IN THE SUNSHINE

Prince / 5'05

Musicians: Prince: vocals, electric guitar, acoustic guitar, bass, drums, programming, piano, synthesizers, backing vocals / **Susannah Melvoin:** backing vocals / **Recording: Sunset Sound, Los Angeles:** 26–28 November 1986; 15 January 1987 / **Technical team: Producer:** Prince / **Recording engineers:** Susan Rogers, Coke Johnson

Play in the Sunshine is as light as a feather, the perfect antithesis to *Sign O' the Times*, even though Prince urges the listener to "dance every dance/Like it's going to be the last time." Its tangy pop rhythm and cheerful lyrics have nothing to do with the dark atmosphere of the previous track. Susan Rogers explained in 2012 that this was one of those songs Prince considered marginal, only important because it acted as a transition between two major songs on a record. Initially recorded for the unreleased album *Crystal Ball*, it was kept for *Sign O' the Times* during editing of the tracklisting. Prince and Susan Rogers finished recording the album at Sunset Sound on 15 January 1987, when they added the noise of the crowd between the first two tracks.

HOUSEQUAKE

Prince / 4'38

Musicians: Prince: vocals, electric guitar, bass, drums, programming, synthesizers, Fairlight CMI, backing vocals / **Eric Leeds:** saxophone / **Atlanta Bliss:** trumpet / **Susannah Melvoin:** backing vocals / **Gilbert Davidson:** backing vocals / **Coke Johnson:** backing vocals / **Todd Herreman:** backing vocals / **Susan Rogers:** backing vocals / **Mike Soltys:** backing vocals / **Brad Marsh:** backing vocals / **Recording: Sunset Sound, Los Angeles:** 18 and 27 October, 7 November 1986 / **Technical team: Producer:** Prince / **Recording engineers:** Susan Rogers, Coke Johnson

Recorded the day after the official announcement of The Revolutions' dissolution, *Housequake* came off as Prince's liberation song. As he quietly arrived at Sunset Sound on the morning of 18 October, Prince was wearing his non-prescription glasses and seemed to be in a sour mood. Susan Rogers, who that day was expecting to record one of Prince's "Sunday songs," which is what she called his sadder compositions recorded during musicians' days off, was surprised by the material they put on tape. The song they recorded that day is one of Prince's funkiest. The rhythmic pattern is bewitching, and the lyrics, as in James Brown's best hits, urge the listener to take to the dance floor. Rogers suggested Prince invite some of his entourage to participate in the backing vocals, including his bodyguard Gilbert Davidson, his drum backliner Brad Marsh, and the assistant recording engineer who prepared the Fairlight CMI samples for Prince, Todd Herreman.

THE BALLAD OF DOROTHY PARKER

Prince / 4'04

Musicians: Prince: vocals, bass, drums, programming, synthesizers, Fairlight CMI, backing vocals / **Susannah Melvoin:** backing vocals / **Recording: Galpin Boulevard Home Studio, Chanhassen, Minnesota:** 13 and 15 March, 15 April 1986 / **Technical team: Producer:** Prince / **Recording engineer:** Susan Rogers

On the morning of 13 March 1986, Susan Rogers was desperately trying to install the new console in Prince's home studio on Galpin Boulevard, in Chanhassen, Minnesota, where he had moved with his fiancé Susannah Melvoin. That day, the famous technician Frank DeMedio, who'd designed the console according to the specifications of the one at Sunset Sound, was busy working on the last cables needed to make the machine work. While everyone was working, Prince entered the studio and demanded to record a song that had come to him in the night. DeMedio was summarily sent home and Rogers asked to take her place at the console. A tape was placed in the recorder, a few faders were hastily inserted, and the song was recorded in next to no time. Susan Rogers later corrected the accidental lack of high frequencies on the console, but in the song, the first one recorded under the Galpin Boulevard label, the muffled atmosphere was retained to match the mood of the piece. "That unusual sound, just through serendipity," explained Rogers, "served the underwater dream state that he was trying to describe."[101]

IT

Prince / 5'10

Musician: Prince: vocals, electric guitar, drums, programming, synthesizers, Fairlight CMI, claps, backing vocals / **Recording: Sunset Sound, Los Angeles:** 11 May 1986 / **Technical team: Producer:** Prince / **Recording engineers:** Susan Rogers, Coke Johnson / **Assistant recording engineer:** Todd Herreman

Like *New Position* and *Do It All Night,* the lyrics of *It* couldn't be more explicit. Prince sings about his constant thirst for sex, and when he says, "I wanna do it baby everyday, all right/In a bed, on the stairs, everywhere, all right," he makes his point even clearer. Recorded at Sunset Sound during a 15-hour session, *It* fits in easily with this dark and raw album.

STARFISH AND COFFEE

Prince, Susannah Melvoin / 2'51

Musicians: Prince: vocals, electric guitar, bass, drums, programming, piano, synthesizers, Fairlight CMI, tambourine, backing vocals / **Susannah Melvoin:** backing vocals / **Recording: Galpin Boulevard Home Studio, Chanhassen, Minnesota:** 19 April 1986 / **Technical team: Producer:** Prince / **Recording engineer:** Susan Rogers

During Prince's long conversations with Susannah Melvoin, he kept seizing on one theme: her childhood memories, especially her friendship with Cynthia Rose, an autistic child who attended elementary school with the Melvoin sisters. Susannah had taken Cynthia Rose under her wing and felt a deep affection for her. Prince often asked about the details of this friendship. He wanted to hear the anecdotes that made this young girl such an interesting character. Susannah was happy to share. So, the couple wrote lyrics based on this story, which Prince added to an instrumental part that he recorded, as usual, in one day. "Cynthia would say, 'Guess what I had for breakfast this morning?'" recounted Susannah. "I'd say, 'What did you have Cynthia?' And she'd say, 'I had starfish and pee pee.'"[104] Prince was reluctant to call his song *Starfish and Pee Pee*, so with Susannah's approval, he called it *Starfish and Coffee*.

HEADPHONES AT THE READY

In *Starfish and Coffee*, Prince's drum line is doubled by a drum machine track that is played backward. This gives it a strange pattern, which pairs beautifully with the song's pop melody.

SLOW LOVE

Prince, Carole R Davis / 4'18

Musicians: Prince: vocals, electric guitar, bass, drums, piano, synthesizers, zills, backing vocals / **Wendy Melvoin:** electric guitar, backing vocals / **Eric Leeds:** saxophone / **Atlanta Bliss:** trumpet / **Novi Novog:** alto violin / **Suzie Katayama:** cello / **Lisa Coleman:** backing vocals / **Recording: Kiowa Trail Home Studio, Chanhassen, Minnesota:** 1 July 1984 / **Galpin Boulevard Home Studio, Chanhassen, Minnesota:** 4 June 1986 / **One On One Recording, Los Angeles:** 11 July 1986 (orchestra) / **Sunset Sound, Los Angeles:** 13 July 1986 / **Technical team: Producer:** Prince / **Recording engineers:** Susan Rogers, Coke Johnson / **Orchestral arrangements:** Clare Fischer

Prince met Carole Davis in 1984 after she responded to a casting call for *Purple Rain*. She was a model, actress, and songwriter in her spare time. Although she did not join the cast, she forged a friendship with the artist. In the summer of 1984, she went to Chanhassen to pitch one of her songs, *Slow Love*, to Prince, who recorded it at his home studio at Kiowa Trail on 1 July. Three years later, as the production for *Sign O' the Times* was coming to an end, Prince and Susan Rogers decided that for the sake of rhythm, the album needed a ballad. Since Prince didn't feel like writing that type of song, he pulled out *Slow Love* from his archives, embellished it with new arrangements, including strings by Novi Novog and Suzie Katayama, and brass parts played by Alan Leeds and Matthew Blistan (aka Atlanta Bliss). He also called on Clare Fischer, whose chord arrangements constitute his only contribution to this record. As Davis explained: "He [Prince] had his lawyers call me, and they offered me $25,000 to own the song outright, and I refused." She went on, "And they got back to me about a month later to give me 50 per cent of publishing and writers, which I accepted for the opportunity to appear on a Prince record."[79] This was a wise decision on Davis' part, who went on to play her own version of the song for her album *Heart of Gold* in 1989.

Susannah Melvoin in 2019. The singer was once Prince's fiancée and would be his muse during the writing of *Sign O' the Times.*

HOT THING

Prince / 5'39

Musicians: Prince: vocals, electric guitar, drums, programming, synthesizers, Fairlight CMI, bell, backing vocals / **Eric Leeds:** saxophone / **Recording:** Galpin Boulevard Home Studio, Chanhassen, Minnesota: 6–7 August 1986 / **Technical team:** Producer: Prince / **Recording engineer:** Susan Rogers

After returning from New York, where he performed at Madison Square Garden for two nights in a row to a packed house, Prince was back in his new home studio at Chanhassen. On 6 August 1986, he recorded the groovy *Hot Thing* in a few hours and filled it with many different arrangements, including a bass line that was later removed during mixing. The next day, he asked Eric Leeds to add a saxophone track, which became a hallmark feature of this cult song. Since The Revolution's backline had left for London for concerts at the Wembley Arena on 12, 13, and 14 August, Prince didn't have his instrument with him. So, he had to rent one at the last minute. "I had to play on some shit-ass horn," said Prince. "And I guess it turned out okay."[95]

FOREVER IN MY LIFE

Prince / 3'38

Musician: Prince: vocals, acoustic guitar, programming, backing vocals / **Recording:** Galpin Boulevard Home Studio, Chanhassen, Minnesota: 8 August 1986 / **Technical team:** Producer: Prince / **Recording engineer:** Susan Rogers

On 7 August 1986, Prince added saxophone overdubs to *Hot Thing*, then recorded a new song, *Make Your Mama Happy*. It was well past midnight when he decided to record an additional song, *Forever In My Life*, which was written for Susannah Melvoin, who was sleeping two floors above. "He had been up all night and he came upstairs," recounted Susannah Melvoin in 2020. "It was like 7:00 in the morning and he grabbed my hand and said 'follow me,' and so I followed him downstairs. The sun was coming through the stained-glass windows and he pressed play, and that song came on and I looked at him and I got teary-eyed. And that was it. He didn't have to say anything."[105]

HEADPHONES AT THE READY

When Prince recorded his voice for *Forever In My Life*, he decided to record the backing vocals before doing the lead vocals. Once this was done, he moved on to the verses and choruses, but he started two bars too late. Prince liked this little accident, and decided not to correct the mistake, which created a strange interval between the vocals and the backing vocals.

Sheena Easton achieved lasting fame singing in a duo with Prince in *U Got the Look*.

Single

U GOT THE LOOK

Prince / 3'58

Musicians: Prince: vocals, electric guitar, synthesizers, Fairlight CMI, backing vocals / **Sheena Easton:** vocals / **Sheila E.:** drums, percussion / **Recording: Sunset Sound, Los Angeles:** 21–23 December 1986 / **Technical team: Producer:** Prince / **Recording engineers:** Susan Rogers, Coke Johnson
Single: A-side: *U Got the Look*/3'58 / **B-side:** *Housequake* (Edit)/3'24 / **Released in the USA by Paisley Park Records/Warner Bros. Records:** 14 July 1987 (single ref.: 7-28289) / **Released in the UK by Paisley Park Records/WEA International:** 3 August 1987 (single ref.: W8289) / **Best chart ranking in the USA:** 2 / **Best chart ranking in the UK:** 11

Even though she'd wanted to spend a few days with her family during the Thanksgiving holidays, Susan Rogers was called back to work when Prince decided to record a new song, whose working title was *The Look*. They recorded relentlessly for three long days before obtaining a satisfying version of what would become the incomparable *U Got the Look*. Unhappy with the first takes, which he thought were too slow, Prince resorted to the *varispeed* process. Well known to recording engineers of the time, this clever studio hack was done by scrolling the tape at a higher or lower speed in the recording, allowing the tempo to be increased or decreased, though it also created a change in pitch, which is why Sheila E.'s drums, recorded on 21 December, sound so punchy and the electric guitar a bit piercing. On the third day, Prince's friend, singer Sheena Easton, stopped by. He'd written *Sugar Walls* for her in 1984. As the singer explained: "He said, 'Do you want to just come in and sing some backup vocals on the choruses?' So I went into the studio, and because I didn't know I was singing against him, I was all over the place—and he said he kind of liked that, so he expanded it into a duet."[106]

FOR PRINCE ADDICTS

In 1987, Lorna Nelson sued her half-brother, Prince, for plagiarism. The subject of the disagreement was the lyrics to *U Got the Look*, which she thought were too similar to those in *What's Cooking in This Book*, a song that she'd written but never recorded. The United States Court of Appeals for the Eighth Circuit sided with Prince on 3 May 1989, after they failed to detect any similarities that could support a ruling of plagiarism.

Single

IF I WAS YOUR GIRLFRIEND

Prince / 4'54

Musician: Prince: vocals, bass, programming, synthesizers, Fairlight CMI, backing vocals / **Recording: Sunset Sound, Los Angeles:** 2 November 1986 / **Technical team: Producer:** Prince / **Recording engineer:** Susan Rogers / **Assistant recording engineer:** Jim Preziosi
Single: A-side: *If I Was Your Girlfriend* (Edit)/3'46 (USA); ***If I Was Your Girlfriend***/3'47 (UK) / **B-side:** *Shockadelica*/3'30 (USA); *Shockadelica* (Extended Version)/6'12 (UK) / **Released in the USA by Paisley Park Records/Warner Bros. Records:** 6 May 1987 (single ref.: 7-28334) / **Released in the UK by Paisley Park Records/WEA International:** 1 June 1987 (single ref.: W8334) / **Best chart ranking in the USA:** 67 / **Best chart ranking in the UK:** 20

Camille (see page 142) is credited as the singer in *If I Was Your Girlfriend*, and observers know that Prince didn't choose this female alter ego by accident. The song was inspired by the end of his friendship with Wendy Melvoin and Lisa Coleman, but also by his breakup with Susannah, Wendy's sister. Susan Rogers, who admired Prince's honesty in these lyrics, pushed Warner Bros. Records to release the song as a single. It was a massive flop, but this didn't take away from the emotional power of the song. During recording, Prince added a flanger from a simple Boss guitar pedal to his Linn LM-1 Drum Computer, but left the snare drum devoid of any effects. Rogers had been in control of the production until then, but when Prince asked her to leave the studio so he could record his voice, she made a rookie mistake. She set the preamplifier for the API console at 10 decibels too high, which is the same as turning the mic input on too high. When she returned to the studio, after Prince had recorded all his vocal lines, she realized with horror that all the takes were saturated. She thought she was going to be fired for this poor manipulation of the console, but Prince quickly reassured her, saying: "We don't sound like those other people. We don't sound like Michael Jackson. We don't spend all that kind of money. We go fast. We make mistakes."[107] The take was kept as it was and quickly mixed to join the tracklisting of the album. Nevertheless, when the record was rereleased in 2020, Susan Rogers said, "I grit my teeth every time I hear it."[108]

STRANGE RELATIONSHIP

Prince / 4'04

Musicians: Prince: vocals, electric guitar, bass, drums, programming, synthesizers, Fairlight CMI, backing vocals / **Wendy Melvoin:** tambourine, Fairlight CMI / **Lisa Coleman:** Fairlight CMI / **Sheila E.:** congas / **Recording: Kiowa Trail Home Studio, Chanhassen, Minnesota:** March 1983 / **Flying Cloud Drive Warehouse, Eden Prairie, Minnesota:** April and May 1984 / **The Complex Studios, Los Angeles:** 15, 17, and 21 June, 1 July 1985 / **Sunset Sound, Los Angeles:** 3, 4, and 5 November 1986 / **Technical team:** **Producer:** Prince / **Recording engineer:** Susan Rogers / **Assistant recording engineer:** Jim Preziosi

Prince wrote *Strange Relationship* for Vanity (see page 72) in 1983, during their tumultuous relationship. Vanity was fed up with her partner and mentor's mood swings and infidelities, and she was getting ready to break free from his grip, which she thought too restrictive. Prince recorded a first version of this song in March 1984, at the same time as *Wonderful Ass*, and played it for Vanity. It was later reworked in the spring of 1984 and reappeared in July 1985, when Wendy and Lisa got the green light to cover some of Prince's songs at The Complex Studios in Los Angeles. Almost a year and a half later, Prince revisited the song and decided to include it on *Dream Factory*, then on Camille's album, and finally on *Sign O' the Times*. He added overdubs in November 1986, notably replacing conga tracks that Lisa and Wendy had pulled from the Fairlight CMI with real takes played by Sheila E.. The final version of the song came out on *Sign O' the Times*, his ninth album.

Single

I COULD NEVER TAKE THE PLACE OF YOUR MAN

Prince / 6'31

Musicians: Prince: vocals, electric guitar, acoustic guitar, bass, programming, synthesizers, Fairlight CMI, claps, backing vocals / **Susannah Melvoin ? (not confirmed):** backing vocals / **Recording: Sunset Sound, Los Angeles:** 16 July 1986 / **Technical team:** **Producer:** Prince / **Recording engineers:** Susan Rogers, Coke Johnson / **Assistant recording engineer:** Todd Herreman
Single: A-side: *I Could Never Take the Place of Your Man* (Fade)/3'39 / **B-side:** *Hot Thing* (Edit)/3'40 / **Released in the USA by Paisley Park Records/Warner Bros. Records:** 3 November 1987 (single ref.: 7-28288) / **Released in the UK by Paisley Park Records/WEA International:** 23 November 1987 (single ref.: W8288) / **Best chart ranking in the USA:** 10 / **Best chart ranking in the UK:** 29

On 16 July 1986, while writing his tenth album, *Lovesexy*, Prince unearthed a song, *I Could Never Take the Place of Your Man*, which had originally been recorded on 23 May 1979. He relistened to the song and decided to overhaul it. He replaced the drums with his precious Linn LM-1 Drum Computer, rerecorded the bass, synthesizers, and guitar tracks, and lastly, he recorded his voice, at once plaintive and powerful. Susannah Melvoin, who wasn't credited on the album, also seems to have recorded her voice for this track. This song became one of the strong points of the album, but it never reached higher than No.10 in the British charts when it came out as a single, which was still better than in the United States, where it only got to No.28. The injustice can be righted by (re)discovering as soon as possible this monument to 1980s pop with its timeless chorus.

THE CROSS

Prince / 4'46

Musician: Prince: vocals, electric guitar, bass, drums, Fairlight CMI, backing vocals / **Recording: Sunset Sound, Los Angeles:** 13 July 1986 / **Technical team: Producer:** Prince / **Recording engineers:** Susan Rogers, Coke Johnson

Prince reveals his faith in God in this very personal, brutally honest song. Hands down the rawest song on the album, *The Cross* was recorded quickly, with Prince settling for a rather shaky drum take, to Susan Rogers' chagrin. "I thought for sure he was going to redo the drums on it, because he played the drums on it all in one take and it just progressively became faster [...], but he was satisfied with it, and he knew what he was doing, so who was I to argue!"[109] On 7 June 2020, Kirk Johnson, Prince's drummer between 1996 and 1999, managed the arduous task of bringing together Prince's most famous musicians to play a virtual cover of *The Cross*. The video, made during the Covid-19 global health crisis and posted online on what would have been Prince's sixty-second birthday, included Donna Grantis, Ida Nielsen, Levi Seacer Jr, Doctor Fink, Mayte Garcia (see page 216), MonoNeon, Morris Hayes, Tommy Barbarella, and Sonny Thompson.

IT'S GONNA BE A BEAUTIFUL NIGHT

Prince, Doctor Fink, Eric Leeds / 8'59

Musicians: Prince: vocals, electric guitar, piano, synthesizers, programming / **Jill Jones:** vocals / **Sheila E.:** rap / **Wendy Melvoin:** electric guitar, backing vocals / **Miko Weaver:** electric guitar / **Brown Mark:** bass / **Bobby Z.:** drums, electronic drums / **Lisa Coleman:** synthesizers, backing vocals / **Doctor Fink:** synthesizers / **Eric Leeds:** saxophone / **Atlanta Bliss:** trumpet / **Susannah Melvoin:** backing vocals / **Greg Brooks:** backing vocals / **Wally Safford:** backing vocals / **Jerome Benton:** backing vocals / **Recording: The Zénith (Dierks Studio Mobile Trucks), Paris:** 25 August 1986 / **Sunset Sound, Los Angeles:** 22, 23, and 26–30 November 1986 / **Technical team: Producer:** Prince / **Recording engineers:** Susan Rogers, Coke Johnson

When Prince arrived at The Zénith, in Paris, on 25 August 1986, during the Parade Tour, he recorded the sound check and concert in their entirety, as usual. Back at Sunset Sound the following November, he decided to rework *It's Gonna Be A Beautiful Night*, the first song he'd played for the encore at the concert. A precious specimen from the end of the The Revolution era, this was also the first live song Prince released. He took care of the song's arrangements in November, asked Jill Jones and Susannah Melvoin to add various vocals, then he called in Eric Leeds and Atlanta Bliss to spruce up the song with better brass tracks. During the night of 26 and 27 November, Prince decided to add a track where Sheila E. rapped a part based on a poem that she recited to him regularly: *The Table and The Chair* by British poet Edward Lear. The problem was that Sheila E. was in a hotel in Cincinnati because she was on The Outrageous Tour with Lionel Richie at the time. Sunset Sound employees used all their available tools to hook up Sheila E.'s phone to the studio console, and the take was done live from the drummer's hotel. The credit given to Sheila E. in the sleeve notes of the record was "Transmississippirap" since she recorded her part from the other side of the Mississippi, in Ohio.

ADORE

Prince / 6'29

Musicians: Prince: vocals, bass, drums, programming, Hammond organ, Fairlight CMI, backing vocals / **Eric Leeds:** saxophone / **Atlanta Bliss:** trumpet / **Novi Novog:** alto violin / **Recording: Sunset Sound, Los Angeles:** 19, 21, 22, 23, and 24 November 1986 / **Technical team: Producer:** Prince / **Recording engineers:** Susan Rogers, Coke Johnson

Disappointed that radios specializing in rhythm and blues (R&B) and soul were no longer playing his music since he had taken a more pop-y turn with *Purple Rain*, Prince decided to add a Motown-influenced track to the end of his ninth album. "He wanted that core audience back," said Susan Rogers. "He talked about that. *Adore* was an attempt to get more R&B radio play [...] Lyrically, as well as the horn arrangements, the tempo and everything about it, was R&B. I loved the high voice he put on the track. It was straight-up soul!"[109] When listening to this languid song in which Prince reassures his beloved that "Until the end of time/I'll be there 4 U," it is clear that his plan worked.

MADHOUSE "8"

1. *One* (Madhouse/7'16)
2. *Two* (Madhouse/5'31)
3. *Three* (Madhouse/3'16)
4. *Four* (Madhouse/2'24)
5. *Five* (Madhouse/1'15)
6. *Six* (Madhouse/4'28)
7. *Seven* (Madhouse/4'09)
8. *Eight* (Madhouse/10'05)

Musicians: Prince: bass, electric guitar, piano, synthesizers, drums / **Eric Leeds:** tenor saxophone, baritone saxophone, flute, synthesizers / **Vanity:** moans (***Four, Seven***) / **Recording: Galpin Boulevard Home Studio, Chanhassen, Minnesota:** 28 September to 1 October 1986 / **Technical team: Producer:** Prince / **Recording engineer:** Susan Rogers / **Released in the USA by Paisley Park Records/Warner Bros. Records:** 19 January 1987 (LP ref.: 9 25545-1; CD ref.: 9 25545-2) / **Released in Europe by Paisley Park Records/WEA International:** 19 January 1987 (LP ref.: 925 545-1; CD ref.: 925 545-2) / **Best chart ranking in the USA:** did not make the charts / **Best chart ranking in the UK:** did not make the charts

MADHOUSE "16"

1. *Nine* (Madhouse/2'06)
2. *Ten* (Madhouse/5'04)
3. *Eleven* (Madhouse/6'14)
4. *Twelve* (Madhouse/5'14)
5. *Thirteen* (Madhouse/4'46)
6. *Fourteen* (Madhouse/5'12)
7. *Fifteen* (Madhouse/3'49)
8. *Sixteen* (Madhouse/4'17)

Musicians: Prince: electric guitar, bass, drums, piano, synthesizers, Fairlight CMI, programming / **Eric Leeds:** tenor saxophone, baritone saxophone, flute, synthesizers / **Sheila E.:** drums (***Ten*, *Eleven*, *Fifteen***) / **Susannah Melvoin:** sampled voice (***Eleven***) / **Recording: Paisley Park Studios, Chanhassen, Minnesota:** July to August 1987 / **Technical team: Producer:** Prince / **Recording engineers:** Eddie Garcia, Eddie Miller / **Released in the USA by Paisley Park Records/Warner Bros. Records:** 18 November 1987 (LP ref.: 9 25658-1; CD ref.: 9 25658-2) / **Released in Europe by Paisley Park Records/WEA International:** 18 November 1987 (LP ref.: 925 658-1; CD ref.: 925 658-2) / **Best chart ranking in the USA:** did not make the charts / **Best chart ranking in the UK:** did not make the charts

MADHOUSE, PRINCE'S JAZZ SIDE

Prince met saxophonist Eric Leeds while making *The Family* album in the mid-1980s, an encounter that had a significant impact on its production. Once St Paul Peterson and Susannah Melvoin's band was defunct, Leeds was able to join The Revolution, bringing with him trumpet player Matthew Blistan. He also joined The Flesh, a short-lived band made up of Leeds, Sheila E., Jonathan and Wendy Melvoin, Lisa Coleman, and Levi Seacer Jr, which recorded some 20 songs with jazz-rock influences. After the project was abandoned, Leeds took advantage of the Parade Tour to share with Prince his love of Miles Davis—he knew every detail of his prolific discography. Also, when Prince found out at the start of the tour that Miles Davis had just signed with Warner Bros. Records, he wrote a song for this trumpet player with the irreplaceable muted sound. The collaboration never took place, and in the autumn of 1986 Prince retired to his home studio on Galpin Boulevard to write eight instrumental jazz songs, for which he played all the instruments. He asked Eric Leeds to join him, and the latter added several saxophone and flute tracks. Madhouse's first album, *8*, came out in January 1987 under Prince's label, Paisley Park Records. Eric Leeds (saxophone), Doctor Fink (synthesizers), Levi Seacer Jr (bass), and Dale Alexander (drums) formed a band to open for Prince during the Sign O' the Times Tour 1987. Prince confirmed the project in the summer of 1987, when he recorded the band's second album, *16*, in his brand-new studio at Paisley Park. These two timeless records have gained cult followings and are not to be missed.

LOVE

PRINCE

LOVESEXY

No · Alphabet St · Glam Slam · Anna Stesia · Dance On · Lovesexy
When 2 R In Love · I Wish U Heaven · Positivity

Released in the USA by Paisley Park Records/Warner Bros. Records:
10 May 1988 (LP ref.: 1-25720; CD ref.: 9 25720-2)
Released in the Europe by Paisley Park Records/WEA International
9 May 1988 (LP ref.: 925 720-1 - WX 164; CD ref.: 925 720-2)
Best chart ranking in the USA: 11
Best chart ranking in the UK: 1

A change of color scheme for Prince who abandoned peach and black in favor of blue, white, and pink.

PRINCE CONFRONTED WITH AN UNPRECEDENTED DUALITY

Although the first Madhouse album was recorded in the summer of 1987 in the Paisley Park studios, the latter were only officially opened on 11 September. Alongside the various productions of his Paisley Park Records label recorded at Paisley Park that autumn, Prince began a compilation of tracks for a new project. He wanted some joyful dance music and was looking to move away from the anxious atmosphere of his previous opus. "We'd been working really hard on *Sign O' the Times* [...]," recalled Susan Rogers, "the topics are deeper, more introspective than your typical dance music. Those songs require a bit of time to write and produce and record. So Prince needed a break from all that. He just wanted to make some funky dance music [...]"[110] Eight tracks recorded between October 1986 and March 1987 were then put together for what would become, paradoxically, a record commonly known as *The Black Album* (it was entirely black in color and had no title or credits on the sleeve at the time, just the names of the songs and their length). Warner Bros. Records set the release date for 8 December 1987. For reasons only Prince himself really understood, he dramatically backtracked on 1 December, believing it wasn't the uplifting album he had originally intended and feeling that it symbolized his darkest self and was inspired by an evil force. He ordered that all copies already distributed to retailers be destroyed, and the "black record" thus passed into the realms of legend. It is estimated that around a hundred copies of the vinyl, along with a dozen CDs, escaped destruction and the whole episode turned the album into a highly sought-after collectors' item. In 2018, an original copy of the monochrome record sold on Discogs.com for $27,500!

From The Black Album to Lovesexy

Once the copies of *The Black Album* had been destroyed, Prince focused on the recording of *Lovesexy*, an album with a more positive message, which he laid down on tape in less than two months from December 1987 to January 1988. "It was clear to everyone that what they were doing was a reaction to and a replacement for *The Black Album*," said Alan Leeds, Prince's tour manager and soon-to-be president of Paisley Park Records. "Anybody who was involved in *Lovesexy* was clear of that. He had had an epiphany and ran around telling how *The Black Album* was the devil's work that wasn't really him. 'I gotta make a record for God now.'"[111] Guided by his faith and inspired by his budding friendship with the young poet Ingrid Chavez, Prince embarked on the production of his tenth album in his Paisley Park studios. Susan Rogers had quit following a disagreement with her employer, who objected to her being unavailable on a rare day off. She was replaced by Joe Blaney, who worked with Prince until 1992, and Eddie Miller, who was only present on *Lovesexy* and *Batman*. The sessions began with long rehearsals involving Prince and his band, which were recorded for Prince to rework later. Prince put the album together in just seven weeks and presented it to Warner Bros. Records, who were stunned with the result. He first showed them the visuals created with the Frenchman Jean-Baptiste Mondino, featuring Prince in the nude against a backdrop of flowers. "It is a religious image par excellence,"[112] the photographer later asserted. The record company executives were no more convinced by the songs than they were by the cover and even less so when they were told that the CD version of the album would only have one track with all the

Prince with Cat Glover—emblematic dancer, rapper, and backing vocalist on the Lovesexy Tour.

Prince during a sound check onstage at the Stadion Feijenoord, in Rotterdam, on 17 August 1988.

songs seguing into one another, thus forcing people to listen to the album in one go (it was generally agreed that listening to *Lovesexy* on CD was a very unpleasant experience). Finally, Prince informed Warner Bros. that, to retain his air of mystery, there would be no music video to accompany the single, *Alphabet St.*

Although the single was well received when it was released on 23 April 1988, the various decisions Prince made explain why *Lovesexy* was a relative flop when released in the United States on 10 May. The album languished at No.11 on the Billboard 200 chart, before gradually slipping down the charts. Not the success Prince had anticipated, and he was forced to postpone his American tour in favor of the European leg of the Lovesexy Tour, where the album made it to No.1 in the UK, Swiss, Dutch, and Swedish charts. The tour got underway on 8 July 1988 in France at the Palais Omnisports, in Paris-Bercy, and ended on 13 February 1989 at the Osaka-Jo Hall in Osaka, Japan. It was a monumental undertaking: over 50 trailer trucks were required to transport the equipment and the two-million-dollar set built by Leroy Bennett (the Ford Thunderbird that appeared onstage—a three-quarter-sized reconstruction because Prince felt too small in the full-sized car—cost $250,000 alone). After a successful run in Europe, the US tour, which ran from 14 September to 29 November 1988, received a mixed reception. Some venues were half-full, the singles *Glam Slam* and *I Wish U Heaven* didn't make the Billboard Hot 100 chart, and a tragic accident plunged the tour into mourning: a man lost control of his car outside Bostons Tower Records and plowed into a line of young people waiting to buy tickets to a Prince concert. Seventeen-year-old Frederick Webber was killed in the crash and five other people were injured. Following this series of incidents, Prince decided to turn his attention to new projects. "*Lovesexy* wasn't as successful compared to the previous albums," said saxophonist Eric Leeds. "It was probably the start of the downturn of the marketability of his career. And it was very frustrating for him, because I think he considered *Lovesexy* his best or at least his most personal record."[25]

Prince's Ford Thunderbird, rebuilt for the Lovesexy Tour, caused Prince a lot of bother. In 1988, Prince's half-brother Duane was also his odd-job man. One of his tasks was to organize the washing of the car in which Prince used to listen to his recordings. It turns out that most of the songs circulating on the black market at the time came from the tapes Prince had left in the Ford, which were stolen by the people who cleaned it.

👁 NO

Prince / 5'46

Musicians

Prince: vocals, electric guitar, synthesizers, claps, backing vocals
Miko Weaver: electric guitar
Levi Seacer Jr: bass
Sheila E.: drums, backing vocals
Boni Boyer: Hammond organ, vocals
Doctor Fink: synthesizers
Eric Leeds: saxophone
Atlanta Bliss: trumpet, spoken voice
Ingrid Chavez: spoken voice
Wally Safford: spoken voice
Greg Brooks: spoken voice

Recording

Washington Avenue Warehouse, Edina, Minnesota: July 1986
Paisley Park, Chanhassen, Minnesota: 11 and 17 December 1987

Technical team

Producer: Prince
Recording engineer: Eddie Miller

Genesis

In July 1986, Prince recorded the funky *The Ball* at Edina's Washington Avenue Warehouse and included it in the tracklist for *Crystal Ball*. At the end of the song, he added the voices of Eric Leeds, Matthew "Atlanta Bliss" Blistan, Wally Safford, and Greg Brooks pretending to be a band talking to one another, but then had to resign himself to setting it aside once *Crystal Ball* was dropped. Just over a year later, with *The Black Album* dead and buried, Prince embarked on the production of its antithesis, the joyful *Lovesexy*. He retrieved *The Ball* from The Vault, his new safe where his musical production lay dormant, and transformed it into *Eye No* (meaning: "I Know"). He added an intro in which he declares "Welcome to The New Power Generation," a sentence that became one of his most famous mantras, and asked his new muse, the poet Ingrid Chavez, whom he had met a few days earlier, to read a short text, which he integrated into the track. The young woman declares: "When love calls, you gotta go," a message of peace that sets the tone for a deeply spiritual album.

Production

While Prince played all the instruments on *The Ball* (except for the saxophone and trumpet, which were supplied by Eric Leeds and Atlanta Bliss, respectively), revising the song was a group effort. Robert "Cubby" Colby, recording engineer for Prince's concerts, did the legwork of preparing the sessions. He set up the band's equipment in Studio C at Paisley Park and prepared the recordings, which were handled by recording engineer Eddie Miller. "Matt Blistan and I immediately realized it was a remake of *The Ball*," explained Eric Leeds, "[...] but no one else understood what we were talking about. I said 'Oh, you'll love it. It's a great song.'"[111] *Eye No* was the first song Prince recorded for *Lovesexy* and also the only one that featured his full band.

FOR PRINCE ADDICTS

What is the meaning of the word "Hundalasiliah" that Prince sings several times on *Eye No*? A subject of much debate among fans, it remains an unsolved mystery, although biographer Per Nilsen, an eminent Prince specialist, stated in 2000 that, slowed down and played backward, the word becomes "*Is it me? Is it not?,*" underlining the duality of a human being, one of the themes Prince frequently addressed at the time.

Doctor Fink, Eric Leeds, Cat Glover, Miko Weaver, Prince, Boni Boyer, Sheila E., Atlanta Bliss, and Levi Seacer Jr made up Prince's new group in 1988.

Prince and Cat Glover leaving the Limelight Club in New York in October 1988.

Single

ALPHABET ST.

Prince / 5'38

Musicians

Prince: vocals, electric guitar, bass, programming, synthesizers, percussion, claps, backing vocals
Cat Glover: rap, backing vocals
Ingrid Chavez: spoken voice
Sheila E.: drums, claps
Boni Boyer: backing vocals
Eric Leeds: saxophone
Atlanta Bliss: trumpet

Recording

Paisley Park, Chanhassen, Minnesota: 30 December 1987

Technical team

Producer: Prince
Recording engineers: Joe Blaney, Eddie Miller

Single version

A-side: ***Alphabet St*** (Edit)/2'25 (USA); ***Alphabet St*** (Album Version)/5'40 (UK)
B-side: ***Alphabet St*** (Cont.)/3'14 (USA); ***Alphabet St (This is Not Music, This Is A Trip)***/7'48 (UK)

CD single version

1. *Alphabet St* (Album Version)/5'40
2. *Alphabet St (This Is Not Music, This Is A Trip)*/7'48

Released in the USA by Paisley Park Records/Warner Bros. Records: 23 April 1988 (single ref.: 7-27900)
Released in the UK by Paisley Park Records/WEA International: 15 April 1988 (single ref.: W7900; CD single ref.: W7900CD)
Best chart ranking in the USA: 8
Best chart ranking in the UK: 9

Genesis

Some observers contend that *Alphabet St* was the track that saved *Lovesexy* from oblivion, giving this underestimated record the posterity that it ultimately deserved. Although it was intended for release as a single, there was to be no music video accompanying the song, an odd but deliberate choice on Prince's part. One day, in March 1988, Prince picked up the phone and called Alan Leeds—his tour manager, who at the time was his unofficial right-hand man—and said: "I want to shoot a video."[113] Leeds, who was enjoying a rare day off with his family, had to make himself available to his employer, who was determined to shoot the *Alphabet St* video that day, with no financial backing from Warner Bros. Records and no one else's input. It was late in the day and snowing in Minneapolis. In other words, assembling a film crew could prove very difficult. But nothing was impossible for Leeds, who called everyone in his address book and finally found a director who was available: Michael Barnard. At 11pm, everyone gathered in the studios of a local television station equipped with a blue screen so that different backgrounds and texts could be inserted. Cat Glover and Sheila E. were both there, and shooting could begin. Although the video now looks extremely dated, at the time it was given a slot on MTV, providing much-needed exposure and propelling the song to No.8 in the Billboard Hot 100 chart on 25 June 1988.

Production

As he was finishing off the recording of *Alphabet St* in Paisley Park, on 30 December 1987, Prince decided to leave Cat Glover alone to record her legendary rap parts on the future single. "When I come back, I want to make sure they sound good," Prince said to her."[103] Just before leaving, Prince explained to Cat how to use the console and gave her one last warning: "You better get it right, because, if you don't, Salt 'n' Pepa are going to rag on you!"[103] Here, he was teasing her with a reference to the New York rap trio whom he greatly admired. Glover took up the gauntlet brilliantly and recorded her part of the track, which would follow on from Prince's famous call: *"Cat! We need you to rap!"*

FOR PRINCE ADDICTS

Prince sends a message to his fans with a hidden phrase at 0'26 of the *Alphabet St* video, which reads: "Don't buy the Black Album, I'm sorry."

HEADPHONES AT THE READY

At 5'02 of *Alphabet St*, Ingrid Chavez is heard slowly and languidly reciting the alphabet, omitting the letter G. When a fan asked Prince in 1997 what the significance of such an omission was, Prince replied, "She was being kissed at the time, and got flustered, I suppose."[114]

Single

GLAM SLAM

Prince / 5'04

Musicians: Prince: vocals, electric guitar, acoustic guitar, bass, drums, programming, synthesizers, percussion, backing vocals / **Cat Glover:** backing vocals / **Recording:** Paisley Park, Chanhassen, Minnesota: December 1987 / **Technical team:** Producer: Prince / Recording engineers: Joe Blaney, Eddie Miller
Single version: A-side: *Glam Slam* (Edit)/3'28 / **B-side:** *Escape* (Edit)/3'31 / **CD single version: 1.** *Glam Slam* (Edit)/3'28 / **2.** *Escape* (Edit)/3'31 / **3.** *Glam Slam* (Remix)/8'52 / **Released in the USA by Paisley Park Records/Warner Bros. Records:** 11 July 1988 (single ref.: 7-27806) / **Released in the UK by Paisley Park Records/WEA International:** 11 July 1988 (single ref.: W7806; CD Single ref.: W7806CD) / **Best chart ranking in the USA:** did not make the charts / **Best chart ranking in the UK:** 29

Here, Prince co-opted a famous expression popularized by David Bowie in his 1972 song *Suffragette City:* "Wham Bam, Thank You Ma'am!" Prince turns it into "Glam Slam, Thank You Ma'am/I pray you always stay." Although the single release of this very pop-sounding song was a resounding flop, *Glam Slam* would remain part of Prince's universe as the name given to the clubs he opened in Minneapolis in May 1990 and in Yokohama, Japan, in 1991, followed by Glam Slam West, in Los Angeles, in 1993, and Glam Slam East in Miami in 1994. The track also marked the beginning of Prince's collaboration with Steve Parke, whom he asked to design the video for the song. Parke would go on to design the monumental stage set for the Lovesexy Tour, before becoming one of the singer's most well-known in-house photographers.

ANNA STESIA

Prince / 4'57

Musicians: Prince: vocals, electric guitar, bass, synthesizers, claps, backing vocals / **Sheila E.:** drums, claps, backing vocals / **Cat Glover:** backing vocals / **Boni Boyer:** backing vocals / **Recording:** Paisley Park, Chanhassen, Minnesota: 13 January 1988 / **Technical team:** Producer: Prince / **Recording engineers:** Joe Blaney, Eddie Miller

Prince met the young Anna Garcia in August 1986 after one of his concerts at Wembley Arena in London. Although Prince fell in love with the teenager at first sight, their relationship remained platonic until she came of age in 1988, at which point they went public about being a couple. The young woman was a major influence during the *Batman* era,

The Glam Slam in Minneapolis, Prince's club where devotees of the Minneapolis Sound used to meet.

Kneeling before Cat Glover onstage at the National Exhibition Centre, in Birmingham on 5 August 1988.

and Prince quickly renamed her Anna Fantastic. It doesn't take much imagination to work out that she was at the forefront of this track as Prince declares "Anna Stesia come to me/Talk to me, ravish me/Liberate my mind," expressing his anguish at this seemingly impossible love. With its famous descending chords played on a Roland D-50 synthesizer, a keyboard that Prince used extensively on his following albums, *Anna Stesia* is undoubtedly the best track on *Lovesexy*. A peak of melancholy with indisputable lyrical power, the song describes its creator's loneliness, something rare in Prince's lyrics. It concludes with a very religious finale, featuring Prince, Ingrid Chavez, Boni Boyer, and Sheila E. singing in unison "Love is God, God is love, girls and boys love God above." During the reunited New Power Generation's Prince tribute concert at La Cigale, Paris, on 1 December 2019, singer Jeanne Added joined the mythical band to deliver a poignant version of *Anna Stesia*.

DANCE ON

Prince / 3'43

Musicians: Prince: vocals, electric guitar, drums, programming, synthesizers, percussion, backing vocals / **Boni Boyer:** vocals, synthesizers, backing vocals / **Miko Weaver:** electric guitar, backing vocals / **Levi Seacer Jr:** bass, backing vocals / **Sheila E.:** percussion, backing vocals / **Doctor Fink:** synthesizers / **Recording: Paisley Park, Chanhassen, Minnesota:** 16 December 1987 / **Technical team: Producer:** Prince / **Recording engineer:** Joe Blaney

The composition of *Dance On* is based on the elusive drum pattern played by Prince on 16 December 1987. One of the funkiest moments on *Lovesexy*, virtuosity is key, as backing vocals are layered to offer listeners hope, urging them to dance away the evils of the world. Prince used a Dynacord ADD-One sampler connected to his snare drums to give a synthetic sound. The snare drum was equipped with a small sensor that turned the striking sound into a MIDI signal. This signal was transferred to the Dynacord, which modified it according to the musician's wishes, before being sent back to the console. Prince could thus change the original sound of his snare drum to be flashier and more modern. This process can also be heard on the bass drum in *Eye No*.

LOVESEXY

Prince / 5'49

Musicians: Prince: vocals, electric guitar, bass, drums, synthesizers, claps, backing vocals / **Eric Leeds:** saxophone / **Atlanta Bliss:** trumpet / **Recording: Paisley Park, Chanhassen, Minnesota:** 29 January 1988 / **Technical team: Producer:** Prince / **Recording engineers:** Joe Blaney, Eddie Miller

Lovesexy opens with a gospel feel before turning into a devilishly sexy funk anthem. It is a reworking of *Luv Sexy*, which was recorded with the band on 14 December 1987. "It was just a whole different song," said Eric Leeds. "The original version was lighter, bouncier. He re-did the song entirely. The second song had a harder edge to it, much more aggressiveness, which I think he felt was more appropriate for the lyrics [...] Personally, I feel the re-make was a better piece of music."[111]

The three Cloud Guitars made by Dave Rusan were repainted many times. Here, the blue version, known as the "Blue Angel," is seen with Prince onstage at Madison Square Garden in New York.

WHEN 2 R IN LOVE

Prince / 4'01

Musician: Prince: vocals, programming, synthesizers, backing vocals / **Recording: Paisley Park, Chanhassen, Minnesota:** October 1987 / **Technical team: Producer:** Prince / **Recording engineer:** Eddie Garcia

When 2 R In Love is the only survivor from *The Black Album*, providing a welcome break in the midst of a production that sometimes overdoes the artifices to the detriment of the melodies. Played entirely by Prince, with technical assistance from recording engineer Eddie Garcia, the song slots perfectly into the album, and would later resurface in 1994 on Warner Bros. Records' official "rerelease" of *The Black Album*.

Single

I WISH U HEAVEN

Prince / 2'43

Musician: Prince: vocals, electric guitar, acoustic guitar, bass, drums, programming, synthesizers, Fairlight CMI, backing vocals / **Recording: Paisley Park, Chanhassen, Minnesota:** 31 January 1988 / **Technical team: Producer:** Prince / **Recording engineer:** Eddie Miller
Single version: A-side: ***I Wish U Heaven*** (LP Version)/2'43 / **B-side:** ***Scarlet Pussy*** (Edit) [Camille]/4'10 / **CD maxi-single version: 1.** ***I Wish U Heaven*** (Part 1, 2 & 3)/10'12 / **2.** ***Scarlet Pussy*** (Hidden Track) [Camille]/ 6'09 / **Released in the USA by Paisley Park Records/Warner Bros Records:** 20 September 1988 (single ref.: 7-27745) / **Released in the UK by Paisley Park Records/WEA International:** 24 October 1988 (single ref.: W7745; CD maxi-single ref.: W7745CD) / **Best chart ranking in the USA:** did not make the charts / **Best chart ranking in the UK:** 24

On 22 December 1987, Prince recorded *The Line* with Boni Boyer, Sheila E., Eric Leeds, and Atlanta Bliss. The song, slated to appear on *Lovesexy*, was ultimately replaced by the ballad *I Wish U Heaven*, recorded on 31 January. It initially featured an omnipresent synthesizer line, but, in the end, Prince preferred a catchy electric guitar riff to the saturated sound. The three guitars in the solo at the end of the track are his famous Hohner Madcat, a Sigma SE-19 acoustic guitar (which had already been used on *Forever In My Life*), and an Epiphone hollow body guitar plugged directly into the console. The single release of the song was a remix by Femi Jiya. The new version was 10 minutes and 12 seconds long, also featured Sheila E., Eric Leeds, and Cat Glover, and was titled *I Wish U Heaven (Part 1, 2 & 3)*.

POSITIVITY

Prince / 7'15

Musicians: Prince: vocals, electric guitar, programming, synthesizers, Fairlight CMI, backing vocals / **Sheila E.:** drums, backing vocals / **Boni Boyer:** backing vocals / **Eric Leeds:** saxophone / **Atlanta Bliss:** trumpet / **Recording: Paisley Park, Chanhassen, Minnesota:** 11 December 1987; 9 January 1988 / **Technical team: Producer:** Prince / **Recording engineers:** Joe Blaney, Eddie Miller

"That's my favorite song on the album," Atlanta Bliss said of *Positivity*. "Not only because we played on it, but because of the color and the sound of it. It sets itself off from the rest of the songs."[111] The song's gospel vibe and message of peace did indeed set the tone for the album when Prince recorded it immediately after *Eye No*. It was as if he were turning the page on *The Black Album*, which he believed was guided by an evil spirit—referred to in the song as Spooky Electric. The track originally featured a rap part borrowed from J M Silk's *Music Is The Key* and already recorded by Cat Glover for *Cindy C.*, one of the highlights of *The Black Album*. When Prince realized that the lyric was not Cat's original creation, he decided to cut it from *Positivity* to avoid having to share his credits with Steve Hurley (aka J M Silk), who wrote *Music Is The Key*.

During rehearsals for the Lovesexy Tour, Prince established a simple rule that James Brown had already tried with his band in the 1960s. If a musician made even a minor mistake, they would be fined fifty dollars. So that everyone understood, Prince had sampled the sound of a cash register, which he could trigger by hitting a pad next to him with a stick—a fine that was impossible to ignore!

PRINCE

BATMAN
(MOTION PICTURE SOUNDTRACK)

The Future · Electric Chair · The Arms of Orion · Partyman · Vicki Waiting
Trust · Lemon Crush · Scandalous · Batdance

Released in the USA by Warner Bros. Records:
20 June 1989 (LP ref.: 1-25936; CD ref.: 9 25936-2)
Released in the UK by WEA International:
19 June 1989 (LP ref.: 9 25936-1; CD ref.: 925 936-2)
Best chart ranking in the USA: 1
Best chart ranking in the UK: 1

A darker atmosphere…a portrait by the photographer Matthew Rolston, shot in 1989.

A TOUCH OF FUNK IN GOTHAM CITY

After the American segment of the Lovesexy Tour came to an end in November 1988, Prince was hit with considerable financial losses. The tour had been enormously expensive and became a financial fiasco, and Prince's last album had also failed to draw a large audience. Having recently parted ways with Bob Cavallo, Prince entrusted his career, which was on shaky ground for the first time, to Albert Magnoli. He had directed the movie *Purple Rain* and become Prince's closest confidant. "I immediately did a forensic kind of financial search as to what was really going on, and it was more horrible than anybody thought. So [the plan] was about trying to bring revenue into the operation without overextending him to the point where no one would be interested in getting involved in anything he wanted to do."[115] It was around this time that Mark Canton, a production manager at Warner Bros. who had worked on *Purple Rain* in 1984, reached out to Magnoli. He proposed a project that would save Prince from bankruptcy and place him back on top of the international pop scene.

A prestigious collaboration

At the end of 1988, Warner Bros. was about to pull off a master stroke with the production of *Batman*, a movie based on the adventures of the DC Comics superheroes created by Bob Kane and Bill Finger in 1939. Tim Burton, who'd made his name with *Pee-Wee's Big Adventure* (1985) and *Beetlejuice* (1988), was the director. Michael Keaton was cast as the lead, while Jack Nicholson was deemed the ideal candidate to play the Joker—some of the most famous actors in Hollywood had tried their hand at the role and failed. Mark Canton told Magnoli that Burton, who was a big Prince fan, wanted to include two of his songs in the movie score: *1999* and *Baby I'm A Star*. When Prince visited Pinewood Studios in Iver, near London, in January 1989, Burton played him a few scenes from the movie. Prince was immediately seduced by its dark universe. Burton and Prince got along well, which helped to seal the deal quickly. The initial agreement was only for two songs, but Prince soon got into the flow, and once his Japanese tour ended in February 1989, he recorded a series of songs for the movie. The matter became complicated when Danny Elfman, the movie's resident composer, refused to collaborate with the Kid from Minneapolis. "I knew what the score was," explained Elfman, "and as much as I love Prince's music, I didn't feel that his score was going to be the right score sound for the *Batman* movie […] My feeling at that point was that Prince was a great, great songwriter, but that he probably was not a movie composer, and that he would come up with melodies, and I would essentially be turning those melodies into a score. And so, my feeling is that I would end up being a glorified orchestrator, or an arranger, not a composer on the project. And I just wasn't willing to do that."[116] After Warner Bros. proposed a collaboration with Prince, Michael Jackson, and George Michael on the whole of the record, Danny Elfman walked out, only to be called back by the production team. A compromise was finally reached: Elfman would write the movie score, which would appear under the name *Batman (Original Motion Picture Score)*, while Prince would write an album inspired by the movie, called *Batman (Motion Picture Soundtrack)*.

Behind the worldwide success of the *Batman* movie was a visionary and uncompromising filmmaker: the brilliant Tim Burton.

The actor Michael Keaton in costume on the set of the movie *Batman*.

At the top of the charts thanks to *Batdance*

The album, commonly known as *Batman*, was recorded at Paisley Park in six weeks, between February and March 1989. Prince made an intensive use of sampling, notably by extracting passages from the movie, which he then incorporated into his songs. To do this, Prince and his recording engineers worked in front of a monitor playing movie scenes sent to them by Warner Bros. *1999* and *Baby I'm A Star* were soon replaced by *Partyman* and *Trust*, and it became impossible to stop our insatiable creator. He recorded *The Arms of Orion, The Future*, and *Lemon Crush* in no time at all, then pulled previously recorded songs, namely *Electric Chair, Scandalous*, and *Vicki Waiting*, out of The Vault. The last song he recorded was the majestic *Batdance*, which was released as a single on 6 June 1989 to a spectacular reception. It was then full-on "Batmania," and the song joined the global craze for the man in the bat costume, making it Prince's fourth No.1 song in the United States, after *When Doves Cry* and *Let's Go Crazy*, in 1984, and *Kiss* in 1986. The movie's release, on 19 June, exceeded Warner Bros.'s expectations. It ran in more than 3,000 movie theaters across the country and everyone was talking about it. This helped to boost Prince's record, which, since its release the day after the movie came out, had shot to the top of the charts. On 24 September, Prince played *Electric Chair* onstage on *Saturday Night Live*, using the occasion to introduce his new band to the world. Newcomers included drummer Michael Bland, saxophonist Candy Dulfer, backing vocalist Margie Cox, and keyboardist Patrice Rushen, with whom Prince had already worked on *Baby*. With this top-notch performance, Prince proved once again that he could surprise his fans and rise from the ashes with an avant-garde album, deemed especially so because of its technoid sounds and chilling riffs, like the laugh of the Joker himself.

FOR PRINCE ADDICTS

Although Prince famously did not make song demos, he did have to capture his ideas as they came to him. To do that, he used two old, low-end tape recorders. With the first one, he recorded a vocal percussion, then he played this while he recorded the bass line on the second. This tape served as the demo he would later rerecord.

Along with Prince and Michael Jackson, Madonna was one of the three greatest pop stars of the 1980s. Fans always dreamed of the three singers forming a trio.

LOVE SONG
(MADONNA FEATURING PRINCE)
Madonna, Prince / 4'52

Musicians
Madonna: vocals, synthesizers, backing vocals
Prince: vocals, electric guitar, bass, programming, synthesizers, backing vocals
Recording
Paisley Park, Chanhassen, Minnesota: March to November 1988
Technical team
Producers: Madonna, Prince
Recording engineers: Eddie Miller, Stephen Shelton, Heidi Hanschu

Madonna *Like A Prayer*
Released in the USA by Sire: 21 March 1989 (LP ref.: 1-25844; CD ref.: 9 25844-2)
Released in the UK by Sire: 21 March 1989 (LP ref.: WX 239; CD ref.: 7599-25844-2)
Best chart ranking in the USA: 1
Best chart ranking in the UK: 1

Genesis
In 1987, thanks to the success of her album *True Blue*, released the previous year, Madonna was at the peak of her glory. She was part of the Holy Trinity of 1980s pop music, alongside Michael Jackson and Prince, with whom she already had a friendly relationship. The two artists had met between tours and hoped to write some songs together, but no project had yet come to fruition. "[...] we've been friends for years and admirers of each other's work," explained Madonna. "So we'd always talked about getting together to write. And, in fact, there was a moment last year when we were possibly going to write a musical together."[121] After a few days trying to write a song at Paisley Park, Madonna became resigned to abandoning the idea. Their collaboration did not turn out to be as successful as she'd hoped. It was also on this occasion that Prince offered her a role in *Graffiti Bridge*, a movie he was writing. But Madonna politely refused the invitation and returned to Los Angeles. Later, in the summer of 1988, Prince attended a performance in New York of *Speed-the-Plow*, a play by David Mamet in which Madonna starred alongside Joe Mantegna and Ron Silver. Prince gave Madonna some recordings and they decided to work separately on *Love Song*, which ended up on *Like A Prayer*, her fourth album. She wanted to release it as a single and make a quick video, but Prince categorically refused, thereby depriving the song of its posterity.

Production
"We ended up writing it long-distance, because I had to be in L.A. and he couldn't leave Minneapolis, and quite frankly I couldn't stand Minneapolis. When I went there, it was like 20 degrees below zero, and it was really desolate. I was miserable and I couldn't write or work under those circumstances."[122] Prince recorded an initial version of the song, which Madonna later worked on with her producers. The Kid recorded his voice in the final mix a few months later. On that occasion, he recorded some guitar lines for *Like A Prayer*, which can be heard in the first few seconds of the song, before the sound of the closing door.

The Sounds of Blackness choir brought depth to certain songs on the album *Batman (Motion Picture Soundtrack)*.

THE FUTURE

Prince / 4'07

Musicians: Prince: vocals, electric guitar, bass, programming, synthesizers, Fairlight CMI, finger snapping / **Sounds of Blackness:** choir / **Recording: Paisley Park, Chanhassen, Minnesota:** February 1989 / **Technical team: Producer:** Prince / **Executive producers:** Jon Peters, Peter Guber, Gary LeMel / **Recording engineer:** Femi Jiya / **Assistant recording engineers:** David Friedlander, Heidi Hanschu, Chuck Zwicky, Eddie Miller

Even though Prince was always one step ahead of the latest musical trend, he played along and used house music in *The Future*. This style of electronic music comes from disco, and its repetitive and throbbing rhythms was taking over nightclubs around the world. Drowning out the rhythmic pattern of his drum machine with different effects plucked from his Boss guitar pedals (including a Dynamic Filter FT-2 and an Overdrive OD-1), Prince launched the song at a danceable but somber pace. He then recorded a funky guitar line and plugged that tape into the Publison Infernal Machine 90, a multi-effect processor with a sampler function. Following that, he triggered, at random, the samples he'd recorded and modified, giving them the synthetic sound that is especially noticeable at 2'29 in. Next, he embellished the song with string parts that Clare Fischer had recorded on 5 August 1986 in Los Angeles for the song *Crystal Ball*, as well as snippets of Jack Nicholson, Michael Keaton, Kim Basinger, Christopher Fairbank, and Robert Wuhl's lines from the movie. Lastly, Prince asked his friend Gary Hines, of the Sounds of Blackness choir, to refine the song with deep, dark vocals, which he also modified with the sampler. "I'll never forget he called and said they had this really important project that he wanted us to work with him on," said Hines. "At the time, he couldn't even tell us what it was, he told us afterward. He said we probably would stay an hour or two in the studio; of course we were there all night [laughs]. We had a great time!"[117] *The Future* was released as a single in Europe, and eminent producers Mark Moore and William Orbit made a remixed version that came out as a maxi-single.

ELECTRIC CHAIR

Prince / 4'07

Musicians: Prince: vocals, electric guitar, bass, programming, synthesizers, backing vocals / **Recording: Paisley Park, Chanhassen, Minnesota:** 6 June 1988 / **Technical team: Producer:** Prince / **Executive producers:** Jon Peters, Peter Guber, Gary LeMel / **Recording engineer:** Femi Jiya / **Assistant recording engineers:** David Friedlander, Heidi Hanschu, Chuck Zwicky, Eddie Miller

Recorded in June 1988 and unearthed specifically for *Batman*, the explosive *Electric Chair* was the only song on the album to have had the privilege of being mixed by Chris Lord-Alge, one of the greatest specialists in this genre. Lord-Alge made the song shine, giving the guitars, recorded masterfully by Femi Jiya and Eddie Miller, all the space they deserved. Prince used his vintage Colorsound Wah-Wah pedal, which gave his solos a welcome warmth amid the torrent of synthetic sounds. "At that time, [the pedal] hadn't been reissued and was somewhat hard to find, and had a very distinctive sound and very distinctive travel compared to a Crybaby pedal [...],"[118] explained recording engineer Chuck Zwicky, referring to the most famous pedals of this kind.

Single

THE ARMS OF ORION

Prince, Sheena Easton / 5'02

Musicians: Prince: vocals, bass, programming, Wurlitzer 200, piano, synthesizers, zills, triangle, backing vocals / **Sheena Easton:** vocals / **Recording: Paisley Park, Chanhassen, Minnesota:** 25 January 1989 / **Technical team: Producer:** Prince / **Executive producers:** Jon Peters, Peter Guber, Gary LeMel / **Recording engineer:** Femi Jiya / **Assistant recording engineers:** David Friedlander, Heidi Hanschu, Chuck Zwicky, Eddie Miller
Single version: A-side: *The Arms of Orion* (Edit) [Prince with Sheena Easton]/3'40 / **B-side:** *I Love U In Me*/4'13 / **CD single version:** / **1.** *The Arms of Orion* (Prince with Sheena Easton)/5'03 / **2.** *I Love U In Me*/4'12 / **3.** *The Arms of Orion* (Edit)/3'52 / **Released in the USA by Warner Bros. Records:** 16 October 1989 (single ref.: 7-22757) / **Released in the UK by WEA International:** 9 November 1989 (single ref.: W2757; CD single ref.: W2757CD) / **Best chart ranking in the USA:** 36 / **Best chart ranking in the UK:** 27

Hoping to reconnect to the 1980s ballad, a trend he'd contributed to setting, Prince took a wrong turn with this sentimental piece, which comes closer to *Take My Breath Away* by Berlin (1986) than the unforgettable *Free*, *Purple Rain*, or *The Ladder*. Recorded as a duo with Sheena Easton, with whom Prince had got on well when they made *U Got the Look* in 1987, the song was nevertheless able to bring a little lightness to a very dark album, in which the spirit of Gotham City reigned supreme. Prince composed the music, but Easton wrote the lyrics. In 2012 she explained their origins: "I sent him the lyrics to *The Arms of Orion*. He really liked it, put music to it, and it ended up being on the *Batman* soundtrack. I'm totally into the stars. Right outside my bedroom window, [...] you looked right into Orion. I loved the concept of two lovers apart, looking up at the same stars and wishing they could be together."[106]

Single

PARTYMAN

Prince / 3'11

Musicians: Prince: vocals, electric guitar, bass, programming, piano, synthesizers, Fairlight CMI, backing vocals / **Anna Garcia:** spoken word / **Femi Jiya:** spoken word / **Recording: Paisley Park, Chanhassen, Minnesota:** March 1989 / **Technical team: Producer:** Prince / **Executive producers:** Jon Peters, Peter Guber, Gary LeMel / **Recording engineer:** Femi Jiya / **Assistant recording engineers:** David Friedlander, Heidi Hanschu, Chuck Zwicky, Eddie Mille
Single: A-side: *Partyman* (LP Version)/3'11 / **B-side:** *Feel U Up* (Short Stroke)/3'42 / **Released in the USA by Warner Bros Records:** 25 August 1989 (single ref.: 7-22814) / **Released in the UK by WEA International:** 18 August 1989 (single ref.: W2814) / **Best chart ranking in the USA:** 18 / **Best chart ranking in the UK:** 16

Prince had proposed *Rave Unto the Joy Fantastic* as a replacement for *1999*, which Tim Burton had initially chosen for the movie, but *Partyman* ended up as the ideal choice for *Batman*. At 61'46 in, it accompanies the scene in which the Joker and his minions come to rob the Flugelheim Museum in Gotham City (keen observers noticed the spelling error on the restaurant menus, where it says: "Fluegelheim Museum"). The choreography of this scene is as charming as Jack Nicholson's character is evil. Prince once said that Nicholson's elegant and nonchalant attitude is what inspired *Partyman*. "He just walked over, sat down and put his foot up on a table, real cool, he had this attitude that reminded me of Morris [Day]—and there was that song."[123] Prince incorporated all sorts of samples into the song, including the voices of his recording engineer Femi Jiya and of his girlfriend Anna Garcia (aka Anna Fantastic). He didn't hesitate to borrow lines from the movie and integrate them into the song, the quick pace of which was maintained by a thunderous, four-string line played on the Auerswald Cleo bass. Prince had picked up this bass guitar again in 2010 and can be seen holding it on the cover of the posthumous album *Welcome 2 America*, which was released in 2021. The 1989 documentary *Prince/Musical Portrait* by Albert Magnoli gives a rare glimpse into the recording sessions for *Partyman*, with Prince slapping his futuristic bass with all the virtuosity for which he was known.

Prince with his partner, the young Anna Garcia, who inspired the songs *Vicky Waiting* and *Pink Cashmere*.

VICKI WAITING

Prince / 4'51

Musicians: Prince: vocals, electric guitar, bass, programming, synthesizers, Fairlight CMI, backing vocals / **Recording: Paisley Park, Chanhassen, Minnesota:** December 1988; February 1989 / **Technical team: Producer:** Prince / **Executive producers:** Jon Peters, Peter Guber, Gary LeMel / **Recording engineer:** Femi Jiya / **Assistant recording engineers:** David Friedlander, Heidi Hanschu, Chuck Zwicky, Eddie Miller

While he waited patiently for his beloved Anna Garcia to reach adulthood in order to enjoy an unconstrained romance with her under American law, Prince decided to record *Anna Waiting* for her, in which he explains—over a synthesizer gimmick reminiscent of *Mountains*, from 1986—their forbidden relationship: "This is where she wants to be/I am what she wants to see/I've never known a love so sweet/Still, I keep Anna waiting." Prince played her the song on her eighteenth birthday, on 31 December 1988, and then asked her if he could change it to *Vicki Waiting*, so he could include it in *Batman*. Once his now official girlfriend greenlighted the modification, he recorded the new lyrics in February and added the song to the album. He imagined Bruce Wayne, aka Batman, as the narrator referring to Vicki Vale, who was played by Kim Basinger.

TRUST

Prince / 4'23

Musicians: Prince: vocals, electric guitar, bass, programming, synthesizers, Fairlight CMI, percussion, tambourine, claps, backing vocals / **Recording: Paisley Park, Chanhassen, Minnesota:** March 1989 / **Technical team: Producer:** Prince / **Executive producers:** Jon Peters, Peter Guber, Gary LeMel / **Recording engineer:** Femi Jiya / **Assistant recording engineers:** David Friedlander, Heidi Hanschu, Chuck Zwicky, Eddie Miller

Tim Burton chose *Baby I'm A Star*, from the *Purple Rain* album, to accompany the scene where the Joker parades through the streets of Gotham City, handing out fistfuls of dollars to people before slaughtering them with nerve gas. This scene inspired Prince to compose *200 Balloons*, which he gave to Burton. But Burton and his producer decided that the song didn't match the atmosphere of the movie, so Prince had to revise his work. He came up with *Trust*, whose disco rhythm recalls *Baby I'm A Star*, while the Caribbean ambience of its introduction is reminiscent of the Brazilian influences found in *New Position*, from the *Parade* album. The song,

The unforgettable Jack Nicholson played a terrifying Joker in Tim Burton's movie.

perfectly synchronized to the Joker's swagger, provided a moment of happiness for Prince fans, who had gone to movie theaters to hear him in the feature movie, even though his music only appears in it three times. As for *200 Balloons*, it came out on the B-side of the single *Batdance*.

LEMON CRUSH

Prince / 4'15

Musicians: Prince: vocals, electric guitar, programming, synthesizers, Fairlight CMI, backing vocals / **Recording:** Paisley Park, Chanhassen, Minnesota: February to April 1989 / **Technical team:** Producer: Prince / Executive producers: Jon Peters, Peter Guber, Gary LeMel / Recording engineer: Femi Jiya / Assistant recording engineers: David Friedlander, Heidi Hanschu, Chuck Zwicky, Eddie Miller

Anna Garcia revealed that Prince was inspired to write this song because of her favorite drink, Lemon Crush, a lemon soda she drank regularly. In the song, Prince calls out her addiction, using slang that was unusual for him, but which allowed him to write some simple and effective rhymes: "If I'm workin' at my jobba/I'm the victim, you're the robba/No matter how much I try to stoppa/I can't help thinkin' about cha." Prince's fans didn't miss a beat: they noticed that *Lemon Crush* contained a few musical elements that Prince used again in 1991, in the stunning *Thunder*: the descending synthesizer at 2'55 and the rise of the keyboard at 3'35 are two hallmarks of the masterful opening to *Diamonds and Pearls*.

Single

SCANDALOUS

Prince, John L Nelson / 6'14

Musicians: Prince: vocals, programming, synthesizer, backing vocals / **Recording:** Paisley Park, Chanhassen, Minnesota: 17 October 1988 / **Technical team:** Producer: Prince / Executive producers: Jon Peters, Peter Guber, Gary LeMel / Recording engineer: Femi Jiya / Assistant recording engineers: David Friedlander, Heidi Hanschu, Chuck Zwicky, Eddie Miller
Single: A-side: *Scandalous!* (Edit)/4'12 / **B-side:** *When 2 R In Love*/3'57 / **Released in the USA by Warner Bros. Records:** 28 November 1989 (single ref.: 7-22824) / **Best chart ranking in the USA:** did not make the charts

Prince reconnected with his love of soul in this piece, which could easily be mistaken for an Otis Redding or Sam Cooke song. Composed and recorded long before Prince's participation in *Batman*, *Scandalous* was nevertheless included in the project and found pride of place in the second part of the movie's closing credits. As he'd done with all the other songs on the record, Prince attributed it to a character in the movie. Here, Batman himself reveals his fantasies to Vicky Vale and urges her to come and throw herself into his strong, superhero arms. Prince hesitated between *Scandalous* and another song, *Still Would Stand All Time*, to appear on the record. On the advice of his recording engineer, Chuck Zwicky, he ended up choosing the first one. Prince returned to the studio in October 1989, this time with Kim Basinger, his new girlfriend, and recorded *The Scandalous Sex Suite*, an almost 20-minute-long version of the song, in which the actress stands out with rather sensual sound bites where she alternates naughty words with moans.

Single

BATDANCE

Prince / 6'13

Musicians

Prince: vocals, electric guitar, bass, programming, synthesizers, Fairlight CMI, backing vocals

Chuck Zwicky: programming

Recording

Paisley Park, Chanhassen, Minnesota: March 1989

Technical team

Producer: Prince

Executive producers: Jon Peters, Peter Guber, Gary LeMel

Recording engineer: Femi Jiya

Assistant recording engineers: David Friedlander, Heidi Hanschu, Chuck Zwicky, Eddie Miller

Single version

A-side: *Batdance* (Edit)/4'06

B-side: *200 Balloons*/5'05

CD single version (UK)

1. *Batdance*/6'13
2. *200 Balloons*/5'05

Released in the USA by Warner Bros. Records: 6 June 1989 (single ref.: 7-22924)

Released in the UK by WEA International: 12 June 1989 (single ref.: W2924; CD single ref.: W2924CD)

Best chart ranking in the USA: 1

Best chart ranking in the UK: 2

Genesis

As Prince was wrapping up his album inspired by the *Batman* movie, Albert Magnoli, his manager, urged him to write a song that could be presented to Warner Bros. Records as a single worth its salt. The two men had established a relationship based on trust, which was all they needed to work together. Their partnership only ended when Magnoli left to replace Andreï Kontchalovski on the feature movie *Tango & Cash*, but Prince was still listening to his manager during recording of *Batman*, so he locked himself in his studios at Paisley Park in March 1989, and only came out again once he'd finished the Dantesque *Batdance*. "He brought it to me in the morning, as he was leaving the studio," recalled Magnoli, "And he said, 'You're probably going to be angry because I kept a crew working overtime, but I've got this six-minute song. Listen to it and I'll come in later on and you can tell me what you think.' He said, 'Do you want me to edit it?' And I said, 'Cut it in half and give me a shorter version, but I'm going to get Warner Brothers to approve this six-minute version to go out with the video we make.'"[115] Thanks to this musical audacity and a video starring Gemini, Prince's half-Batman, half-Joker avatar, *Batdance* became a colossal success. It remains one of Prince's greatest global hits.

Production

Created from samples of *The Future* and *Electric Chair*, but also from a range of extracts from the movie, *Batdance* pushes the use of the sampling technique as far as it can go. You can hear all sorts of samples within the song, including the voices of Jack Nicholson, Michael Keaton, Kim Basinger, Christopher Fairbank, and Robert Wuhl. One of Prince's technicians, Matthew Larson, appears at 0'27 singing "Get The Funk Up," then at 5'14, shouting: "Don't Stop Dancing." Every once in a while, there is a nod to Neal Hefti's Batman theme, which accompanied the original 1966 series, and voices from the recording of the Sounds of Blackness chorale for *The Future* are also audible in parts. At a time when artists had to provide a megamix (a sort of mishmash of their hits played back to back), Prince was able to surf the wave of this trend without being pulled under it. This was a unique song made up of a series of quotes, providing fans with an additional masterpiece and closing the 1980s with a bang.

HEADPHONES AT THE READY

At 4'21 into *Batdance*, Prince tells a certain "Duckie" that he's about to stick a "7-inch in the computer." Then he draws on an extract from a previously unreleased song recorded in 1988: *We Got The Power*. At 4'31, you can hear him sing, "Hey, we got the power/Oh, we got the soul/Hey we got the sho'nuff get off/To make the devil go go."

Although he normally avoided being photographed during studio sessions, Prince agreed to have his photograph taken during his visit to Olympic Studios in Barnes, London, in 1988.

THE SCANDALOUS SEX SUITE

1. *The Crime* (Prince/6'24) * / 2. *The Passion* (Prince/6'17) * / 3. *The Rapture* (Prince/6'39) * / 4. *Sex "The 80's Are Over and the Time Has Come 4 Monogamy and Trust"* (Prince, Levi Seacer Jr / 7'02) / 5. *When 2 R In Love* (Prince/4'02) **

Released in the USA by Warner Bros. Records: 1 December 1989 (CD maxi-single ref.: 9 21422-2)
Released in Europe by WEA International: 1 December 1989 (CD maxi-single ref.: 927 491-2)
Best chart ranking in the USA: did not make the charts
Best chart ranking in the UK: did not make the charts

* Conceived as elements of a single song, these three tracks are covered together here.
** Previously released as *Lovesexy*, in 1988.

After taking part in the shooting of *Batman*, the actress Kim Basinger succumbed to Prince's charms and had a passionate relationship with him.

THE CRIME

Prince / 6'24

THE PASSION

Prince / 6'17

THE RAPTURE

Prince / 6'39

Musicians: Prince: vocals, electric guitar, bass, programming, synthesizers, backing vocals / **Kim Basinger:** spoken word, moans / **Eric Leeds:** saxophone / **Recording:** Paisley Park, Chanhassen, Minnesota: 17 October 1988; 1 October 1989 / **Technical team: Producer:** Prince / **Executive producers:** Jon Peters, Peter Guber / **Recording engineer:** Femi Jiya / **Assistant recording engineers:** David Friedlander, Heidi Hanschu, Chuck Zwicky, Eddie Miller

October 1989. Although the *Batman* era was already behind him, Prince decided to give American fans one last single from the album: the languorous *Scandalous*, recorded a year before. He reworked the song at Paisley Park, this time with Kim Basinger, who played Vicki Vale in the movie. She and Prince had started dating after he kicked out Anna Fantastic for having the bad idea—according to Prince—of posing nude for Dutch *Playboy* magazine. Prince created an almost 20-minute-long version of the song and divided it into three distinct sections: *The Crime*, *The Passion*, and *The Rapture*, all bundled together as a maxi-single called *The Scandalous Sex Suite*, which was released internationally. Lenny Waronker, of Warner Bros. Records, remembers discovering the song during a listening session Prince himself had organized. Kim Basinger was there too: "She's sitting in front of me; she has her legs crossed. He gives me the cassette. About five, six minutes into it, he taps me on the shoulder, and he says, 'That's good enough.'"[119] The actress with the wavy blonde hair brings a good dose of sensuality to the piece, alternating between naughty words to her lover ("What do I look like?" she asks at 2'46, to which Prince replies, "Overdressed") and drawn-out moans. In a 2015 interview, when asked about her romantic relationship with Prince and their collaboration on *The Scandalous Sex Suite*, Kim Basinger responded: "I don't really have boundaries, so I enjoyed that time of my life. It was a really special moment in time, and I have great memories. I don't put a lot of restrictions on myself, let's just put it that way. If there's someone I connect with, we'll go on these rides together."[120]

SEX « THE 80'S ARE OVER AND THE TIME HAS COME 4 MONOGAMY AND TRUST »

Prince, Levi Seacer Jr / 7'02

Musicians: Prince: vocals, electric guitar, bass, tambourine, programming, synthesizers / **Recording:** Paisley Park, Chanhassen, Minnesota: 1989 / **Technical team: Producer:** Prince / **Recording engineer:** Michael Koppelman? (not confirmed)

Recorded in the summer of 1989, *Sex* (subtitled *The 80's Are Over And the Time Has Come 4 Monogamy and Trust*), ended up on the B-side of the maxi-single *The Scandalous Sex Suite*. Strangely, Prince also included a song from *Lovesexy*: *When 2 R In Love*, which had been previously recorded for the mysterious *Black Album*. Against the backdrop of a simple but effective groove, Prince explains what he believes is the true meaning of the word sex. In the chorus he sings: "S is for scandalous/E is for exciting/X is for adults only/Let's do something frightening." In 1992, Prince gave the song to the band Lois Lane. They included it on their album *Precious*, the vocal tracks for which were recorded at Paisley Park.

PRINCE

GRAFFITI BRIDGE

Can't Stop This Feeling I Got* · New Power Generation* · Release It—The Time
The Question of U* · Elephants & Flowers* · Round and Round—Tevin Campbell
We Can Funk—George Clinton and Prince* · Joy in Repetition* · Love Machine—The Time
Tick, Tick, Bang* · Shake! —The Time · Thieves in the Temple* · The Latest Fashion —The Time
with Prince* · Melody Cool—Mavis Staples · Still Would Stand All Time* · Graffiti Bridge*
New Power Generation (Pt. II)*

** Since Graffiti Bridge contains songs by multiple artists, only those by Prince are covered here.*

Released in the USA by Paisley Park Records/Warner Bros. Records:
21 August 1990 (LP ref.: 1-27493; CD ref.: 9 27493-2)
Released in the UK by Paisley Park Records/WEA International:
20 August 1990 (LP ref.: 7599-27493-1 – WX 361; CD ref.: 7599-27493-2)
Best chart ranking in the USA: 6
Best chart ranking in the UK: 1

Funk, glamor, and big bikes: the Kid is back!

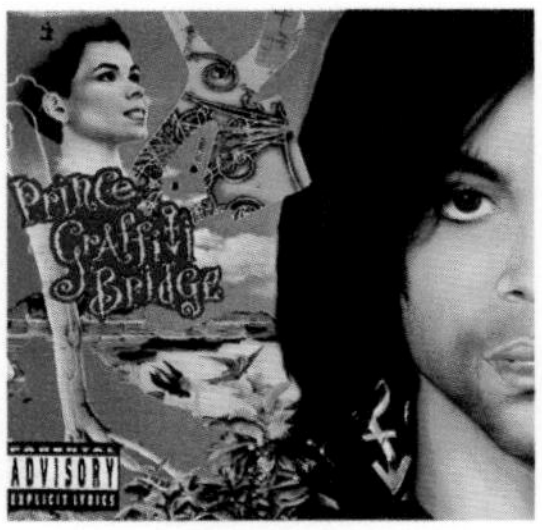

A REUNION WITH THE KID

Despite the commercial flop of *Under the Cherry Moon* in 1986, Prince still felt drawn to the world of movies. The following year, he started work on a new screenplay called *Graffiti Bridge*. During a meeting in Minneapolis, Prince asked Madonna to join the project, which she curtly refused after reading the script because she felt it was mediocre. Focused on the movie/concert event *Sign O' the Times*, whose release in movie theaters on 20 November 1987 gave American fans something they'd missed (since the tour had been limited to 34 concerts in Europe), Prince shelved the project for a while. At the time, each new idea of his chased out the one before. Between 1987 and the start of 1989, Prince recorded *The Black Album*, then *Lovesexy*, which was immediately followed by the Lovesexy Tour, and, finally, he joined the *Batman* adventure. But despite the multitude of projects, *Graffiti Bridge* remained in Prince's thoughts during that prolific period.

Between old songs and novelties

Before he got involved with *Batman*, Prince started compiling songs from The Vault to create the original score for *Graffiti Bridge*, even though the movie only existed in his imagination. *Melody Cool*, *Bloody Mouth*, *Big Tall Wall*, *Pink Cashmere*, *The Grand Progression*, and *The Question of U* were among the songs selected for the record. Two songs written for *Rave Unto the Joy Fantastic*, the production of which was abandoned in favor of *Batman*, were also selected: *Rave Unto the Joy Fantastic* and *Elephants & Flowers*. Prince later decided to record two new songs inspired by the script he was working on—*New Power Generation*, *Round and Round*, and *Thieves in the Temple*. He also rehashed other old songs, including *Can't Stop This Feeling I Got* and *Joy in Repetition*. The pace of work at Paisley Park was as sustained as ever, as reported by Chuck Zwicky, one of Prince's many recording engineers at the time: "He would come in the studio in the morning, between 10am and noon, then rehearse with the band until 6 or 7 at night, go home, have dinner, come back, and record until 3 or 4 in the morning, go home and watch the videotapes of the rehearsal from the day. Then get up the next day, rehearse 6 or 7 hours, go into the studio and record 6 or 7 hours, go home, and watch 4 or 5 hours of videotapes—the same thing, day in and day out."[118]

A collective adventure

When Prince set out to direct *Graffiti Bridge*, he wanted to work with a limited budget and finish the movie in a very short timeframe, hoping to release it 12 months later. Albert Magnoli, his manager, who'd gone to shoot *Tango & Cash*, was replaced by Arnold Stiefel and Randy Phillips. They both promised Prince their unconditional support in this new cinematic adventure. Even though it wasn't presented as such, the movie was the follow-up to *Purple Rain*. The plot follows the misadventures of the Kid—who co-owns a club called Glam Slam with Morris Day—as he struggles to retain control of the place since his financial partner puts profitability above his soulful songs. The movie has a sort of déjà-vu feeling. Kim Basinger had also been asked to star in it, but turned the role down, and the part was finally given to Ingrid Chavez, Prince's muse during recording for the *Lovesexy* album. She played Aura, an imaginary character who guides Prince's character on his way to success. Shooting began at Paisley Park in February 1990 under Prince's

Prince triumphant... onstage at the Stadio Flaminio, in Rome, on 17 July 1990.

Jill Jones, a major artist in Prince's circle and a close friend of the singer.

direction. Onstage, Prince's friends mixed with the extras. Among them were Jill Jones, Mavis Staples, George Clinton, and 14-year-old Tevin Campbell. The choreographies were by singer and dancer Paula Abdul and the original score, unlike that of *Purple Rain*, was performed by the various artists appearing on screen. On 2 June 1990, Prince launched the highly lucrative Nude Tour in Europe and Japan. It comprised a reinterpretation of his hits and was intended to refill his coffers after the financial disaster of the Lovesexy Tour. Once the tour was over, the following 10 September, *Graffiti Bridge* came out in the US to general indifference. After disastrous reviews and a torrent of horrific criticisms, it disappeared from the bill in just a few weeks.

Prince's last movie

While *Graffiti Bridge* is pleasant in many ways, especially because of Prince's on-screen reunion with Morris Day, the movie was a bitter failure for the singer, who then abandoned his cinematographic dreams for good. As for the album, its style resembles *Batman*, especially because of the old drum machine sounds and the frequent use of synthesizers. The album marks the ending of an unofficial trilogy that started with *Lovesexy* and was followed by *Batman*, and it is imbued with equal amounts of spirituality, a concept that was very dear to Prince and echoed his faith in God. Made up of songs from Prince's various periods, this catch-all record struggles to live up to his greatest albums, although it does contain a few hidden gems, such as the timeless *Joy in Repetition*. It became a part of Prince's discography and marks the introduction of his new group, The New Power Generation (often simply called NPG), who would go on to accompany him in various ways until the end of his career.

CAN'T STOP THIS FEELING I GOT

Prince / 4'24

Musician: Prince: vocals, electric guitar, bass, drums, programming, synthesizers, claps, backing vocals / **Recording: Paisley Park, Chanhassen, Minnesota:** 1989 / **Technical Team: Producer:** Prince / **Recording engineers:** Michael Koppelman, David Friedlander, Tom Garneau

First recorded in 1982, *Can't Stop This Feeling I Got* was reworked in June 1986 for inclusion on the *Dream Factory* album. After abandoning this project, Prince offered it to the band The Three O'Clock, but they ended up preferring another Prince song: *Neon Telephone*. However, quite proud of the song, Prince rerecorded it in 1989 for *Graffiti Bridge* and released it as a single in the Philippines. During the recording of this piece, Paisley Park became the site of a friendly competition. Susan Rogers had jumped ship, so the other recording engineers were lining up to replace her. Prince had decided to work with a multitude of technicians, whom he judged based on their skills and availabilities. Michael Koppelman was among them. While he was busy recording *Can't Stop This Feeling I Got*, Prince told him that none of the hopefuls for the role could mix any of his songs. Koppelman reminded him that he'd never given him the chance to prove himself, to which the singer responded he could always test his mettle on that song. Koppelman spent the night mixing the song, which he then put on a tape he slipped under Prince's door the next morning. That very morning, Prince congratulated Koppelman for his work. He soon became one of Prince's official recording engineers.

Single

NEW POWER GENERATION

Prince / 3'39

Musicians: Prince: vocals, electric guitar, bass, synthesizers, claps, backing vocals / **Rosie Gaines:** vocals, backing vocals / **Morris Day:** drums / **The New Power Generation:** vocals, spoken words / **Recording: Sunset Sound, Los Angeles:** 12 January 1982 / **Paisley Park, Chanhassen, Minnesota:** December 1989 / **Technical Team: Producer:** Prince / **Recording engineers:** Michael Koppelman, Tom Garneau
Single version: A-side: *New Power Generation*/3'39 / **B-side:** *New Power Generation* (Part II)/2'57 / **CD single version (UK)** / **1.** *New Power Generation*/3'39 / **2.** *New Power Generation* (Pt. II)/2'57 / **3.** *Melody Cool* (Extended Remix) [Mavis Staples]/6'04 / **Released in the USA by Paisley Park Records/Warner Bros. Records:** 23 October 1990 (single ref.: 7-19525) / **Released in the UK by Paisley Park Records/WEA International:** 22 October 1990 (single ref.: W9525; CD single ref.: W9525CD) / **Best chart ranking in the USA:** 64 / **Best chart ranking in the UK:** 26

Drum rolls for The New Power Generation, Prince's new band, whose many lineups contributed to his success in the 1990s. "We are The New Power Generation/We want to change the World," sings Prince in this very funky song, whose first version, initially called *Bold Generation*, was recorded in January 1982 during sessions for the second album produced by The Time (see page 64). The song even has Morris Day on drums, as on the original version. During sessions for *Graffiti Bridge*, Prince kept the original track, to which he added a drum machine, thereby doubling the rhythmic pattern. The song was released as a single in the autumn of 1990 and a maxi-single with several remixes was also created for the occasion.

Like the great Sister Rosetta Tharpe before him, Prince knew how to combine syncopated music with pious praise.

THE QUESTION OF U

Prince / 4'00

Musician: **Prince:** vocals, electric guitar, bass, claps, programming, synthesizers, backing vocals / **Recording:** **Galpin Boulevard Home Studio, Chanhassen, Minnesota:** 6 July 1986 / **Paisley Park, Chanhassen, Minnesota:** 1987 / **Technical Team:** **Producer:** Prince / **Recording engineers:** Eddie Garcia, Tom Garneau, Chuck Zwicky

The Question of U was created and recorded during sessions with the short-lived band The Flesh in December 1985. It was reworked the following July at the Galpin Boulevard Home Studio, before being shelved in The Vault. Partly rerecorded at the end of 1987 at Paisley Park, the song ended up on the album, as well as appearing at the fifty-second minute of the movie, in a kitsch erotic scene between the Kid and Aura, played by Ingrid Chavez.

HEADPHONES AT THE READY

The strange flute in the introduction to *The Question of U* is an extract from Claude Debussy's *Prélude à l'Après-midi d'un Faune* (Prelude to the Afternoon of a Faun), which Prince added to his Publison Infernal Machine 90 rack before reshuffling it to create an unrecognizable sample.

ELEPHANTS & FLOWERS

Prince / 3'54

Musician: **Prince:** vocals, electric guitar, drums, programming, tambourine, synthesizers, backing vocals / **Recording:** **Paisley Park, Chanhassen, Minnesota:** 6 October 1988; autumn 1989 / **Technical Team:** **Producer:** Prince / **Recording engineers:** Michael Koppelman, Tom Garneau

The strange name of this song conceals a real hymn beneath what appears to be a rock 'n' roll song. Like Sister Rosetta Tharpe, who serenaded God with a Gibson SG, in this song Prince declares his unbreakable faith: "Love the one who is love/The one who gives us the power/The one who made everything/Elephants and flowers." Prince stood by this declaration of faith in 1997. When a fan asked him about the meaning of the song, he replied: "The gratitude we give 2 God 4 everything God gives 2 us."[114]

George Clinton, the eccentric inventor of p-funk, would cross paths numerous times with Prince.

WE CAN FUNK

(George Clinton and Prince)—Prince / 5'28

Musicians: Prince: vocals, electric guitar, acoustic guitar, bass, synthesizers, backing vocals / **George Clinton:** vocals / **Wendy Melvoin:** electric guitar, backing vocals / **Lisa Coleman:** synthesizers, backing vocals / **Joseph "Amp" Fiddler:** synthesizers, backing vocals / **Gary "Mudbone" Cooper:** drums / **David Coleman:** zills, backing vocals / **Eric Leeds:** saxophone / **Atlanta Bliss:** trumpet / **Susannah Melvoin:** backing vocals / **Jonathan Melvoin:** backing vocals / **Jill Jones:** backing vocals / **Garry Shider:** backing vocals / **Steve Boyd:** backing vocals / **William Payne:** backing vocals / **Belita Woods:** backing vocals / **Tracey Lewis:** backing vocals / **Mike Harris:** backing vocals / **Pat Lewis:** backing vocals / **Sandra Dance:** backing vocals / **Recording: Sunset Sound, Los Angeles:** 31 December 1983 / **Washington Avenue Warehouse, Edina, Minnesota:** 17 June 1986 / **Paisley Park, Chanhassen, Minnesota:** 1989–1990 / **United Sound Systems, Detroit:** 1989–1990 / **Technical Team: Producer:** Prince / **Recording engineers:** Michael Koppelman (Paisley Park), David Friedlander (Paisley Park), Larry Fergusson (United Sound Systems)

On 31 December 1983, at Sunset Sound, Prince and The Revolution recorded a song they had created the day before during a jam session. *We Can Fuck*—which became *We Can Funk*—expresses Prince's irrepressible desire to make love to his partner. He sings to her using explicit words: "I could tell you things to get you excited, things you never heard/You know the Kama Sutra?/I could re-write it with half as many words." As Susan Rogers explained in 2016, "One of the things that was lost on some people, not on his fans, but on a lot of people, they didn't really get that when Prince was singing songs about sex, he was giving power to women [...]" She continued, "He's saying how much he loves it when she has all the power."[107] It was a done deal with this song, which Prince partially rerecorded in 1986 and reworked in 1990 for *Graffiti Bridge*. On that occasion, he worked with the leader of Parliament-Funkadelic, George Clinton, who played himself in the movie. Clinton recorded his voice and a few overdubs with his musicians at Paisley Park and at United Sound Systems studios in Detroit, giving the piece an atmosphere reminiscent of his two legendary groups: Parliament and Funkadelic. In 1985, Prince declared his admiration for the godfather of psychedelic funk in the pages of *Rolling Stone* magazine: "Not long ago I talked to George Clinton, a man who knows and has done so much for funk. George told me how much he liked *Around the World in a Day*. You know how much more his words meant than those from some mamma-jamma wearing glasses [...] behind a typewriter?"[27]

In 2011, Prince recorded several songs with singer Andy Allo, including a cover of *We Can Funk*, renamed *Oui Can Luv* for the occasion. In this sublime version, Prince accompanies Allo on the acoustic guitar. Although nine songs from this session were made available on the streaming platform Tidal in November 2015, they were permanently pulled from the site after only a few hours.

JOY IN REPETITION

Prince / 4'53

Musicians: Prince: vocals, electric guitar, bass, drums, percussion, programming, synthesizers, backing vocals / **Susannah Melvoin:** backing vocals / **Recording: Sunset Sound, Los Angeles:** 17 July 1986 / **Paisley Park, Chanhassen, Minnesota:** 1990 / **Technical Team: Producer:** Prince / **Recording engineers:** Susan Rogers, Chuck Zwicky

Recorded in July 1986 for *Dream Factory*, the beautiful *Joy in Repetition* was luckily retrieved from the shelves of The Vault to appear in *Graffiti Bridge*. The lyrics contain a reference to another song, an instrumental, recorded five days later: *Soul Psychodelicide*. Chuck Zwicky, the recording engineer, talked about his work on the song's understated arrangements, when Prince decided to add a few overdubs in 1990: "I recorded *Joy in Repetition*, and as a producer, I do a lot of atmospheric and trippy-sounding stuff, and I've always loved that sort of thing."[119]

HEADPHONES AT THE READY

The chattering crowd at the start of *Joy in Repetition* was not made up of members of The New Power Generation. It was a recording of Matthew "Atlanta Bliss" Blistan, Wally Safford, and Greg Brooks from 1988. The same recording can be heard at the very end of *Eye No*, on the *Lovesexy* album.

TICK, TICK, BANG

Prince / 3'30

Musician: Prince: vocals, electric guitar, bass, programming, synthesizers, tambourine, backing vocals / **Recording: Paisley Park, Chanhassen, Minnesota:** 1989 / **Technical Team: Producer:** Prince / **Recording engineers:** Michael Koppelman, David Friedlander, Tom Garneau

Written in 1981 for the *Controversy* album, *Tick, Tick, Bang* was rerecorded in 1989 at Paisley Park for *Graffiti Bridge*. This time, Prince didn't play the drums himself, nor did he opt for a feature from his legendary Linn LM-1 Drum Computer. Instead, he chose to sample the drum part that Mitch Mitchell had recorded at Olympic Studios in Barnes, near London, for the song *Little Miss Lover*, the twelfth track on *Axis: Bold as Love*, the second album by The Jimi Hendrix Experience. Prince didn't bother noting this in the album credits, however, since the use of samples was common at the end of the 1980s. But a wave of lawsuits for plagiarism or the illegal use of sound samples shook the music world some time later and kept musicians from pursuing their "artistic citation" initiatives.

Single

THIEVES IN THE TEMPLE

Prince / 3'20

Musician: Prince: vocals, electric guitar, programming, synthesizers, backing vocals / **Recording: Paisley Park, Chanhassen, Minnesota:** 11 February 1990 / **Technical Team: Producer:** Prince / **Recording engineers:** Michael Koppelman, Tom Garneau
Single: A-side: *Thieves in the Temple* (Album Version)/3'20 / **B-side:** *Thieves in the Temple* (Part II)/1'41 / **Released in the USA by Paisley Park Records/Warner Bros. Records:** 24 July 1990 (single ref.: 7-19751) / **Released in the UK by Paisley Park Records/WEA International:** 23 July 1990 (single ref.: W9751) / **Best chart ranking in the USA:** 6 / **Best chart ranking in the UK:** 7

"I feel good most of the time, and I like to express that by writing from joy," explained Prince in 1990. "I still do write from anger sometimes, like *Thieves in the Temple*. But I don't like to. It's not a place to live."[123] *Thieves in the Temple* was the last song recorded for *Graffiti Bridge*, which had to be slightly rearranged to accommodate it. A wise decision since the song was also the first single to be released from the album and was warmly received by both the public and critics. As proof, in 1996, the famous jazzman Herbie Hancock himself gave a very interesting reinterpretation of the song for his cover album *The New Standard*.

On 11 February 1990, Michael Koppelman was the first recording engineer to work with Prince on producing this song. After the first night working together, the two men left Paisley Park for a well-deserved break. One hour later, Prince turned back and called in Tom Garneau, another recording engineer. When Koppelman returned to work at around 6pm, he took up the song again. Prince was still alert, after having only slept for an hour. Once the mixing was finished, Prince began shooting the video the following day. On the evening of 13 February 1990, after three days of intense work, *Thieves in the Temple* and its video were complete.

HEADPHONES AT THE READY

Prince did not play the harmonica heard at 1'43 into *Thieves in the Temple*. This was a sample borrowed from *I Can't Stand It* by The Chambers Brothers, from the 1967 album *The Time Has Come*. Prince used the work of harmonica player Lester Chambers again in 1993, in the groovy *Black M.F. in the House* from the *Gold Nigga* album by The New Power Generation (see page 231).

THE LATEST FASHION

(The Time with Prince)—Prince / 4'02

Musicians: Prince: vocals, rap, electric guitar, bass, drums, percussion, programming, synthesizers, claps, backing vocals / **Morris Day:** vocals, spoken word / **Candy Dulfer:** saxophone / **Jerome Benton:** spoken word, crowd chatter / **Tom Garneau:** crowd chatter / **Michael Koppelman:** crowd chatter / **Recording: Sunset Sound, Los Angeles:** 27 March 1983 / **Galpin Boulevard Home Studio, Chanhassen, Minnesota:** April 1987 / **Paisley Park, Chanhassen, Minnesota:** summer 1989 / **Technical Team: Producers:** Prince, The Time / **Recording engineers:** Femi Jiya, Tom Garneau, Michael Koppelman

Prince recorded *My Summertime Thang* at Sunset Sound on 27 February 1983. It was supposed to appear on The Time's third album, *Ice Cream Castle*, but was set aside and later offered to singer Dale Bozzio for her album *Riot in English*, produced by Paisley Park Records. Preferring *So Strong*, another Prince composition, Bozzio politely refused it. Prince reworked the song again, with Morris Day, for *Corporate World*, The Time's new album, which they made with Prince in 1989. But Warner Bros. Records blocked the recording of the song because they wanted something by the original band rather than yet another Prince production, so the song was revisited for the movie *Graffiti Bridge*—resulting in a rare Prince/Morris Day duet—and renamed *The Latest Fashion*. When The Time finally released its fourth album, *Pandemonium*, on 10 July 1990, *My Summertime Thang* was included on it, in a nod to this song with many lives.

1990

STILL WOULD STAND ALL TIME

Prince / 5'23

Musicians: Prince: vocals, bass, drums, percussion, programming, synthesizers, claps, backing vocals / **Jevetta Steele:** backing vocals / **Fred Steele:** backing vocals / **J D Steele:** backing vocals / **Jearlyn Steele:** backing vocals / **Jill Jones:** backing vocals / **Jellybean Johnson:** backing vocals / **Jesse Johnson:** backing vocals / **Jimmy Jam:** backing vocals / **Monte Moir:** backing vocals / **Terry Lewis:** backing vocals / **Jerome Benton:** backing vocals / **Recording: Paisley Park, Chanhassen, Minnesota:** 6 October 1988; winter 1989; winter 1990 / **Technical Team: Producer:** Prince / **Recording engineers:** Femi Jiya, Tom Garneau, Chuck Zwicky

Prince and recording engineer Chuck Zwicky recorded *Still Would Stand All Time* in 1988 for the *Batman* album, but the

Morris Day in 1988, shortly before the shooting of *Graffiti Bridge*, where he met up again with the musicians of The Time.

song was ultimately replaced by *Scandalous*. The following year, however, it replaced *The Grand Progression*, a melancholic song reminiscent of some of Prince's other splendid ballads, for the tracklisting for *Graffiti Bridge*. *Still Would Stand All Time* is a perfect fit for the spirituality that permeates the record, especially thanks to the choir made up of The Steeles, The Time, and Jill Jones. Since Prince hadn't asked Clare Fischer to work on the arrangements for this song, he once again used a sample from Claude Debussy's *Prélude à l'Après-midi d'un Faune*, which he slowed down before adding it during mixing. Then he decided to rummage through his archives and add some string arrangements Fischer had recorded for another song, which proved once again that with Prince nothing is wasted, everything is transformed!

GRAFFITI BRIDGE

Prince / 3'51

Musicians: Prince: vocals, electric guitar, synthesizers, claps, backing vocals / **Boni Boyer:** vocals, backing vocals / **Tevin Campbell:** vocals, backing vocals / **Mavis Staples:** vocals, claps, backing vocals / **Levi Seacer Jr:** bass, backing vocals / **Sheila E.:** drums, claps, backing vocals / **Recording: Paisley Park, Chanhassen, Minnesota:** 11 July 1987; winter 1989; winter 1990 / **Technical Team: Producer:** Prince / **Recording engineers:** Michael Koppelman, David Friedlander, Tom Garneau

Continuing with the gospel choir, *Graffiti Bridge* closes the trilogy started two years earlier with the albums *Lovesexy* and *Batman*. Prince and his choir sing about peace and love, providing the movie with end credits consistent with the spirituality that pervades the storyline and these three albums. For the introduction to this track, one of the first recorded at Paisley Park in July 1987, Prince used the string arrangements Clare Fischer had written in 1985 for an unreleased Jill Jones song, *Killin' at the Soda Shop*, instead of the ones recorded specifically for this song in February 1990.

NEW POWER GENERATION (PT. II)

Prince / 2'57

Musicians: Prince: vocals, electric guitar, bass, synthesizers, tambourine, claps, backing vocals / **T C Ellis:** rap / **Morris Day:** drums / **Tevin Campbell:** backing vocals / **Mavis Staples:** backing vocals / **Robin Power:** backing vocals / **The New Power Generation:** backing vocals, spoken words / **Recording: Sunset Sound, Los Angeles:** 12 January 1982 / **Paisley Park, Chanhassen, Minnesota:** December 1990 / **Technical Team: Producer:** Prince / **Recording engineers:** Michael Koppelman, David Friedlander, Tom Garneau

Prince's reinterpretation of *New Power Generation* closes his twelfth album. It includes many samples—extracts from songs by artists who orbited around him. From the start, between 0'04 and 0'16, you can hear an extract from *My Tree (A Positive Place)*, which was recorded as a duet with Robin Power in October 1990. At 2'04, the singer asks Prince, "You Want Me To What?" To which he responds: "Shake!" A sample from *Oobey Doop*, a duet recorded the previous June with Elisa Fiorillo, makes a few subtle appearances between 0'35 and 0'56, before giving way to T C Ellis's rap song, *True Confession*, which he reused on his own album *True Confessions*, in 1991. Lastly, at 2'29, Prince's slowed-down voice announces the start of a new era, when he says: "New Power Generation has just taken control." With that, Prince was calling on his fans to join the coming artistic revolution.

NEW POWER GENERATION

1. *N.P.G. (Funky Weapon Remix)* (5'01)
2. *T.C.'s Rap (Featuring T.C. Ellis)* (3'11)
3. *Brother With A Purpose (Featuring Tony Mosley)* (4'18)
4. *Get Off* (4'41)
5. *The Lubricated Lady* (2'39)
6. *Loveleft, Loveright* (5'00)

Released in the USA by Paisley Park Records/Warner Bros. Records: 29 November 1990 (maxi-single ref.: 0-21783; CD maxi-single ref.: 9 21783-2)
Best chart ranking in the USA: did not make the charts

After *New Power Generation* came out as a single in October 1990, Prince decided to remix it at the Larrabee Sound Studios, in Los Angeles, with recording engineer Sylvia Massy. They worked on multiple versions and compiled them into a maxi-single that came out in the US the following 29 November. *N.P.G. (Funky Weapon Remix)* isn't all that different from its original version, except for the biting electric guitar, which fans greatly enjoyed. *T.C.'s Rap (Featuring T.C. Ellis)* highlights T C Ellis's rap, which had already been heard on *New Power Generation (Part II)*. Meanwhile, *Brother With A Purpose (Featuring Tony Mosley)* showcases rapper Tony Mosley, a soon-to-be key member of the NPG, who discharges a brutal but pleasant flow on a

The singers of the New Power Generation soon became stars, thanks above all to the support of their mentor, Prince.

slowed-down version of the single, hinting that we will see him again on Prince's next album. As for *Get Off*, which is not to be confused with *Gett Off*, one of the hits from the *Diamonds and Pearls* album, it comes off more as a draft of Prince's future single. *The Lubricated Lady* was Prince's chance to make an instrumental interpretation of *Get Off*, where he blended various elements heard in the maxi-single without really adding anything new. *Loveleft, Loveright* is the only previously unreleased song on the maxi-single, which is why it's the only one covered in these pages.

LOVELEFT, LOVERIGHT

Prince / 5'00

Musician: Prince: vocals, synthesizers, programming, backing vocals / **Recording: Larrabee Sound Studios, Los Angeles:** November 1989 / **Technical Team: Producer:** Prince / **Recording engineers:** Michael Koppelman, Sylvia Massy

Loveleft, Loveright is the only track to bear no similarity to the original single, aside from the reprisal of the melody, "Love to the left of me, love to the right," from 1'42 into *New Power Generation (Part II)*, the last song on *Graffiti Bridge*. An undeniable sensuality emanates from this piece, where our sexually insatiable artist recounts his exploits with not one, but two women, to whom he promises a passionate night. "Thinkin' 'bout the way things might have been/In another life, if you were my wife/And I don't mean one, but the two of you every night," sings the incorrigible Prince. No doubt it was no accident that the following year, Prince appeared at the promotion of the *Diamonds and Pearls* album on the arm of two women, Lori Elle and Robia LaMorte. A song to be urgently (re)discovered, at maximum volume, if possible.

PRINCE AND THE NEW POWER GENERATION

DIAMONDS AND PEARLS

Thunder · Daddy Pop · Diamonds and Pearls · Cream
Strollin' · Willing and Able · Gett Off · Walk Don't Walk · Jughead
Money Don't Matter 2 Night · Push · Insatiable · Live 4 Love

Released in the USA by Paisley Park Records/Warner Bros. Records:
1 October 1991 (CD ref.: 9 25379-2)
Released in the UK by Paisley Park Records/WEA International:
1 October 1991 (LP ref.: 7599-25379-1 – WX 432; CD ref.: 7599-25379-2)
Best chart ranking in the USA: 3
Best chart ranking in the UK: 2

Prince (and his New Power Generation) performed *Diamonds and Pearls* and *Baby I'm A Star* at the opening ceremony of the Special Olympics in Minneapolis–Saint Paul on 20 July 1991.

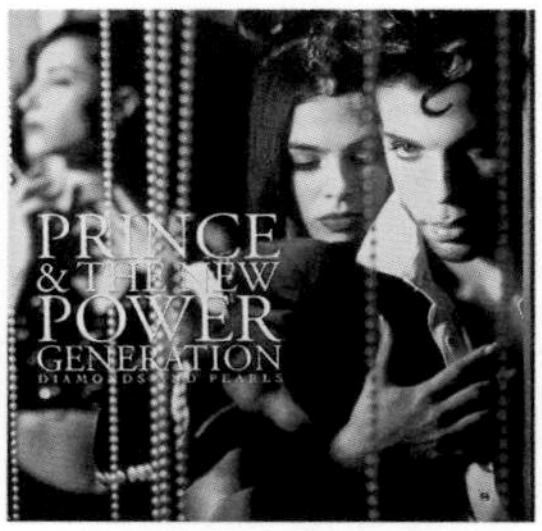

THE FIRST PANEL OF A RAP DIPTYCH

After having spent an entire decade trying to seduce a white public bent on pop and rock music, Prince decided to launch an artistic revolution, which surprised a lot of people. He had heavily criticized rap in *Dead On It*, a largely unknown song that was recorded for *The Black Album*, but this style clearly gradually grew on him in *Lovesexy* (*Alphabet St*) and *Graffiti Bridge* (*The Latest Fashion, New Power Generation [Pt. II]*). Tony Mosley, a dancer on the Nude Tour in 1990, came to support his interest in the hip- hop movement, which was quite popular at the time. Mosley had captured Prince's attention during sound checks by launching into a rap of his own, called *The Flow*. Prince suggested including it each night in the live version of *The Future*. He soon fell in love with this music, which was being broadcast across the airwaves. Whether it was FM (Vanilla Ice, MC Hammer), glamor (TLC), or protest (Public Enemy, N.W.A), the hip-hop movement was in full swing, and Prince saw his chance to reconnect with the African-American community, from whom he'd distanced himself in favor of mainstream rock. "Prince got interested in rap during the late '80s, when rappers started having more things to say besides 'throw your hands in the air and wave 'em like you just don't care,'" explained Tony Mosley, who soon started going by the name of Tony M. "Prince listens to a lot of other things and keeps up on what's going on."[124] Prince and his new partner decided to work together. "We sat down and talked about it, and he said it was an avenue he wanted to go down," he confirmed. "He realized that rap has changed, and the culture has changed. It was more socially conscious and topical at that time, and he began to take notice and wanted to dip into that area."[85]

Recording in the four corners of the world

Recording for *Diamonds and Pearls* began in December 1989, before the Nude Tour. For the first time in a while, Prince started off with a blank slate, without drawing from The Vault and reworking old songs. He knew that he could only truly be reborn through spontaneous work, so he created new songs during multiple recording sessions across the world, which continued until May 1991. After recording *Diamonds and Pearls* and *Live 4 Love* at Paisley Park during a session with the future members of the New Power Generation—Michael Bland, Sonny Thompson, and Thomas Elm—Prince took advantage of his stay at Wembley Arena (19–27 June 1990) to record some new songs at the legendary Olympic Studios in Barnes, near London. When the Nude Tour reached Japan in late August, he set up shop at the Warner-Pioneer studios in Tokyo and recorded *Willing and Able, Money Don't Matter 2 Night*, and *Strollin'*. The album's production lasted until May 1991, when Prince finally recorded *Gett Off*, just as recording for his next work was starting. Most songs contained hip-hop elements, so Prince established a balance in the record's tracklisting by archiving many of them in The Vault, including *Schoolyard, Something Funky (This House Comes), Call the Law*, and *The Flow*.

Prince's return to grace

Determined to get back on top after the painful failure of the movie *Graffiti Bridge*, Prince increased his media appearances in 1991. He hadn't gone to such lengths to promote himself since *Dirty Mind*. Ahead of the release of *Diamonds and Pearls*, on 20 July 1991, the singer and his band took part in the opening ceremony of the Special Olympics,

1991

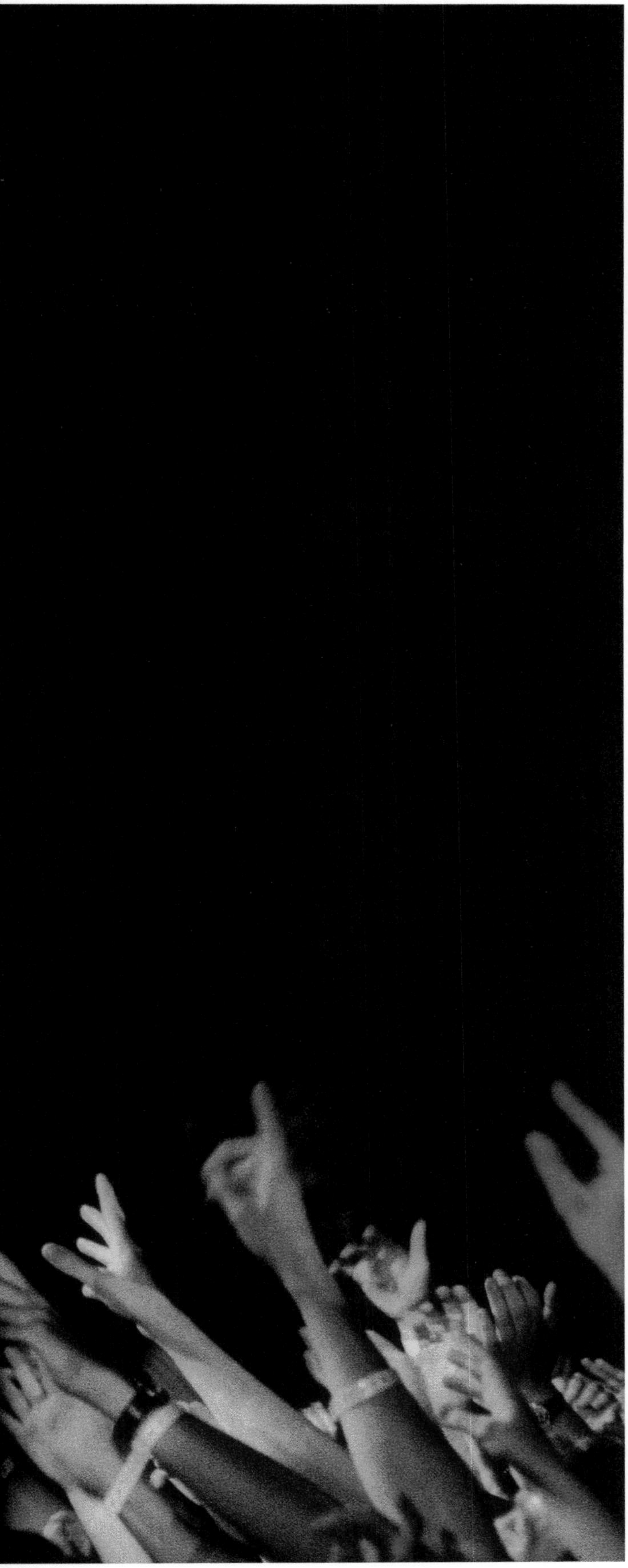

The Diamonds and Pearls Tour was the crowning success of an exceptional album.

FOR PRINCE ADDICTS

In the credits for *Diamonds and Pearls*, Tommy Barbarella and Rosie Gaines were featured as Purpleaxxe musicians. This was a MIDI keyboard that took the form of a guitar-synthesizer, which Prince invented for his two keyboardists. Barbarella made a notable use of it at 4'07 into the music video for *Gold*, in 1995, a few months after the patent was officially filed.

Jon Bon Jovi fell in love with the power and virtuosity of the New Power Generation and dared to ask Prince if he could record with his musicians. "I went, 'What? No!' It was like he wanted to make love to my woman," explained Prince.[125]

held in the Twin Cities (Minneapolis and Saint Paul), playing two songs live at the Hubert H. Humphrey Metrodome in Minneapolis. He used these appearances to introduce his new band, The New Power Generation, made up of Michael B. (Michael Bland) on drums, Sonny T. (Sonny Thompson) on bass, and Rosie Gaines on synthesizers and providing backing vocals. Doctor Fink was no longer on the team, having been replaced by Thomas Elm (who was nicknamed Tommy Barbarella) on the synthesizers, while Levi Seacer Jr was on the 6-string guitar. Rappers and dancers Tony M. (Tony Mosley) and Damon Dickson enlivened the bunch, as did percussionist Kirk Johnson, who was also a dancer in the trio known as the Game Boyz. Prince launched the promotion for his thirteenth album, which was released on 1 October 1991, after the singles *Gett Off* and *Cream* came out on 29 July and 9 September, respectively. Although Tony M.'s rap parts received a lukewarm response, the record was a global success, which was a good sign for the upcoming Diamonds and Pearls Tour. Despite the album's success, Prince didn't want to promote it on tour in America—the cost did not make this seem financially viable. Still hampered by the astronomical losses from the Lovesexy Tour, Prince chose Japan, Australia, and Europe instead. He unveiled his new songs onstage between 3 April and 12 July 1992.

Some of the members of the NPG, the 1992 lineup. From left: Damon Dickson, Lori Elle, Tony Mosley, Robia LaMorte, Kirk Johnson, and Tommy Barbarella.

THUNDER

Prince and The New Power Generation / 5'45

Musician: Prince: vocals, electric guitar, bass, drums, programming, synthesizers, percussion, zills, backing vocals / **Recording: Paisley Park, Chanhassen, Minnesota:** January 1991 / **Technical team: Producer:** Prince / **Recording engineer:** Michael Koppelman / **Assistant recording engineers:** Brian Poer, Steve Noonan

Like *3 Chains O' Gold*, Prince's *Bohemian Rhapsody* that came out the following year on the [symbol] album, *Thunder* is structured around several distinct sequences. In the space of five minutes and 45 seconds, this incredible song delivers a rare flood of emotions. Prince was inspired to write it on seeing the American bombing of Iraq on 17 January 1991, when George Bush launched Operation Desert Storm upon invading Iraq from Kuwait. As a tribute to the region, Prince included several Arabic sounds, such as the main riff of the song (played on a synthesizer modeling a sitar, which is not actually Iraqi but works nevertheless) and the melody that appears at 4'34. Prince reworked the song in October 1991 to create an almost 11-minute-long version, which was embellished with piano and called *The Thunder Ballet*. He then offered this to the Joffrey Ballet dance troupe of Chicago, founded by Robert Joffrey and Gerald Arpino in 1956, for *Billboards*, their new play whose first showing was on 27 January 1993 at the Hancher Auditorium at the University of Iowa, in Iowa City. It included many Prince songs, including *Sometimes It Snows In April* and *Purple Rain*.

DADDY POP

Prince and The New Power Generation / 5'16

Musicians: Prince: vocals, electric guitar, synthesizers, backing vocals / **Elisa Fiorillo:** vocals / **Tony M.:** rap / **Levi Seacer Jr:** bass / **Michael B.:** drums / **Rosie Gaines:** Hammond organ, backing vocals / **Tommy Barbarella:** synthesizers / **Damon Dickson:** backing vocals / **Kirk Johnson:** backing vocals / **Recording: Olympic Studios, Barnes, London:** June 1990 / **Paisley Park, Chanhassen, Minnesota:** winter 1990–1991 / **Technical team: Producer:** Prince / **Recording engineer:** Michael Koppelman / **Assistant recording engineer:** Timothy Penn

Daddy Pop was recorded with the group while the Nude Tour was in the UK and later embellished with several overdubs at Paisley Park. Initially provided with a powerful drum line that demonstrated all of Michael Bland's virtuosity, the song was later covered with a drum sample by Bernard Purdie from *Rock Steady*, a song that appears on Aretha Franklin's 1972 album *Young, Gifted and Black*. Purdie's pattern blends elegantly with Bland's, creating an intoxicating sound in a very nice meeting of minds. Meanwhile, Tommy Barbarella had the difficult task of activating the samples onstage (until Michael B. was able to launch them with electronic pads). Years later, he said that this hadn't been in his contract when he joined the New Power Generation. He had wanted to play his own lines rather than release a constant stream of samples. "[It was] the first loop I guess Prince ever played with," he explained. "[It] was played with my, with this finger on a low F, and I had to hold it the whole time."[126]

Single

DIAMONDS AND PEARLS

Prince and The New Power Generation / 4'43

Musicians: Prince: vocals, electric guitar, synthesizers, backing vocals / **Rosie Gaines:** vocals, backing vocals / **Sonny T.:** bass / **Michael B.:** drums / **Tommy Barbarella:** synthesizers / **Sheila E.:** synthesizers / **Recording: Paisley Park, Chanhassen, Minnesota:** December 1989 / **Technical team: Producer:** Prince / **Recording engineer:** Michael Koppelman / **Assistant recording engineer:** Timothy Penn
Single version: A-side: *Diamonds and Pearls* (Edit)/4'20 / **B-side:** *X-cerpts From The Songs: Thunder, Daddy Pop, Strollin', Jughead, Money Don't Matter 2 Night, Push, Live 4 Love*/5'04 (USA); *Q In Doubt*/4'00 (UK) / **CD single version (UK)** / **1.** *Diamonds and Pearls*/4'44 / **2.** *2 The Wire (Creamy Instrumental)*/3'13 / **3.** *Do Your Dance (KC's Remix)*/5'56 / **Released in the USA by Paisley Park Records/ Warner Bros. Records:** 25 November 1991 (single ref.: 7-19083) / **Released in the UK by Paisley Park Records/WEA International:** 25 November 1991 (single ref.: W0075; CD single ref.: W0075CDX) / **Best chart ranking in the USA:** 3 / **Best chart ranking in the UK:** 25

In mid-December 1989, Prince invited singer and keyboardist Rosie Gaines to Paisley Park. She was to sing backing vocals for *I Want U*, a song Prince had written and Levi Seacer Jr had produced for The Pointer Sisters. Prince was impressed by Gaines' vocal power, and immediately asked her to join the band he was forming for the Nude Tour. A few days later at Paisley Park, he ran into his drummer, Michael Bland, coming

out of a rehearsal with Margie Cox, whom he also accompanied. Bassist Sonny Thomas, a veteran of Minneapolis's funk scene, and keyboardist Tommy Barbarella were with him. Prince asked them if they could come and play a song he was producing with Rosie Gaines. This was how *Diamonds and Pearls* was recorded, before Prince finally released his musicians. Determined to take advantage of a night in the city, the three men made their way to the Bunker's club, where they were approached by one of Prince's bodyguards, who told them to return to Paisley Park immediately. They did so and the band recorded *Live 4 Love*, the last track on the album in something of a hurry. "He encouraged us to do whatever we felt with it," explained Barbarella. "And everything we did that day ended up on the final version."[85] The artistic freedom Prince gave to these exceptional musicians was the basis of his collaboration with his new band: The New Power Generation.

Michael Koppelman, the recording engineer who worked on most of the songs on the record, also mixed *Diamonds and Pearls*. Koppelman preferred refined productions awash with all sorts of sound effects, so he made an initial version of this song by removing a good number of tracks in favor of the melody. When Prince returned, he took back control of the song and reinserted the deleted instruments before ironing it out. "Prince came in and grabbed every fader that had a return effect and turned them all down 10 DB each, and that song is still just ridiculously wet when I listen to it today, it cracks me up!"[118] A few overdubs were quickly added to what later became a popular single, including the drum rolls played by Sheila E. on the synthesizer.

After having recorded two of Prince's most famous ballads with him (*Diamonds and Pearls* and the live version of *Nothing Compares 2 U*), Rosie Gaines left the New Power Generation at the end of the Diamonds and Pearls Tour. Prince promised her he'd never sing *Diamonds and Pearls* with another singer. He kept that promise until his death in 2016.

The two dancers who never left Prince's side in 1991, and are inseparable from the album's visual universe, were both given nicknames during the promotion of the album and the tour that followed: Lori Elle became known as "Diamond" and Robia LaMorte was called "Pearl."As Elle explained: "[Prince] said that I was a diamond because diamonds are very hard to find, but once you find them, all you have to do is polish 'em, and they shine."[127]

Lori Elle and Robia LaMorte, aka Diamond and Pearl—the two dancers on the Diamonds and Pearls Tour.

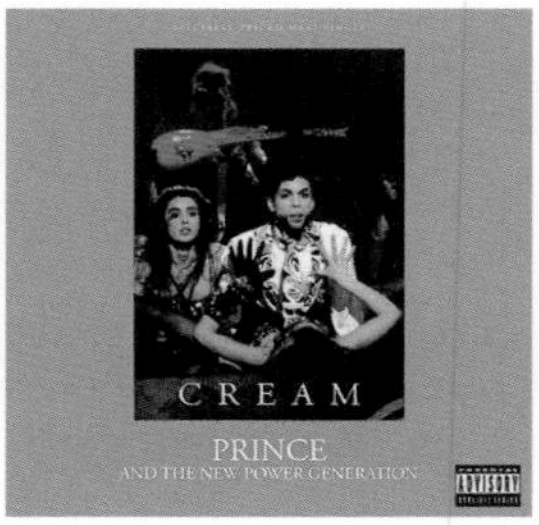

Single

CREAM

Prince and The New Power Generation / 4'12

1991

Musicians: Prince: vocals, electric guitar, backing vocals / **Levi Seacer Jr:** electric guitar / **Sonny T.:** bass / **Michael B.:** drums / **Rosie Gaines:** Hammond organ, backing vocals / **Tommy Barbarella:** synthesizers / **Recording:** **Paisley Park, Chanhassen, Minnesota:** December 1990 / **Technical team:** **Producer:** Prince / **Recording engineer:** Michael Koppelman / **Assistant recording engineer:** Timothy Penn
Single version: A-side: *Cream*/4'12 / **B-side:** *Horny Pony*/4'17 / **CD maxi-single version (UK)** / **1.** *Cream*/4'12 / **2.** *Horny Pony*/4'17 / **3.** *Gangster Slam*/5'06 / **Released in the USA by Paisley Park Records/ Warner Bros. Records:** 9 September 1991 (single ref.: 7-19175) / **Released in the UK by Paisley Park Records/WEA International:** 9 September 1991 (single ref.: W0061; CD maxi-single ref.: W0061CD) / **Best chart ranking in the USA:** 1 / **Best chart ranking in the UK:** 15

This was another No.1 hit in the Billboard Hot 100 chart for Prince, whose new single was all over American airwaves. Endowed with a straight and powerful rhythm hammered out by the unflappable Michael Bland, the song is based on a repetitive blues. Meanwhile, Prince ramps up his sexual innuendoes with a warm and sensual voice, making an obvious reference to male ejaculation in the chorus when he sings, "Cream, Get On Top/Cream and u will cop/Cream, don't u ever stop." When he arrived at the studio on 3 December 1990, Prince already had an outline for the song in mind. He recorded the backing tracks with Michael B. and Levi Seacer Jr, before adding several overdubs over the following days. "We recorded it in studio A at Paisley," explained recording engineer Michael Koppelman. "And I'd say it was probably 95% done by the end of the first day of the recording of the song."[118] The mixing (as well as that for *Daddy Pop*) was later assigned to Keith Cohen, the recording engineer at Larrabee Sound Studios in Los Angeles, and the song was released as a single on 9 September 1991.

STROLLIN'

Prince and The New Power Generation / 3'46

Musicians: Prince: vocals, electric guitar, synthesizers, backing vocals / **Levi Seacer Jr:** bass / **Michael B.:** drums / **Recording: Warner-Pioneer Studios, Tokyo:** August to September 1990 / **Paisley Park, Chanhassen, Minnesota:** autumn 1990 / **Technical team: Producer:** Prince / **Recording engineers:** Matthew Larson (Warner-Pioneer Studios), Michael Koppelman (Paisley Park)

While Prince was in Tokyo giving two concerts at the Tokyo Dome on 30 and 31 August 1990, he took advantage of some rare free time to record a few songs at the Warner-Pioneer Studios, the label's Japanese branch. Michael B., the group's drummer, had been struck down by a stomach flu and wanted to rest until the evening concert. But he hadn't taken his employer's impatience into consideration. Prince drafted him on the spot, and they held an improvised recording session in the small Japanese studio. Along with Matthew Larson, the technician on the tour, Prince, Bland, and Levi Seacer Jr recorded the backing tracks for three songs for *Diamonds and Pearls*: *Willing and Able*, *Money Don't Matter 2 Night*, and *Strollin'*, the melody of which is very close to that of *Yellow*, a duet recorded with Sheila E. in 1985. This experience left Michael Bland with a bitter taste in his mouth. Years later, he said: "To this day, when I hear those songs I feel nauseous."[21]

WILLING AND ABLE

Prince and The New Power Generation / 4'59

Musicians: Prince: vocals, electric guitar / **Levi Seacer Jr:** bass / **Michael B.:** drums / **Rosie Gaines:** Hammond organ, backing vocals / **Tommy Barbarella:** synthesizers / **Tony M.:** rap / **Damon Dickson:** percussion / **Kirk Johnson:** congas / **Jevetta Steele:** backing vocals / **Fred Steele:** backing vocals / **J D Steele:** backing vocals / **Jearlyn Steele:** backing vocals / **Janice Steele:** backing vocals / **Recording: Warner-Pioneer Studios, Tokyo:** August to September 1990 / **Paisley Park, Chanhassen, Minnesota:** autumn 1990 / **Technical team: Producer:** Prince / **Recording engineers:** Matthew Larson (Warner-Pioneer Studios), Michael Koppelman (Paisley Park) / **Assistant recording engineer:** Timothy Penn (Paisley Park)

"We were just tuning up our guitars and stuff and I just started messing around with this little bass line," recounted Levi Seacer Jr. "And Prince just said 'wait a minute, wait a minute, yeah that's cool,' and he starts to add some chords and Michael Bland started shuffling. And then Prince turned around and said 'you ready to record? Here we go.' So from just messing around to getting the basic idea on tape was 20 minutes."[124] Recorded in Tokyo on the same day as *Strollin'* and *Money Don't Matter 2 Night*, *Willing and Able* later crossed the Pacific Ocean to be reworked at Paisley Park, wtih Prince and his musicians bringing their personal touches: Rosie Gaines added backing vocals and the Hammond organ, Tommy Barbarella the Korg T3 synthesizer arpeggio with the classic guitar sound we hear throughout the song, and Tony M. contributed a well-chosen rap, contrasting with the gospel ambience created by the backing vocals of the Steele siblings, with whom Prince had already worked on *Still Would Stand All Time*, in 1990.

On 5 September 1991, Prince and The New Power Generation performed *Gett Off* on the set of the MTV Video Music Awards.

Single

GETT OFF

Prince and The New Power Generation / 4'31

Musicians

Prince: vocals, rap, electric guitar, programming, backing vocals
Rosie Gaines: vocals, backing vocals
Tony M.: rap
Levi Seacer Jr: electric guitar, backing vocals
Sonny T.: bass
Michael B.: drums
Tommy Barbarella: synthesizers
Eric Leeds: transverse flute
Damon Dickson: percussion, backing vocals
Kirk Johnson: percussion, backing vocals

Recording

Paisley Park, Chanhassen, Minnesota: 10 May 1991

Technical team

Producer: Prince
Recording engineer: Michael Koppelman
Assistant recording engineers: Steve Noonan, Ray Hahnfeldt

Single

A-side: ***Gett Off*** (Single Remix)/4'27 (USA); ***Gett Off*** (Single Remix)/3'59 (UK)
B-side: ***Horny Pony***/4'17
Released in the USA by Paisley Park Records/Warner Bros. Records: 29 July 1991 (single ref.: 7-19225)
Released in the UK by Paisley Park Records/WEA International: 19 August 1991 (single ref.: W0056)
Best chart ranking in the USA: 21
Best chart ranking in the UK: 4

1991

Genesis

On Friday 10 May 1991, Prince finished recording *Diamonds and Pearls* and was waiting to hear Warner Bros. Records' opinion of the album. After carefully listening to all 13 tracks, the label's managers decided that despite its forays into hip-hop, which was a very popular musical genre at the time, the album lacked a single that could reach hip-hop audiences. Lenny Waronker, the label's president, revealed his doubts that day about the album's commercial potential. Prince's categorical response: "Well, sounds like you got a marketing problem, figure it out."[128] Accustomed to inflated egos, Waronker decided to let the storm pass. Three days later, Prince came back to him. "The following Monday," explained Waronker, "I get a call from him. He said 'You got a new baby. I got something to play you.' He came in and he played *Gett Off*."[128] The song replaced *Horny Pony* in the tracklisting for *Diamonds and Pearls* and was released as a single in July 1991. Despite the contributions of rapper Tony M., which unsettled fans from the outset, the song became a Prince classic. Prince made several remixes of the song in August 1991.

Production

Prince recorded *Gett Off* immediately after Waronker's call. Over the weekend, he finetuned his future single by following hip-hop codes to the letter, to the point of bordering on caricature. He asked Rosie Gaines and Tony Mosley to go along with a call and response, which was a common feature of rap, but in NPG style. He then multiplied the samples in the song. While there are doubts as to the possible sampling of the rhythmic pattern from *Hold On*, sung by En Vogue in 1989, you can easily recognize the extract from *Mother Popcorn (You Got to Have a Mother for Me)* by James Brown (1969), at 2'38. Prince openly pays tribute to him by turning the "Some like 'em fat and some like 'em tall" into "I like 'em fat/I like 'em proud." Finally, Rosie Gaines quotes the 1969 Dykes & The Blazers hit when she proclaims: "Let a woman be a woman and a man be a man" in each chorus.

Prince loved making fun of his bodyguard Harlan "Hucky" V. Austin for his habit of wearing a bandana on his head with the tip in front of his face, adding that he looked like the African-American activist Harriet Tubman, who always wore her famous head covering. The day Prince shot the video for *Gett Off*, he arrived onstage with a red bandana on his forehead. "I thought I looked like Harriet?" said Austin. "You do, but I wear it sexy,"[21] responded Prince, amused.

WALK DON'T WALK

Prince and The New Power Generation / 3'07

Musicians: Prince: vocals, electric guitar, acoustic guitar, programming, tambourine, backing vocals / **Rosie Gaines:** vocals, backing vocals / **Elisa Fiorillo:** vocals, backing vocals / **Levi Seacer Jr:** bass / **Michael B.:** drums / **Tommy Barbarella:** synthesizers / **Recording: Olympic Studios, Barnes, London:** June 1990 / **Paisley Park, Chanhassen, Minnesota:** 1991 / **Larrabee Sound Studios, Los Angeles:** ? (not confirmed) / **Technical team: Producer:** Prince / **Recording engineers:** Michael Koppelman, Sylvia Massy

Recorded in Barnes during Prince's stay in the UK in June 1990, the song was reworked at Paisley Park and with Sylvia Massy, the recording engineer for Larrabee Sound Studios in Los Angeles. Massy was only credited for *Insatiable*, even though her work for *Diamonds and Pearls* was much more extensive. One of her jobs was to record the acoustic guitar parts for *Walk Don't Walk*. On the day of her first session with Prince, she decided to bring a range of 6-string guitars to the studio. Among them was a low-end, Korean-made acoustic Fender Gemini II bought for $200 at Guitar Center (an American music retail chain). Massy left it standing in a corner of the room. In part because he was a Gemini, in part because he liked the look of the guitar, Prince decided to use this folk instrument on the song. "It was untuned, had old strings and no stand,"[129] confessed Massy, worried about the result. Prince somehow used the instrument and when it was time to leave, he quietly asked his roadies to pack it up with his own guitars. "I don't think he realized it was mine and assumed the rental company would just charge him for it," said Massy, forgivingly. "I noticed what Prince was doing, and said, 'Excuse me, you can buy one of your own for $200; they aren't that expensive.' He smiled at me, and said, 'But I want this one.'"[129] Massy chose to keep her 6-string guitar and only parted from it at an auction in 2020.

HEADPHONES AT THE READY

For the post-chorus bridges in *Walk Don't Walk*, Prince decided to rehash the melody from *Rebirth of the Flesh*, which had been recorded in October 1986 for the unreleased *Camille* project (see page 142). Fans had to wait for the 2020 re-edition of *Sign O' the Times* to hear the original version of the famous "Sha-na-na-na-na."

JUGHEAD

Prince and The New Power Generation / 4'56

Musicians: Prince: rap, electric guitar, synthesizers, backing vocals / **Tony M.:** rap, backing vocals / **Rosie Gaines:** rap, synthesizers, backing vocals / **Levi Seacer Jr:** bass / **Michael B.:** drums / **Damon Dickson:** percussion, backing vocals / **Kirk Johnson:** percussion, backing vocals / **Recording: Paisley Park, Chanhassen, Minnesota:** 11 September 1990 / **Technical team: Producer:** Prince / **Recording engineer:** Michael Koppelman / **Assistant recording engineers:** Brian Poer, Steve Noonan

Prince gave free reign to Tony Mosley, his rapper, on this song, which was heavily revisited in 1993 to become the brilliant *Black M.F. in the House* (see page 231), on the *Gold Nigga* album (see page 230). While the songs credited Prince and The New Power Generation on the disc jacket, Prince, the only author and composer of the album, filed all of them in his name except for *Jughead*. Prince shared the royalties with Kirk Johnson and Tony Mosley for this song because the rap parts came from *Money Matters*, a song by their group, M.P.L.S. Prince's former manager, Steve Fargnoli, didn't like the last part of *Jughead*, in which Tony M. tells his agent that he doubts his honesty. Fargnoli, guessing the dialogue was a reproduction of a private exchange between himself and his former client, sued Prince in December 1991 for breach of confidentiality and asked for $5 million in compensation.

Single

MONEY DON'T MATTER 2 NIGHT

Prince and The New Power Generation / 4'46

Musicians: Prince: vocals, electric guitar, synthesizers, backing vocals / **Levi Seacer Jr:** bass / **Michael B.:** drums / **Recording: Warner-Pioneer Studios, Tokyo:** August to September 1990 / **Paisley Park, Chanhassen, Minnesota:** autumn 1990 / **Technical team: Producer:** Prince / **Recording engineers:** Matthew Larson (Warner-Pioneer Studios), Michael Koppelman (Paisley Park) / **Assistant recording engineer:** Timothy Pen (Paisley Park)

Single: A-side: *Money Don't Matter 2 Night* (Edit)/4'12 / **B-side:** *Call the Law*/4'19 / **Released in the USA by Paisley Park Records/Warner Bros. Records:** 3 March 1992 (single ref.: 7-19020) / **Released in the UK by Paisley Park Records/WEA International:** 16 March 1992 (single ref.: W0091; CD single ref.: W0091CDX) / **Best chart ranking in the USA:** 23 / **Best chart ranking in the UK:** 19

"What's the use of money if you ain't gonna break the mold?," wondered Prince in 1995 in the single *Gold*. In 1991, he was already questioning Western capitalism and the imperial politics of his country, which had gone to war in Iraq for obscure reasons. "Hey now, maybe we can find a good reason/ To send a child off to war/So what if we're controllin' all the oil/Is it worth a child dying for?" he says in the last verse. After writing and recording the song during the Japanese sessions for *Diamonds and Pearls*, Prince worked on the melody and lyrics with Rosie Gaines at the Paisley Park Studios. The day they recorded the vocals, before Michael Koppelman left the room to let Prince record alone as usual, he made a tuning error. Eager to get to work, Prince had rushed him and Koppelman had pushed the preamp to its limits, not suspecting that the audio signal would be permanently saturated. When he returned to the control room, all gauges were in the red. But against all expectations, Prince approved the take, even though his voice verges on saturation throughout.

PUSH

Prince and The New Power Generation / 5'52

Musicians: Prince: vocals, electric guitar, bass, drums, programming, synthesizers, backing vocals / **Rosie Gaines:** vocals, rap, backing vocals / **Tony M.:** rap / **Recording:** **Paisley Park, Chanhassen, Minnesota:** 5 February 1991 / **Technical team: Producer:** Prince / **Recording engineer:** Michael Koppelman / **Assistant recording engineers:** Brian Poer, David Friedlander, Steve Noonan

Prince pulled out his falsetto voice for the very funky *Push*, on which he plays all the instruments. Prince, Tony M., and Rosie Gaines each perform a high-caliber rap that is enough to silence their most virulent detractors. "Rosie is like a tornado," explained Prince. "There's never enough hours in the day for her voice. There's never enough tape for her voice."[130] For this rap and funk song, Prince blended string arrangements that Clare Fischer had recorded for an old song, and which had remained unused. Scott McCullough, who shot the video for *Daddy Pop* (which ended up in The Vault), had the privilege of filming some rehearsals for the Diamonds and Pearls Tour. These images, gathered under the name *Prince—Diamonds and Pearls Tour Rehearsals: Uncut Gems*, showed the making of an astonishing show, especially by revealing a perfectly executed version of *Push* performed during a sound check. Whether you love or hate Prince's rap period, it proves once again that no matter what musical style he tried his hand at, he only ever strived for excellence.

Single

INSATIABLE

Prince and The New Power Generation / 6'39

Musicians: Prince: vocals, bass, drums, programming, synthesizers, backing vocals / **Recording: Larrabee Sound Studios, Los Angeles:** October 1990 / **Technical team: Producer:** Prince / **Recording engineers:** Michael Koppelman? (not confirmed), Sylvia Massy / **Assistant recording engineers:** Timothy Penn, Brian Poer
Single: A-side: *Insatiable* (Edit)/4'01 / **B-side:** ***I Love U In Me***/4'12 / **Released in the USA by Paisley Park Records/Warner Bros. Records:** 4 November 1991 (single ref.: 7-19090) / **Best chart ranking in the USA:** 77

Insatiable returns us to the realm of soul music, with a song that recalls the languorous *Adore* on the *Sign O' the Times* album. While the single bombed in the United States, the song provided a welcome moment of calm amid the many hip-hop songs that permeate the record. Recording engineer Sylvia Massy, who worked with Prince on several songs on the album, has a clear memory of her collaboration with Prince: "The minute that he walks in the studio, you better be ready to record," she explained. "The minute he picked up an instrument, you better be in record, and if you miss one thing, you're outta there. So I learned how to be really fast and really on the ball."[118]

LIVE 4 LOVE

Prince and The New Power Generation / 6'59

Musicians: Prince: vocals, electric guitar, synthesizers, backing vocals / **Tony M.:** rap / **Sonny T.:** bass / **Michael B.:** drums / **Recording: Paisley Park, Chanhassen, Minnesota:** December 1989 / **Technical team: Producer:** Prince / **Recording engineer:** Michael Koppelman / **Assistant recording engineers:** Timothy Penn, Brian Poer

A strong criticism of the war in Iraq, *Live 4 Love* initially described the day-to-day life of a fighter pilot, without sufficiently pointing out the misfortune he caused. "How can I let a song out that is sort of glorifying war when this is going on and people's kids are dying out there? I can't release that song,"[118] Prince told his recording engineer Michael Koppelman, before rewriting the lyrics and rerecording his vocals. The keenest observers can read between the lines of these lyrics, in which a pilot seems to become aware of his sad reality. "My mission, so they said, was just to drop the bombs," he says, while realizing he would be wiser to choose love over war.

HORNY PONY

Prince and The New Power Generation / 4'17

Musicians: Prince: vocals, electric guitar, bass / **Michael B.:** drums / **Rosie Gaines:** Hammond organ, backing vocals / **Robin Power:** spoken word / **Tony M.:** backing vocals / **Kirk Johnson:** backing vocals / **Damon Dickson:** backing vocals / **Recording: Warner-Pioneer Studios, Tokyo:** September 1990 / **Paisley Park, Chanhassen, Minnesota:** 1991 / **Technical team: Producer:** Prince / **Recording engineers:** Matthew Larson (Warner-Pioneer Studios), Michael Koppelman (Paisley Park)
Gett Off (single) / Released in the USA by Paisley Park Records/Warner Bros. Records: 29 July 1991 (single ref.: 7-19225) / **Released in Europe by Paisley Park Records/WEA International:** 29 July 1991 (single ref.: W0056; CD single ref.: W0056CD)

Recorded for *Diamonds and Pearls*, *Horny Pony* was replaced by *Gett Off* in May 1991. The song did, however, appear on the B-side of *Gett Off* when it came out as a single in the July and on the single *Cream* the following September. In the song, Prince introduces us to a new dance called the *Horny Pony* and provides some details about it, singing: "I'm talking about the dance that every parent fears the most." Played onstage at the Glam Slam club in Minneapolis, on 6 January 1991, for the very first concert Prince gave with The New Power Generation, *Horny Pony* was a key feature of the *Diamonds and Pearls* era. As proof, the title of the song was written in red watermark inside that of *Gett Off*, on the back of the disc jacket.

VIOLET THE ORGAN GRINDER

Prince and The New Power Generation / 4'59

Musicians: Prince: vocals, rap, electric guitar, piano, programming, claps, backing vocals / **Rosie Gaines:** vocals, backing vocals / **Levi Seacer Jr.:** electric guitar, backing vocals / **Sonny T.:** bass / **Michael B.:** drums / **Tommy Barbarella:** synthesizers / **String orchestra / Recording: Paisley Park, Chanhassen, Minnesota:** 10 May 1991, spring 1991 / **Larrabee Sound Studios, Los Angeles:** 1991 / **Technical team: Producer:** Prince / **Recording engineers:** Michael Koppelman (Paisley Park), Keith Cohen (Larrabee Sound Studios) / **Assistant recording engineers:** Steve Noonan (Paisley Park), Ray Hahnfeldt (Paisley Park), Sylvia Massy (Larrabee Sound Studios) / **String arrangements:** Clare Fischer
Gett Off (maxi-single) / Released in the USA by Paisley Park Records/Warner Bros. Records: 12 August 1991 (maxi-single ref.: 0-40138; CD maxi-single ref.: 9 40138-2) / **Best chart ranking in the USA:** did not make the charts

Prince decided to add *Gett Off* to *Diamonds and Pearls* even though the album was already finished. He also decided to play the remix game, creating numerous versions with the intention of distributing them across various media. Some of them, such as *Gett Off (Urge Mix)* and *Gett Off (Thrust Mix)*, appeared on the maxi-single. Others, like *Gett Off (Extended Remix)*, *Gett Off (Houstyle)*, *Gett Off (Flutestramental)*, *Clockin' the Jizz (Instrumental)*, *Violet the Organ Grinder*, and *Gangster Glam*, were included on the maxi-single released in the US on

Lori Elle, Robia LaMorte, and the rappers of the NPG, pictured in 1991.

12 August 1991. As the last two could be considered songs in their own right, they are treated as such in these pages. While *Violet the Organ Grinder* retains the musical part from *Gett Off*, it also contains a new vocal line by Prince, who compares his orgasms to the notes coming from a pump organ: "I took all the pictures you gave me/And I placed them right under my bed/And I pumped and I pumped/'Til the 'gasm much as jumped." Sylvia Massy, who was helping recording engineer Keith Cohen mix these different versions, did not like the song, and wrote her thoughts in her diary, which she kept in the recording booth at Larrabee Sound Studios in Los Angeles. In a flash, Prince got hold of the diary and read it out loud in front of her. "There's Prince. He's sitting on his purple throne, taking a perfectly good record and ruining it with this song."[131] Amused, Prince did not hold it against her. Instead, she became one of his closest partners.

HEADPHONES AT THE READY
The female moan that can be heard at 0'25 into *Violet the Organ Grinder* belongs to Kim Basinger and was taken during the recording for *The Scandalous Sex Suite*. Prince used it again for *Peach*, in 1993.

GANGSTER GLAM

Prince and The New Power Generation / 6'04

Musicians: Prince: vocals, rap, electric guitar, programming, backing vocals / **Tony M.:** rap / **Rosie Gaines:** vocals, backing vocals / **Levi Seacer Jr:** electric guitar, programming, backing vocals / **Sonny T.:** bass / **Michael B.:** drums / **Tommy Barbarella:** synthesizers / **Kirk Johnson:** backing vocals / **Damon Dickson:** backing vocals / **Recording: Paisley Park, Chanhassen, Minnesota:** 10 May 1991, spring 1991 / **Larrabee Sound Studios, Los Angeles:** 1991 / **Technical team: Producer:** Prince / **Recording engineers:** Michael Koppelman (Paisley Park), Keith Cohen (Larrabee Sound Studios) / **Assistant recording engineer:** Sylvia Massy (Larrabee Sound Studios)
Gett Off (maxi-single) / Released in the USA by Paisley Park Records/ Warner Bros. Records: 12 August 1991 (maxi-single ref.: 0-40138; CD maxi-single ref.: 9 40138-2) / **Best chart ranking in the USA:** did not make the charts

In the spring of 1991, Prince gave Tony M. and Levi Seacer Jr the keys to his studio, along with free reign to produce different versions of *Gett Off*. "We just started off with different bass lines and things that we might throw in to give it a different flavor," explained Tony M. "We'll get the 48-track master and we'll get to pulling up different things."[124] Director Scott McCullough was put in charge of making videos for this collection of remixes, including one for *Gangster Glam*, which was shot in the Paisley Park parking lot, and in which Prince is on top of his "rap attitude." Wads of cash, shiny muscle cars, and pretty girls, no stereotype was spared, which must have angered some fans at the time (and no doubt some women's rights defenders). Despite its clichés, the video is a testimony to Prince's brief dalliance with hip-hop, which he embraced, it must be said, with a very infectious energy.

THINGS HAVE GOTTA CHANGE (TONY M. RAP)

Prince and The New Power Generation / 3'56

Musicians: Tony M.: rap / **Prince:** vocals / **Rosie Gaines:** synthesizers, backing vocals / **Levi Seacer Jr:** electric guitar, synthesizers, programming / **Sonny T.:** bass / **Tommy Barbarella:** synthesizers / **Recording: Paisley Park, Chanhassen, Minnesota:** autumn 1991 / **Technical team: Producer:** Prince / **Recording engineer:** Michael Koppelman? (not confirmed)
Cream (maxi-single) / Released in the USA by Paisley Park Records/ Warner Bros. Records: 4 November 1991 (maxi-single ref.: 0-40197; CD maxi-single ref.: 9 40197-2) / **Best chart ranking in the USA:** did not make the charts

Prince followed the same direction as *Gett Off* when he released the single *Cream* in November 1991. While many remixes of this song were distributed across the single's different formats, only *Things Have Gotta Change (Tony M. Rap)* offers a real reinterpretation of the song. Mosley showcases his talents as a rapper, and several sound samples are taken from all sorts of places, including a saxophone sample recorded by Eric Leeds for *Love or Money* in 1985 and an extract from *Chocolate Buttermilk*, from the first eponymous album of Kool & The Gang (released in 1969), which is audible at 0'18 into *Things Have Gotta Change (Tony M. Rap)*. Prince soon tired of this catalog of musical extracts, and even said, not long before the release of the single: "Nobody's learning how to make music, how to read and write it, and how to play. I worry that we're raising a whole generation that's going to turn out nothing but samples and rehashes."[125]

LOVE

PRINCE AND THE NEW POWER GENERATION

My Name Is Prince · Sexy M.F. · Love 2 the 9's · The Morning Papers
The Max · Segue · Blue Light · 👁 Wanna Melt With U · Sweet Baby · The Continental
Damn U · Arrogance · The Flow · 7 · And God Created Woman
3 Chains O' Gold · Segue · The Sacrifice of Victor

Released in the USA by Paisley Park Records/Warner Bros. Records:
13 October 1992 (CD ref.: 9 45037-2)
Released in the UK by Paisley Park Records/WEA International:
5 October 1992 (LP ref.: 9362-45037-1 - WX 490; CD ref.: 9362-45037-2)
Best chart ranking in the USA: 5
Best chart ranking in the UK: 1

Shortly before he renounced his birth name, the singer declared loud and clear: "My Name Is Prince."

On 25 February 1993, Prince appeared on The Arsenio Hall Show. After he had performed *My Name Is Prince*, The *Morning Papers, Blue Light*, and *The Max*, his golden gun-microphone was stolen. The stage manager had to threaten to run a metal detector over every audience member before the famous mic reappeared as if by magic.

THE ALBUM CALLED "LOVE SYMBOL"

1992

Recording of Prince's fourteenth album began in December 1991 with a number of tracks including *Sexy M.F., And God Created Woman*, and *The Sacrifice of Victor*. Prince had surrounded himself with a powerhouse team that was more united than ever and ready to hit the road on the Diamonds and Pearls Tour. He completed his band with a brass section consisting of Michael B Nelson (trombone), Kathy Jensen (baritone saxophone), Brian Gallagher (tenor saxophone), Dave Jensen (trumpet), and Steve Strand (trumpet). A new recruit also appeared on the winter 1991–1992 recordings: Mayte Garcia, a dancer whom Prince had recently discovered in a video. As well as being a major influence on this new album, the young woman would completely change Prince's life. Not only would Mayte's vocals, choreography, and image profoundly mark Prince's new productions, but she would become much more than just another newcomer in the New Power Generation. She was soon to become Prince's first wife.

Three chains of gold

Mayte Garcia was born on 12 November 1973, at Fort Rucker Army Base in Alabama, where her father was a serving US Air Force pilot. She is of Puerto Rican origin, but was raised in Germany and the United States, and she developed a passion for belly dancing. While Prince was on the Nude Tour, Mayte's mother, via Kirk Johnson, sent him a video showcasing her daughter's talents. Prince immediately fell for the charms of the 17-year-old, but once again, despite being strongly attracted to her, refused to meet her until she came of age. They kept in touch over a period of months and he congratulated her every time she sent him a new videotape. He took their discussions and the story of Beauty and the Beast and used them as the inspiration for the concept album that would become his fourteenth opus. Once he had most of the melodies on tape, Prince wrote the lyrics to a story that he had been carrying around in his head for months: It's Minneapolis, 1997. A young boy finds a box containing the Three Chains of Turin, a precious treasure that he hurries to take to his mother, an Egyptian princess called Mayte. When the princess sees the box, she starts telling him the story of an adventure that began five years earlier when she met the boy's father, Prince, a star who regularly featured in articles written by the journalist Vanessa Bartholomew. The new album incorporated long, spoken-word tracks called segues in which listeners could follow the story behind the songs, but the concept was truncated when Prince decided to include one last track—*Eye Wanna Melt With U*—to the album's final tracklist. As the time available on a CD is limited, in the end Prince retained only two segue tracks and inserted some dialogue between the songs instead. While listeners no longer have the story as initially intended, these changes made the album much more digestible. However, the original concept had become blurred and, as critics pointed out when the record was released on 31 October 1992, a track as monumental as *3 Chains O' Gold* is better suited to a musical than a pop album.

The end of the Prince era

Despite its unpronounceable name, ⚥ was a success on all fronts. Prince alternates pop songs (*The Morning Papers, 7*), funk (*Sexy M.F., Love 2 the 9's*), and hip-hop (*My Name Is Prince, The Flow*). He even ventures into electro with the

Putting the concept of the album ⚥ onstage during the Act I Tour in 1993.

FOR PRINCE ADDICTS

In 1992, Prince recorded a dozen songs for the James L Brooks' movie *I'll Do Anything*. Despite his total investment in the project, the movie was extremely badly received by the public at test screenings, so he simply withdrew his songs from the final cut. Most remain unreleased to this day.

technoid *Eye Wanna Melt With U*, a style of music that he would adopt more fully for *Come* in 1994. As for the New Power Generation, Rosie Gaines quit to focus on her solo album and was replaced by Morris Hayes, a musician who would become one of Prince's key collaborators. The brass section became The NPG Hornz (sometimes also called the Hornheads or Hornheadz) and Mayte became a permanent fixture in the group. Prince had just renewed his contract with his record company and his fans loved ⚥—he was at the top of his artistic game, but could see the storm clouds gathering on the horizon. His detractors accused him of megalomania and were convinced that *My Name Is Prince* was the death rattle of a star whose glory days were behind him as he struggled to find a path through the mid-1990s. Observers remained unconvinced by the concept behind the album, many were troubled by the vulgarity of the lyrics in *Sexy M.F.*, and added to all that was his romance with a girl barely out of childhood. Prince prepared to navigate his way through the 1990s as if piloting a plane through thick cloud. But this only increased his appetite for self-transformation and his endless creativity. Prince and The New Power Generation hit the road again on 8 March 1993 for two consecutive tours: Act I, which would take them across America until 17 April 1993, followed by Act II in Europe from 26 July to 7 September 1993.

A black version of Prince's famous police cap with chains, from the private collection of Mayte Garcia, sold for €9,244 at auction in November 2021.

Single

1992

MY NAME IS PRINCE

Prince, Tony M. / 6'38

Musicians: **Prince:** vocals, electric guitar, bass, programming, synthesizers, backing vocals / **Tony M.:** rap / **Recording:** **Paisley Park, Chanhassen, Minnesota:** 18 September 1991 / **Technical team:** **Producer:** Prince / **Recording engineers:** Michael Koppelman, David Friedlander, Steve Noonan, Ray Hahnfeldt, Brian Poer / **Assistant recording engineers:** Dave Aron, Airiq Anest, Steve Durkee
Single: **A-side:** *My Name Is Prince* (Edit)/4'05 / **B-side:** *Sexy Mutha*/3'55 (USA); *2 Whom It May Concern*/4'02 (UK) / **Released in the USA by Paisley Park Records/Warner Bros. Records:** 29 September 1992 (single ref.: 7-18707) / **Released in the UK by Paisley Park Records/WEA International:** 28 September 1992 (single ref.: W0132) / **Best chart ranking in the USA:** 36 / **Best chart ranking in the UK:** 7

With all due respect to the critics of Prince's rap period, this is an explosive track by a singer who proclaims his identity loud and clear, as he hides behind the chains hanging from the peak of his cap. The video for *My Name Is Prince* was filmed in Minneapolis and Los Angeles in August 1992 and features actress Kirstie Alley as reporter Vanessa Bartholomew covering a breaking news story for the fictitious KLCA station. She reports back to the show's anchorwoman on rioting that has erupted in the singer's hometown following the announcement of a Prince concert at the Glam Slam club. Tony Mosley delivers 40 bars of razor-sharp rap, hence his credit as the track's cowriter. Mosley nevertheless ended up suing Prince for unpaid royalties. The lawsuit was settled in 1998, after Prince paid out $40,000 in compensation to Mosley and to Levi Seacer Jr (who also sued for $800,000 in unpaid royalties for *Sexy M.F.*). Observers pointed out that many of the punchlines in Tony M.'s rap number were aimed at the person often described as Prince's arch-enemy: Michael Jackson. When Prince said, "U must become a prince before u're a king, anyway," it was hard not to see it as a dig at the King of Pop. Mosley confirmed in 2018 in an interview with *Uncut* magazine that this was indeed his intention.

HEADPHONES AT THE READY

Connoisseurs of Prince's discography will have noticed samples in *My Name Is Prince* taken from previous songs, including *I Wanna Be Your Lover* and *Controversy* (from 0'56).

The guitarist Levi Seacer Jr brought a blues touch to the song *Sexy M.F.*

Single

SEXY M.F.

Prince, Tony M., Levi Seacer Jr / 5'24

Musicians: Prince: vocals / **Levi Seacer Jr:** vocals, electric guitar / **Tony M.:** rap / **Sonny T.:** bass / **Michael B.:** drums / **Tommy Barbarella:** synthesizers, Hammond organ / **Michael B Nelson:** trombone / **Kathy Jensen:** baritone saxophone / **Brian Gallagher:** tenor saxophone / **Dave Jensen:** trumpet / **Steve Strand:** trumpet / **Kirk Johnson:** percussion, backing vocals / **Damon Dickson:** percussion, backing vocals / **D J Graves:** scratching / **Recording: Paisley Park, Chanhassen, Minnesota:** December 1991 / **Technical team: Producer:** Prince / **Recording engineers:** Michael Koppelman, David Friedlander, Steve Noonan, Ray Hahnfeldt, Brian Poer / **Assistant recording engineers:** Dave Aron, Airiq Anest, Steve Durkee

Single version: A-side: *Sexy M.F.* (Album Version)/5'25 / **B-side:** ***Strollin'*** (Album Version)/3'46 / **CD single version / 1.** ***Sexy M.F.***/5'25 / **2.** ***Strollin'***/3'46 / **3.** ***Daddy Pop***/5'16 / **Released in the USA by Paisley Park Records/Warner Bros. Records:** 30 June 1992 (single ref.: 7-18817) / **Released in the UK by Paisley Park Records/WEA International:** 6 July 1992 (single ref.: W0123; CD single ref.: W0123CD) / **Best chart ranking in the USA:** 66 / **Best chart ranking in the UK:** 4

Sexy M.F. was recorded in one take during the prolific sessions of December 1991. It started out as a jam session. "Levi was running around the studio, singing in that [high voice]: 'Sexy Motherfucker!'" Sonny Thompson would recall. "Prince said, 'alright, we're going to make a song out of this!' We just started grooving and it all came together."[85] What would go on to become one of Prince's best-known songs shows the New Power Generation at its funkiest, hitting that spot where blues (Levi Seacer Jr's delectable guitar solo) meets jazz (Michael Bland's rhythmic pattern and Tommy Barbarella's Hammond organ solo). And how can we fail to be captivated by the heady melody of the Game Boyz—Damon Dickson, Kirk Johnson, and Tony Mosley—when they sing the irresistible "Sexy motherfucker, shakin' that ass! Shakin' that ass!" in unison? In June 1992, when Prince decided to release the song as a single, he knew censorship was inevitable, which is why he asked his recording engineer, Tom Garneau, to replace the word "fuckers" with his famous scream, heard notably in the intro to *D.M.S.R.* (1982). The engineer used an Akai S1100 sampler to paste the sensual growl over each "fucker." That's how the ludicrous *Sexy M.F. (Clean Version)* came into being, proof that censorship was still alive and kicking. Prince eventually disowned *Sexy M.F.* in the 2000s, when his commitment to the Jehovah's Witnesses prevented him from swearing in his songs. "I was there in '92–'93 with the band that made *Sexy MF*," Prince said in 2004. "I know what it's like to hear 70,000 people yelling that at me, and I don't need to hear that anymore."[132]

LOVE 2 THE 9'S

Prince / 5'44

Musicians: Prince: vocals, electric guitar, finger snapping, backing vocals / **Mayte:** vocals, spoken voice / **Tony M.:** rap, spoken voice / **Levi Seacer Jr:** electric guitar / **Sonny T.:** bass / **Michael B.:** drums / **Tommy Barbarella:** synthesizers / **Michael B Nelson:** trombone / **Kathy Jensen:** baritone saxophone / **Brian Gallagher:** tenor saxophone / **Dave Jensen:** trumpet / **Steve Strand:** trumpet / **Kirk Johnson:** percussion, backing vocals / **Damon Dickson:** percussion, backing vocals / **D J Graves:** scratching / **Recording: Paisley Park, Chanhassen, Minnesota:** December 1991 / **Technical team: Producer:** Prince / **Recording engineers:** Michael Koppelman, David Friedlander, Steve Noonan, Ray Hahnfeldt, Brian Poer / **Assistant recording engineers:** Dave Aron, Airiq Anest, Steve Durkee

Love 2 the 9's (from the expression "dressed to the nines") was recorded during sessions involving the New Power Generation's full lineup. This track sees Prince and his band venturing into a mishmash of musical styles. Funk, jazz, rock, rap, it's all there. It also features Mayte's very first appearance in Prince's discography, during a question-and-answer section with Tony M. that is a particular standout. The NPG Hornz get the opportunity to showcase their skills on this high-quality track, too.

Single

THE MORNING PAPERS

Prince / 3'57

Musicians: Prince: vocals, electric guitar, percussion, backing vocals / **Levi Seacer Jr:** electric guitar / **Sonny T.:** bass / **Michael B.:** drums / **Tommy Barbarella:** synthesizers / **Michael B Nelson:** trombone / **Kathy Jensen:** baritone saxophone / **Brian Gallagher:** tenor saxophone / **Dave Jensen:** trumpet / **Steve Strand:** trumpet / **Recording: Paisley Park, Chanhassen, Minnesota:** December 1991 / **Technical team: Producer:** Prince / **Recording engineers:** Michael Koppelman, David Friedlander, Steve Noonan, Ray Hahnfeldt, Brian Poer / **Assistant recording engineers:** Dave Aron, Airiq Anest, Steve Durkee
Single version: A-side: *The Morning Papers* (Album Version)/3'57 / **B-side:** *Live 4 Love* (Album Version)/6'58 / **CD single version (UK)** / **1.** *The Morning Papers*/3'57 / **2.** *Live 4 Love*/6'58 / **3.** *Love 2 the 9's*/5'46 / **Released in the USA by Paisley Park Records/Warner Bros. Records:** 3 April 1993 (single ref.: 7-18583) / **Released in the UK by Paisley Park Records/WEA International:** 1 March 1993 (single ref.: W0162; CD single ref.: W0162CD) / **Best chart ranking in the USA:** 44 / **Best chart ranking in the UK:** 52

Like *Sexy M.F.*, *The Morning Papers* was recorded in one take at Paisley Park in December 1991. Although he doesn't mention her name, Prince is clearly singing about his relationship with the young Mayte. She had just turned 18 and was in a serious relationship with the artist, who sings at the beginning of the track: "He realized that she was new 2 love/Naive in every way/Every schoolboy's fantasy she was/That's why he had 2 wait." As Mayte wrote in her memoir in 2017, "Something had been shifting in our relationship since I became my newly emancipated self." She continued, "I was an interesting adult instead of a charming kid [...] The connection was becoming more personal. A different kind of flirtation began to go both ways."[134]

THE MAX

Prince / 4'30

Musicians: Prince: vocals, electric guitar, bass, programming, claps, synthesizers, backing vocals / **Tony M.:** rap / **Mayte:** spoken voice / **D J Graves:** scratching / **Airiq Anest:** programming / **Recording: Paisley Park, Chanhassen, Minnesota:** winter 1991–1992 / **Technical team: Producer:** Prince / **Recording engineers:** David Friedlander, Steve Noonan, Ray Hahnfeldt, Brian Poer / **Assistant recording engineers:** Dave Aron, Airiq Anest, Steve Durkee

Prince sticks to the idea of a concept album and inserts various Arabic sounds into *The Max*, including the famous riff in *Rave Unto the Joy Fantastic* (at 2'10), which was written and recorded in 1988, but put aside until the album of that name was released in 1999. A trumpet sample from Matthew "Atlanta Bliss" Bliss follows, then it's over to Tony M.'s rap and Mayte's sensual vocals. As ever, the piano parts are played on Prince's Roland D-50 synthesizer, adding a jazzy note to this track which also mixes in some funk and hip-hop.

SEGUE

Prince / 0'21

Musicians: Prince: spoken voice / **Kirstie Alley:** spoken voice / **Recording: Paisley Park, Chanhassen, Minnesota:** winter 1991–1992 / **The Record Plant, Sausalito, Los Angeles:** winter 1991–1992 (voice: Kirstie Alley) / **Technical team: Producer:** Prince / **Recording engineers:** David Friedlander, Steve Noonan, Peter Arata (The Record Plant)

Only three of the nine segues (transitional spoken-word segments) that Prince recorded for [Love Symbol] were retained on the album's final edit in order to leave room for *Eye Wanna Melt With U*. Two of the segues appear on the album's tracklist, while the third comes in at the end of *Damn U*. The dialogue between Prince and Kirk Johnson at the end of *My Name Is Prince* was taken from one of the segues that disappeared during the mixing. Here, reporter Vanessa Bartholomew, played by Kirstie Alley—at the height of her fame following her roles in *Look Who's Talking*, *Look Who's Talking Too*, and *Look Who's Talking Now*—calls Prince for an interview, only to be hung up on after she asks permission to record the conversation. One of the fundamental rules in Prince's world: never record a Prince interview.

BLUE LIGHT

Prince / 4'37

Musicians: Prince: vocals, electric guitar, drums, programming, synthesizers, backing vocals / **Mayte:** backing vocals / **Michael Koppelman:** bass, synthesizers / **Eric Leeds:** saxophone / **Recording:** **Paisley Park, Chanhassen, Minnesota:** 12 May 1991 / / **Technical team:** **Producer:** Prince / **Recording engineer:** Michael Koppelman

Here, Prince ventures into a music genre rarely seen in his discography: reggae. And, with the help of his recording engineer, Michael Koppelman, he rises to the challenge brilliantly. This was one of Koppelman's last productions, as he was fired by his employer in late December 1991 for refusing to cancel his family Christmas vacation. However, Koppelman was delighted to discover that Prince kept his arrangements, including the bass track and some synthesizer overdubs. "That is the only Prince record that has me playing music,"[135] he said. Prince never used reggae again, but two tracks mentioning reggae reappeared years later: *Ripopgodazippa*, recorded in 1993 and included on *Crystal Ball* in 1998, and *Splash* with its reverse guitar rhythm, recorded in 1985 and released on the NPG Music Club in *2001* (see page 386).

The dancer Mayte Garcia, pictured when she joined the NPG in 1992.

WANNA MELT WITH U

Prince / 3'50

Musicians: Prince: vocals, electric guitar, bass, programming, synthesizers, backing vocals / **D J Graves:** scratching / **Airiq Anest:** programming / **Recording:** **Paisley Park, Chanhassen, Minnesota:** July 1992 / **Technical team:** **Producer:** Prince / **Recording engineers:** David Friedlander, Steve Noonan, Ray Hahnfeldt, Brian Poer / **Assistant recording engineers:** Dave Aron, Airiq Anest, Steve Durkee

Although he had recorded *Eye Wanna Melt With U* in July 1992 for the 7 maxi-single, Prince ultimately chose to include it on at the expense of six of the nine spoken-word sections between the tracks that told the story of the concept album. The singer declares his intention to "groove until the earth moves" with his girlfriend, who we guess is the young Mayte, a recurring character in his songs. "Don't look now, but there's a river of blood/You must have been a virgin/What am I guilty of?/Are you afraid? Then take me to the next phase," he sings in this techno-influenced track. Techno was a genre that developed in the second half of the 1990s, and Prince would regularly revisit it, notably in *Loose!* (*Come*, 1994) and in the various versions of his classic *1999* on the EP *1999 The New Master*.

HEADPHONES AT THE READY

At 2'23 of *Eye Wanna Melt With U*, Prince resorts to animal analogy to emphasize the bestiality of his sexual relationship with his girlfriend. He inserts the barks recorded for the 1987 track *La, La, La, He, He, Hee* that featured as the B-side of the single *Sign O' the Times* the same year.

A perfect hairstyle for the actress Carmen Electra in 1993.

SWEET BABY

Prince / 4'01

Musicians: Prince: vocals, tambourine, synthesizers, backing vocals / **Levi Seacer Jr:** electric guitar / **Sonny T.:** bass / **Michael B.:** drums / **Tommy Barbarella:** synthesizers / **Recording: Paisley Park, Chanhassen, Minnesota:** 1 October 1991 / **Technical team: Producer:** Prince / **Recording engineers:** Michael Koppelman, David Friedlander, Steve Noonan, Ray Hahnfeldt, Brian Poer / **Assistant recording engineers:** Dave Aron, Airiq Anest, Steve Durkee

Prince considered releasing *Sweet Baby,* one of the album's two ballads, as a single. A test pressing was done and a music video was made from images of Mayte filmed by Randee St Nicholas in Cairo in 1991, when the two women traveled there to work on the planned movie *3 Chains O' Gold.* This was before Prince and his future wife had even officially met. Prince subsequently decided to cancel the plan to use this track as a single and focus on other projects instead.

THE CONTINENTAL

Prince / 5'30

Musicians: Prince: vocals, electric guitar, bass, programming, synthesizers, backing vocals / **Carmen Electra:** rap / **Michael B Nelson:** trombone / **Kathy Jensen:** baritone saxophone / **Brian Gallagher:** tenor saxophone / **Dave Jensen:** trumpet / **Steve Strand:** trumpet / **D J Graves:** scratching / **Airiq Anest:** programming / **Recording: Paisley Park, Chanhassen, Minnesota:** January 1992 / **Technical team: Producer:** Prince / **Recording engineers:** David Friedlander, Steve Noonan, Ray Hahnfeldt, Brian Poer / **Assistant recording engineers:** Dave Aron, Airiq Anest, Steve Durkee

The first album by Carmen Electra, Prince's new protégée (and occasional girlfriend), was recorded in Paisley Park and London in 1991 and 1992, and officially released on 9 February 1993, after the young woman had had the honor of opening for Prince on his Diamonds and Pearls Tour, which ran from April to July 1992. Despite the energy and effort Prince put into making Electra (real name, Tara Leigh Patrick) his new Vanity (see page 72), he had to abandon the idea after the album proved a resounding failure. The young woman decided to move to Los Angeles rather than stay at Paisley Park and the collaboration between the two artists went no further. Electra nevertheless participated on the [Love Symbol] album, rapping on *The Continental.* She still has fond memories of the years she spent working with Prince: "He controlled everything, but I loved that about him," she later said. "How I dressed, the music, hairstyles. He was genius at all that [...] He made me who I am today. He inspired me. He believed in me. He picked a select few to believe in and taught us everything."[136]

Single

DAMN U

Prince / 4'24

Musicians: Prince: vocals, electric guitar, finger cymbals, synthesizers / **Kirstie Alley:** spoken voice / **Levi Seacer Jr:** electric guitar / **Sonny T.:** bass / **Michael B.:** drums / **String orchestra / Recording: Paisley Park, Chanhassen, Minnesota:** January 1992 / **Ocean Way Recording, Los Angeles:** February 1992 / **The Record Plant, Sausalito, Los Angeles:** winter 1991–1992 (voice: Kirstie Alley) / **Technical team: Producer:** Prince / **Recording engineers:** David Friedlander, Steve Noonan, Ray Hahnfeldt, Brian Poer, Larry Mahn (Ocean Way Recording), Peter Arata (The Record Plant) / **Assistant recording engineers:** Dave Aron, Airiq Anest, Steve Durkee / **String arrangements:** Clare Fischer
Single: A-side: *Damn U* (Album Version)/4'04 / **B-side:** *2 Whom It May Concern*/4'01 / **Released in the USA by Paisley Park Records/Warner Bros. Records:** 17 November 1992 (single ref.: 7-18700; CD single ref.: 2-18700) / **Best chart ranking in the USA:** did not make the charts

Damn U is a syrupy ballad that Prince said was "dedicated to all lovers." It was released as the fourth single from [symbol] but failed to convince or even make it into the bottom reaches of the Billboard Hot Singles chart. An instrumental version, on which saxophonist Brian Gallagher played the vocal line, was even recorded as a B-side for the single, but Prince finally opted for *2 Whom It May Concern*, a medley of songs from the album mixed with the instrumentals from *7*.

ARROGANCE

Prince, Tony M. / 1'35

Musicians: Prince: vocals, electric guitar, claps, synthesizers / **Kirstie Alley:** spoken voice / **Tony M.:** backing vocals, spoken voices / **Levi Seacer Jr:** electric guitar / **Sonny T.:** bass / **Michael B.:** drums / **Tommy Barbarella:** synthesizers / **Michael B Nelson:** trombone / **Kathy Jensen:** baritone saxophone / **Brian Gallagher:** tenor saxophone / **Dave Jensen:** trumpet / **Steve Strand:** trumpet / **D J Graves:** scratching / **Kirk Johnson:** backing vocals, spoken voices / **Damon Dickson:** backing vocals, spoken voices / **Recording: Paisley Park, Chanhassen, Minnesota:** December 1991 / **The Record Plant, Sausalito, Los Angeles:** winter 1991–1992 (voice: Kirstie Alley) / **Technical team: Producer:** Prince / **Recording engineers:** Michael Koppelman, David Friedlander, Steve Noonan, Ray Hahnfeldt, Brian Poer, Peter Arata (The Record Plant) / **Assistant recording engineers:** Dave Aron, Airiq Anest, Steve Durkee

"Why are you so arrogant?" yells reporter Vanessa Bartholomew at the start of the track, as Prince ignores all her questions. "I always see myself described as arrogant or pretentious. I just do what I want," Prince said in his own defense. "I don't consider that arrogance."[125] While the booklet accompanying the album indicates that the song contains samples from *Jazz It Up (Jazz Mix)* by C.F.M. Band, *I Know You Got Soul* by Eric B. & Hakim, and *Niggaz 4 Life* by N.W.A, it's difficult, if not impossible, to locate these snippets in the track. By 1992, the days when Prince could borrow samples here or there were well and truly over. A wave of lawsuits for plagiarism (Killing Joke vs. Nirvana, Ingrid Chavez vs. Madonna...) had sent ripples through the record industry, and everyone had decided, quite justifiably, to assert their rights and not let their repertoires be plundered by all-comers.

THE FLOW

Prince, Tony M. / 2'25

Musicians: Prince: rap, vocals, electric guitar / **Tony M.:** rap / **Michael B Nelson:** trombone / **Kathy Jensen:** baritone saxophone / **Brian Gallagher:** tenor saxophone / **Dave Jensen:** trumpet / **Steve Strand:** trumpet / **Kirk Johnson:** backing vocals / **Damon Dickson:** backing vocals / **D J Graves:** scratching / **Airiq Anest:** programming / **Recording: Paisley Park, Chanhassen, Minnesota:** winter 1991–1992 / **Technical team: Producer:** Prince / **Recording engineers:** David Friedlander, Steve Noonan, Ray Hahnfeldt, Brian Poer / **Assistant recording engineers:** Dave Aron, Airiq Anest, Steve Durkee

Tony Mosley, one of the three Game Boyz, caught Prince's attention when he performed a rap version of *The Flow* during sound checks on the Nude Tour, and in so doing effectively introduced Prince to hip-hop. Soon after, *The Flow* was added to the end of *The Future* on the tour, and Tony M. also regularly performed *The Humpty Dance*, a 1990 Digital Underground track, in the middle of *Partyman*. *The Flow* was recorded on 11 September 1990 with Mosley and Rosie Gaines, and for a while was considered a serious candidate for *Diamonds and Pearls*, but it was eventually dropped from the tracklist, as the album already contained several hip-hop songs. It was reworked at Paisley Park in early 1992 and ultimately found a place on [symbol].

Prince during the Act II Tour, at the Flanders Expo, in Ghent, on 4 September 1993.

Single

7

Prince, Lowell Fulson, Jimmy McCracklin / 5'12

Musician: Prince: vocals, acoustic guitar, bass, finger cymbals, programming, synthesizers, percussion, claps, backing vocals / **Recording: Paisley Park, Chanhassen, Minnesota:** winter 1991–1992 / **Technical team: Producer:** Prince / **Recording engineers:** Michael Koppelman, David Friedlander, Steve Noonan, Ray Hahnfeldt, Brian Poer / **Assistant recording engineers:** Dave Aron, Airiq Anest, Steve Durkee
Single version: A-side: *7* (Album Edit)/4'23 / **B-side:** *7* (Acoustic Version)/3'54 / **CD single version (US)** / **1.** *7* (Album Version)/5'09 / **2.** *7* (Acoustic Version)/3'54 / **CD single version (UK)** / **1.** *7* (Album Edit)/4'23 / **2.** *7* (Acoustic Version)/3'54 / **3.** *7* (After 6 Edit)/4'20 / **4.** *7* (After 6 Long Version)/5'15 / **Released in the USA by Paisley Park Records/Warner Bros. Records:** 17 November 1992 (single ref.: 7-18824; CD single ref.: 9 18824-2) / **Released in the UK by Paisley Park Records/ WEA International:** 23 November 1992 (single ref.: W0147; CD single ref.: 9362-40732-9) / **Best chart ranking in the USA:** 7 / **Best chart ranking in the UK:** 27

"In the beginning, God made the sea/But on the 7th day, he made me," our artist proclaims loud and clear in *My Name Is Prince*, referencing both the Book of Genesis and *The Hippo Song* as sung by American scouts. Prince used to sing in a Seventh Day Adventist choir as a child, so it's understandable that this particular number was important to him. In 7, Prince assures his beloved that the two of them will annihilate the seven deadly sins as proof of their faith and love. The song 7 can also be seen as a reference to the seven seals, seven trumpets, and seven bowls, three sets of divine judgments that, according to the Book of Revelation, the last book in the New Testament, will take place at the end of time. When Prince decided to release this marvel of pop as one of the singles from [symbol], he launched production of a grandiose video in which he and Mayte play the heroes. A set was built in Los Angeles, and on the day the video was shot, Mayte wore her famous dress by Madame Alba, a well-known designer in the oriental world. In the video, Mayte and Prince are surrounded by seven boys and seven girls dressed in the same clothes as them. That was the day the couple realized they wanted to start a family. After the last scene was shot, Prince said to Mayte "I think it's time."[134] This desire to have a child was new for him, and Mayte was the woman with whom he wanted to make the dream come true. For this story and for the quality of its writing, 7 remains a major track in Prince's discography.

1992

7 was constructed around a drum sample borrowed from *Tramp* by Lowell Fulson (1967), which also inspired the instrumental part (the bass line in particular). Prince was careful to add the songwriters Lowell Fulson and Jimmy McCracklin to the credits, so he wouldn't be sued for plagiarism. Prince rarely played acoustic guitar on his songs, and 7, along with *Forever In My Life* and *Walk Don't Walk* that preceded it, delight fans, who always enjoy this kind of experimentation. David Friedlander, one of the many recording engineers who worked on the album, provided more detail about the acoustic guitar recordings: "When he did his acoustic guitar tracks, he wouldn't kick us out of the room [...] We'd mic up his acoustic right there behind the board, between the sound hole and the bottom of the neck of the guitar."[118]

AND GOD CREATED WOMAN

Prince / 3'18

Musicians: Prince: vocals, backing vocals / **Levi Seacer Jr:** electric guitar / **Sonny T.:** bass / **Michael B.:** drums / **Tommy Barbarella:** synthesizers / **Michael B Nelson:** trombone / **Kathy Jensen:** baritone saxophone / **Brian Gallagher:** tenor saxophone / **Dave Jensen:** trumpet / **Steve Strand:** trumpet / **Kirk Johnson:** percussion / **Mayte:** backing vocals / **Recording: Paisley Park, Chanhassen, Minnesota:** December 1991 / **Technical team: Producer:** Prince / **Recording engineers:** Michael Koppelman, David Friedlander, Steve Noonan, Ray Hahnfeldt, Brian Poer / **Assistant recording engineers:** Dave Aron, Airiq Anest, Steve Durkee

Inspired by one of his favorite movies, Roger Vadim's *Barbarella* (1968), Prince decided to call Thomas Elm, his new keyboardist, Tommy Barbarella. In 1991, he borrowed the title of another of Vadim's movies, *And God Created Woman*, for one of his new songs. Recorded in a single take with the New Power Generation, the song is pop perfection with its velvety-smooth melody and a bridge of incredible harmonic power. "I did all of that ornate drumming, almost unconsciously, on my first pass," says Michael Bland. "Prince was like 'Thank you, sir!' Not only is he imbued with this

spirit, it gets into you as well. You are sharing a space. You get into an unconscious plane. That is what I remember most about that time."[21]

3 CHAINS O' GOLD

Prince / 6'02

Musicians: Prince: vocals, electric guitar, piano, tambourine, backing vocals / **Levi Seacer Jr:** electric guitar / **Sonny T.:** bass / **Michael B.:** drums / **Tommy Barbarella:** synthesizers / **Michael B Nelson:** trombone / **Kathy Jensen:** baritone saxophone / **Brian Gallagher:** tenor saxophone / **Dave Jensen:** trumpet / **Steve Strand:** trumpet / **Kirk Johnson:** percussion / **Mayte:** spoken voice / **Orchestra** / **Recording:** **Paisley Park, Chanhassen, Minnesota:** January 1992 / **Ocean Way Recording, Los Angeles:** February 1992 / **Technical team:** **Producer:** Prince / **Recording engineers:** David Friedlander, Steve Noonan, Ray Hahnfeldt, Brian Poer, Larry Mahn (Ocean Way Recording) / **Assistant recording engineers:** Dave Aron, Airiq Anest, Steve Durkee / **String arrangements:** Clare Fischer

3 Chains O' Gold is the highlight of ♀, and ranks among Prince's greatest songs. Rightly considered as Prince's *Bohemian Rhapsody* or *Stairway to Heaven*, *3 Chains O' Gold* is a masterpiece in more ways than one. Its structure in particular takes the listener on an emotional rollercoaster, alternating operatic sections with pop passages, then rising to a heavy-metal climax and impressive finale, sustained by Clare Fischer's orchestral arrangements. It will send a shiver down your spine from the first listening! The press, however, had a different opinion, judging the production pompous, to the detriment of the song's obvious creativity. "[Prince] tends to go for spontaneous, first take, live-in-the-studio tracks even when he's cutting a complex, episodic piece like *Three Chains O' Gold* [...]," Michael Bland recalls. "That's one of many we had to do in one take. We had to cut that all in one big hunk, and it was murder, man. All [Prince] had was all these little sections [...] We had to piece it all together and then play it."[137]

FOR PRINCE ADDICTS

Prince loved the comic book *Prince: Alter Ego* by Dwayne McDuffie and Denys Cowan (published in 1991) and commissioned the two men to create a book inspired by the original story of his concept album ♀. The book was entitled *Three Chains of Gold* and published in 1994.

1992

SEGUE

Prince / 1'29

Musicians: Prince: spoken voice / **Kirstie Alley:** spoken voice / **Recording:** Paisley Park, Chanhassen, Minnesota: winter 1991–1992 / The Record Plant, Sausalito, Los Angeles: winter 1991–1992 (voice: Kirstie Alley) / **Technical team:** Producer: Prince / Recording engineers: David Friedlander, Steve Noonan, Ray Hahnfeldt, Brian Poer, Peter Arata (The Record Plant) / Assistant recording engineers: Dave Aron, Airiq Anest, Steve Durkee

In this second interlude on the album, when reporter Vanessa Bartholomew finally manages to interview Prince, he once again evokes *Barbarella*, the Roger Vadim movie starring Jane Fonda. In the movie, Barbarella says to two weird twin sisters who are speaking a foreign language, "Wait, let me adjust my Tongue Box"; Prince refers to this scene to explain his peculiar tone of voice to the puzzled reporter. Prince recorded his spoken-word segments for the album at Paisley Park, while Kirstie Alley's parts were recorded at the Record Plant studios, in Los Angeles, by Peter Arata and sent from there to Chanhassen.

The unforgettable Jane Fonda in the movie *Barbarella*, directed by Roger Vadim, in 1968.

Prince (back row, left) posing with the family of André Cymone in the mid-1970s.

THE SACRIFICE OF VICTOR

Prince / 5'41

Musicians: Prince: vocals, electric guitar, programming, backing vocals / **Tony M.:** rap / **Levi Seacer Jr:** electric guitar / **Sonny T.:** bass / **Michael B.:** drums / **Tommy Barbarella:** synthesizers / **Michael B Nelson:** trombone / **Kathy Jensen:** baritone saxophone / **Brian Gallagher:** tenor saxophone / **Dave Jensen:** trumpet / **Steve Strand:** trumpet / **D J Graves:** scratching / **Kirk Johnson:** backing vocals / **Damon Dickson:** backing vocals / **Jevetta Steele:** backing vocals / **Jearlyn Steele:** backing vocals / **J D Steele:** backing vocals / **Fred Steele:** backing vocals / **Recording: Paisley Park, Chanhassen, Minnesota:** December 1991 / **Technical team: Producer:** Prince / **Recording engineers:** Michael Koppelman, David Friedlander, Steve Noonan, Ray Hahnfeldt, Brian Poer, Peter Arata (The Record Plant) / **Assistant recording engineers:** Dave Aron, Airiq Anest, Steve Durkee

Until he delivered his memoirs to the author Dan Piepenbring, who would help write his unfinished autobiography *The Beautiful Ones* (published posthumously in 2019), Prince had rarely spoken about his childhood. References to his father John L Nelson pop up here and there in interviews in the mid-1980s, and veiled memories of his early years in Minneapolis are identifiable in his songs. This song is a tribute to Bernadette Anderson (alias Queen Bernie), the mother of André "Cymone" Anderson, Prince's childhood friend. Bernadette played a fundamental role in the life of the teenage Prince, notably for her open-mindedness, patience, and the moral values that she tried to instil in him—during the period he stayed at her house—and in her own children. "Education got important, so important to Victor/A little more important than ripple and weed/Bernadette's a lady and she told me/Whatever you do son/A little discipline is what you need/Is what you need, you need to sacrifice," Prince sings.

The Sacrifice of Victor also guides the listener through a Minneapolis rife with discrimination and social inequality, while emphasizing Prince's love for his hometown, where the hope of a fairer life was never far away. "I'm as much a part of the city where I grew up as I am anything," Prince explained in 1997. "I was very lucky to be born here because I saw both sides of the racial issue, the oppression, and the equality. I got the best of all worlds here [...] I used to be part of a busing program that took me through Kenwood every day to John Hay Elementary School and then Lincoln Junior High. You can check it out in the song *The Sacrifice of Victor*."[138]

THE NPG *GOLD NIGGA* (ALBUM)

Released by NPG Records: 31 August 1993
(sold during the Act II Tour) [CD ref: none]
Best chart ranking in the USA: did not make the charts
Best chart ranking in the UK: did not make the charts

The 1993 lineup of The New Power Generation, photographed with The NPG Hornz. Mayte Garcia, wearing Prince's police cap with chains, is in the center.

1. *Goldnigga Pt. 1*
2. *Guess Who's Knockin'*
3. *Oilcan*
4. *Segue*
5. *Deuce & A Quarter*
6. *Segue*
7. *Black M.F. in the House*
8. *Goldnigga Pt. 2*
9. *Goldie's Parade*
10. *Segue*
11. *2gether*
12. *Segue*
13. *Call the Law*
14. *Johnny*
15. *Segue*
16. *Goldnigga Pt. 3*

Morris Hayes was known for his humor and his impressions of American ministers. After he joined the New Power Generation as a keyboardist, he was given a handful of nicknames based on the characters he portrayed in his sketches. Prince chose the definitive one: Mr Hayes.

THE CULMINATION OF PRINCE'S HIP-HOP

On 24 April 1992, the Diamonds and Pearls Tour reached Sydney, Australia, for six concerts at the Sydney Entertainment Center and a final night at the Sydney Cricket Ground on 3 May. Prince made the most of this stopover to record some new songs at Studios 301, including several for the James L Brooks' movie *I'll Do Anything* (1994), a project that Prince eventually disassociated himself from. At the same time, the idea was mooted to do an album recorded entirely by the NPG, the acronym of the New Power Generation, Prince's famous backing band. Prince therefore began recording songs with the full band, featuring Tony M. as lead vocalist. *Goldnigga*, *Deuce & A Quarter*, and *Goldie's Parade* were laid down on tape. Once the tour was over, the musicians returned to Paisley Park to continue producing the record, adding *Call the Law* (already on the B-side of the March 1992 single *Money Don't Matter 2 Night*) and a new track, *2gether*, which came out of a session in spring 1993. As Paisley Park Records would be ceasing operations after Prince signed a new contract with Warner Bros. Records in September 1992, he decided to launch a new label, NPG Records, whose first release would be *Gold Nigga*. NPG Records had no access to Warner Bros. Records' distribution channels, so the album was sold exclusively on merchandising stands—starting with the concert, on 31 August 1993, at the Palais Omnisports in Paris-Bercy during the Act II Tour—and became a highly coveted collectors' item. A second pressing was done at a later date, this time without the track *Guess Who's Knockin'* (probably because of its similarity to *Let 'Em In* by Wings, which was released in 1976).

Although the album wouldn't go down in history, it is nevertheless an undeniably high-quality blend of funk, jazz, and rap, bringing together all Prince's influences at that time. Despite the visual universe in the promotional material resorting to all the hip-hop clichés of the day (Tony M. at the wheel of a Buick Electra 225 with a scantily clad woman perched on the trunk, and so on), the album is a total success, especially for its instrumental tracks and the vocals delivered by the much-underrated Tony Mosley. Although a discreet presence, Prince is very much behind every single track on the LP, and a careful listen reveals that he is never far away. Despite him singing on two of the tracks (hence their inclusion here), *Gold Nigga* should be seen as a genuine New Power Generation record, not a Prince album.

BLACK M.F. IN THE HOUSE

The New Power Generation / 5'08

Musicians: Tony M.: rap, vocals / Prince: rap, vocals, electric guitar / Levi Seacer Jr: electric guitar / Sonny T.: bass, backing vocals / Michael B.: drums / Tommy Barbarella: synthesizers, electric piano, backing vocals / Mr Hayes: synthesizers, backing vocals / Michael B Nelson: trombone / Kathy Jensen: baritone saxophone / Brian Gallagher: tenor saxophone / Dave Jensen: trumpet / Steve Strand: trumpet / Kirk Johnson: rap, percussion, backing vocals / Damon Dickson: rap, backing vocals / D J Graves: scratching / **Recording:** Paisley Park, Chanhassen, Minnesota: winter 1991–1992 / **Technical team:** Producer: Prince / Recording engineer: ? (not confirmed)

In this quintessential anti-racist track, Prince plays a customer who is unhappy that there are African-Americans in his bar. "Next time we need a big white sign at the door that says/'No black motherfuckers in the house,'" exclaims the detestable character he plays. The purpose of these lyrics is, of course, to draw attention to discrimination against African-Americans in the United States. The track ends with the Game Boyz (Tony M., Damon Dickson, and Kirk Johnson) shouting in unison "Stop racism now!" Besides the strength of its message, *Black M.F. in the House* stands out for its unstoppable groove. Note the almost total absence of synthesizers on the album, lending a funk authenticity that was extremely rare in the mid-1990s. A real gem.

JOHNNY

The New Power Generation / 10'19

Musicians: Tony M.: rap, vocals / Prince: rap, vocals, electric guitar / Levi Seacer Jr: electric guitar / Sonny T.: bass, backing vocals / Michael B.: drums / Tommy Barbarella: synthesizers, backing vocals / Mr Hayes: synthesizers, backing vocals / Michael B Nelson: trombone / Kathy Jensen: baritone saxophone / Brian Gallagher: tenor saxophone / Dave Jensen: trumpet / Steve Strand: trumpet / Kirk Johnson: rap, percussion, claps, backing vocals / Damon Dickson: rap, claps, backing vocals / **Recording:** Paisley Park, Chanhassen, Minnesota: winter 1991–1992 / **Technical team:** Producer: Prince / Recording engineer: ? (not confirmed)

Ten minutes of an irresistible groove, that's what the NPG offers us here live from Glam Slam, the club Prince opened in Minneapolis in 1990. Prince plays the role of Johnny, an amateur singer who comes on stage to sing a verse with the New Power Generation. This is the first track featuring Morris Hayes, a talented keyboardist, backing vocalist, and arranger, who went on to become Prince's longest-serving musician. Mayte is the only member of the NPG who is not present on *Gold Nigga*. She later gave her candid view of this track, which is a little racy to say the least, as Johnny spouts out obscenities. "Truthfully, I wasn't a huge fan of it—particularly the song *Johnny*, which is this crude song about condoms. The first time I heard it, I wrinkled my nose and said, 'What's up with that? My father's name is John. Your father's name is John. I don't like that.'"[134]

THE HITS / THE B-SIDES

Released in the USA by Paisley Park Records/Warner Bros. Records: 14 September 1993 (CD ref.: 9 45440-2)
Released in the UK by Paisley Park Records/WEA International: 13 September 1993 (CD ref.: 9362-45440-2)
Best chart ranking in the USA: 19
Best chart ranking in the UK: 4

Disc 1 (The Hits 1)

1. *When Doves Cry*
2. *Pop Life*
3. *Soft and Wet*
4. *I Feel For You*
5. *Why You Wanna Treat Me So Bad?*
6. *When You Were Mine*
7. *Uptown*
8. *Let's Go Crazy*
9. *1999*
10. *I Could Never Take the Place of Your Man*
11. *Nothing Compares 2 U*
12. *Adore*
13. *Pink Cashmere*
14. *Alphabet St*
15. *Sign O' the Times*
16. *Thieves in the Temple*
17. *Diamonds and Pearls*
18. *7*

Disc 2 (The Hits 2)

1. *Controversy*
2. *Dirty Mind*
3. *I Wanna Be Your Lover*
4. *Head*
5. *Do Me, Baby*
6. *Delirious*
7. *Little Red Corvette*
8. *I Would Die 4 U*
9. *Raspberry Beret*
10. *If I Was Your Girlfriend*
11. *Kiss*
12. *Peach*
13. *U Got the Look*
14. *Sexy M.F.*
15. *Gett Off*
16. *Cream*
17. *Pope*
18. *Purple Rain*

Disc 3 (The B-Sides)

1. *Hello*
2. *200 Balloons*
3. *Escape*
4. *Gotta Stop (Messin' About)*
5. *Horny Toad*
6. *Feel U Up*
7. *Girl*
8. *I Love U In Me*
9. *Erotic City*
10. *Shockadelica*
11. *Irresistible Bitch*
12. *Scarlet Pussy*
13. *La, La, La, He, He, Hee*
14. *She's Always in My Hair*
15. *17 Days*
16. *How Come U Don't Call Me Anymore*
17. *Another Lonely Christmas*
18. *God*
19. *4 The Tears in Your Eyes*
20. *Power Fantastic*

THE FIRST PRINCE ANTHOLOGY

On 13 September 1993, Christmas came early for British Prince fans (those on the other side of the pond would have to wait until 14 September). It was the day that Warner Bros. Records released three compilations by its protégé. *The Hits 1* and *The Hits 2* brought together the artist's greatest hits since 1978, while *The Hits/The B-Sides* bolstered the two aforementioned compilations with a third disc containing the songs that had appeared on the B-sides of Prince's singles. A real goldmine for fans but also for newcomers to Prince's discography, who could (re)discover nuggets such as *Another Lonely Christmas, Feel U Up, How Come U Don't Call Me Anymore*, and two of his greatest songs: *17 Days* and *She's Always in My Hair.* The tracklist of the boxset contains some unreleased songs of note, including a live version of *Nothing Compares 2 U*, recorded as a duet with Rosie Gaines at Paisley Park in 1992, and *Pink Cashmere* which was written for Anna Garcia, the singer's girlfriend in 1988. An indispensable triple album for anyone wishing to acquaint themselves with Prince's musical genius spanning the period 1978–1993, or simply appreciate this salvo of rare and precious songs.

The inimitable Rosie Gaines who was to sing in a duo with Prince in the live version of *Nothing Compares 2 U*.

NOTHING COMPARES 2 U

Prince / 4'57

Musicians: **Prince:** vocals, piano, electric guitar / **Rosie Gaines:** vocals, synthesizers / **Levi Seacer Jr:** electric guitar / **Sonny T.:** bass / **Michael B.:** drums / **Tommy Barbarella:** synthesizers / **Kathy Jensen:** baritone saxophone / **Recording:** **Paisley Park, Chanhassen, Minnesota:** 27 January 1992 / **Technical team:** **Producer:** Prince / **Recording engineer:** ? (not confirmed)

In 1984, when Sandy Scipioni quit her job as Prince's personal assistant to attend to her father's funeral arrangements, Prince was inconsolable. Legend has it that he wrote *Nothing Compares 2 U* for Scipioni after her departure, as Don Batts, Prince's recording engineer at the time and Scipioni's one-time boyfriend, claimed: "Line for line, it's pretty accurate about what happened. He spoke about the flowers dying and all that. Sandy was 'mama' in the song; she took care of him everyday [...] Sandy was kind of honored to have a song written about her."[88] Performed by The Family on their only album in 1984, Prince gave the song to Sinéad O'Connor who recorded an unforgettable version of it in 1990. On 26 January 1992, Minneapolis hosted a Super Bowl game between the Washington Redskins and the Buffalo Bills at the Hubert H. Humphrey Metrodome. After the game, Prince and The New Power Generation gave a private concert for around two hundred lucky spectators (including future president Donald J. Trump), and it was after midnight when *Nothing Compares 2 U* was recorded. It was a track worthy of a Prince anthem. And with this live version recorded at Paisley Park in 1992, that's what it became. As for the original version of the song, it remained unreleased until the *Originals* compilation that came out posthumously in 2019.

Anna "Fantastic" Garcia, pictured at the time of her love affair with Prince in 1988.

Single

PINK CASHMERE

Prince / 6'13

Musician: **Prince:** vocals, electric guitar, acoustic guitar, bass, programming, synthesizers, claps, backing vocals / **Orchestra** / **Recording:** **Paisley Park, Chanhassen, Minnesota:** 10 June 1988 / **Mad Hatter Studios, Los Angeles:** summer 1990 (orchestra) / **Technical team:** **Producer:** Prince / **Recording engineers:** Eddie Miller, Arne Frager (Mad Hatter Studios) / **String arrangements:** Clare Fischer
Single: A-side: *Pink Cashmere*/6'12 / **B-side:** *Soft and Wet*/3'01 / **Released in the USA by Paisley Park Records/Warner Bros. Records:** 31 August 1993 (single ref.: 7-18371; CD single ref.: 2-18371) / **Best chart ranking in the USA:** 50

On 31 December 1988, Anna Garcia celebrated her eighteenth birthday by joining Prince at Paisley Park. To mark the day she came of age, Prince gave his then-girlfriend two priceless gifts. The first was a pink cashmere coat with the word "Fantastic" written on it, after Prince's nickname for her: Anna Fantastic. The second was a song, which the artist played for her as she arrived: "I walked into the house from a long trip visiting my family [...] to spend my 18th bday [sic] with Prince, there was a beautiful song playing I didn't realize what it was about until moments later when he brought out the coat as my 18th bday gift. It was the most romantic thing I've ever experienced till this day and my best bday ever! I will never forget that day or any of the time spent with him."[139] Prince ended their relationship a few months later, after Anna posed naked in *Playboy* magazine.

Single

PEACH

Prince / 3'48

Musicians: **Prince:** vocals, electric guitar, backing vocals / **Michael B.:** drums / **Sonny T.:** bass / **Mayte:** backing vocals / **Recording:** **Olympic Studios, Barnes, London:** June 1992 / **Technical team:** **Producer:** Prince / **Recording engineers:** Steve Noonan, Mark Forrester
Single: A-side: *Peach*/3'48 / **B-side:** *Nothing Compares 2 U* (Edit) [Prince featuring Rosie Gaines]/4'17 (USA); ***My Name Is Prince*** (Edit)/4'05 (UK) / **Released in the USA by Paisley Park Records/Warner Bros. Records:** 18 November 1993 (single ref.: 7-18372; CD single ref.: 2-18372) / **Released in the UK by Paisley Park Records/WEA International:** 4 October 1993 (single ref.: W0210) / **Best chart ranking in the USA:** did not make the charts / **Best chart ranking in the UK:** 14

The Diamonds and Pearls Tour called into London from 15 June to 24 June 1992 for a series of eight concerts at the Earls Court Exhibition Center. Prince also took the opportunity to record some new songs in the legendary Olympic Studios in Barnes, ten miles from the British capital. Some of the tracks appeared on *Gold Nigga*, the New Power Generation's first album. A track titled *Shhh* was given to Tevin Campbell before being rerecorded for *The Gold Experience*. The hard rock-tinged blues number *Peach* was also recorded during these sessions, with a band reduced to a strict minimum: Michael Bland on drums and Sonny Thompson on bass. Prince and Mayte later added some overdubs, including a sample of a Kim Basinger moan recorded for *The Scandalous Sex Suite* in 1989. *Peach* was a foretaste of the rock 'n' roll fury Prince would soon unleash with tracks like *Endorphinmachine*.

Prince with his bodyguard Charles "Big Chick" Huntsberry in 1985.

POPE

Prince / 3'28

Musicians: Prince: vocals, programming, synthesizers, backing vocals / **Mayte:** vocals / **D J Graves:** scratching / **Recording:** Paisley Park, Chanhassen, Minnesota: May 1993 / **Technical team: Producer:** Prince / **Recording engineer:** Ray Hahnfeldt

Pope was recorded in 1993—among 12 other new songs—for the *Glam Slam Ulysses* project. Prince hired Jamie King, Michael Jackson's choreographer for the Dangerous World Tour, to create the dance parts for this production which was inspired by Homer's *The Odyssey*. This was an opportunity for the singer to put new songs out there without requiring his record company's approval. The two men planned to produce a complete musical by working together on one new track each week and showcasing them onstage at the Glam Slam club, in Minneapolis, every Friday night. *Glam Slam Ulysses* premiered on 21 August 1993, but it was quickly abandoned due to poor reviews. Hence, *Pope* ended up on this compilation. With an effective chorus carried by Mayte's sensual vocals as well as some fairly successful rap parts, *Pope* is a pleasant song, typical of Prince's hip-hop era. Note the samples of American comedian Bernie Mac's voice in the intro and throughout the track, taken from his legendary appearance on *Def Comedy Jam* during which he got the audience onside by repeating: "I ain't scared of you motherfuckers." Interestingly, "The Pope" was also Bernie Mac's nickname at the time.

HELLO

Prince / 3'23

Musicians: Prince: vocals, electric guitar, bass, drums, programming, synthesizers, Fairlight CMI, backing vocals / **Jill Jones:** backing vocals / **Recording:** Sunset Sound, Los Angeles: 24–25 May 1985 / **Technical team: Producer:** Prince / **Recording engineers:** Peggy McCreary, David Leonard, Susan Rogers

After an article appeared in *The National Enquirer* in which Prince's former bodyguard Charles "Big Chick" Huntsberry described certain aspects of Prince's personality, the singer picked up his pen and began writing *Hello* as a revenge piece. It also gave him the opportunity to respond to press criticisms as to why he did not participate in the single *We Are The World*. "I think once he wrote the song and recorded it, he put the whole thing behind him," said Susan Rogers. "He could have gotten on his high horse and written a whole album around it: 'I was misunderstood.' But he didn't. He knew how these things work and I think he was very happy to get the song out of his system."[95] *Hello* was recorded with Jill Jones in 1985 and featured as the B-side of *Pop Life*.

200 BALLOONS

Prince / 5'05

Musician: Prince: vocals, electric guitar, bass, programming, synthesizers, backing vocals / **Recording: Paisley Park, Chanhassen, Minnesota:** February 1989 / **Technical team: Producer:** Prince / **Recording engineer:** Femi Jiya / **Assistant recording engineers:** David Friedlander, Heidi Hanschu, Chuck Zwicky, Eddie Miller

Originally recorded for the scene in the *Batman* movie where the Joker parades through Gotham City handing out banknotes to passersby, *200 Balloons* didn't appeal to the director Tim Burton who decided to use *Trust* instead. *200 Balloons* subsequently appeared as the B-side of *Batdance*.

ESCAPE

Prince / 3'30

Musicians: Prince: vocals, electric guitar, acoustic guitar, bass, programming, synthesizers, backing vocals / **Eric Leeds:** saxophone / **Atlanta Bliss:** trumpet / **Sheila E.:** backing vocals / **Boni Boyer:** backing vocals / **Recording: Paisley Park, Chanhassen, Minnesota:** 5 May 1988 / **Technical team: Producer:** Prince / **Recording engineer:** Eddie Miller

Escape, the B-side of *Glam Slam* (1988), is a robotic funk with the kind of wind instrument lines typical of the *Lovesexy* era. Prince and his backing singers, Sheila E. and Boni Boyer, turn it into an ode to freedom when they sing: "Glam Slam, free yo mind from this rat race." The song, written to accompany the single and reproducing some of the single's musical elements, such as the bass line, slots perfectly into the *Lovesexy* album's spirit of freedom and peace.

Boni Boyer, Sheila E., and Cat Glover during the Lovesexy Tour in 1988.

HORNY TOAD

Prince / 2'12

Musician: Prince: vocals, electric guitar, bass, programming, synthesizers, claps, backing vocals / **Recording: Kiowa Trail Home Studio, Chanhassen, Minnesota:** 5 June1982 / **Technical team: Producer:** Prince / **Recording engineer:** Don Batts

Horny Toad takes us back to Prince's 1982 experiments with rockabilly and is not dissimilar to *Delirious*, the A-side of the single, or *Jack U Off*, which was released in 1981. Prince gives his guitar some real bite here as he delivers the staccato melody throughout the track. An enjoyable pop treat in the midst of the barrage of funk and synthpop numbers in this compilation.

FEEL U UP

Prince / 3'44

Musicians: Prince: vocals, bass, programming, synthesizers, Fairlight CMI, backing vocals / **Eric Leeds:** saxophone / **Atlanta Bliss:** trumpet / **Recording: Sunset Sound, Los Angeles:** 26 October 1986 / **Technical team: Producer:** Prince / **Recording engineers:** Susan Rogers, Coke Johnson

On this track previously recorded in 1981, Prince makes way for Camille, his new female alter ego (see page 142). The track was rerecorded in 1986 (in the same sessions that gave rise to *Housequake*) with the intention of including it on the *Camille* album. In the end, the album was never finalized, although some tracks were subsequently used in the production of *Sign O' the Times*. *Feel U Up* and *Housequake* share similar synthetic arrangements, achieved using the mythical Linn LM-1 Drum Computer and numerous synthesizers, including the Oberheim OB-8 and the Prophet VS. The horns of Eric Leeds and Atlanta Bliss give the song its typical *Sign O' the Times* era feel; it appeared on the B-side of *Partyman* in August 1989. Listen to this track with the volume turned up to enjoy its unstoppable groove.

GIRL

Prince / 3'47

Musicians: Prince: vocals, programming, synthesizers, finger snapping, backing vocals / **Vanity:** backing vocals / **Recording: Kiowa Trail Home Studio, Chanhassen, Minnesota:** 1982–1984 / **Washington Avenue Warehouse, Edina, Minnesota:** July 1985 / **Technical team: Producer:** Prince / **Recording engineers:** Don Batts (Kiowa Trail Home Studio), Susan Rogers (Washington Avenue Warehouse), David Tickle (Washington Avenue Warehouse)

"He sometimes would phone me and give me a list of tapes and say: 'Pull these out and give me rough mixes of them so I can listen to them,'" said Susan Rogers. "*Girl* was one of them."[95] So, Prince plucked this track, which had been recorded in the early 1980s, out of his bag of goodies and worked with Rogers to produce a revised version. *Girl*, the B-side of *America* (1985), takes us back to Prince's racy *Lady Cab Driver* (1982) or *Darling Nikki* (1984) period. By using the multiple synthesizers at his disposal, he creates a totally 1980s-sounding track that fans love.

I LOVE U IN ME

Prince / 4'12

Musician: Prince: vocals, synthesizers, backing vocals / **Recording: Paisley Park, Chanhassen, Minnesota:** 1989 / **Technical team: Producer:** Prince / **Recording engineer:** ? (not confirmed)

"When she makin' love it's like surgery/And she say, ooh, I love you in me," Prince sings in this ballad, which is powered by the Yamaha DX7 synthesizer, the instantly recognizable synthesizer that produced the unmistakable sounds of the late 1980s. *I Love U In Me* featured as the B-side of *The Arms of Orion* (1989) and *Insatiable* (1991), and is a real success, notably for its lack of embellishment and beautiful melody.

The relationship between Prince and Sheila E., which was both romantic and professional, was to develop into a profound friendship over the years.

EROTIC CITY

Prince / 3'55

Musicians: Prince: vocals, acoustic guitar, bass, programming, synthesizers, backing vocals / **Sheila E.:** vocals, backing vocals / **Recording: Sunset Sound, Los Angeles:** 25 March, 4 April 1984 / **Technical team: Producer:** Prince / **Recording engineer:** Peggy McCreary

Sheila E. recorded the drum part of *Pop Life* in February 1984 and, on 25 March, she received a call from Prince. It was the end of the day in Los Angeles and the drummer responded to the Kid's invitation to join him at Sunset Sound. When she got there, there was no drum kit in the studio and no sign of any percussion instruments. Instead, there was a microphone, set up and ready to record her vocals. The young woman, who had even refused to accompany Lionel Richie on *Endless Love* when she was his drummer, couldn't imagine singing with Prince. "'You've been singing behind everyone for years, Sheila,' Prince said softly, brushing back a fallen strand of my hair. 'You know just what to do,'"[140] the musician recalls. She went along with it but categorically refused to sing the line: "We can fuck until the dawn." Although Prince happily sang the line as it was, Sheila E. replaced "fuck" with "funk." The two takes were superimposed and, thanks to the last-minute change in lyrics, the track was subsequently played in clubs and on the radio without being censored. *Erotic City* appeared on the B-side of *Let's Go Crazy*.

Prince used the VariSpeed process for his vocals and guitar on this track, as explained by Susan Rogers a few years later: "He had discovered that if you put the tape machine down to half speed, you can sing in your normal voice and play guitar, and when you put the tape machine back to regular speed, it's going to be higher and thinner [...] It wasn't done with a pitch shifter."[2] This was the technique that led to the appearance of Camille, Prince's female alter ego in the mid-1980s to whom he planned to devote an entire album. When the project was shelved in favor of *Sign O' the Times*, Camille would nevertheless become an essential figure in Prince's discography, starting with *Shockadelica*, the first track officially released under this pseudonym. Miles Davis, a Prince fan himself, gave an amusing account of his listening experience in his 1989 autobiography: "When he's singing that funky X-rated shit that he does about sex and women, he's doing it in a high-pitched voice, in almost a girl's voice. If I said 'Fuck you' to somebody, they would be ready to call the police. But if Prince says it in that girl-like voice he uses, then everybody says it's cute."[141]

SHOCKADELICA

Prince / 3'30

Musicians: Prince: vocals, electric guitar, bass, programming, synthesizers, Fairlight CMI, backing vocals / **Jill Jones:** backing vocals / **Recording: Galpin Boulevard Home Studio, Chanhassen, Minnesota:** 16 September 1986 / **Technical team: Producer:** Prince / **Recording engineer:** Susan Rogers

When Jesse Johnson, the guitarist for The Time (see page 64), showed Prince the album he was working on in the summer of 1986, Prince picked up on the title *Shockadelica*, yelling at Johnson: "Man, I gotta tell you, that's the album title of the century. Boy I wish I had thought of that. Why in hell isn't there a song on the album with that title?"[95] Prince suggested that Johnson write a song with that name, but the guitarist wasn't interested. Not to be deterred, Prince kept the enchanting *Shockadelica* for himself and it appeared on the B-side of *If I Was Your Girlfriend* in 1987. The lyrics portray a love affair with a scary woman—"This girl must be a witch," sings Prince—and was inspired by his affair with the actress Troy Byera, who starred in *Dynasty*. "Prince said directly to me that she was somewhat 'witch-like' and that she scared him because she was kind of spooky"[2] Susan Rogers recounted.

IRRESISTIBLE BITCH

Prince / 4'11

Musicians: Prince: vocals, bass, drums, programming, synthesizers, backing vocals / **Lisa Coleman:** backing vocals / **Wendy Melvoin:** backing vocals / **Recording: Kiowa Trail Home Studio, Chanhassen, Minnesota:** 7 September 1982 / **Sunset Sound, Los Angeles:** 15–18 September 1983 / **Technical team: Producer:** Prince / **Recording engineers:** Peggy McCreary, David Leonard

First recorded in 1981 before being reworked by Prince in September 1982, then again in September 1983, *Irresistible Bitch* appeared on the B-side of *Let's Pretend We're Married* the following November. The song loses (a little) of its macho side with the addition of vocals from Lisa Coleman and Wendy Melvoin in a typically cunning move by Prince. Rumor has it that Morris Day recorded the drums for the track, but no one has been able to confirm this. That said, if you listen closely to *Tricky*, a song recorded by Day and Prince in 1984 and on which the vocalist from The Time played drums, you can hear the similarity between the two rhythmic patterns, so this assumption would appear to be correct.

SCARLET PUSSY

Prince / 4'18

Musicians: Prince: vocals, electric guitar, bass, drums, programming, synthesizers, backing vocals / **Sheila E.:** vocals, backing vocals / **Eric Leeds:** flute, saxophone / **Recording: Paisley Park, Chanhassen, Minnesota:** December 1987 / **Technical team: Producer:** Prince / **Recording engineer:** Eddie Miller

"Why must I chase the cat?" asked George Clinton in his 1982 song *Atomic Dog*. Prince took this idea of an analogy between his insatiable quest for sexual pleasure and the games cats and dogs play to reveal something of himself in *Scarlet Pussy*, a song attributed to Camille when it appeared on the B-side of *I Wish U Heaven* in 1988. *Scarlet Pussy* is a groovy duet recorded with Sheila E. in late December 1987 that gets all the animals in the menagerie dancing.

LA, LA, LA, HE, HE, HEE

Prince, Sheena Easton / 3'21

Musicians: Prince: vocals, electric guitar, bass, drums, programming, synthesizers, sound effects, backing vocals / **Sheila E.:** backing vocals, percussion / **Eric Leeds:** saxophone / **Atlanta Bliss:** trumpet / **Recording: Galpin Boulevard Home Studio, Chanhassen, Minnesota:** January 1987 / **Technical team: Producer:** Prince / **Recording engineer:** Susan Rogers

Recorded a year before *Scarlet Pussy*, *La, La, La, He, He, Hee* had already used the imagery of animal courtship to describe the love play between humans. Cowritten with Sheena Easton who had recorded *U Got the Look* with Prince a month earlier, the track appeared on the B-side of *Sign O' the Times*. Sheena Easton spoke about it in 2012: "It was about a cat up in a tree teasing a dog. I was actually being sarcastic. He said, 'Ya, that could be a song,' and I was like 'Oh ya, like what do you want me to sing? La La La, He He He—I love you, you love me? That's how talented I am?' He said, 'Actually, that'd be kind of cute! Go ahead and write it' [...] Then, all my songs were little stories. I liked storytelling songs. He used to think they were amusing. I don't think other people did but he used to think they were."[106]

Jill Jones at the time of the release of her eponymous album in 1987.

SHE'S ALWAYS IN MY HAIR

Prince / 3'27

Musician: Prince: vocals, electric guitar, bass, drums, programming, synthesizers, finger cymbals, percussion, backing vocals / **Recording: Sunset Sound, Los Angeles:** 29 December 1983; 8 January 1984 / **Flying Cloud Drive Warehouse, Eden Prairie, Minnesota:** August 1984 / **Technical team: Producer:** Prince / **Recording engineer:** Bill Jackson

Although it doesn't appear on any Prince album, *She's Always In My Hair* is one of Prince's greatest songs. Fans love this song and it was frequently performed at concerts right up to Prince's death in 2016. He recorded all the instrumental tracks for this anthem, which is characteristic of the *Purple Rain* era, on 29 December 1983, at Sunset Sound. He wrote the lyrics in his room at Le Parc Hotel in West Hollywood, before recording the vocals on 8 January 1984. Written for Jill Jones, his close friend in the 1980s, Prince rerecorded this mid-tempo wonder in August 1984 at Eden Prairie with Susan Rogers. Dissatisfied with the reworked version, he put it in store and it remains unreleased to this day. *She's Always In My Hair* appeared on the B-side of the single *Raspberry Beret* in May 1985.

17 DAYS

Prince and The Revolution / 3'54

Musicians: Prince: vocals, electric guitar, bass, drums, programming, synthesizers, backing vocals / **Wendy Melvoin:** backing vocals / **Lisa Coleman:** backing vocals / **Jill Jones:** backing vocals / **Recording: Sunset Sound, Los Angeles:** 8 January, 18 March 1984 / **Technical team: Producer:** Prince / **Recording engineers:** Bill Jackson, Peggy McCreary

Another essential B-side, full title *17 Days (The Rain Will Come Down, Then U Will Have 2 Choose. If U Believe, Look 2 The Dawn And U Shall Never Lose)*, is also another song beloved of fans. It emerged from a rehearsal with The Revolution in August 1983 during which the musicians were working on the writing of *Purple Rain*. The song initially featured a vocal sample recorded by Brenda Bennett of Vanity 6 (see page 72). Following Vanity's departure, the song was then earmarked for the Apollonia 6 album (see page 91), before Prince retrieved and reworked it on 8 January 1984 in Sunset Sound while the overdubs for *She's Always In My Hair* were being added. A day to remember! On 18 March 1984, Prince decided to remove Bennett's contributions to the track, which would ultimately become the B-side of the single *When Doves Cry*.

HOW COME U DON'T CALL ME ANYMORE

Prince / 3'50

Musician: Prince: vocals, piano / **Recording: Sunset Sound, Los Angeles:** 28 April 1982 / **Technical team: Producer:** Prince / **Recording engineer:** Peggy McCreary

Before it was made popular by Alicia Keys in 2002 with the title *How Come You Don't Call Me*, Prince recorded *How Come U Don't Call Me Anymore* in 1982, then gave it to Stephanie Mills, who released it as a single on Casablanca Records the following year. The song impresses for its lack of embellishment and feels out of place in Prince's productions at the time, as the artist accompanies himself alone on piano, which was highly unusual in his discography back then. Peggy McCreary, who had the honor of recording the only two takes of this song, recalls the evening with Prince. He asked her to order a bottle of Rémy Martin cognac for her and a bottle of Asti Spumante for him. "There was a deli that delivered and put it on the work order. And we had a couple of drinks and he started playing the piano, and we cut this song, and I kept thinking I knew I was a little buzzed, and I kept thinking this is really amazing."[142] Once the song was laid down on tape, McCreary heard no more of it until one day she came across *The Hits/The B-Sides* in the Amoeba Records store in Los Angeles. The song had been used as the B-side of *1999* in 1982.

ANOTHER LONELY CHRISTMAS

Prince / 4'51

Musician: Prince: vocals, electric guitar, bass, drums, synthesizers, piano, backing vocals / **Recording: Sunset Sound, Los Angeles:** 18–19 February 1984 / **Technical team: Producer:** Prince / **Recording engineer:** Peggy McCreary

Another Lonely Christmas, the B-side of the single *I Would Die 4 U*, is a ballad cut from the same cloth as *Purple Rain* and *Electric Intercourse*. Prince sings about his lover dying on 25 December and recounts different memories of her in the lyrics. Although he admitted that the song was just a "work of fiction,"[114] he nonetheless delivers a powerful performance on this track that ranks among the most moving songs in his discography.

GOD

Prince / 4'02

Musicians: Prince: vocals, synthesizers, piano, backing vocals / **Recording: Flying Cloud Drive Warehouse, Eden Prairie, Minnesota:** 19–20 August 1984 / **Technical team: Producer:** Prince / **Recording engineer:** Susan Rogers

One Saturday evening on 19 August 1984, Prince placed candles around his Eden Prairie studio and started recording a piano-vocal version of *God (Love Theme From Purple Rain)*, recorded in February with Sheila E. on drums for the upcoming movie. Susan Rogers was having trouble getting the equipment in the control room to work, and it was the middle of the night before Prince managed to lay down on tape a single take of *God*, after which he left the studio without a word. The next day, he added some overdubs to the track, which appeared on the B-side of the single *Purple Rain*. It was a Sunday, and Prince had just recorded a new "Sunday Song," intimate songs he liked to get on tape in the hushed weekend atmosphere with the loyal Susan Rogers.

4 THE TEARS IN YOUR EYES

Prince / 3'23

Musicians: Prince: vocals, 12-string acoustic guitar, backing vocals / **Wendy Melvoin:** electric guitar, backing vocals / **Lisa Coleman:** electric piano, backing vocals / **Recording: SIR Studios, Los Angeles:** 4 June 1985 / **Technical team: Producer:** Prince / **Recording engineers:** Susan Rogers, David Tickle

After refusing to appear alongside Michael Jackson in the video for *We Are the World*, Prince decided to contribute to the USA for Africa project in his own way. He recorded the track *4 The Tears In Your Eyes* with The Revolution during the sound check for his concert at the Louisiana Superdome, in New Orleans, in February 1985. He decided to provide an acoustic version for the video, which was shot on 4 June 1985 at SIR Studios, in Los Angeles, and broadcast during Live Aid, on 13 July 1985, in Philadelphia. It is this version, recorded by Susan Rogers and David Tickle during the shooting of the video, which appeared on *The Hits/The B-Sides*. Susan Rogers gave an emotional account of the February session, during which Prince brought the track to life, far from the cameras that filmed the video for *We Are the World*. "Later on, when I read about the USA for Africa session and how those people had $15,000 worth of food during the session at A&M, I thought about how Prince and I on our day off, and we hadn't had a day off for a long time, sat in that truck by ourselves and he ate this horrible salami and cheese and crackers and drank that warm coke. He put in his time for the cause in a very noble and gracious way although no one was there to see it."[143]

POWER FANTASTIC

Prince / 4'45

Musicians: Prince: vocals, percussion, finger cymbals / **Wendy Melvoin:** electric guitar / **Lisa Coleman:** piano / **Bobby Z.:** drums / **Eric Leeds:** flute / **Atlanta Bliss:** trumpet / **Recording: Galpin Boulevard Home Studio, Chanhassen, Minnesota:** 19 March 1986 / **Technical team: Producer:** Prince / **Recording engineer:** Susan Rogers

On a March afternoon in 1986, scattered around the Galpin Boulevard house for what would be the first recording session in Prince's new studio, the singer and his musicians recorded this jazz-sounding ballad in one take, having only rehearsed it a few times. Although it was created from *Carousel*, a song written by Lisa Coleman and Wendy Melvoin, Prince claimed credit for *Power Fantastic* on *The Hits/The B-Sides*. This did little to improve relations between Prince and his musicians at the time.

COM

PRINCE

COME

Come · Space · Pheromone · Loose! · Papa
Race · Dark · Solo · Letitgo · Orgasm

Released in the USA by Warner Bros. Records:
16 August 1994 (CD ref.: 9 45700-2)
Released in the UK by WEA International:
15 August 1994 (LP ref.: 9362 45700-1; CD ref.: 9362-45700-2)
Best chart ranking in the USA: 15
Best chart ranking in the UK: 1

Prince photographed in black and white, as in the shot (left) for the album *Come*, in which he is seen in front of Antoni Gaudí's *Sagrada Família* in Barcelona.

THE ALBUM OF DISSENT

1994

Despite selling three million copies around the world, Prince felt that the ⚥ album had not enabled him to achieve his goals. He thought Warner Bros. Records hadn't provided a strong enough promotion for the record and no longer felt supported enough by the label, despite having renewed his contract with them in September 1992. In February 1993, the bitter failure of Carmen Electra's first album was also blamed on Warner Bros. Records due to their lack of investment in the project. Then, in the spring, the label refused to release *Gold Nigga*, the New Power Generation's first LP (see page 230). Prince was sufficiently upset by this to announce his temporary retirement that April, during which time he would develop new projects. The reality was quite different because, while Prince did disappear, it was only to yield the floor to his new alter ego. On 7 June 1993, the day of his thirty-fifth birthday, Prince announced in a press release that he wanted to be called by his new stage name, the unpronounceable ⚥. Prince developed the name from the symbols ♂ and ♀, which represent masculine and feminine, respectively. In fact, Prince had an idea. Since he still owed Warner Bros. Records five more albums, he would let the label publish his records (which were mostly comprised of songs from The Vault) under the name Prince, while his new songs would appear under another name. The label's managers obviously rejected this idea from the very beginning.

Chronicle of a breakup foretold

Although relations were not ideal between Prince and Warner Bros. Records, tensions soon went up a notch. On 14 June 1993, Prince called Michael Bland and Sonny Thompson to Paisley Park for a night session on the main stage. In one hour, the Paisley Park Power Trio, which is what Prince called them at the time, recorded a complete live album called *The Undertaker*, which gave pride of place to both blues and rock 'n' roll. As Michael Bland explained, "Picture this: A DAT machine, a 32-channel board, two techs, and three players. It was about three o'clock in the morning. We got our sounds together and just let the DAT roll. We took about an hour to make that record, from start to finish, playing straight through with no overdubs. The sequence of songs on the record is exactly the way we played it. The guitar segues from one song to the next, like when we do live stuff."[137] Prince then wanted to feature *The Undertaker* in an upcoming issue of *Guitar World*, which Warner Bros. Records firmly opposed, preferring to release three compilations of his greatest hits: *The Hits 1, The Hits 2*, and *The Hits/The B-Sides*. On 31 July 1993, while launching the Act II Tour, Prince addressed the audience at Wembley Stadium: "The only reason why I retired is because I can no longer give the music to someone else to give to you. I wanna come to your house and give it to you myself. You don't need no records."[144] The managers at Warner Bros. Records did not take this well.

The birth of ⚥

In September 1993, he who now went by the name of ⚥ (sometimes even Love Symbol, The Artist, or The Artist Formerly Known As Prince) recorded *The Most Beautiful Girl in the World* at Paisley Park. Produced by NPG Records and distributed by Bellmark Records, the song was a small taste of freedom for Prince. In an effort to defuse tensions, Warner had given Prince free reign on this project. A global

Prince performing *Peach* at the first MTV European Music Awards, in Berlin, on 24 November 1994.

success from its release in February 1994, the single confirmed Prince's desire to release his music at his own pace. In the months before, not only had he produced this hit, but he had also worked on two new albums. While Prince wanted to release the first of these albums, *The Gold Experience*, under his new pseudonym, it wasn't ready yet and so he gave Warner Bros. Records *Come* in March. The label hated it and immediately demanded a new version, which should include *The Most Beautiful Girl in the World* and a new single worth its salt. So, Prince recorded *Letitgo*, which was a resounding failure when it came out on 9 August 1994. "But again, it's the record company," he explained. "If they don't want to promote a song, they don't make the effort to cross it over into other markets and the fans don't get to know it. It's the same with my albums. People say, 'Why did he drop Rosie Gaines after one album?' But I did three albums with her in between which nobody heard because the record company never released them!"[145]

End of the state of grace

When *Come* came out in the United States on 16 August 1994, its reception was a disaster. The record, which mainly featured songs recorded for the ballet *Glam Slam Ulysses* and a few new tracks, was heavily criticized. Cold and dark and containing songs that tackled sex in a far too explicit manner, *Come* sounded the death knell of its author's omnipotence in the music business. Mocked for his new unpronounceable name, ridiculed for what the media wrongly believed was a celebrity whim, Prince was more isolated than ever, even though he was still surrounded by his loyal musicians and had Mayte, his dancer and girlfriend (see page 216). The disc jacket, illustrated by a melancholy shot that Terry Gydesen had taken of Prince in front of Antoni Gaudí's *Sagrada Família* in Barcelona, and accompanied by the funereal inscription "Prince 1958 1993," sets the tone for the album. *Come* sold less than 400,000 copies in the US, which is the worst rating Prince ever received in the land of Uncle Sam. The following 30 September, the video for *Dolphin*, a song that had been scrapped from the tracklisting for the album, aired on American music channels, even though no single of this name had been released at the time. It features Prince singing happily, with a strange inscription scribbled upside down on his right cheek: slave. The message was clear: the artist formerly known as Prince was no longer master of his music, nor of his own destiny. He was shackled to the label that had made him successful. The artist put all his frustration and anger into his dazzling next album: *The Gold Experience*.

FOR PRINCE ADDICTS

Two cameramen filmed the June 1993 recording session that led to *The Undertaker*. On 6 March 1995, Warner Music Vision released a recording of this exceptional night on VHS, which was directed by Parris Patton.

THE MOST BEAUTIFUL GIRL IN THE WORLD

⚥ / 4'25

Musicians
⚥: vocals, acoustic guitar, electric guitar, bass, drums, programming, percussion, piano, synthesizers, backing vocals
Ricky Peterson: synthesizers, sound effects
James Behringer: electric guitar

Recording
Paisley Park, Chanhassen, Minnesota: 20 September 1993; January 1994

Technical team
Producers: ⚥, Ricky Peterson
Recording engineers: David "Chronic Freeze" Friedlander, Ray Hahnfeldt, Tom Tucker, Steve Durkee

Single
A-side: *The Most Beautiful Girl in the World*/4'07
B-side: *Beautiful*/3'57
Released in the USA by NPG Records/Bellmark Records: 9 February 1994 (CD single ref.: BR 72514-2)
Released in the UK by NPG Records/Grapevine: 28 March 1994 (single ref.: NPG6015-7; CD single ref.: NPG 6015-5)
Best chart ranking in the USA: 3
Best chart ranking in the UK: 1

A year after the colossal success of *The Most Beautiful Girl in the World*, two Italian composers, Bruno Bergonzi and Michele Vicino, sued Prince for plagiarism, claiming that a resemblance between the song and their single *Takin' Me To Paradise*, which was released in 1983, was no coincidence. The two artists won their case in Italy's Supreme Court of Cassation in 2015, and their names were added to the song credits in Italy.

Genesis

In September 1993, three months after announcing his "identity change," Prince was everywhere. In Minneapolis, the first NPG Store opened on 3 August, allowing the *Gold Nigga* album to be sold freely without other distribution channels, while NPG Records, of which Levi Seacer Jr was now the owner, was developing its artistic partnerships and preparing the release of a compilation of Minneapolis Sound artists: *1-800 NEW FUNK*, named after the hotline where you could order one hundred percent Paisley Park songs. The contentious relationship between Prince and his record label made friendly collaboration difficult, but Mo Ostin made an exception for NPG Records, allowing them to produce and distribute a single Prince song with total independence. On 23 September, NPG Records seized their chance and recorded *The Most Beautiful Girl in the World* at Paisley Park. This smooth ballad was perfectly suited to the airwaves. Produced by NPG Records and distributed by the independent label Bellmark Records in the United States, the song came out as a single in February 1994. "We're gonna definitely learn a lot from putting out *The Most Beautiful Girl in the World*," explained Levi Seacer Jr at the time. "We're gonna find out what's all the work involved in marketing a song, getting distribution, all that. We're gonna do it with other artists, but it's definitely a plus to do it with the boss [...] All thanks to Warner Brothers."[149]

Much to the chagrin of Warner's managers, the single became one of Prince's greatest hits of all time and allowed him to get his first No.1 in the UK. "Do you know what a sense of freedom it gave me to release *The Most Beautiful Girl in the World* on an independent label?" he said in 1995. "When I released that I didn't have to give [Warner Bros. Records] the master, I could keep the master. I can release that record again next year if I want to."[145]

Production

After recording the first version of the song, the artist entrusted the tape to a musician he liked and with whom he had worked since the late 1970s, but who had never joined the group: keyboardist Ricky Peterson, brother of Paul Peterson, the former front man for The Family (see page 110). "He handed me a cassette tape of him playing the guitar part and singing the vocals of that song," recounted Peterson. "[...]

A successful gamble for Prince, who with *The Most Beautiful Girl in the World* achieved the biggest success in the history of his label, NPG Records.

and he just said 'Fix this! [...] Let me see if you can, you know, fix this for me.' [...] I took it, and I ended up rearranging and pretty much writing those changes."[150] At one point, Prince decided to record many versions of the song, sung in different languages by female singers from different countries. Mayte sang a Spanish version called *¿Quieres Ser El Mas Bello De Este Mundo?*, then a version called *The Most Beautiful Boy in the World* for her album *Child of the Sun* in 1995, while singer Ophélie Winter, who was close to Prince at the time, recorded a version at Studio Guillaume Tell, in Suresnes, near Paris. It was called *Le Garçon Le Plus Beau Dans l'Univers* and it was never released. Ophélie Winter, who'd returned from Paisley Park with the instrumental tapes of the song, asked the singer Zazie to help her record backing vocals. Lastly (except for the multiple remixes released in different formats at the time), Prince made slight arrangements to the song so it could appear on the *The Gold Experience* album in 1995.

HEADPHONES AT THE READY

At 1'08 into the song, after Prince sings "I will cry tears of joy," you can hear drops of water fall to the ground. These were not recorded near a tap, but by Ricky Peterson, who created the sound effect himself—with his mouth!

COME

Prince / 11'13

Musicians: Prince: vocals, bass, programming, percussion, synthesizers, backing vocals / **Michael B** Nelson: trombone / **Kathy Jensen:** baritone saxophone / **Brian Gallagher:** tenor saxophone / **Dave Jensen:** trumpet / **Steve Strand:** trumpet / **Recording: Paisley Park, Chanhassen, Minnesota:** April 1994 / **Technical team: Producer:** Prince / **Recording engineers:** David "Chronic Freeze" Friedlander, Ray Hahnfeldt, Tom Tucker / **Assistant recording engineers:** Xanex Bess, Tom Garneau, Kimm James

On 26 March 1993, Prince gave a concert at the Radio City Music Hall in New York. He was in the middle of his Act I Tour, and the three concerts held in that city were a resounding success. As per usual, Prince gave his fans an after show. It was held on the night of the 26th at Club USA, one of the trendiest establishments in the Big Apple at the time. When he took the stage after midnight, Prince started his set with a new song: *Come*. A demo version of the song was then regularly played before the start of each concert on the tour, and it quickly became the new unreleased song all the fans were talking about. Prince later reworked it for the ballet *Glam Slam Ulysses*, and in the end, it appeared on Prince's fifteenth album. Equipped with a three-minute-long instrumental part in which The NPG Hornz proved their virtuosity once again, the song joined the ranks of R&B, which was very popular in 1994.

Single

SPACE

Prince / 4'28

Musicians: Prince: vocals, programming, synthesizers, finger snapping, backing vocals / **Sonny T.:** bass / **Michael B.:** drums / **Tommy Barbarella:** synthesizers / **Mr** Hayes: synthesizers / **Recording: Paisley Park, Chanhassen, Minnesota:** May 1993 / **Technical team: Producer:** Prince / **Recording engineers:** David "Chronic Freeze" Friedlander, Ray Hahnfeldt, Tom Tucker / **Assistant recording engineers:** Xanex Bess, Tom Garneau, Kimm James
Single: A-side: *Space* (Universal Love Radio Remix)/3'58 / **B-side:** *Space* (Album Version)/4'28 / **Released in the USA by Warner Bros. Records:** 1 November 1994 (single ref.: 7-18012; CD single ref.: 18012-2) / **Best chart ranking USA:** did not make the charts

After the explicit lyrics in *Come*, in which Prince says he wants to give his partner an orgasm, he continues in the same vein, using the image of space as the place of ultimate pleasure, where he'd like to take his young woman. While the album was partly based on a simple concept (a sexual encounter in multiple stages put to song), the single *Space*, which came from writing sessions for the ballet *Glam Slam Ulysses*, struggled to gain a wide audience and didn't even make the Billboard Hot 100 chart when it came out in November 1994.

PHEROMONE

Prince / 5'08

Musician: Prince: vocals, spoken word, bass, drums, programming, synthesizers, backing vocals / **Recording: Paisley Park, Chanhassen, Minnesota:** January 1993 / **Technical team: Producer:** Prince / **Recording engineers:** David "Chronic Freeze" Friedlander, Ray Hahnfeldt, Tom Tucker / **Assistant recording engineers:** Xanex Bess, Tom Garneau, Kimm James

On 27 April 1993, the audience of the musical show *Video LP*, which aired on BET (Black Entertainment Television), heard the new song for the closing credits of their favorite program. It was an instrumental by Prince called *Pheromone*. In the lyrics, he plays an unwilling witness to the rape of a captive woman by her jailer. The song, the words of which border on bad taste (the narrator revels in this disturbing scene), did not help the press support Prince in his lewd experiments. The song appeared in the ballet *Glam Slam Ulysses*, and was then inserted in the tracklisting of *Come* without any changes.

FOR PRINCE ADDICTS

On 5 June 1993, the Glam Slam club in Minneapolis invited its patrons to hear two new Prince songs in its VIP listening booths, equipped with headphones. One of them was *Pheromone*, this time presented with the vocals. A fan stole the two sheets containing the lyrics to the songs, which led Prince to cancel a party planned at Paisley Park that same evening.

LOOSE!

Prince / 3'27

Musician: Prince: vocals, electric guitar, bass, drums, programming, synthesizers, backing vocals / **Recording: Paisley Park, Chanhassen, Minnesota:** February 1993; 1994 / **Technical team: Producer:** Prince / **Recording engineers:** David "Chronic Freeze" Friedlander, Ray Hahnfeldt, Tom Tucker / **Assistant recording engineers:** Xanex Bess, Tom Garneau, Kimm James

Loose! was a rare Prince incursion into the fast-growing techno genre. An initial version was played during the Act I Tour, in the middle of a medley that also included *Partyman*. Embellished with an edgy guitar riff, it was later included in the ballet *Glam Slam Ulysses,* then remodeled around a technoid rhythm to rival that of The Prodigy, a British band who had just released their first album, *Experience*—one of the greatest hits in the UK at the end of 1992. A very welcome rarity in Prince's discography.

PAPA

Prince / 2'48

Musicians: Prince: vocals, electric guitar, programming, synthesizers, backing vocals / **Sonny Thompson:** bass / **Michael Bland:** drums / **Recording: Paisley Park, Chanhassen, Minnesota:** 2 January 1993 / **Technical team: Producer:** Prince / **Recording engineers:** David "Chronic Freeze" Friedlander, Ray Hahnfeldt, Tom Tucker / **Assistant recording engineers:** Xanex Bess, Tom Garneau, Kimm James

It's hard not to hear *Papa* and see a reference to the violent father of the Kid, a character Prince played in *Purple Rain* in 1984. Here, the narrator describes a man who comes home from work, tears up dandelions from the garden, hits his four-year-old son before locking him in a closet, and then shoots himself in the head. In order to dispel rumors on this subject, Prince stressed many times that this aspect of *Purple Rain* was not autobiographical and that John L Nelson had never been a violent man. Perhaps Prince was referring to the dandelions in the family garden that his stepfather, Hayward Baker, would make him pull up to punish him for bad behavior. Recorded with Prince's Paisley Park Power Trio, the occasional band he'd formed with Michael B. and Sonny T., *Papa* is by far the most interesting song on *Come.* It stands out for its structure with two very distinct stages: verses and choruses as dark as can be and a rock grand finale.

No one argues with Prince when he is toting his micro-pistol!

RACE

Prince / 4'28

Musicians: Prince: vocals, rap, electric guitar, bass, programming, percussion, synthesizers, backing vocals / **Michael B** Nelson: trombone / **Kathy Jensen:** baritone saxophone / **Brian Gallagher:** tenor saxophone / **Dave Jensen:** trumpet / **Steve Strand:** trumpet / **Mayte:** backing vocals / **Recording: Paisley Park, Chanhassen, Minnesota:** May 1993 / **Technical team: Producer:** Prince / **Recording engineers:** David "Chronic Freeze" Friedlander, Ray Hahnfeldt, Tom Tucker / **Assistant recording engineers:** Xanex Bess, Tom Garneau, Kimm James

Race enjoyed many lives before ending up on *Come.* Initially recorded on 8 November 1991 at the Record Plant studios in Los Angeles (the same day as *Go Go Dancer,* which was given to Carmen Electra), the song was recorded again—this time with the members of NPG—at the Paisley Park Studios in May 1993. Not satisfied with this second version, Prince did a third one on his own, which ended up on his fifteenth album. The song is notable for the samples from the "group version" and a recurring sample of Jearlyn Steele-Battle singing "Face the music." The line "Cut me, cut you, both the blood is red" refers to the very first edition of William Shakespeare's play *The Merchant of Venice,* in which the Prince of Morocco tells Portia, who hates the darkness of his skin: "Bring me the fairest creature northward born/Where Phoebus' fire scarce thaws the icicles/And let us make incision for your love/To prove whose blood is reddest, his or mine."[146] An elegant quote to highlight that racism, unfortunately, is still going strong.

HEADPHONES AT THE READY

Prince's keenest observers will have recognized a sample from *Girls & Boys* (1986) at 0'30, 1'30, and 2'30 into *Race.* Prince had played it at the time on his Roland G-707 Guitar-Synthesizer.

The playwright David Henry Hwang wrote the poem on which the song *Solo* is based.

1994

DARK

Prince / 6'10

Musicians: Prince: vocals, acoustic guitar, backing vocals / **Sonny T.:** bass / **Michael B.:** drums / **Tommy Barbarella:** synthesizers / **Mr Hayes:** Hammond organ / **Michael B** Nelson: trombone / **Kathy Jensen:** baritone saxophone / **Brian Gallagher:** tenor saxophone / **Dave Jensen:** trumpet / **Steve Strand:** trumpet / **Recording:** **Paisley Park, Chanhassen, Minnesota:** 2 January 1993 / **Technical team:** **Producer:** Prince / **Recording engineers:** David "Chronic Freeze" Friedlander, Ray Hahnfeldt, Tom Tucker / **Assistant recording engineers:** Xanex Bess, Tom Garneau, Kimm James

The *Come* album was partially comprised of songs from the ballet *Glam Slam Ulysses*, but a January 1993 recording session gave rise to other album songs. "Sonny [Thompson] and I were the only two cats in the band who hung around Minneapolis during Christmas vacation," remembered Michael Bland. "And [Prince] got bored, as he usually does. Because when he's not creating, he's not alive, you know. So he went down to the soundstage where we were set up for rehearsal before vacation began. And he just played by himself all day; they say he stayed in there for like eight, ten hours, just messing around with ideas. And then the second day he got up the courage to call us and ask, 'You guys bored, too?' So we came out and worked on a good half dozen tunes. And we went in the studio and started cutting them. We cut the rhythm tracks for *Dark, Come, Papa*, and a few other things like that."[137]

SOLO

Prince, David Henry Hwang / 3'48

Musician: Prince: vocals, synthesizer / **Recording:** **Paisley Park, Chanhassen, Minnesota:** May 1993 / **Technical team:** **Producer:** Prince / **Recording engineers:** David "Chronic Freeze" Friedlander, Ray Hahnfeldt, Tom Tucker / **Assistant recording engineers:** Xanex Bess, Tom Garneau, Kimm James

After seeing a Broadway production of *M. Butterfly*, by playwright David Henry Hwang, Prince decided to develop his own creation: *Come*. He met Hwang at the Rihga Royal Hotel, in Manhattan, and explained his vision: a musical about the epistolary relationship between a rock star and a fan, which becomes obsessive. Prince asked Hwang to write him a poem that could be recited between two songs. Something about loss. As Hwang explained: a poem on "The way you feel when you've lost someone you love. And you know they're never coming back. And that, for the rest of your life, you're going to be alone."[147] A few days later, Hwang faxed the poem to Paisley Park. But he never heard anything about a possible collaboration until *Come* came out in August 1994. "I checked the writing credit on the CD case: 'Prince with David Henry Hwang,'" he recounted in 2016. "No contracts between us, nothing on paper. But he remembered. That we had Worked Together."[147]

Single

LETITGO

Prince / 5'33

Musicians: Prince: vocals, electric guitar, programming, tambourine, synthesizers, backing vocals / **Kathleen Bradford:** vocals, backing vocals / **Sonny T.:** bass / **Michael B.:** drums / **Tommy Barbarella:** synthesizers / **Mr** Hayes: synthesizers / **Ricky Peterson:** synthesizers / **Michael B** Nelson: trombone / **Kathy Jensen:** baritone saxophone / **Brian Gallagher:** tenor saxophone / **Dave Jensen:** trumpet / **Steve Strand:** trumpet / **Eric Leeds:** transverse flute / **Mayte:** backing vocals / **Recording: Paisley Park, Chanhassen, Minnesota:** 16 March 1994 / **Technical team: Producer:** Prince / **Recording engineers:** David "Chronic Freeze" Friedlander, Ray Hahnfeldt, Tom Tucker / **Assistant recording engineers:** Xanex Bess, Tom Garneau, Kimm James
Single: A-side: *Letitgo* (Edit)/4'15 / **B-side:** *Solo*/3'48 / **Released in the USA by Warner Bros. Records:** 9 August 1994 (single ref.: 7-18074; CD single ref. 5439-18074-2) / **Released in the UK by WEA International:** 9 August 1994 (single ref.: W0260P) / **Best chart ranking in the USA:** 31 / **Best chart ranking in the UK:** 30

When Prince proposed *Come* to Warner Bros. Records in March 1994, the reaction was final: "The company was so upset with that album. People said it was a piece of shit,"[144] confided Marylou Badeaux, a long-time partner of Warner Bros. Prince resolved to record another song for the album, replacing *Strays of the World*, which would appear on the *Crystal Ball* album in 1998. *Letitgo*, with its very R&B sound and undeniable FM rock potential, nevertheless failed to convince American fans, to Prince's chagrin. "That was a great pop song," he complained in 1995. "If Warner had promoted it properly it would have been a huge hit. Now I don't have any control over that."[148] In the song, Prince sang alongside Kathleen Bradford, sister of Kirk Johnson and wife of Michael Bradford, a Paisley Park employee.

HEADPHONES AT THE READY

The young lady we hear in the introduction to *Letitgo* is none other than Vanity (see page 72). While producing the album, Prince dipped into The Vault and retrieved a vocal track that Vanity had recorded for *Vibrator* in 1983 (which remains unreleased to this day). He weaved extracts from it throughout the record, including the "Ready or Not, Here I Come," at 5'23 into the original song.

ORGASM

Prince / 1'39

Musician: Prince: spoken word, electric guitar, synthesizers / **Recording: Paisley Park, Chanhassen, Minnesota:** 1993 / **Technical team: Producer:** Prince / **Recording engineers:** David "Chronic Freeze" Friedlander, Ray Hahnfeldt, Tom Tucker / **Assistant recording engineers:** Xanex Bess, Tom Garneau, Kimm James

Unsurprisingly to those who knew Prince, the *Come* album could only end with a song called *Orgasm*. Without asking for the permission, or even advice, of the person in question, Prince incorporated the moans that Vanity had recorded for *Vibrator* in 1983, in which she simulates an orgasm after having replaced the batteries in her vibrator. There was no guarantee that Vanity, who'd converted to Christianity in 1994 and had quickly become a seasoned evangelist, would appreciate her forced participation in the album. There was also no guarantee that Mayte, Prince's then girlfriend, would appreciate the "I Love You" Prince utters to Vanity at the end of the song, after giving her the long-awaited orgasm which builds up throughout the album. Despite the irreverence of Prince's songs, he once again managed to transform a dirty concept-album into a romantic declaration of love.

FOR PRINCE ADDICTS

The saturated guitar at the start of *Orgasm* was not recorded by Prince in 1993. It was, in fact, a 6-string guitar track that was recorded on 14 August 1981 for the feedback-filled solo from *Private Joy*, which Prince integrated into the last song on *Come*.

Nona Gaye, daughter of the famous soul singer, at Midem, in Cannes, in January 1993.

LOVE SIGN

(NONA GAYE AND ⚥)

⚥ / 4'33

Musicians

Nona Gaye: vocals
⚥: vocals, rap, electric guitar, synthesizers
Paul Peterson: bass
Statik: programming
Ricky Peterson: synthesizers

Recording

Paisley Park, Chanhassen, Minnesota: January 1994
The Record Plant, Los Angeles: 1994

Technical team

Producers: ⚥, Ricky Peterson
Recording engineers: David "Chronic Freeze" Friedlander, Ray Hahnfeldt, Tom Tucker
Assistant recording engineers: Kyle Bess, Kimm James, Brian Poer

1-800 NEW FUNK (compilation)

Released in the USA by NPG Records/Bellmark Records: 12 August 1994 (LP ref.: BR 71006-1; CD ref.: BR 71006-2)
Released in the UK and Europe by NPG Records/Edel: 12 August 1994 (LP ref.: 0060511NPG; CD ref.: NPG 6051-2)
Best chart ranking in the USA: did not make the charts

Genesis

In 1994, if you dialled 1-800-NEW-FUNK on your phone (American businesses sometimes use phone numbers made up of numbers and letters), you'd reach the voice service of NPG records, Prince's new label. Totally independent of Warner Bros. Records, the little platform, managed by Levi Seacer Jr and unofficially by Prince, had already produced the New Power Generation's first album, *Gold Nigga*. After some initial hurdles, NPG Records had managed to get its distribution under control, notably thanks to a partnership with Bellmark Records, which had been created in 1989 by Al Bell, a veteran of Stax Records. Prince used his new platform to champion artists he'd been supporting for years but that Warner Bros. Records hadn't wanted to distribute, never mind produce.

Production

Mavis Staples, George Clinton, and M.P.L.S. were some of the artists included in the label's first compilation, *1-800 NEW FUNK*, in August 1994. Among them was Nona, the daughter of the late singer Marvin Gaye. She and Prince had been friendly for more than two years. At the start of the year, the young singer (who already had an album, *Love for the Future*, under her belt, released in 1992 by Third Stone/Atlantic) was invited to Paisley Park, where Prince made her an offer she couldn't refuse. "It was a surprise," she later explained. "He brought me over to the studio and said, 'Listen to this.' I was like, 'That's amazing, I love it.' And he said, 'Well, go sing on it.' So we did a duet."[151] *Love Sign*, with its anti-violence and anti-gun messages, came out as a promotional single for the compilation, and a video was directed by Ice Cube, a former member of N.W.A., one of America's greatest hip-hop bands. On the back of the success of *The Most Beautiful Girl in the World*, keyboardist Ricky Peterson was asked to produce *Love Sign*. He soon became a house producer at Paisley Park. Prince let him work with total freedom on some of his songs (*Letitgo*, *319*, and *Gold*) and on other NPG Records projects, such as Mayte's songs (*If I Love U 2night*, on *Child of the Sun*, in 1995); Chaka Khan's (*Don't Talk 2 Strangers*, on *Come 2 My House*, in 1998); and Graham Central Station's (*Just B My Lady*, on *GCS 2000*, in 1999).

BLAC

PRINCE

THE BLACK ALBUM

Le Grind · Cindy C. · Dead On It · When 2 R In Love* · Bob George
Superfunkycalifragisexy · 2 Nigs United 4 West Compton · Rockhard in a Funky Place

** Already on Lovesexy (1988)*

Released in the USA by Warner Bros. Records:
22 November 1994 (LP ref.: 1-45793; CD ref.: 2-45793)
Released in the UK by WEA International:
21 November 1994 (LP ref.: 9362-45793-1); CD ref.: 9362-45793-2)
Best chart ranking in the USA: 47
Best chart ranking in the UK: 36

Prince and his Purple Cloud Guitar in 1988.

FOR PRINCE ADDICTS

Alongside the numerous bootlegs of *The Black Album* in circulation between 1987 and 1994, a plethora of fake records flooded the black market. These included an edition produced by the German label TNT Records in which a group called The Black Album Band delivers an (almost) identical version of the famous album. As a joke, a free sticker reading "I Own The Black Album" was slipped inside the cover. To find your way around the multiple versions of the record, refer to the-black-album.info website.

THE BEST-KNOWN BOOTLEG

1994

In November 1987, while Prince was surfing the wave of success of *Sign O' the Times*, Warner Bros. Records began promoting his new album. It had no title and no author or tracklist credits, and was slated for release on 8 December 1987, shrouded in mystery. The album cover was entirely black, and so it was referred to as *The Black Album*. The eight tracks that featured on the album were dance numbers which alternated between 1980s funk and synthpop. Some had been recorded a year earlier, while Prince was working on bringing a personal touch to Sheila E.'s twenty-ninth birthday party at Vertigo, a Los Angeles club, on 11 December 1986. "*The Black Album* was recorded [...] in order to make music to dance to at Sheila's birthday party [...]," explained Susan Rogers. "So he took some time and recorded all that fun stuff and then set it aside and forgot about it [...]"[110] The idea of an album came about gradually, but by the time Prince decided to cancel the marketing of the record on 1 December 1987, nearly 500,000 copies had already been pressed and distributed to American retailers. "I suddenly realized that we can die at any moment, and we'd be judged by the last thing we left behind. I didn't want that angry bitter thing to be the last thing,"[152] Prince said of the album, which incorporated the saucy *Cindy C.*, the vulgar *Bob George*, and the acerbic hip-hop *Dead On It*. Warner Bros. Records raced to recall all the copies scattered around the country, for which Prince picked up the bill.

Inevitably, the opus became the most exchanged, bought, and sold bootleg Prince album, to the despair of Alan Leeds, the head of Paisley Park Records. "[We] captained a major investigation, along with the R.I.A.A. and the F.B.I., into the black market CD's that were showing up all over the U.S. and Europe," he explained. "No legal action resulted, other than to confiscate illegal product from dealers. The proliferation of bootlegged material suggested someone who had regular access to the tape vault and suspicion was directed toward several Paisley Park associates and employees. But because Prince himself was so generous (and careless) with cassettes of his unissued material, it was impossible to legally prove guilt in any one direction."[153]

A late release

Seven years later, tensions between Prince and Warner Bros. Records were at their height and the end of the collaboration between the two parties was only five albums away. Just five more records and Prince would have his artistic freedom. On 22 November 1994, the record company chose to release what—according to stickers affixed to it—would officially be called *The Black Album*. There was no single to accompany the opus, and it incited very little interest, as the black market had already been flooded with bootlegs in the intervening years. *The Black Album* therefore appeared to general indifference, and its impeccable tracks, which fly in the face of its detractors—and there were many of those—vanished into the dark recesses of Prince's discography. A grave injustice that needs to be urgently remedied by getting your hands on one of the very rare official copies of the album!

The top model Cindy Crawford who took center stage in *Cindy C.*, the second song on *The Black Album*.

1994

LE GRIND

Prince / 6'44

Musicians: **Prince:** vocals, electric guitar, bass, drums, programming, Fairlight CMI, synthesizers, backing vocals / **Eric Leeds:** saxophone / **Atlanta Bliss:** trumpet / **Boni Boyer:** backing vocals / **Sheila E.** backing vocals / **Susannah Melvoin:** backing vocals / **Jill Jones:** backing vocals / **Recording:** **Sunset Sound, Los Angeles:** 10 December 1986 / **Galpin Boulevard Home Studio, Chanhassen, Minnesota:** December 1986 / **Paisley Park, Chanhassen, Minnesota:** 18 October 1987 / **Technical team:** **Producer:** Prince / **Recording engineer:** Susan Rogers

In the rush to deliver new songs—preferably that were good to dance to—for Sheila E.'s twenty-ninth birthday party, Prince and Susan Rogers worked on a number of sessions that produced three new songs: *Bob George*, *2 Nigs United 4 West Compton*, and *Le Grind*. The French-influenced title of the the last song is borrowed from Chic's *Le Freak*, one of the biggest disco hits of the late 1970s, and it follows on from *Housequake* recorded a few weeks earlier. Once this funk triplet was laid down on tape, it was entrusted to Bernie Grundman at Sunset Boulevard, who was responsible for mastering it in record time. He burned acetates from the master, which he delivered to Prince. "We would take a stack of these acetates to the party," Rogers recalls, "and the DJ could play them and we could dance to them."[110]

CINDY C.

Prince / 6'14

Musicians: **Prince:** vocals, spoken voice, electric guitar, bass, drums, programming, Fairlight CMI, synthesizers, percussion, claps, backing vocals / **Cat Glover:** rap / **Eric Leeds:** saxophone / **Atlanta Bliss:** trumpet / **Boni Boyer:** backing vocals, claps / **Sheila E.:** backing vocals, percussion, claps / **Susannah Melvoin:** backing vocals, claps / **Jill Jones:** backing vocals, claps / **Recording:** **Galpin Boulevard Home Studio, Chanhassen, Minnesota:** March 1987 / **Technical team:** **Producer:** Prince / **Recording engineer:** Susan Rogers

Prince and the heroine of this song met on the dance floor at Nell's club in the heart of Manhattan. That night, the young lady in question was dancing with a girlfriend when a man began shimmying beside her. She recognized Prince and danced with him for a while. Months later, a friend told her that Prince had written a song about her for his upcoming album. The title was *Cindy C.*, in reference to Cindy Crawford, superstar model and the young lady who had caught Prince's eye that evening. The lyrics are explicit about Prince's attraction to Cindy C.: "Where'd you get that beauty mark?/Maybe you and I should be undressing." As a clearly amused Cindy Crawford said in 2016: "Now I know what was going through his mind as we were dancing."[154]

DEAD ON IT

Prince / 4'37

Musician: Prince: vocals, electric guitar, bass, programming, Fairlight CMI, synthesizers, backing vocals / **Recording: Galpin Boulevard Home Studio, Chanhassen, Minnesota:** March 1987 / **Technical team: Producer:** Prince / **Recording engineer:** Susan Rogers

The message is loud and clear in *Dead On It*: Prince denounces rappers and their music. "Riding in my Thunderbird on the freeway/I turned on my radio to hear some music play/I got a silly rapper talking silly shit instead/And the only good rapper is one that's dead on it," he sings, paradoxically in the style he's openly attacking. Prince stridently criticizes a musical movement that he would fully embrace a few years later when three rappers, including the underrated Tony Mosley, joined his band. "Well, first I never said I didn't like rap," Prince said in an attempt to justify himself in 1991. "[...] I didn't used to like all that braggadocio stuff. 'I'm bad, I'm this. I'm that.' Anyway, everybody has the right to change their mind."[155]

HEADPHONES AT THE READY

At 3'02 of *Dead On It*, Prince slips in a sample from *Holly Rock*, a rap song he had written for Sheila E. in 1985. "I'm worse than a wicked witch," we hear her say, playing with the kind of hip-hop lyrics that were trendy at the time.

BOB GEORGE

Prince / 5'36

Musician: Prince: spoken voice, electric guitar, drums, programming, Fairlight CMI, synthesizers / **Recording: Sunset Sound, Los Angeles:** 7 and 9–10 December 1986 / **Technical team: Producer:** Prince / **Recording engineer:** Susan Rogers

Journalist Nelson George, a Prince fan from the early days, attended the first concert on the Purple Rain Tour at the Joe Louis Arena, in Detroit, on 4 November 1984. He was not impressed with the show and published a withering critique in *Billboard* magazine on 17 November, accusing Prince of having lost his brilliance and complaining that he didn't play some of the classics. This did not please Prince one bit. In December 1986, the singer used his legendary Publison Infernal Machine 90 to transform his voice (this time making it lower rather than higher) to lay down on tape the scathing *Bob George*, a song about a man hellbent on taking his revenge by killing a rock manager. The surname George is borrowed from the rock critic, while the first name Bob is a vengeful nod to Bob Cavallo, the singer's ex-manager, with whom relations had become strained over time. "When [*The Black Album*] got an official release in November 1994 someone called and said: '*Bob George* was partially about me,'" Nelson George later commented, "and, I must sadly admit, the line 'that skinny motherfucker with the high-pitched voice' was an apt 1987 description."[156]

Back to the year 1988 with Cat Glover, the iconic dancer on the Lovesexy Tour.

1994

SUPERFUNKYCALIFRAGISEXY

Prince / 5'55

Musician: **Prince:** vocals, rap, electric guitar, bass, drums, programming, percussion, Fairlight CMI, synthesizers, backing vocals / **Recording:** **Galpin Boulevard Home Studio, Chanhassen, Minnesota:** January 1987 / **Washington Avenue Warehouse, Edina, Minnesota:** January 1987 / **Technical team:** **Producer:** Prince / **Recording engineer:** Susan Rogers

Borrowing from Julie Andrews' famous "Supercalifragilistic-expialidocious," a word she used in the movie *Mary Poppins* to define a feeling of intense joy, Prince created the excellent *Superfunkycalifragisexy* that would have made a great single had *The Black Album* been released in 1987. The song was performed during the Lovesexy Tour in 1988 and 1989, and included in a medley with *Controversy* in the concerts. A memento of this live version, which saw Cat Glover tying Prince to his chair every night, is available on the *Lovesexy Live 2* VHS tape, which was released by Granada International Ltd. in 1988. It is a precious video keepsake, never released as a DVD, of Prince's last European concert on this classic tour.

Prince's albums are punctuated by the unsurpassable solos of the saxophonist Eric Leeds.

2 NIGS UNITED 4 WEST COMPTON

Prince / 7'00

Musicians: Prince: spoken voice, bass, Hammond organ, synthesizers / **Cat Glover:** spoken voice / **Sheila E.:** drums / **Eric Leeds:** saxophone / **Atlanta Bliss:** trumpet / **Recording: Sunset Sound, Los Angeles:** 7 and 9 December 1986 / **Technical team: Producer:** Prince / **Recording engineer:** Susan Rogers

2 Nigs United 4 West Compton, an instrumental version (but with a spoken intro and outro), which was recorded along with *Bob George* and *Le Grind* for Sheila E.'s birthday party, is a perfect dancefloor track powered by the frenetic pace of Sheila E.'s drums, mixed with electronic percussion played by Prince.

ROCKHARD IN A FUNKY PLACE

Prince, Eric Leeds / 4'30

Musicians: Prince: vocals, electric guitar, bass, drums, percussion, synthesizers, Fairlight CMI, claps, backing vocals / **Eric Leeds:** saxophone, flute / **Atlanta Bliss:** trumpet / **Susannah Melvoin:** backing vocals, claps / **Recording: Sunset Sound, Los Angeles:** 28–29 October 1986 / **Technical team: Producer:** Prince / **Recording engineer:** Susan Rogers

Structured around a saxophone line written by Eric Leeds, *Rockhard in a Funky Place* was included in the tracklist for *Camille*, then *Crystal Ball*, before being rescued from The Vault in extremis for inclusion in the untitled work that would become *The Black Album* in 1994. During the sessions, Prince asked recording engineer Susan Rogers to record her voice at the end of the track. He wanted to hear her say: "Yes, I agree. Now start all over and this time, be beautiful." After a few unsuccessful attempts, Prince decided instead to add his own voice to the outro, where he can be heard saying: "What kind of fuck ending was that?"

GOLD

THE GOLD EXPERIENCE

P. Control · NPG Operator · Endorphinmachine · Shhh · We March · NPG Operator
The Most Beautiful Girl in the World · Dolphin · NPG Operator · Now · NPG Operator · 319
NPG Operator · Shy · Billy Jack Bitch · 👁 Hate U · NPG Operator · Gold

Released in the USA by NPG Records/Warner Bros. Records:
26 September 1995 (CD ref.: 9 45999-2)
Released in the UK by NPG Records/WEA International:
25 September 1995 (LP ref.: 9362-45999-1; ref. CD: 9362-45999-2)
Best chart ranking in the USA: 6
Best chart ranking in the UK: 4

The singer sports his brand-new Love Symbol Guitar, designed by the German guitar maker Jerry Auerswald.

FOR PRINCE ADDICTS

In 1994, like a proudly brandished standard, Prince presented his new custom-made 6-string guitar to the world: The Love Symbol Guitar. It was made by the German luthier Jerry Auerswald from the finest wood available. "The body was cut out of 90-years-old storage Rock Maple," says Zeke Clark, Prince's guitar technician. "The neck was cut out of 120-year-old storage Curly Maple, and the fingerboard was cut from 120-years-old ebony [...] We consider this guitar to be priceless, beyond value."[161]

COME'S LUMINOUS TWIN

1995

Like its twin *Come* in the chronological order of Prince albums, *The Gold Experience* had a long and painful gestation period. Already in January 1994, fans were spreading a rumor that the two albums would be released simultaneously, the first under the name Prince and the second under his new name: ⚥. Warner Bros. Records dismissed the idea out of hand, and *The Gold Experience* was returned to The Vault. Over the next 18 months, Prince gradually disclosed songs from the album whenever he made a public appearance. On 3 April 1994, *Now* and *Days of Wild* were featured in the short movie *The Beautiful Experience*, which was directed by Prince himself and broadcast on the British channel Sky One. On 5 May, he set the world alight when he unveiled the rock 'n' roll number *Endorphinmachine* on a French TV show called *Nulle part ailleurs*. In August, when he should have been promoting the release of *Come*, he was distributing snarky flyers at the NPG Store in Minneapolis that referred to Warner Bros. Records' as-yet undetermined release date for *The Gold Experience*. The flyers revealed the final tracklist for the album and urged fans to contact the record company and express their dissatisfaction.

The conflict intensifies

After the enforced departure of Mo Ostin and Lenny Waronker, two long-standing bosses at Warner Bros. Records and ardent Prince supporters, nothing was working any more between the record company and The Artist Formerly Known As Prince. "What's happened is that the people who signed me, and the people I had a relationship with there, have moved on and been replaced by people I don't know," Prince said. "And I can't do business with those people [...] Guys like Mo Ostin, who built the industry with people like Clive Davis, Ahmet Ertegun, Berry Gordy—they're moving out and there are guys coming in who don't understand me, they don't understand music. All they know is marketing. I mean, I haven't met some of them."[160] In May 1995, against all the odds, and despite the tension between the two parties, Prince and his record label reached an agreement on the marketing plan for his new album.

24-carat Prince

The Gold Experience was released in the United States on 26 September 1995. Although fans already knew most of the tracks, the album was nonetheless remarkably well received and sold over 500,000 copies in a few weeks. This was Prince back to his best, equaling the quality of his greatest albums and showing his capacity to rise from the ashes after the relative failure of *Come*. Everything is majestic on this record, on which Mayte repeats the words "*Prince está muerto*" (Prince is dead). The compositions are inspired, the production polished, and the New Power Generation supply music of breathtaking virtuosity: this is an album of endless surprises. Prince takes the concept used in the short movie *The Beautiful Experience* and inserts spoken segments called *NPG Operator* which guide listeners on a tour of the Prince universe, 1995 vintage. *The Gold Experience* was the first album released under the name ⚥. It is a pure marvel and recommended to anyone seeking to discover Prince's music. Essential and revolutionary.

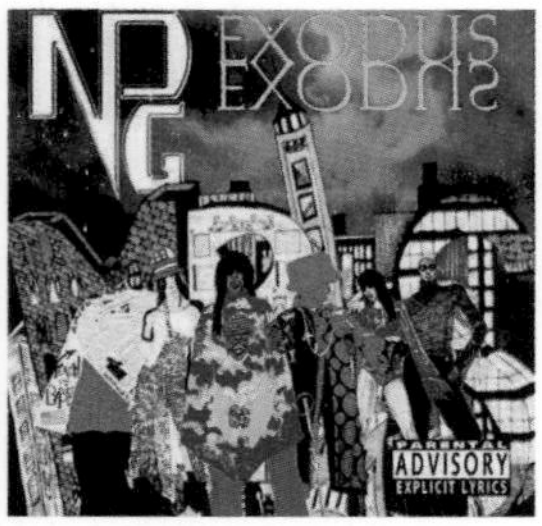

THE NEW POWER GENERATION *EXODUS* (ALBUM)

Released in the UK by NPG Records/Edel: 27 March 1995
(LP ref.: 0061031NPG - NPG 6103-1; CD ref.: EDL 4710-2)
Best chart ranking in the UK: 11

1. *GNPG Operator Intro*
2. *Get Wild*
3. *Segue*
4. *DJ Gets Jumped*
5. *New Power Soul*
6. *DJ Seduces Sonny*
7. *Segue*
8. *Count the Days*
9. *The Good Life*
10. *Cherry, Cherry*
11. *Segue*
12. *Return of the Bump Squad*
13. *Mashed Potato Girl Intro*
14. *Segue*
15. *Big Fun*
16. *New Power Day*
17. *Segue*
18. *Hallucination Rain*
19. *NPG Bum Rush the Ship*
20. *The Exodus Has Begun*
21. *Outro*

THE CALL TO EXODUS

On 15 May 1994, as he was preparing to present *Come* to the Warner Bros. Records team, Prince launched production of The New Power Generation's new album. Over the next few days, several tracks were recorded live at Paisley Park without the Game Boyz, who had departed by then, leaving the job of lead vocalist to bass player Sonny Thompson, accompanied by a very discreet Prince. In August 1994, the NPG recorded a new song for the soundtrack of Mike Binder's *Blankman* movie. Originally a 1992 Prince composition for Earth, Wind & Fire called *Super Hero,* the song was recorded this time around by the NPG, featuring The Steeles, and released as a single.

In December 1994 and January 1995, Prince continued producing his band's new album with the recording of new songs, including *The Good Life* and *Return of the Bump Squad. Exodus* was released on 27 March 1995 in just a few countries, including the UK and Australia, and Prince and Levi Seacer Jr (the head of NPG Records) decided not to release it in the USA. Only the single *The Good Life* was released in the US, where it failed to convince listeners, despite its unquestionable commercial potential. *Exodus*, with its strong emphasis on effective funk pop, partly jettisoned the hip-hop feel that used to ruffle fans' feathers, although Prince and Sonny T. occasionally let rip with some well-chosen rap parts. Of the 21 tracks on the album, only nine are songs, while the other 12 are segues, the spoken interludes that Prince was fond of at the time, but which tend to disturb the listening experience to the point of completely spoiling it. Prince gave various interviews to promote the album—during which he unveiled his new avatar Tora Tora (after the Japanese war cry uttered during the attack on Pearl Harbor), who generally wore a red, green, or black-and-white face veil. *Exodus* is a grain of sand in Prince's discography, but it marked another step toward Prince's emancipation as he strove for full artistic freedom. In the album's final track, *The Exodus Has Begun*, he implicitly calls on all artists to extricate themselves from their record companies and embrace independence.

FOR PRINCE ADDICTS

According to the sleeve notes, *Exodus* is dedicated to the memory of "His Royal Badness." This was a nickname given to Prince in 1984 by journalist Martin Keller of *City Pages*, a Minneapolis weekly.

Prince, aka Tora Tora, at a New Power Generation signing at the Virgin Megastore, in London, on 5 April 1995.

> In 1995, Michael B. and Sonny T., drummer and bass player for the New Power Generation, released a CD called *Funky-Ass Loops* on East West Communication. The disc, comprising 190 musical loops, was priced at $99.95. Why so expensive? Anyone who bought the CD could use any number of samples whenever they wanted in their own productions, without paying royalties to the two musicians.

Single

GET WILD

The New Power Generation / 4'33

Musicians: O(+>: rap, vocals, electric guitar / **Sonny T.:** vocals, bass / **Michael B.:** drums / **Tommy Barbarella:** synthesizers / **Mr Hayes:** Hammond organ / **Michael B Nelson:** trombone / **Kathy Jensen:** baritone saxophone / **Brian Gallagher:** tenor saxophone / **Dave Jensen:** trumpet / **Steve Strand:** trumpet / **Mayte:** spoken voice / **Recording:** **Paisley Park, Chanhassen, Minnesota:** 15 May 1994 / **Technical team:** **Producer:** O(+> / **Recording engineers:** David "Chronic Freeze" Friedlander, Ray Hahnfeldt, Steve Durkee / **Assistant recording engineers:** Kimm James, Shane T Keller, Kyle Bess
Single: 1. *Get Wild* (Single Version)/4'31 / **2.** ***Beautiful Girl*** (Single Mix)/4'31 / **3.** ***Hallucination Rain***/5'52 / **Released in the UK and Europe by NPG Records:** 20 March 1995 (CD single ref.: 0061045NPG - NPG 6104-5) / **Best chart ranking in the UK:** did not make the charts

Cowritten with Sonny Thompson but credited—like all the songs on the record—to The New Power Generation, *Get Wild* was recorded live during the first work session for *Exodus*. Prince then reworked it, adding his voice to Sonny T.'s. It was released as a promotional record in the US and as a single in the UK, having previously appeared on the soundtrack of the Robert Altman movie *Ready to Wear* (1994). When the movie was released in movie theaters in the US on 23 December 1994, the distributors opted for an Americanized name (*Ready to Wear*), but the soundtrack for the movie featuring *Get Wild* kept the original French title *Prêt à Porter*.

Single

COUNT THE DAYS

The New Power Generation / 3'24

Musicians: O(+>: vocals, acoustic guitar, electric guitar / **Sonny T.:** vocals, bass, backing vocals / **Michael B.:** drums / **Tommy Barbarella:** synthesizers / **Mr Hayes:** Hammond organ / **Recording:** **Paisley Park, Chanhassen, Minnesota:** May 1994 / **Technical team:** **Producer:** O(+> / **Recording engineers:** David "Chronic Freeze" Friedlander, Ray Hahnfeldt, Steve Durkee / **Assistant recording engineers:** Kimm James, Shane T Keller, Kyle Bess
Single: 1. *Count the Days* (Edit)/3'24 / **2.** ***Count the Days*** (Album Version)/3'24 / **3.** ***New Power Soul*** (Edit)/4'09 / **Released in the UK and Europe by NPG Records:** 25 September 1995 (CD single ref.: 0061335 NPG) / **Best chart ranking in the UK:** did not make the charts

Sung in unison by Prince and Sonny T., *Count the Days* is a soulful ballad that, thanks to its stripped-down arrangements, does not sound dated. The song was released as a single in the UK and Europe in an edited form, with the word "Motherfucker" in the verses replaced by thumps on the guitar and drums. It was one of the songs selected by Prince and Spike Lee for the soundtrack of the movie *Girl 6* (1996).

The bass player Sonny Thompson, the dancer Mayte, and the keyboard player Mr Hayes: three vital members of the NPG in 1995.

Single

THE GOOD LIFE

The New Power Generation / 5'48

Musicians: [symbol]: vocals, electric guitar, programming, backing vocals / **Sonny T.:** vocals, rap, bass, backing vocals / **Michael B.:** drums / **Tommy Barbarella:** synthesizers / **Mr Hayes:** Hammond organ / **Recording: Paisley Park, Chanhassen, Minnesota:** December 1994 to January 1995 / **Technical team:** Producer: [symbol] / Recording engineers: David "Chronic Freeze" Friedlander, Ray Hahnfeldt, Steve Durkee / **Assistant recording engineers:** Kimm James, Shane T Keller, Kyle Bess
CD single version (USA) / 1. ***The Good Life***/5'48 / **2.** ***Get Wild*** (Money Maker Remix)/6'01 / **CD single version (UK) / 1.** ***The Good Life*** (Edit)/4'01 / **2.** ***The Good Life*** (Platinum People Edit)/4'22 / **Released in the USA by NPG Records/Warner Bros. Records:** 13 June 1995 (CD single ref.: 9 17859-2) / **Released in the UK and Europe by NPG Records:** 7 August 1995 (CD single ref.: 0061835 NPG) / **Best chart ranking in the USA:** did not make the charts / **Best chart ranking in the UK:** 29

In the same vein as *Love Sign*, *Letitgo*, or *Pope*, *The Good Life* is a hip-hop nugget, flirting with the New Jack Swing style that was in vogue in the mid-1990s. Despite being released as a single in the US and the UK, the track did not go down in posterity, which is a shame because Prince gave the NPG one of his best songs here. It has a compelling chorus and an unassailable groove, but alas did not make the Billboard Hot 100 chart when it was released in June 1995.

RETURN OF THE BUMP SQUAD

The New Power Generation / 7'20

Musicians: [symbol]: singing, electric guitar, claps, programming / **Sonny T.:** vocals, bass / **Michael B.:** drums / **Tommy Barbarella:** synthesizers / **Mr Hayes:** Hammond organ / **Eric Leeds:** saxophone, flute / **Eric Bradford:** backing vocals / **James McGregor:** backing vocals / **Kathleen Bradford:** backing vocals / **Michael Bradford:** backing vocals / **Mayte:** spoken voice / **Recording: Paisley Park, Chanhassen, Minnesota:** December 1994 to January 1995 / **Technical team:** Producer: [symbol] / Recording engineers: David "Chronic Freeze" Friedlander, Ray Hahnfeldt, Steve Durkee / **Assistant recording engineers:** Kimm James, Shane T Keller, Kyle Bess

With a title worthy of a gangster movie, *Return of the Bump Squad* refers more to the Bible than to the world of besuited thugs and employs various choice expressions. "Bow Down Motherfucker, surrender your rod," sing Prince and Sonny T. in reference to the rod that Moses took from God's hands to perform wonders in Exodus, the second book of the Old Testament. Prince (or rather his avatar Tora Tora) systematically carried a walking stick when promoting the record, inevitably drawing a parallel between Moses leading his people to the Promised Land and Prince guiding his people to freedom, far from the clutches of the all-powerful record companies. The album's original title was *The Exodus Has Begun*.

The vocal group The Steeles appeared in several Prince songs, including *Still Would Stand All Time*, *Willing and Able*, *The Sacrifice of Victor*, and *The Exodus Has Begun*, by the New Power Generation.

BIG FUN

The New Power Generation / 7'26

Musicians: ♀: rap, electric guitar, percussion, claps, backing vocals / **Sonny T.**: vocals, bass / **Michael B.**: drums / **Tommy Barbarella:** synthesizers / **Mr Hayes**: organ / **Eric Leeds:** saxophone, flute / **Recording: Paisley Park, Chanhassen, Minnesota:** December 1994 to January 1995 / **Technical team:** Producer: ♀ / Recording engineers: David "Chronic Freeze" Friedlander, Ray Hahnfeldt, Steve Durkee / **Assistant recording engineers:** Kimm James, Shane T Keller, Kyle Bess

Although Prince's vocals are under-mixed throughout the track, they become more obvious from 6'38 and in the catchy line "Get freaky, let the head bob," which resurfaces in *Newpower Soul* in 1998. A version of *Big Fun* was recorded during NPG's appearance on The White Room in London, on 5 April 1995, which featured Angelo Moore, the legendary lead singer of Fishbone, on saxophone. The collaboration was cut in the final edit and only *Count the Days* was broadcast.

THE EXODUS HAS BEGUN

The New Power Generation / 10'06

Musicians: ♀: rap, spoken voice, vocals, electric guitar / **Sonny T.**: vocals, bass, backing vocals / **Michael B.**: drums, backing vocals / **Tommy Barbarella:** synthesizers, backing vocals / **Mr Hayes:** Hammond organ / **Statik:** programming / **Michael B Nelson:** trombone / **Kathy Jensen:** baritone saxophone / **Brian Gallagher:** tenor saxophone / **Dave Jensen:** trumpet / **Steve Strand:** trumpet / **Brother Jules:** scratching / **Jevetta Steele:** backing vocals / **Jearlyn Steele:** backing vocals / **J D Steele:** backing vocals / **Fred Steele:** backing vocals / **Kimm James:** spoken voice / **Levi Seacer Jr:** spoken voice / **Recording: Paisley Park, Chanhassen, Minnesota:** 15 May 1994 / **Technical team:** Producer: ♀ / Recording engineers: David "Chronic Freeze" Friedlander, Ray Hahnfeldt, Steve Durkee / **Assistant recording engineers:** Kimm James, Shane T Keller, Kyle Bess

The psychedelic funk of George Clinton at his best combined with the lyrical flights of the Steele brothers conclude *Exodus* in a mood of joyful chaos (the musical part ends here but the track is followed by a spoken outro). The Steeles, specialists in a gospel style that proves a perfect fit for Prince's religious references, offer a worthy follow-up to *Still Would Stand All Time* (*Graffiti Bridge*, 1990), while adapting to the hip-hop and funk textures of *Exodus*. Prince and his acolytes are convinced the exodus has begun and that freedom lies at the end of the road. We had to wait until the *Emancipation* album was released in 1996 to savor the taste of liberty.

PURPLE MEDLEY

Prince / 11'00

Musicians
Prince: vocals, electric guitar, acoustic guitar, bass, drums, programming, percussion, synthesizers, backing vocals
Sonny T.: bass
Michael B.: drums
Tommy Barbarella: synthesizers
Mr Hayes: synthesizers
Kirk Johnson: programming

Recording
Paisley Park, Chanhassen, Minnesota: spring 1994

Technical team
Producer: Prince
Recording engineers: Ray Hahnfeldt, Steve Durkee
Assistant recording engineer: Shane T Keller

Single version
A-side: ***Purple Medley*** (Edit)/3'14
B-side: ***Kirk J's B Sides Remix***/7'01

CD single version (UK)
1. *Purple Medley* (Edit)/3'14
2. *Purple Medley*/11'00
3. *Kirk J's B Sides Remix*/7'00
Released in the USA by Warner Bros. Records: 14 March 1995 (single ref.: 7-17903; CD single ref.: 2-17903)
Released in the UK by WEA International: 6 March 1995 (CD single ref.: W0289CD)
Best chart ranking in the USA: 84
Best chart ranking in the UK: 33

Genesis

In the early spring of 1994, in the middle of a personal artistic revolution, Prince decided to embark on a new project: producing a medley of the most famous songs in his repertoire. Under the supervision of technicians Ray Hahnfeldt, Steve Durkee, and Shane T Keller, who started as a night receptionist in Paisley Park and ended up as Prince's recording engineer, Prince brought elements of the following songs together in a *Purple Medley*, which is somewhat superfluous, granted, but fun nonetheless: *Batdance, When Doves Cry, Kiss, Erotic City, Darling Nikki, 1999, Baby I'm A Star, Diamonds and Pearls, Purple Rain, Let's Go Crazy, Sexy Dancer, Let's Work, Irresistible Bitch, Sexy M.F., I Wanna Be Your Lover, Alphabet St, Thieves in the Temple, 777-9311A Love Bizarre, If I Was Your Girlfriend, Raspberry Beret, Little Red Corvette, Peach, Cream*, and *It's Gonna Be A Beautiful Night*. In the UK, fans had to buy the 11-minute-long version of the track on a maxi-single, while in the US a version lasting three minutes and 14 seconds was released as a single.

Production

Not one to do things in the same way as everyone else, Prince chose to rerecord each part of the medley rather than create a montage of existing songs. With the exception of *Batdance*, which was inserted into the track using an E-Mu EMAX II sampler, all the tracks were reworked by the artist, sometimes accompanied by members of the New Power Generation. Had he decided to release the *Purple Medley* under his NPG Records label, he would have been able to recover the rights to his old songs (at least, for this single). This was the approach Taylor Swift took when she rerecorded her hit album *Fearless* in 2021. Instead, our artist decided to release *Purple Medley* on Warner Bros. Records, under the name Prince.

94 EAST FEATURING PRINCE SYMBOLIC BEGINNING (COMPILATION)

Released in the UK by Charly Records, London: 16 May 1995 (CD ref.: CPCD 8104-2)
Best chart ranking in the UK : did not make the charts

Disc 1

1. *Just Another Sucker*
2. *If You Feel Like Dancin'*
3. *Lovin' Cup*
4. *Games*
5. *Dance to the Music of the World*
6. *One Man Jam*

Disc 2

1. *If You See Me*
2. *Games (Original Version)*
3. *I'll Always Love You*
4. *Better Than You Think*
5. *If We Don't*
6. *You Can Be My Teacher*
7. *Love, Love, Love*
8. *Dance to the Music of the World (Practice Session)*
9. *If You See Me (Instrumental Version)*
10. *Games (Instrumental Version)*
11. *Better Than You Think (Instrumental Version)*

RINCE'S FIRST RECORDINGS

In 1974, Prince met his cousin Shauntel Manderville's new husband, Linster "Pepé" Willie, the nephew of Clarence Collins, baritone singer with Little Anthony and The Imperials. Pepé Willie's uncle had taught him how record companies functioned as well as the tricks of the trade to transform an ordinary song into a hit. Willie was therefore able to give Prince's band, Grand Central Corporation, valuable advice that the musicians followed to the letter, anxious to improve enough to land a recording contract as soon as they could. In late 1975, it was Prince's turn to do Willie a favor, when the latter, astounded by the young Prince's virtuosity, asked him to come and play on some demos he wanted to record at the Cookhouse Studios in Minneapolis. On 4 December, Prince met up with 94 East, the band Pepé Willie had put together for the occasion. Willie sings and plays the 6-string, with Pierre Lewis on synthesizers, Wendell Thomas on bass, Dale Alexander on drums, and backing singers Kristie Lazenberry and Marcy Ingvoldstad. Prince laid down numerous guitar lines on the tracks: *Better Than You Think*, *Games*, *If We Don't*, *I'll Always Love You*, and *If You See Me*. "That was the first time that he ever played in a studio and got paid," Willie recalled in 1995. "I thought he was the perfect guitar player to make my stuff work for me. I was playing mostly acoustic guitar, but he played the hell out of electric guitar. He was very funky and I liked his style and his input. He had a lot of creative ideas."[157]

After landing a contract with Polydor, Willie returned to Minneapolis in March 1977 to record two new songs at Sound 80 with Prince: *Fortune Teller* and *10:15*. At subsequent sessions, Prince recorded guitar, synthesizers, drums, or clavinet.

From 94 East to The Cookhouse Five

In 1995, with Pepé Willie's agreement, the label Charly Records released a compilation of tracks recorded almost twenty years earlier, on which Prince is credited as a musician. Although Prince does not sing on *Symbolic Beginning*, the songs are testament to a time when Prince Rogers Nelson was an unknown genius trying to make his way in the music business. Multiple, mostly unofficial, editions were released over the years, but *Minneapolis Genius*, the first compilation released in January 1985, and *Symbolic Beginning* (as well as its vinyl version, released by Charly Records in 2016) are the only versions approved by Pepé Willie.

In 2010, Willie returned to the Cookhouse Studios in Minneapolis with his old friend Matt "Doctor" Fink to remix the five songs recorded there 35 years earlier. He would go on to release them under the name The Cookhouse Five.

P. CONTROL

⚥ / 5'59

Musicians: ⚥: rap, vocals, bass, drums, programming, percussion, finger snapping, synthesizers, backing vocals / **Mayte:** spoken voice / **Recording: Paisley Park, Chanhassen, Minnesota:** 25 July 1994 / **Technical team: Producer:** ⚥ / **Recording engineer:** ⚥ / **Assistant recording engineer:** Shane T Keller

The term "pussy" being a metaphor for female genitalia, Prince decided to change the title of his song to *P. Control*. Behind the use of this vulgar word, there lurks a feminist song that deserves attention. Our artist, once criticized for the apparently misogynistic aspects of the movie *Purple Rain*, tells the story of a young girl who, in the first verse, is beaten up by her schoolmates, on whom she swears to take revenge when she grows up. As a woman, she goes for the more gratifying option of forgiving them their misdeeds, arguing that as boys they had not enjoyed such a stable upbringing as her and that their mothers had never taught them self-control. Beyond the story told by the song, which is narrated by Prince in an impeccable, flowing style, *P. Control* is an ambitious hip-hop track that catapults listeners into a multifaceted album.

1995

ENDORPHINMACHINE

⚥ / 4'06

Musicians: ⚥: vocals, rap, electric guitar, percussion, backing vocals / **Sonny T.:** bass / **Michael B.:** drums / **Tommy Barbarella:** synthesizers / **Mr Hayes:** Hammond organ / **Mayte:** spoken voice / **Recording: Paisley Park, Chanhassen, Minnesota:** 2 January 1993 / **Technical team: Producer:** ⚥ / **Recording engineer:** ⚥ / **Assistant recording engineer:** Shane T Keller

On 5 May 1994, the singer now sometimes known as The Artist walked onto the stage of *Nulle part ailleurs*, the flagship program of the French TV channel Canal +. Prince had left his fans on an R&B note with his single *The Most Beautiful Girl in the World*, which had been released three months earlier, so viewers couldn't believe their ears when he launched into *Endorphinmachine* in a deluge of saturated guitars, standing straight as a die behind his mic stand. Prince had never given his fans such a frenetic rock track, but the song is fully convincing right from the first note. With his Love Symbol Guitar slung over his shoulder (which alas ends up being thrown to the ground), our hero hammers out the growling chords while his beloved Mayte (see page 216) dances at his side. *Endorphinmachine* was initially slated to appear on the *Come* album but was postponed when the artist decided that it was a track for ⚥ rather than Prince, and its presence on the *Interactive* CD-Rom, released in June 1994, underscores this. The Endorphin Machine started out as the name given to the set Prince presented to fans on 7 June 1994, at a concert in Glam Slam Miami. "It's funny, I didn't really realize until I stood back away from it and looked at it, [...] and really saw what it was," Morris Hayes explains. "I'm like hey, wait a minute, like this is all like sexual parts. It's like there's that, and there's a womb here and there's this thing here, and it was really crazy. And everything just kind of went around that theme, like Endorphin machine, and we were playing in this Endorphinmachine, and so Prince is coming out of this womb with the curtain open on a conveyor belt [...]!"[162]

SHHH

⚥ / 7'16

Musicians: ⚥: vocals, electric guitar, backing vocals / **Sonny T.:** bass / **Michael B.:** drums / **Tommy Barbarella:** synthesizers / **Mr Hayes:** Hammond organ / **Mayte:** moans, choruses / **Recording: Paisley Park, Chanhassen, Minnesota:** 1994 / **Technical team: Producer:** ⚥ / **Recording engineer:** ⚥ / **Assistant recording engineer:** Shane T Keller

Michael Bland's drumming was never as powerful as on this soulful ballad from 1992. Written for Tevin Campbell for his 1993 album *I'm Ready*, the song was reworked by Prince, who added the majestic introductory drum rolls, a bridge, and an outro, inspired by the Ohio Players' *I Want To Be Free* from their 1974 album *Fire*. Mr Hayes, whose omnipresent Hammond B-3 organ lends color to the song, talked about how fond he was of this superb track. "I'm a church cat, and so Prince liked that influence from me [...] When he heard what I was doing, organ-wise, he really made that a central piece of the sound from that era [...] That's—when I came on, the Hammond came in. And so that got to be my thing, and so he just kind of let me do my thing as far as that, and just really put that at the forefront on that record. *Shhh* was crazy. I loved that because I can really hear it in the mix," he says.[162]

Martin Luther King Jr at the March on Washington for Jobs and Freedom, which took place on 28 August 1963.

WE MARCH

⚥ / 4'49

Musicians: **⚥:** vocals, electric guitar, bass, programming, tambourine, synthesizers, backing vocals / **Nona Gaye:** vocals, backing vocals / **Sonny T.:** vocals, backing vocals / **Kirk Johnson:** programming / **Ricky Peterson:** synthesizers / **Mayte:** spoken voice / **Recording:** **Guillaume Tell Studio, Suresnes, Paris:** November 1993 / **Paisley Park, Chanhassen, Minnesota:** spring 1994 / **Technical team:** **Producers:** ⚥, Ricky Peterson / **Recording engineer:** ⚥ / **Assistant recording engineer:** Shane T Keller

Twenty years before Prince recorded *Baltimore* as a tribute to the young Freddie Gray who died as a result of police violence during his arrest, *We March* in 1995 was a call for justice and equality between Americans, regardless of their skin color. "We ain't got no time for excuses, the promised land belongs to all/We can march in peace but you best watch your back if another leader falls," he sings in unison with Nona Gaye, referring to Martin Luther King and Malcolm X, the spiritual leaders who fought for the rights of African-Americans and were both assassinated for their beliefs. Prince had previously collaborated with Nona Gaye on *Love Sign*, and she cowrote *We March*, although this is not made explicit in the sleeve notes. Prince recorded some songs (including an early version of *Hide the Bone*, which subsequently featured on *Crystal Ball* in 1998), at the Studio Guillaume Tell in Suresnes, a Parisian suburb, between 10 November and 22 November 1993. *We March* was first recorded during these sessions before being reworked with Nona Gaye at Paisley Park.

1995

DOLPHIN

⚥ / 4'59

Musicians: ⚥: vocals, electric guitar, acoustic guitar, backing vocals / **Sonny T.:** bass / **Michael B.:** drums / **Tommy Barbarella:** synthesizers / **Mr Hayes:** synthesizers / **Lenny Kravitz:** backing vocals / **Recording: Paisley Park, Chanhassen, Minnesota:** 2 January 1993; 1993–1994 / **Technical team: Producer:** ⚥ / **Recording engineer:** ⚥ / **Assistant recording engineer:** Shane T Keller

Dolphin was unveiled to the general public on 30 September 1994 in a music video that saw Prince sporting the word "slave" on his cheek for the first time, as a sign that he would not be controlled by his record company. *Dolphin* expresses the artist's anger with Warner Bros. Records, which was refusing to release *The Gold Experience*. "You can cut off all my fins/But to your ways I will not bend/I'll die before I let you tell me how to swim/And I'll come back again as a dolphin," sings Prince, who a few years later confirmed that it was, indeed, his intention to settle the score with this song. "At the time EYE [I] felt oppressed by people who claimed 2 b charitible [sic] and proved just the opposite,"[114] he said. Keen observers will have noticed the presence of the singer Lenny Kravitz, taking his role of VIP backing vocalist very seriously. *The Gold Experience* was released in 1995, but it was several years before Kravitz's contribution to *Always On The Run* (and also *Billy Jack Bitch*) became known to fans. In 1999, Kravitz revealed to the British magazine *Touch* and the Catalan daily *El Periódico* his secret collaboration with Prince, who made no mention of him in the album credits. "You'd have to really listen and say 'oh that's Lenny,' you know what I mean? They were just like little secret momentoes,"[163] said the dreadlocked rocker sid.

NOW

⚥ / 4'30

Musicians: ⚥: rap, electric guitar, bass, drums, programming, tambourine, synthesizers, piano, backing vocals / **Michael B Nelson:** trombone / **Kathy Jensen:** baritone saxophone / **Brian Gallagher:** tenor saxophone / **Dave Jensen:** trumpet / **Steve Strand:** trumpet / **Recording: Paisley Park, Chanhassen, Minnesota:** 10 October 1993 / **Technical team: Producer:** ⚥ / **Recording engineer:** ⚥ / **Assistant recording engineer:** Shane T Keller

Unquestionably Prince's best hip-hop song (although there is stiff competition from *Days of Wild*, which was recorded during the same period), *Now* shines as much for his impeccable, flowing delivery as for the NPG Hornz' contributions, which bring an irresistible groove to the track. Prince's legendary humor comes through in the song's lyrics, when he tells listeners, "Don't worry about my name, it's too long to remember/I could tell you now but we'd be here 'til next September," as does his aversion to drugs, when he states (as he had previously in *Pope*) that his music is stronger than all the illicit substances in the world: "Fill us with the dope track, lick us, twist us, roll us in your mouth/Light us up and take a hit, light us up and take a hit," he sings, comparing his band to a joint. An essential track in Prince's 1990s' discography.

Elizabeth Berkley gave an unforgettable performance in the much-misjudged movie *Showgirls* by Paul Verhoeven (1995).

319

O(+> / 3'05

Musicians: O(+>: vocals, electric guitar, backing vocals / **Sonny T.:** bass / **Michael B.:** drums / **Tommy Barbarella:** synthesizers / **Mr Hayes:** synthesizers / **Ricky Peterson:** synthesizers / **Michael B Nelson:** trombone / **Kathy Jensen:** baritone saxophone / **Brian Gallagher:** tenor saxophone / **Dave Jensen:** trumpet / **Steve Strand:** trumpet / **Recording:** Paisley Park, Chanhassen, Minnesota: 25 October 1993 (brass) / **Technical team: Producers:** O(+>, Ricky Peterson / **Recording engineer:** O(+> / **Assistant recording engineer:** Shane T Keller

How can you forget Elizabeth Berkley's torrid pole dance in Paul Verhoeven's 1995 movie *Showgirls*? Because it was, of course, to the sound of *319* that the actress appeared onstage at Cheetah's Club in Las Vegas for the first time, performing her legendary dance routine that left actors Gina Gershon and Kyle MacLachlan (not to mention the audience) speechless. Prince stated in a 1997 chat hosted by Internet service provider AOL that the track was inspired by the former *Saved by the Bell* star. According to the Dutch director, there was a plan for Prince to do the whole soundtrack for the movie, but Prince never confirmed this. Instead, he wrote a second track for the movie, the very reggae-sounding *Ripopgodazippa* which was included on *Crystal Ball* in 1998.

FOR PRINCE ADDICTS

The voices of the operators that guide listeners through *The Gold Experience* album are those of Mayte and Ivana Raina, a receptionist at the Record Plant studios in Los Angeles. However, when Prince asks to be put though on the *NPG Operator* track that precedes *319*, it is Franco-Dutch singer Ophélie Winter that we hear saying: "*Un instant je vous connecte*" (One moment while I connect you).

Angelo Moore, Fishbone's charismatic singer, was very reluctant to be sampled in *Billy Jack Bitch*.

1995

SHY

[symbol] / 5'04

Musician: [symbol]: vocals, electric guitar, acoustic guitar, bass, tambourine, synthesizers, backing vocals / **Recording:** Paisley Park, Chanhassen, Minnesota: 10 October 1993 / **Technical team:** Producer: [symbol] / Recording engineer: [symbol] / **Assistant recording engineer:** Shane T Keller

In this tambourine-led acoustic ballad, Prince tells the story of a lonely man who meets a young woman. Her shy demeanor hides a deadly secret. She once killed a man by firing two bullets into his head after he murdered a friend of hers. Despite not being the type of woman he should mix with, the lonely man falls for her charms and throws caution to the wind. *Shy* was recorded at Paisley Park in the same set of sessions as *Now* and *Ripopgodazippa*, and gives listeners a welcome breather before the outstanding *Billy Jack Bitch*.

BILLY JACK BITCH

[symbol] / 5'32

Musicians: [symbol]: vocals, electric guitar, Fender Rhodes piano, backing vocals / **Sonny T.:** bass / **Michael B.:** drums / **Tommy Barbarella:** synthesizers / **Mr Hayes:** Hammond organ / **Michael B Nelson:** trombone / **Kathy Jensen:** baritone saxophone / **Brian Gallagher:** tenor saxophone / **Dave Jensen:** trumpet / **Steve Strand:** trumpet / **Lenny Kravitz:** backing vocals / **Ivana Raina:** spoken voice / **Recording:** Paisley Park, Chanhassen, Minnesota: October 1993 / **Technical team:** Producer: [symbol] / Recording engineer: [symbol] / **Brass arrangements:** [symbol], Michael B Nelson / **Assistant recording engineer:** Shane T Keller

Unhappy with being nicknamed Symbolina by gossip columnist Cheryl Johnson in the Minneapolis *Star Tribune*, Prince retaliated by writing a song called *Billy Jack Bitch* in which he addresses the journalist directly: "What if I called you silly names/Just like the ones that you call me?/What if I filled your eyes with tears/So many that you cannot see?" Prince only partially accepted responsibility for his lyrics, backtracking during an interview with the journalist in question in June 1997, claiming his diatribe was directed at all the Johnsons he had met in his life who had betrayed his trust. The unforgettable brass score by The NPG Hornz on the track combines a line created for the occasion with lines from a track called *New Dell Inn*, previously composed by trombonist Michael B Nelson. *New Dell Inn* would feature on the first album by the Hornheads in 1994. Prince inserted another extract into the track, sampled from *Lyin' Ass Bitch* by the Californian band Fishbone. This song featured on their first self-titled EP released in 1985. "He didn't ask permission," explained Angelo Moore, Fishbone's lead singer, "and we didn't get paid, but I thought 'Fine, he felt like a sample of my voice was good enough to convey what he wanted. I was ok with it.'"[21]

When the singer decided to change his name in June 1993, his entourage had to resort to various ruses to communicate with him. Staff at Paisley Park either called him The Artist Formerly Known As Prince (sometimes shortened to TAFKAP) or simply The Artist or sometimes even The Boss. Others would simply say "him" when talking about him, while Tommy Barbarella opted for "hey man" when addressing his employer. "I wish I had a dollar for every time someone asked me that,"[25] the keyboardist laughs when asked what he called Prince at the time.

Single

HATE U

/ 5'54

Musicians: : vocals, spoken voice, electric guitar, backing vocals / **Sonny T.:** bass / **Michael B.:** drums / **Tommy Barbarella:** synthesizers / **Mr Hayes:** Hammond organ / **Ricky Peterson:** synthesizers / **Ivana Raina:** spoken voice / **Recording:** **Paisley Park, Chanhassen, Minnesota:** 1994 / **Technical team:** **Producers:** , Ricky Peterson / **Recording engineer:** / **Assistant recording engineer:** Shane T Keller
Single: A-side: *Eye Hate U* (Edit)/4'27 / **B-side:** *Eye Hate U* (Quiet Night Mix by Eric Leeds)/3'55 / **Released in the USA by NPG Records/Warner Bros. Records:** 12 September 1995 (single ref.: 7-17811; CD single ref.: 5439-17811-2) / **Best chart ranking in the USA:** 12 / **Best chart ranking in the UK:** 20

Prince settles scores with an ex-girlfriend in this soulful ballad, which incorporates a particularly successful trial scene. In *Witness 4 The Prosecution* (1986), Prince was on the side of the witnesses in a sordid affair of the heart, but this time he takes on the role of the prosecutor presenting the facts before the accused: "U're being charged with one too many counts of heartbreaking in the 1st degree/I don't give a damn about the others/My main concern is U and me," he tells Carmen Electra, with whom he had had a brief romance a few years earlier. "And I was too young to really communicate with him," confides the young woman, "so I just kind of pulled away. And during that time I went out with a guy—I hadn't slept with this person—and Prince found out. He said, 'I wrote this song about you,' and then he played 'I Hate U.' It was hard to hear [...] I literally screamed in front of him. I think he just wanted me to hear it and know that he was really upset. Then he flew me back to Los Angeles."[30]

GOLD

/ 7'23

Musicians: : vocals, electric guitar, acoustic guitar, shaker, backing vocals / **Sonny T.:** bass / **Michael B.:** drums / **Tommy Barbarella:** synthesizers / **Mr Hayes:** synthesizers / **Ricky Peterson:** synthesizers / **Rain Ivana:** spoken voice / **Recording:** **Paisley Park, Chanhassen, Minnesota:** October 1993 / **Technical team:** **Producers:** , Ricky Peterson / **Recording engineer:** / **Assistant recording engineer:** Shane T Keller
Single version: A-side: *Gold* (Edit)/4'43 / **B-side:** ***Rock 'N' Roll Is Alive! (And It Lives In Minneapolis)***/4'34 / **CD single version** / **1.** *Gold* (Edit)/4'43 / **2.** ***Rock 'N' Roll Is Alive! (And It Lives In Minneapolis)***/4'34 / **3.** *Eye Hate U* (Extended Remix)/6'17 / **Released in the USA by NPG Records/Warner Bros. Records:** 30 November 1995 (single ref.: 7-17715; CD single ref.: 9 17715-2) / **Released in the UK by NPG Records/WEA International:** 30 November 1995 (CD single ref.: W0325CD) / **Best chart ranking in the USA:** 88 / **Best chart ranking in the UK:** 10

"I happen to think *Gold* is the best song I've ever done, but you'll never hear it,"[148] Prince told journalist Adam Mattera. When he gave this interview in March 1995, *The Gold Experience* was still owned by Warner Bros. Records, which was categorically refusing to release it. *Gold* had been recorded 18 months earlier, and at this rate risked being little more than a reflection of the past. However, once the entente cordiale between Prince and his record company had been signed, and the opus planned for release the following September, Prince was able to lift the lid on one of the major works in his discography. The high point of the album was *Gold*, a track made for stadiums and American FM rock stations. The song was released as a single in November, accompanied by a music video shot in Paisley Park, on 10 October 1995, in front of a crowd of lucky spectators. They were also the first to hear the B-side of *Gold*, entitled *Rock 'N' Roll Is Alive! (And It Lives In Minneapolis)* for which a video was shot the same day.

The irreplaceable Mayte Garcia, dancer and backing vocalist for the New Power Generation from 1992 to 1997.

HOWEVER MUCH U WANT

(DUET WITH [Love Symbol])

[Love Symbol] / 4'33

Musicians

Mayte: vocals, finger cymbals, backing vocals
[Love Symbol]: vocals, acoustic guitar, programming, synthesizers, claps, backing vocals
Sonny T.: bass
Michael B.: drums
Tommy Barbarella: synthesizers
Kirk Johnson: percussion, backing vocals
Damon Dickson: percussion, backing vocals
Levi Seacer Jr: backing vocals
D J Graves: scratching

Recording

Paisley Park, Chanhassen, Minnesota: December 1991; 1993–1995

Technical team

Producer: [Love Symbol]
Recording engineers: Michael Koppelman, Ray Hahnfeldt, Steve Durkee
Assistant recording engineers: Steve Noonan, Shane T Keller, Hans-Martin Buff

Mayte *Child of the Sun* (album)

Released in the USA by NPG Records/Phantom Sound & Vision: 27 November 1995 (CD ref.: 226202)
Released in the UK by NPG Records/Edel: 27 November 1995 (CD ref: Edel 0061622NPG)
Best chart ranking in the USA: did not make the charts
Best chart ranking in the UK: did not make the charts

Genesis

A talented dancer, amateur singer, and respected member of the New Power Generation, Mayte would be Prince's muse before becoming his wife in 1996. Inevitably, Prince produced an album for her. He launched the project on 13 September 1993 with an initial selection of tracks from The Vault that he thought would suit her. "I didn't want to do an album [...]," she explained in 2018. "I was content being in the band, and then later on starting my dance company and moving forward with that, but to do an album...I'll never forget it, we were in Spain, and he looked at me onstage and [he said] we're gonna do an album [...]"[158]

Production

After Mayte had recorded several covers from Prince's catalog, the artist began writing new songs for the album, which he continued producing until late 1994. Prince brought out a song he had first worked on with his protégée in 1991: *However Much U Want*. "That was a duet that we did when I first came to Minneapolis [...]," Mayte recalled. "It was supposed to be on the [Love Symbol] album, but it didn't make it. Well, he just remembered it. I loved that song and I really wanted it. So, we did it again and put it on my album."[159]

Just like *Exodus*, Mayte's album, *Child of the Sun*, was rejected by Warner Bros. and would be distributed by Phantom Sound & Vision in the US and Edel in the UK and Europe. The album, which was not as successful as hoped, bore all the hallmarks of the albums that Prince wrote and produced for his various protégés, including Vanity (see page 72), Sheila E., Jill Jones, Ingrid Chavez, and Carmen Electra.

Lenny Kravitz, a close friend of Prince, appeared as a discreet backing vocalist in several of his songs. Many of the numbers they made together are still lying dormant in The Vault.

ROCK 'N' ROLL IS ALIVE (AND IT LIVES IN MINNEAPOLIS)

Prince / 4'34

Musicians
♱: vocals, electric guitar, acoustic guitar, backing vocals
Sonny T.: bass
Michael B.: drums, tambourine
Tommy Barbarella: synthesizers
Mr Hayes: Hammond organ, synthesizers
Mayte: backing vocals

Recording
Paisley Park, Chanhassen, Minnesota: 9 and 12 September 1995

Technical team
Producer: ♱
Recording engineer: ♱

♱ ***Gold* (US single version)**
1. *Gold* (Edit)/4'43
2. *Rock 'N' Roll Is Alive (And It Lives In Minneapolis)*/4'34

♱ ***Gold* (UK maxi-single version)**
1. *Gold* (Edit)/4'43
2. *Rock 'N' Roll Is Alive (And It Lives In Minneapolis)*/4'34
3. *Eye Hate U* (Extended Remix)/6'17

Released in the USA by NPG Records/Warner Bros. Records: 30 November 1995 (single ref.: 7-17715; CD single ref.: 9 17715-2)
Released in the UK by NPG Records/WEA International: 30 November 1995 (maxi-single ref.: W0325CD - 9362-43571-2)
Best chart ranking in the USA: 88
Best chart ranking in the UK: 10

Genesis

On 9 September 1995, a concert was thrown at Paisley Park. The fans gathered and waited for their idol to show up. Electricity crackled in the air that night because the show would be filmed and broadcast on a special program, *Love 4 One Another*, which was scheduled to air on VH1 on 27 January 1996. Prince and The New Power Generation took to the stage at 11:45pm and played a typical set of the period, featuring *Purple Medley* and two tracks from *Exodus*: *Return of the Bump Squad* and *Get Wild*.

Production

It was the early hours of the morning of 10 September when the singer concluded his show by calling on his audience to shout out "*Rock 'N' Roll Is Alive (And It Lives In Minneapolis).*" Prince clearly had something in mind when he did so, as that day he couldn't stop talking about his friend Lenny Kravitz's new single *Rock 'n' Roll Is Dead*. The next day, he presented his musicians with a new song: *Rock 'N' Roll Is Alive! (And It Lives In Minneapolis)*, which was recorded on 12 September, with the addition of the spectators' chants from the concert. This song then appeared on the B-side of the single *Gold* as a shoutout to his rocker friend. Kravitz, not one to bear grudges, was in fact amused by this musical riposte and would frequently appear onstage with Prince, notably for the *Rave Un2 the Year 2000* concert, where they were filmed performing the classic *American Woman* together. On 17 December 2016, Lenny Kravitz posted on his Facebook page a photo of the lyrics of *Rock 'N' Roll Is Alive! (And It Lives In Minneapolis)*, along with the comment: "This was Prince's answer to *Rock 'n' Roll is Dead*. The inspiration we got from each other was a Godsend."[165]

CHAO

CHAOS AND DISORDER

Chaos and Disorder · I Like It There · Dinner with Delores
The Same December · Right the Wrong · Zannalee · I Rock, Therefore I Am
Into the Light · I Will · Dig U Better Dead · Had U

Released in the USA by Warner Bros. Records:
9 July 1996 (CD ref.: 9 46317-2)
Released in the UK by WEA International:
9 July 1996 (CD ref.: 9362-46317-2)
Best chart ranking in the USA: 26
Best chart ranking in the UK: 14

Prince and Mayte entwined in a photograph that featured in the program handed out to guests on their wedding day.

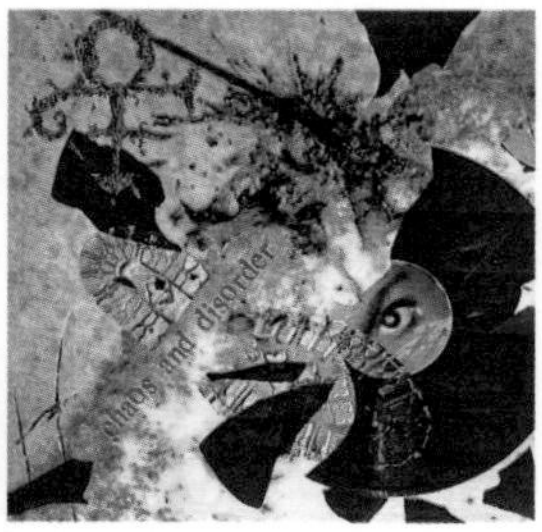

1996

PASSION AND FURY AT PAISLEY PARK

After completing *The Black Album* and *The Gold Experience* for Warner Bros. Records, Prince still needed to deliver three more albums to the label before he could gain his independence. With this in mind, while waiting impatiently for the label to give the green light for the release of *The Gold Experience*, in 1994 the singer started putting together some songs unearthed from The Vault (*Chaos and Disorder* and *Right the Wrong*) and chose others that had just been recorded (*I Like It There* and *The Same December*). Most would be reworked at Paisley Park in 1995 and 1996, with the aim of ending the collaboration between the two parties, which had become impossible to continue.

A funk-themed marriage

On 14 February 1996, Prince married Mayte (see page 216) in the United Methodist Church, Minneapolis. The extravagant ceremony (doves were released at the moment the vows were exchanged and the order of service was entitled *Coincidence or a sign of fate?*) was held in the presence of the couple's entourage, including the musicians Michael Bland and Morris Hayes, Prince's mother and her spouse, and various members of the couple's families. On 1 April a press release announced that the singer's young wife was pregnant and that the happy event would take place in November. The father-to-be then decided to make a large number of changes in his personal and professional life. First of all, he parted company from his group The New Power Generation, even though he included its musicians in some projects during that year. He also decided to transform Paisley Park into a more welcoming home for his family, and planned to slow down, for a while at least, the rate at which recordings, parties, and concerts were held there. He had only one project to complete: the album *Chaos and Disorder*, the final work he would record for Warner Bros. Records (even though his contract only ended officially after the release of *The Vault...Old Friends 4 Sale*—a compilation of unreleased songs which the record label released in 1999).

A raw and very rock record

To finish the production of this work, Prince took advantage of his stay in Florida at the end of March 1996, recording at South Beach Studios in Miami Beach. Over two days the singer, in the company of Michael Bland and Sonny Thompson, recorded new songs and revisited certain others. The songs had a rock sound, giving prominence to saturated guitars. "Even though I was working with an artist of this magnitude, he made me feel totally at ease by his ability to focus and get the heart of the matter which was laying down some of the most natural, fun and funkiest grooves I've heard in some time," explained César Sogbe, the recording engineer who worked on the Florida sessions.[166] In the album's final tracklist, some hip-hop moments also give an idea of the singer's state of mind when making other solo recordings. *Chaos and Disorder* was released on 9 July 1996 to general indifference, selling barely 150,000 copies and attaining one of the worst sales figures among Prince's records. However, far from having any interest in its success, during the summer of 1996 Prince was engaged in producing the album that would celebrate his new-found freedom: *Emancipation*.

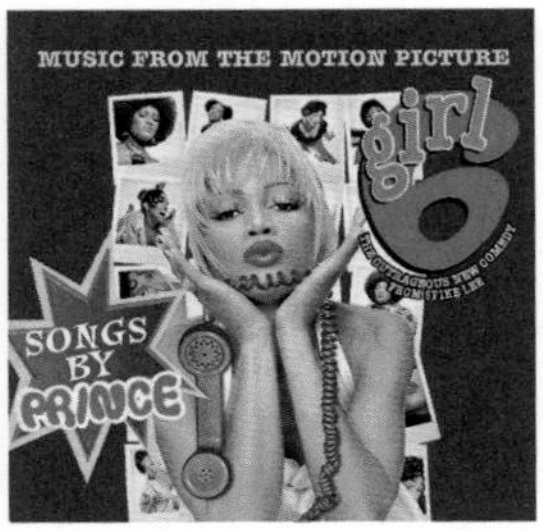

MUSIC FROM THE MOTION PICTURE GIRL 6 *

Released in the USA by Warner Bros. Records: 19 March 1996 (CD ref.: 9 46239-2)
Released in the UK by WEA International: 19 March 1996 (CD ref.: 9362-46239-2)
Best chart ranking in the USA: 75
Best chart ranking in the UK: did not make the charts

1. *She Spoke 2 Me* (Prince)
2. *Pink Cashmere* (Prince)
3. *Count the Days* (New Power Generation)
4. *Girls & Boys* (Prince and The Revolution)
5. *The Screams of Passion* (The Family)
6. *Nasty Girl* (Vanity 6)
7. *Erotic City* (Prince and The Revolution)
8. *Hot Thing* (Prince)
9. *Adore* (Prince)
10. *The Cross* (Prince)
11. *How Come U Don't Call Me Anymore* (Prince)
12. *Don't Talk 2 Strangers* (Prince)
13. *Girl 6* (New Power Generation)

* Music from The Motion Picture Girl 6 comprises songs by several artists; only unreleased songs performed by Prince are dealt with here.

WHEN SPIKE LEE GAVE PRINCE PRIDE OF PLACE

When Spike Lee met Prince in 1986, there was an immediate connection. The singer, who had greatly enjoyed *She's Gotta Have It*—at the time the director's latest feature-length movie—invited him to his complex at Paisley Park, which was about to open its doors. It was the start of a long friendship between the two artists, who vowed to work together in the future.

In the mid-1990s, Spike Lee mentioned to his friend that he wanted to make a movie built around his songs. The singer showed interest, even though his battle with Warner Bros. Records and the feeling of losing control over his own catalog did not make him inclined to work on new songs—which would, yet again, be the property of the record company. Spike Lee then embarked on the production of the movie *Girl 6*, about the adventures of a young actor who succumbs to the lure of well-paid work as an operator on a telephone sex hotline. With a screenplay by Suzan-Lori Parks and careful casting—including cameos by Quentin Tarantino, Madonna, and Naomi Campbell—the movie had everything that would appeal to Prince, who agreed that his music could be used. Eventually, once the movie was finished, the director and the singer made a compilation of songs from Prince's catalog. Although viewers were able to (re)discover *17 Days*, *Power Fantastic*, *Oilcan* (by NPG), and *4 The Tears in Your Eyes* when watching the movie, the original soundtrack, released in March 1996, was reduced to just 13 tracks, numbering various songs by Prince and his satellite groups, such as Vanity 6 (*Nasty Girl*) and The Family (*The Screams of Passion*). These included two unreleased songs from The Vault—*She Spoke 2 Me* and *Don't Talk 2 Strangers*—as well as a new piece written by Tommy Barbarella, with Prince singing as a duo with Nona Gaye, and performed by The New Power Generation: *Girl 6*. Derided by the critics, the movie was a resounding failure for the director who had made *Do the Right Thing* (1989) and *Mo' Better Blues* (1990). The movie's original soundtrack was also released to general indifference—all the more since it bore the name of Prince at a time when the singer was trying to get the media to use his new name, ⚥. Although fans shunned it from the outset, *Music From the Motion Picture Girl 6* is nevertheless an album recommended for listeners who wish to discover the many facets of our singer.

FOR PRINCE ADDICTS

Spike Lee was profoundly affected by the death of Prince on 21 April 2016. That same evening, he decided to organize a gathering in his friend's honor in front of the offices of his production company on South Elliott Place, Brooklyn. At 8pm fans came together to dance to their idol's music and celebrate—alongside the director, who was entirely dressed in purple—an unparalleled musical career.

SHE SPOKE 2 ME

Prince / 4'19

Musicians: Prince: vocals, backing vocals / **Levi Seacer Jr**: electric guitar / **Sonny T.:** bass / **Michael B.:** drums / **Kirk Johnson:** percussion / **Michael B** Nelson: trombone / **Kathy Jensen:** baritone saxophone / **Brian Gallagher:** tenor saxophone / **Dave Jensen:** trumpet / **Steve Strand:** trumpet / **Recording: Paisley Park, Chanhassen, Minnesota:** October 1991 / **Technical team: Producer:** Prince / **Recording engineers:** Michael Koppelman, David Friedlander, Steve Noonan, Ray Hahnfeldt, Brian Poer

Even though he was working on recording the album ⚥ in October 1991, Prince recorded this jazz number, in a similar vein to *Sexy M. F.* and *Love 2 the 9's*, with NPG. The version of *She Spoke 2 Me* used for the opening credits of the movie *Girl 6* is shortened to four minutes and 19 seconds, whereas the original version, lasting eight minutes and 20 seconds, would appear in 1999 on the album *The Vault...Old Friends 4 Sale*—the last released by Warner Bros. Records under the contract between Prince and his record label. It features numerous instrumental parts, including the solos by the virtuosi Levi Seacer Jr, Michael Bland, and Sonny Thompson, accompanied by the quintet The NPG Hornz on top form.

DON'T TALK 2 STRANGERS

Prince / 3'11

Musician: Prince: vocals, electric guitar, bass, drums, piano, synthesizers, claves, chimes, backing vocals / **Recording: Platinum Studios, Melbourne:** 16 April 1992 / **Technical team: Producer:** Prince / **Recording engineer:** ? (not confirmed)

While on his Diamonds and Pearls Tour in Australia, in April 1992, Prince took advantage of a break in Melbourne to work on recording new songs for the movie *I'll Do Anything*, directed by James L Brooks. The singer made *Don't Talk 2 Strangers* at Platinum Studios before continuing with the production of the original soundtrack at Studios 301 in Sydney from 25 April. Influenced by the screenplay of the movie, in which a mother is imprisoned and must entrust her young daughter to her ex-partner, Prince wrote a moving song with lyrics in which the narrator offers advice to her child, informing her in passing of her imminent departure. The actor Tracey Ullman, who plays the jailed mother, recorded her own version for the movie which was shelved when Prince left the project following disastrous test screenings. The song, which is delightful, replaced *Darling Nikki* in the selection of songs for *Girl 6*. It was rerecorded by Chaka Khan in early 1998 for her album *Come 2 My House*, which was released by NPG Records a few months later.

Single

GIRL 6

(THE NEW POWER GENERATION)

Prince, Tommy Barbarella / 4'04

Musicians: Prince: vocals, electric guitar, bass, programming, synthesizers, toy piano, backing vocals / **Nona Gaye:** vocals, backing vocals / **Kirk Johnson:** programming / **Recording: Paisley Park, Chanhassen, Minnesota:** December 1995 / **Technical team: Producer:** Prince / **Recording engineer:** ? (not confirmed)
Vinyl single and CD single version (USA): A-side: *Girl 6*/4'04 / **B-side:** *Nasty Girl* (Vanity 6)/5'14 / **CD single version (UK)** / **1.** *Girl 6*/4'04 / **2.** *Nasty Girl* (Vanity 6)/5'14 / **3.** *Erotic City* (Prince and The Revolution)/3'55 / **Released in the USA by NPG Records/Warner Bros. Records:** 26 March 1996 (single ref.: 7-17710; CD single ref.: 2-17710) / **Released in the UK and Europe by Warner Music International:** 26 March 1996 (CD single ref.: WO 346 CD) / **Best chart ranking in the USA:** did not make the charts / **Best chart ranking in the UK:** did not make the charts

In December 1995, Tommy Barbarella, one of the two keyboard players for the New Power Generation, wrote the instrumental part of what would become *Girl 6*. When the outline of the song was shown to Prince, he rerecorded it in its entirety, then gave it lyrics that fitted the movie being made and a title which, with its echoes of his former protégés Vanity 6 (see page 72) and Apollonia 6 (see page 91), would amuse his fans. Prince then invited Nona Gaye, who had already featured in *Love Sign* (on *1-800 NEW FUNK*, in 1994) and *We March* (on *The Gold Experience*, in 1995), to sing alongside him. He offered Spike Lee the only new song to feature on the original soundtrack of *Girl 6*, heard with the movie's closing credits. It includes spoken extracts from the movie, as well as samples from *Raspberry Beret* and *Housequake*. In 2019, the composer James Brandon sued The Prince Estate and Spike Lee, claiming that the chorus of *Girl 6* was a copy of his song *Phone Sex*, which he had suggested to the director some time previously. In December 2020, the Florida court of appeal dismissed the case, freeing The Prince Estate from any further legal proceedings. Although the pronunciation of the titles *Phone Sex* and *Girl 6* is the only slight similarity between the two songs, it should be pointed out that Brandon's song does contain choruses that are strongly "inspired" by another Prince song: *Gett Off*.

HEADPHONES AT THE READY

The introduction of *Chaos and Disorder* features a short extract from the animated series *Beavis & Butt-Head*, in which Beavis says: "Check, check. Cool. OK, rolling." At the end, between 3'45 and 4'00, Ophélie Winter says, in French, then in Spanish, and finally in English: "I'm not going to tolerate you sleeping with another woman." Listen carefully—it is definitely her, buried in the mixing!

After a brief romantic liaison with Prince, the singer Ophélie Winter was to remain a faithful friend with whom he met every time he stayed in Paris.

1996

CHAOS AND DISORDER

⚥ / 4'18

Musicians: ⚥: vocals, electric guitar, backing vocals / **Sonny T.:** bass / **Michael B.:** drums / **Tommy Barbarella:** synthesizers / **Mr** Hayes: Hammond organ / **Rosie Gaines:** backing vocals / **Mayte:** backing vocals / **Ophélie Winter:** spoken voice / **Recording: Paisley Park, Chanhassen, Minnesota:** October 1993; winter 1995–1996 / **Studios Davout, Paris**: 1993 (voice of Ophélie Winter) / **Technical team: Producer:** ⚥ / **Recoding engineers:** David "Chronic Freeze" Friedlander, Ray Hahnfeldt, Shane T Keller, Steve Durkee

Fans who bought the videocassette *Prince Live!—The Sacrifice of Victor*, released on 6 March 1995 and featuring the aftershow given by Prince at Bagley's Warehouse, London, on the morning of 8 September 1993, will recognize the guitar riff in *Chaos and Disorder*. Indeed, at this time Prince was in the habit of adding this lively figure on a 6-string guitar at the end of the song *Peach*. Using this riff to make a new song, he created a true rock 'n' roll moment worthy of *Endorphinmachine* (on *The Gold Experience*, 1995) or *Interactive*, which featured on *Crystal Ball* in 1998. Before revealing this song on the *Chaos and Disorder* album, Prince published the lyrics in the form of a poem in the first issue of *New Power Generation Magazine*, which was published by Paisley Park Enterprises in 1994. In this statement, he lists the evils of the world (third-rate journalism, pervasive sadness, betrayal, AIDS, and more), which are "ruining my world today." After rerecording this unreleased song with Michael Bland and Sonny Thompson during some sessions in Florida during the spring of 1996, Prince finally opted for the original version, recorded with all the members of NPG in October 1993.

Prince introduces his promotional single *Dinner with Delores* on the *Late Show with David Letterman* on 2 July 1996.

I LIKE IT THERE

[symbol] / 3'15

Musicians: [symbol]: vocals, electric guitar, backing vocals / **Sonny T.:** bass / **Michael B.:** drums / **Recording:** Paisley Park, Chanhassen, Minnesota: 1994 / **Technical team:** Producer: [symbol] / **Recording engineers:** David "Chronic Freeze" Friedlander, Ray Hahnfeldt, Shane T Keller, Steve Durkee

Recorded with the Paisley Park Power Trio, which Prince formed with Michael B. and Sonny T., *I Like It There* is a perfect example of the virtuosity of the musicians with whom the singer associated. Prince later added only vocal overdubs to the song, in which he declares his desire to his lady love, adding with a touch of humor: "U know how much I love you/More than I love my hair."

Single

DINNER WITH DELORES

[symbol] / 2'45

Musicians: [symbol]: vocals, electric guitar, acoustic guitar, synthesizers, backing vocals / **Sonny T.:** bass / **Michael B.:** drums / **Recording:** South Beach Studios, Miami Beach, Florida: March to April 1996 / **Technical team:** Producer: [symbol] / **Recording engineer:** César Sogbe / **Assistant recording engineer:** Femio Hernandez

Single: 1. *Dinner with Delores*/2'46 / **2.** *Had U*/1'27 / **3.** *Right the Wrong*/4'40 / **Released in the UK by WEA International:** 29 July 1996 (CD single ref.: 9362 43742-2 – W0360CD) / **Best chart ranking in the UK:** 36

Released as a single in the UK, Japan, and Germany, *Dinner with Delores* describes a dinner with a woman who is hungry... for sex and finds no favor in Prince's eyes. It was doubtful whether American radio stations would have appreciated the image of this greedy young woman, which is why the song was given only a promotional release in the US. The song was first recorded at Paisley Park, and then a second time in Miami Beach, during the sessions in March and April 1996. This revisited version was retained for *Chaos and Disorder*.

Prince performed *Dinner with Dolores* and *Zannalee* on *The Today Show*, which was filmed outside the Rockefeller Center Plaza, in New York, on 9 July 1996.

THE SAME DECEMBER

[symbol] / 3'23

Musicians: [symbol]: vocals, electric guitar, backing vocals / **Sonny T.:** bass / **Michael B.:** drums / **Tommy Barbarella:** synthesizers / **Mr** Hayes: Hammond organ / **Recording: Paisley Park, Chanhassen, Minnesota:** 1994 / **Technical team: Producer:** [symbol] / **Recording engineers:** David "Chronic Freeze" Friedlander, Ray Hahnfeldt, Shane T Keller, Steve Durkee

Alternating rhythmic motifs throughout the song, Prince goes from rock to blues in the middle of *The Same December*, concluding with a flourish of soul worthy of Tina Turner at the time of her recordings with her brilliant (and violent) husband, Ike. The singer clearly references Jesus Christ, born on 25 December, when he states: "We all come from the same December/And in the end that's where we'll go." Behind this biblical image is a pacifist message, which again takes center stage in the song *Last December* on *The Rainbow Children*, an album that Prince would release in 2001 and in which he sings: "In the name of the Father/In the name of the Son/We need to come together/Come together as one."

RIGHT THE WRONG

[symbol] / 4'38

Musicians: [symbol]: vocals, spoken voice, electric guitar, acoustic guitar, claps, backing vocals / **Sonny T.:** bass / **Michael B.:** drums, tambourine / **Tommy Barbarella:** synthesizers / **Mr** Hayes: Hammond organ / **Michael B** Nelson: trombone / **Kathy Jensen:** baritone saxophone / **Brian Gallagher:** tenor saxophone / **Dave Jensen:** trumpet / **Steve Strand:** trumpet / **Recording: Paisley Park, Chanhassen, Minnesota:** October 1993 / **Technical team: Producer:** [symbol] / **Recording engineers:** David "Chronic Freeze" Friedlander, Ray Hahnfeldt, Shane T Keller, Steve Durkee

Prince adopts a Texan accent to tell the story of a young Native American woman who has buried her grandfather in the Black Hills, which stretch from South Dakota to eastern Wyoming. Rumor had it that there was gold in this mountain range, so the Black Hills were annexed by the American settlers in violation of the Treaty of Fort Laramie (1868), even though the latter safeguarded the territory of Native Americans from invasion by colonizers—an episode that bears witness to the lack of respect for the indigenous peoples. The singer exhorts the listener—and people in positions of power in general—to correct their mistakes for a better tomorrow. Perfectly in keeping with the rest of the album, this song is marked by numerous rhythmic changes and a stirring melody.

ZANNALEE

[symbol] / 2'43

Musicians: [symbol]: vocals, spoken voice, electric guitar, backing vocals / **Sonny T.:** bass / **Michael B.:** drums / **Tommy Barbarella:** synthesizers / **Mr** Hayes: synthesizers / **Recording: Paisley Park, Chanhassen, Minnesota:** May 1993 / **South Beach Studios, Miami Beach, Florida:** March to April 1996 / **Technical team: Producer:** [symbol] / **Recording engineers:** David "Chronic Freeze" Friedlander, Ray Hahnfeldt, Shane T Keller, Steve Durkee, César Sogbe (South Beach Studios), / **Assistant recording engineer:** Femio Hernandez (South Beach Studios)

Initially recorded at Paisley Park, *Zannalee* was reworked at South Beach Studios in spring 1996. In the meantime, Prince, Michael Bland, and Sonny Thompson recorded a bluesy version during the sessions for *The Undertaker*, an album that was recorded on 14 June 1993, but then put away in The Vault because Warner Bros. Records refused to distribute it. The only way to experience this other interpretation of the song is to unearth, via the Internet, a VHS of those sessions, filmed by Parris Patton and enlivened by images of the actor Vanessa Marcil, who was a close friend of Prince's at the time. The version released on *Chaos and Disorder* is nonetheless one of the most interesting, not least because it features the whole of the NPG (apart from Mayte). Mayte made known her feelings about the sessions for the album to journalist Christophe Geudin of the French website Funk U: "Prince was really angry with his record label, and he was to complete his contractual commitment with this album commission," she explained. "He was always going on about things like 'I have to do this thing, but I really don't want to.' One day, we were in Miami with Sonny T. and Michael B. to finish the album, and this really got to him. He listened to the playbacks again and said: 'I don't want to work on these songs.' But he went at it with all his aggressiveness and anger, and you can hear that in the music. I really love this album."[164]

I ROCK, THEREFORE I AM

[symbol] / 6'14

Musicians: [symbol]: vocals, electric guitar, bass, drums, programming, synthesizers, Hammond organ, backing vocals / **Scrap D.:** rap / **Steppa Ranks:** rap / **Michael B** Nelson: trombone / **Kathy Jensen:** baritone saxophone / **Brian Gallagher:** tenor saxophone / **Dave Jensen:** trumpet / **Steve Strand:** trumpet / **Rosie Gaines:** backing vocals / **Recording: Paisley Park, Chanhassen, Minnesota:** March 1996 / **Technical team: Producer:** [symbol] / **Recording engineers:** David "Chronic Freeze" Friedlander, Ray Hahnfeldt, Shane T Keller, Steve Durkee

Here, Prince has adapted philosopher René Descartes's famous maxim, "I think, therefore I am." It sounds like an outtake from the time of *Diamonds and Pearls*, yet *I Rock, Therefore I Am* was recorded in 1996, in the company of the vocalists Scrap D. and Steppa Ranks. With a raggamuffin feel to it that was already dated at the time, the song only stands out by virtue of the fact that it features a reunion of Prince with Rosie Gaines, whose voice is very prominent.

INTO THE LIGHT

[symbol] / 2'46

Musicians: [symbol]: vocals, electric guitar, backing vocals / **Sonny T.:** bass / **Michael B.:** drums / **Tommy Barbarella:** synthesizers / **Mr Hayes:** Hammond organ / **Michael B** Nelson: trombone / **Kathy Jensen:** baritone saxophone / **Brian Gallagher:** tenor saxophone / **Dave Jensen:** trumpet / **Steve Strand:** trumpet / **Rosie Gaines:** backing vocals / **Recording: Paisley Park, Chanhassen, Minnesota:** February 1996 / **Technical team: Producer:** [symbol] / **Recording engineers:** David "Chronic Freeze" Friedlander, Ray Hahnfeldt, Shane T Keller, Steve Durkee

When asked about his taste in literature, Prince told a journalist from *Vox Magazine* that the latest book he had read, *Embraced by the Light* by Betty Jean Eadie, had touched him profoundly. The novel, which deals with the experience of imminent death, had enlightened him regarding facts of life that are not to be overlooked, and so he decided to put this experience into a song, *Into the Light*, which is imbued with spirituality. The song is also significant in the story of the New Power Generation, since it was recorded during the last sessions Prince held with his musicians, before their contract came to an end (although Michael B. and Sonny T. would nonetheless take part in the Florida sessions in 1996).

I WILL

[symbol] / 3'35

Musicians: [symbol]: vocals, electric guitar, backing vocals / **Rosie Gaines:** vocals, backing vocals / **Sonny T.:** bass / **Michael B.:** drums / **Tommy Barbarella:** synthesizers / **Mr** Hayes: synthesizers / **Michael B** Nelson: trombone / **Kathy Jensen:** baritone saxophone / **Brian Gallagher:** tenor saxophone / **Dave Jensen:** trumpet / **Steve Strand:** trumpet / **Recording: Paisley Park, Chanhassen, Minnesota:** February 1996 / **Technical team: Producer:** [symbol] / **Recording engineers:** David "Chronic Freeze" Friedlander, Ray Hahnfeldt, Shane T Keller, Steve Durkee

Recorded during the final sessions Prince held with his musicians in the NPG, the ballad *I Will* was made at the same time as *Sarah* (which features on *The Vault...Old Friends 4 Sale*) and *Da Bang*, on the triple album of previously unreleased songs *Crystal Ball*, which would be released in 1998. The feeling of urgency can be felt through the course of the album, and, despite its creator's bitterness, some real gems were made during those sessions—notably *I Will*, in which the voice of Rosie Gaines is even more delicate than usual.

Portrait by the photographer Tony Bock of the *Toronto Star*, which was taken on 16 December 1996.

DIG U BETTER DEAD

⚥ / 4'00

Musicians: ⚥: vocals, programming, synthesizers, backing vocals / **Rosie Gaines:** backing vocals / **Recording:** **Paisley Park, Chanhassen, Minnesota:** 1996 / **Technical team:** **Producer:** ⚥ / **Recording engineers:** David "Chronic Freeze" Friedlander, Ray Hahnfeldt, Shane T Keller, Steve Durkee

Here is a return to the rhythms of the hip-hop period of *Diamonds and Pearls* or ⚥. *Dig U Better Dead* would have been the perfect single to promote the highly underrated *Chaos and Disorder*. In the song, Prince describes yet again a society in which individualism is king, and urges us to take a more altruistic path, looking after our neighbor instead. Spirituality, together with a certain amount of reflection on a more open society, is an integral part of Prince's output during the second half of the 1990s. It runs beneath the surface in *Chaos and Disorder*, and would be a constituent element of *Emancipation* a few months later.

HAD U

⚥ / 1'25

Musician: ⚥: vocals, electric guitar, synthesizers / **Recording:** **Paisley Park, Chanhassen, Minnesota:** 1996 / **Technical team:** **Producer:** ⚥ / **Recording engineers:** David "Chronic Freeze" Friedlander, Ray Hahnfeldt, Shane T Keller, Steve Durkee

Prince concluded his final submission to Warner Bros. Records with this brief, mysterious song, the lyrics of which are simply a series of verbs preceding a personal pronoun in the second person. The singer manages to summarize brilliantly, in a few lines, the feeling of love and the relationship between two lovers, singing: "Called U/Found U/Begged U/Convinced U/Saw U/Held U/Kissed U," and concluding with "Hurt U/Disappoint U/Fuck U/Had U."

EMANCIPATION

DISC 1

Jam of the Year · Right Back Here in My Arms · Somebody's Somebody · Get Yo Groove On
Courtin' Time · Betcha By Golly Wow! · We Gets Up · White Mansion · Damned If 👁 Do
👁 Can't Make U Love Me · Mr. Happy · In This Bed 👁 Scream

DISC 2

Sex in the Summer · One Kiss At A Time · Soul Sanctuary · Emale · Curious Child
Dreamin' About U · Joint 2 Joint · The Holy River · Let's Have A Baby · Saviour
The Plan · Friend, Lover, Sister, Mother/Wife

DISC 3

Slave · New World · The Human Body · Face Down · La, La, La Means 👁 Love U · Style
Sleep Around · Da, Da, Da · My Computer · One of Us · The Love We Make · Emancipation

Released in the USA by NPG Records/EMI-Capitol:
19 November 1996 (CD regular version ref.: 7243 8 54982 2 0 – E2-54982;
CD clean version ref.: 7243 8 55063 2 1 – E2-55063)
Released in the UK by NPG Records/EMI-Capitol:
18 November 1996 (CD ref.: 7243 8 54982 2 0)
Best chart ranking in the USA: 11
Best chart ranking in the UK: 18

Prince asked the photographer Steve Parke to create this montage himself for the promotion of the *Emancipation* album.

BREAKING HIS CHAINS

Eager to free himself from the clutches of Warner Bros. Records, in 1996 Prince delivered to the label the disturbing, and to say the least divisive, *Chaos and Disorder*. Compiled mostly of songs unearthed from The Vault, the album lacked freshness and was not convincing when it was released on 9 July, all the more so since the artist carried out no promotional work to help it achieve any kind of success. However, the year 1996 was an important one for the singer, who was preparing for many changes, both personal and professional. While *Chaos and Disorder* was a mere footnote in Prince's output, a major album was already in production: the monumental *Emancipation*, which would celebrate our artist's new-found artistic freedom. Here is a look back at a pivotal year in Prince's story.

Early upheavals

Following the European The Ultimate Live Experience Tour, the Japan '96 Tour allowed Prince to show his Japanese fans all the energy condensed into his albums *Come* (1994) and *The Gold Experience* (1995). In February 1996, the singer returned to Paisley Park and made a series of major changes. On 14 February he married Mayte Garcia (see page 216) and launched his first website, TheDawn.com. The site's name was not chosen by chance, since it was used by Prince to announce his forthcoming artistic rebirth. As well as pages giving information on his catalog and containing video and audio clips, the website featured a hidden page entitled *Message from the Artist*, where Prince gave fans his version of the battle with Warner Bros. Records. "I would never be able to leave the legacy of my music to my family, my future children, or anyone," he explained "because 'Prince' did not own the Masters—I did not, and still do not, own my Art."[167]

On 8 March, the artist announced the breakup of the New Power Generation and did not renew the contracts of the group's musicians and technicians. On 19 April, the *Star Tribune*, a Minneapolis daily, announced in its pages the temporary closure of the studios at Paisley Park and informed musicians who had booked sessions there that they should seek other recording venues. Paisley Park also let go of numerous employees, as part of budget cuts that were explained by Julie Knapp-Winge, one of the complex's two directors (the other was Therese Stoulil, the former archivist at Paisley Park who had become Prince's personal assistant) in the following terms: "Paisley Park is moving in a new direction as it prepares for the challenges of the 21st century and the aggressive corporate goals we have set for ourselves."[168]

Paisley Park, a family cocoon

As Paisley Park closed its doors to the public, Prince was preparing to accommodate his family there. Indeed, Mayte had announced her pregnancy via a press release on 1 April, and the premises would soon welcome the newlyweds' child. Prince transformed his complex in Chanhassen into a cocoon where his child would be born and he could work calmly on his next album. Now with no official group, the singer unleashed a seemingly endless creative flow, with the help of his closest associates. Kirk Johnson, who was first a dancer and then a remixer for Prince, became the album's co-arranger. He said: "We worked nonstop. We'd cut three or four songs in one day. He'd come in with a new song or a new idea every day."[169] Of the various recording engineers

emancipation

Arms raised in protest... the singer in search of freedom, February 1997.

On 22 July 1997, the singer held a press conference at the Millennium Hotel Broadway, in New York, to promote his Jam of the Year Tour.

who would work on the record, Hans-Martin Buff, the newcomer who initially helped Tom Tucker before securing his place as Prince's official studio technician, would unquestionably be one of the most important creators of the artist's sound during the second half of the 1990s. In June 1996, the singer began to rehearse with the musicians who would form the third lineup of the New Power Generation. While Morris Hayes was still on keyboards, Kirk Johnson replaced Michael Bland on drums and the veteran Eric Leeds intermittently returned to his role as saxophonist. Two new recruits, recommended to Prince by Sheila E., joined the ranks: the guitarist Kathleen "Kat" Dyson, who had got herself noticed playing alongside Dave Stewart, and the bass guitarist Rhonda Smith. These two musicians joined the group following a jam session organized at Paisley Park in the company of Prince and Kirk Johnson. More often than not working alone with his technician, or sometimes accompanied by one of his musicians, Prince would go on to record a multitude of songs until the following autumn, when the album *Emancipation* was finished.

EMI-Capitol, a partner for the duration of one album

Finally free of his contractual commitments to Warner Bros. Records, in September 1996 Prince assessed the options open to him. After meeting with the management of Sony, Polygram, and BMG, he settled on EMI-Capitol; the partnership was officially announced on 17 October via a press release issued by the company's CEO, Charles Koppelman. He stated: "We're thrilled and deeply honored to begin a relationship with the Artist Formerly Known As Prince. He's a ground-breaker, a risk-taker, and a genius. People in our industry overuse the word 'artist,' but he is one in every sense of the word. This is a moment in time that will last forever."[170] EMI-Capitol was responsible for the distribution and promotion of the album, which was produced by NPG Records, while Prince, naturally, would retain ownership of the rights to the songs as well as of the master tapes.

A family drama

Prince had hoped that the release of *Emancipation* would coincide with the birth of his first child—a sequence of happy events bearing witness to the rebirth not only of the artist, but also of the man he was at that time. Amiir Nelson was born on 16 October at the Northwestern Hospital in Minneapolis. He had a serious skull deformity, which was the result of Pfeiffer syndrome. The child was operated on twice, but died on 23 October from complications linked to his illness. His parents had given their consent for life

support to be withdrawn. Prince and his young bride were devastated by this tragedy. Yet, incomprehensibly, the artist decided to keep the ordeal he was suffering from the media and told journalists that his child was in good health. Finding refuge in his art, Prince decided to work on the promotion of his album, while remaining profoundly affected by this episode. "I didn't really know what to do, other than to just try to comfort him," said his friend and musician Morris Hayes. "[...] It was very heartbreaking. It was really tough. And he had to continue after that. That was so difficult because he was trying to do all these things to get himself back into the headspace [...], and that's when you see the mental fortitude of somebody who is able to absorb all of that grief and find some way to keep going."[54]

Three hours of love, sex, & liberty

It was past midnight on 25 October 1996 when Prince and the new lineup of NPG went on stage at Paisley Park for a concert aimed at introducing his new songs to eager fans. Despite his personal pain, the artist performed for three evenings in succession and in the process settled in his new recruits so they would be ready for the colossal tour that he would embark on a few months later. On 18 November, *Emancipation* was launched in the UK (it appeared the next day in the US) with the slogan: "Three hours of love, sex, & liberty." Released as a triple album, it is a monumental work. Each CD contains an hour of music to enchant fans, who were much satisfied to hear 36 new songs by their idol. "This is my most important record. I'm free, and my music is free,"[171] Prince told Jon Bream of the *Star Tribune*, Minneapolis. "I worked on it for a year and I must admit I'm amazed by the results. I think *Emancipation* is, without a doubt, the best album of my whole career,"[172] he proudly announced to Solange Plamondon of *Hello!* magazine. Although the press acknowledged the scale of the production, it was more critical regarding the triple album's content, emphasizing the lack of artistic risk-taking and a certain weakness in the writing of the songs, which are chiefly R&B in style. Remaining defiant in the face of the negative reviews, on 7 January 1997 Prince embarked on The Love 4 One Another Charities Tour, a charitable initiative that had been launched with two evenings at Paisley Park on the 27 and 28 December, the goal of which was to raise funds for various American foundations.

On 21 July 1997, the Jam of the Year World Tour was launched; despite its name, it never left North America. With the support of EMI-Capitol, Prince undertook an unprecedented promotion of *Emancipation*, giving multiple interviews and being unusually open with journalists. With all due respect to fans of this album, which is a major one in Prince's career because of its message of freedom, few of its songs stand out among Prince's output. Once its calming effect had worn off, Prince was able to renew himself with a funk style that he mastered to perfection in the *Newpower Soul* album in 1998.

JAM OF THE YEAR

⚥ / 6'09

Musicians: ⚥: vocals, electric guitar, bass, piano, synthesizers, finger cymbals, backing vocals / **Eric Leeds:** saxophone, flute / **Walter Chancellor Jr:** saxophone / **Rosie Gaines:** backing vocals / **Recording: Paisley Park, Chanhassen, Minnesota:** winter 1995–1996 / **Technical team: Producer:** ⚥ / **Arrangements:** ⚥, Kirk Johnson / **Recording engineers:** Tom Tucker, Ray Hahnfeldt, Steve Durkee, Shane T Keller

Recorded during the same period as *Chaos and Disorder*, the sessions for which often saw the reappearance of Rosie Gaines, *Jam of the Year* makes an ideal introduction to the album, showing as it does its author's more R&B side. In 1997 it was remixed and enlivened with a rap by Doug E Fresh for release as a single, but was eventually shelved before being reworked to be reborn as *Push It Up*, one of the standout songs on *Newpower Soul*, in 1998.

RIGHT BACK HERE IN MY ARMS

⚥ / 4'33

Musicians: ⚥: vocals, rap, beat box, bass, percussion, piano, synthesizers, backing vocals / **Michael Mac:** scratching / **Recording: Paisley Park, Chanhassen, Minnesota:** 1995–1996 / **Technical team: Producer:** ⚥ / **Arrangements:** ⚥, Kirk Johnson / **Recording engineers:** Tom Tucker, Ray Hahnfeldt, Steve Durkee, Shane T Keller, Hans-Martin Buff, Peter Mokran

When she arrived at Paisley Park to record some new songs in 1993, the poet Dietra Moses, better known by the name Ninety-9, knew what she wanted...and above all what she did not want: to be considered a rapper. At college she had sold love poems to her classmates for $10, and she did not want to perform the kind of hip-hop from which her idols, such as the New Yorker Rakim, had quickly managed to break free; instead, she preferred to describe herself as a writer of poems. Although the song *Three Shots*, written with Prince in 1993, has remained unreleased, the latter extracted a sample from it to use in *Right Back Here in My Arms*. It can be heard in several passages in the song, where Ninety-9 is heard to say: "and that's my only mission." With a beat box and flawless flow, Prince here deploys the whole panoply of the perfect rapper, to the great pleasure of the listener.

SOMEBODY'S SOMEBODY

⚥, Brenda Lee Eager, Hilliard Wilson / 4'43

Musician: ⚥: vocals, electric guitar, bass, percussion, synthesizers, backing vocals / **Recording: Paisley Park, Chanhassen, Minnesota:** 1994 / **Technical team: Producer:** ⚥ / **Arrangements:** ⚥, Kirk Johnson / **Recording engineers:** Tom Tucker, Ray Hahnfeldt, Steve Durkee, Shane T Keller

In 1992, while she was working on recording her album *The Voice* at Paisley Park, Mavis Staples suggested to her old friend Brenda Lee Eager that she could send her a few song lyrics. Eager, a legendary soul singer who had campaigned for civil rights during her youth, was also a respected composer, having written hits for The Carpenters and Jerry Butler. "She didn't use them, but about a year later she calls me, and she was whispering, she says, 'Prince is in his office and he's reading your lyrics. And Brenda, he says you're one of the best writers that he knows. He wants you to send him more lyrics.' [...] So I did, and later he got in touch with me and said that he had recorded one of my songs, and he said, 'Do you approve of this?' He asked for my approval! I wouldn't have cared what it sounded like...it was Prince!"[173] Although it was not released as a single, *Somebody's Somebody* benefited from a promotional release in the US, aimed at publicizing the release of *Emancipation*.

The saxophonist Paul Gonsalves who was an influence on Prince when he wrote *Courtin' Time*.

GET YO GROOVE ON

⚥ / 6'31

Musicians: ⚥: vocals, electric guitar, bass, programming, synthesizers, backing vocals / **Rhonda Smith:** bass, spoken voice / **Eric Leeds:** saxophone / **Kat Dyson:** backing vocals / **Mr Hayes:** backing vocals / **Recording:** **Paisley Park, Chanhassen, Minnesota:** summer 1996 / **Technical team:** **Producer:** ⚥ / **Arrangements:** ⚥, Kirk Johnson / **Recording engineers:** Tom Tucker, Ray Hahnfeldt, Steve Durkee, Shane T Keller, Hans-Martin Buff, Peter Mokran

Freed from the endless adjustments required for the operation of his drum machines, Prince took advantage, during the production of *Emancipation*, of the skills of his associate Kirk Johnson, as he described in 1997: "He's good at using the computer to put a rhythm track together. I don't like setting that kind of stuff up, because a lot of times the song will leave me while I'm doing it. But when Kirk and I work together, we can keep each other excited [...] Technology used to play a big part in my music; it only plays a very little part now."[174] *Get Yo Groove On* demonstrates this synergy, to which the voice of the guitarist Kat Dyson adds a familiar sound—you could swear you're listening to Vanity (see page 72) when she says, at 2'15, "Hey Girl, let's hang tonight."

COURTIN' TIME

⚥ / 2'46

Musicians: ⚥: vocals, electric guitar, bass, piano, synthesizers, claps, backing vocals / **Michael B** Nelson: trombone / **Kathy Jensen:** baritone saxophone / **Brian Gallagher:** tenor saxophone / **Dave Jensen:** trumpet / **Steve Strand:** trumpet / **Recording:** **Paisley Park, Chanhassen, Minnesota:** 1992 / **Technical team:** **Producer:** ⚥ / **Arrangements:** ⚥, Kirk Johnson / **Recording engineers:** Tom Tucker, Ray Hahnfeldt

Inspired by his discovery of Duke Ellington's album *Ellington at Newport*—and especially by Paul Gonsalves's saxophone solo in *Diminuendo and Crescendo in Blue*, which the saxophonist Eric Leeds had played to him during the sessions for *Emancipation*—Prince decided to record his own swing hymn, and so made *Courtin' Time*. "I wanted it to be a dance record. Eric Leeds [...] was telling me that one reason the solo went as long as it did was that this lady jumped up on a table and started dancing to the rhythm, so naturally nobody wanted to quit. That's the vibe I'm trying to capture."[174]

The influence of Sylvester Stewart, aka Sly Stone, was a dominant one throughout Prince's albums.

Single

BETCHA BY GOLLY WOW!

Thomas Randolph Bell, Linda Creed / 3'30

Musicians: ⚥: vocals, backing vocals / **Sonny T.**: bass / **Michael B.**: drums / **Mr** Hayes: synthesizers / **Tommy Barbarella**: synthesizers / **Recording:** Paisley Park, Chanhassen, Minnesota: 1995–1996 / **Technical team:** Producer: ⚥ / **Arrangements:** ⚥, Kirk Johnson / **Recording engineers:** Tom Tucker, Ray Hahnfeldt, Steve Durkee, Shane T Keller, Hans-Martin Buff, Peter Mokran

Single: 1. *Betcha by Golly Wow!*/3'30 / **2.** *Right Back Here in My Arms*/4'33 / **Released in the UK by NPG Records/EMI-Capitol Music:** 2 December 1996 (CD single ref.: 7243 8 83560 2 2) / **Best chart ranking in the UK:** 11

Written by Thomas Randolph Bell and Linda Creed for Connie Stevens under the title *Keep Growing Strong* in 1970, this song became popular when it was recorded by The Stylistics in 1972 with its new title: *Betcha by Golly, Wow*. Having played it regularly with Grand Central during his younger years, this song always stayed with Prince, who delivers here a (let's be honest) somewhat syrupy cover. But the singer's thinking—as he explained when asked about this odd choice of single—was entirely honorable and overshadows the crooner aspect of this unremarkable version. "I choose artists who are not able to support themselves. I'm glad to be in this position that I do this not for money, but to give something to artists from the past."[175] Despite its undeniably kitsch quality, the video clip of the single, in which the gymnast Dominique Dawes, who had just won a gold medal at the Olympic Games in Atlanta, Georgia, dazzles alongside 50 dancers, is poignantly touching, as it shows Prince and his bride Mayte, happier than ever having discovered that she is pregnant. A video that, with hindsight, fans would unquestionably find moving.

WE GETS UP

⚥ / 4'17

Musicians: ⚥: vocals, electric guitar, drums, synthesizers, claps, backing vocals / **Rhonda Smith:** bass / **Eric Leeds:** saxophone / **Brian Lynch:** trumpet / **Recording:** Paisley Park, Chanhassen, Minnesota: summer 1996 / **Technical team:** Producer: ⚥ / **Arrangements:** ⚥, Kirk Johnson / **Recording engineers:** Tom Tucker, Ray Hahnfeldt, Steve Durkee, Shane T Keller, Hans-Martin Buff, Peter Mokran

"Inspired by the face one makes when Jordan dunks!"[176] Prince explains in the sleeve notes for *Emancipation* when describing this very funky number, which reconnects with the tradition of the singer's most authentic songs. Rhonda Smith, who joined the group in June 1996, had barely had time to put down her bags at Paisley Park before she recorded a stunning line of walking bass in *We Gets Up*. There is no rhythm programmed on a sequencer here—just a drums line recorded by Prince himself, enriched by sharp funk plucking on the guitar. This song reminds the listener that, behind its R&B façade, *Emancipation* is still an album by Prince that combines various musical styles.

HEADPHONES AT THE READY

At 2'07 in *We Gets Up*, Prince pays homage to his idol Sly Stone, letting fly with "Boom Lakalakalaka Boum," which is reminiscent of the famous motif in *I Want to Take You Higher*, recorded by Sly and the Family Stone in 1969.

Nine years before he recorded one of her songs, Prince had already worked with the guitarist Bonnie Raitt in April 1987.

WHITE MANSION

O(+> / 4'47

Musicians: O(+>: vocals, acoustic guitar, bass, tambourine, synthesizers, backing vocals / **Janice Garcia:** spoken voice / **Recording: Paisley Park, Chanhassen, Minnesota:** 1995–1996 / **Technical team: Producer:** O(+> / **Arrangements:** O(+>, Kirk Johnson / **Recording engineers:** Tom Tucker, Ray Hahnfeldt, Steve Durkee, Shane T Keller, Hans-Martin Buff, Peter Mokran

Janice Garcia, Mayte's sister, makes a brief appearance on this R&B number in which Prince sings of the hard struggle faced by musicians who arrive in New York dreaming of a career that allows them to afford that "big white mansion at the top of the road." Prince takes pleasure in telling the song's narrator that a return to Minneapolis, a city covered in snow, would be more appropriate. Prince reinforced the point on the Oprah Winfrey show on 20 November 1996 (the program went out the following day), stating: "I'll always live in Minneapolis [...] It's so cold it keeps the bad people out."[177]

DAMNED IF 👁 DO

O(+> / 5'20

Musicians: O(+>: vocals, electric guitar, acoustic guitar, bass, drums, programming, percussion, synthesizers, piano, backing vocals / **Michael B** Nelson: trombone / **Kathy Jensen:** baritone saxophone / **Brian Gallagher:** tenor saxophone / **Dave Jensen:** trumpet / **Steve Strand:** trumpet / **Mayte:** spoken voice / **Recording: Paisley Park, Chanhassen, Minnesota:** February 1996 / **Technical team: Producer:** O(+> / **Arrangements:** O(+>, Kirk Johnson / **Recording engineers:** Tom Tucker, Ray Hahnfeldt, Steve Durkee, Shane T Keller

Although *Damned If Eye Do* is a pop rock song like those that featured on *Rave Un2 the Joy Fantastic* three years later, it is its Cuban influence that gets the listener's attention. Built around a dialogue between Prince, the piano, and The NPG Hornz at their best, the song's break is a resounding success—with all due respect to the rock press, which criticized Prince for no longer experimenting, as he had in the past. Mayte—who, it should be remembered, is of Puerto Rican descent—regales us with interjections in Spanish, taking the listener back to the era of *The Gold Experience*, which already seems so long ago.

👁 CAN'T MAKE U LOVE ME

Mike Reid, Allen Shamblin / 6'37

Musicians: O(+>: vocals, programming, synthesizers, backing vocals / **Rhonda Smith:** bass / **Todd Burrell:** synthesizers / **Eric Leeds:** saxophone / **Recording: Paisley Park, Chanhassen, Minnesota:** summer 1996 / **Technical team: Producer:** O(+> / **Arrangements:** O(+>, Kirk Johnson / **Recording engineers:** Tom Tucker, Ray Hahnfeldt, Steve Durkee, Shane T Keller, Hans-Martin Buff, Peter Mokran

When Rhonda Smith appeared before Prince in the spring of 1996, she knew that her future would be decided by this first meeting. That day, the Canadian had brought along a fretless bass guitar, which surprised the singer. The instrument enabled her to play glissandos reminiscent of the sound of the bass parts played on a synthesizer. "I guess he liked the instrument, because he had me play on the *Emancipation* album," Rhonda Smith explained. "It was maybe 95 percent done, not completely finished, and he asked me to play the fretless on two songs. One was *I Can't Make U Love Me*, [...] and the other one was *Dreamin' About U*."[178] Written by Mike Reid and Allen Shamblin for the singer Bonnie Raitt, who recorded a first version of it for her *Luck of the Draw* in 1991, *I Can't Make You Love Me* became *Eye Can't Make U Love Me* in the hands of Prince, who added it to the three other covers that feature on *Emancipation*.

The twin sisters Susannah and Wendy Melvoin in July 1990.

1996

IN THIS BED 👁 SCREAM

[symbol] / 5'40

Musicians: [symbol]: vocals, electric guitar, bass, programming, percussion, synthesizers, backing vocals / **Michael Mac:** scratching / **Recording:** **Paisley Park, Chanhassen, Minnesota:** 1995–1996 / **Technical team:** **Producer:** [symbol] / **Arrangements:** [symbol], Kirk Johnson / **Recording engineers:** Tom Tucker, Ray Hahnfeldt, Steve Durkee, Shane T Keller, Hans-Martin Buff, Peter Mokran

Ten years after The Revolution split up (see page 126), Prince made *In this Bed Eye Scream* as a song of reconciliation meant for his former associates Lisa Coleman and Wendy Melvoin, but also for his ex-girlfriend Susannah Melvoin. In the sleeve notes, beneath the song's title, are the words "2 Wendy and Lisa and Susannah"—which, even though the text is printed backward, clearly conveys the writer's message. At the heart of the song (one of the best on the album) Prince sings of his regrets, declaring: "How did we ever lose communication?/ How did we ever lose each other's sound?/Baby, if you wanna, we can fix the situation." Prince went further than a mere song buried in the middle of his triple album, as he asked those in question to think about working together on the piece. "We gave him some suggestions about it, and it sounded like he was into it," Wendy Melvoin explained, "but then we never heard from him again on the subject."[2] Prince never returned to the studio with his former friends and associates from The Revolution.

MR. HAPPY

[symbol] / 4'46

Musicians: [symbol]: vocals, rap, bass, programming, synthesizers, backing vocals / **Scrap D.:** rap / **Michael Mac:** scratching / **Recording:** **Paisley Park, Chanhassen, Minnesota:** 1996 / **Technical team:** **Producer:** [symbol] / **Arrangements:** [symbol], Kirk Johnson / **Recording engineers:** Tom Tucker, Ray Hahnfeldt, Steve Durkee, Shane T Keller, Hans-Martin Buff, Peter Mokran

After being closed for several months, the recording studios at Paisley Park reopened for business on 23 August 1996. That evening, a party was held in the renovated complex, and more than 150 guests were lucky enough to receive an invitation after having got wind of the event on the local radio station KMOJ Minneapolis. The party only got going after midnight, when the DJ played, exclusively, some pieces from Prince's forthcoming album. These included *Mr. Happy*, an R&B number containing a rap part by Scrap D., who had already featured on *I Rock, Therefore I Am* (*Chaos and Disorder*, 1996), and a sample from Ice Cube, borrowed from his song *What Can I Do?* (*Lethal Injection*, 1993).

HEADPHONES AT THE READY

During the recording of *In this Bed Eye Scream*, Prince put his guitar on the floor and recorded the feedback from it, which can be heard from 4'26. "Does this mean that instruments have a soul or a life of their own?" he asked. "Will they end up writing the song?"[174]

The drummer of Funkadelic, Ramon "Tiki" Fulwood, who is heard at the start of the song *Sex in the Summer*.

SEX IN THE SUMMER

⚥ / 5'56

Musicians: ⚥: vocals, electric guitar, tambourine, synthesizers, backing vocals / **Kat Dyson:** electric guitar / **Rhonda Smith:** bass / **Ricky Peterson:** piano / **Eric Leeds:** saxophone / **Recording: Paisley Park, Chanhassen, Minnesota:** summer 1996 / **Technical team: Producer:** ⚥ / **Arrangements:** ⚥, Kirk Johnson / **Recording engineers:** Tom Tucker, Ray Hahnfeldt, Steve Durkee, Shane T Keller, Hans-Martin Buff, Peter Mokran

The introduction to this song is a drum sample by Ramon "Tiki" Fulwood from the song *Good Old Music* by Funkadelic (*Funkadelic*, 1970). *Sex in the Summer* (the original title of which was *Conception*) is in the great tradition of American songs that celebrate summer and its many pleasures. Here, Prince created a number that's perfectly suited to an evening on the beach or as the soundtrack of a movie for teenagers featuring quarterbacks and cheerleaders in a predictable romance. However, during the summer of 1996, the singer was not in the frame of mind of an aspiring lover, since he was preparing for the birth of his first child with his wife Mayte. There was, therefore, a family atmosphere at Paisley Park, as confirmed by Ricky Peterson, who was asked to enliven the second part of the song with a well-judged piano line alongside the guitarist Kat Dyson. He described in moving terms his memory of this timeless period: "[The Paisley staff] had to turn in all our keys. So we'd come to the door and have to buzz it. Mayte answered the door. It was the sweetest thing. Pregnant, basketball out to here. Barefoot and pregnant. And he came down the stairs by the front door in these big bunny slippers. He said, 'Come on in.' He was so happy. I've never seen him happier than when she was pregnant."[25]

FOR PRINCE ADDICTS

From 0'12 in *Sex in the Summer*, the sound of a damaged soundtrack can be heard in the background of the mix. It is a recording of the heartbeat of Mayte and Prince's unborn baby, as the latter explained in 1996: "What we did was take a microphone and place it on Mayte's stomach and move it around with the gel till we get the right spot. And then [imitates heartbeat], you know, you start to hear that and then we put the drums around that."[179]

ONE KISS AT A TIME

⚥ / 4'40

Musician: ⚥: vocals, bass, synthesizers, backing vocals / **Recording: Paisley Park, Chanhassen, Minnesota:** 1995–1996 / **Technical team: Producer:** ⚥ / **Arrangements:** ⚥, Kirk Johnson / **Recording engineers:** Tom Tucker, Ray Hahnfeldt, Steve Durkee, Shane T Keller, Hans-Martin Buff, Peter Mokran

"This is something every man should see/Give your woman what she wants and give her what she needs," sings Prince, in a romantic, rather syrupy tone, as only he knows how. The singer often wrote this kind of ballad, typical of American soul singers, which places him in the same tradition as James Brown, who sang in 1966: "This is a man's world/But it wouldn't be nothing, nothing without a woman or a girl."

1996

SOUL SANCTUARY

⚥, Sandra St Victor / 4'41

Musician: ⚥: vocals, bass, tambourine, percussion, synthesizers, backing vocals / **Recording: Paisley Park, Chanhassen, Minnesota:** spring 1995 / **Technical team:** Producer: ⚥ / Arrangements: ⚥, Kirk Johnson / **Recording engineers:** Tom Tucker, Ray Hahnfeldt, Steve Durkee, Shane T Keller

Supported by Bob Krasnow, then CEO of Elektra Records, the Texan Sandra St Victor was due to release her first record, *Sanctuary*, in 1993. After Krasnow left the record company, and despite the $700,000 already spent on its production, the singer's album project was simply dropped. After meeting Prince in Los Angeles in 1995, St Victor sent Prince a series of songs (*Nothing Left to Give*, *How We Livin'*, *I'll Never Open My Legs Again*, *Love Is*, and *Sanctuary*) in the hope that they might work together soon. However, without her agreement, Prince recorded his own version of *Sanctuary*, which then became *Soul Sanctuary* on *Emancipation*, for which the song's cowriter, Johnny Kemp, did not even receive a credit. As for *I'll Never Open My Legs Again*, it was recorded at Paisley Park by Chaka Khan under the title *I'll Never Be Another Fool* in 1998, while *Love Is* became *Van Gogh*, which Prince offered to the group of the same name, then rerecorded himself to put on the NPG Music Club (see page 384) in July 2001.

EMALE

⚥ / 3'37

Musician: ⚥: vocals, bass, synthesizers, backing vocals / **Kat Dyson:** electric guitar / **Eric Leeds:** saxophone / **Brian Lynch:** trumpet / **Recording: Paisley Park, Chanhassen, Minnesota:** 1996 / **Technical team:** Producer: ⚥ / Arrangements: ⚥, Kirk Johnson / **Recording engineers:** Tom Tucker, Ray Hahnfeldt, Steve Durkee, Shane T Keller, Hans-Martin Buff, Peter Mokran

On 2 July 1996, Prince was in New York, where he gave interviews to the *Los Angeles Times* and the UK edition of *The Times*. The same day, he played his new single *Dinner with Delores* on the *Late Show with David Letterman*. Never one to miss an opportunity to connect with the new soul scene, the following day he treated himself to a jam session at Battery Studios in the company of Eric Leeds, Brian Lynch, and the singer Meshell Ndegeocello. The instrumental written during this session became *Emale* a few weeks later. Relishing the pun of E-mail and E-male, Prince created a song that sang the praises of cybersex, which was booming at the time. When asked in 1997 by the journalist Ben Greenman whether he had ever tried cybersex, Prince replied categorically: "Ain't nothin' like the real thang."[180]

CURIOUS CHILD

⚥ / 2'57

Musician: ⚥: vocals, acoustic guitar, bass, synthesizers, piano, backing vocals / **Recording: Paisley Park, Chanhassen, Minnesota:** 1995–1996 / **Technical team:** Producer: ⚥ / Arrangements: ⚥, Kirk Johnson / **Recording engineers:** Tom Tucker, Ray Hahnfeldt, Steve Durkee, Shane T Keller, Hans-Martin Buff, Peter Mokran

Although no one can say who this "curious child" is, in whose memory Prince sings here, this poignant ballad in triplets, which was recorded in 1995, clearly has a very special resonance for the listener, who is now aware of the tragedy that befell the artist and his wife in October 1996. "A simple ballet 4 an old friend...or 2 whomever it may concern," writes the singer in the sleeve notes, leaving fans totally in the dark about what this could mean.

DREAMIN' ABOUT U

⚥ / 3'52

Musicians: ⚥: vocals, spoken voice, synthesizers, backing vocals / **Kat Dyson:** classical guitar / **Rhonda Smith:** bass / **Eric Leeds:** saxophone / **Recording: Paisley Park, Chanhassen, Minnesota:** summer 1996 / **Technical team:** Producer: ⚥ / Arrangements: ⚥, Kirk Johnson / **Recording engineers:** Tom Tucker, Ray Hahnfeldt, Steve Durkee, Shane T Keller, Hans-Martin Buff, Peter Mokran

Rehearsals with the new lineup of the New Power Generation were in full swing when the guitarist Kat Dyson recorded her part in this song, using Prince's nylon-stringed Godin

A poster for *Bring in 'da Noise, Bring in 'da Funk*, a tap-dancing show with Savion Glover that delighted Prince in 1996.

guitar: "I remember, we were messing around once in a rehearsal, and I was playing something on acoustic guitar, and the next thing I know, I'm in the studio. He says, 'I like that pattern you're playing. Can you put it on this song?' And it turned into *Dreamin' About U*."[181] Rhonda Smith was also asked to leave her mark on the piece: "That was his own composition, a very beautiful ballad—and he asked me to take a solo on it, with the fretless. I was thinking 'What? I must have done something right.' So there's a lot of special moments there. It was the most amazing musical experience that I have ever had."[178]

JOINT 2 JOINT

[symbol] / 7'51

Musicians: [symbol]: vocals, electric guitar, bass, synthesizers, backing vocals / **Michael Mac:** scratching / **Hans-Martin Buff:** spoken voice, sound effects / **Recording:** Paisley Park, Chanhassen, Minnesota: 1996 / **Technical team:** Producer: [symbol] / Arrangements: [symbol], Kirk Johnson / **Recording engineers:** Tom Tucker, Ray Hahnfeldt, Steve Durkee, Shane T Keller, Hans-Martin Buff, Peter Mokran

The result of various experiments conducted by Prince during the making of *Emancipation*, *Joint 2 Joint* is, without a doubt, one of the most interesting songs on the album. For almost eight minutes, it takes the listener on an emotional rollercoaster, like those of *Batdance*, *Thunder*, and *3 Chains O' Gold* before it. As well as the presence of the poet Ninety-9, who between 2'28 and 2'48 unleashes a well-crafted flow, it is the appearance of the tap dancer Savion Glover that surprises the listener. Prince, who had attended a performance of the musical *Bring in 'da Noise, Bring in 'da Funk*, written by George C Wolfe, in which Glover took the lion's share, suggested the young man come and meet him at Paisley Park. It was during the visit that Glover recorded some 30 seconds of tap-dancing, which the singer divided into two distinct parts before incorporating them into *Joint 2 Joint*. It was the last song recorded for the album, and one of the first to be worked on by Prince's new recording engineer, Hans-Martin Buff.

Although the technicians who worked on *Emancipation* are so numerous that it is impossible to detail the contribution of every individual to each song, Buff rapidly earned his spurs with Prince, who made him into an invaluable associate in the months that followed. The young man, who during the making of the song was allowed carte blanche with regard to adding sound effects, as well as the green light for all kinds of tinkering with sounds, added a recording of his voice to the song and another of the door to his bedroom at Paisley Park, which creaked when he closed it.

HEADPHONES AT THE READY

While Prince was recording the vocal parts of *Joint 2 Joint*, alone in the control room of the studio, Hans-Martin Buff was waiting in the adjoining room when he suddenly heard Prince's voice on the intercom between the two asking him to bring in his favorite breakfast cereal, Quaker Cap'n Crunch. The recording engineer complied, assuming Prince simply wanted a little snack. But, totally unexpectedly, the singer recorded himself enjoying his cereal and included this sequence at 5'55 in *Joint 2 Joint*!

Prince photographed by Steve Parke during the shooting of the clip of *The Holy River.*

Single

THE HOLY RIVER

⚥ / 6'55

1996

Musicians
⚥: vocals, electric guitar, acoustic guitar, bass, tambourine, piano, synthesizers, backing vocals
Kirk Johnson ? (not confirmed): drums

Recording
Paisley Park, Chanhassen, Minnesota: 1995–1996

Technical team
Producer: ⚥
Arrangements: ⚥, Kirk Johnson
Recording engineers: Tom Tucker, Ray Hahnfeldt, Steve Durkee, Shane T Keller, Hans-Martin Buff, Peter Mokran

CD 1/2
1. *The Holy River* (Radio Edit)/4'00
2. *Somebody's Somebody* (Edit)/4'30
3. *Somebody's Somebody* (Livestudio Mix)/3'47
4. *Somebody's Somebody* (Ultrafantasy Edit)/3'45

CD 2/2
1. *The Holy River* (Radio Edit)/4'00
2. *The Most Beautiful Girl in the World* (Mustang Mix)/6'19
3. *Somebody's Somebody* (Radio Edit)/4'30
4. *On Sale Now!*/0'48

Released in the UK by NPG Records/EMI-Capitol Music: 13 January 1997 (CD single ref. 1/2: 7243 8 83765 2 5; CD single ref. 2/2: 7243 8 83760 2 0)
Best chart ranking in the UK: 19

Genesis

Here, Prince created a song that is imbued with spirituality. He relates how he asked his girlfriend to marry him, with his feet in the holy river—a reference to Hinduism, which considers seven Indian rivers, the Ganges, Yamuna, Godavari, Sarasvati, Narmada, Kaveri, and Indus, to be sacred. The singer, who would soon become a fervent Jehovah's Witness, was at this time embarking on a spiritual transformation, which would intensify after the death of his son, Amiir. Prince first asserted his belief in the rebirth of souls in an interview with Spike Lee for the magazine *Interview* in 1997, in which he declared: "I am a firm believer in reincarnation for people who either have more work to do or have so much debt to pay back that they have to be here."[182] In the same article, the singer revealed his desire to be surrounded only by vegetarian musicians—a dietary rule that was soon enforced at Paisley Park. He also became interested in reading about personal development after Oprah Winfrey gave him the best-seller *The Seat of the Soul* by Gary Zukav, an interest which continued with his discovery of *The Celestine Prophecy* by James Redfield. "I'm studying religion and philosophy; that's what I want my music to reflect," he said. "It's hard to put that in a pop song."[183]

Production

Taking advantage of his complete artistic and spiritual freedom, Prince declared, quoting the third verse of *The Holy River*, "Now I can write a song that says, 'If u ask God 2 love u longer, every breath u take will make u stronger, keepin' u happy and proud 2 call His name: Jesus' and not have to worry about what *Billboard* magazine will say."[174] Prince also imbued the song with a strong element of lyricism, which is sustained by the use of acoustic instruments (folk guitar, piano, tambourine, and drums played with rimshots) and verses that are more melodic than ever. The song's mounting harmonic progression, accompanied by the proliferation of vocal harmonies until the entry of a booming solo, followed in turn by backing vocals at 5'35, leads the listener to the high points of an album that we could only have dreamed would be so pop as the magnificent *The Holy River.*

Prince receiving the Brit Award for International Male Solo Artist on 20 February 1995.

1996

LET'S HAVE A BABY

⚥ / 4'07

Musician: ⚥: vocals, bass, piano / **Recording:** **Paisley Park, Chanhassen, Minnesota:** January 1996 / **Technical team:** **Producer:** ⚥ / **Arrangements:** ⚥, Kirk Johnson / **Recording engineers:** Tom Tucker, Ray Hahnfeldt, Steve Durkee, Shane T Keller

It is difficult to believe the album's sleeve notes, which do not credit Rhonda Smith on this song, because the sound of the fretless bass guitar, typical of that musician at the time, is recognizable from the outset. Although Prince doubtless reworked the song with the bass player during the summer of 1996, it was initially only recorded with piano and vocals, and played to his bride on their wedding night, on 14 February 1996. "Just before our wedding", he said, "Mayte spent a few days away from our home so I made a lot of changes to our house—especially in our bedroom, where I placed a crib. It was beautiful. Then, on our wedding night, Mayte was still wearing her long white dress when I brought her into the room and played her *Let's Have A Baby* for the first time. She couldn't stop crying—it was an unforgettable moment."[172]

SAVIOUR

⚥ / 5'48

Musicians: ⚥: vocals, electric guitar, claps, backing vocals / **Sonny T.:** bass / **Michael B.:** drums / **Mr** Hayes: Hammond organ / **Tommy Barbarella:** synthesizers / **Ricky Peterson:** synthesizers / **Michael B** Nelson: trombone / **Kathy Jensen:** baritone saxophone / **Brian Gallagher:** tenor saxophone / **Dave Jensen:** trumpet / **Steve Strand:** trumpet / **Recording:** **Paisley Park, Chanhassen, Minnesota:** February 1996 / **Technical team:** **Producer:** ⚥ / **Arrangements:** ⚥, Kirk Johnson / **Recording engineers:** Tom Tucker, Ray Hahnfeldt, Steve Durkee, Shane T Keller

Recorded during the final sessions with Michael Bland, Tommy Barbarella, and Sonny Thompson, *Saviour* sounds like a relic from the era of *The Gold Experience*, in which the most formidable lineup of the NPG gave one last demonstration of their virtuosity, accompanied on that occasion by The NPG Hornz. It is a song that marks the end of a cycle, or an artistic rebirth, of which Prince would say, in a mystical declaration that was typical of him at the time: "*Saviour* is about being born again. The day that every living thing accepts that fact that God can and does exist—outside of religion—is the day when all will begin 2 welcome the dawn. The awakening will occur among those who beckon it and the new kingdom we've heard so much about will become apparent. Needless 2 say—we will have 2 build it, but 1st it must be born in our hearts."[184]

THE PLAN

⚥ / 1'46

Musician: ⚥: synthesizers / **Recording:** **Paisley Park, Chanhassen, Minnesota:** 1994; 1996 / **Technical team:** **Producer:** ⚥ / **Arrangements:** ⚥, Kirk Johnson / **Recording engineers:** Tom Tucker, Ray Hahnfeldt, Steve Durkee, Shane T Keller

The first track of the instrumental album *Kamasutra*, which Prince would release the following year in cassette format via his platform for ordering by telephone, 1-800-NEW-FUNK, *The Plan* appears here as an edited version that has been shortened from 2'03 to 1'46. *Kamasutra* went on sale the same day that Prince and Mayte were married, 14 February 1996, and was released under the name The NPG Orchestra, even though Prince had worked alone on most of its songs.

FRIEND, LOVER, SISTER, MOTHER/WIFE

⚥ / 7'37

Musicians: ⚥: vocals, electric guitar, acoustic guitar, bass, synthesizers, backing vocals / **Kathleen Bradford:** backing vocals / **Rhonda Johnson:** backing vocals / **Recording:** **Paisley Park, Chanhassen, Minnesota:** January 1996 / **Technical team:** **Producers:** ⚥, Kirk Johnson / **Recording engineers:** Tom Tucker, Ray Hahnfeldt, Steve Durkee, Shane T Keller

According to the sleeve notes of *Emancipation*, where Prince offers us a few precious clues, *Friend, Lover, Sister, Mother/Wife* was written in a hotel room in Tokyo, Japan, while Mayte was asleep, and was subsequently revealed to her at their wedding. Showing the singer once again in the role of future husband completely fulfilled by the idea of starting a family, the song bears the marks of that blessed period in Prince's life when all the planets were aligned.

SLAVE

O(+> / 4'51

Musician: O(+>: vocals, beat box, bass, synthesizers, backing vocals / **Recording:** Paisley Park, Chanhassen, Minnesota: 1995 / **Technical team:** Producer: O(+> / Arrangements: O(+>, Kirk Johnson / **Recording engineers:** Tom Tucker, Ray Hahnfeldt, Steve Durkee, Shane T Keller

Although *Emancipation* celebrated the singer's new-found freedom, the memory of his years of struggle with Warner Bros. Records was never far away. When the album was released, Prince made a U-turn, to general surprise, stating that his self-proclaimed condition of slave was not, after all, connected to his record label. "The Warner Bros. thing had very little to do with it," he announced, even though this meant confusing his fans. "When I started writing 'Slave' on my face, I did it because I had become a slave to myself. We don't know how we get here. I had to figure out my origins and where I'm headed. How did I want the story to end? And I started writing 'Slave' on my face, because I felt like I was in a box spiritually, not creatively."[185] It was a disconcerting declaration, which the artist would contradict a few months later in an interview given when the Jam of the Year World Tour came to the Miami Arena, on 15 August 1997: "Every contracted musician who doesn't own the rights to their work should cover the song *Slave*."[186]

HEADPHONES AT THE READY

Although it bears an uncanny resemblance to the snare drum roll at 4'22 in *Sign O' the Times*, the rhythmic pattern of *Slave* is actually borrowed from another song written and produced by Prince, the excellent *Ain't No Place Like U*, which was sung by Mayte on her album *Child of the Sun* in 1995.

1996

NEW WORLD

⚥ / 3'42

Musician: ⚥: vocals, electric guitar, synthesizers, backing vocals / **Recording: Paisley Park, Chanhassen, Minnesota:** January 1994 / **Technical team: Producer:** ⚥ / **Arrangements:** ⚥, Kirk Johnson / **Recording engineers:** Tom Tucker, Ray Hahnfeldt, Steve Durkee, Shane T Keller

In 1996, while he was the artistic director of Paisley Park, Michael Van Huffel was in charge of visual development for his employer. Having worked on the sleeves for *Exodus*, *The Gold Experience*, and *Purple Medley*, the artist was a close associate of Prince's. When Mayte handed him a CD containing ten new songs by the singer, under the enigmatic title *Emancipation* and illustrated with a collage made the day before, he received a priceless gift which would guide him through the visual world to come with the next album. Some of these songs would remain unreleased (*2020*, *D. J.*), while others would end up on *Crystal Ball* (*Goodbye*) or be recorded by artists connected to Paisley Park, such as *Journey 2 the Center of Your Heart*, which was recorded by Chaka Khan in 1998. Van Huffel also encountered *New World*, in second place on the tracklisting of this first version of *Emancipation*, which would make it onto the final album. The song celebrates the rise of the Internet—of which Prince, like David Bowie, was a pioneer within the music industry. Indeed, in the song he mentions the name of his future website, Love 4 One Another, which would be managed by Kathy Adams and Sam Jennings from 1997.

THE HUMAN BODY

⚥ / 5'41

Musicians: ⚥: vocals, synthesizers, backing vocals / **César Sogbe:** programming, synthesizers / **Joe Galdo:** programming, synthesizers / **Recording: Paisley Park, Chanhassen, Minnesota:** 1995–1996 / **South Beach Studios, Miami Beach, Florida:** summer 1996 / **Technical team: Producer:** ⚥ / **Arrangements:** ⚥, Kirk Johnson / **Recording engineers:** Tom Tucker, Ray Hahnfeldt, Steve Durkee, Shane T Keller, Hans-Martin Buff, Peter Mokran, César Sogbe (South Beach Studios), Joe Galdo (South Beach Studios)

Exhilarating and made for nightclubs, *The Human Body* is a new foray into the techno style, which Prince had previously visited with *Eye Wanna Melt with U* and *Pheromone*. Unlike those songs, *The Human Body* is not entirely Prince's work because, after being recorded at Paisley Park, it was entrusted to the recording engineers and producers at South Beach Studios, in Miami, namely César Sogbe and Joe Galdo. These two technicians took charge of the programming of the song and added many synthesizer tracks. "The body of a human (when healthy) runs like a sequencer," Prince explained in 1997. "It was obviously programmed a long time ago by an absolute genius. This was the notion behind the groove *Human Body* on *Emancipation*. Every track of the song is its own 'cell' [...]"[174]

FACE DOWN

⚥ / 3'16

Musician: ⚥: rap, electric guitar, bass, synthesizers / **Recording: Paisley Park, Chanhassen, Minnesota:** 1995 / **Technical team: Producer:** ⚥ / **Arrangements:** ⚥, Kirk Johnson / **Recording engineers:** Tom Tucker, Ray Hahnfeldt, Steve Durkee, Shane T Keller

Prince settles some scores with this high-quality rap in which humor is combined with a certain aggressiveness. The lyrics of *Face Down* were inspired by a discussion with his keyboard player Morris Hayes. Shortly after *The Gold Experience* was released, in 1995, Prince came across a bad review of his album in the press, which infuriated him. Hayes, who was present in the singer's office at the time, launched into an angry tirade against journalists, who were not always kind to his employer and friend. "They can kiss my butt—matter of fact they can lay us all in caskets face-down and kiss our butts on the way out."[162] Laughing at his friend's outburst, Prince immediately let him go and hastened to create this vigorous rap, one of the most effective of his career. "Two days later, we had a thing you could call and hit the intercom, and I hear, 'Morris come to my office,' and I go up to his office. He's got this song done, mixed, mastered, everything is done in two days, and it's all the cussing I did the day in his studio, like all the stuff that I said was on that record, and he just called it *Face Down* [...]"[162] Prince added a sample from *Stained Glass*, a song by Ninety-9 recorded at Paisley Park in 1993, and some strings recorded by Clare Fischer in 1985 for the song *Killin' at the Soda Shop* by Jill Jones. Prince hoped to release this hard-hitting number as a single the following year, but because several departments of EMI were undergoing restructuring in 1997, he eventually stopped promoting *Emancipation*, and so only a promotional version of the song was released in Europe, in maxi-single format. On it were several remixes, including the excellent *X-Tended Rap Money Mix*, featuring vocals by Jacqui Thompson, the then sales director at NPG Records and the future general manager of Paisley Park Enterprises.

LA, LA, LA MEANS 👁 LOVE U

Thomas Randolph Bell, William Hart / 3'58

Musicians: ⚥: vocals, bass, tambourine, piano, synthesizers, backing vocals / **Mike Scott:** electric guitar / **Eric Leeds ? (not confirmed):** saxophone / **Brian Lynch ? (not confirmed):** trumpet / **Chanté Moore:** backing vocals / **Recording:** **Paisley Park, Chanhassen, Minnesota:** spring 1995 / **Technical team:** **Producer:** ⚥ / **Arrangements:** ⚥, Kirk Johnson / **Recording engineers:** Tom Tucker, Ray Hahnfeldt, Steve Durkee, Shane T Keller

Exactly reproducing this standard by The Delphonics, released in 1968 with original title *La La Means I Love You*, here Prince allowed himself a moment of nostalgia. Even sampling the drum roll that introduces the original version for his cover, Prince plays the tribute card to the full. He also intersperses backing vocals by singer Chanté Moore, whom he had met a few months earlier through Alan Leeds and who had come to Paisley Park to take part in the recording of Chaka Khan's song *Journey 2 the Center of Your Heart*.

STYLE

⚥ / 6'40

Musicians: ⚥: vocals, electric guitar, bass, percussion, synthesizers, backing vocals / **Eric Leeds:** saxophone / **Walter Chancellor Jr:** saxophone / **Brian Lynch:** trumpet / **Scrap D.:** backing vocals / **Michael Mac:** backing vocals / **Smooth G.:** backing vocals / **Recording:** **Paisley Park, Chanhassen, Minnesota:** 1996 / **Technical team:** **Producer:** ⚥ / **Arrangements:** ⚥, Kirk Johnson / **Recording engineers:** Tom Tucker, Ray Hahnfeldt, Steve Durkee, Shane T Keller, Hans-Martin Buff, Peter Mokran

Who could be better placed to talk about style and elegance than Prince, an artist who, it is said, even wore his stage outfits in private? The singer had elegance stitched into his very body and makes sure he reminds us of the importance of looking smart in this most significant R&B number: "Style don't get drunk on a Saturday night/Try to dress up every Sunday morning bright." Prince used a sample from *Atomic Dog*, a funk anthem recorded by George Clinton in 1982 and frequently quoted (even pirated) in R&B music (*D. O. G. in Me* by Public Announcement, in 1998), in hip-hop (*Who Am I? [What's My Name?]* by Snoop Doggy Dogg, in 1993), and by the French band FFF in *Marco*, the second song on their album *Blast Culture*, released in 1991.

SLEEP AROUND

⚥ / 7'41

Musicians: ⚥: vocals, electric guitar, bass, synthesizers, Hammond organ, backing vocals / **Michael B** Nelson: trombone / **Kathy Jensen:** baritone saxophone / **Brian Gallagher:** tenor saxophone / **Dave Jensen:** trumpet / **Steve Strand:** trumpet / **César Sogbe:** programming / **Joe Galdo:** programming / **Recording:** **Paisley Park, Chanhassen, Minnesota:** July 1996 / **South Beach Studios, Miami Beach, Florida:** summer 1996 / **Technical team:** **Producer:** ⚥ / **Arrangements:** ⚥, Kirk Johnson / **Recording engineers:** Hans-Martin Buff, Peter Mokran, César Sogbe (South Beach Studios), Joe Galdo (South Beach Studios)

Like *The Human Body*, *Sleep Around* was worked on at Paisley Park before being entrusted to César Sogbe and Joe Galdo of South Beach Studios in Miami. It was the recording engineer Hans-Martin Buff who was entrusted, from his first day at Chanhassen, with recording The NPG Hornz wind parts for the song, one of the most danceable in Prince's 1990s repertoire. It was a song made for the dance floor, but did not stand the test of time, despite its potential appeal to radio stations.

DA, DA, DA

⚥ / 5'15

Musicians: ⚥: vocals, electric guitar, bass, synthesizers, backing vocals / **Scrap D.:** rap / **Recording:** **Paisley Park, Chanhassen, Minnesota:** March 1996 / **Technical team:** **Producer:** ⚥ / **Arrangements:** ⚥, Kirk Johnson / **Recording engineers:** Tom Tucker, Ray Hahnfeldt, Steve Durkee, Shane T Keller

Having distinguished himself on *I Rock, Therefore I Am* (*Chaos and Disorder*, 1996) and then on *Mr. Happy*, the rapper Scrap D., a close associate of the DJ Michael Mac, whose scratches enliven *Emancipation* in places, was again asked to record his voice for *Da, Da, Da*. Built around a rhythmic pattern produced by a Roland TR-808—a legendary drum machine much loved by rappers—*Da, Da, Da* marks a new foray into the hip-hop style, which was dear to Prince's heart in the mid-1990s, even though he was keen to emphasize that he was a musician first and foremost: "I need to remind you that I'm not a rapper. I'll do rhythmic speaking [...] It's like James Brown: he'll talk his whole song, but he's not a rapper either. There's music behind my groove; it's not just loops and sample."[174]

Prince and Kate Bush shared a certain addiction for their computer, a window on to the world and a creative tool that was essential to both artists.

and went online only three or four times a week. Once the song had been produced at Paisley Park, Prince sent it to Kate Bush, with whom he had worked in 1991, recording backing vocals and some overdubs on the British singer's song *Why Should I Love You?*, which was released in 1993.

Since Prince was a keen fan of Bush, it is worth pointing out the connection between *My Computer* and the song *Deeper Understanding*, which she recorded in 1989 for her album *The Sensual World* and in which she declares: "As the people here grow colder/I turn to my computer/And spend my evenings with it/Like a friend." Prince received the backing vocals recorded by the singer in her home studio in Kent, in the UK, and added in the background to his song. In 2019, The Prince Estate offered the single of *My Computer* to buyers of the October issue of the German magazine *Musikexpress*.

FOR PRINCE ADDICTS

The voice that is heard saying "welcome," "you've got mail," and, finally, "goodbye" at the end of *My Computer* is that of the American Elwood Edwards, a dubbing specialist famous in the US for being the voice of the email service of the Internet provider America Online (AOL) from 1989.

MY COMPUTER

[symbol] / 4'36

Musicians: [symbol]: vocals, electric guitar, acoustic guitar, bass, synthesizers, backing vocals / **Kate Bush:** vocals / **Recording:** **Paisley Park, Chanhassen, Minnesota:** 1995–1996 / **Wickham Farm Home Studio, Welling, United Kingdom:** 1996 (Kate Bush's voice) / **Technical team:** **Producer:** [symbol] / **Arrangements:** [symbol], Kirk Johnson / **Recording engineers:** Tom Tucker, Ray Hahnfeldt, Steve Durkee, Shane T Keller, Hans-Martin Buff, Peter Mokran

With its rhythm built around the sounds of an Internet still in its infancy, audible in the song's opening bars, *My Computer* presents a picture of Prince alone in front of his screen on a Sunday evening, weary of a world where violence reigns and friends are in ever shorter supply. The narrator can no longer communicate via the web, as he is not receiving emails, and is in despair because he only has two real friends. When he was asked about his relationship with the Internet, and with IT in general, in an interview with the monthly *Yahoo! Internet Life* in October 1997, Prince divulged some details, explaining that he only used an IBM machine, had surfed the Internet for the first time at the beginning of that year,

ONE OF US

Eric M Bazilian / 5'19

Musicians: [symbol]: vocals, electric guitar, backing vocals / **Sonny T.:** bass / **Michael B.:** drums / **Mr Hayes:** Hammond organ / **Tommy Barbarella:** synthesizers / **Mayte:** backing vocals / **Recording:** **Paisley Park, Chanhassen, Minnesota:** 1995 / **Technical team:** **Producer:** [symbol] / **Arrangements:** [symbol], Kirk Johnson / **Recording engineers:** Tom Tucker, Ray Hahnfeldt, Steve Durkee, Shane T Keller

When the American singer Joan Osborne released the *Relish* album in 1995, it was an immediate success, driven by the triumph of its single *One of Us*, which was written by Eric M Bazilian, the vocalist for The Hooters. The song, which places God at the center of society and urges the listener to treat their neighbor as if they were the Almighty, went to No.1 in Australia, Belgium, Canada, and Sweden, and was a colossal success worldwide—a fact that did not elude Prince. He was delighted by its lyrics, in which the young woman asks: "What if God was one of us?/Just a slob like one of us/Just a stranger on the bus/Tryin' to make his way home?" Prince was unhesitatingly enthusiastic about the song when talking to the press, declaring: "It's nice to hear God mentioned on the radio. To me, spiritual music is the new alternative music because alternative always means 'that which isn't spoken about.' And nobody speaks about God in music."[187] In another interview he said: "I think it's important for every musician to cover that song. And every person of color should cover it, too."[188] That is exactly what he did, including a cover of the song, recorded at the end of 1995 with the whole lineup of the NPG, on *Emancipation*. When she was invited to a party thrown by Prince in New York after the song's release, Joan Osborne showed herself to be rather touchingly euphoric and naïve. "The security people came over and said, 'Prince would like to meet you now [...],'" the singer recalled. "I went over to meet Prince, and he was standing there just very calm and cool and collected, [...] sitting there, just him and Lenny Kravitz. They said, 'Oh, Joan is here to meet you,' and I started gushing about what a great fan I was. I was all sweaty and I'd been on the dance floor and I must have looked a mess, and I said, 'I just want to give you a hug!' He said, 'Well, you know, words can say a lot.'"[189]

When he appeared at the Zénith in Paris, on 21 August 1998, Prince reused his introduction to *One of Us* for an unforgettable version of *Love... Thy Will Be Done*. He played the song, written for Martika in 1990, live only rarely.

THE LOVE WE MAKE

[symbol] / 4'38

Musicians: [symbol]: vocals, bass, drums, piano, synthesizers, backing vocals / **Kat Dyson:** electric guitar / **Recording:** Paisley Park, Chanhassen, Minnesota: summer 1996 / **Technical team:** Producer: [symbol] / Arrangements: [symbol], Kirk Johnson / **Recording engineers:** Tom Tucker, Ray Hahnfeldt, Steve Durkee, Shane T Keller, Hans-Martin Buff, Peter Mokran

At the end of the album Prince delivers a sermon in the shape of a piece of gospel singing, in which he provides all the harmonies. "The only love there is, is the love we make," he sings, alone, at the end of the song. As he explained: "2 me, *Emancipation* is a gospel record! God is in everything! *The Love We Make* [...] is about the acceptance of the divine plan."[184] The song was incidentally recorded at the same time as the unreleased *The Divine*, which, as of today, is still gathering dust on the shelves of The Vault. This song also deals with the loss of self as a result of drug use; the singer exhorts the listener to: "Put down the needle, put down the spoon." Prince gave an invaluable clue as to whom this song was addressed during an exchange with fans on the website Love4OneAnother.com, on 17 November 1997, when he wrote: "[I] was speaking 2 the spirit of a friend lost 2 drugs."[114] In all probability the song was written in homage to Jonathan Melvoin, the brother of Susannah and Wendy Melvoin, who died of a heroin overdose in New York on 12 July 1996. At the time, he was a keyboard player on The Smashing Pumpkins' Infinite Sadness Tour. Melvoin, who had left his mark on the Prince albums *Around the World in a Day*, *Parade*, and *Graffiti Bridge*, was at the height of his career when he succumbed to a dangerous cocktail of heroin and alcohol on the eve of the group's concert at Madison Square Garden.

EMANCIPATION

[symbol] / 4'12

Musician: [symbol]: vocals, electric guitar, bass, synthesizers, backing vocals / **Recording:** Paisley Park, Chanhassen, Minnesota: 1995 / **Technical team:** Producer: [symbol] / Arrangements: [symbol], Kirk Johnson / **Recording engineers:** Tom Tucker, Ray Hahnfeldt, Steve Durkee, Shane T Keller

During the night, between 8 and 9 September 1995, Prince performed a concert at Paisley Park. The images from the concert would be included in the program *Love 4 One Another*, which went out on 27 January 1996 on VH1. The whole of the New Power Generation were present, together with Walter Chancellor Jr on saxophone and Kirk Johnson on percussion. As was his wont, Prince did not go on stage until after midnight and distributed among the audience some pink sheets of paper bearing a poem entitled *Emancipation*. In the poem, Prince exhorted the audience to follow the path that led to freedom and asked himself about his situation in the conflict with his record label. "Is it reality or just a dream?/2 your spirit Eye say Eye love U in spite of my slavery/We're both 2 blame 4 this lesson in life/'Cuz this is the path we choose." Although this poem was not set to music, Prince nevertheless retained its title for the following album and its title track, in which he commands: "Break the chain." It is an ideal closing track, at the end of which the sound effects of an explosion suggest that the singer has freed himself of his shackles—a point that is made explicitly by the photograph on the album sleeve, which shows his wrists finally free of their chains.

THE NPG ORCHESTRA *KAMASUTRA*

Distributed for NPG Music Club by NPG Records: 14 February 1997 (cassette and CD ref.: none)
Best chart ranking in the USA: did not make the charts
Best chart ranking in the UK: did not make the charts

Mayte hoped to perform the ballet *Kamasutra* all over the world, but unfortunately had to abandon the project.

1. *The Plan* (⚥ / 2'03)
2. *Kamasutra* (⚥ / 11'49)
3. *At Last…"The Lost Is Found"* (⚥ / 3'37)
4. *The Ever Changing Light* (⚥ / 2'59)
5. *Cutz* (⚥ / 3'03)
6. *Serotonin* (⚥ / 0'47)
7. *Promise/Broken* (⚥ / 3'46)
8. *Barcelona* (⚥ / 2'16)
9. *Kamasutra/Overture #8* (⚥ / 3'11)
10. *Coincidence or Fate?* (⚥ / 3'24)
11. *Kamasutra/Eternal Embrace* (⚥ / 4'02)

Musicians: ⚥: piano, synthesizers, Synclavier, sound effects / **Eric Leeds:** saxophone / **Michael B** Nelson: trombone / **Kathy Jensen:** baritone saxophone / **Brian Gallagher:** tenor saxophone / **Dave Jensen:** trumpet / **Steve Strand:** trumpet / **Murray Adler, Israel Baker, Bette Byers, Russel Cantor, Isabelle Daskoff, Yvette Devereaux, Assa Drori, Pamela Gates, Edward P Greene Jr, Norma Leonard, Robert S** Lezin, **Yoko Matsuda, Calabria McChesney, Donald Palmer, James V** Ross, **Gladys Secunda, Harry Scorzo, Harry Shirinian, Benjamin Simon, Ross Shub, Robert Sushel, Marshall Daniel Thomason, Anita A. Thompson, Pam Tomkins, Mari Tsumura, Gerald Vinci, Francine Walsh:** violin / **Marilyn Baker, Suzanna Giordano, Peter Hatch, Margot MacLaine, Jorge Moraga, Carole Mukogawa, Nancy Roth, Herschel Wise:** viola / **Douglas Davis, Marie Fera, Judith Johnson, Anne Karam, Raymond Kelley, Frederick Seykora, Cécilia Tsan:** cello / **Robert D Carr, Lisa Edelstein, David Randall Stone, James R Walker:** flute / **Árni Egilsson, James David Hughart, Morton Klanfer:** double bass / **Charles Boito, Jon Christopher Clarke, Don Shelton:** clarinet / **Robert Tricarico:** oboe / **C Terry Harrington, Daniel L Higgins, Jack Nimitz:** saxophone / **Charles A Coker, Jenice Rosen:** bassoon / **David Duke, Marilyn Johnson, Joseph Meyer, Yvonne Suzette Moriaty:** horn / **Leslie Benedict, Alexander Iles, Andrew M Martin, Morris Repass:** trombone / **Larry Bunker:** percussion, vibraphone / **Dennis Budimir, John J Mitchell, John F Reilly:** guitar / **Gayle Levant:** harp / **Thomas John Ranieri:** piano, saxophone, flute / **Brent Fischer, Richard Hamilton, Richard Mitchell:** ? (not confirmed) / **Clare Fischer:** conductor / **Recording:** **Paisley Park, Chanhassen, Minnesota:** 1994–1995 / **The Record Plant, Sausalito, California:** 1995 / **Mad Hatter Studios, Los Angeles:** 1995 (orchestra) / **Technical team:** **Producer:** ⚥ / **Recording engineers:** Ray Hahnfeldt, Steve Durkee, Shane T Keller, Larry Mah, Arne Frager / **Orchestral arrangements:** Clare Fischer

A BALLET TO THE GLORY OF MAYTE

In 1994, Prince embarked on the production of a ballet, which would take him two years to write. Equipped with a brand new Synclavier synthesizer, which enabled him to produce all sorts of orchestral instruments, he polished this artistic work and, after many long months, sent Clare Fischer a cassette recording, so that his son Brent could transcribe each of the 48 tracks on to a score—the goal being that it should be played by real musicians. "It was difficult to hear everything that was on there. I transcribed a lot of it track by track. I was on tour at the time so, with a Walkman, I transcribed on planes, trains, buses, and whenever I would find the time. I faxed back the transcripts to my father and he started work on it in L.A."[21] At the beginning of 1996, the ballet *Kamasutra* was complete, and it was distributed when Prince and Mayte were married in Minneapolis on 14 February 1996. Very quickly, it was decided that it would be released via 1-800-NEW-FUNK, NPG Records' telephone sales service; Prince felt this would be an effective way to celebrate the couple's first wedding anniversary on 14 February 1997. "We can probably expect a deluge of releases," Prince said the day before it went on sale in cassette format. "To find out more, you can call 1-800-NEW-FUNK."[191] A pressing of *Kamasutra* in CD format was also offered in 1998 to buyers of the *Crystal Ball* box set. Although Mayte's original wish that the ballet should be performed first in Puerto Rico, then in New York, and finally all over the US, *Kamasutra* was never performed onstage. Listening to it offered Prince fans an unprecedented experience, through which the brilliant musician once again demonstrated his ability to reinvent himself. A quality vinyl pressing of this work would be greatly appreciated by fans!

CRYS

CRYSTAL BALL

DISC 1

Crystal Ball · Dream Factory · Acknowledge Me · Ripopgodazippa
Love Sign (Shock G's Silky Remix) · Hide the Bone · 2morrow · So Dark
Movie Star · Tell Me How U Wanna B Done

DISC 2

Interactive · Da Bang · Calhoun Square · What's My Name · Crucial · An Honest Man
Sexual Suicide · Cloreen Bacon Skin · Good Love · Strays of the World

DISC 3

Days of Wild · Last Heart · Poom Poom · She Gave Her Angels
18 & Over · The Ride · Get Loose · P. Control (Remix)
Make Your Mama Happy · Goodbye

Released in the USA by NPG Records:
29 January 1998 (CD box set ref. *Crystal Ball/The Truth*: none)
Best chart ranking in the USA: 62

Prince sporting an unusual hat, photographed by Steve Parke.

1998

THE VAULT REVEALED TO FANS

In April 1997, Prince stopped promoting the *Emancipation* album to work on a new project: the release of a triple album that brought together a multitude of unreleased songs. He was determined to expand the sale of his records via his label, NPG Records, and the telephone sales platform 1-800-NEW-FUNK. He brought in the recording engineer Hans-Martin Buff, who had become his official technician since the previous summer's sessions, to help him work on a selection of unreleased songs that would delight his admirers. "It was fun for me as a fan, of course, you know, I virtually got a list of songs, and he opened the Vault for me and then I went shopping. It was like one of those little trolleys you have in hospitals and such, and I just filled that sucker up and brought it upstairs [...]"[192] The next stage was to digitize the analog tracks, which Buff proceeded to do before embarking on a complete edit of the selected songs. Among them were many tracks from the sessions in 1986 for the albums *Camille* and *Dream Factory* which had been dropped (*Sexual Suicide*, *Good Love*, *Dream Factory*, *Movie Star*), as well as more recent pieces from the time of *The Gold Experience* album (*Acknowledge Me*, *Ripopgodazippa*, and the inevitable *Days of Wild*). Although the future box set's tracklisting also included some remnants from the ballet *Glam Slam Ulysses* (*What's My Name*, *Interactive*, and *Strays of the World*) and just a few other tracks from the 1980s (*Cloreen Bacon Skin* and *An Honest Man*), no song recorded with The Revolution was selected, since at the time Prince was planning to release a compilation of unreleased songs that he had made with his legendary group: *Prince and The Revolution's Roadhouse Garden*. To the great disappointment of fans, the singer abandoned the idea.

Four unreleased discs

Apart from the interest in this avalanche of unreleased songs brought together in the box set's first three discs, it was, of course, the album called *The Truth*, added as a bonus on the release of *Crystal Ball*, which aroused the curiosity of fans. Recorded by Prince using an acoustic guitar between December 1996 and March 1997, this album was a curiosity offered to his admirers, notably those who had supported him in his move to become an independent artist. *Crystal Ball* was completed in April 1997 and, from May onward, the first pre-orders came in from fans via 1-800-NEW-FUNK, with delivery planned for June. However, distribution was delayed, and the unfortunate buyers had to wait until the end of January 1998 to receive their precious orders, enhanced by the addition of a copy of *Kamasutra*, the instrumental album made by the short-lived The NPG Orchestra, which was released on 14 February 1997. To complement the album's sleeve notes, in which Prince included information or anecdotes on the selected songs, a website—Crystal Ball Online Lyric Book—was also set up by two fans, Steffen Bieker and Alice Männl. "Our goal was very simple: We wanted to create something which reflected our love for Prince's music," they explained years later. "We wanted to give something back to him [...] We were lucky enough to meet Prince at an afterparty here in Germany, some months later: he tapped his chest and told us that he could see the big heart behind the website."[193] From March, *Crystal Ball* went on sale in the US in Best Buy, Musicland, and Blockbuster. Prince sold almost 100,000 copies, which only reinforced his desire to distribute his music himself—which he would do again with *Newpower Soul*, the last New Power Generation album (released in June 1998).

1998

Libyans demonstrate furiously following the USA's bombing of Tripoli on 15 April 1986.

CRYSTAL BALL

Prince / 10'28

Musicians: Prince: vocals, electric guitar, bass, drums, synthesizers, Fairlight CMI, percussion, finger cymbals, backing vocals / **Susannah Melvoin:** vocals, spoken voice, recorder, backing vocals / **Wendy Melvoin:** recorder / **Orchestra** / **Recording: Galpin Boulevard Home Studio, Chanhassen, Minnesota:** 17 April, June, August 1986 / **Ocean Way Recording, Los Angeles:** 4 August 1986 (strings) / **Technical team: Producer:** Prince / **Recording engineer:** Susan Rogers / **Assistant recording engineer:** Todd Herreman / **String arrangements:** Clare Fischer

On 5 April 1986, a bomb exploded in a discotheque in West Berlin frequented by American soldiers serving in West Germany. The United States president, Ronald Reagan, blamed the Libyan leader Muammar Gaddafi, who for several years had engaged in provocation against the United States and appeared to be behind this malevolent act. By way of reprisal, on 15 April, the US launched Operation El Dorado Canyon, which involved the bombing of the Libyan capital, Tripoli, and the cities of Benina, Benghazi, and Jamahiriya. Two days after the attacks, which killed 60 Libyan citizens, Prince recorded this song, lasting almost 11 minutes, in which he describes the terror he experienced: "As bombs explode around us and hate advances on the right/The only thing that matters, baby, is the love that we make tonight." Like other songs recorded in 1986, which would produce the monumental *Sign O' the Times*, *Crystal Ball* reveals the artist's anguish when faced with a world where armed conflict shatters an international diplomatic equilibrium that is more fragile than ever. He also references his soulmate, Susannah Melvoin, who is engaged in decorating their love nest on Galpin Boulevard, Chanhassen: "As soldiers draw swords of sorrow/My baby draws pictures of sex." Susan Rogers, who was at the controls during the recording sessions, recalled: "He'd given her this blank wall in his downstairs den." Rogers continued, "She was sketching a mural on the wall with fairies and nymphs—slender, lithe female nude bodies with wings."[22] The young woman's voice is also audible at several points during the song.

After recording all the song's instruments on his own, Prince let the sisters Susannah and Wendy Melvoin complete it with a few clumsy recorder lines which, surprisingly, found their way into the introduction. In the months that followed, the singer went on to cover his work with multiple sound effects and overdubs, before sending it to Brent Fischer, so that he could transcribe his ideas on to a score before passing this to his father, Clare, the man behind the orchestration of many of Prince's songs. "Prince wrote a note saying that it was one of the most important things he had done in his life [...] We had a 60-piece orchestra, including eight French horns, and we overdubbed 12 or 13 separate percussion parts on top of that."[2] In the hope of releasing the song as a single some day, Prince made an edited version lasting 3'29. This version could finally be heard on the prestigious box set *Sign O' the Times* Super Deluxe Edition, which was released in September 2020.

DREAM FACTORY

Prince / 3'07

Musicians: Prince: vocals, electric guitar, bass, drums, synthesizers, backing vocals / **Susannah Melvoin:** spoken voice, backing vocals / **Recording:** Washington Avenue Warehouse, Edina, Minnesota: 30 November, December 1985 / **Technical team:** Producer: Prince / **Recording engineers:** Susan Rogers, Peggy McCreary

Before it became the title of an album that would never see the light of day, the expression "Dream Factory" had been used many times by Prince. Indeed, in 1979, the young artist had used it when talking about success in the pages of the *Twin Cities Reader*: "I don't think about it. It's all just part of the dream factory. If it happens, it happens. It's best not to even worry about that, 'cuz if you strive for it and don't get it, you'll be disappointed and feel like a failure."[15] Two years later, in 1981, he chose that expression to describe the city of Los Angeles: "I can't stand L.A., so I would never move there. . . Every time I have to go out there, I dread it [...] I lose sight of what I'm doing when I'm there, it's like a dream factory. . .They spend so much money! They make it and spend it, and for crazy reasons . . ."[194] A song that is credited to Prince's ephemeral pseudonym Camille (see page 142)—of which a sample was detected by the most perceptive listeners in the introduction of *D J Gets Jumped*, the second interlude on *Exodus* (1995)—*Dream Factory* is a funk delight, to be listened to again at the earliest opportunity!

ACKNOWLEDGE ME

⚥ / 5'27

Musician: ⚥: vocals, rap, electric guitar, bass, programming, synthesizers, backing vocals / **Recording:** Paisley Park, Chanhassen, Minnesota: October 1993 / **Technical team:** Producer: ⚥ / **Recording engineers:** David "Chronic Freeze" Friedlander, Ray Hahnfeldt, Shane T Keller, Steve Durkee

Featuring in the short movie *The Beautiful Experience*, broadcast on the British channel Sky One on 3 April 1994, *Acknowledge Me* is a pure product of the *Come/The Gold Experience* era, in which the singer blends the rock power of his new musicians with remnants of his hip-hop phase, then drawing to a close. There is something of *Gett Off*, *Pope*, and *Now* in this unmissable song, which is typical of this Prince period. Worth noting are several vocal samples from *The Line*, a song recorded on 22 December 1987 (the instrumental part) and 16 January 1988 (the vocals and brass) with Boni Boyer and Sheila E., and which has remained unreleased at the time of writing. Noticeable in the introduction is the powerful voice of Boyer, who included in *The Line* a moving interpretation of the famous traditional gospel number *Take My Hand, Precious Lord*. As for the brass parts in *Acknowledge Me*, they were also recorded by Eric Leeds and Matthew "Atlanta" Bliss during the sessions for *The Line*.

HEADPHONES AT THE READY

At 5'11 in *Acknowledge Me*, Prince's distorted voice—saying "Welcome, this is where I live"—is a sample taken from the song *All My Dreams*, which was recorded between 1985 and 1986 and featured on the Super Deluxe edition of *Sign O' the Times* (released September 2020).

RIPOPGODAZIPPA

⚥ / 4'39

Musicians: ⚥: vocals, electric guitar, synthesizers, backing vocals / **Sonny T.:** bass / **Michael B.:** drums / **Michael B** Nelson: trombone / **Kathy Jensen:** clarinet / **Brian Gallagher:** tenor saxophone / **Dave Jensen:** trumpet / **Steve Strand:** trumpet / **Mayte:** spoken voice / **Recording:** Paisley Park, Chanhassen, Minnesota: 10 October, end October 1993 (wind) / **Technical team:** Producer: ⚥ / Recording engineer: ⚥

Recorded during the sessions for *The Gold Experience*, *Ripopgodazippa* was retained by the director Paul Verhoeven for his movie *Showgirls*, for which Prince also provided *319*. Perfectly synchronized with a rehearsal scene during which, at 47' into the movie, Elizabeth Berkley wraps her arms around the actor Glenn Plummer, the presence of the song in the feature-length movie was eclipsed by the Berkley's passionate dancing. It is nonetheless very well put together and a reminder that Prince was, for the second time since *Blue Light* (⚥, 1992), capable of flirting with the reggae style and producing very respectable results.

Gregory "Shock G." Jacobs, a super-talented producer and public entertainer.

LOVE SIGN (SHOCK G'S SILKY REMIX)

Nona Gaye and [symbol] / 3'53

Musicians: Nona Gaye: vocals / [symbol]: vocals, electric guitar, synthesizers / Paul Peterson: bass / Statik: programming / Ricky Peterson: synthesizers / Shock G.: synthesizers / **Recording:** Paisley Park, Chanhassen, Minnesota: January 1994 / The Record Plant, Sausalito, California: 1994 / **Technical team:** Producers: [symbol], Ricky Peterson / Remix: Shock G. / Recording engineers: David "Chronic Freeze" Friedlander, Ray Hahnfeldt, Tom Tucker / Assistant recording engineers: Kyle Bess, Kimm James, Brian Poer

It was 1994. *Love Sign* had just been recorded in Chanhassen and Los Angeles. The rapper Gregory "Shock G." Jacobs, the producer and leader of the hip-hop group Digital Underground, was taken on at Paisley Park to do a remix of the song. "When we sent the track back to Prince it never came out. At that time, we just thought it was the closest we would ever get to Prince like, 'Wow, we touched the same tape that Prince touched.'"[195] Nevertheless, Shock G. heard nothing from the singer for several years, and forgot about it until he went back to *Love Sign*. Worse still, he reworked this remix, slowed it down, and used it as the basis for working on a new song, *Fuck the World*, which he suggested to his friend 2Pac in 1994. The latter accepted, and added it to his next album, *Me Against the World*, which was released on 14 March 1995. When *Crystal Ball* appeared in 1998, Shock G. was the last to learn of his participation in Prince's new work. "People are coming up to me going, 'Yo, good to see you on that song with Prince,'" the rapper recalled. "So I would turn around and look at whoever I was with and say, 'I ain't never did no song with Prince...' Then I get to the studio and the engineer is like, 'I like the work you did on that *Crystal Ball* album with Prince.' I'm like, 'Why does everybody keep saying that?' So I went to the store and sure enough a remix for *Love Sign* produced by Shock G. was on there. I thought I took too much ecstasy and acid because I couldn't remember doing that song."[195]

HIDE THE BONE

[symbol], Brenda Lee Eager, Hilliard Wilson / 5'04

Musicians: [symbol]: vocals, electric guitar, backing vocals / Sonny T.: bass / Michael B.: drums / Tommy Barbarella: synthesizers / Mr Hayes: Hammond organ / Mayte: backing vocals / **Recording:** Studios Davout, Paris: November 1993 / Paisley Park, Chanhassen, Minnesota: 1994–1995 / **Technical team:** Producer: [symbol] / Recording engineers: Tom Tucker, Ray Hahnfeldt, Steve Durkee, Shane T Keller

After having worked with the singer and songwriter Brenda Lee Eager on the song *Somebody's Somebody* in 1994, Prince asked her and Hilliard Wilson, the uncredited cowriter of the song's lyrics, to write some new ones for him. It was the start of a new partnership and produced the formidable *Hide the Bone*—which has the distinction of being the most effective groove among Prince's records, notably thanks to Michael Bland's direct, powerful playing and the rhythm of Prince's sharp guitar work. Although it is certain that the latter had recorded an initial version of the song during a stay in Paris in the second half of November 1993, for a long time there were doubts as to which studio he had used at that time. The singer definitely visited the Studio Guillaume Tell in Suresnes, a suburb of Paris, in November 1993, but he also went to Studios Davout, where he specifically recorded the voice of Ophélie Winter in the song *Chaos and Disorder* as well as her contribution to the fourth track, *NPG Operator*, on *The Gold Experience* album. The Parisian studio is mentioned in the sleeve notes of *Crystal Ball*, so it can be confirmed that the artist laid down the foundations of *Hide the Bone* at Studios Davout. He would then rework the song the following year with the musicians of the New Power Generation at Paisley Park.

2MORROW

 / 4'14

Musicians: : vocals, electric guitar, bass, programming, synthesizers, Fender Rhodes piano, percussion, backing vocals / **Michael B** Nelson: trombone / **Kathy Jensen:** baritone saxophone / **Brian Gallagher:** tenor saxophone / **Dave Jensen:** trumpet / **Steve Strand:** trumpet / **Recording: Paisley Park, Chanhassen, Minnesota:** November 1996 / **Technical team: Producer:**  / **Recording engineer:** Hans-Martin Buff

On 20 November 1996, Prince went on the hugely popular *Oprah Winfrey Show*. He took advantage of his stay in Chicago to take part in the recording of the *Tom Joyner Morning Show*, as a way of promoting the release of his new album. The program, entitled *Emancipation Special* for the occasion, allowed listeners to hear some of the artist's new songs, as well as an interview with Tom Joyner, the show's star presenter. The songs broadcast that day included an unreleased one for the benefit of fans: *2morrow*, the one and only track recorded by Prince since the release of *Emancipation*. The reason for this creative famine was a promise he had made to his wife Mayte (see page 216) that he would slow down his productivity with the aim of spending more time with her, as he admitted to Joyner. It was a commitment Prince did not honor for long, as he embarked on the production of *The Truth* on 1 December 1996.

SO DARK

Prince / 5'14

Musicians: Prince: vocals, synthesizers, programming, finger cymbals, backing vocals / **Sonny T.:** bass / **Michael B.:** drums / **Mr Hayes:** Hammond organ / **Michael B** Nelson: trombone / **Kathy Jensen:** baritone saxophone / **Brian Gallagher:** tenor saxophone / **Dave Jensen:** trumpet / **Steve Strand:** trumpet / **Recording: Paisley Park, Chanhassen, Minnesota:** 2 January 1993; 1994 / **Technical team: Producer:** Prince / **Recording engineers:** David "Chronic Freeze" Friedlander, Ray Hahnfeldt, Tom Tucker / **Assistant recording engineers:** Xanex Bess, Tom Garneau, Kimm James

Originally recorded in January 1993 for the ballet *Glam Slam Ulysses*, *Dark* was kept to one side so that it could be included on the *Come* album. Prince made a remix of the song during 1994, which he entitled *So Dark*, and he included it on his *Crystal Ball* box set. The classical guitar part, played on a synthesizer by Prince, gives this remake of *Dark* a more melancholy tinge, which, in fact, sets it apart from the dark world of *Come*.

MOVIE STAR

Prince / 4'26

Musicians: Prince: vocals, electric guitar, Roland G-707 Guitar-Synthesizer, bass, drums, programming, synthesizers, finger snapping, backing vocals / **Susannah Melvoin:** spoken voice / **Recording: Galpin Boulevard Home Studio, Chanhassen, Minnesota:** March to April 1986 / **Technical team: Producer:** Prince / **Recording engineer:** Susan Rogers

Despite the breakup of The Time (see page 64) two years earlier, in early 1986 Prince still seemed to be attached to his former buddy Morris Day and the comic, funk world he had created with him for the group. The only other group member who still found favor with Prince, Jerome Benton, remained a close friend whom he included in the project The Family, before offering him a tailor-made part in the movie *Under the Cherry Moon*. The sleeve notes for *Crystal Ball*, written by Prince (and typed out on a typewriter by the recording engineer Hans-Martin Buff!), state that the inspiration for the song came to him from The Time. Indeed, it clearly displays the kind of production that Prince liked to realize with Morris Day in songs such as *Chili Sauce* (*Ice Cream Castle*, 1984) and *Tricky*, which was released on the B-side of the single *Ice Cream Castles* in 1984. Although it remained unreleased until 1998, *Movie Star* would be played onstage by the jazz musician Miles Davis, along with two other bootlegs by Prince: *Penetration* and *Jailbait*. Before including this rarity from the time of the *Parade* album on *Crystal Ball*, Prince added a sample from *Jam of the Year*, the first song on *Emancipation*, as an introduction.

TELL ME HOW U WANNA B DONE

Prince / 3'16

Musicians: Prince: vocals, electric guitar, bass, programming, synthesizers, backing vocals / **Carmen Electra:** spoken voice / **Kirk Johnson:** programming / **Recording: Paisley Park, Chanhassen, Minnesota:** January 1992 / **Technical team: Producer:** Prince / **Remix:** Kirk Johnson / **Recording engineers:** David Friedlander, Steve Noonan, Ray Hahnfeldt, Brian Poer / **Assistant recording engineers:** Dave Aron, Airiq Anest, Steve Durkee

Kirk Johnson, a faithful associate of Prince in the mid-1990s, revisited the final part of *The Continental* (on the  album, released in 1992) in 1994, and took on the task of remixing the song, which was renamed *Tell Me How U Wanna 2 B Done* for the occasion. Johnson removed the "lo-fi" effect from Carmen Electra's voice, which made the lyrics easier to understand, and took the opportunity to add a more danceable rhythmic pattern to the song. This remix was confined to these two slight changes; nothing else about it is new.

The Calhoun Square shopping mall in Minneapolis, which inspired a song of the same name by Prince.

INTERACTIVE

[Love Symbol] / 3'04

Musicians: [Love Symbol]: vocals, electric guitar, claps, backing vocals / **Sonny T.:** bass / **Michael B.:** drums / **Tommy Barbarella:** synthesizers / **Mr** Hayes: Hammond organ / **Recording:** Paisley Park, Chanhassen, Minnesota: June 1993 / **Technical team:** Producer: [Love Symbol] / Recording engineer: [Love Symbol]

Developed in partnership with the multimedia publisher Graphix Zone Inc. and distributed by Compton's NewMedia, the CD-ROM *Interactive* went on sale on 7 June 1994. Prince offered his fans an immersive experience of his colorful and musical world, taking them through scenery worthy of Paisley Park. The user can visit various rooms—the entrance hall, library, and "Candle Room," and even a specially designed recording studio. As well as featuring a puzzle that urges the most determined to find the five constituent parts of the "Love Symbol" logo, the CD-ROM also contains videos and several songs by Prince, two of them unreleased: *Endorphinmachine* and *Interactive*. Using a standard CD player, fans can also enjoy an audio version of the latter song, which features on *Crystal Ball*, released in 1998. Written in the same vein as *Endorphinmachine* and *Chaos and Disorder*, *Interactive* narrowly missed being featured first on the *Come* album and then on *The Gold Experience*, especially for its strongly rock sound—something Prince opted for (all too) rarely.

DA BANG

[Love Symbol] / 3'20

Musician: [Love Symbol]: vocals, electric guitar, bass, drums, tambourine, backing vocals / **Recording:** Larrabee Sound Studios, Los Angeles: 1995 / **Technical team:** Producer: [Love Symbol] / Recording engineer: ? (not confirmed)

In the same vein as the most rock numbers on *Chaos and Disorder*, *Da Bang* was recorded during one of Prince's stays in Los Angeles in 1995. The only information available about this song appears on the sleeve notes to *Crystal Ball*, which state: "Bored in L.A., the Artist in the studio, recorded and mixed this little ditty in one day, rode around in a limo, and heard it back 32 times."[196]

CALHOUN SQUARE

[Love Symbol] / 4'47

Musicians: [Love Symbol]: vocals, electric guitar, bell, backing vocals / **Sonny T.:** bass / **Michael B.:** drums / **Tommy Barbarella:** synthesizers / **Mr** Hayes: Hammond organ / **Recording:** Paisley Park, Chanhassen, Minnesota: 15 June 1993 / **Technical team:** Producer: [Love Symbol] / Recording engineers: David "Chronic Freeze" Friedlander, Ray Hahnfeldt, Tom Tucker

In this funk anthem with an unstoppable riff, Prince references the Calhoun Square shopping mall, which was opened in 1984 at the intersection of Hennepin Avenue and

West Lake Street, in the heart of Minneapolis. It was there that the singer opened his first NPG Store, on 3 August 1993, before opening a second one in London on 30 April 1994. A song with the energy typical of the time of *Chaos and Disorder*, *Calhoun Square* is based on a guitar riff that true fans will have recognized. A careful listen to the famous pirate recordings, *The Loring Park Sessions*, containing spectacular instrumental passages by Prince, Bobby Z., Robbie Paster, and André Cymone, which were recorded during their nighttime sessions in the offices of Owen Husney in 1976, reveals this famous riff at 3'18 in track No.6—logically entitled *Instrumental #6* by the bootleggers.

FOR PRINCE ADDICTS

On 3 July 2016, the famous keyboard player Robi Botos—accompanied by the trumpet player Ingrid Jensen, guitarist Lionel Loueke, organist Cory Henry, bass player Mike Downes, drummer Larnell Lewis, and saxophonist Seamus Blake—recorded a very jazzy cover of *Calhoun Square*, filmed from multiple angles. It was put online on his YouTube page on 21 April 2017, to commemorate the first anniversary of Prince's death.

WHAT'S MY NAME

Prince / 3'04

Musicians: Prince: vocals, bass / **Sonny T.:** bass / **Michael B.:** drums, shaker / **Mr** Hayes: Hammond organ / **Recording: Paisley Park, Chanhassen, Minnesota:** May 1993 / **Technical team: Producer:** Prince / **Recording engineers:** David "Chronic Freeze" Friedlander, Ray Hahnfeldt, Tom Tucker

Recorded in May 1993, a few weeks before the official announcement of Prince's change of name, *What's My Name* was the music people heard while on hold that June on the "Paisley Park Hotline," a telephone number for fans who were curious to know the reason for their idol's change of identity. Lacking a guitar—Prince plays the bass guitar solo between 1'53 and 1'57, complementing the lines played by Sonny Thompson—the song is an appeal by the artist who wishes to explain the reason for his decision. "Take my name, I don't need it/Nothing stays the same anyway/Take my fame, I can't use it," he sings in this number which is driven full tilt by the powerful, precise drumming of Michael Bland. Accompanied by his female group 3rdEyeGirl, on 30 September 2014 Prince performed a definitive version of *What's My Name* onstage at Paisley Park, with the rapper Kendrick Lamar.

CRUCIAL

Prince / 5'06

Musician: Prince: vocals, electric guitar, acoustic guitar, bass, drums, tambourine, programming, synthesizers, piano, backing vocals / **Recording: Galpin Boulevard Home Studio, Chanhassen, Minnesota:** 13 and 15 September 1986 / **Technical team: Producer:** Prince / **Recording engineer:** Susan Rogers

Returning to the theme of rivalry between two musical groups, addressed previously in the movie *Purple Rain*, Prince worked on writing a musical between June and September 1986. On 17 and 18 June, he recorded several songs with all the members of The Revolution, who were gathered together at the Washington Avenue Warehouse. These included *Data Bank*, *Girl O' My Dreams*, *Can't Stop this Feeling I Got*, and a new version of *We Can Fuck* (renamed *We Can Funk* in 1989). In September 1986, he recorded three new songs—*The Cocoa Boys*, *When the Dawn of the Morning Comes*, and *Crucial*—for the project, whose working title was *The Dawn*. Engrossed in multiple projects, Prince eventually abandoned the musical idea, but retained certain elements when writing the movie *Graffiti Bridge*. *Crucial* was given saxophone lines by Eric Leeds and string arrangements by Clare Fischer, but the lyrics were finally rewritten and rerecorded by Prince. It was eventually made available in a version from which the above overdubs had been removed on the *Crystal Ball* box set in 1998. The song, with its original lyrics, appeared on the *Sign O' the Times* Super Deluxe edition, released in September 2020.

AN HONEST MAN

Prince / 1'13

Musician: Prince: vocals, synthesizers, backing vocals / **Recording:** **Sunset Sound, Los Angeles:** 17 December 1985 / **Technical team:** **Producer:** Prince / **Recording engineers:** Susan Rogers, Coke Johnson

On 2 July 1986, as the lights dimmed in movie theaters across the United States, viewers saw the first images of *Under the Cherry Moon*. Prince appeared on the screen, playing the instrumental *An Honest Man* on the piano and soon to be joined by Clare Fischer's orchestral arrangements. Although this first version was recorded in France during the shooting of the movie in November 1985, the singer recorded an alternative version of it with his group on 30 November, when he returned to Edina. On 17 December, at the Sunset Sound studios in Los Angeles, he recorded a final version of the song with piano and vocals, to which he added various sound effects. Finally, he removed the piano track and replaced it with multiple vocal harmonies, sung *a cappella*, which were eventually embellished with discreet synth pads at the end of the song. It was the last interpretation of the song that Prince chose to add to the tracklist of *Crystal Ball* in 1998.

Prince, aka Christopher Tracy, playing *An Honest Man* on the piano in the movie *Under the Cherry Moon* in 1986.

SEXUAL SUICIDE

Prince / 3'40

Musicians: Prince: vocals, spoken voice, Roland G-707 Guitar-Synthesizer, bass, drums, synthesizers, backing vocals / **Eric Leeds:** saxophone / **Susannah Melvoin:** backing vocals / **Recording: Washington Avenue Warehouse, Edina, Minnesota:** 10–11 August 1985 / **Technical team: Producer:** Prince / **Recording engineer:** Susan Rogers

When Prince called on the services of his faithful musician Eric Leeds, on 10 August 1985, he had just recorded *Sexual Suicide*, a funk number with a frenetic pace and strange sounds, straight out of his Roland G-707 guitar-synthesizer, which fans would soon discover on the single *Girls & Boys*. Leeds arrived at the Washington Avenue Warehouse and recorded a few saxophone lines, which did not satisfy his boss. Next day he was asked to start from scratch. He used a clever blend of tenor and baritone saxophones, to which Susan Rogers added a Harmonizer effect in order to thicken the sound considerably. "He just got thrilled with it," the saxophonist said of Prince. "He thought it was the greatest thing in the world he'd ever heard. Of course, the song didn't come out until like 10 years later!"[95]

CLOREEN BACON SKIN

Prince / 15'37

Musicians: Prince: spoken voice, bass / **Morris Day:** drums / **Recording: Sunset Sound, Los Angeles:** 27 March 1983 / **Technical team: Producer:** Prince / **Recording engineer:** Peggy McCreary

Fans were doubtless happy to come across the name of Jamie Starr, the mysterious producer of The Time at the start of the 1980s, on *Crystal Ball*. It is public knowledge that Starr was, in fact, a pseudonym used by Prince for some of his ancillary projects. On 15 October 2021, the vocalist of The Time, Morris Day, posted on his Instagram account the famous photograph by Allen Beaulieu which showed him recording the song with Prince—the latter sporting a wig, a pair of sunglasses, and a false beard—at the console, where a few banknotes lay around. "We had the room smelling real funky that day..." Day commented with his post.[197]

GOOD LOVE

Prince / 4'55

Musicians: Prince: vocals, bass, drums, programming, synthesizers, backing vocals / **Jill Jones:** backing vocals / **Susannah Melvoin:** backing vocals / **Recording: Sunset Sound, Los Angeles:** 30–31 October, 1 November 1986 / **Technical team: Producer:** Prince / **Recording engineers:** Susan Rogers, Coke Johnson, David Rivkin

After recording *Good Love* during the night with the recording engineers, on the morning of 31 October 1986 Prince delivered a cassette of the song to his fiancée, Susannah Melvoin, with the request that she think about various backing vocals she could add to the recording. The song, which is as pop as you could wish for, features effective lyrics, sung with a shrill voice by Prince's female identity: Camille. Jill Jones is called on as backup for the more powerful lines and, directed by Melvoin, leaves her mark on the song. A longer version features on the original soundtrack of the 1988 movie *Bright Lights, Big City* by James Bridges, and an edited version, cut to 4'55, was offered to buyers of *Crystal Ball* ten years later.

STRAYS OF THE WORLD

[symbol] / 5'07

Musicians: [symbol]: vocals, electric guitar, acoustic guitar, bass, drums, synthesizers, Hammond organ, backing vocals / **Sonny T.:** bass / **Michael B.:** drums / **Tommy Barbarella:** synthesizers / **Mr** Hayes: Hammond organ / **Recording: Paisley Park, Chanhassen, Minnesota:** May 1993 / **Technical team: Producer: [symbol]** / **Recording engineers:** David "Chronic Freeze" Friedlander, Ray Hahnfeldt, Tom Tucker

In May 1993, deeply involved in the ballet *Glam Slam Ulysses*, which he aimed to stage in the summer, Prince embarked on a recording marathon, which would produce *Space*, *Pope*, *What's My Name*, *Interactive*, and *Strays of the World*. All these songs would be included in *Glam Slam Ulysses*, the première of which was held on 21 August at the Glam Slam club in Minneapolis. Although *Strays of the World*, which was recorded with the New Power Generation, was a strong contender for inclusion on *Come* (1994), it finally appeared on *Crystal Ball* in 1998.

FOR PRINCE ADDICTS

The famous synthesizer riff in *Days of Wild*, played by Mr Hayes and audible from 0'49 into the song, is a reinterpretation of the main theme of *Caravan*, a jazz standard written by the trombonist Juan Tizol in 1936 for Duke Ellington's orchestra, of which he was a member.

DAYS OF WILD

[symbol] / 9'19

Musicians: [symbol]: vocals, electric guitar, bass, backing vocals / **Sonny T.:** bass / **Michael B.:** drums / **Tommy Barbarella:** synthesizers / **Mr** Hayes: Hammond organ / **Rain Ivana:** spoken voice / **Recording:** **Paisley Park, Chanhassen, Minnesota:** 9 December 1995 (live version); 1995–1996 (overdubs) / **Technical team:** **Producer:** [symbol]

On 30 March 1994, when Prince was fighting with Warner Bros. Records to release *The Gold Experience*, the musicians of NPG answered questions from the journalist Raven Worrell of *New Power Generation Magazine*, which was published by Paisley Park Enterprises. The group gave details of the songs on the future album, including a certain *Days of Wild*, which had been recorded by Prince in January. "Among the many songs recorded," said the group's keyboard player, Morris Hayes, "is *Days of Wild*, a piece with a strong beat driven by a killer groove. The beat alone is enough to make you lose your head."[198] As Mayte confirmed: "It's just crazy." She went on to explain, "I can't place it in this or that category, for it's way too complex."[198] Four days later, the song—one of the most hip-hop numbers Prince ever recorded—appeared in the short movie *The Beautiful Experience*, which was broadcast on the British channel Sky One. When the singer and his record company finally reached an agreement in the summer of 1995, and prepared to release *The Gold Experience*, *Days of Wild* was eventually removed from the album's tracklist—despite the group's fondness for the song. An impressive version of the song was recorded on 9 December 1995 onstage at Paisley Park. Later, with a few overdubs added (including samples from two songs by the poet Ninety-9, *The Mood for Love* and *Simlac*, as well as a string introduction borrowed from *Violet the Organ Grinder*), this muscular interpretation of *Days of Wild* ended up on *Crystal Ball*—a precious testament to Prince's hip-hop period.

The jazz standard *Caravan* by the Duke Ellington Orchestra inspired Prince to come up with the main riff in the discordant song *Days of Wild* in 1995.

LAST HEART

Prince / 3'02

Musicians: Prince: vocals, electric guitar, bass, drums, synthesizers, backing vocals / **Eric Leeds:** saxophone / **Susannah Melvoin:** backing vocals / **Recording: Sunset Sound, Los Angeles:** 12 January 1986 / **Technical team: Producer:** Prince / **Recording engineers:** Susan Rogers, Coke Johnson

"Baby, if you break my heart one more time/It'll be the last heart you'll ever break," Prince tells his girlfriend menacingly in this outtake from the time of the *Parade* album. Recorded in the early hours of 12 January 1986, after a night spent mixing the songs that would soon appear on *Under the Cherry Moon*, *Last Heart* (whose working title was *Baby, My Heart*) was in the running to feature on the album *Dream Factory*, which would never see the light of day. In the sleeve notes to *Crystal Ball*, Prince explained the version featured was only a first version, which he aimed to rework later—an idea that fell by the wayside. Given that Prince never made demos but preferred to record his songs without producing preliminary versions, this fact left fans puzzled as to what a definitive version of this very pleasant pop funk number might have been like.

POOM POOM

O(+> / 4'32

Musician: O(+>: vocals, rap, beat box, bass, programming, claps, backing vocals / **Recording: Paisley Park, Chanhassen, Minnesota:** 1995 / **Technical team: Producer:** O(+> / **Recording engineer:** ? (not confirmed)

An outtake from the time of *Emancipation*, *Poom Poom* is an intense hip-hop number, thanks to a chorus in which Prince repeats this onomatopoeic sound countless times as a way of evoking the sex he dreams of having with the woman who haunts his dreams. Calling to mind the singer's hilarious and daring imitations in some songs of the 1980s (a restaurant waiter in *Chili Sauce* with The Time, a salesman selling batteries for Vanity's vibrator in *Vibrator*, and more), here Prince plays the part of a lecherous producer with a cigar clamped between his teeth, telling a young female singer that she need only pass an audition to become his top choice—an audition that the song's words make clear is based more on her sexual performance than talents as an artist.

SHE GAVE HER ANGELS

O(+> / 3'53

Musician: O(+>: vocals, electric guitar, bass, programming, synthesizers, piano, backing vocals / **Recording: Paisley Park, Chanhassen, Minnesota:** 1996 / **Technical team: Producer:** O(+> / **Recording engineer:** Hans-Martin Buff

On 1 April 1996, Prince announced in a press release that his wife, Mayte, was expecting their first child. The two artists, who had been blissfully happy since their wedding and seemed thrilled by the prospect of parenthood, also told their fans that they aimed to work together on writing a musical album for children, accompanied by a book, and made up of eight songs and three short stories. Prince recorded *She Gave Her Angels* with this in mind, but the project, whose working title was *Happy Tears*, never saw the light of day following the death of their newborn child in October 1996. Although it was also destined for the tracklist of *Emancipation*, the song was then shelved in The Vault until 1998. A few days after the tragedy that befell the two newlyweds, Prince decided, while appearing on the program *Muppets Tonight* on 28 October 1996, to perform the song at the end of the show, demanding that angels fly over him during the song. Although the death of his child had been kept secret, that day the singer revealed a part of the tragedy he had suffered. Sadly, it was not until 13 September 1997 that the program—which was quite surprising in terms of the singer's involvement—was broadcast in the United States.

18 & OVER

O(+> / 5'40

Musicians: O(+>: vocals, rap, electric guitar, bass, synthesizers, tambourine, backing vocals / **Mike Scott:** electric guitar / **Kirk Johnson:** programming / **Recording: Paisley Park, Chanhassen, Minnesota:** 1994 / **Technical team: Producer:** O(+> / **Recording engineers:** David "Chronic Freeze" Friedlander, Ray Hahnfeldt, Tom Tucker

Built around the backing tracks of *Come*, *18 & Over* is a declaration of desire on the part of Prince for his young bride, Mayte—he had waited until she reached the age of consent before declaring his love. It is assumed that she is the female voice in the song, even though no official information has ever confirmed this. Although the lyrics, which are extremely explicit, would be out of place in these pages, credit is due to the singer's hip-hop performance—he shines yet again with his impeccable flow, which overlays an instrumental reminiscent of the languor of *Love Sign*, a song that was recorded during the same period. A clip of the song was shot in November 1995 at Paisley Park, but the song remained unreleased until it appeared on *Crystal Ball* in 1998.

Prince and his Purple Sadowsky Guitar, designed by Roger Sadowsky and based on the singer's Hohner Madcat, which would later be given to Sheila E.

THE RIDE

⚥ / 5'14

Musicians: ⚥: vocals, electric guitar / **Sonny T.:** bass / **Michael B.:** drums / **Tommy Barbarella:** synthesizers / **Mr Hayes:** Hammond organ / **Recording: Paisley Park, Chanhassen, Minnesota:** 29 October 1995 / **Technical team: Producer: ⚥ / Recording engineer:** ? (not confirmed)

The lucky owners of a copy of Parris Patton's short movie *The Undertaker*, released in VHS format on 6 March 1995 and featuring the recording sessions held on 14 June 1993 for the eponymous album, with Michael Bland on drums and Sonny Thompson on bass guitar, know this Prince blues number well. During the night of 28 and 29 October 1995, Prince and his musicians gave a mini concert at Paisley Park, and after midnight played *Return of the Bump Squad*, *The Jam*, *The Ride*, and *Bambi*. As was his wont, Prince recorded the show and offered this version of *The Ride* to his fans on *Crystal Ball* in 1998.

GET LOOSE

Prince / 3'31

Musician: Prince: vocals, electric guitar, bass, drums, programming, synthesizers, backing vocals / **Recording: Paisley Park, Chanhassen, Minnesota:** February 1993; 1994 / **Technical team: Producer:** Prince / **Recording engineers:** David "Chronic Freeze" Friedlander, Ray Hahnfeldt, Tom Tucker / **Assistant recording engineers:** Xanex Bess, Tom Garneau, Kimm James

A remix of *Loose!* made in 1995, whose original title was *Lemme See Your Body (Get Loose)*, this song—which features on the tracklist of *Crystal Ball*—is of little interest, in view of the many precious unreleased songs that could have replaced it.

P. CONTROL (REMIX)

⚥ / 6'00

Musicians: ⚥: rap, vocals, bass, drums, programming, percussion, finger snapping, synthesizers, backing vocals / **Mayte:** spoken voice / **Recording: Paisley Park, Chanhassen, Minnesota:** 25 July 1994 / **Technical team: Producer: ⚥ / Recording engineer: ⚥**

Like *Get Loose*, *P. Control (Remix)* is an uninteresting reworking of the original classic, which opens the monumental album *The Gold Experience*. Never has the maxim "if it ain't broke, don't fix it" been more apt than in the case of this insipid remix.

MAKE YOUR MAMA HAPPY

Prince / 4'01

Musicians: Prince: vocals, electric guitar, bass, drums, synthesizers, backing vocals / **Eric Leeds:** saxophone / **Susannah Melvoin:** backing vocals / **Recording: Galpin Boulevard Home Studio, Chanhassen, Minnesota:** 7–8 August 1986 / **Technical team: Producer:** Prince / **Recording engineer:** Susan Rogers

In the midst of recording what would become the album *Sign O' the Times*, Prince recorded two final songs before traveling to Europe, where he would kick off his Parade Tour at Wembley Arena on 12 August 1986. On 7 August, he had recorded *Forever in My Life*, written in honor of Susannah Melvoin, as well as *Make Your Mama Happy*, a funk number with gospel touches in which he advocates personal success as a goal for the characters in the song to attain. The next day, Eric Leeds enhanced the song with his saxophone, and Prince shelved it before flying to London.

GOODBYE

⚥ / 4'35

Musicians: ⚥: vocals, bass, programming, synthesizers, piano, backing vocals / **Orchestra** / **Recording: Paisley Park, Chanhassen, Minnesota:** December 1991; 1995 / **Ocean Way Recording, Los Angeles:** December 1994 (strings) / **Technical team: Producer: ⚥ / Recording engineers:** Michael Koppelman, David Friedlander, Steve Noonan, Ray Hahnfeldt, Brian Poer, Shane T Keller, Steve Durkee / **String arrangements:** Clare Fischer

Although Prince had started working on the soul ballad *(Excuse Me Is This) Goodbye* during the recording sessions for the ⚥ album, it was only once Clare Fischer's string arrangements had been recorded onto the song, in December 1994, that he finished mixing it. A number in the same vein as the most languorous tracks on *Emancipation*, it was eventually replaced by *The Holy River* when the album's final tracklist was drawn up—a decision that Prince clearly regretted because he ended *Crystal Ball* with this song, renamed *Goodbye* for the occasion.

THE TRUTH

The Truth · Don't Play Me · Circle of Amour · 3rd 👁 · Dionne · Man in a Uniform
Animal Kingdom · The Other Side of the Pillow · Fascination
One of Your Tears · Comeback · Welcome 2 the Dawn (Acoustic Version)

Released in the USA by NPG Records:
29 January 1998 (CD box set ref. *Crystal Ball/The Truth*: none)
Best chart ranking in the USA: 62

With *The Truth*, Prince embarked on a significant transitional phase, revealing a little more of himself in each of the songs on the album.

1998

THE ACOUSTIC INTERLUDE

The Truth is inseparable from *Crystal Ball* as it is the fourth CD in the box set of the same name. Prince recorded *The Truth* between December 1996 and late March 1997. He takes the acoustic guitar lead on this album, showing himself in his most melancholic light (*Don't Play Me, Comeback, Circle of Amour*), but also gracing us with some exceptional blues tracks (*The Other Side of the Pillow, The Truth*). It is an incongruous but nonetheless very pleasing work in Prince's discography, whether you happen to be a specialist or a complete novice in Minneapolis Sound. Shortly after the release of the *Emancipation* album, and after a break that Mayte had insisted on because they were grieving after the death of their newborn son, Prince decided to get back in the saddle and, on 1 December, began recording what would be his only acoustic album. Although the adjective "acoustic" is not entirely accurate since electronic instruments do occasionally pop up, the *MTV Unplugged* style that was very popular in the United States at the time encouraged Prince to leave his Love Symbol guitar in its case. Hans-Martin Buff, by then the official Paisley Park recording engineer, was put in charge of the sessions and these continued into the early spring of 1997. Prince planned to release *The Truth* as a CD album for international distribution, but Virgin Records' takeover of EMI Records that year put a stop to the promotion of *Emancipation* as well as to any new collaborative projects with EMI. The single *The Truth* was released in February 1997, but the album of the same name fetched up in The Vault.

A precious bonus disc

Never one to let a good idea go to waste, in the summer of 1997 Prince sent copies of the album to various journalists who had been long-time supporters, including Jon Bream of the Minneapolis *Star Tribune* and Jim Walsh of the *St. Paul Pioneer Press*. After some positive feedback, he decided to include the album in the box set of unreleased material he was then producing: the famous *Crystal Ball*. Pre-orders had opened in May 1997, but deliveries were considerably delayed (Prince wanted to achieve a minimum of 100,000 pre-orders before he began pressing *Crystal Ball*). Therefore, he was able to add *The Truth* to the box set, much to the delight of fans. The record did not come out on its own until 2021 when The Prince Estate released a limited-edition vinyl version on Record Store Day, which fell on 12 June that year. Although *The Truth* is an integral part of the *Crystal Ball* box set, it is very much an album in its own right and will be approached as such here.

Single

THE TRUTH

[symbol] / 3'35

Musician: [symbol]: vocals, acoustic guitar, finger snapping, synthesizers / **Recording:** **Paisley Park, Chanhassen, Minnesota:** 1 December 1996 / **Technical team:** **Producer:** [symbol] / **Recording engineer:** Hans-Martin Buff
Single: 1. ***The Truth***/3'32 / **2.** ***Don't Play Me***/2'50 / **Released in the USA by NPG Records:** 14 February 1997 (CD single ref.: none) / **Best chart ranking in the USA:** did not make the charts

"If you abide in My word, you are My disciples indeed. And you shall know the truth, and the truth shall make you free."[199] These are Jesus's words from the Gospel according to John in the New Testament (John 8: 31–32) and they remained with Prince throughout 1996, the year he began a profound spiritual conversion that grew in intensity after he met the musician Larry Graham. Like *The Dawn* during *The Gold Experience* era, *The Truth* became Prince's new mantra, and he inserted it into every one of his spiritual flights of fancy, which tended to leave journalists somewhat bemused. "The Bible has taught me the Truth," he declared at the time. "Only once I realized that I couldn't resist the Truth, I learned the true meaning of freedom. Once you've reached that point, all your senses of creativity will reveal itself."[200] As Prince turned to faith to help him recover from the tragedy he had just experienced, the only possible name for his new album, as well as this the first track recorded for it on 1 December 1996, was the one he gave it. Released as a single through NPG Records on 14 February 1997 (the same day as the *Kamasutra* album; see page 318), *The Truth* presents Prince at his most bluesy, with the reverb-drenched chords on his acoustic guitar giving way to singing worthy of the best American gospel preaching. Those who first heard this track after ordering it on the 1-800-NEW-FUNK platform must have been totally astonished as Prince had never seemed so close to his listeners...you can just reach out and touch the wood of his acoustic 6-string guitar! *The Truth* is very much a spiritual track set in a velvet-lined casket by recording engineer Hans-Martin Buff, who was the most talented technician to work with Prince since the departure of Susan Rogers in 1987.

DON'T PLAY ME

[symbol] / 2'48

Musician: [symbol]: vocals, acoustic guitar, synthesizers, backing vocals / **Recording:** **Paisley Park, Chanhassen, Minnesota:** 1 December 1996 / **Technical team:** **Producer:** [symbol] / **Recording engineer:** Hans-Martin Buff

Immediately after *The Truth* was recorded, Hans-Martin Buff kept the tape machine running and Prince laid down *Don't Play Me* in that same session, thus capturing a rare moment in which he sings in a pure and unadorned way. As he had previously stated in *My Name Is Prince* in 1992: "I've seen the top, and it's just a dream/Big cars and women and fancy clothes/Will save your face, but it won't save your soul." Prince now reminds his audience of his vision of success with the metaphorical line in *Don't Play Me*: "I've been to the mountain top and it ain't what U say." *Don't Play Me* was unveiled to fans on 14 February 1997 as the B-side—a misnomer if ever there was one, especially as CD singles only have one side—of *The Truth*.

CIRCLE OF AMOUR

[symbol] / 4'44

Musicians: [symbol]: vocals, acoustic guitar, electric guitar, bass, synthesizers, backing vocals / **Kirk Johnson:** programming / **Recording:** **Paisley Park, Chanhassen, Minnesota:** December 1996 to March 1997 / **Technical team:** **Producer:** [symbol] / **Recording engineer:** Hans-Martin Buff

Here, Prince gives us a rare insight into his time at Central High School, in Minneapolis, in the mid-1970s. This is a moving description of "The Original Gang of 4"—four girls called Mary, Claire, Denise, and Belle, teenagers on the cusp of womanhood who form a close-knit group that Prince calls "the circle of amour." Any memories of Prince's youth are always worth their weight in gold in his discography because apart from this sweet acoustic ballad, *The Sacrifice of Victor* on the [symbol] album, a song that mentions Bernadette Anderson, his surrogate mother from when he was friends with André

Had Prince succumbed to the charms of Dionne Farris? Yet another secret that contributed to the artist's mystery!

Cymone, and *Musicology* in 2004 which listed his music idols, Prince revealed very little about his teenage years during his prolific career.

3RD 👁

♀ / 4'54

Musicians: ♀: vocals, beat box, acoustic guitar, drums, Hammond organ, synthesizers, backing vocals / **Rhonda Smith:** bass / **Recording:** Paisley Park, Chanhassen, Minnesota: December 1996 to March 1997 / **Technical team:** Producer: ♀ / Recording engineer: Hans-Martin Buff

In 2012, Prince called his final all-female band 3rdEyeGirl in reference to the Eastern metaphor of the Third Eye, or sixth chakra, the center of spiritual awareness and intuition. But he had already used the esoteric allegory for this bluesy fourth track on *The Truth*. *3rd Eye* emerged from a collaboration with bassist Rhonda Smith (who is not credited on the track) and features a breathtaking, fretless 4-string line with glissandos and beautifully executed harmonics. "She played him a cassette with six riffs/chord progressions," recalls Hans-Martin Buff. "Right in front of me, he would add to what she wrote and sketch out a song."[21]

DIONNE

♀ / 3'14

Musician: ♀: vocals, acoustic guitar, piano, synthesizers, backing vocals / **Recording:** Paisley Park, Chanhassen, Minnesota: December 1996 to March 1997 / **Technical team:** Producer: ♀ / Recording engineer: Hans-Martin Buff

Dionne was written in honor of Dionne Farris, a singer with Arrested Development, the hip-hop group famous for the 1992 singles *Tennessee* (which samples Prince's *Alphabet St*) and *People Everyday*, an adaptation of Sly and the Family Stone's hit *Everyday People*. Prince met Farris in 1995, after a concert she had given while launching her solo career. "We met, talked, exchanged numbers, and we kept in touch I'd say for about three years having conversations about the music industry," she said. "I listened, giving him my full attention, and because of that I'm sure about the artist I am today. It opened me up to a lot of knowledge."[202] In 1999, when a fan on the website Love4OneAnother.com chat asked Prince who the track was inspired by, he teasingly replied, "Dionne lives in London, and is well aware of the heart she broke. All Dionnes are heartbreakers!"[201] in reference to the song *Heartbreaker* by another singer called Dionne (Warwick). In 2016, Dionne Farris recorded *Revelation*, an album dedicated to the memory of Prince.

The traditional martial tune *Reveille* was used in two pieces recorded by Prince in 1996: *Chaos and Disorder* and *Man in a Uniform*.

MAN IN A UNIFORM

[symbol], Rhonda Smith / 3'08

Musician: [symbol]: vocals, acoustic guitar, bass, percussion, synthesizers, backing vocals / **Recording:** Paisley Park, Chanhassen, Minnesota: December 1996 to March 1997 / **Technical team:** Producer: [symbol] / Recording engineer: Hans-Martin Buff

This is Prince back to his sassy style, recounting the story of a night spent with a woman who insists he wear a uniform and tells him: "Man in a uniform do funny things to me." The track incorporates the melody from the *Reveille*, a bugle call traditionally played to wake up soldiers (already heard on the track *Chaos and Disorder* in 1995). It sees Prince digging deep into military imagery and the popular fantasy of the male uniform as an object of seduction, to offer us a very successful folk track.

ANIMAL KINGDOM

[symbol], Rhonda Smith / 4'01

Musicians: [symbol]: vocals, acoustic guitar, electric guitar, piano, synthesizers, backing vocals / **Rhonda Smith**: bass / **Recording:** Paisley Park, Chanhassen, Minnesota: March 1997 / **Technical team:** Producer: [symbol] / Recording engineer: Hans-Martin Buff

"Who told us we should eat the swine?" Prince asks in this ode to vegetarianism. This song advocates a sensible diet and was inspired by a conversation Prince had with movie director Spike Lee on 7 February 1997 for *Interview* magazine, in which Prince said: "Our people have the worst diet of anybody. I'm ready to put a farmer on my payroll. We've got to get back to growing our own food. You are what you eat!"[182] He even suggested that he only wanted to work with vegetarian musicians from then on. In answer to a question from journalist Catherine Censor Shemo of *Vegetarian Times* magazine, who asked him how he thought fans would react to this, Prince restated his position: "I'm not sure how many are meat eaters but soon all will know the consequences of a barbarian lifestyle. It's called karma! My music is dictated by the spirit. Not worrying about people's reaction is what has sustained me."[203]

THE OTHER SIDE OF THE PILLOW

[symbol] / 3'22

Musician: [symbol]: vocals, whistles, acoustic guitar, synthesizer, backing vocals / **Recording:** Paisley Park, Chanhassen, Minnesota: December 1996 to March 1997 / **Technical team:** Producer: [symbol] / Recording engineer: Hans-Martin Buff

Lucky owners of the ultra-limited vinyl edition of *The Truth*, which was made available sparingly in record stores on the 2021 Record Store Day (12 June), will have noticed the obvious mistake in the booklet notes of this long-awaited version of the acoustic album. The musicians John Blackwell, Rhonda Smith, Renato Neto, Greg Boyer, and Najee, who were not involved in any way, shape, or form with the recording of this track, which was exclusively Prince playing the acoustic 6-string. However, they did perform on the live version recorded for the *One Nite Alone...Live!* album on 24 November 2002. A mistake that everyone thinks warrants a new vinyl edition of *The Truth* (and which would certainly delight the poor unfortunates who couldn't get their hands on a copy!). Despite this error, *The Other Side of the Pillow* is unquestionably one of the best songs on the album, shining out for its sobriety and Prince's sensuous vocals.

FASCINATION

O(+> / 4'55

Musicians: O(+>: vocals, acoustic guitar, electric guitar, synthesizers, backing vocals / **Mike Scott:** electric guitar / **Rhonda Smith:** bass / **David "Fingers" Haynes:** drums / **Kat Dyson:** percussion, backing vocals / **Kirk Johnson:** percussion, backing vocals / **Recording: Paisley Park, Chanhassen, Minnesota:** 29–31 March 1997 / **Technical team:** Producer: O(+> / Recording engineer: Hans-Martin Buff

Over the Easter weekend of 1997, Prince invited some musician friends round to jam with him at Paisley Park. Mike Scott was on guitar, Rhonda Smith on bass, Kat Dyson and Kirk Johnson on percussion and backing vocals, while a certain David Haynes was on drums. After starting out on a Yamaha RX11 programmable drum machine in 1986, the drummer was a past master of digital pads which model drum sounds. His mastery of drum machines of all kinds would even influence the Korg brand in the development of its famous NanoPad in the early 2010s. Despite the prolific sessions over the three days in Paisley Park, which Hans-Martin Buff archived in The Vault as *Jams One to Six*, Prince decided that to stay true to the album's folky spirit, he would only keep Haynes's bass drum for this song, which became *Fascination*.

ONE OF YOUR TEARS

O(+> / 3'27

Musicians: O(+>: vocals, acoustic guitar, synthesizers, backing vocals / **Rhonda Smith:** bass / **Kirk Johnson:** programming / **Recording: Paisley Park, Chanhassen, Minnesota:** December 1996 to March 1997 / **Technical team:** Producer: O(+> / Recording engineer: Hans-Martin Buff

In the lyrics for this song, Prince is upset at the woman who mailed him a used condom in response to a song he had written about her. He tells us he wants to come back as one of her tears. Some observers maintain the song was intended for Dionne Farris for whom he had written the track *Dionne* shortly before, although neither party ever confirmed this.

COMEBACK

O(+> / 2'00

Musician: O(+>: vocals, acoustic guitar, finger snapping, backing vocals / **Recording: Paisley Park, Chanhassen, Minnesota:** December 1996 / **Technical team:** Producer: O(+> / Recording engineer: Hans-Martin Buff

Comeback is the highlight of the album and was written by Prince in memory of his child who had died a few weeks earlier. "It was hard to listen to it for many years [...]," Mayte said in 2019. "When I first heard it, I thought it was amazing and beautiful. I told [Prince] that I could smell [Amiir], and he used that in the beautiful lyrics that he wrote. He would put his emotions in his songs [...] I hear intense sadness, but with that sadness, for me now, I acknowledge it, and turn it into something positive."[204] The title of the song was inspired by the spirituality that was ever-present in the couple's lives during the traumatic ordeal of their infant's death, as Mayte explained in 2006: "We believed he was going to come back, that souls come back. We didn't want to acknowledge he was gone, it was our way of grieving."[205] During the recording of *Comeback* (the third track to be laid down on tape for the album, in December 1996), Prince added a short, four-sentence *a cappella* called *Mindblow* as an intro. His decision to delete it was a sign of the extreme discretion he was exercising at the time. "Even just thinking about it, I'm getting goosebumps," said Hans-Martin Buff, who was there to witness this deeply spiritual moment in December 1996. "[...] That was deeply personal, that was just crazy..."[192]

WELCOME 2 THE DAWN (ACOUSTIC VERSION)

O(+> / 3'18

Musician: O(+>: vocals, acoustic guitar, synthesizers, backing vocals / **Recording: Paisley Park, Chanhassen, Minnesota:** December 1997 / **Technical team:** Producer: O(+> / Recording engineer: Hans-Martin Buff

In January 1997, Prince released the single *The Holy River*. A special audio cassette version was then made for Borders Books and Music stores and given to customers at the checkout. In addition to Prince's new single, the promotional item included a new, entirely acoustic, track: *Welcome 2 the Dawn*. This beautiful version features on *The Truth*, but recording engineer Hans-Martin Buff has also confirmed the existence of another funkier version of the track in The Vault which was recorded around the same time.

THE NEW POWER GENERATION

NEWPOWER SOUL

Newpower Soul · Mad Sex · Until U're in My Arms Again · When U Love Somebody
Shoo-Bed-Ooh . Push It Up . Freaks on this Side . Come On · The One
(👁 Like) Funky Music · Wasted Kisses (Hidden track)

Released in the USA by NPG Records:
30 June 1998 (CD ref.: none)
Released in the UK by NPG Records/BMG:
30 June 1998 (CD ref.: 74321 60598 2)
Best chart ranking in the USA: 22
Best chart ranking in the UK: 38

No doubt about it —the Newpower Soul movement is up and running!

1998

THE REBIRTH OF FUNK

A few months after *Crystal Ball*, Prince could take pride in the success of this independent album, as sales were approaching 150,000. Not being the kind of person to rest on his laurels, the singer announced in the spring that *Newpower Soul*, the third album by the New Power Generation, would be released on 30 June 1998. Recorded during the months when *Crystal Ball* was being conceived, the group's next album was described as a return to funk with, at its heart, an irresistible groove and catchy melodies—the very opposite of the spiritual *Emancipation*.

Here we look back over the timeline of an album whose release would coincide with numerous changes in Prince's personal life.

Larry Graham, the "guru" of funk

During the summer of 1997, Mayte (see page 216) gave Prince the most precious of gifts, informing him that she was once again pregnant with their child. The trauma of losing their infant Amiir, in October 1996, was still raw; the news delighted the couple, who were then on the road for the Jam of the Year Tour. However, a series of ordeals would play havoc with their stability. On 22 August 1997, Prince went on stage at the Nashville Arena with the new lineup of the New Power Generation, which notably included the guitarist Mike Scott and the backing vocalist Marva King. On hearing that the bass player Larry Graham, the idol of his youth, was performing in town that same evening, Prince organized a meeting at his aftershow at the Music City Mix Factory. The connection between the two artists was instant. The legendary bass player of Sly and the Family Stone from 1967 to 1972, Graham was also the leader, since 1974, of Graham Central Station, one of the most famous American funk groups—Prince never made a secret of the major influence this band had on his music. *Hair* (*Graham Central Station*, 1974), as well as *The Jam* and *It's Alright* (*Ain't No 'Bout-A-Doubt It*, 1975), were all songs that Prince had covered onstage over the years in homage to the bass player who invented slapping, a revolutionary bass guitar technique that was adopted by all the instrument's devotees. "The connection my husband felt with Larry was spiritual, not just musical," Mayte recalled. "[...] I was happy for him. I thought this friendship would be a healthy, positive influence."[134]

Indeed, the two men quickly became inseparable. Prince offered his new songs to Graham and, in return, received recommendations as to what to read from the bass player, who was an active member of the Jehovah's Witnesses community—a movement that considers itself to be Christian, while also having its own precepts, based above all on an in-depth study of the Bible. "I sent a book called *You Can Live Forever In Paradise On Earth* [a study of the Bible that is an important text for Jehovah's Witnesses]," Graham related. "He called me and asked if he could make seven copies for the members of his band. I told him I'd bring him some books myself and we met up again in New York."[21] From then on, Prince's spiritual quest knew no limits. He came out with arcane pronouncements that were sometimes unfathomable, even eccentric, and gradually drew apart from his wife, who struggled to follow him on this path, which led him to join the Jehovah's Witnesses two years later. The crisis affecting the couple worsened considerably with the arrival on the scene of a young Canadian woman, Manuela Testolini, who was hired by Paisley Park Enterprises to work within the Love 4 One Another foundation, an organization with which Mayte had been involved previously.

new newpower

"The Artist" onstage at the Flanders Expo in Ghent, Belgium, on 28 December 1998.

1998

Since he considered that *Newpower Soul* was inextricably linked to the albums by Chaka Khan and Graham Central Station, which were produced at the same time, in 1998 Prince released a box set containing all three albums with the title *Newpowerpak*, which was available through 1-800-NEW-FUNK.

Prince with Mayte, Larry Graham, and the singer Chaka Khan in 1998.

The road to Newpower Soul

On 19 November 1997, Mayte found out via the routine scan carried out in the third month of pregnancy that she was carrying a "blighted ovum," a term used to describe a fertilized embryo that has stopped developing early in pregnancy. Despite the pain caused by this news, which would progressively defeat the couple, Prince threw himself into producing three albums simultaneously in November 1997: *Come 2 My House*, the new album by Chaka Khan, whom he had always considered an influence; *GCS 2000*, Graham Central Station's new CD; and the new album by the New Power Generation, *Newpower Soul*. The recording of the latter, which Prince decided would bear the name of his group—even though he was the only musician playing on it, bar the odd guest here and there—conveyed a precious piece of information to fans. It was, in fact, a digression in his career: an extremely funky album, to be regarded as a moment of madness right in the middle of an output of the highest craftsmanship. When *Newpower Soul* was released on 30 June 1998, it was panned by the critics, who did not appreciate the album's regressive side, in which the artist seemed to have reconnected with his two past obsessions: sex and partying. Barely 138,000 copies were sold in the US in the months that followed, despite a New Power Soul Tour that crossed the country and Europe until 28 August 1998, followed by the New Power Soul Festival Tour, from 23 September to 28 December the same year. With all due respect to the critics—who failed to notice the charm of this sensual, groovy album—on its release, *Newpower Soul* marked a rebirth for the artist, offering a collection bursting with energy and full of potential hits that were just made for live performance and the dance floor. Its credo: "Get freaky, let the head bob!"

FOR PRINCE ADDICTS

In 1998, Prince revealed on his website Love4OneAnother.com that he was producing a compilation of unreleased songs recorded in the mid-1980s with The Revolution. The project's name, which varied from one interview he gave to another, was *Prince and The Revolution's Roadhouse Garden*, or simply *Roadhouse Garden*, from the title of a song recorded in 1984 that had never been released. After various discussions with Wendy Melvoin on the subject, Prince finally announced that the project was being dropped, to the great displeasure of fans.

1998

NEWPOWER SOUL

The New Power Generation / 5'00

Musicians: ⚥: vocals, rap, electric guitar, bass, synthesizers, backing vocals / **Kirk Johnson:** programming / **Michael B** Nelson: trombone / **Kathy Jensen:** baritone saxophone / **Kenni Holmen:** saxophone / **Dave Jensen:** trumpet / **Steve Strand:** trumpet / **Marva King:** backing vocals / **Kim Berry:** backing vocals / **Recording:** **Paisley Park, Chanhassen, Minnesota:** May 1997 to February 1998 / **Technical team:** **Producer:** ⚥ / **Recording engineer:** Hans-Martin Buff

The strident *Newpower Soul* makes a fine opening to the album and will buzz around in your head for hours after just one hearing. To achieve this result, Prince reused the motif "Get freaky, let the head bob," which had already been heard in *Big Fun*, on the *Exodus* album, in 1995. The wind section of the NPG, now dubbed the Hornheadz and featuring a new saxophonist in the shape of Kenni Holmen, who replaced Brian Gallagher, makes its mark in this song with its power and constant presence, reminding us of Prince's admiration for funk groups with wind instruments such as Tower of Power, whose numbers he had already sampled in the past. Worthy of note is a lo-fi rap by Prince, in which he lists all the songs on the album in order of appearance with the exception of the hidden track, *Wasted Kisses*, which was doubtless added to the tracklist after the recording of the irresistible *Newpower Soul*, to which so many of us danced in the summer of 1998.

MAD SEX

The New Power Generation / 5'12

Musicians: ⚥: vocals, rap, spoken voice, bass, synthesizers, piano, backing vocals / **Kirk Johnson:** programming / **Michael B** Nelson: trombone / **Kathy Jensen:** baritone saxophone / **Kenni Holmen:** saxophone / **Dave Jensen:** trumpet / **Steve Strand:** trumpet / **DJ Brother Jules:** scratching / **Recording:** **Paisley Park, Chanhassen, Minnesota:** November to December 1997 / **Technical team:** **Producer:** ⚥ / **Recording engineer:** Hans-Martin Buff / **Arrangements:** Kirk Johnson

Prince worked closely with Kirk Johnson, who was already responsible for programming on the album, to put together *Mad Sex*—a funky gem driven by the Hornheadz who here reveal all their musical skill, with the muted trumpets of Dave Jensen and Steve Strand leading the charge. The singer gave Kirk Johnson free rein to demonstrate his ability to produce, with panache, this kind of relentless groove, which is remarkable. "I allowed other sounds made by other individuals," Prince said. "*Mad Sex* is a creation of Kirk's. I let that dictate how I wrote and arranged it."[206] The song relates the misfortunes of a man whose mistress has left him. The lyrics, which are strongly reminiscent of those of *Dionne*, on *The Truth* album, recorded a year earlier, have a particular resonance because in this song Prince describes his former lover as "A bird from London." Whether friendly or romantic, real or imagined, Prince's relationship with the singer Dionne Farris appears to have inspired some deeply felt lyrics.

No wind ensemble was more inspiring than Tower of Power, a legendary soul-funk group from Oakland, California.

Sometimes called The NPG Hornz, sometimes The Hornheadz or the Hornheads, Michael B Nelson's wind section stayed with Prince until his final album in 2015.

UNTIL U'RE IN MY ARMS AGAIN

The New Power Generation / 4'47

Musicians: [symbol]: vocals, bass, chimes, synthesizers, backing vocals / **Kirk Johnson:** drums, programming / **Orchestra** / **Recording:** **Paisley Park, Chanhassen, Minnesota:** May 1997 to February 1998 / **O'Henry Sound Studios, Burbank, California:** 1998 (orchestra) / **Technical team:** **Producer:** [symbol] / **Recording engineers:** Hans-Martin Buff, Arne Frager (O'Henry Sound Studios) / **Assistant recording engineer:** Brett Swain (O'Henry Sound Studios) / **Orchestral arrangements:** Clare Fischer

Although on the surface *Until U're in My Arms Again* is a love song in the purest tradition of the doo-wop hits of the 1950s, it was, according to some commentators, written by Prince in memory of his child who had died in October 1996. "Every night Eye said a prayer 2 God and his angels/I'm sure they knew/The many tears that Eye'd have 2 cry/If Eye ever had 2 leave your side," he sings. One can imagine him being deeply moved by the memory. A little later in the song he adds: "Every morning when Eye awaken/Eye imagine U sleepin' in your bed/Wrong or right—the reason U were taken/From my embrace, well—it's never said." On listening to this song, it is this context—which was never confirmed by the artist—that gives it all its charm and touches our hearts, in the process effacing its slightly sugary character.

WHEN U LOVE SOMEBODY

The New Power Generation / 5'56

Musicians: [symbol]: vocals, rap, electric guitar, bass, synthesizers, backing vocals / **Kirk Johnson:** programming / **Michael B** Nelson: trombone / **Kathy Jensen:** baritone saxophone / **Kenni Holmen:** saxophone / **Dave Jensen:** trumpet / **Steve Strand:** trumpet / **Pierre Baptiste:** saxophone / **Clark Gayton:** trombone / **Wayne Dumaine:** trumpet / **Marva King:** backing vocals / **Recording:** **Paisley Park, Chanhassen, Minnesota:** August 1997, autumn 1997 (wind) / **Technical team:** **Producer:** [symbol] / **Recording engineer:** Hans-Martin Buff

A love song with somewhat over-the-top lyrics, *When U Love Somebody* is a number that is pure Paisley Park, featuring a coda lasting almost two minutes in which Prince launches into a highly effective rap, accompanied by wah-wah guitar lines on the left-hand side of the stereo recording, with saturated lines on the right. Three new musicians bolster the wind section, consisting of the Hornheadz: the trumpet player Wayne Dumaine, the trombonist Clark Gayton, and the saxophonist Pierre Baptiste.

The rapper Doug E Fresh recorded his rhythmic flow for the irresistible song *Push It Up* in 1997.

SHOO-BED-OOH

The New Power Generation / 3'23

Musicians: [symbol]: vocals, bass, synthesizers, backing vocals / **Kirk Johnson:** programming / **Recording:** Paisley Park, Chanhassen, Minnesota: May 1997 / **Technical team:** Producer: [symbol] / Recording engineer: Hans-Martin Buff

Apart from the programming, Prince once again plays every instrument on this R&B number, which would not have looked out of place on *Emancipation*, an album released two years earlier. The expert hand of the discreet Hans-Martin Buff masterminded *Newpower Soul* and, especially, *Shoo-Bed-Ooh*, one of the first tracks recorded for the album. Buff declared—without complaining—that some sessions could last up to 40 hours and that, during his years at Paisley Park, he had spent more time with Prince than with his own wife. During a chat on the website Love4OneAnother.com in 1999, Buff explained what his role alongside Prince had been. "An engineer is the fellow that captures a musician's performance on tape and makes sure it all sounds good in the end. Eye'm responsible 4 making sure that the musicians and the producers can follow their muse without getting stuck in technical hassle. As a result of my work, the CD that U all will buy at 1-800-Newfunk hopefully sounds like what the recording artist(s) envisioned b4 they were at my mercy in the recording studio."[207]

PUSH IT UP

The New Power Generation / 5'28

Musicians: [symbol]: vocals, rap, bass, synthesizers, backing vocals / **Larry Graham:** rap / **Chaka Khan:** vocals / **Doug E Fresh:** rap, beat box / **Kirk Johnson:** programming / **DJ Brother Jules:** scratching / **Marva King:** backing vocals / **Recording:** Paisley Park, Chanhassen, Minnesota: 12 August 1997 / **Technical team:** Producer: [symbol] / Recording engineer: Hans-Martin Buff

The hip-hop legend Doug E Fresh—who was especially famous for his mastery of the beat box (of which he was one of the inventors) and world-renowned for hits such as *The Show* and *La-Di-Da-Di*, both performed as a duo with M. C. Ricky D in 1985—is the distinguished guest on *Push It Up*. This is an addictive number and marks the climax of the album, in which Doug E Fresh unleashes a top-notch duo with Prince. The rapper came to Prince's attention when the famous *Sinbad's Summer Jam Festival* was broadcast on the HBO network and he hurried to invite him to come and jam with him, before proposing that he take part in the recording of two songs on *Newpower Soul*. "Despite its party mood, *Push It Up* does not really come alive on record, probably working much better in a concert situation," the excellent magazine *Uptown* reported in September 1998. That view is questioned, entirely subjectively, in these pages, where it is strongly felt that *Push It Up* is a remarkably well-produced song, in which flows intertwine without ever clashing and the sole message conveyed by the artist—an invitation to party—is perfectly well understood by fans. A must-hear song in Prince's output at the end of the decade.

The singer Marva King, a newcomer to the New Power Generation who was with the group between 1997 and 1999.

FREAKS ON THIS SIDE

The New Power Generation / 5'42

Musicians: ⚥: vocals, bass, Hammond organ, synthesizers, backing vocals / **Marva King:** vocals, backing vocals / **Kirk Johnson:** programming / **Michael B** Nelson: trombone / **Kathy Jensen:** baritone saxophone / **Kenni Holmen:** saxophone / **Dave Jensen:** trumpet / **Steve Strand:** trumpet / **Recording:** Paisley Park, Chanhassen, Minnesota: May 1997 to February 1998 / **Technical team:** Producer: ⚥ / Recording engineer: Hans-Martin Buff

"Congratulations... U're in The New Power Generation," sing Prince and Marva King together in this funk number, led by the shouts of a crowd recorded during a concert at Paisley Park, just as the singer had done with the introduction to *Rock 'N' Roll Is Alive (and It Lives in Minneapolis)* in 1995. Marva King, whose powerful voice timbre had delighted Prince, was invited to join the NPG on the Jam of the Year World Tour on 2 August 1997, and recorded numerous backing vocals for *Newpower Soul*. "Prince encouraged total performance freedom," she said. "I learned to get wild onstage without an ounce of embarrassment. And that we did!"[209] Prince would start work on a Marva King album at Paisley Park in 1997, but the recording of those by Chaka Khan and Graham Central Station, on top of that of *Newpower Soul*, prevented him from bringing the project to fruition. Marva King left the New Power Generation in 1999.

Single

COME ON

The New Power Generation / 5'59

Musicians: ⚥: vocals, bass, synthesizers, piano, backing vocals / **Kat Dyson:** acoustic guitar / **Kirk Johnson:** programming / **Chaka Khan:** backing vocals / **Recording:** Paisley Park, Chanhassen, Minnesota: May 1997 to February 1998 / **Technical team:** Producer: ⚥ / Recording engineers: Hans-Martin Buff, Fred Harrington
Single: 1. *Come On* (Radio Edit)/4'30 / **2.** *Come On* (Remix)/8'13 / **3.** *Come On* (Late Nite Mix)/4'10 / **Released in the UK and Europe by NPG Records/RCA:** 16 October 1998 (CD single ref.: 74321 63472 2) / **Best chart ranking in the UK:** 65

Chaka Khan, who at the time was in the middle of recording her album *Come 2 My House* at Paisley Park, recorded some backing vocals for the very funky *Come On*, in which Prince returns to his voice pitched as it was during the Camille period (see page 142) and Kat Dyson plays bottleneck on her acoustic guitar, giving the song a folk/country sound never heard before on a Prince record. Used as a promotional aid in the United States, *Come On* was released as a single in the UK and Europe, and enjoyed the benefit of a most surprising clip. When he was in London for a concert at the Wembley Arena on 26 August 1998 and at the Brixton Academy two days later, Prince asked his right-hand person Jacqui Thompson to hastily make a video for his forthcoming single *Come On*. He urged her to meet him in Hyde Park, where the sun was shining that day and there were many passersby, and demanded Thompson put together a small film crew. Once the camera was running, Prince emerged from his limousine sporting a false beard, a pair of round glasses, and an old cap, then let fly a torrent of nonsense at the gawking onlookers who, naturally, had no idea who they were looking at. "We filmed him saying 'I've got the butter for your muffin,' a line of the song, to hot girls like some old pervert,"[21] Thompson recalled. It is true that seeing the greatest pop singer of the 20th century giving the finger to passersby or improvising all sorts of sketches while disguised as a grandfather is a fairly disconcerting experience!

THE ONE

The New Power Generation / 7'04

Musicians: [symbol]: vocals, percussion, synthesizers, backing vocals / **Rhonda Smith:** bass / **Kirk Johnson:** programming / **String orchestra** / **Recording:** **Paisley Park, Chanhassen, Minnesota:** November 1996 / **O'Henry Sound Studios, Burbank, California:** 1998 (orchestra) / **Technical team:** **Producer:** [symbol] / **Recording engineers:** Hans-Martin Buff, Arne Frager (O'Henry Sound Studios) / **Assistant recording engineer:** Brett Swain (O'Henry Sound Studios) / **String arrangements:** Clare Fischer

In the spring of 1998, Prince asked his wife, Mayte, to take charge of making a clip for the song *The One*, recorded two years earlier, to which Clare Fischer had just added some sublime string arrangements. The project allowed the couple to get together at a time when their relationship had been falling apart. "*The One* is the truest work we created together," Mayte confided in her autobiography, which was published in 2017. "When you look at it, even if you don't know the backstory, the love between us is tangible. There's a shadow of sadness in the music, but the sensuality overwhelms it."[134] Answering the journalist Ben Edmonds of *Mojo* magazine, who asked him what he had done for his fortieth birthday, Prince did not show himself to be as romantic as poor Mayte: "Making a video for *The One*. Maybe we went bowling. I don't really remember. I stopped celebrating those things a while back."[217] Having formed a friendship with the mystical Larry Graham, Prince ended up denying the song's romantic side, saying at the time: "[*The One*] started as an ordinary love song, but it turned out to be a respectful hymn to the creator, God. *The One* now has a kind of Garden of Eden feel to it. It's one of the purest songs I've ever written."[210] So much for romance.

(👁 LIKE) FUNKY MUSIC

The New Power Generation / 4'31

Musicians: [symbol]: vocals, electric guitar, bass, synthesizers, backing vocals / **Doug E** Fresh: rap, beat box / **Kirk Johnson:** programming / **Dave Jensen:** trumpet / **Steve Strand:** trumpet / **Pierre Baptiste:** saxophone / **Clark Gayton:** trombone / **Wayne DuMaine:** trumpet / **Recording:** **Paisley Park, Chanhassen, Minnesota:** May 1997 / **Technical team:** **Producer:** [symbol] / **Recording engineer:** Hans-Martin Buff

You could swear that *(Eye Like) Funky Music* came straight out of a time capsule buried in 1986 by Camille, Prince's feminine persona, in order to make way for the album *Sign O' the Times*. Yet this song is totally contemporary with the rest of the *Newpower Soul* album. High-pitched vocals and guitars guide our ears toward a time gone by, reviving the memory of *Shockadelica* and *Erotic City* and proving a joy to listen to. Doug E Fresh adds his mark to this very funky number, which was produced with the assistance of the recording engineer Hans-Martin Buff and Kirk Johnson, NPG's drummer, who was responsible for rhythmic programming on *Newpower Soul*. "It's amazing," Johnson said, explaining what it was like to work with The Artist. "I have an idea, some beats. So me and our engineer leave some ideas on the board and when we come back it's a whole new beast."[206]

WASTED KISSES

The New Power Generation / 2'58

Musicians: [symbol]: vocals, acoustic guitar, bass, synthesizers, backing vocals / **Kirk Johnson:** programming / **Recording:** **Paisley Park, Chanhassen, Minnesota:** 1997 / **Technical team:** **Producer:** [symbol] / **Recording engineer:** Hans-Martin Buff

Here is a song that is really difficult to dig out—the 49th track on the compact disc of *Newpower Soul*. After *(Eye Like) Funky Music*, the tenth track on the album, the listener must click through 37 silent, five-second tracks, then a 48th, equally silent, 44-second track, before being able to enjoy this excellent song, which is perhaps the best on the album.

The 49th track on *Newpower Soul*, *Wasted Kisses* is nevertheless named on page 21 of the album's sleeve notes, appearing on the elastic of the shorts worn by the character drawn by Debbie McGuan, alongside two logos that users of CDs know well: the arrow indicating fast forward and the one indicating a change of track. Although it is difficult to say whether this song of regret (that of a lover who feels he has wasted his kisses on a woman who did not deserve them) was destined for Mayte, the heartbeat sound effect at the end of the track, followed by the sound of a flatlining heart, to which are added a man's cries of pain, have a special resonance given the tragedy that had just befallen Prince and his wife (having lost their baby). A touching song that marked in an inescapable way the end of an era for the singer and the vulnerable Mayte.

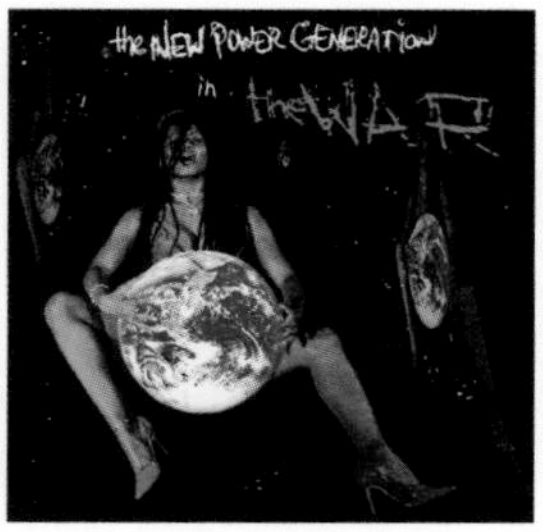

THE WAR

(THE NEW POWER GENERATION)

The New Power Generation / 26'00

Musicians
⚥: vocals, electric guitar, synthesizers, piano, percussion
Mike Scott: electric guitar
Rhonda Smith: bass
Kirk Johnson: drums
Mr Hayes: Hammond organ, synthesizers, programming
Marva King: backing vocals, percussion

Recording
Paisley Park, Chanhassen, Minnesota: 20 June 1998 (live), summer 1998 (overdubs)

Technical team
Producer: ⚥
Recording engineer: ? (not confirmed)

Promotional version (cassette and CD single)
1. *The War* /26'00
Digital release on Love4OneAnother.com: 21 July 1998

Genesis

Distributed to buyers of *Crystal Ball* during the summer of 1998 as a cassette, then released in CD format and distributed via the telephone order line 1-800-NEW-FUNK, this single by The New Power Generation was recorded onstage at Paisley Park in the early hours of 20 June 1998, before a crowd of lucky listeners. *The War* contains a mantra—"The Evolution will be colorized"—which recalls *The Revolution Will Not Be Televised* by Gil Scott-Heron (1971), a poem that was set to music and harshly attacks the media for their lack of interest in poor people. *The War* also appears to be a sermon by a Jehovah's Witness describing the Apocalypse, a subject often mentioned by members of the movement, in which Prince was becoming increasingly interested. The singer describes the signs of a world heading for perdition and the unavoidable end of humanity, with a highly organized life underground as the sole solution. The song, which is mystical to say the least, could also be heard on the website Love4OneAnother.com in 1998, in return for a symbolic contribution of one dollar, accompanied by this warning: "The peril of pestilence come to those who download for free. Download at your own risk."[211]

Production

A total of 46 minutes of this jam session were recorded during the concert on 20 June 1998 (it was planned for the evening of 19 June, but eventually began after midnight); Prince edited this down to a version lasting 26 minutes. Using the version recorded in concert, in which the new musicians of the NPG launch into an improvisation that is as insistent as it is long, Prince later added numerous overdubs, especially in the final segment, from 23'25 in the piece. Rather than a song in its own right, *The War* is essentially a bonus track distributed to fans in return for their loyalty, as demonstrated by Prince's message to his admirers on the back of the promotional CD: "Thanks 2 those of U who support the dreams of freedom..."[212]

PRINCE

THE VAULT... OLD FRIENDS 4 SALE

The Rest of My Life · It's About That Walk · She Spoke 2 Me (Extended Remix)
5 Women · When the Lights Go Down · My Little Pill · There Is Lonely
Old Friends 4 Sale · Sarah · Extraordinary

Released in the USA by Warner Bros. Records:
24 August 1999 (CD ref.: 9 47522-2)
Released in the UK by Warner Bros. Records:
24 August 1999 (CD ref.: 9362-47522-2)
Best chart ranking in the USA: 85
Best chart ranking in the UK: 47

Prince poses at his property in Marbella, Spain, in 1999.

THE LAST ALBUM FOR WARNER

In April 1996, tensions between Prince and Warner Bros. Records were at their highest. In November 1995, the singer had revealed to Julie Baumgold from *Esquire* magazine that he was working on a revolutionary album, which he would only release after his contract with Warner had expired. This announcement angered the record company's management who refused to release *Exodus*, the new album by the New Power Generation. Hostility between the two sides increased further before they reached a compromise, with Prince producing, in the spring of 1996, the last two albums he owed the record company: *Chaos and Disorder* and *The Vault... Old Friends 4 Sale*. The former was released on 9 July 1996 to general indifference, while the latter was shelved by Warner Bros. Records, who would release it quietly at the end of August 1999. As the singer explains in the notes (released with the definitive visuals for each album), both albums are merely compilations of old songs "Originally intended 4 private use only."[219] Nevertheless, they allow fans to rediscover some rare tracks by their idol, sometimes heard live and often swapped among bootleggers.

From rock to jazz

While *Chaos and Disorder* reflected Prince's more rock side, The *Vault... Old Friends 4 Sale* reveals more jazzy numbers, with a softer mood, recorded by an accomplished artist who now abandoned drum machines and other synthetic instruments in favor of tracks created in the company of his virtuoso musicians, led by Michael Bland and Sonny Thompson. With all due respect to Prince's detractors, there is a coherence to the selection made for the album by the singer within his legendary strongroom of Paisley Park. As a whole, the album is very pleasing, even though it is the diametric opposite of the groovy *Emancipation* and the partying *Newpower Soul*. Warner Bros. Records—who did not know that Prince had agreed distribution to great fanfare of his next album, *Rave un2 the Joy Fantastic* (planned for release two months later), with Arista—suffered a crushing failure in the summer of 1999 with this compilation of unreleased tracks, which were disowned by the singer and not promoted upon release. This is an injustice that can be righted by listening once more to the songs on this misjudged album, which contains many treasures. Worthy of note is the portrait of Prince on the cover by French photographer Claude Gassian, taken in the Mirano green room in Brussels where Prince held a legendary aftershow during the night of 4 and 5 September 1993. "I stayed close to him for five days, but there were few moments when I could photograph him—it was very frustrating. The last evening [...] I told him I would really like him to pose in the green room, which was fantastic [...] After a few minutes, he made a sign to follow him. He sat on a chair long enough for 12 shots, and left without a word. I had my picture, and was overjoyed."[220]

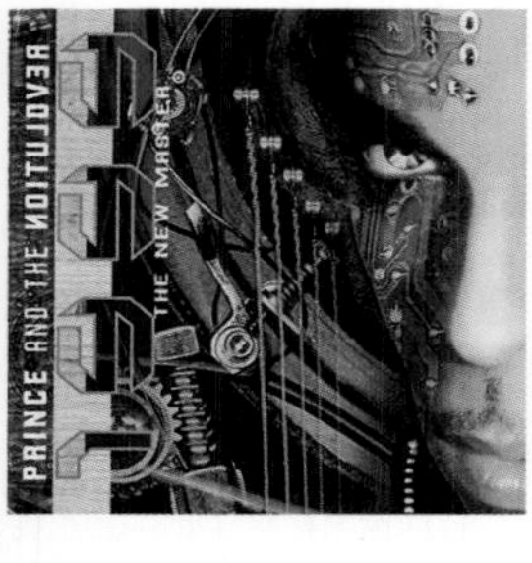

The singer's ambition of rerecording his entire repertoire quickly gave way to the production of new songs.

1999: THE NEW MASTER

(PRINCE AND THE REVOLUTION)

1. *1999 (The New Master)* **(7'09)**
2. *Rosario (1999)* **(1'19)**
3. *1999 (The Inevitable Mix)* **(5'46)**
4. *1999 (Keep Steppin')* **(4'33)**
5. *1999 (Rosie & Doug E. In A Deep House)* **(6'23)**
6. *1999 (The New Master: Single Edit)* **(4'30)**
7. *1999 (Acapella)* **(5'11)**

Released in the USA by NPG Records: 2 February 1999 (maxi-single ref.: 7-85337-19991-6; CD ref.: 7-85337-19992-3)
Best chart ranking in the USA: 150

Musicians

Prince: vocals, electric guitar, bass, programming, piano, synthesizers, percussion, claps, backing vocals
Lisa Coleman: vocals
Dez Dickerson: vocals
Rosie Gaines: vocals, backing vocals
Doug E Fresh: rap, backing vocals
Jill Jones: vocals, backing vocals
Jesse Johnson: backing vocals
DJ Brother Jules: scratching

Recording

Paisley Park, Chanhassen, Minnesota: 1998

Technical team

Producer: Prince
Recording engineer: Hans-Martin Buff

Genesis

Taking advantage of the euphoria over the fast-approaching end of the millennium, Warner Bros. Records decided to reissue the single *1999*, which had originally been released by Prince in 1982. So, a maxi-single appeared on 28 December 1998 in Europe and in a promotional format in the United States. This enraged Prince who had naturally not been consulted on the decision—his former record label, it must be remembered, were in possession of his old master tapes. The furious Prince had the brilliant idea of rerecording his entire catalog. "I wanted to buy my masters back from Warner Bros," he explained in June 1999. "They said no way. So I'm going to rerecord them. All of them. Now you will have two catalogs with pretty much exactly the same music—except mine will be better—and you can either give your money to WB, the big company, or to NPG. You choose."[213] Happily, Prince would abandon this project after making the new version of *1999*, which he released, accompanied by various remixes, in maxi-single format on 2 February 1999.

Production

Apart from the fact that this reinterpretation of the 1983 classic belonged to him completely, here Prince did something unprecedented: he brought together The Revolution and The New Power Generation. Indeed, during the production of the song the singer decided to rerecord all the instruments, but to keep the original voices of Lisa Coleman, Dez Dickerson, and Jill Jones, to which he added those of Rosie Gaines and Doug E Fresh. The song was made all the more suitable for the millennium celebrations because it contained a beautifully put together "Latin part" led by a talented percussionist who, it might be surmised, was Sheila E. "I always thought 'what a weird idea to stick that in there.' And then I cut the original tape out to take a good listen to it, and there's a Latin part in there, so he, in that version, put it out, but it had been thought about before."[192] Prince also gave Doug E Fresh the opportunity to carry out a remix for the maxi-single and invited the actor

Rosario Dawson, who had just distinguished herself in *He Got Game* (1998), the latest movie by Spike Lee, to read a text for one of the reinterpretations of the song entitled *Rosario (1999)*. "He randomly called me when I was nineteen years old," Dawson recalled "[...] and said 'You're a voice of the generation, I want you to do this monologue I've written for my *1999* remix album. You must come to Paisley Park!' [...] I went there, and then I completely embarrassed myself [...]"[214] The actor was far too modest here because her performance was totally respectable and, in fact, enabled new talents to be discovered in Prince's songs.

Although he soon left the New Power Generation, Larry Graham remained a close friend of the singer.

Despite briefly being available via streaming, the cover of *You're Still the One* by Shania Twain, buoyed by the voice of Marva King, was a success.

U'RE STILL THE ONE

(♀ AND MARVA KING)

Robert John "Mutt" Lange, Shania Twain / 3'09

Musicians: **Prince:** vocals, electric guitar, bass, drums, synthesizers, backing vocals / **Marva King:** vocals, backing vocals / **Recording:** **Paisley Park, Chanhassen, Minnesota:** June 1998 / **Technical team:** **Producer:** ♀ / **Recording engineer:** Hans-Martin Buff

When *You're Still the One*—the third single from *Come On Over*, the new album by the Canadian singer Shania Twain—was released on 27 January 1998, success was on the cards. Admittedly, she had to wait until May for her song to reach the top of the American charts and a further year for her hit *Man! I Feel Like a Woman!* to make her an international star, but the fact remains that on hearing this ballad written with the celebrated producer Robert John "Mutt" Lange—the man behind AC/DC's *Highway to Hell* in 1979 and Bryan Adams' *(Everything I Do) I Do it for You* in 1991—Prince was immediately seduced by the irresistible melody. He quickly recorded a cover of the song in a duo with Marva King, who also sang on his new album, *Newpower Soul*, the release of which was planned to coincide with the first days of summer. In a similar vein to the song's original version, but logically retitled *U're Still the One*, the number's reinterpretation has nevertheless shed its original country-pop flavor and taken on a more Prince-like sound. Featuring a catchy final riff and more rock-like vocal lines, the song is a real success. "*U're Still the One* is a well-written pop song that begged 4 VOLUME. We gave it that,"[215] Prince explained in 1999. The song, which would be played onstage at Paisley Park on the night of 19 and 20 June 1998 (the day *The War* was recorded), was released, only for streaming, on the website Love4OneAnother.com on 26 January 1999, but sadly never enjoyed a physical release, nor was it even offered for sale by download. Several years later, Prince would contact Shania Twain and suggest she produce her new album in the studios at Paisley Park. "I just wasn't ready, I was afraid of working with a new producer. I was feeling insecure about sharing my songwriting [...] In the end, I never did get to work with Prince. He ended up as we all know, leaving us way too early, and before we could work together."[216]

FREE

(GRAHAM CENTRAL STATION FEATURING ⚥ AND CHAKA KHAN)

Larry Graham / 7'04

Musicians: Larry Graham: vocals, spoken voice, bass, backing vocals / **⚥:** vocals, spoken voice, electric guitar, programming, synthesizers, backing vocals / **Chaka Khan:** vocals, backing vocals / **Michael B** Nelson: trombone / **Kathy Jensen:** baritone saxophone / **Kenni Holmen:** saxophone / **Dave Jensen:** trumpet / **Steve Strand:** trumpet / **Recording: Paisley Park, Chanhassen, Minnesota:** November 1997 to January 1998 / **Technical team: Producer:** Larry Graham, ⚥ / **Recording engineer:** Hans-Martin Buff / **Wind arrangements:** Michael B Nelson
Graham Central Station GCS 2000 / Released in the USA by NPG Records: 2 February 1999 (CD ref.: none) / **Released in the UK by NPG Records:** 2 February 1999 (CD ref.: none) / **Best chart ranking in the USA:** did not make the charts / **Best chart ranking in the UK:** did not make the charts

Although Prince's input to this song by Graham Central Station, the group of his new associate Larry Graham, from whom he was now inseparable, is confined simply to backing vocals, he is fully at the controls for this song—as funk-sounding as can be—which he produced. Led by the Hornheadz, who unleash a wall of wind sound that would be the envy of Dennis Thomas, Otha Nash, Larry Gittens, and Robert Mickens (members of the unforgettable wind section of Kool & the Gang in *Open Sesame*, in 1976), the number sings the praises of having total artistic autonomy, a subject close to Prince's heart at the time since he was fully celebrating his long-desired creative freedom. As a result, he did not even sign a contract with Larry Graham and Chaka Khan, whose respective albums would be released by NPG Records. "We don't need to [sic] piece of paper telling us who we are to each other,"[217] Prince explained in August 1998 to the journalist Ben Edmonds, before answering in response to a question about potential return on investment: "What costs? I own this studio, all I have to pay for is the electricity [...] All I'm doing is offering my time and friendship, and some of the tools I'm blessed to have at my disposal."[217] A true lesson in humility on the part of the singer, in a music business where money was king, as confirmed by Larry Graham: "Eye had complete freedom 2 do whatever eye want 2 do...No one saying eye can't do this or eye can't do that...No time limit...No budget worries... So when we finish with a song...It's becuz we're actually finished...Not becuz we ran out of $ or time."[218] Prince would also contribute to *Raise Up*, a song in the same vein on the eponymous album by Larry Graham & Graham Central Station, which was released in 2012.

The movie *I'll Do Anything* opened in US movie theaters on 4 February 1994—without any songs by Prince.

THE REST OF MY LIFE

Prince / 1'38

Musicians: Prince: vocals, piano, tambourine, backing vocals / **Levi Seacer Jr:** electric guitar / **Sonny T.:** bass / **Michael B.:** drums / **Tommy Barbarella:** synthesizers / **Michael B** Nelson: trombone / **Kathy Jensen:** saxophone / **Brian Gallagher:** saxophone / **Dave Jensen:** trumpet / **Steve Strand:** trumpet / **Recording: Platinum Studios, Melbourne:** 16–22 April 1992 / **Technical team: Producer:** Prince / **Recording engineer:** Mark Forrester

On 16 April 1992 the Diamonds and Pearls Tour paused in Melbourne, Australia, for five concerts at the National Tennis Center in Flinders Park (renamed the Rod Laver Arena in 2000). Prince, who was also working on writing the original soundtrack to *I'll Do Anything* by James L Brooks, used his free time to record a few songs for the movie at Platinum Studios. He then got started on the NPG's first album, *Gold Nigga* (see page 230), at Studios 301 when he arrived in Sydney a few days later. The first sessions in Melbourne yielded several pieces destined for Brooks's movie, some of which would end up on *The Vault... Old Friends 4 Sale*, such as *There Is Lonely* and *The Rest of My Life*. With its syncopated jazz rhythm and walking bass line, played with virtuosity by Sonny Thompson, the song sets the tone for an album that was mostly recorded live with the most remarkable lineup of the New Power Generation.

IT'S ABOUT THAT WALK

Prince / 4'26

Musicians: Prince: vocals, electric guitar, backing vocals / **Levi Seacer Jr:** electric guitar / **Sonny T.:** bass / **Michael B.:** drums / **Tommy Barbarella:** synthesizers / **Mr** Hayes: Hammond organ / **Michael B** Nelson: trombone / **Kathy Jensen:** saxophone / **Brian Gallagher:** saxophone / **Dave Jensen:** trumpet / **Steve Strand:** trumpet / **Recording: Studio Davout, Paris:** 2 September 1993 / **Technical team: Producer:** Prince / **Recording engineer:** ? (not confirmed)

Recorded at Studio Davout in Paris, the day after Prince's second concert that year at the Palais Omnisports in Paris-Bercy (now the Accor Arena), *It's About That Walk* continues the singer's jazzy vein for this last album delivered to Warner Bros. Records. Michael Bland leads the song with his masterly shuffle—confirmation, if any were needed, of his status as the NPG's best drummer of all time. The song, which was inspired by Mayte (see page 216) according to some members of the group, paints the portrait of a young woman who, from Paris to New York, steals the singer's heart thanks to her gait and "ass like a fine cut diamond." Whether it is a nod to the event or simply a coincidence, that day Prince also recorded, in Paris's 20th district, the voice of the 18-year-old model Ophélie Winter (whom he met on the night of 12 and 13 July 1992 during an aftershow at Bains Douches), for the song *Chaos and Disorder*.

SHE SPOKE 2 ME (EXTENDED REMIX)

Prince / 8'19

Musicians: Prince: vocals, spoken voice, backing vocals / **Levi Seacer Jr:** electric guitar / **Sonny T.:** bass / **Michael B.:** drums / **Tommy Barbarella:** synthesizers / **Kirk Johnson:** percussion / **Michael B** Nelson: trombone / **Kathy Jensen:** saxophone / **Brian Gallagher:** saxophone / **Dave Jensen:** trumpet / **Steve Strand:** trumpet / **Recording: Paisley Park, Chanhassen, Minnesota:** October 1991 / **Technical team: Producer:** Prince / **Recording engineers:** Michael Koppelman, David Friedlander, Steve Noonan, Ray Hahnfeldt, Brian Poer

The French actress Mathilda May inspired Prince's song *5 Women* without being aware of it.

After releasing this song for the soundtrack of the movie *Girl 6* (Spike Lee, 1996), Prince felt duty-bound to release the long version on this album of jazz sounds. It features a series of solos by his exceptional and multitalented musicians. Drums, bass guitar, saxophone, synthesizer, and electric guitar: each instrument is showcased here, in a few delicious bars.

5 WOMEN

Prince / 5'12

Musicians: Prince: vocals, spoken voice, electric guitar, Hammond organ, piano, bass / **Levi Seacer Jr:** electric guitar / **Michael B.:** drums / **Ricky Peterson:** synthesizers / **Michael B** Nelson: trombone / **Kathy Jensen:** saxophone / **Brian Gallagher:** saxophone / **Dave Jensen:** trumpet / **Steve Strand:** trumpet / **Recording: Warner-Pioneer Studios, Tokyo:** August to September 1990 / **Paisley Park, Chanhassen, Minnesota:** autumn 1990 (wind) / **Technical team: Producer:** Prince, Ricky Peterson / **Recording engineers:** Matthew Larson (Warner-Pioneer Studios), Michael Koppelman (Paisley Park)

Who, then, is this woman who haunts Prince's nights in 1990, when he sings: "May was her name, she was jumpin'/Jumpin' from plane to plane/She was an actress or model or somethin'/Can't even remember her first name"? Let us help out the artist, who declares to the beautiful stranger that "It took five women to getcha off of my mind." She is the French actor Mathilda May, whom Prince met at his aftershow at the Bains Douches, in Paris, during the night of 8 and 9 July 1988. The young woman, whom Prince had seen in Jean-Claude Sussfeld's *La Passerelle* (*The Catwalk*), which was released in 1988, formed a friendship with the singer and was even invited to Paisley Park the following December to record her voice for *The Dopamine Rush*, a song written and produced by Prince for Eric Leeds's first solo album, *Times Squared*. "We stayed friends, despite the fact that he is a UFO, but when he came through Paris, we met up, at the cinema, or in a club...," declared the actor, who had subsequently become a theater director. "[...] I was lucky enough to have seen real talent, freedom, creativity at work. He changed my life. There is a 'before Prince' and an 'after Prince.'"[221] The singer offered this blues song to Joe Cocker, who recorded it at A&M Studios in Los Angeles for his album *Night Calls*, which was released in the UK in 1991, and renamed it *Five Women*.

WHEN THE LIGHTS GO DOWN

Prince / 7'10

Musician: Prince: vocal, electric guitar, bass, drums, piano, percussion, synthesizers, Fender Rhodes piano / **Recording: Paisley Park, Chanhassen, Minnesota:** ? (not confirmed) / **Technical team: Producer:** Prince / **Recording engineer:** ? (not confirmed)

This song is wrapped in mystery because Prince aficionados have been unable to pinpoint an exact recording date. There is no trace of the sessions that produced this instrumental jazz number or any indication as to the identity of the musician who plays the conga part throughout the song. The drummer Sheila E. is credited in the album's notes, so perhaps she is playing percussion, but this is far from certain. The only thing we can be sure of is that the song clearly belongs on this album. It was much appreciated by fans, who were thrilled by the high-caliber live version performed at Club Nokia, in L.A., on 29 March 2009. It featured the drummer John Blackwell, bass player Rhonda Smith, and keyboard player Renato Neto who, for this occasion, played the percussion solo using the keys of his synthesizer.

MY LITTLE PILL

Prince / 1'08

Musician: Prince: spoken voice, electric guitar, bass, drums, piano, percussion, synthesizers / **Recording:** Paisley Park, Chanhassen, Minnesota: March 1992 / **Technical team:** Producer: Prince / Recording engineers: David Friedlander, Steve Noonan, Ray Hahnfeldt, Brian Poer

Written for the original soundtrack of *I'll Do Anything* (1994), *My Little Pill* does not sing the praises of medicines and drugs, but was written for the character Nan Mulhanney, who abuses pills in order to forget her troubles. Nan is played by the actor Julie Kavner, who even recorded her own version of the song, which declares: "All my cares and troubles dive right off my windowsill/Everytime I pop my little pill."

THERE IS LONELY

Prince / 2'29

Musicians: Prince: vocals, piano, percussion / Levi Seacer Jr: electric guitar / Sonny T.: bass / Michael B.: drums / Tommy Barbarella: synthesizers / **Recording:** Platinum Studios, Melbourne: 16–22 April 1992 / **Technical team:** Producer: Prince / Recording engineer: Mark Forrester

Recorded in Melbourne during the sessions for *I'll Do Anything*, *There Is Lonely* tells of the loneliness suffered by the producer Burke Adler, a character played by Albert Brooks in the movie. The actor recorded a version of the song and this featured in the first edit of *I'll Do Anything*. The edit was dropped after disastrous test screenings, which led to the director cutting all songs performed by actors from his feature-length movie.

OLD FRIENDS 4 SALE

Prince / 3'27

Musicians: Prince: vocals, drums, backing vocals / Mari Botnick, Oscar Chausow, Ron Clark, Isabelle Daskoff, Assa Drori, Henry Ferber, Pam Gates, Janice Gower, Endre Granat, Ed Green, Reginald Hill, Bill Hybel, William Hymanson, Pat Johnson, Karen Jones, Betty Moor, Irma Neumann, Donald Palmer, Sheldon Sanov, Joseph Schoenbrun, Terry Schoenbrun, Francine Walsh, Harold Wolf: violin / Myer Bello, Alan DeVeritch, Norman Forrest, Pamela Goldsmith, Allan Harshman, Margot MacLaine, Jorge Moraga, Carole Mukogawa, David Stock: viola / James Arkatov, Ray Kelley, Raphael Kramer, Frederick Seykora: cello / Chuck Domanico, Árni Egilsson: double bass / Don Ashworth, Gene Cipriano, Jon Clarke, Dave Edwards, Gary Foster, Jim Kanter, Dick Mitchell, Jack Nimitz: clarinet / John Lowe, Joe Soldo, Bob Tricarico: flute / Ray Brown, Rich Cooper, Bob Findley, Larry Ford, Bob O'Donnell, Allen Vizzutti: trumpet / Garnett Brown, Charles Loper, Morris Repass, Bill Watrous: trombone / David Duke, Marni Johnson, Joe Myer, Brian O'Connor, Calvin Smith, James Thatcher: French horn / Tommy Johnson: tuba / Brent Fischer: timpani, percussion / **Recording:** Sunset Sound, Los Angeles: 20 April 1985 / Monterey Sound Studios, Glendale, California: 3 July 1985 (orchestra) / Paisley Park, Chanhassen, Minnesota: 1991 / **Technical team:** Producer: Prince / Recording engineers: Peggy McCreary (Sunset Sound), Susan Rogers (Sunset Sound), Michael Koppelman (Paisley Park) / Orchestral arrangements: Clare Fischer

The future producers Jimmy Jam and Terry Lewis in the offices of the magazine *Right On!* in 1982, when The Time were active.

On 7 May 1985, a month to the day after the Purple Rain Tour ended, the *National Enquirer*, one of the most famous US tabloids, ran an interview with Prince's former bodyguard, Charles "Big Chick" Huntsberry. The latter revealed certain secrets about his former employer (these came at a price—some $3,000), as well as personal details about the person who considered him one of his few friends. Some time before the article came out, on 20 April 1985, Prince already knew that Huntsberry had given the interview and, having begun the sessions for *Parade* two days earlier, recorded the first version of *Old Friends 4 Sale*. In it, he refers to his former bodyguard, but also to the firing of two musicians from The Time (see page 64) in 1983: Terry Lewis and Jimmy Jam, who did not hesitate to divulge the story to the press. The following July, Clare Fischer added his orchestration to the song, but Prince finally decided not to include it on *Parade*. Following Huntsberry's death in 1990 (Prince had remained close to him despite their disagreements), the singer rewrote the song's lyrics and reworked it in 1991, before adding it to the tracklist of *The Vault... Old Friends 4 Sale* in 1996. On 30 April 1990, Prince had performed a concert at Rupert's Nightclub in Los Angeles with the aim of raising funds for the family of his late friend. More than $50,000 was donated to his wife and children, thanks to that evening.

SARAH

Prince / 2'52

Musicians: Prince: vocals, electric guitar / **Sonny T.:** bass / **Michael B.:** drums / **Tommy Barbarella:** synthesizers / **Mr** Hayes: synthesizers / **Michael B** Nelson: trombone / **Kathy Jensen:** saxophone / **Brian Gallagher:** saxophone / **Dave Jensen:** trumpet / **Steve Strand:** trumpet / **Recording: Paisley Park, Chanhassen, Minnesota:** February 1996 / **Technical team: Producer:** Prince / **Recording engineers:** David Friedlander, Ray Hahnfeldt, Shane T Keller, Steve Durkee

Sarah was recorded in February 1996 at Paisley Park, during the very last sessions involving the New Power Generation musicians Michael Bland, Sonny Thompson, Tommy Barbarella, and Morris Hayes. Recorded at the same time as *Into the Light* and *I Will* (which would be included on the *Chaos and Disorder* album) and *Da Bang* (which would end up on *Crystal Ball*), *Sarah* is in the same vein, filled with the same jazz-rock sounds and a million miles from the powerful *The Gold Experience* and the dark *Come* album. Although the journalists Per Nilsen, David Magdziarz, and Alex Hahn suggested in *Uptown* magazine (November 1999), that Prince was inspired to write the song by the singer Tina Turner, whose biopic had come out in 1993, Prince never confirmed this.

EXTRAORDINARY

Prince / 2'27

Musicians: Prince: vocals, piano, backing vocals / **Sonny T.:** bass / **Michael B.:** drums / **Tommy Barbarella:** synthesizers / **Mr Hayes:** synthesizers / **Recording: Paisley Park, Chanhassen, Minnesota:** September 1992 / **Technical team: Producer:** Prince / **Recording engineers:** David Friedlander, Steve Noonan, Ray Hahnfeldt, Brian Poer

Recorded after the Diamonds and Pearls Tour ended in 1992, this soul ballad was offered to Rosie Gaines, who at the time was in the middle of recording her album *Concrete Jungle*. Gaines recorded a version, but since in the end the record never saw the light of day, Prince decided to retrieve the song and in 1996 added it to the tracklist of *The Vault... Old Friends 4 Sale*. *Extraordinary* is a misnomer: the song is merely a hitherto unseen curiosity for fans on the lookout for rarities, and a timid ending to this excellent album.

RAVE

RAVE UN2 THE JOY FANTASTIC

Rave Un2 the Joy Fantastic · Undisputed · The Greatest Romance Ever Sold · Segue
Hot Wit U · Tangerine · So Far, So Pleased · The Sun, the Moon and Stars
Everyday is a Winding Road · Segue · Man'O'War · Baby Knows
👁 Love U, But 👁 Don't Trust U Anymore · Silly Game · Strange But True
Wherever U Go, Whatever U Do · Segue (Hidden track) · Prettyman (Hidden track)

Released in the USA by NPG Records/Arista:
9 November 1999 (LP ref.: 07822-14624-1; CD ref.: 07822-14624-2)
Released in the UK and Europe by NPG Records/Arista/BMG:
9 November 1999 (LP ref.: 07822 14624 1; CD ref.: 07822-14624-2)
Best chart ranking in the USA: 18
Best chart ranking in the UK: did not make the charts

Prince in 1999: long hair, Andalusian sun, and no apocalypse on the horizon.

1999

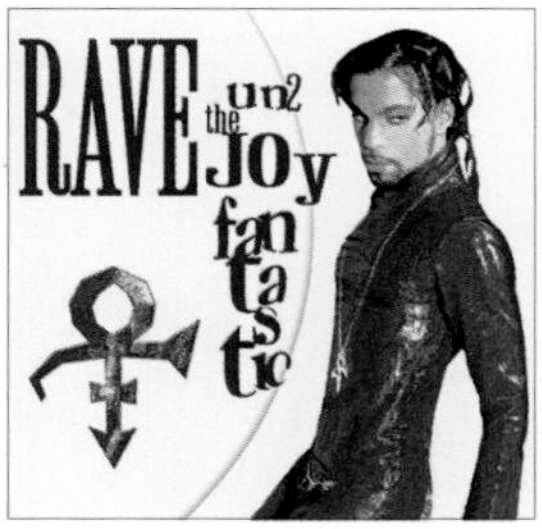

ATTRACTING A NEW GENERATION

Before launching the European leg of the New Power Soul Festival Tour, Prince gathered journalists at the Santo Mauro hotel, in Madrid, on 11 December 1998 and held an impromptu press conference. No one knew what he was about to announce. Only Mayte, his wife, had been informed of the reason for the press conference on the way to the luxury hotel. With his wife at his side, Prince announced the annulment of their marriage, explaining that their prenuptial contract contained some gray areas and they would be renewing their vows on 14 February 1999, which would allow them to live their union in a "less traditional fashion."[134] However, the marriage wasn't actually annulled until after their divorce in May 2000. Their breakup was inevitable—it couldn't even be avoided by the purchase of a luxurious home in Marbella, Spain, where Prince went to rest after his many musical productions in 1998. "I go there for the serenity and the warmth of the people," he explained. "It's always beautiful and the people are very hands on [...] I don't go there for creation. I go for a break from it. It's very chilled out and laid back. I love the culture, the food, the discos."[222] As Mayte added: 'It's so relaxed, so different from here." Explaining further, she said, "We have cats, dogs, birds. You walk into a room and you just feel at peace."[223] Despite this idyllic picture and the image of a happy marriage—which photographer Steve Parke tried to depict during a legendary photo session at Prince's Spanish residence—the relationship had gradually started to crumble. While Mayte lived in the house in Spain, Prince more often lived in Minneapolis, where he quickly got back to work.

Partnering with Clive Davis

In early April 1999, Prince was in New York for a meeting with his lawyer, L. Londell McMillan, and Clive Davis, the founder of the Arista record label. Davis was known in the record industry for his ability to discover talent and his visionary qualities. He'd earned great respect from his artists, including Carlos Santana, who was working with him to prepare a big comeback, with the late 1999 hit album *Supernatural*. McMillan told Davis that Prince was looking for a partner to distribute his next album. He wanted to let go of limited productions for a while, rise back to the top with an album full of hits, and obtain the exposure that only a major label could provide. Prince imposed two conditions: he demanded full ownership of the master tapes and wanted Davis to commit to only one album. That same day, McMillan and Davis met Prince, who played a few new songs for Davis in his limousine while driving through the streets of New York. On 12 April, Prince announced the name of his next album on his website: *Rave Un2 the Joy Fantastic*.

A full-scale pop renaissance

Like Carlos Santana with *Supernatural*, Prince multiplied his collaborations while recording his new album, notably with a new generation of artists. Thanks to hits like *Smooth* (a duet with Rob Thomas) and especially *Maria Maria*, produced by rapper Wyclef Jean and producer Jery Duplessis, both on the back of the success of the Fugees, in 1996, Santana's album topped the charts around the world. For his part, Prince brought in young artists like Ani DiFranco, Gwen Stefani of No Doubt, and Eve, a rapper known in the hip-hop world for working with DMX and the label Ruff Ryders. Prince

Despite the disintegration of their relationship, Prince and Mayte posed one last time for Steve Parke in the peace of their Spanish home.

also enlisted the services of renowned musicians like Maceo Parker and Sheryl Crow. Loyal recording engineer Hans-Martin Buff was at the console and provided the album with a modern, powerful sound that matched the spirit of the times. Everything seemed poised to give Prince the album he needed to make his big comeback. On 25 August 1999, a press conference was held to inform journalists that the singer's new album would come out under the Arista flag on 9 November. They were also told that while the artist with the unpronounceable name had indeed written the album, it would be produced by...Prince. In fact, the singer spread the rumor that the album was being produced by "his favorite producer from the 80s."[21] As the artist explained, "I think in a lot of ways I still sound like I did before." He went on: "So by having Prince produce it, it helps make that connection."[222] This mishmash of pseudonyms was starting to become completely incomprehensible, so the following year the artist permanently re-adopted his original stage name, Prince.

The start of the jazz-funk shift

Despite a warm welcome when *Rave Un2 the Joy Fantastic* came out in November 1999, thanks in part to Arista's prowess, it did not meet Prince's expectations. The album's first single, *The Greatest Romance Ever Sold*, did not appeal to its intended audience, and the album sold barely 450,000 copies in the first few months after its release in the United States. Despite the energy put into reaching new generations of potential fans, Prince struggled to capture their attention with this overproduced album which was sorely lacking in artistic coherence. Again, Prince dived into new projects, including the production of two new albums, *High* and *Madrid 2 Chicago*, which he ultimately put off in favor of a more ambitious plan: writing the formidable album *The Rainbow Children*. This album illustrated Prince's ability to reinvent himself, this time as an orchestra conductor at the helm of a reinvigorated New Power Generation performing exceptional compositions. While waiting for the release of this new album, Prince launched the Hit n Run Tour on 25 August, which showed fans the new NPG lineup: Rhonda Smith (bass), Morris Hayes (keyboards), Kip Blackshire (keyboards), Najee (saxophone and transverse flute), Geneva (backing vocals and dance), and John Blackwell on drums. Without an album to promote on this tour, Prince rehashed his entire repertoire and gave fans a very interesting retrospective, playing songs such as *Scandalous*, *Sexy Dancer*, *Come On*, *Diamonds and Pearls*, and *Uptown* side by side.

FOR PRINCE ADDICTS

The Special Edition of *Rave Un2 the Joy Fantastic* was intended to contain remixes and outtakes from recording sessions, such as *I Ain't Gonna Run*, *R U Ready?*, *This Is Your Life*, or the Shania Twain cover *U're Still the One*. The website NPGOnlineLtd.com announced that it would be postponed until 10 March 2000. *Rave In2 the Joy Fantastic* finally went on sale on Prince's new site, NPG Music Club, and was delivered to fans in April 2001.

The rapper Chuck D was one of the star guests on *Rave Un2 the Joy Fantastic*.

RAVE UN2 THE JOY FANTASTIC

⚥ / 4'19

Musician: ⚥: vocals, electric guitar, bass, programming, synthesizers, backing vocals / **Recording:** Paisley Park, Chanhassen, Minnesota: June 1988; 1999 / **Olympic Studios, Barnes, London:** 24 July 1988 / **Technical team:** **Producer:** Prince / **Recording engineers:** Femi Jiya (Olympic Studios), Hans-Martin Buff, ⚥

In June 1988, Prince embarked on the production of his new album, *Rave Unto the Joy Fantastic*, at Paisley Park. He started by recording three new songs: *God is Alive*, *If I Had A Harem*, and the album's title song. Joy Fantastic was the nickname Prince had given his new conquest, the young Anna Garcia, but she hadn't liked giving up her name, so Prince modified the nickname to Anna Fantastic. After *Pink Cashmere* and *Vicki Waiting*, this was the third song written for her. Since Prince had decided to take on the *Batman* project at the start of 1989, he abandoned the album he was producing, and *Rave Unto the Joy Fantastic*—once intended for the movie's original score—was replaced with *Partyman*. "The title track is one I did twelve years ago," Prince explained in 1999. "But it sounded so much like *Kiss* that I wanted to put it in The Vault and let it marinate for a while."[224] The Arabic riff resurfaced in 1992 in *The Max*, on the ⚥ album, then the song was completely reworked in 1999 and renamed *Rave Un2 the Joy Fantastic*.

"That's one of the amazing things about Prince, I think, is that he could just pull stuff out of The Vault and you would never know that it was from earlier,"[192] confessed recording engineer Hans-Martin Buff. It's true that when listening to this song from 1988 everything points to it having just been recorded. In reality, only a few overdubs were done on the song, which Buff mixed in one day. Prince played the legendary guitar riff, recorded in 1988, with two different guitars. The first was his famous Hohner Madcat and the second his Auerswald Model C, which was given to him by German princess Gloria von Thurn und Taxis in 1986 and made by luthier Jerry Auerswald, who also made the Love Symbol Guitar a few years later. The two instruments were plugged into a Leslie console, traditionally used to give Hammond organs their characteristic rotating sound, then put through stereo to give the song a very interesting panoramic.

UNDISPUTED

⚥, Chuck D / 4'20

Musicians: ⚥: vocals, electric guitar, bass, programming, synthesizers, piano, backing vocals / **Chuck D:** rap / **Kirk Johnson:** vocals, programming / **Morris Hayes:** vocals / **Kip Blackshire:** vocals / **Adele C.:** spoken word / **Bros. Jules:** scratching / **Recording:** Paisley Park, Chanhassen, Minnesota: 1999, August 1999 (Chuck D's vocals) / **Technical team:** **Producer:** Prince / **Recording engineers:** Hans-Martin Buff, ⚥

Prince never hid his admiration for the rapper Chuck D. Before paying tribute to him in the lyrics to *Musicology*, in 2004, he asked the frontman of Public Enemy to perform on this hip-hop song, which also includes Morris Hayes, Kirk Johnson, and Kip Blackshire, who became a backing vocalist

A leading group of the R&B movement at the end of the 1990s, TLC mourned the death of the singer Lisa Lopes (right) in 2002.

and keyboardist on the Hit n Run Tour in 2000 and 2001. "It was a gigantic vibe session," reported the rapper. "I guess Prince has his particular way, because he's first and foremost a musician, and second and foremost a master producer. So we gelled on many ideas and mutually expressed our admiration for each other."[225] Not long before this session, on 10 July 1999, Prince had performed one of Public Enemy's cult pieces, *Fight the Power* (from the wonderful *Fear of a Black Planet* album, released in 1990), onstage at Paisley Park. Prince had recorded the song three days before, but this studio version remains unknown to this day.

Single

THE GREATEST ROMANCE EVER SOLD

⚥ / 5'30

Musicians: ⚥: vocals, electric guitar, acoustic guitar, bass, programming, synthesizers, backing vocals / **Kirk Johnson:** programming / **Mike Scott:** electric guitar / **Recording:** Paisley Park, Chanhassen, Minnesota: summer 1999 / **Technical team:** Producer: Prince / Recording engineers: Hans-Martin Buff, ⚥
Single: 1. *The Greatest Romance Ever Sold* (Radio Edit)/4'26 / **2.** *The Greatest Romance Ever Sold* (Adam & Eve Remix) featuring Eve/4'30 / **Released in the USA by NPG Records/Arista:** 5 October 1999 (CD single ref.: 0782213749-2) / **Released in the UK and Europe by NPG Records/ Arista/BMG:** 15 November 1999 (CD single ref.: 74321-706652) / **Best chart ranking in the USA:** 63 / **Best chart ranking in the UK:** 65 /

Those who lived through it can confirm that 1999 was the year of the advent of contemporary R&B. Never again did the American record industry produce as many R&B hits as they did that year. The charts were completely taken by storm, featuring singles by Whitney Houston (*Heartbreak Hotel*, *It's Not Right But It's Okay*, *My Love Is Your Love*), Destiny's Child (*Say My Name*, *Bills, Bills, Bills*), Christina Aguilera (*Genie in a Bottle*), and Jennifer Lopez (*If You Had My Love*). Leading the pack was TLC, who dominated the market with their breathtaking *FanMail*, an album produced with the amazing Dallas Austin. The main single from this album, *No Scrubs*, is a feminist appeal in which the singers proclaim their disgust for loser men who can't get a grip and learn to treat their girlfriends properly. Despite the undisputable quality of the song, and his long-time admiration for TLC, Prince, who was at that point working to become a Jehovah's Witness, no longer liked vulgarity in general, especially the kind found in women's R&B. "I just hear a lot of negativity in the songs of today, especially in the R&B field. I was trying to reverse that single-handedly."[226] So Prince wrote *The Greatest Romance Ever Sold*, a syrupy ballad—whose title was inspired by *The Greatest Story Ever Told*, a book by Fulton Oursler about Jesus Christ—with the support of Clive Davis, who thought he was dealing with the biggest hit of his career as a producer. Alas, the song instead showed a singer trying to attract new generations of fans and falling short, and then getting lost in the reeds of the international charts. This shock forced Prince to reinvent himself again, and to create more mature music that better suited his status as the ultimate funk reference.

When, in an apparent fit of schizophrenia, the artist decided to have Prince produce *Rave Un2 the Joy Fantastic*, it was because he thought the public wanted to rediscover the sounds that had made him successful in the 1980s. His first decision, when he started producing the album, was to pull out his famous Linn LM-1 Drum Machine, which was notably used for *Batman* and *Graffiti Bridge*. After a good dusting off and a complete overhaul, the machine was ready to get to work. Once the song was recorded (in a single day), Prince sent a version to Clive Davis, who tried many times to convince him to rework the song more thoroughly. Prince, as succinct as ever, simply said: "Ok, Clive, I understand. I'd rather be dragged through nails."[21]

The paths of the trumpeter Miles Davis and Prince would cross many times.

SEGUE

None / 0'04

Musician: None / **Recording:** None / **Technical team:** None

Prince and Miles Davis began a friendly and mutually respectful relationship in the mid-1980s. In the last years of his life, the trumpetist often mentioned Prince in interviews, comparing him to Jimi Hendrix for his virtuosity and to Charlie Chaplin for his aptitude for showmanship. As with the New Power Generation albums, Prince decided in 1999 to include segues—those curious short transition segments—in *Rave Un2 the Joy Fantastic*. He wanted the first interlude to contain a sample, repeated several times, of Miles Davis's voice saying "Prince, Prince, Prince." Since Davis's estate categorically refused to allow such an instrumentalization of the musician's voice, Prince decided to leave four seconds of silence in its place. He included a dedication to his friend's memory in the sleeve notes.

HOT WIT U

[symbol] / 5'11

Musicians: [symbol]: vocals, bass, synthesizers, backing vocals / **Eve:** rap / **Kirk Johnson:** programming / **Michael B Nelson:** trombone / **Kathy Jensen:** baritone saxophone / **Kenni Holmen:** baritone saxophone / **Dave Jensen:** trumpet / **Steve Strand:** trumpet / **Bros. Jules:** scratching / **Recording:** **Paisley Park, Chanhassen, Minnesota:** 1999, 17 May 1999 (brass) / **Electric Lady Studios, New York:** 10 September 1999 (Eve's voice) / **Technical team:** **Producer:** Prince / **Recording engineers:** Hans-Martin Buff, [symbol] / **Brass arrangement:** Michael B Nelson, [symbol]

"When Larry walks in the room, we all become more aware," Prince explained in 1999, referring to bass player Larry Graham. "Not only of swearing but even of what we talk about. He's gotten us to the point where nobody swears in the building anymore."[227] No such level of submission could have ever been imaginable for Prince before meeting Larry Graham, a devoted Jehovah's Witness. The new rule in Prince's world was that there should be no swearing—and any violators would be fined. Eve, a rapper signed with the Ruff Ryder label (for which L. Londell McMillan also worked as a lawyer), had to bend to this rule when she came to sing for *Hot Wit U*. "Eve cleaned her rap up to be on my record,"[227] Prince confirmed proudly. Prince soon followed this same path by undertaking a purification of his repertoire. He never again played songs onstage that contained profanities. Eve, who soon let her vocabulary run wild again in hits like *Let Me Blow Ya Mind* (2001) and *Gangsta Lovin'* (2002), performs here a sensible but successful rap, proving once again that rap isn't just for men.

TANGERINE

[Love Symbol] / 1'31

Musicians: [Love Symbol]: vocals, acoustic guitar, synthesizers, backing vocals / **Kirk Johnson:** programming / **Rhonda Smith:** acoustic bass / **Recording: Paisley Park, Chanhassen, Minnesota:** 1999 / **Technical team: Producer:** Prince / **Recording engineers:** Hans-Martin Buff, [Love Symbol]

Fleeting and delicate, *Tangerine* paints a picture of a man who wants to draw a curtain over a past romantic relationship. "Some days I just wanna black out/Everything I felt for you," sings Prince, echoing his relationship with his wife, Mayte, from whom he'd separated for good. But then, "Some days I miss you too," he'd sometimes assure the young woman, locked away in her palace in Marbella. Rhonda Smith is on the acoustic fretless bass for this song, which provides the perfect accompaniment to Kirk Johnson's syncopated programming.

SO FAR, SO PLEASED

[Love Symbol] / 3'24

Musicians: [Love Symbol]: vocals, electric guitar, synthesizers, percussion, backing vocals / **Gwen Stefani:** vocals, backing vocals / **Rhonda Smith:** bass / **Kirk Johnson:** drums / **Marva King:** backing vocals / **Recording: Paisley Park, Chanhassen, Minnesota:** 1999 / **Technical team: Producer:** Prince / **Recording engineers:** Hans-Martin Buff, [Love Symbol]

In order to reconnect with the pop of *When You Were Mine* (*Dirty Mind*, 1980) or *I Could Never Take the Place of Your Man* (*Sign O' the Times*, 1987), Prince called in Gwen Stefani for this song. No Doubt, her band from California, had won over the world with their ska, rock, and pop hits. While Marva King and Jennifer Lopez were initially considered for the duet, the collaboration with the glamorous Stefani was a good choice, as her band at the time was riding the wave of success after the hits *Don't Speak* and *Just a Girl*. Prince discovered the power of Stefani's stage presence at the Target Center, in Minneapolis, on 1 July 1997, when No Doubt were promoting their second album, *Tragic Kingdom*, in Prince's hometown. A jam session was held that very night with the Kid and three members of the band (Stefani, bass player Tony Kanal, and guitarist Tom Dumont) in the Paisley Park studios, and in July 1999 Prince recorded his vocals for the song *Waiting Room*. Initially slated for the album *Return of Saturn* (2000), the song was ultimately retained for the very successful *Rock Steady* album, which was released in 2001. Although the idea of releasing *So Far, So Pleased* as a single was quickly abandoned, the song nevertheless stands out for its very rock feel, notably thanks to Prince's biting guitar lines: he plugged his 6-string guitar into Boss vibrato and flanger pedals, then into his precious Zoom 9030 Multi-Effects Processor, creating octave and delay effects. A most effective mix, which provides Prince's solo with textures worthy of his historic guitar exploits.

THE SUN, THE MOON AND STARS

[Love Symbol] / 5'16

Musicians: [Love Symbol]: vocals, rap, bass, synthesizers, backing vocals / **Kirk Johnson:** programming / **NPG Orchestra:** strings / **Recording: Paisley Park, Chanhassen, Minnesota:** 1999 / **O'Henry Sound Studios, Burbank, California:** 18 June 1999 (strings) / **Technical team: Producer:** Prince / **Recording engineers:** Hans-Martin Buff, [Love Symbol], Arne Frager (O'Henry Sound Studios) / **Assistant recording engineers:** Jeff Shannon (O'Henry Sound Studios), Victor Carrillo (O'Henry Sound Studios) / **String arrangements:** Clare Fischer

Prince stated that this song with seaside noises came to him one night as he stood on the balcony of his home in Marbella, but it's difficult to say with any certainty whether his imminent breakup with Mayte is at the heart of this song, in which he says, "It's late and I think it's 'bout time for you and me to get closer/...closer than we ever did before." If Prince wanted to give his all to winning back the heart of his woman, then the allusion to Canada at the end of the song ("You come like a cold winter due in Montreal"), the native country of Manuela Testolini, with whom Prince was probably in love, sounds a bit out of place. Hans-Martin Buff, who did not like this song, tried to convince Prince to pull it from the album. Prince retorted that the song was written to appeal to women, like *Silly Game* and *The Greatest Romance Ever Sold*.

The folk singer Sheryl Crow, undisputed star of America's new folk-country scene.

EVERYDAY IS A WINDING ROAD

Sheryl Crow, Jeff Trott, Brian Mcleod / 6'13

Musicians: [symbol]: vocals, electric guitar, bass, synthesizers, backing vocals / **Kirk Johnson:** programming / **Larry Graham:** backing vocals / **Kip Blackshire:** backing vocals / **DuJuan Blackshire:** backing vocals / **Johnnie Blackshire:** backing vocals / **Recording:** **Paisley Park, Chanhassen, Minnesota:** 1999 / **Technical team:** **Producer:** Prince / **Recording engineers:** Hans-Martin Buff, [symbol]

In 1988, the young Sheryl Crow was a backing vocalist for Michael Jackson on the Bad World Tour. She took advantage of a day off to see Prince onstage at a concert for his Lovesexy Tour. Eleven years later, after she'd become an international star, thanks to an exemplary discography punctuated with incredible hits (such as *All I Wanna Do, Run, Baby, Run, If It Makes You Happy*), Prince contacted her and told her that he wanted to cover her single *Everyday is a Winding Road*, from her second album. The two artists developed a friendly relationship, which was strengthened further when Crow recorded some backing vocals and harmonica lines for *Baby Knows*. Their friendship was cemented further when Prince joined her onstage on 22 August 1999 during the traveling festival Lilith Fair, which was in Toronto that night. Crow, who's from Missouri, impulsively invited Prince to come and sing by her side at her big concert in Central Park on 14 September, an invitation Prince politely refused for the simple reason that the show was sponsored by American Express. "He just had very, very staunch beliefs about ownership," explained Cheryl Crow. "He came down on me pretty hard and it just hit me at a moment when I was feeling super fragile."[228] The two artists never spoke to each other again, which Crow regretted after Prince's death. "You have to seize the moment, every opportunity, to tell the people that you care about that you care about them," she said on the subject. "And I wish I would have done that more."[228']

SEGUE

[symbol] / 0'19

Musicians: **NPG Orchestra:** strings / **Recording:** **O'Henry Sound Studios, Burbank, California:** 18 June 1999 / **Technical team:** **Producer:** Prince / **Recording engineer:** Arne Frager / **Assistant recording engineers:** Jeff Shannon, Victor Carrillo / **String arrangements:** Clare Fischer

This instrumental segment was arranged by Clare Fischer and recorded during the string arrangement sessions for *Man'O'War.*

MAN'O'WAR

[symbol] / 5'15

Musicians: [symbol]: vocals, electric guitar, bass, programming, synthesizers, backing vocals / **Kirk Johnson:** programming, percussion / **Michael B Nelson:** trombone / **Kathy Jensen:** baritone saxophone / **Kenni Holmen:** saxophone / **Dave Jensen:** trumpet / **Steve Strand:** trumpet / **NPG Orchestra:** strings / **Recording:** **Paisley Park, Chanhassen, Minnesota:** 1999, 17 May 1999 (brass) / **O'Henry Sound Studios, Burbank, California:** 18 June 1999 (orchestra) / **Technical team:** **Producer:** Prince / **Recording engineers:** Hans-Martin Buff, [symbol], Arne Frager (O'Henry Sound Studios) / **Assistant recording engineers:** Jeff Shannon (O'Henry Sound Studios), Victor Carrillo (O'Henry Sound Studios) / **String arrangements:** Clare Fischer / **Brass arrangements:** Michael B Nelson, [symbol]

Initially slated for the album *Madrid 2 Chicago*, which was abandoned in favor of the production of *Rave Un2 the Joy Fantastic*, *Man'O'War* contains some particularly meticulous arrangements, combining harmonies based on 14 different vocal lines. To give his 6-string solo that special sound between 3'54 and 4'22, Prince plugged his guitar into his Boss DS-2 Turbo Distortion, Boss DD-3 Digital Delay, and Dunlop Cry Baby wah-wah pedals and blocked them halfway. He then re-added his solo to the synthesizer one octave higher, which created this muffled yet powerful sound.

Ani DiFranco, an independent, politically committed musician, left her mark on *Eye Love U, But Eye Don't Trust U Anymore.*

BABY KNOWS

[symbol] / 3'19

Musicians: [symbol]: vocals, electric guitar, bass, Hammond organ, synthesizers, claps, backing vocals / **Sheryl Crow:** harmonica, backing vocals / Michael B.: drums / **Recording:** Paisley Park, Chanhassen, Minnesota: summer 1999 / **Technical team:** Producer: Prince / Recording engineers: Hans-Martin Buff, [symbol]

With its Chuck Berry-inspired Hohner Madcat guitar solo and its harmonica part recorded in a single take by Sheryl Crow, *Baby Knows* is perfectly suited to Crow's repertoire—she also contributed to the backing vocals for this song. Unfortunately, she did not have the time to realize the meaning of the recorded words before she sang them, and she later kicked herself for it. "I'm kinda singing nasty lyrics," reported Crow. "I didn't really think about it until I got home, and when I played it back to myself, I went 'My parents are going to be so bummed out!'"[229] Crow paid tribute to Prince after the recording session, giving her impressions of the day she spent with him: "It's not only his ability to play so many instruments, it's the level at which he plays them. I've heard him play piano like Chick Corea or Herbie Hancock, move over to bass and play like Larry Graham, then play guitar like Jimi Hendrix or Buddy Guy."[230]

👁 LOVE U, BUT 👁 DON'T TRUST U ANYMORE

[symbol] / 3'36

Musicians: [symbol]: vocals, synthesizers, piano / **Ani DiFranco:** acoustic guitar / **Recording:** Paisley Park, Chanhassen, Minnesota: 1999, 3 June 1999 (Ani DiFranco's guitar) / **Technical team:** Producer: Prince / Recording engineers: Hans-Martin Buff, [symbol]

This song would have been a perfect fit for the "Sunday Songs" catalog, which Susan Rogers and Prince liked to record on lazy Sundays, when their musicians were enjoying a day off. Recalling the melancholic *Sometimes It Snows In April*, *Eye Love U, But Eye Don't Trust You Anymore* exists to remind persistent sceptics that Prince is an amazing showman and even better songwriter. Echoing the collapse of his marriage to Mayte—which the tabloids suspected was due to adultery because the lyrics describe a man who doubts the faithfulness of his spouse—the song is a marvel, played on the Paisley Park studio's Steinway B7. Prince also recorded the vocals and piano at the same time, which gives the song a live feeling that suited him perfectly. On 3 June 1999, Prince went to an Ani DiFranco concert at the Midway Stadium in Saint Paul, Minnesota. That night, Prince enjoyed the feminist folk music of this fervent defender of gay rights just as much as he appreciated her artistic independence. In the end, he was won over by the tribute that DiFranco paid him with her cover of *When You Were Mine* in the encore. Right after the show, Prince invited DiFranco to Paisley Park and suggested she record a few acoustic guitar lines for *Eye Love U, But Eye Don't Trust You Anymore*. "He knew I was in mortal panic and he was messing with me," reported DiFranco. "I managed to play a very basic lunk-headed fingerpicked accompaniment to his song...The whole thing was over in five minutes."[231] As Prince later confessed: "I showed her the chords to the song, but I didn't tell her how it actually went." He went on, "If I'd told her too much, then silence wouldn't have been one of the sounds."[232] By way of a thank you, Prince recorded some backing vocals for *Providence*, which appears on *To The Teeth*, DiFranco's tenth album.

SILLY GAME

⚥ / 3'30

Musicians: ⚥: vocals, acoustic guitar, bass, synthesizers, percussion, backing vocals / **Kirk Johnson:** programming / **NPG Orchestra:** strings / **Recording:** Paisley Park, Chanhassen, Minnesota: 1999 / O'Henry Sound Studios, Burbank, California: 18 June 1999 (orchestra) / **Technical team:** Producer: Prince / Recording engineers: Hans-Martin Buff, ⚥, Arne Frager (O'Henry Sound Studios) / Assistant recording engineers: Jeff Shannon (O'Henry Sound Studios), Victor Carrillo (O'Henry Sound Studios) / String arrangements: Clare Fischer

Prince came up with *Rave Un2 the Joy Fantastic* to maximize his radio appearances. Undoubtedly, he wrote songs like *Silly Game* to achieve this objective, and who could blame him. He was in the middle of a personal crisis. That said, this saccharine ballad, led by the synthesizers, immediately leaves the listener dumbfounded given how outdated the sounds are. Since Prince preferred to use the preset options on his keyboard, and rarely modified them, his recording engineers could only hope he wouldn't come across a poor-quality prefab sound, as was the case here. "I don't ever read manuals," confirmed Prince. "I don't want to have a preconception about what a piece of gear should or shouldn't do. I just start using it, I start pushing buttons, and I discover the sounds that I can make with it. Sometimes a particular sound will give me a whole song, like the harpsichord sound on *Manic Monday*,"[233] he added, referring to The Bangles' hit that he wrote in 1985.

STRANGE BUT TRUE

⚥ / 4'13

Musicians: ⚥: rap, bass, programming, synthesizers, backing vocals / **Bros. Jules:** scratching / **Recording:** Paisley Park, Chanhassen, Minnesota: 1999 / **Technical team:** Producer: Prince / Recording engineers: Hans-Martin Buff, ⚥

Prince checked his rear-view mirror for this rap song with sounds from the 1980s, modifying his voice in the bass (a process he used excessively in his following album, *The Rainbow Children*) and pulling out his Linn LM-1 Drum Machine from the cellar. "He showed me how it worked with a lot of pride," said Hans-Martin Buff. "He would put guitar pedals behind the toms and create those weird fills you get on tunes like *The Ballad of Dorothy Parker*."[21] In a very effective way, and undoubtedly with a bit of nostalgia, Prince created *Strange But True*, which would not have been unworthy of a place on the *Sign O' the Times*, in 1988.

WHEREVER U GO, WHATEVER U DO

⚥ / 8'51

Musician: ⚥: vocals, electric guitar, acoustic guitar, bass, programming, percussion, synthesizers, backing vocals / **Recording:** Paisley Park, Chanhassen, Minnesota: 1999 / **Technical team:** Producer: Prince / Recording engineers: Hans-Martin Buff, ⚥ /

With similar sounds to *Love...Thy Will Be Done*, this mid-tempo ballad is carried by the Linn LM-1 Drum Machine, on which Prince records a few well-placed slapped bass lines. As for the 4-string, Prince used Larry Graham's Moon Bass, equipped with Bartolini pickups, or his own Warwick Thumb, nicknamed Warwick Eye Bass after Steve Parke decorated the instrument by painting it white and then drawing an eye on it. While the whole track lasts for 8'51, the song actually stops at 3'16 and is then followed by a period of silence 5'33 long.

SEGUE

⚥ / 0'44

Musician: ⚥: spoken word, programming, synthesizers / **Recording:** Paisley Park, Chanhassen, Minnesota: 1999 / **Technical team:** Producer: Prince / Recording engineer: Hans-Martin Buff

In this last segment of the album, Prince uses a low voice to advertise his websites Love4OneAnother.com and 1800NewFunk.com, and the phone service 1-800-NEW-FUNK. "Call Now, before I start laughing," he says, before bursting out laughing and showing more light-heartedness than at the time of *The Gold Experience* segues, which announced the fatal "*Prince esta muerto*" (Prince is dead).

PRETTYMAN

⚥ / 4'25

Musicians: ⚥: vocals, electric guitar, bass, synthesizers, backing vocals / **Kirk Johnson:** drums / **Maceo Parker:** saxophone / **Bros. Jules:** scratching / **Recording:** Paisley Park, Chanhassen, Minnesota: 1999, 3 June 1999 (Maceo Parker saxophone) / **Technical team:** Producer: Prince / Recording engineers: Hans-Martin Buff, ⚥

Prince wrote the lyrics to *Prettyman* while thinking about the social-dandy character that Morris Day played in his band. "Everywhere I go, people stop and stare/They just wanna see me swing this pretty hair," he sings, before adding

The song *Prettyman* marked the arrival of Maceo Parker in the world of Prince.

synth pads typical of *Ice Cream Castle* at 1'40 in. This was an album by The Time (see page 64), and it was full of hits, including *Jungle Love* and *The Bird*. "It was so good I kept it," Prince said, referring to *Prettyman*. "In fact, I wish I had kept some other songs I gave them."[200] Later in the song—no doubt the funkiest Prince ever recorded at the time—the singer emits some James Brown-style shouts at 3'53, then calls on the legendary saxophonist to the Godfather of Soul, Maceo Parker, and asks him to blow in his instrument, just as Brown had done in *Cold Sweat*, in 1967. Prince never hid his boundless admiration for James Brown, and explained that when he was ten years old, his stepfather had taken him to one of his concerts and he'd danced with him for a few moments. "He influenced me by his control of his group... and his dancing girls,"[234] Prince confessed in 1985. "Maceo, can you blow?" Prince shouts. Soon, his wish is granted. In fact, on the night of 3 June 1999 (the one where Ani DiFranco came to record her acoustic guitar for *Eye Love U, But Eye Don't Trust You Anymore*), Maceo Parker was invited to a jam session at Paisley Park. As Prince explained: "I called him and he came in and laid down an eight-minute solo that just killed. He came down for two to three hours of jamming and by the end Maceo was lying on his back on the stairs playing, and everyone just stopped and we were just near tears."[225] Prince added: "Then he said [impersonating Maceo] 'If you wanna jam, call me at the hotel!'"[222] This last proposition did not fall on deaf ears, since Maceo Parker joined the New Power Generation from 2002 to 2008. An ideal transition toward Prince's jazz/funk manifesto *The Rainbow Children*, which came out the following year, *Prettyman* was the piece that saved a very interesting album from oblivion, though it lacks any artistic coherence.

FOR PRINCE ADDICTS

In the introduction to *Prettyman*, Prince puts on a strange accent and says: "Don't hate me 'cause I'm beautiful." This is a nod to the actress Kelly LeBrock, who used this slogan in Pantene shampoo ads in 1986.

The Staples Singers in 1968, shortly before they recorded the soul anthem *When Will We Be Paid?*.

ONE SONG

⚥ / 9'01

Musician: ⚥: spoken word, vocals, electric guitar, bass, programming, synthesizers, backing vocals / **Recording:** Paisley Park, Chanhassen, Minnesota: 1999 / **Technical team:** Producer: Prince / Recording engineer: Hans-Martin Buff / **Video aired on Love4OneAnother.com:** 1 January 2000

On 1 January 2000, Prince closed down the website Love4OneAnother.com, but retained its URL, which only contained a nine-minute video divided into two separate parts. In it, Prince delivers an unfathomable speech for more than six minutes, making multiple references to the Bible and explaining that human beings must unite around a common song. He criticizes the music industry and the creations of man, which he believes are harmful to the natural evolution of the world, and asks his listeners to be one with God. The follow-up to the video is a pop song called *One Song*, whose lyrics are an extension of Prince's sermon. "I believe it had everything to do with the year 2000 and a sense of rebirth and renewal for the new millennium," explained webmaster Sam Jennings, Prince's close collaborator at the time. "That was the energy around that time in the world. Let's start over! But that led to Prince pulling me aside and starting work on our next project together, NPG Online LTD."[235]

CYBERSINGLE (2000)

⚥ / 2'43

Musicians: ⚥: vocals, electric guitar, bass, drums, synthesizers, backing vocals / **Bros. Jules:** scratching / **Recording:** Paisley Park, Chanhassen, Minnesota: 2000 / **Technical team:** Producer: ⚥ / Recording engineer: Hans-Martin Buff / **Released online at NPGOnlineLtd.com:** 14 July 2000

Cybersingle was an MP3 Prince made available to his fans via the website NPGOnlineLtd.com on 14 July 2000 (an extract lasting 1'04 was released on 1 June). It's a rock song reminiscent of Prince's *The Gold Experience* days. The song also takes up the famous drum roll breaks from *Shhh*. Uploaded on 4 March, the website became a launch pad for Prince, who always gave his subscribers lots of unreleased content in the years to come. Like *One Song*, this track urges people to free themselves of their shackles and attachment to the media. "Television got your mind but you got to get free," Prince sings wisely in this high-quality rock song.

Single

U MAKE MY SUN SHINE (PRINCE AND ANGIE STONE)

Prince / 7'06

Musicians: Prince: vocals, electric guitar, bass, programming, synthesizers, piano, claps, backing vocals / **Angie Stone:** vocals, claps, backing vocals / **Kip Blackshire:** backing vocals / **Niyoki White:** backing vocals / **"Mikki White":** backing vocals / **Tia White:** backing vocals / **Malikah White:** backing vocals / **Recording:** Paisley Park, Chanhassen, Minnesota: 2000, July 2000 (Angie Stone's vocals) / **Technical team:** Producer: Prince / Recording engineer: Femi Jiya
Single: 1. *U Make My Sun Shine*/5'52 / **2.** *When Will We B Paid?*/4'06 / **Digital release on NPGOnlineLtd.com:** 21 December 2000 / **Released in the USA by NPG Records/Wingspan Records:** 10 April 2001 (CD single ref.: WS-00102) / **Best chart ranking in the USA:** did not make the charts

A gospel singer in her church choir at 11 years old, frontwoman of the rap trio The Sequence at 17, saxophonist to Lenny Kravitz, then backing vocalist for D'Angelo, Angie Stone had already lived many lives by the time she met Prince in 2000. The latter, impressed by her first solo album *Black Diamond*, invited her in late July 2000 to sing the soul *U Make My Sun Shine* with him, which was released on the website NPGOnlineLtd.com before coming out as a single four months later. According to Stone, their good relationship hadn't been a given, since she'd long been shocked by Prince's provocative outfits and attitude. "When I first saw Prince in his little tight undies I was offended," she explained in 2004. "I went to the concert and I was hurt, I was disappointed, and I failed to realize that he was a great artist who felt that he had to take his clothes off *[...]* I walked away and for nearly ten years I did not want to support Prince. [He] asked me to

come to his studio [...] Now I have discovered an amazing, wonderful person who is my good friend."[236]

To accompany Angie Stone on this delicate ballad, the four White sisters, who made up the band Milenia, came to support Kip Blackshire's backing vocals. The singers, who accompanied Prince on *The Rainbow Children* and on the second part of the Hit n Run Tour, had only just joined the Prince universe. Without a base in Chanhassen, the sisters had arrived one morning at Paisley Park without being invited, knocked on the door, and asked for an audition. Determined to carry on the myth of the American dream, the master of the house immediately granted them a trial. They joined his team that same day. Once the song was recorded, Prince decided to make it into a single.

The night of 13 October 2000, during a party at Paisley Park, Prince slipped behind the console and inserted a cassette with the video for *U Make My Sun Shine* into the tape recorder, unveiling his new song to his 50 guests. Presenter Donnie Simpson aired it on his radio show on 2 November. Initially slated for the album *High*, the song was ultimately uploaded to NPGOnlineLtd.com on 21 December, but was only accessible after engaging in a little treasure hunt. Fans had to click on different sun-shaped icons hidden within the pages of the site, which revealed the word "truth." This was the password that allowed fans to download the song.

WHEN WILL WE B PAID?

Randall Stewart / 4'07

Musician: Prince: vocals, electric guitar, bass, drums, programming, percussion, claps, synthesizers, backing vocals / **Recording:** Paisley Park, Chanhassen, Minnesota: 1999–2000 / **Technical team:** Producer: Prince / **Recording engineer:** Femi Jiya / **Digital release on NPGOnlineLtd.com:** 21 December 2000

Prince moved away from the original gospel feel of this soul hymn, which was initially sung by The Staples Singers in 1969, and turned it into a deeply serious piece, perfectly suited to its lyrics. This song champions the history of the African-American population when it asks: "When will we be paid/For the work we've done?" These words revive the sad memory of slavery and show indignation for the injustices that this part of society still face every day. "We have worked this country from shore to shore/Our women cooked all your food and washed all your clothes/We picked all your cotton and laid the railroad steel/Worked our hands to the bone at your lumber mill," sings a rebellious Prince. The songs' important lyrics highlight persistent inequalities in the land of Uncle Sam. *When Will We B Paid?* appeared on the single *U Make My Sun Shine* when it came out in CD format on 10 April 2001.

Prince poses proudly in front of his Plymouth Prowler, bought in 1999.

FROM FUNK TO CIRCUIT COURT

After various attempts to distribute his albums on the Love4OneAnother.com and NPGOnlineLtd.com websites, Prince decided he had to ramp things up and so asked his collaborator Sam Jennings to develop a new tool that would allow him to sell or give his fans unreleased songs, live songs, or remixes at a pace he alone would decide on. In pursuit of his quest for artistic freedom, Prince launched the NPG Music Club on 14 February 2001. The first version of the website only contained a downloadable audio player, allowing fans access to unreleased songs like *When Eye Lay My Hands On You*, *Mad*, *Funky Design*, *Splash*, and *Peace*. Soon, webmaster Jennings realized that a full-blown website would be more appropriate for fans and abandoned the idea of the audio play in favor of a complete site. When NPG Music Club V2 came out a few months later, it revealed the Prince universe to his followers, allowing them to access a wide range of content for a monthly fee of $7.77. Members could also opt for a Premium membership (costing a lump sum of $100) and enjoy privileges such as pre-sales for concerts, a multitude of unreleased songs for download, and many other advantages. Before Prince launched this revolutionary site, no artist had ever released so many musical works online.

WHEN 👁 LAY MY HANDS ON U

(THE NEW POWER GENERATION)

Prince / 3'41

Musician: **Prince:** vocals, electric guitar, bass, programming, synthesizers, backing vocals / **Recording:** **Paisley Park, Chanhassen, Minnesota:** 2000 / **Technical team:** **Producer:** Prince / **Recording engineer:** Femi Jiya / **Digital release on NPG Music Club:** 18 February 2001

Slated to close the album *High*, abandoned in favor of *The Rainbow Children*, and gathered into the compilation *The Chocolate Invasion* in 2004, *When Eye Lay My Hands On You* reveals a mischievous Prince, reconnecting with his old ways when he asks his partner if she is "ready for the touch that makes you go insane."

Single

PEACE

(THE NEW POWER GENERATION)

Prince / 5'33

Musicians: **Prince:** vocals, electric guitar, bass, programming, synthesizers, piano, backing vocals / **Larry Graham:** vocals / **Johnnie Blackshire:** backing vocals / **Morris Hayes:** spoken word / **Recording:** **Paisley Park, Chanhassen, Minnesota:** 1999–2000 / **Technical team:** **Producer:** Prince / **Recording engineer:** Hans-Martin Buff / **Digital release on NPG Music Club:** 18 February 2001 / **CD single sales during Hit n Run Tour concerts:** 14 April 2001 (ref.: none)

Recorded to appear on *Peace*, the New Power Generation's fourth album, this eponymous song is full of bouncy pop. In it, Prince declares loud and clear that "Peace, that's what we're here for, and not to war"—in a snub to one of the band's previous singles, *The War* (1998). Prince, the only author of this song, warns his sweetheart of his naughty intentions with a rather comical image when he sings, "I will touch thee in the softest manner/Like Europa in the hands of Santana," referring to the hit by the band led by the famous guitarist, Carlos Santana: *Europa (Earth's Cry Heaven's Smile)*, which was released in 1976.

MAD

⚥ / 5'32

Musician: **⚥:** vocals, electric guitar, bass, programming, synthesizers, backing vocals / **Recording:** **Paisley Park, Chanhassen, Minnesota:** November 1994 / **Technical team:** **Producer:** ⚥ / **Recording engineers:** David "Chronic Freeze" Friedlander, Ray Hahnfeldt, Steve Durkee / **Digital release on NPG Music Club:** 18 February 2001

With a similar rhythm to *Now* (*The Gold Experience*, 1995), *Mad*'s arrangements, which include samples from the poet Ninety-9 (here, an excerpt from *Simlac*), make it a pure hip-hop song. Recorded in 1994, it was initially intended for the New Power Generation's second album *Exodus*. Ultimately placed in The Vault, the song was made available for download on the website NPGOnlineLtd.com on 17 July 2000, then on 18 February 2001 on the NPG Music Club, the website launched by Prince four days earlier.

FUNKY DESIGN

⚥ / 3'46

Musician: **⚥:** rap, bass, programming, synthesizers, backing vocals / **Recording:** **Paisley Park, Chanhassen, Minnesota:** November 1994 / **Technical team:** **Producer:** ⚥ / **Recording engineers:** David "Chronic Freeze" Friedlander, Ray Hahnfeldt, Steve Durkee / **Digital release on NPG Music Club:** 18 February 2001

In the same vein as *Now* or *Mad*, *Funky Design* has similar origins as it was once intended for the *Exodus* album. Presented in the form of a short excerpt on NPGOnlineLtd.com on 17 July 2000, it became available via the NPG Music Club on 18 July 2001. "[NPGOnlineLtd.com] was kind of a transition phase for Prince," explained Sam Jennings. "We really began the discussions of how to make a legit online music business with this site. In a way, it was like an incubator for what would become the NPG Music Club. There was a sense that anything was possible, so what were we going to do? For its brief existence we managed to make a fun little site that paved the way for what was to come."[237] Here Prince delivers an impeccable flow, which he accompanies with a brilliant bass solo. When listening to *Mad* and *Funky Design*, fans of *The Gold Experience* can imagine what a "Super Deluxe" edition of their favorite album might sound like if The Prince Estate ever decide to publish one in the future.

SPLASH
(PRINCE AND THE REVOLUTION)
Prince and The Revolution / 4'05

Musicians: Prince: vocals, electric guitar, bass, drums, synthesizers, piano, backing vocals / **Wendy Melvoin:** backing vocals / **Lisa Coleman:** backing vocals / **Recording: Washington Avenue Warehouse, Edina, Minnesota:** 1 August 1985 / **One On One Recording, Los Angeles:** 11 and 13 July 1986 (strings) / **Paisley Park, Chanhassen, Minnesota:** September 1998 (overdubs) / **Technical team: Producer:** Prince / **Recording engineer:** Susan Rogers / **Digital release on NPG Music Club:** 18 February 2001

Recorded on 1 August 1985 in Edina, the lyrics to *Splash* were partially inspired by a pack of Wrigley's chewing gum swiped from Susan Rogers' bag. The wrapping contained the word "wintergreen" (a plant used to make menthol chewing gum), which Prince inserted at 0'45 into the song. When he says: "Oh when you make love to me/There's things I never thought I'd see/Cherry blue wintergreen, fireworks, and rain in every scene," Rogers realized he'd rummaged through her things, but she didn't hold it against him. Embellished with the voices of Wendy Melvoin and Lisa Coleman, then with Clare Fischer's string arrangements, the song was once intended for the *Crystal Ball* album in 1998, an idea that was abandoned in favor of making *Roadhouse Garden*, the compilation of unreleased songs from The Revolution era. Since this project was also dropped, *Splash* was uploaded to the NPG Music Club on 18 February 2001.

Single

THE DAISY CHAIN
Prince / 6'15

Musicians: Prince: vocals, electric guitar, bass, programming, synthesizers, backing vocals / **DVS:** rap, vocals / **Kip Blackshire:** vocals, backing vocals / **Recording:** Paisley Park, Chanhassen, Minnesota: 2000 / **Technical team: Producer:** Prince / **Recording engineer:** Femi Jiya / **Video release on NPG Music Club:** 22 March 2001 / **CD single sold during Hit n Run Tour concerts:** 14 April 2001 (ref.: none)
Single: 1. *The Daisy Chain*/6'15 / **2.** *Gamillah*/3'18

Torn between his sexual appetite and his growing faith, Prince sings: "Bless my soul, save my name, I ain't never going down to the daisy chain." Due to appear on *High*, this funk song contains a rap part by David Max "DVS" Schwartz, a young musician and graphic designer from Minneapolis who did not have a fixed abode or job. "I didn't want a regular day job," explained the rapper, who was then 19 years old. "I just wanted to spend all of my time creating and not waste it working. I would crash on couches or with a girlfriend."[238] In 2000, he met Morris Hayes, who asked him to work on the visuals for a demo by the singer Bria Valente. It was at Hayes's place that DVS met Kip Blackshire, who soon introduced him to Prince. A video was shot for the song, in which the singers are seen performing with a ball, Blackshire, Prince, and DVS being great basketball players. "We must have played over a hundred games within those years," remembered DVS. "He [Prince] really could hoop! He had all kinds of tactics for distracting me when I was shooting, getting really low to the floor and tapping on the ground by my feet or running around me or under my legs. He would use his height and quickness to his advantage."[239] *The Daisy Chain* was the last single The New Power Generation released in Prince's lifetime.

Single

SUPERCUTE
Prince / 4'19

Musician: Prince: vocals, bass, programming, synthesizers, piano, backing vocals / **Recording: Paisley Park, Chanhassen, Minnesota:** 2000 / **Technical team: Producer:** Prince / **Recording engineer:** Femi Jiya / **CD single sold during Hit n Run Tour concerts:** 14 April 2001 (ref.: none) / **Digital release on NPG Music Club:** 11 June 2001 / **Single: 1.** *Supercute*/4'18 / **2.** *Underneath The Cream*/4'00

A survivor of the *High* adventure, the irresistible *Supercute*, with its haunting groove and effective choruses, is by far the most remarkable song from this abandoned project. Prince decided to release it as a single during the second half of the Hit n Run Tour in April 2001, then in MP3 format on the NPG Music Club on 11 June. The song was included in the tracklisting for *The Chocolate Invasion*, in 2004.

The saxophonist Najee was one of the key elements of the return to his roots that Prince would soon embark on.

UNDERNEATH THE CREAM

Prince / 4'01

Musicians: Prince: vocals, rap, bass, programming, synthesizers, backing vocals / **Mr** Hayes: synthesizers, Fender Rhodes piano / **Recording:** Paisley Park, Chanhassen, Minnesota: 2000 / **Technical team:** Producer: Prince / Recording engineer: Femi Jiya / Sold as a CD single during Hit n Run Tour concerts: 14 April 2001 (ref.: none) / Digital release on NPG Music Club: 15 November 2001

On the B-side of the single *Supercute, Underneath the Cream* is an R&B song that sounds as if it came straight out of 1994, a time when Jodeci, Blackstreet, and Wreckx-N-Effect's New Jack Swing dominated the charts. An NPG veteran, keyboardist Morris Hayes (who's mentioned in the credits under his pseudonym Mr Hayes) contributed to the song and embellished it with delicate Fender Rhodes lines. Initially intended for *High, Underneath the Cream* became available for download on 15 November 2001 from the NPG Music Club.

NORTHSIDE

Prince / 6'34

Musicians: Prince: vocals, rap, electric guitar, bass, programming, synthesizers, Hammond organ, backing vocals / **Najee:** saxophone / **Kip Blackshire:** backing vocals / **Recording:** Paisley Park, Chanhassen, Minnesota: 2000–2001 / **Technical team:** Producer: Prince / Recording engineer: ? (not confirmed) / Digital release on NPG Music Club: 22 April 2001

Northside, in which New York saxophonist Najee makes his first appearance, represents a return to funk. The creator of seven studio albums, the renowned musician met Prince on 25 September 1998, when the New Power Soul Festival Tour was being held at Madison Square Garden in New York. Doug E Fresh, who was on the tour, invited Najee to the concert, then—the ultimate privilege—he invited him backstage. "I didn't know Prince was actually a fan of mine," confessed the musician. "I didn't find out until we started working together. I found out he would come to my shows and be backstage but never announce he was there. After the show, I was invited to perform at one of the after parties which were his tradition. So after that [the concert at Madison Square Garden], I got a call from him inviting me out to Paisley Park. We started jam sessions, and after about three days, he asked me to join NPG for a two-week tour. Before I knew it, we had three years of working together."[240]

HABIBI

Prince / 4'58

Musicians: Prince: vocals, electric guitar / ? (not confirmed): bass / ? (not confirmed): drums / **Recording:** Paisley Park, Chanhassen, Minnesota: 1998 / **Technical team:** Producer: Prince / Recording engineer: ? (not confirmed) / Digital release on NPG Music Club: 22 April 2001

Habibi means "my love" in Arabic. Perhaps Prince had heard this term when in Marbella, in Spain, after declaring he wanted to discover North African culture (Morocco is very close to the Andalusian Coast). The fact remains that the word inspired a declaration of affection for...his guitar. In fact, Habibi is the name of the purple version of his gold Love Symbol Guitar, the copy being made by American brand Schecter in 1999. The song is a liberal adaptation of *Machine Gun* by Jimi Hendrix, which he recorded live with his Band of Gypsys in 1970.

BEAUTIFUL STRANGE

♀ / 4'56

Musicians: ♀: vocals, electric guitar, bass, synthesizers, backing vocals / Mike Scott: electric guitar / Kirk Johnson: percussion, programming / Marva King: backing vocals / **Recording:** Paisley Park, Chanhassen, Minnesota: 1998 / **Technical team:** Producer: Prince / Recording engineers: Hans-Martin Buff, ♀ / Digital release on NPG Music Club: 30 April 2001

When *Rave In2 the Joy Fantastic*, the Special Edition of *Rave Un2 the Joy Fantastic*, finally came out on 30 April 2001 on the NPG Music Club, fans were able to listen to an unreleased song: *Beautiful Strange*. The song was not completely unknown to Prince's most loyal fans, as it had featured in *Beautiful Strange*, a TV special that brought together images from the live performance at the Café de Paris, in London, on 28 August 1998 and an interview of Spice Girl Mel B. from that 30 July. Aired in England on Channel 4 on 24 October 1998, the TV special was later released as a VHS on 24 August 1999 and distributed via the website 1800NewFunk.com, as well as in the NPG Store in Minneapolis.

The recording engineer Hans-Martin Buff (left) and Kirk Johnson (right) with Prince in the intimate setting of the studios at Paisley Park.

PROPS N' POUNDS

Prince / 4'36

Musician: Prince: vocals, electric guitar, bass, programming, synthesizers, backing vocals / **Recording: Paisley Park, Chanhassen, Minnesota:** 2000–2001 / **Technical team: Producer:** Prince / **Recording engineer:** ? (not confirmed) / **Digital release on NPG Music Club:** 15 May 2001

"Love 4 one another is the only sound 2day/Positivity is the only way," says our singer in this song, which was released on the NPG Music Club on 15 May 2001. A keen self-congratulator, Prince decided to insert excerpts from *MTV News* in which presenter Kurt Loder talks about him in a very flattering way. They can be found in the introduction and closing of the song.

SEX ME SEX ME NOT

Prince / 5'42

Musician: Prince: vocals, rap, bass, programming, synthesizers, backing vocals / **Recording: Paisley Park, Chanhassen, Minnesota:** 2000 / **Technical team: Producer:** Prince / **Recording engineer:** ? (not confirmed) / **Digital release on NPG Music Club:** 11 June 2001

Despite the déjà-vu quality that brings us back to Prince's past hip-hop periods, *Sex Me Sex Me Not* is a real guilty pleasure. When listening to his naughty words, in which Prince boasts of being a sexually irresistible star, you can glean the reasons that pushed him to abandon the *High* project as well as other songs recorded around the same time, such as this one. Most of these songs have something in common: a return to irreverent lyrics that extoll the pleasures of the flesh, or of other pleasures deemed futile by the Jehovah's Witness evangelist Prince was becoming at the time. Putting an end to this out-of-control schizophrenia, Prince chose instead to produce the spiritual *The Rainbow Children*.

Y SHOULD 👁 DO THAT WHEN 👁 CAN DO THIS?

Prince / 4'31

Musicians: Prince: rap, spoken word, electric guitar, bass, synthesizers, claps, backing vocals / **Michael B.:** drums / **Michael B Nelson:** trombone / **Kathy Jensen:** baritone saxophone / **Kenni Holmen:** saxophone / **Dave Jensen:** trumpet / **Steve Strand:** trumpet / **Recording: Paisley Park, Chanhassen, Minnesota:** 1999, 17 May 1999 (brass) / **Technical team: Producer:** Prince / **Recording engineer:** Hans-Martin Buff / **Digital release on NPG Music Club:** 11 June 2001

The Hornheadz recorded their brass parts for this very funky song during the same session as *Hot With U* and *Man'O'War*, on 17 May 1999. Two other songs, which have remained unreleased, were also wrapped up that same day with the famous quintet: *I Ain't Gonna Run* and *R U Ready?*

S&M GROOVE

Prince / 5'08

Musicians: Prince: vocals, rap, electric guitar, acoustic guitar, bass, programming, synthesizers, backing vocals / **Marva King:** vocals, rap / **Recording: Paisley Park, Chanhassen, Minnesota:** 1997 / **Technical team: Producer:** Prince / **Recording engineer:** Hans-Martin Buff / **Digital release on NPG Music Club:** 7 July 2001

Made available for streaming on Love4OneAnother.com in June 2001, *Sado-Masochistic Groove* was renamed *S&M Groove* when it was uploaded that 7 July. It came out on the compilation *The Slaughterhouse* in March 2004.

HYPNOPARADISE

Prince / 6'03

Musician: Prince: vocals, spoken word, bass, programming, synthesizers, backing vocals / **Recording: Paisley Park, Chanhassen, Minnesota:** 1998–1999 / **Technical team: Producer:** Prince / **Recording engineer:** Hans-Martin Buff / **Digital release on NPG Music Club:** 7 July 2001

A song that sounds as if it came from the 1990s, *Hypnoparadise* is danceable but stodgy—this is as much a result of the arrangements as the soulless melody. A special mention goes to the synthesizer that comes in at 2'32, which brings you back to the mad years of dance music and makes you think of forgotten bands, such as 2 Unlimited, Ice MC, or Black Box. A moment of distraction for Prince, but he can easily be forgiven.

VAN GOGH

⚥ / 5'59

Musician: ⚥: vocals, bass, programming, synthesizers, backing vocals / **Recording:** Paisley Park, Chanhassen, Minnesota: 1995 / **Technical team:** Producer: ⚥ / Recording engineer: ? (not confirmed) / **Digital release on NPG Music Club:** 7 July 2001

In 1995, Prince asked Michael Van Huffel, then artistic director at Paisley Park, to work on an ad for an album he wanted to give to Gianni and Donatella Versace. Several unreleased songs appeared on the album, including *Van Gogh*, which was based on *Love Is*, a song by Sandra St Victor with whom Prince collaborated on *Soul Sanctuary*. With a pop spirit that's very reminiscent of the 1990s, the song is blessed with a quality chorus and undoubtedly explains why the only copy of this album, called *Playtime By Versace* from Van Huffel's personal collection, sold for $3,288 at an auction organized by RR Auction in 2017. The song became available for download on the NPG Music Club on 7 July 2001. A second version of the song, containing a saxophone part played by Eric Leeds, later circulated on the web.

JUDAS SMILE

Prince / 6'34

Musician: Prince: vocals, electric guitar, bass, programming, synthesizers, backing vocals / **Recording:** Paisley Park, Chanhassen, Minnesota: 2001 / **Technical team:** Producer: Prince / Recording engineer: ? (not confirmed) / **Digital release on NPG Music Club:** 28 August 2001

With its slick production, *Judas Smile* is a powerful song that blends modern sounds (synthesizer riffs played on the arpeggiator, a percussion drum machine) with Prince's natural-sounding 6-string guitar, which delivers violent power chords throughout the song. This is an exceptional song, in which the narrator declares, "You've been bamboozled," referring to Spike Lee's movie *Bamboozled*, released in 2000 and for which Prince wrote the song *2045: Radical Man*.

MY MEDALLION

Prince / 5'07

Musician: Prince: vocals, spoken word, rap, bass, programming, synthesizers, backing vocals / **Recording:** Paisley Park, Chanhassen, Minnesota: 2000 / **Technical team:** Producer: Prince / Recording engineer: Femi Jiya / **Digital release on NPG Music Club:** 28 August 2001

Let's say that the resemblance between *You Got It (The Right Stuff)*, the 1988 hit by boy band New Kids On The Block, and the main synthesizer line from *My Medallion*, is pure coincidence. That said, there is no other similarity to point out between these two songs, since Prince here uses a formula he had tried out while producing *High*, the album for which *My Medallion* was initially composed: a powerful groove, loads of synthetic instruments, vocals mixed with rap parts, and effective melodies.

GOLDEN PARACHUTE

Prince / 5'36

Musicians: Prince: vocals, electric guitar, bass, programming, synthesizers, backing vocals / Najee: transverse flute, trumpet / **Recording:** Paisley Park, Chanhassen, Minnesota: May 2000 / **Technical team:** Producer: Prince / Recording engineer: Femi Jiya / **Digital release on NPG Music Club:** 28 August 2001

In addition to being a high-quality R&B song, *Golden Parachute* is a critique of "golden parachutes," the bonuses given to directors when they leave their companies. Well-known to insiders, and only revealed to the larger public during the 2000s, these nauseating practices, which are in stark contrast to employees' low salaries, outraged people and inspired Prince to write this song, in which he addresses the departing directors: "Here's 50 million dollars, 2 go along with this boot!/Just keep your mouth shut, and never tell of the plan/2 conquer and control the very soul of man."

The fashion designer Gianni Versace and his sister Donatella, who was a close friend of Prince.

There was no meeting of minds between Prince and the pop diva Mariah Carey who did not like the songs the artist suggested to her.

VAVOOM

Prince / 4'36

Musician: Prince: vocals, electric guitar, bass, programming, synthesizers, backing vocals / **Recording: Paisley Park, Chanhassen, Minnesota:** 1999 / **Technical team: Producer:** Prince / **Recording engineer:** Hans-Martin Buff / **Digital release on NPG Music Club:** 15 November 2001

When Mariah Carey visited Prince at Paisley Park in 1999, he played *Vavoom* for her, a pop song that seemed to fit her repertoire. Hans-Martin Buff, the recording engineer at Chanhassen, recalled the scene: "I remember Prince and I in the studio shooting each other looks and thinking 'Is that really what superstars are like?' Prince had written a song, *Vavoom*, with a distinct 80s vibe. He played it to Mariah and her entourage for consideration. Mariah didn't look impressed and she never covered the song."[21]

SILICON

Prince / 4'15

Musician: Prince: vocals, spoken word, rap, bass, programming, synthesizers, backing vocals / **Recording: Paisley Park, Chanhassen, Minnesota:** 1999 / **Technical team: Producer:** Prince / **Recording engineer:** Hans-Martin Buff / **Digital release on NPG Music Club:** 15 December 2001

As with *The War*, the NPG single released in 1998, or *One Song*, the video for which came out on 1 January 2000 on the website Love4OneAnother.com, *Silicon* contains dystopian lyrics that tell listeners about the miserable conditions they will soon face if they don't change their ways. "You can bet that they'll be chillin' in Babylon/Thinking about a way that they can split the proton/While you eating all the bloody chicken and dead prawn," sings Prince in an apparent pro-vegetarian apocalyptic sermon. *Silicon* is a brilliant song that recalls the icy textures of *Undisputed* or *Strange But True* from *Rave Un2 the Joy Fantastic*, which was recorded during the same period.

CONTEST SONG

Prince / 3'34

Musician: Prince: electric guitar, bass, drums, synthesizers, Hammond organ / **Recording: Paisley Park, Chanhassen, Minnesota:** 2001 / **Technical team: Producer:** Prince / **Recording engineer:** ? (not confirmed) / **Digital release on NPG Music Club:** 28 August 2001 /

Rehashing the concept of the "Cyber Song Contest," a writing competition initiated by David Bowie in 1998 on his website BowieNet, where fans were asked to write lyrics to an instrumental track, Prince asked his fans to write lyrics for a song provisionally called *Contest Song*. Uploaded to the NPG Music Club on 28 August 2001, the game was a huge success. On 15 November, the three winners were announced, and their versions became available for download on Prince's site: Dana D. with *Where Are Your Dandelions?*, *How Could I Love You More?* by Miles Rivers, and *No War* by The Muse.

THE VERY BEST OF PRINCE

Released in the USA by Warner Bros. Records:
30 July 2001 (CD ref.: R2 74272)
Released in the UK by WEA International:
21 May 2001 (CD ref.: 8122-74272-2)
Best chart ranking in the USA: 66
Best chart ranking in the UK: 2

1. *I Wanna Be Your Lover* (2'57)
2. *1999* (3'35)
3. *Little Red Corvette* (4'58)
4. *When Doves Cry* (3'49)
5. *Let's Go Crazy* (4'39)
6. *Purple Rain* (8'45)
7. *I Would Die 4 U* (2'57)
8. *Raspberry Beret* (3'31)
9. *Kiss* (3'46)
10. *Sign O' the Times* (3'44)
11. *U Got the Look* (3'58)
12. *Alphabet St* (5'38)
13. *Thieves in the Temple* (3'19)
14. *Gett Off* (4'27)
15. *Cream* (4'12)
16. *Diamonds and Pearls* (4'20)
17. *Money Don't Matter 2 Night* (4'48)

AN UNSURPRISING COMPILATION

Almost eight years after the release of the essential triptyque *The Hits/The B-Sides*, Warner Bros. Records decided to release a new Prince compilation in 2001. It did not include any unreleased songs, not even a live or remixed curiosity. This CD was nothing but a commercial object used to fill the record label's coffers at the expense of the artist who'd left the inner circle after years of open war. In fact, when Prince's former label found out that he was planning to release a "best-of" album with rerecorded versions of his songs, as he'd done for *1999: The New Master*, they released this compilation in a hurry. As a result, Prince abandoned the project *A Celebration* and the tour of the same name that had started on 15 June 2001. On the NPG Music Club, Prince did not hesitate to say what he really thought of this album released by Warner Bros. Records without his consent, mentioning that this product would not bring him much money—an untruth that was quickly rectified by observers who highlighted the fact that he was still the author, composer, performer, and publisher of all the songs on the album. Fans would have appreciated the presence of hits such as *The Most Beautiful Girl in the World*, but since this song was the exclusive property of NPG Records, the record company had no financial incentive to include it, other than to attract a wider audience. So then where the heck were the singles from *Batman (Motion Picture Soundtrack)*, including the wonderful *Batdance* or the very funky *Partyman*?; *My Name Is Prince*, *7*, or *Sexy M.F.* from *Love Symbol;* or other 1990s gems by Prince (*Letitgo*, *Gold*, *Endorphinmachine*, and *Dinner with Delores*)? These songs would have covered a wide range of Prince's career until his separation from Warner Bros. Records. But it wasn't to be, to the great disappointment of fans who would have been equally happy to find one or two unreleased songs. The CD, which includes the most successful Prince singles from 1979 to 1991, presents one hit after another (*Little Red Corvette, Purple Rain, Kiss...*) and while it doesn't surprise, it does manage to introduce Prince to a new generation of music lovers.

PRINCE

THE RAINBOW CHILDREN

Rainbow Children · Muse 2 the Pharaoh · Digital Garden · The Work Pt. 1
Everywhere · The Sensual Everafter · Mellow · 1+1+1 Is 3
Deconstruction · Wedding Feast · She Loves Me 4 Me · Family Name
The Everlasting Now · Last December · Last December (Reprise)

Digital release on NPG Music Club:
16 October 2001
Released in the USA and UK by NPG Records/Redline Entertainment:
20 November 2001 (LP ref.: 70004; CD ref.: 70004-2)
Best chart ranking in the USA: 109
Best chart ranking in the UK: did not make the charts

Now comfortable with his age and advocating music that was more authentic, Prince gained credibility with *The Rainbow Children* album.

FOR PRINCE ADDICTS

For the cover of *The Rainbow Children*, Prince decided to use a painting by the artist Cbabi Bayloc called *The Queen Keis Quintet*. It was reminiscent of the cover for Marvin Gaye's 1976 album *I Want You*. Note, however, that here the album cover is not a reproduction of the painting but a photograph of Prince standing next to it.

THE JAZZ-FUNK RAINBOW

On 16 May 2000, Prince gave a press conference in New York. He announced that his contractual obligations with Warner Bros. Records had ended on 31 December 1999 and that he would once again be using his birth name as his stage name. Prince might have been back, but having just finalized his divorce from Mayte and after the failure of his new single *The Greatest Romance Ever Sold*, he said he wanted to take some time off. "My main concern right now is to take time to study things of a spiritual nature," he said, "[...] so I'm going to go away for awhile and do that, and then I'm hoping to go on the road by July or early August."[241] The break would be a short one, as he also announced the creation of an annual event called *Prince: A Celebration*. The idea was to open Paisley Park to his "fams" (his name for his most loyal fans) for a week from the 7 to 13 June, so they could visit the location and attend concerts. "People who have supported my music through the years never really got a chance to go inside Paisley Park, he explained. "[...] I'd like for them to see what they helped create—the interaction that went on with us throughout the years that actually painted the joint."[241]

The short-lived High adventure

Prince didn't hit the road again until November 2000, when he launched his famous Hit n Run Tour. He spent the summer producing *High*, a new album in the same smooth and modern vein as *Rave Un2 the Joy Fantastic*. With the help of recording engineer Femi Jiya, who had come in to replace Hans-Martin Buff, Prince laid down a quality album on tape, featuring tracks with risqué lyrics that harked back to classics such as *Cream*, *Sexy M.F.*, and *Pheromone*. But this change of tack was short-lived. By then a convert to the Jehovah's Witness movement, Prince reverted to a doctrine that prohibited swearing and racy themes in his songs. Although an official reason was never given, it is highly likely this was why he decided to drop *High* and immerse himself in a new project: an album entitled *The Rainbow Children*. Come autumn, Prince shut himself away at Paisley Park with Femi Jiya and a handful of session musicians to start recording his most spiritual album to date. Drumming virtuoso John Blackwell, a newcomer to Prince's stable who was discovered when Prince heard him on tour with Patti LaBelle, proved key to the sound of the forthcoming album. "One night after Patti's show at New York's Madison Square Garden, he came up to me and asked if I would come to Minneapolis to jam with him and Larry [Graham] [...]," Blackwell reports. "The tour was about to end. And it was right before I was committed to start a short one-month tour with Hikaru Utada, Japan's number one pop star. Prince waited until that tour ended and then we got together. I officially signed with Prince on 2 September 2000."[242] In early 2001, once the album had been recorded, Prince called on saxophonist and flautist Najee as well as Milenia, the female vocal quartet with whom he had collaborated on *U Make My Sun Shine* that summer, to add various embellishments. He also brought in Kip Blackshire and Morris Hayes to boost the number of backing vocal tracks, before adding horn scores by the Hornheadz to several of the songs.

Jazz for the 'fams

On 6 April 2001, Prince once again surprised fans by making a song called *The Work Pt. 1.* available to users of Napster, the

peer-to-peer file-sharing service. This flew in the face of his previous hostility to pirate records that his fans used to share in the 1980s and 1990s, and people were surprised to see him collaborating with the illegal site. However, Prince was pleased with the outcome when the song became one of the most downloaded tracks in the platform's history. He saw it as a counter-offensive against the record companies, which he felt were unfair to artists and turned a deaf ear to the expectations of music consumers. With summer came the second edition of *Prince: A Celebration*, held in Paisley Park from the 11 to 16 June 2001, which gave Prince an opportunity to unveil his new album *The Rainbow Children* to his "fams." Listening sessions were organized and the lyrics were also revealed. It is a complex and exciting album, tinged with jazz and funk. A formidable groove adds color to the mix of pure 1970s acoustic funk (the influence of James Brown and his J.B.'s can be felt throughout) and instruments that add warm, electric sound textures such as the Fender Rhodes or the few synthesizers scattered here and there. But beyond this return to the musical sources of Prince's youth, the record is a concept album like 1992's ⚥. Reading between the lines, Prince hints at his devotion to the Jehovah's Witness movement and tells a story that is nothing if not mystical.

From left to right: Candy Dulfer, Greg Boyer, John Blackwell, Prince, Renato Neto, Maceo Parker, and Rhonda Smith—the musicians that formed a revitalized NPG on the One Nite Alone…Tour.

In 2003, Prince invited Sam Jennings to work on the cover for *The Rainbow Children 2.* He also asked Argentine artist Pablo Lobato to paint his wife, Manuela, in the same style as he had sketched Prince for the *Hartford Courant*, a Connecticut newspaper. The album project was dropped in 2004, when the *Musicology* album brought a wider audience back into the Prince fold.

Manuela Testolini, sent by God

A deep-voiced narrator (played by Prince with the pitch of his voice altered in a way reminiscent of the intros to *1999* in 1982 and *Bob George* in 1987) tells the story of the Rainbow Children, a people led by a king called The Wise One whose wife has been tempted by the devil (called The Resistor). God rewards the king for his loyalty by giving him a new wife who will become queen. This is an obvious analogy to Prince's separation from Mayte and, lurking behind the preposterous twists and turns that we'll come to shortly, the album's main theme is the chastisement of humankind for turning away from God, Prince's obsession at the time. In early October, Prince bought a $5.5-million home in Toronto, the hometown of his new girlfriend, Manuela Testolini, and, on 16 October, he made his new album available for download as an MP3 on the NPG Music Club (see page 384). In November, he restructured the New Power Generation, which now featured John Blackwell on drums, Rhonda Smith on bass, and Renato Neto on keyboards. Mike Scott, Kip Blackshire, Morris Hayes, and backing vocalist and dancer Geneva all left the band. It was the start of a new era for Prince, and he subsequently launched one of his most ambitious tours: the jazzy One Nite Alone...Tour. Prestigious brass players followed one another thick and fast onstage throughout the nine months of the tour. Greg Boyer was ever-present on trombone, accompanied on various dates by saxophonists Najee, Maceo Parker, Candy Dulfer, and Eric Leeds, as well as D.J. Dudley D. The American press gave *The Rainbow Children* a lukewarm reception when it was released, but Europe rolled out the red carpet for Prince, praising his artistic risk-taking and his jazz-funk audaciousness. This enabled him to reconnect with audiences and, wherever he went, people were won over. Once the One Nite Alone...Tour was over, Prince flew to Hawaii where he married Manuela Testolini on 31 December 2001 in a Jehovah's Witness ceremony held in the utmost secrecy.

The influence of James Brown's jerky funk became ever more palpable in Prince's new songs.

RAINBOW CHILDREN

Prince / 10'04

Musicians: Prince: vocals, spoken voice, electric guitar, bass, synthesizers, Fender Rhodes piano, claps, backing vocals / **John Blackwell**: drums / **Najee**: soprano saxophone, flute / **Niyoki White**: claps, backing vocals / **"Mikki White"**: claps, backing vocals / **Tia White**: claps, backing vocals / **Malikah White**: claps, backing vocals / **Recording: Paisley Park, Chanhassen, Minnesota**: autumn 2000; January to February 2001 / **Technical team: Producer**: Prince / **Recording engineers**: Femi Jiya, Prince

The imagery of the king (The Wise One) whose wife is tempted by the devil (here called The Resistor) had not escaped the notice of Prince's ex-wife Mayte. According to the narrative of *The Rainbow Children*, the young woman joins The Banished Ones and will soon be replaced by a pure woman, sent to the king by God himself. Mayte refused to embrace her husband's faith, so he considered her a pagan, and this disagreement over their spirituality was one of the reasons for their estrangement. On the album, Prince-as-narrator adopts the same deep voice that he used in the intro to *1999* as well as the intro to *Bob George*, which was performed on the Lovesexy Tour and released on *The Black Album* in 1994.

MUSE 2 THE PHARAOH

Prince / 4'21

Musicians: Prince: vocals, rap, electric guitar, bass, Fender Rhodes piano, backing vocals / **John Blackwell**: drums / **Recording: Paisley Park, Chanhassen, Minnesota**: autumn 2000; January to February 2001 / **Technical team: Producer**: Prince / **Recording engineers**: Femi Jiya, Prince

"She could become Pharaoh's muse," Prince sings in this delightful jazz ballad, perfectly suited to the Fender Rhodes electric piano. The guitar is discreet, almost inaudible, although a few chords played using the Whammy pedal pop up here and there. If the young woman wants to become the new wife of the king (called The Pharaoh in this song), she will have to read Proverbs 31 verse 10 over and over—a passage from the Bible praising virtuous women. After she has performed her task, perhaps this woman sent by God will be lucky enough to become The Wise One's wife. Let's ignore the old-fashioned misogyny of this song and just enjoy its fine production.

DIGITAL GARDEN

Prince / 4'07

Musicians: Prince: vocals, spoken word, electric guitar, bass, synthesizers, programming, backing vocals, screams / **John Blackwell**: drums / **Niyoki White**: screams / **"Mikki White"**: screams / **Tia White**: screams / **Malikah White**: screams / **Kip Blackshire**: screams, backing vocals / **Recording: Paisley Park, Chanhassen, Minnesota**: autumn 2000; January to February 2001 / **Technical team: Producer**: Prince / **Recording engineers**: Femi Jiya, Prince

While Prince makes an implicit reference to his faith in *Rainbow Children* when he cites the new translation (The New World Translation is a 1950 version of the Bible used by Jehovah's Witnesses to study holy scripture), he is more explicit at the end of *Digital Garden* when he refers to " The Work"—in other words, the door-to-door evangelism carried out by Jehovah's Witnesses to spread their message and their beliefs. Prince himself once went house to house in Minneapolis, much to the surprise of one particular mother who spoke to the *Star Tribune* about her encounter with him and Larry Graham. "They start in on this Jehovah's Witnesses stuff. I said, 'You know what? You've walked into a Jewish household, and this is not something I'm interested in.' He says, 'Can I just finish?' Then the other guy, Larry Graham, gets out his little Bible and starts reading scriptures about being Jewish and the land of Israel [...] He was very kind [...] Curiously, they did not visit any other homes on the block. It was so bizarre, you would have just laughed."[243]

Single

THE WORK PT. 1

Prince / 4'28

Musicians: Prince: vocals, spoken voice, electric guitar, synthesizers, Hammond organ, Fender Rhodes piano, backing vocals / **Larry Graham**: bass / **John Blackwell**: drums / **Michael B Nelson**: trombone / **Kathy Jensen**: baritone saxophone / **Dave Jensen**: trumpet / **Steve Strand**: trumpet / **Niyoki White**: backing vocals / **"Mikki White"**: backing vocals / **Tia White**: backing vocals / **Malikah White**: backing vocals / **Kip Blackshire**: backing vocals / **Recording: Paisley Park, Chanhassen, Minnesota**: autumn 2000; January to February 2001 / **Technical team: Producer**: Prince / **Recording engineers**: Femi Jiya, Prince
Single: 1. ***The Work Pt. 1***/3'40 / **2.** ***U Make My Sun Shine***/5'52 / **Digital distribution via Napster**: 6 April 2001 / **CD single distribution via NPG Music Club**: summer 2001 (CD single ref.: 27Y61 7135 THEWORK)

Prince resurrects the spirit of The J.B.'s (James Brown's band in the 1970s) with *The Work Pt. 1* (titled *The Work Part 1* when it was released on Napster on 6 April 2001), which is in some ways reminiscent of *Sexy M.F.* from 1992. More than just a tribute to his idols, *The Work Pt. 1* is a funk manifesto that testifies to Prince's artistic renaissance. Its syncopated rhythms and thumping brass parts, as well as the title itself, are a nod to James Brown's *Cold Sweat*, which was released in 1967 in two parts: *Cold Sweat Part 1* and the B-side, *Cold Sweat Part 2*. John Blackwell's score, performed on his six-piece Tama Starclassic, is every bit as formidable as the performance by the Brown clan's Clyde Stubblefield, with Blackwell's remarkable playing giving Larry Graham free rein to let rip with his lively bass line. A marvel of pure funk, to be listened to again and again.

EVERYWHERE

Prince / 2'55

Musicians: Prince: vocals, bass, synthesizers, Fender Rhodes piano, backing vocals / **John Blackwell**: drums / **Michael B Nelson**: trombone / **Kathy Jensen**: baritone saxophone / **Dave Jensen**: trumpet / **Steve Strand**: trumpet / **Niyoki White**: backing vocals / **"Mikki White"**: backing vocals / **Tia White**: backing vocals / **Malikah White**: backing vocals / **Recording: Paisley Park, Chanhassen, Minnesota**: autumn 2000; January to February 2001 / **Technical team: Producer**: Prince / **Recording engineers**: Femi Jiya, Prince

One morning in Paisley Park, while recording engineer Femi Jiya was setting up the Audix mics on his drum kit for a recording session, John Blackwell was warming up with a rhythmic pattern of his own invention. "I started doing this crazy uptempo Latin fusion beat and Prince was like, 'Keep that going,'" Blackwell recalls. "And they pressed 'record' and he immediately started adding things, like a bass line. The next day I came in and he said, 'Check this out,' and it was a whole song. I mean, it had everything. My mouth just dropped. I've always heard stories like that about him, but until you see it for your own eyes, you can't grasp the whole picture."[244] While *Everywhere* stands out for its atypical genesis, it is also shines for the contribution from Milenia, a group of female vocalists consisting of the White sisters, whose warm, crystalline layers add color to the track.

MELLOW

Prince / 4'24

Musicians: Prince: vocals, bass, Fender Rhodes piano, backing vocals / **John Blackwell**: drums / **Najee**: soprano saxophone, flute / **Michael B Nelson**: trombone / **Kathy Jensen**: baritone saxophone / **Dave Jensen**: trumpet / **Steve Strand**: trumpet / **Recording: Paisley Park, Chanhassen, Minnesota**: autumn 2000; January to February 2001 / **Technical team: Producer**: Prince / **Recording engineers**: Femi Jiya, Prince

Despite his willingness to abandon his racy lyrics, Prince returns to his old ways when he dons the guise of The Wise One and tells of his burning desire for the woman at his side, informing her—in his own inimitable fashion—of the pleasure he will bring her. "Can I sing to you while you bring yourself to joy?/I'll go slow at first, while you quench your thirst/Wet circles round the toy," sings the artist in his most languid voice, accompanied by the sexiest instrument in the perfect crooner's toolkit: a Fender Rhodes electric piano with its soft, velvety sound textures that could melt an ice floe. Najee adds a discreet flute score to the track, making the most of the small measure of confidence Prince had in her. "I had some room to improvise, but a lot of the melodies were how he heard it," Najee said. "So I would come up with stuff and then he would say, 'Yeah, that's what I want right there.' And then in some cases, he would just sing exactly what it is he wanted."[245]

THE SENSUAL EVERAFTER

Prince / 2'58

Musicians: Prince: spoken voice, electric guitar, bass, synthesizers, programming, piano, percussion / **John Blackwell**: drums / **Recording: Paisley Park, Chanhassen, Minnesota**: autumn 2000; January to February 2001 / **Technical team: Producer**: Prince / **Recording engineers**: Femi Jiya, Prince

The Sensual Everafter is a short musical interlude introduced by a narrator's monologue. It is an instrumental piece dedicated to The Muse, the new sweetheart of The Wise One, who is becoming ever more devoted to God.

1+1+1 IS 3

Prince / 5'17

Musicians: Prince: vocals, spoken voice, electric guitar, bass, backing vocals / **John Blackwell**: drums / **Niyoki White**: backing vocals / **"Mikki White"**: backing vocals / **Tia White**: backing vocals / **Malikah White**: backing vocals / **Kip Blackshire**: backing vocals / **Recording: Paisley Park, Chanhassen, Minnesota**: autumn 2000; January to February 2001 / **Technical team: Producer**: Prince / **Recording engineers**: Femi Jiya, Prince

With its *Erotic City* feel, *1+1+1 Is 3* invites us into a love triangle between The Wise One, The Muse, and God, whose presence in the lovers' bedroom is necessary because they are now living under a "theocratic order," according to the leader of

Although famous primarily for his virtuosity, drummer John Blackwell was recognizable on the One Nite Alone...Tour for his distinctive black hat. "When you're with Prince, you got to look cool," he confided in 2001. "He personally gave me that hat right off his head. Now it's my trademark."[242]

The much-missed John Blackwell, NPG's virtuoso drummer, sporting the hat Prince gave him when he joined the group.

the Rainbow Children. Behind the story is a funky track, led by John Blackwell's straight, metronomic drumming. Blackwell had to adapt quickly when Prince wanted to integrate different loops or sounds into the drum lines, which had to be triggered by pads next to his drums. Those lucky enough to see the One Nite Alone...Tour will remember hearing the famous claps that often replaced the snare drum hits on the last beat of many bars in a way reminiscent of 1984's *I Would Die 4 U*. Blackwell explained the difficulties involved: "When I first came out to jam with Prince, Takumi [Suetsugu, Prince's guitar technician] would show me how to work it. He'd say 'This button turns the loops on. This button turns on the claps [...] Prince wants you to play around and get used to it.'"[242] Blackwell then decided to place the loop trigger pedal next to his hi-hat pedal, which was not without its issues. "The only time it gave me a problem was when I did a solo. Sometimes I like to take my foot off the hi-hat pedal, but then my foot would land on the trigger pedal. All of sudden you'd hear 'crash-bing-boom-boom,' all this stuff going off, and I'm like, Oh, no! And Prince would look over at me, like Oh, that's funny."[242]

The keyboard player rad. (left) joined the NPG for the World Tour 2003.

DECONSTRUCTION

Prince / 2'00

Musicians: Prince: spoken voice, electric guitar, synthesizers / **Niyoki White**: backing vocals / **"Mikki White":** backing vocals / **Tia White**: backing vocals / **Malikah White**: backing vocals / **Kip Blackshire**: backing vocals / **Recording: Paisley Park, Chanhassen, Minnesota**: autumn 2000; January to February 2001 / **Technical team: Producer**: Prince / **Recording engineers**: Femi Jiya, Prince

This mainly instrumental interlude is narrated over by The Wise One celebrating The Muse's awakening as a queen.

WEDDING FEAST

Prince / 0'54

Musicians: Prince: vocals, synthesizers, electric guitar, backing vocals / **Kip Blackshire**: vocals / **Niyoki White**: vocals / **"Mikki White":** vocals / **Tia White**: vocals / **Malikah White**: vocals / **Recording: Paisley Park, Chanhassen, Minnesota**: autumn 2000; January to February 2001 / **Technical team: Producer**: Prince / **Recording engineers**: Femi Jiya, Prince

Prince gave Kip Blackshire a special spot on *The Rainbow Children:* 15 seconds of a beautiful *a cappella* reminiscent of Terence Trent D'Arby's impressive vocal performance on *Introducing the Hardline According to Terence Trent D'Arby* in 1987. Prince and the White sisters from the Milenia quartet then join in and the song takes a surprising direction, comparable to Queen's famous operatic break in their 1975 *Bohemian Rhapsody*.

SHE LOVES ME 4 ME

Prince / 2'50

Musicians: Prince: vocals, electric guitar, bass, Fender Rhodes piano / **John Blackwell**: drums / **Recording: Paisley Park, Chanhassen, Minnesota**: autumn 2000; January to February 2001 / **Technical team: Producer**: Prince / **Recording engineers**: Femi Jiya, Prince

Prince's ex-wife Mayte might not have appreciated the lyrics of this gentle ballad, in which the singer says that his new sweetheart "loves him for who he really is." This song was given to American radio stations as a promotional single, and was recorded entirely by Prince, who was accompanied only by John Blackwell, his loyal drummer. Blackwell, a left-handed musician, explained how he managed to adapt and become the virtuoso musician that he was. "There were a lot of things I couldn't do. Then I realized it was because I'm a lefty. When I see things right-handed drummers do, I have to remember to reverse certain techniques. But I still play right-handed on ballads, R&B, and jazz when I use brushes. So I'm living two lives. It can be a little crazy."[242]

79

The intimate aftershows Prince held on the One Nite Alone...Tour were famous—here, onstage at the Nighttown in Rotterdam on 3 November 2002.

FAMILY NAME

Prince / 8'17

Musicians: Prince: vocals, spoken voice, electric guitar, bass, Hohner clavinet, synthesizers, tambourine / **John Blackwell**: drums / **Niyoki White**: vocals / **"Mikki White"**: vocals / **Tia White**: vocals / **Malikah White**: vocals / **Recording: Paisley Park, Chanhassen, Minnesota**: autumn 2000; January to February 2001 / **Technical team: Producer**: Prince / **Recording engineers**: Femi Jiya, Prince

Here, Prince tells people they have nothing to worry about when it comes to family names or origins, unlike the poor slaves who arrived from Europe in the 17th century and were frequently renamed. Before incorporating an excerpt from Martin Luther King Jr's famous speech of 28 August 1963 in Washington, D.C., the narration begins with a robotic voice. This arose from a surprising collaboration with Morris Hayes, the New Power Generation's ex-keyboardist, who had remained close friends with Prince. One day, Hayes demonstrated to Prince the VoiceOver function designed for the visually impaired on the latest version of the iBook. When activated, this tool enables the computer to describe aloud what appears on the screen and speak any text. "When he figured out I could do that it blew his mind," Hayes recalled in 2018. "He was like wait, you just type this out and you hit play and then the computer talks back? And he went bananas. He was like oh this is great. We're going to go in the studio and he said, 'Write this out.' And we wrote out all of this dialogue, and then he got this like this low voice thing that he wanted to do all over it."[246]

THE EVERLASTING NOW

Prince / 8'18

Musicians: Prince: vocals, spoken voice, electric guitar, acoustic guitar, bass, synthesizers, piano, percussion, backing vocals / **John Blackwell**: drums / **Michael B Nelson**: trombone / **Kathy Jensen**: baritone saxophone / **Dave Jensen**: trumpet / **Steve Strand**: trumpet / **Recording: Paisley Park, Chanhassen, Minnesota**: autumn 2000; January to February 2001 / **Technical team: Producer**: Prince / **Recording engineers**: Femi Jiya, Prince

When *The Tonight Show with Jay Leno* aired on NBC on 13 December 2002, America held its breath. As far as the press was concerned, Prince was back to his best, thanks to the high-profile One Nite Alone...Tour. However, those who hadn't been lucky enough to attend one of the concerts knew nothing of the "new Prince," who was wearing a sober suit designed by his faithful stylist Debbie McGuan (whom he had described as "strange and gifted"[247] in 1997) and surrounded by the latest incarnation of the NPG. When he appeared on screen and launched into *The Everlasting Now*, he had the whole country on its feet and in the four minutes it took him to perform the song he had regained his crown. The simple elegance of the musicians' clothing, which only served to emphasize their virtuosity, Maceo Parker and Eric Leeds on saxophones, as well as an old friend on percussion in the person of Sheila E. (who changes the pitch of her snare drum by putting a high heel on the drumhead!), made this unforgettable performance sheer perfection. A performance more than worthy of this equally perfect song in which Prince pays homage to his idol Carlos Santana by slipping in a Latin break at 4'55.

LAST DECEMBER

Prince / 7'58

Musicians: **Prince**: vocals, electric guitar, synthesizers, tambourine, backing vocals / **Larry Graham**: bass / **John Blackwell**: drums / **Niyoki White**: backing vocals, claps / **"Mikki White"**: backing vocals, claps / **Tia White**: backing vocals, claps / **Malikah White**: backing vocals, claps / **Recording:** **Paisley Park, Chanhassen, Minnesota**: autumn 2000; January to February 2001 / **Technical team:** **Producer**: Prince / **Recording engineers**: Femi Jiya, Prince

Last December is a song with no verse or chorus that is more than a match for *Thunder*, *3 Chains O' Gold*, or *Rock'N'Roll Is Alive! (And It Lives In Minneapolis)*. It is undoubtedly the most rock-sounding track on the album, despite starting off as a gospel ballad with a pious "In the name of the Father/In the name of the Son/We need to come 2gether/Come 2gether as one."

(LAST DECEMBER REPRISE)

Prince / 0'38

Musicians: **Niyoki White**: backing vocals / **"Mikki White"**: backing vocals / **Tia White**: backing vocals / **Malikah White**: backing vocals / **Recording:** **Paisley Park, Chanhassen, Minnesota**: autumn 2000; January to February 2001 / **Technical team:** **Producer**: Prince / **Recording engineers**: Femi Jiya, Prince

This short, hidden track samples and repeats the backing vocals of the White siblings from the very end of *Last December*, which is why fans unofficially call it the *Last December (Reprise)*.

George Clinton was on top form when he worked with Prince on the song *Paradigm* in 1999.

In 1999, Prince had banned the consumption of meat at Paisley Park. George Clinton, who attended the *Rave Un2 the Year 2000* concert on 18 December, had no intention of following this rule and decided to sit next to Prince in the kitchen of the Paisley Park complex with a huge tub of chicken wings he'd bought at the local KFC. Out of respect for his idol, Prince made an exception for the funk ogre and his voracious appetite!

PARADIGM

(GEORGE CLINTON FEATURING [symbol])

George Clinton, Prince / 6'50

Musicians: **George Clinton**: vocals, backing vocals / **[symbol]**: electric guitar, vocals, backing vocals / **Brian "Kool-Ace" Fleming ? (not confirmed)**: bass, programming / **Recording:** **DARP Studios, Atlanta, Georgia**: 1992 / **Paisley Park Studio, Chanhassen, Minnesota**: 1999 / **Technical team:** **Producer**: George Clinton, **[symbol]** / **Recording engineers**: Larry Fergusson (DARP Studios), Hans-Martin Buff (Paisley Park) / **CD-R distributed at Paradiso, Amsterdam**: 12 July 2001 / **George Clinton presents The P-Funk Allstars *"How Late Do U Have 2BB4UR Absent?"*** (album) / **Released in the USA by The C Kunspyruhzy**: 6 September 2005 (ref. TCK 0010-2) / **Best chart ranking in the USA**: did not make the charts

Prince and George Clinton, the master of p-funk, a musical and theatrical movement invented by the brilliant producer in the early 1970s, had already crossed paths when Clinton was invited to play in *Graffiti Bridge* and sing on *We Can Funk* in 1990. The p-funk style, as performed by his two bands Funkadelic and Parliament, broke away from traditional funk, injecting albums with a healthy dose of psychedelia, complete with strong visuals and remarkable costumes—the best-known records include Funkadelic's *Maggot Brain* (1971) and *One Nation Under A Groove* (1978) and Parliament's *Up For The Down Stroke* (1974) and *Mothership Connection* (1975). Nine years after their first collaboration, Prince gave a classic concert at Paisley Park on 18 December 1999, which was broadcast on 31 December on In Demand, an American video-on-demand cable channel. Among the guests that day was George Clinton, who came to jam with the band and catch up with Prince, whom he subsequently invited to do some arrangements on a previously recorded track called *Paradigm*. In the space of four hours, Prince laid down his vocals and a few electric guitar lines, and sent the tapes back to Clinton who, in his own inimitable way, explained the spontaneous nature of the collaboration: "I peed on it, sent it to him, he peed on it, and sent it back."[248] A CD-R featuring the song was sold at George Clinton's concert in Amsterdam on 12 July 2001, and the track appeared on the *Sneak Peek EP* on iTunes on 30 August 2005, before being added to the tracklist of Clinton's new album, *How Late Do U Have 2BB4UR Absent?* on 6 September.

The members of the Californian group No Doubt—Adrian Young, Gwen Stefani, Tony Kanal, and Tom Dumont—at the peak of their fame in 2000.

WAITING ROOM
(NO DOUBT FEATURING ♀)

Gwen Stefani, Tony Kanal, Tom Dumont, Prince / 4'27

Musicians: Gwen Stefani: vocals, backing vocals / ♀: vocals, electric guitar, synthesizers, programming, backing vocals / Tom Dumont: electric guitar, synthesizers / Tony Kanal: bass, synthesizers / / **Recording: 11AD, Los Angeles**: 1999 / **Paisley Park, Chanhassen, Minnesota**: 10 July 1999 / **Technical team:** Producer: ♀, No Doubt / Recording engineers: Alan Johanness (11AD), Hans-Martin Buff (Paisley Park) / Assistant recording engineer: Steve Mandel (11AD) / **No Doubt *Rock Steady* (album)** / **Released in the USA by Interscope Records**: 11 December 2001 (LP ref.: 069493158-1; CD ref.: 0694931582) / **Released in Europe by Interscope Records**: 11 December 2001 (LP ref.: 493 195-1; CD ref.: 493 158-2) / **Best chart ranking in the USA**: 9 / **Best chart ranking in the UK**: 43

After a successful first collaboration on *So Far, So Pleased*, the seventh track of *Rave Un2 the Joy Fantastic*, Prince and the No Doubt singer Gwen Stefani quickly decided to work together again. While the band was busy producing their fourth album, *Return of Saturn*, guitarist Tom Dumont, bassist Tony Kanal, and Stefani recorded *Waiting Room*, a rock song with lyrics that recount a young woman's despair as she waits for a sign from her loved one—heartbreak being a recurring theme in the quartet's songs. The tapes were then sent to Paisley Park, where Prince decided to do new arrangements for the track. He replaced Adrian Young's powerful drums with a glacial drum machine, taking the track a world away from the punk-rock spirit of the new No Doubt album that was earmarked as a comeback after the global success of *Tragic Kingdom* in 1995. This was why the song ended up being shelved, only resurfacing in 2001 when the Californian band released the brilliant *Rock Steady*, an album where synthetic textures were omnipresent. Nevertheless, the song failed to convince fans and wasn't a coherent fit for the reggae and acid pop-style album. In 2015, by which time No Doubt had disappeared from the radar (despite a few comeback attempts), Prince paid tribute to this 1990s cult group in *Ebony* magazine: "No Doubt, you know that group? Friends of mine. Came in here and jammed together. They don't know how to jam. They don't know nothing about that. You get them to play one of their songs? Girl jumping on top of tabletops and all of that, all kinds of stuff."[249]

Prince and his second wife, Manuela Testolini, in 2004.

HIGH

Prince / 5'05

Musicians: Prince: vocals, electric guitar, bass, programming, synthesizers, backing vocals / **DVS**: backing vocals / **Kip Blackshire:** spoken voice / **Recording: Paisley Park, Chanhassen, Minnesota**: 2000 / **Technical team: Producer**: Prince / **Recording engineer**: Femi Jiya / **Digital release on NPG Music Club**: 19 December 2001

On 7 June 2001, Tony Fly, a host on KDWB, a Minneapolis radio station, played an unreleased Prince track called *High*. Prince immediately posted a comment on website NPGOnlineLtd.com urging his fans to ask Fly to play the song on heavy rotation, something that never happened. Whether it was a sign or just coincidence, Prince dropped the album of the same name and held on to this track until December, when it was made available as a download on the NPG Music Club. It is an upbeat song about the pleasures of partying that falls somewhere between funk and New Jack Swing. It takes us back to the Prince of the mid-1990s when he states unequivocally in the lyrics: "Prince gonna get you high." Guesting on the track (and on *The Daisy Chain*), the hard-up rapper DVS was disappointed that both the song and the album of the same name ended up in The Vault, especially as he had designed the cover. "There's a song called *High* on there and I'm doing a chorus, chant-kinda breakdown on there [...] Once he finished the album, he decided not to release it. This was big for me, because it would have been my most high-profile design job at the time and for a long time after that. He asked me to design the CD packaging for *High* because I came up with a transparent idea for my CD and he really liked it. He already had the cover designed, but he wanted me to do something really trippy with it. I was crushed it didn't come out."[238]

GAMILLAH

Prince / 3'18

Musicians: Prince: electric guitar, bass, drums, synthesizers, percussion / **Najee**: saxophone / **Recording: Paisley Park, Chanhassen, Minnesota:** 2000 / **Technical team: Producer**: Prince / **Recording engineer**: Femi Jiya / **Digital release on NPG Music Club**: 19 December 2001

In October 2001, businessman Kenneth Gertner and his wife, Sandra, put their lavish home in Bridle Path, an upmarket suburb of Toronto, Canada, up for sale for $5.5 million. The house was quickly acquired by a company called Gamillah Holdings Inc. and an initial down payment of $1.375 million was made before Christmas, followed by the balance of $4.125 million on 1 January 2002. The president of this real estate company was none other than Manuela Testolini, who had been Prince's second wife since 31

December when the two were wed during a trip to Hawaii. The name Gamillah was not unfamiliar to Prince's fans since an instrumental track of the same name had been released on the NPG Music Club on 19 December. Gamillah is an insipid track, perfect background music for a seaside wedding (or even a beach cocktail party). It was one of only two songs officially written by Prince for Manuela Testolini, the second being *Another Girl*, which remains unreleased to this day.

POORGOO

[Symbol] / 4'38

Musicians: [Symbol]: vocals, electric guitar / **Sonny T.**: bass / **Michael B.**: drums / **Recording:** Paisley Park, Chanhassen, Minnesota: 14 June 1993 / **Technical team:** Producer: [Symbol] / **Recording engineer**: ? (not confirmed) / **Digital release on NPG Music Club**: 19 December 2001

Poorgoo was recorded on 14 June 1993 during a mythical night session with Prince's Paisley Park Power Trio, a short-lived band he had formed with Michael Bland and Sonny Thompson. It was previously only available as a VHS video released on 6 March 1995, called *The Undertaker*, which was essentially a recording of this memorable recording session. Prince wanted to turn the session into an album to be offered to buyers of a future issue of *Guitar World* magazine, but Warner Bros. Records flatly refused. So *Poorgoo* was shelved and made available on the NPG Music Club on 19 December 2001. Legend has it that the track, more of a blues improvisation than a fully fledged song, was inspired by a member of Prince's technical team, James McGregor (known as McGoo), who was a drum technician for the New Power Generation from 1993 to 1995.

BREATHE

[Symbol] / 2'01

Musician: [Symbol]: vocals, programming, synthesizers / **Recording:** Paisley Park, Chanhassen, Minnesota: 1998 / **Technical team:** Producer: Prince / **Recording engineer**: Hans-Martin Buff / **Digital release on NPG Music Club**: 17 January 2002

Breathe was recorded in 1998 for the *Madrid 2 Chicago* album, a project that was finally abandoned in favor of *The Rainbow Children*. It is a track bordering on trip-hop, a musical genre that Prince had never previously touched. Light as a feather and not the most interesting of songs, it eventually ended up on the NPG Music Club on 17 January 2002.

MADRID 2 CHICAGO

[Symbol] / 3'14

Musician: [Symbol]: vocals, bass, programming, synthesizers, backing vocals / **Recording:** Paisley Park, Chanhassen, Minnesota: 1998 / **Technical team:** Producer: Prince / **Recording engineer**: Hans-Martin Buff / **Digital release on NPG Music Club**: 17 January 2002

Madrid 2 Chicago was composed during the production of *Rave Un2 the Joy Fantastic*, then reworked by Prince to become *Man'O'War*. The title was the inspiration behind the name of one of his two next albums (*High* being the other), before the project was shelved and ended up in The Vault. Inspired by Prince's flights between Spain and the United States, the song was featured as a short music video on Love4OneAnother.com on 26 January 1999 and made available for download on the NPG Music Club on 17 January 2002.

ONE NITE ALONE...

Released in the USA and UK by NPG Records: 14 May 2002 (CD ref: none)
Best chart ranking in the USA: did not make the charts
Best chart ranking in the UK: did not make the charts

1. *One Nite Alone...*
2. *U're Gonna C Me*
3. *Here On Earth*
4. *A Case of U*
5. *Have A ♥*
6. *Objects in the Mirror*
7. *Avalanche*
8. *Pearls B4 the Swine*
9. *Young and Beautiful*
10. *Arboretum*

A TÊTE-À-TÊTE WITH PRINCE

On 14 May 2002, the NPG Music Club presented the album *One Nite Alone...* to Prince fans. Premium members of the site could download the ten-song album, which was available exclusively on the platform. Recorded in early spring while Brian Gardner was doing the final master for *The Rainbow Children*, the album takes a similar approach to *The Truth* with Prince mainly using just one instrument in its production (in this case, the piano). Although a few overdubs were subsequently put in to add color, the album nevertheless offers us a moment of intimacy with the artist, who was clearly set on swapping his 6-string for the velvety touch of Paisley Park's piano. Some tracks were not unknown to fans, as they had previously been made available for download as individual songs on the NPG Music Club. These included *Pearls B4 the Swine*, *U're Gonna C Me*, and *A Case of U*, a Joni Mitchell cover that Prince frequently performed onstage. On 27 June 2002, after midnight, the singer took to the stage for the last Xenophobia: 7 Nights Alone with Prince concert (a big gathering organized for his fans from the 21 to 27 June in Paisley Park) and started with a short piano-vocal set, during which fans were treated to a delicious version of *One Nite Alone...*

ONE NITE ALONE...

Prince / 3'35

Musician: Prince: vocals, piano, synthesizers / **Recording: Paisley Park, Chanhassen, Minnesota**: March 2001 / **Technical team: Producer**: Prince / **Recording engineers**: Femi Jiya, Joseph Lipinski

"Do U like it fast? Or do U like it slow?" the narrator of the song asks the girl he is about to undress. Like most tracks on the *One Nite Alone...* album, it is a mini-scene depicting two lovers who have just met and the burning passion that gradually overcomes them. Prince's voice is languorous, and one can guess that Manuela Testolini's slim figure was very much on his mind during the recording of this lithe song.

An unavoidable routine after every live performance: viewing the show with the aim of eliminating any weaknesses or mistakes going forward.

U'RE GONNA C ME

Prince / 5'16

Musician: Prince: vocals, piano, synthesizers / **Recording:** Paisley Park, Chanhassen, Minnesota: March 2001 / **Technical team:** Producer: Prince / Recording engineers: Femi Jiya, Joseph Lipinski

Enhanced by a few discreet synthesizer layers, *U're Gonna C Me* is one of Prince's most beautiful piano-vocal ballads. Prince pays tribute to his lovely wife when he says: "There's never a minute that Eye find/That u don't ever cross my mind." The artist's voice is fragile, hesitant, and less adventurous than on other tracks of the same ilk, such as *How Come U Don't Call Me Anymore* or *Eye Love U But Eye Don't Trust You Anymore*.

HERE ON EARTH

Prince / 3'22

Musicians: Prince: vocals, spoken voice, piano, bass, synthesizers, backing vocals / John Blackwell: drums / **Recording:** Paisley Park, Chanhassen, Minnesota: March 2001 / **Technical team:** Producer: Prince / Recording engineers: Femi Jiya, Joseph Lipinski

Prince summons drummer John Blackwell to play on this ephemeral and delicate track, in which he sings about a bad dream and wakes up to find himself safe in the arms of his beloved.

Although Prince frequently covered the American singer Joni Mitchell's song *A Case of You*, he claimed the entirety of her work was a major influence.

A CASE OF U

Joni Mitchell / 3'39

Musicians: **Prince**: vocals, piano, bass, organ / **John Blackwell**: drums / **Recording:** **Paisley Park, Chanhassen, Minnesota**: March 2001 / **Technical team:** **Producer**: Prince / **Recording engineers**: Femi Jiya, Joseph Lipinski

"Another big influence was Joni Mitchell," Prince said back in 1986. "She taught me a lot about color and sound, and to her, I'm very grateful."[250] The artist had always expressed his admiration for the Canadian singer and guitarist, and he sang this ballad from her 1971 album *Blue* (originally called *A Case of You*) on numerous occasions. "[It's] one of my favorite songs 2 sing because the melody is so heartbreaking,"[251] he commented a few years later. The song was first recorded at the Kiowa Trail Home Studio in Chanhassen in 1983 (and later appeared on the posthumous album *Piano & A Microphone* in 2018). It was even played on 3 August 1983 during the mythical First Avenue concert in Minneapolis when *Purple Rain* was recorded. Officially released for the first time on *One Nite Alone...*, *A Case of U* is a vibrant tribute from a fan to his idol, whose performances and qualities he praised once again in 2004: "I love all Joni's music." He went on: "Joni's music should be taught in school, if just from a literature standpoint."[252] This version of *A Case of U* also featured on the compilation *A Tribute To Joni Mitchell*, which was released by the Nonesuch label in April 2007.

HAVE A ♥

Prince / 2'03

Musician: **Prince**: vocals, piano, backing vocals / **Recording:** **Paisley Park, Chanhassen, Minnesota**: March 2001 / **Technical team:** **Producer**: Prince / **Recording engineers**: Femi Jiya, Joseph Lipinski

Although the spirit of Keith Jarrett's *The Köln Concert* (1975) hovers over the piano score of *Have A Heart*, the comparison with the jazz genius ends there, as Prince transforms his piano score into a real song about a painful breakup with a woman, in which he asks her if she really has a heart.

OBJECTS IN THE MIRROR

Prince / 3'26

Musician: **Prince**: vocals, piano, synthesizers / **Recording:** **Paisley Park, Chanhassen, Minnesota**: March 2001 / **Technical team:** **Producer**: Prince / **Recording engineers**: Femi Jiya, Joseph Lipinski

Prince tells his sweetheart of the carnal pleasures that still await her as the two lovers look at each other in their bedroom mirror after making love. Is he also trying to slip in a dirty metaphor by repeating the warning engraved on car rear-view mirrors when he sings that "the objects in the mirror r closer than they appear"? Subtle metaphor or incomprehensible nod to the listener? Either way, he issues a warning to listeners in the very first verse of the song when he says to his girl, "That's my favorite time with u/Just after we make a movie/The kind that requires the title/Parental advisory."

AVALANCHE

Prince / 4'24

Musician: **Prince**: vocals, piano, backing vocals / **Recording:** **Paisley Park, Chanhassen, Minnesota**: March 2001 / **Technical team:** **Producer**: Prince / **Recording engineers**: Femi Jiya, Joseph Lipinski

Prince rarely took a political or social stand in the 1980s and 1990s. However, he did sing about the suffering of minority groups in Louisiana after Hurricane Katrina in August 2005 (the single *S.S.T.*) and denounced police violence in Baltimore in 2015. *Avalanche* is his take on a part of American history. Quoting from Abraham Lincoln's State of the Union address to the House of Representatives and the Senate on 1 December 1862, Prince denounces the racism of the 16th American president, even though he was responsible for abolishing slavery in the United States. This is a gospel-sounding track of undeniable quality, and it's interesting to see a politically committed Prince expressing his convictions loud and proud.

PEARLS B4 THE SWINE

Prince / 3'00

Musician: **Prince**: vocals, acoustic guitar, bass, percussion, piano, synthesizers, backing vocals / **Recording:** **Paisley Park, Chanhassen, Minnesota**: March 2001 / **Technical team:** **Producer**: Prince / **Recording engineers**: Femi Jiya, Joseph Lipinski

Here Prince takes another biblical quote, this time from the Gospel according to Matthew in the New Testament (Matthew 7:6): "Do not give what is holy to the dogs; nor cast your pearls before swine, lest they trample them under their feet, and turn and tear you in pieces."[253] He draws on this quote for the title of this gentle ballad: *Pearls B4 the Swine*. Released on the NPG Music Club on 18 September 2001, the song was included on *One Nite Alone...*, and would have made a perfect single for promoting this intimate album.

YOUNG AND BEAUTIFUL

Prince / 2'44

Musician: **Prince**: vocals, piano, synthesizers, backing vocals / **Recording:** **Paisley Park, Chanhassen, Minnesota**: March 2001 / **Technical team:** **Producer**: Prince / **Recording engineers**: Femi Jiya, Joseph Lipinski

A track with Japanese sounds (a first in Prince's discography), *Young and Beautiful* would have made an excellent single had it been played with a full band, not dissimilar to Prince's future incursions into pop-rock in the late 2000s. Listening to the melody of *Young and Beautiful,* it's impossible not to compare it to some of Prince's tracks from the late 2000s such as *Fury* (2006), *Guitar* (2007), and especially *Rock and Roll Love Affair*, which was released as a single in 2012. *Young and Beautiful* is a track that saw Prince returning to rock 'n' roll after the success of *Musicology* in 2004.

ARBORETUM

Prince / 3'16

Musician: **Prince**: piano, synthesizers / **Recording:** **Paisley Park, Chanhassen, Minnesota**: March 2001 / **Technical team:** **Producer**: Prince / **Recording engineers**: Femi Jiya, Joseph Lipinski

After two minutes and 16 seconds of this instrumental track, let's savor the sound of Prince closing the lid of his piano and listen to his footsteps receding as he leaves the studio after recording his score. A full minute of silence follows, as if to give us time to rest our ears after an album of rare gentleness in the artist's discography. For *One Nite Alone...*

Prince was not on his usual Steinway B7. Instead, he played a Schimmel K208 Pegasus whose curved forms were the brainchild of the German designer Luigi Colani. Prince replaced the standard Pegasus statue on the piano lid with an imposing Love Symbol, thus marking his territory on this unusually shaped instrument.

ONE NITE ALONE... LIVE!

Distribution via NPG Music Club: 24 November 2002 (longbox box set ref.: none)
Released in the USA and the UK by NPG Records: 17 December 2002 (longbox box set ref.: none)

Disc 1 One Nite Alone...Live!

1. *Rainbow Children* (11'45)
2. *Muse 2 the Pharaoh* (4'49)
3. *Xenophobia* (12'39)
4. *Extraordinary* (5'01)
5. *Mellow* (4'30)
6. *1+1+1 Is 3* (6'05)
7. *The Other Side of the Pillow* (4'47)
8. *Strange Relationship* (4'12)
9. *When U Were Mine* (3'47)
10. *Avalanche* (6'04)

Disc 2 One Nite Alone...Live!

1. *Family Name* (7'16)
2. *Take Me With U* (2'53)
3. *Raspberry Beret* (3'26)
4. *Everlasting Now* (7'40)
5. *One Nite Alone...* (1'12)
6. *Adore* (5'32)
7. *I Wanna B Ur Lover* (1'21)
8. *Do Me, Baby* (1'56)
9. *Condition of the ♥ (Interlude)* (0'39)
10. *Diamonds & Pearls* (0'40)
11. *The Beautiful Ones* (2'10)
12. *Nothing Compares 2 U* (3'47)
13. *Free* (1'06)
14. *Starfish & Coffee* (1'07)
15. *Sometimes It Snows In April* (2'40)
16. *How Come U Don't Call Me Anymore* (5'06)
17. *Anna Stesia* (13'12)

Disc 3 One Nite Alone...The Aftershow: It Ain't Over!

1. *Joy in Repetition* (10'55)
2. *We Do This* (4'41)
3. *Medley: Just Friends (Sunny) / If You Want Me To Stay* (4'26)
4. *2 Nigs United 4 West Compton* (6'14)
5. *Alphabet Street* (2'54)
6. *Peach (Xtended Jam)* (11'18)
7. *Dorothy Parker* (6'16)
8. *Girls & Boys* (6'59)
9. *The Everlasting Now (Vamp)* (1'49)

Musicians: Prince: vocals, electric guitar, bass, synthesizers, piano, Fender Rhodes piano / **George Clinton**: vocals / **Musiq Soulchild**: vocals / **Doug E Fresh**: Rap / **Rhonda Smith**: bass, backing vocals / **Larry Graham**: bass, backing vocals / **John Blackwell**: drums / **Questlove**: drums / **Renato Neto**: synthesizers, organ / **Maceo Parker**: saxophone / **Candy Dulfer**: saxophone / **Greg Boyer**: trombone / **Najee**: saxophone / **Recording: *One Nite Alone... Live!*** / Murat Theatre, Indianapolis: 11 March 2002 (tracks 1/2, 1/5, 1/7, 1/8) / Warner Theatre, Washington D.C.: 31 March 2002 (track 1/1) / Youkey Theatre (Lakeland Center), Lakeland: 6 April 2002 (track 1/6) / Verizon Wireless Theater, Houston: 14 April 2002 (tracks 2/6, 2/8, 2/9) / Kodak Theatre, Los Angeles: 20 April 2002 (track 1/9) / Paramount Theatre, Oakland: 24 April 2002 (track 2/2) / Paramount Theatre, Seattle: 29 April 2002 (tracks 2/5, 2/13, 2/14, 2/15) / Arlene Schnitzer Concert Hall (Portland Center for the Performing Arts), Portland: 30 April 2002 (tracks 1/3, 1/4, 1/10, 2/1, 2/3, 2/4, 2/7, 2/10, 2/11, 2/12, 2/16) / Paisley Park, Chanhassen: 2002 (overdubs) / ***One Nite Alone...The Aftershow: It Ain't Over!*** / The World, New York: 10 April 2002* (tracks 1, 2, 3) / The Highlands Hollywood, Los Angeles: 20 April 2002* (tracks 4, 5, 8, 9) / House of Blues Sunset Strip, Los Angeles: 21 April 2002* (track 7) / Roseland Theater, Portland: 1 May 2002* (track 6) / Paisley Park, Chanhassen: 2002 (overdubs) / **Technical team: Producer**: Prince / **Recording engineers**: Scott Michael "Scottie P." Pakulski (live), Joseph Lipinski (overdubs), Femi Jiya (overdubs)

* All aftershows started between midnight and 1am.

Prince with his irreplaceable Hohner Madcat on the One Nite Alone...Tour.

A JAZZ-TINGED LIVE DEBUT

One Nite Alone...Live! was released as a longbox box set via the NPG Music Club on 24 November 2002. It was Prince's first ever live album. The first two discs in the box set were recorded on eight American dates of the One Nite Alone... Tour and saw Prince returning to his funk and jazz roots. He adeptly mixed his classics (*When You Were Mine*, by then renamed *When U Were Mine*, *Raspberry Beret*, *Adore*...) with the most prominent tracks from *The Rainbow Children* (*Family Name*, *Muse 2 the Pharaoh*...), thus bringing several generations of fans together on this tour (which was a favorite of the "fams"), as he lined up hits and rarities from his wide repertoire (*One Nite Alone...*, *Avalanche*). The box set, available in stores from 17 December, included the live album double CD and another disc entitled *One Nite Alone... The Aftershow: It Ain't Over!* This album featured songs from four different aftershows, nights when Prince and his musicians performed in small, intimate venues, including the legendary House of Blues Sunset Strip in Los Angeles, which was closed in 2015 and demolished to make way for a soulless apartment complex. As well as the reprises in the tracklist, it's worth pointing out the one unreleased Prince song on this must-have box set, namely *Xenophobia*, which was written after the attacks of 11 September 2001, shows how America withdrew into itself due to fear of certain foreigners. The track, based on a riff from an Eric Leeds' song *Overnight, Every Night*, which appeared on the 1991 CD version of *Times Squared*, was played on every date of the US leg of the tour which ended in Portland on 30 April 2002. On 29 May 2020, The Prince Estate released *Up All Nite With Prince: The One Nite Alone Collection*, a five-vinyl box set featuring *One Nite Alone...Live!*, *One Nite Alone...The Aftershow: It Ain't Over!*, the *One Nite Alone...* album, and the *Live At The Aladdin Las Vegas* DVD, which was originally released on 19 August 2003.

XPECTATION

Candy Dulfer, the essential saxophonist of the New Power Generation from 1998 to 2004.

Digital distribution via NPG Music Club:
1 January 2003 (CD ref: NPGMC13)

1. *Xhalation* **(Prince / 2'04)**
2. *Xcogitate* **(Prince / 3'34)**
3. *Xemplify* **(Prince / 5'53)**
4. *Xpectation* **(Prince / 4'01)**
5. *Xotica* **(Prince / 3'05)**
6. *Xogenous* **(Prince / 4'12)**
7. *Xpand* **(Prince / 6'11)**
8. *Xosphere* **(Prince / 3'34)**
9. *Xpedition* **(Prince / 8'24)**

Musicians
Prince: electric guitar, Fender Rhodes piano, synthesizers
Rhonda Smith: bass
John Blackwell: drums
Candy Dulfer: saxophone
Vanessa Mae: violin
Recording
Paisley Park, Chanhassen, Minnesota: October to December 2001
Technical team
Producer: Prince
Recording engineer: ? (not confirmed)

Before she became a top-class skier, Vanessa-Mae was a brilliant violinist.

FOLLOWING ON FROM THE RAINBOW CHILDREN

Building on the instrumental experimentation of Madhouse's two 1987 jazz albums *8* and *16* (see page 153), Prince returned to this particular genre by offering NPG Music Club members this incredible, multifaceted album on 1 January 2003. Alongside drummer John Blackwell (note his awesome drum rolls on *Xpectation*), saxophonist Candy Dulfer, and bassist Rhonda Smith (who switches from bass to double bass), he recorded nine breathtaking tracks on an album that to date has not been made available in record stores. Prince also invited classical violinist Vanessa Mae, who had never played jazz before, to participate in the recording sessions at Paisley Park, advising her beforehand to study the work of Weather Report and Herbie Hancock's legendary *Head Hunters* (1973). The woman who would later compete in the 2014 giant slalom ski event at the Sochi Olympics shines on four tracks on the record, adding a shot of tension that perfectly suits the dynamic rhythms of the Blackwell/Smith duo. When journalist Gary Graff asked Prince why he decided to produce a record like this, the artist unassumingly replied: "That's for dinner parties [...] I have dinner parties sometimes, and I wanted to have something I could play that kept things in a place I like. I'm not trying to shock the world with every record."[254]

N.E.W.S.

Distribution via NPG Music Club: 30 June 2003 (CD ref: NPGNEWS)
Released in the USA by NPG Records: 29 July 2003 (CD ref.: NPGNEWS)
Released in the UK by NPG Records: 29 July 2003 (CD ref.: NPGNEWS)
Best chart ranking in the USA: did not make the charts
Best chart ranking in the UK: did not make the charts

1. *North* **(Prince / 14'00)**
2. *East* **(Prince / 14'00)**
3. *West* **(Prince / 14'00)**
4. *South* **(Prince / 14'00)**

Musicians
Prince: electric guitar, Fender Rhodes piano, synthesizers, percussion
Rhonda Smith: bass, acoustic bass
John Blackwell: drums
Renato Neto: piano, synthesizers
Eric Leeds: saxophone
Recording
Paisley Park, Chanhassen, Minnesota: 6 February 2003
Technical team
Producer: Prince
Recording engineer: Jess Sutcliffe

ALL OVER THE WORLD

Prince's shift to jazz, which began with *The Rainbow Children* and continued with *Xpectation*, seemed to carry on into early 2003, as the artist recovered from an exhausting One Nite Alone...Tour. On 6 February, he summoned Rhonda Smith, John Blackwell, Renato Neto, and Eric Leeds to a recording session in Paisley Park, at which each of them was given free rein for their improvisations, as long as they followed the structure of the songs previously prepared by Prince. Shortly before the session, Prince had grouped together the songs, which were all instrumental, and restructured them so that the musicians would only be laying four tracks down on tape. Eric Leeds recalls the day's recording: "I can say the total amount of time it took to make the album was the duration of the finished record. It was probably mixed as we recorded it. The band was in studio B at Paisley [...] Prince had a talkback mic that didn't go to tape. It just went into our headphones. He said, 'Here's the key, here is the groove, start to play.' We'd be in D minor for 5 minutes and he'd say, 'Go for F,' or 'Eric, start the solo.' It was that simple."[21] While *Xpectation* had only been distributed through the NPG Music Club, Prince decided to go for a big release for this session in the form of a prestigious digipack disc that unfolds like a compass rose. Appropriate packaging given the title of the album, *N.E.W.S.*, an acronym taken from the four tracks, each named after a cardinal point: North, East, West, and South.

C-NOTE

Digital distribution via NPG Music Club: 29 March 2004

1. *Copenhagen* **(10'07)**
2. *Nagoya* **(8'53)**
3. *Osaka* **(5'53)**
4. *Tokyo* **(5'09)**
5. *Empty Room* **(4'01)**

Musicians
Prince: vocals, electric guitar
Rhonda Smith: bass
John Blackwell: drums
Renato Neto: synthesizers
Candy Dulfer: saxophone
Eric Leeds: saxophone
Greg Boyer: trombone
Dudley D.: scratching

Recording
Falconer Salen, Copenhagen, Denmark: 25 October 2002 (tracks 1 and 5)
Nippon Budokan, Tokyo, Japan: 18 November 2002 (track 4)
Osaka-jō Hall, Osaka, Japan: 28 November 2002 (track 3)
Century Hall (Nagoya Congress Center), Nagoya, Japan: 29 November 2002 (track 2)

Technical team
Producer: Prince
Recording engineer: Scott Michael "Scottie P." Pakulski (live)

INTIMATE MOMENTS WITH THE "FAMS"

Prince's sound checks were always recorded by his recording engineers, and he frequently allowed premium members of the NPG Music Club to attend these legendary events, where he sometimes played entire shows for his "fams" before the venue opened to the public. A few weeks before the release of his next album, Prince was determined to catch the bootleggers off guard, so he decided to offer NPG Music Club members the opportunity to download a compilation of improvisations recorded during the sound checks of the One Nite Alone...Tour. The sessions were recorded in Denmark and Japan, and the album also includes a live performance of *Empty Room*, a track well known to fans, although never officially released. Bobby Z. recalls the genesis of this song that is characteristic of the *Purple Rain* and *Around the World in A Day* eras: "I got married, but I had a party three months later. Then the night before my huge party, I had a party in my mother's party room at her apartment complex that Prince came to [...] He was having some sort of fight with Susannah, and at the end of this party he asked if we could rehearse. It was August 1985. We rehearsed and recorded it."[255] *Empty Room* was rerecorded at Paisley Park in 1992 as a piano-vocal for the soundtrack of the movie *I'll Do Anything*, and then put away again. A video of the 1985 version was filmed in 1994, but never officially released. After circulating illegally on numerous pirate records in the 1980s and 1990s, *Empty Room* finally appeared on a Prince album, in a very successful live version that has similar sonorities to the ballads of *The Gold Experience* era.

THE CHOCOLATE INVASION (TRAX FROM THE NPG MUSIC CLUB VOLUME ONE)

Digital distribution via NPG Music Club, at NPG Records:
29 March 2004

1. *When 👁 Lay My Hands On U* (3'41)*
2. *Judas Smile* (6'34)*
3. *Supercute* (4'19)*
4. *Underneath the Cream* (4'01)*
5. *Sexmesexmenot* (5'42)*
6. *Vavoom* (4'36)*
7. *High* (5'05)*
8. *The Dance* (4'40)
9. *Gamillah* (3'18)*
10. *U Make My Sun Shine* (7'06)*

***tracks previously discussed.**

THE SLAUGHTERHOUSE (TRAX FROM THE NPG MUSIC CLUB VOLUME 2)

Digital distribution via NPG Music Club, at NPG Records:
29 March 2004

1. *Silicon* (4'15)*
2. *S&M Groove* (5'08)*
3. *Y Should 👁 Do That When 👁 Can Do This?* (4'31)*
4. *Golden Parachute* (5'36)*
5. *Hypnoparadise* (6'03)*
6. *Props N' Pounds* (4'36)*
7. *Northside* (6'34)*
8. *Peace* (5'33)*
9. *2045: Radical Man* (6'35)
10. *The Daisy Chain* (6'15)*

***tracks previously discussed.**

THE FINAL RELEASE ON THE NPG MUSIC CLUB

On 29 March 2004, Prince decided to release two compilations of tracks that had originally appeared on the NPG Music Club website between 2001 and 2002. While most of the tracks on *The Chocolate Invasion* were recorded with the intention of including them on the *High* album (*Supercute, Underneath the Cream, Gamillah...*), others emerged from isolated sessions and were given to people that Prince knew. The second opus, *The Slaughterhouse*, also released in digital format, is cut from the same cloth and brings together the other tracks from this period. These two compilations give listeners the choice between essential songs (*Supercute, Props N' Pounds*) and rarities, some of which have only archival value. As most of the songs on *The Chocolate Invasion* and *The Slaughterhouse* have been covered earlier in the book, here we only consider the tracks that were never previously offered for download on the site. These two compilations were the last albums that Prince would share on the NPG Music Club, a revolutionary website that allowed him to develop his artistic independence, but which he would close in 2006.

Spike Lee's 2000 movie *Bamboozled*, a satire on the racism endured daily by African-Americans, included Prince's song *2045: Radical Man*.

THE DANCE

Prince / 4'43

Musician: Prince: vocals, electric guitar, bass, programming, synthesizers, backing vocals / **Recording:** Paisley Park, Chanhassen, Minnesota: ? (not confirmed) / **Technical team:** Producer: Prince / Recording engineer: ? (not confirmed)

Although by 2004, punk rock, nu metal, and guitar pop made R&B sound old hat (the record industry has the nasty habit of steamrollering everything in its path), Prince clung to the genre like ivy to an oak tree. Glacial drum machines and soulless synthesizers color this languid, featureless track, in which Prince tells a woman he would rather forget her than succumb to her charms. Prince rerecorded the song in 2005, and it appeared on his hit album *3121*, which was released in the US on 21 March 2006.

2045: RADICAL MAN

Prince / 6'35

Musicians: Prince: vocals, spoken voice, electric guitar, bass, synthesizers, backing vocals / Kirk Johnson: programming / Kip Blackshire: backing vocals / **Recording:** Paisley Park, Chanhassen, Minnesota: 2000 / **Technical team:** Producer: Prince / Recording engineer: Hans-Martin Buff

A short excerpt of *2045: Radical Man* appeared on the website NPGOnlineLtd.com in March 2000 along with the announcement that it was one of the planned tracks on the New Power Generation's fourth album. No release date was given, and it was eventually dropped. The full version of the song was played on Chicago radio station WGCI on 11 August and finally featured on the soundtrack for Spike Lee's new movie *Bamboozled/The Very Black Show* on 26 September. The song, which questions the future of humankind if our obsession with possession continues, also accompanied the New Power Generation's single *Peace* when it was sold on select dates of the Hit n Run Tour in April 2001.

PRINCE

MUSICOLOGY

Musicology · Illusion, Coma, Pimp & Circumstance · A Million Days
Life 'O' the Party · Call My Name · Cinnamon Girl · What Do U Want Me 2 Do?
The Marrying Kind · If Eye Was the Man in Ur Life · On the Couch
Dear Mr. Man · Reflection

Offered to buyers of tickets for the Musicology Live 2004ever Tour: 27 March 2004
Digital distribution via NPG Music Club: 29 March 2004
Released in the USA by NPG Records/Columbia: 20 April 2004 (CD ref.: CK 92560)
Released in the UK by NPG Records/Columbia:
19 April 2004 (CD ref.: COL 517165 2)
Best chart ranking in the USA: 3
Best chart ranking in the UK: 3

A return to funk basics by Prince who was determined to educate the biggest music lovers among us.

A MUSIC LESSON WITH NPG

Although *The Rainbow Children* did not give Prince a No.1 hit in the American charts, it did play a part in his return to favor in the eyes of the press. As for the One Nite Alone... Tour, this reconnected him with his audience, and after the intimate jazz excursion of his previous album, Prince prepared to make a new about-turn, which would shoot him to the top of the world's charts. Once the tour was over, Prince embarked on the World Tour 2003, a series of eight concerts that took him to Australia and Hawaii, where he now had a house. Before that, the singer and his wife had spent 2003 in their house in Toronto, where the artist had been inspired to move toward an artistic and professional rebirth. After recording the bulk of his new album in the Canadian studios MetalWorks, in Mississauga, and at Paisley Park, Prince wanted to reach a wider audience and regain his place at the top of the Billboard charts.

Spotlight on Prince

From September 2003, Prince enlisted the services of the Lippin Group, an advertising agency whose founder, Ronnie Lippin, had distinguished herself through her work with Elton John, Mark Knopfler, and Eric Clapton. With a new album in the bag, the singer was ready to regain his status as the supreme star; and the planets lined up in his favor when, on 20 November, the selection committee of the prestigious Rock & Roll Hall of Fame announced that he would be inducted into the famous institution on 15 March 2004, alongside the likes of Bob Seger and ZZ Top. The distinction—which is a real reward for any artist who has made a noteworthy contribution to the history of American rock—was most welcome. Prince was then able to begin negotiations to find a distributor for the album that was fitting for his return to fame, a choice quickly narrowed down to Sony Music and its label, Columbia. Don Ienner, the company's CEO, allowed the singer complete freedom in the production of *Musicology* and offered support that perfectly complemented his return to grace. "Sony has graciously agreed 2 augment the *Musicology* project with worldwide promotion and distribution," he explained. "They r cool because they do not restrict NPG's ability 2 sell the product as well. It's a win-win situation."[256] On 8 February, Prince appeared at a Grammy Awards ceremony for the first time, and performed a medley of songs with the occasion's top star, Beyoncé, who would end the evening crowned with five awards for her first solo album, *Dangerously in Love*, which had been released the previous 24 June. "I get asked every year to play at the Grammys," he said. "This year I did it because I have an album out that I want to promote and a concert tour that I want to promote."[257]

In the pantheon of rock 'n' roll

On 15 March 2004, on his induction into the Rock & Roll Hall of Fame, Prince took part in a tribute to George Harrison in the company of Tom Petty, Jeff Lynne, and the ex-Beatle's son, Dhani Harrison. The supergroup played The Beatles' song *While my Guitar Gently Weeps*. That evening Prince stole the limelight from his fellow musicians with a version of Eric Clapton's legendary original solo, giving the

Since she was in the middle of promoting her first solo album, Beyoncé hesitated to share the stage with Prince at the Grammy Awards on 8 February 2004. Their performance together became the stuff of legend.

Right : Prince listens to his audience on the Musicology Live 2004ever Tour.

audience a moment of unforgettable television. The highlight came at the end of the song when he hurled his famous Hohner Madcat into the air; no one, neither the audience nor the musicians onstage, saw it land or get caught by some roadie. "Everybody wonders where that guitar went, and I gotta tell you, I was on the stage, and I wonder where it went, too," said Steve Ferrone, Tom Petty's drummer."[258] No doubt about it: the Prince legend was alive and kicking.

The Musicology Live 2004ever Tour

From 27 March to 11 September 2004, Prince was on the Musicology Live 2004ever Tour, which was extravagant in every way. Accompanied by a New Power Generation who were on top form, the singer performed no fewer than 88 concerts in the United States, as well as two performances in Canada, at the Air Canada Center in Toronto. In a stroke of genius, Prince decided to distribute to each audience member a copy of *Musicology*, which was only released on the American market on 20 April. Taking advantage of a gray area in the regulations governing the way album sales were counted by the two main chart organizations, SoundScan and Billboard, he drove his album to the top of the sales rankings from the time of its release, thanks to this massive distribution at his concerts. More than 50,000 copies of *Musicology* were distributed during each week of the tour, and this tactic inevitably made the record climb in the charts because each disc given away counted as an album sold. Although SoundScan changed its rules immediately after this episode, Prince took advantage of the loophole to promote his album, as a complement to an impressive tour. "I didn't do this to usurp power from Billboard or SoundScan," he said in July 2004. "But the real power is in community, in actually connecting with people."[259]

Prince looking more elegant than ever for his induction into the Rock & Roll Hall of Fame on 15 March 2004.

Single

MUSICOLOGY

Prince / 4'24

Musician

Prince: vocals, spoken voice, beat box, electric guitar, bass, drums, synthesizers, Hammond organ, backing vocals

Recording

Paisley Park, Chanhassen, Minnesota: 2003
MetalWorks Studios, Mississauga, Canada: 2003

Technical team

Producer: Prince
Recording engineers: Jess Sutcliffe, L Stu Young, Prince
Assistant recording engineer: Joseph Lipinski

Single

1. *Musicology*/4'26
2. *On the Couch*/3'33

Digital distribution via NPG Music Club: 29 March 2004
Released in the UK and Europe by NPG Records/Columbia: 3 May 2004 (CD single ref.: 67 4923 1)
Best chart ranking in the USA: did not make the charts
Best chart ranking in the UK: did not make the charts

Like Doug E Fresh and Sly Stone, the DJ Jam Master Jay, of Run-D.M.C., was quoted in the single *Musicology.*

Genesis

This first single from the eponymous album did not make it into the American charts, but it helped Prince enormously in finding his way back into the hearts of the wider public. Unquestionably one of the most personal songs in his repertoire, it paints the portrait of a singer who is nostalgic for the years of his youth, during which he discovered the artists who later contributed, following an in-depth study of their repertoires, to the formation of his own musical identity. The singer reels off a jumbled list of names: Sly Stone, James Brown, Chuck D. of Public Enemy, Jam Master Jay of Run-D.M.C., and Earth, Wind & Fire. To emphasize his point, Prince decided to shoot, on 10 and 11 October 2003, a clip in which the young actor Colton "Lil' C" Burton plays the role of the young Prince, practicing the splits and footwork using a vacuum cleaner—a nod to Prince's future acrobatics with his microphone stands. Directed by Sanaa Hamri and featuring stunning choreography by Fatima Robinson and Aakomon Jones, the clip is highly effective and takes us back to the 1970s, when the singer grew up.

It is worth mentioning the presence of the keyboard player Rose Ann Dimalanta in the NPG in the scene shot at the Tower Theatre in Los Angeles on 11 October. The young woman, whose stage name was rad., took part in the World Tour 2003, before being removed from the group because she was temperamentally incompatible with Prince.

Production

Musicology was one of the first Prince albums to be recorded using Pro Tools. The software, developed by Avid Technology, which would revolutionize musical practice and allow millions of musicians to record their songs in their own home studios, opened new horizons for Prince. Indeed, the singer could put together, using a sequencer, all manner of musical parts and revise them endlessly. The same applied to mixing, which was entrusted to Jess Sutcliffe and subsequently reworked by Prince at Paisley Park, before being sent for mastering to Bernie Grundman, who did this at The Hit Factory, the legendary New York studios that closed in 2005. It is therefore difficult to know precisely which recording engineer worked on this or that song on the album, which is why Jess Sutcliffe and L Stu Young are named in every case.

HEADPHONES AT THE READY

Here is proof that Prince liked to confuse listeners by reusing old fragments of songs. The riff in the break of *Musicology*, which comes at 2'36 into the song, is not new because it had already featured in 1996—at 3'42 in *My Computer*, on the *Emancipation* album!

The group Mint Condition, ambassadors of the Minneapolis Sound during the 1990s.

The philanthropist Doris Duke and her boyfriend, the jazz musician Joe Castro.

ILLUSION, COMA, PIMP & CIRCUMSTANCE

Prince / 4'46

Musician: Prince: vocals, rap, spoken voice, electric guitar, bass, programming, synthesizers, backing vocals / **Recording: Paisley Park, Chanhassen, Minnesota:** 2003 / **MetalWorks Studios, Mississauga, Canada:** 2003 / **Technical team: Producer:** Prince / **Recording engineers:** Jess Sutcliffe, L Stu Young, Prince / **Assistant recording engineer:** Joseph Lipinski

In this song, which calls to mind the funk and hip-hop sound texture of *Newpower Soul* (1998), Prince tells the story of a passionate romance between a wealthy woman, whose figure—which he regards as ungainly—he describes in extravagant terms, and a much younger man. The singer appears to take as his reference point the actor Doris Duke, who was as well known for her philanthropy as for her romantic escapades, and was the heiress to the tobacco empire of her father, James Buchanan Duke, who died in 1925 when she was 13 years old. "She knew which fork to use/But she couldn't dance/So he hipped her 2 the funk/In exchange 4 the finance," Prince sings, describing the relationship Duke had from 1951 to 1966 with the jazz pianist Joe Castro. Duke formed the Clover Records company for Castro, and had a recording studio built at Falcon Lair, her Beverly Hills home, which hosted a procession of jazz greats, including Zoot Sims, Billy Higgins, and Oscar Pettiford. "'Doris's money opened a lot of doors for him," the famous jazz producer Daniel Richard said of Castro, "but when jazz musicians talked about him, they didn't talk about him as a jazz musician but as Doris Duke's friend."[260]

A MILLION DAYS

Prince / 3'50

Musician: Prince: vocals, electric guitar, acoustic guitar, bass, drums, synthesizers, backing vocals / **Recording: Paisley Park, Chanhassen:** December 1996 to March 1997; 2003 / **Technical team: Producer:** Prince / **Recording engineer:** Hans-Martin Buff

A Million Days was recorded by Hans-Martin Buff, who worked on the song during the period when *The Truth* album was being made, from December 1996. In fact, in contrast to *The Rainbow Children*, the *Musicology* album was not written in a continuous artistic outpouring, as desired by Prince—which is why the record lacks a certain coherence of sound, alternating between pure funk and pop typical of the mid-1990s. Prince recorded numerous songs from 2003, then retrieved some from The Vault, such as *A Million Days* and *If Eye Was the Man in Ur Life*.

LIFE 'O' THE PARTY

Prince / 4'30

Musicians: Prince: vocals, rap, bass, programming, percussion, piano, synthesizers, backing vocals / **Candy Dulfer:** vocals, saxophone, backing vocals / **Chance Howard:** backing vocals / **Recording: Paisley Park, Chanhassen, Minnesota:** 2003 / **MetalWorks Studios, Mississauga, Canada:** 2003 / **Technical team: Producer:** Prince / **Recording engineers:** Jess Sutcliffe, L Stu Young, Prince / **Assistant recording engineer:** Joseph Lipinski

The talented saxophonist Candy Dulfer, who had already featured on *Graffiti Bridge* (1990), was invited to join the New Power Generation for the start of the One Nite Alone... Tour in March 2002. A distinguished member of Prince's tribe, the Dutch musician then became indispensable in the sound balance of the wind section, alongside Maceo Parker,

Eric Leeds, Najee, and Greg Boyer, the five musicians alternating on different dates of the tour. In 2003, Dulfer received the ultimate accolade when Prince called on her to take a major role in the song *Life 'O' the Party*, in which she sang the choruses. An acknowledged virtuoso, a member of the NPG, and appreciated by fans, Dulfer revealed some confidential information in 2017 regarding her professional relationship with Prince. "If [he] wasn't there, I don't know if I would play the saxophone. Working with [him] was such an inspiration, such a stamp of approval. Whenever I get insecure about my playing or me being a musician, I think that Prince wanted me. Prince wanted me back and he wants me in his band and to record with him. It was my go-to place when I was telling myself I was going to stop. I'll never be Coltrane, but I found my sense of purpose and a lot of that comes with him."[261]

CALL MY NAME

Prince / 5'16

Musicians: Prince: vocals, electric guitar, bass, drums, piano, synthesizers, backing vocals / **Stokley Williams:** backing vocals / **Chance Howard:** backing vocals / **Kip Blackshire:** backing vocals / **Recording:** **Paisley Park, Chanhassen, Minnesota:** 2003 / **MetalWorks Studios, Mississauga, Canada:** 2003 / **Technical team:** **Producer:** Prince / **Recording engineers:** Jess Sutcliffe, L Stu Young, Prince / **Assistant recording engineer:** Joseph Lipinski

In order to enliven this languorous soul ballad with backing vocals worthy of the name, in 2003 Prince invited his new keyboard player, Chance Howard, and Kip Blackshire to record their voices on *Call My Name*. He also called on Stokley Williams, who was a former drummer with Janet Jackson and Blu Cantrell, and a singer with Mint Condition, an R&B group from Saint Paul of which Prince was particularly fond. When Stokley came on board, he was unaware that from 2017 to 2019 he would go on stage for the grand return of The Revolution, which would lead to him singing a few songs in the place of the Kid, such as *Let's Work*, *When Doves Cry*, and *Baby I'm A Star*. Prince added a few string samples from The Vault to *Call My Name*, which were inevitably written by the discreet figure of Clare Fischer. In 2003, when the two men had still not met, Fischer was once again summoned for an important mission: Prince asked him to compose orchestral arrangements for *Purple Rain*, which he would play, along with other songs, at the Grammy Awards on 8 February 2004. Brent Fischer, the composer's son and associate, recalled that evening: "I did meet him [Prince] and talk to him and I found him very easy to work [with], and we just talked for a few minutes [...] But even though they were together in The Staples Center, he didn't meet Dad [...], not wanting to jinx the relationship because it was still working so well all these years later. I understand his reasoning, but just thought it was perhaps sad that Prince did not get to meet Clare Fischer."[79]

It was all going amazingly well for Gil Moore, owner of the MetalWorks studios in Mississauga, Canada, where Prince went for a few unforgettable sessions.

Single

CINNAMON GIRL

Prince / 3'57

Musicians: Prince: vocals, electric guitar, acoustic guitar, bass, drums, tambourine, synthesizers, backing vocals / **Candy Dulfer:** backing vocals / **Rhonda Smith:** backing vocals / **Chance Howard:** backing vocals / **Recording: Paisley Park, Chanhassen, Minnesota:** 2003 / **MetalWorks Studios, Mississauga, Canada:** 2003 / **Technical team: Producer:** Prince / **Recording engineers:** Jess Sutcliffe, L Stu Young, Prince / **Assistant recording engineer:** Joseph Lipinski
CD single version (US): 1. ***Cinnamon Girl***/3'56 / + ***Cinnamon Girl*** (video)/4'04 / **+** ***Cinnamon Girl**: **Xposed*** (making of the video)/5'15 / **CD single version (UK): 1.** ***Cinnamon Girl***/3'56 / **2.** ***Dear Mr. Man*** (live at Webster Hall)/4'14 / **3.** ***United States of Division***/6'18 / **4.** ***Dear Mr. Man*** (live at Webster Hall video)/4'14 / **Released in the USA by NPG Records:** 28 September 2004 (CD single ref.: 1056569) / **Released in the UK by NPG Records/Columbia:** 8 November 2004 (CD single ref.: COL 675142-2) / **Best chart ranking in the USA:** did not make the charts / **Best chart ranking in the UK:** 43

Behind the pop appeal of *Cinnamon Girl* lurks a virulent condemnation of the United States. The wounds of 11 September 2001 were still raw in 2004 when the singer wrote these lyrics, and the US, which had invaded Iraq in March 2003, is accused of mismanaging the war, withdrawing into itself, and stigmatizing its Muslim citizens. The song emphasizes injustice against these minorities, who for many years suffered a dubious form of integration because of their beliefs. The song's initial message got rather lost when the clip, made by Phil Harder, was released. It shows a young woman of Asian descent, who has suffered bullying because of her background, planning a terrorist attack on an American airport before changing her mind. Despite its obvious clumsiness, Prince's song was significant from a social point of view, at a time when his country was at war on the other side of the world, as well as within its own borders. "We live in a real xenophobic place," Prince declared in June 2004. "They talk about all these terrorists. But I didn't feel no terror until the media told me to feel it. Who am I supposed to be feeling terrified of?"[262]

WHAT DO U WANT ME 2 DO?

Prince / 4'15

Musicians: Prince: vocals, electric guitar, acoustic guitar, bass, programming, synthesizers, backing vocals / **Ornella Bonaccorsi:** spoken voice / **Recording: Paisley Park, Chanhassen, Minnesota:** 2003 / **MetalWorks Studios, Mississauga, Canada:** 2003 / **Technical team: Producer:** Prince / **Recording engineers:** Jess Sutcliffe, L Stu Young, Prince / **Assistant recording engineer:** Joseph Lipinski

Released via streaming on the NPG Music Club on 13 November 2003, *What Do U Want Me 2 Do?* revisits the R&B conventions that were used for the songs on the album *Rave Un2 the Joy Fantastic* in particular, as well as those on the album *High*, which was shelved. The song, which ends with a monologue in Italian recited by the actor Ornella Bonaccorsi (real name Ornella Bonaccorsi Testolini—she is the sister of Manuela), highlights the album's real lack of artistic coherence, which is the result of it having been made over multiple sessions. "I record all the time. I like to think of my songs as timeless," Prince said. "*What Do U Want Me 2 Do* could be on my album *Sign 'O' the Times*. Or *Cinnamon Girl* could be from *Dirty Mind*. I consider the whole thing one song anyway, from the beginning of my career on."[263]

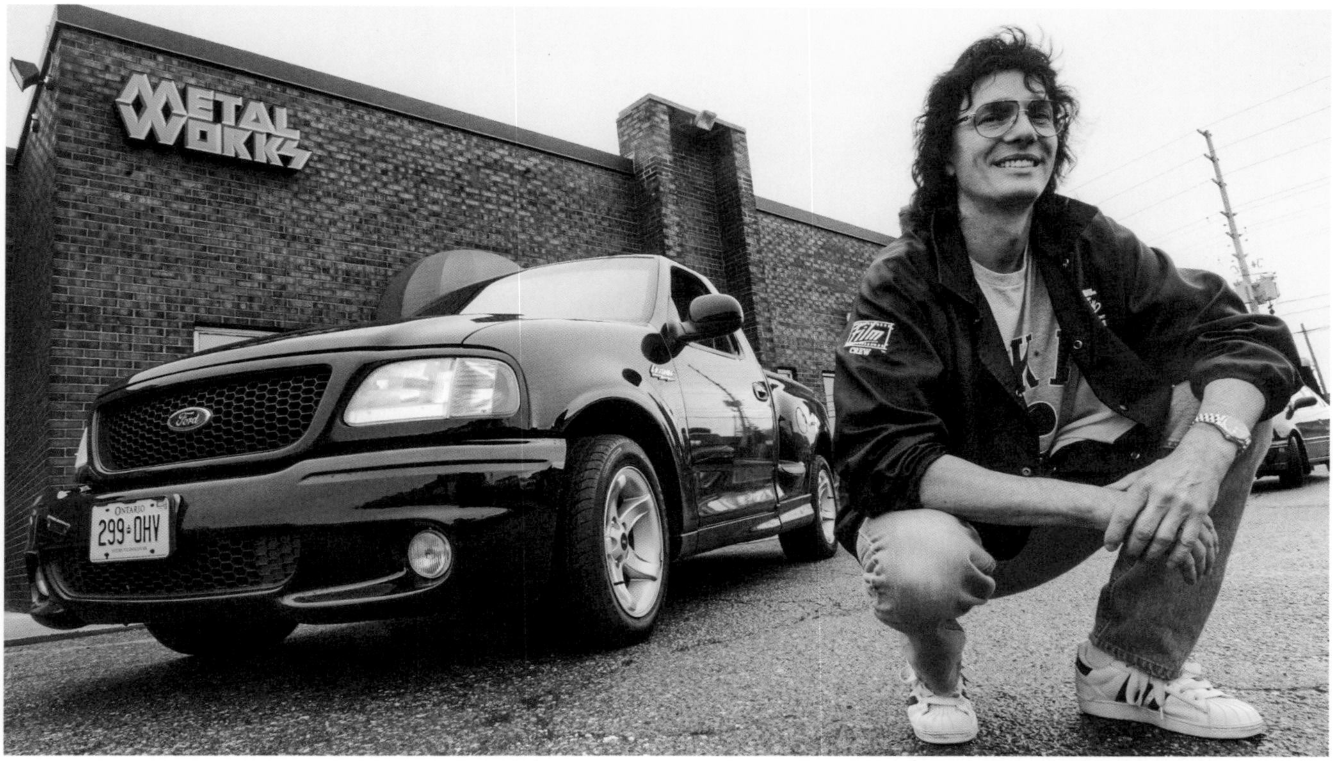

THE MARRYING KIND

Prince / 2'49

Musicians: Prince: vocals, electric guitar, acoustic guitar, bass, synthesizers, backing vocals / **John Blackwell:** drums / **Candy Dulfer:** saxophone / **Maceo Parker:** saxophone / **Greg Boyer:** trombone / **Recording: MetalWorks Studios, Mississauga, Canada:** 2003 / **Paisley Park, Chanhassen, Minnesota:** 2003 / **Technical team: Producer:** Prince / **Recording engineers:** Jess Sutcliffe, L Stu Young, Prince / **Assistant recording engineer:** Joseph Lipinski

When Prince visited MetalWorks Studios in Mississauga, near Toronto, he immediately announced to the boss, Gil Moore, that he wanted to record some new songs. L Stu Young, then the studio's recording engineer, was requisitioned by Prince, and would also work for him on *3121*, shuttling between Los Angeles, Paisley Park, and Mississauga. On the first day at MetalWorks Studios, Prince recorded *The Marrying Kind* and *On the Couch*. He stayed there for two months, taking advantage of the place's peaceful atmosphere to record the backing tracks for other songs, or adding a few arrangements to them. "*Musicology* is the first record I've recorded in Toronto and I can really feel the difference," Prince explained. "It has a completely unique sound that came from the total disregard for what's happening in American music, and for the workings of the American music industry. It doesn't sound like anything else that's out there right now."[257]

IF EYE WAS THE MAN IN UR LIFE

Prince / 3'09

Musicians: Prince: vocals, electric guitar, bass, piano, synthesizers, backing vocals / **John Blackwell:** drums / **Candy Dulfer:** saxophone / **Maceo Parker:** saxophone / **Greg Boyer:** trombone / **Recording: Paisley Park, Chanhassen, Minnesota:** 2003 / **MetalWorks Studios, Mississauga, Canada:** 2003 / **Technical team: Producer:** Prince / **Recording engineers:** Jess Sutcliffe, L Stu Young, Prince / **Assistant recording engineer:** Joseph Lipinski

This song was recorded for the first time with the recording engineer Hans-Martin Buff at the end of the 1990s and benefited from a new version made when Prince went to MetalWorks Studios in Mississauga. John Blackwell's drums play a major role, and the singer wasted no time in emphasizing this, while at the same time highlighting his own special affinity with the instrument and his idea of directing the musicians that surrounded him: "On some songs, I just like the way I play drums and keys better than anyone I know. My drummer, John Blackwell, can certainly do things I can't do, but, if I bring him into the studio, there are things he'll do differently than how I envisioned them [...] You know how Billy Wilder got such a seamless quality to his films? It was because he wrote and directed everything himself. It's the same for me."[264]

Prince and his Taylor 612-CE, which he played especially during the acoustic sets on the Musicology Live 2004ever Tour.

Cornel West, a passionate defender of African-Americans, proposed an interesting reinterpretation of *Dear Mr. Man* in 2007.

ON THE COUCH

Prince / 3'34

Musicians: Prince: vocals, electric guitar, bass, piano, Hammond organ, backing vocals / **John Blackwell:** drums / **Candy Dulfer:** saxophone / **Maceo Parker:** saxophone / **Greg Boyer:** trombone / **Recording:** **MetalWorks Studios, Mississauga, Canada:** 2003 / **Paisley Park, Chanhassen, Minnesota:** 2003 / **Technical team:** **Producer:** Prince / **Recording engineers:** Jess Sutcliffe, L Stu Young, Prince / **Assistant recording engineer:** Joseph Lipinski

In this soul ballad par excellence the singer begs his beloved not to make him sleep on the couch and declares that he would like to "go down south" on her body. On 27 April 2004, when singing the song onstage at Jacksonville Veterans Memorial Arena, in Florida, the singer stopped the song after that phrase and told the audience with characteristic humor: "What? I mean down south to Jacksonville..."[262] The journalist Mick Brown, who was in the auditorium at the time, reported the audience's reaction in the pages of *The Telegraph Magazine*: "Beside me, a woman groans involuntarily. 'He is sex...'"[262]

DEAR MR. MAN

Prince / 4'15

Musicians: Prince: vocals, electric guitar, backing vocals / **Rhonda Smith:** bass / **John Blackwell:** drums / **Renato Neto:** Fender Rhodes / **Sheila E.:** shaker / **Maceo Parker:** saxophone / **Candy Dulfer:** saxophone / **Recording:** **MetalWorks Studios, Mississauga, Canada:** 2003 / **Paisley Park, Chanhassen, Minnesota:** 2003 / **Technical team:** **Producer:** Prince / **Recording engineers:** Jess Sutcliffe, L Stu Young, Prince / **Assistant recording engineer:** Joseph Lipinski

Prince quotes both the Bible and the United States constitution in this attack on "Mr Man" who, it is supposed, is the president, George W Bush Jr, or simply a figure representing the country's ruling class. The singer deplores politicians' lack of interest in economic, healthcare, social, and ecological problems, listing all sorts of disasters sweeping the world during the mid-2000s. In 2007, Cornel West, a philosopher and then professor of African-American studies at the prestigious Princeton University, in New Jersey, suggested to Prince that he, West, make a second recording of his song in order to include it on his second

album, *Never Forget: A Journey of Revelations*. West wrote some lyrics for *Dear Mr.* Man and the song was included on the album, on which various artists, such as André 3000, Jill Scott, and Lenny Williams, question the listener about the situation of African Americans.

REFLECTION

Prince / 3'05

Musician: **Prince:** vocals, electric guitar, acoustic guitar, bass, drums, synthesizers, backing vocals / **Recording:** **MetalWorks Studios, Mississauga, Canada:** 2003 / **Paisley Park, Chanhassen, Minnesota:** 2003 / **Technical team:** **Producer:** Prince / **Recording engineers:** Jess Sutcliffe, L Stu Young, Prince / **Assistant recording engineer:** Joseph Lipinski

Originally offered for download on NPG Music Club from 29 May 2003, *Reflection* was retained for inclusion on the tracklist of *Musicology* ten months later. On 12 February 2004, Prince appeared on *The Tavis Smiley Show* and played a pared-down version of *Reflection* for the occasion, accompanied by Wendy Melvoin. When the program was broadcast, on 19 February on PBS, the singer could be seen playing his Schecter acoustic guitar, and a photograph of his performance was included in the sleeve notes of *Musicology*. Next to him, Wendy Melvoin played her delicate part on a 6-string guitar—which would be passed on, as Prince would use it for the acoustic sets on his Musicology Live 2004Ever Tour—a Taylor 612-CE with a crystal-clear sound. The prestigious instrument would be sold by its owner, Scottie Baldwin (Prince's drum technician from 1990 to 2016) on 18 May 2019, at an exceptional auction held by the American house Julien's Auctions. The lucky buyer had to splash out €78,634 to treat themselves to that piece of contemporary pop music history.

Jimi Hendrix with the bass guitarist Noel Redding (left) and the drummer Mitch Mitchell (right).

PURPLE HOUSE

Jimi Hendrix / 3'39

Musicians
Prince: vocals, electric guitar, drums, synthesizers, Fender Rhodes piano, backing vocals
Larry Graham: bass
Recording
Paisley Park, Chanhassen, Minnesota: 1999? (not confirmed)
Technical team
Producer: Prince
Recording engineer: ? (not confirmed)

Power of Soul: A Tribute to Jimi Hendrix (compilation)
Released in the USA by Experience Hendrix: 4 May 2004 (LP ref.: RTH 2012; CD ref.: EXP2281)
Released in the UK by Experience Hendrix /Legacy/Sony: 4 May 2004 (CD ref.: 88697631052)
Best chart placing in the USA: did not make the charts
Best chart placing in the UK: did not make the charts

Genesis

In 1981, it was not advisable to compare Prince to the creator of *Purple Haze*. When a journalist wrote that "Prince is 'the first black rocker to gain mass acceptance since (Jimi) Hendrix,'"[37] the artist's response was virulent. "'That's baloney,'" Prince said. "'First of all, they don't even know if I'm black. What would they say if I was Chinese? The first Chinese rocker? Also, I know nothing about Jimi Hendrix.'"[37] As Prince confirmed in 1985, "It's only because he's black." He went on to eleborate: "That's really the only thing we have in common. He plays different guitar than I do. If they really listened to my stuff, they'd hear more of a Santana influence than Jimi Hendrix. Hendrix played more blues; Santana played prettier."[27] In support of his argument, Prince explained at the time that he had no record player as a child and that, moreover, the artists of Hendrix's generation were already dead when he started seriously being involved in music—he played his first notes on a guitar in 1974. Whatever he may have said in his younger years, his guitar playing was undeniably influenced, little by little, by Hendrix's blues gimmicks, going as far as to fill his solos with the sound of the legendary wah-wah pedal used by the latter. When the producers of the tribute compilation *Power of Soul: A Tribute to Jimi Hendrix* contacted him in 2004, Prince supplied a cover of *Red House*, which featured on the UK edition of *Are You Experienced*, a cult album by the trio The Jimi Hendrix Experience (with Mitch Mitchell on drums and Noel Redding on bass guitar), which was released in 1967. Perfectly logically, referencing his house in Kiowa Trail, which he had repainted in purple at the start of the 1980s, Prince renamed the song *Purple House*.

Production

With an undeniable funk tinge to it, *Purple House* is nevertheless a blues gem that could have been recorded during the legendary sessions for *The Undertaker* with the Paisley Park Power Trio on 14 June 1993, when he was accompanied by the drummer Michael Bland and bass player Sonny Thompson. The latter offered a pretty fair analysis of the differences between the two virtuoso guitarists in 1994: "His vibrato is different. Just the way he attacks the guitar is different. I think his guitar sound is coming into its own at this point. I think he incorporates whatever he hears into

his guitar playing, like from different instruments and all. It's like his absorbing all this stuff and spitting it back out."[137] In *Purple House*, his friend Larry Graham plays bass guitar, while Prince plays all the other instruments. By adding a few discreet, carefully judged synth pads to his cover, Prince gives the piece a certain modernity, without really departing from the original version and still paying tribute to Hendrix, the maestro of the Fender Stratocaster.

The American people were more divided than ever when the country became bogged down in war in the Middle East.

XYLOPHONE

Prince / 0'26

Musician: Prince: electric guitar, bass, drums, percussion, programming, synthesizers / **Recording: Paisley Park, Chanhassen, Minnesota:** ? (not confirmed) / **Technical team: Producer:** Prince / **Recording engineer:** ? (not confirmed) / **Digital release on NPG Music Club:** 19 May 2003

Only 26 seconds of this instrumental were revealed on NPG Music Club on 19 May 2003. The sound was reminiscent of some tracks on the album *Xpectation*. As the song has never reappeared since it was quietly released on the singer's website, and there is no further information on its production.

MAGNIFICENT

Prince / 4'30

Musician: Prince: vocals, bass, programming, synthesizers, backing vocals / **Recording: Paisley Park, Chanhassen, Minnesota:** 2003–2004 / **Technical team: Producer:** Prince / **Recording engineer:** ? (not confirmed) / **Digital release on NPG Music Club:** 5 April 2004

After the single *Musicology* went online on NPG Music Club, on 29 March 2004, Prince decided to make a virtual B-side, offering *Magnificent* for download on 5 April. A million miles from the authentic funk number that bears the name of the coming album, the song follows R&B convention, and Prince plays no acoustic instruments on it, preferring the ice-cold sounds of synthesizers and his soulless rhythmic programming.

UNITED STATES OF DIVISION

Prince / 6'18

Musicians: Prince: vocals, spoken voice, electric guitar, bass, programming, percussion, synthesizers, backing vocals / **Rhonda Smith:** backing vocals / **Candy Dulfer:** saxophone, backing vocals / **Recording: Paisley Park, Chanhassen, Minnesota:** 2003–2004 / **Technical team: Producer:** Prince / **Recording engineer:** ? (not confirmed) / **Digital distribution via NPG Music Club:** 4 July 2004

On 4 July 2004, the United States' national holiday, Prince released a new manifesto for peace on NPG Music Club. *United States of Division* emphasizes the country's paradox: that of a nation whose population declares itself to be more united than ever since the attacks of 11 September 2001, but within which the stigmatization of the gay, Muslim, and African-American communities is at its height. The song begins with a gloomy statement, with the singer declaring: "2004/Still at War/And everybody hates Americans." At a time when diplomatic relations between the word's great powers were in a fragile state, the song questioned voters on their role, including their influence on successive governments. "Look at the reality and the truth," Prince declared. "They're our supposed 'elected' officials who are supposed to take care of us. Some people are benefiting, and some aren't."[252]

The singer Nikka Costa made her own version of *Silver Tongue* in 2017, a song written by both her and Prince in 2003.

SILVER TONGUE (DEMO)

Prince, Nikka Costa / 4'56

Musician: **Prince:** vocals, piano, synthesizers, backing vocals / **Recording:** **Paisley Park, Chanhassen, Minnesota:** 2003–2004 / **Technical team:** **Producer:** Prince / **Recording engineer:** ? (not confirmed) / **Digital distribution via NPG Music Club:** 13 July 2004

When *Everybody Got Their Something*, Nikka Costa's fifth album, was released in 2001, Prince fell under the spell of the soul-tinted pop of the singer, who is the daughter of the renowned producer Don Costa. The two artists quickly made contact, and the young, red-haired woman rapidly became part of Prince's closed circle, with the latter even asking her to join him onstage during the One Nite Alone... Tour for a high-quality duet. Costa supplied the original lyrics for this track. Once Prince had set these words to music, they would become the magnificent *Silver Tongue*, a melancholy ballad with vocals and piano, although a few synthesizer overdubs were added here and there. The friendship between the two artists would endure, and Nikka Costa went so far as to rerecord *Silver Tongue* for her album *Nikka & Strings: Underneath and in Between*, in 2017. "We've developed a relationship, you know, a friendship," Costa said of Prince in 2020. He mentored me for like 15 years. He was so generous with advice and support and everything."[265]

GLASSCUTTER (2004)

Prince / 4'39

Musician: **Prince:** vocals, rap, beat box, electric guitar, bass, drums, claps, Hammond organ, synthesizers, backing vocals / **Recording:** **Paisley Park, Chanhassen, Minnesota:** September 2004 / **Technical team:** **Producer:** Prince / **Recording engineer:** ? (not confirmed) / **Digital distribution via NPG Music Club:** 5 April 2005

When the Musicology Live 2004ever Tour paused for a few days during the winter of 2004, Prince and his assistant Ruth Arzate returned to Chanhassen and to the below-freezing temperatures of Minnesota. The young woman called one of her friends, to whom she said: "It's so cold here my nipples could cut glass."[266] Years later, in 2018, Arzate related how the following day, entering studio A at Paisley Park, she came upon Prince listening to his new song, *Glasscutter*, which had been inspired directly by her telephone conversation the day before. Furious that Prince had eavesdropped on her, she told her boss: "You motherfucker, we need to put a cowbell on you!"[266]

S.S.T.

Prince / 3'39

Musician

Prince: vocals, beat box, electric guitar, acoustic guitar, bass, programming, Fender Rhodes piano, synthesizers, backing vocals

Recording

Paisley Park, Chanhassen, Minnesota: 2 September 2005

Technical team

Producer: Prince

Recording engineer: George Ian Boxill

CD single version (US)

1. *S.S.T.*/3'39
2. *Brand New Orleans*/6'37

Digital version, on NPG Music Club

1. *S.S.T.*/ 3'39
2. *Brand New Orleans*/6'37
3. *You Will Be Moved*/4'12

Digital release on NPG Music Club: 3 September 2005

Released worldwide by NPG Records/Columbia: 25 October 2005 (CD ref.: 38K 675152)

Best chart ranging in the USA: did not make the charts

Best chart ranging in the UK: did not make the charts

Genesis

The trail of destruction left by Hurricane Katrina's passage through New Orleans, Louisiana, in August 2005 was tragic. Hundreds of people lost their lives and dozens more went missing. More than 140,000 were left homeless, and the mostly poor population was devastated by the violence of this natural disaster, one of the worst in the history of the United States. The slow response of the authorities was quickly condemned by the inquiries that followed, which concluded that the people affected, who were poor and mostly African Americans, did not receive the support they deserved, because the powers that be held their social status in contempt. On 2 September 2005, Prince recorded this deeply moving song entitled *S.S.T.*, an acronym for "Sade's Sweetest Taboo," which is a reference to Sade's 1985 hit *The Sweetest Taboo*. In this, she sings, with heavy irony: "There's a quiet storm/And it never felt like this before/There's a quiet storm/I think it's you." Prince exhorts the listener to hear this song and to fully appreciate its gentleness in the face of a world filled with danger.

Production

In producing this single, the profits of which were donated to the charity Hurricane Katrina Relief, Prince penned one of his most beautiful pieces of the 2000s. The touchingly melancholic melody of this song is accompanied by lyrics that suggest to someone at the end of their life that they should take stock of what they have achieved in their lifetime. "Are you gonna be happy with how your life has been spent?/Did you have open arms 4 each and everybody you met/Or did you let them die in the rain? Endless war, poverty, or hurricane..." An exceptional song with an unstoppable groove that was recorded for a noble cause.

As well as doing immense physical damage, which left the poorest deprived of resources, Hurricane Katrina created a sense of abandonment in Louisiana's African-American community who felt they had been neglected by the government.

BRAND NEW ORLEANS

Prince / 6'37

Musician: Prince: beat box, electric guitar, acoustic guitar, bass, programming, Fender Rhodes piano, synthesizers. / **Recording:** Paisley Park, Chanhassen, Minnesota: 2 September 2005 / **Technical team:** Producer: Prince / **Recording engineer:** ? (not confirmed)

Revisiting the instrumental coda of *S.S.T.*, *Brand New Orleans* is a track without vocals, but it features a delicate Fender Rhodes part. The solos (guitar, synthesizer, and more) follow one another and make the listener forget the sad reason for the existence of this single, until the rain-sound effects arrive in the finale, taking us back to the dark reality of New Orleans's stricken inhabitants.

PRINCE

3121

3121 · Lolita · Te Amo Corazón · Black Sweat · Incense and Candles
Love · Satisfied · Fury · The Word · Beautiful, Loved and Blessed
The Dance · Get On the Boat

Released in the USA by NPG Records/Universal Records:
21 March 2006 (CD ref.: B0006296-02)
Released in the UK by NPG Records/Universal Records:
20 March 2006 (CD ref.: 0602498520727)
Best chart ranking in the USA: 1
Best chart ranking in the UK: 9

Prince asked the photographer Afshin Shahidi to come to the filming of the clip of *Te Amo Corazón* in Morocco in order to take pictures of him.

FOR PRINCE ADDICTS

Like a Willy Wonka of groove, Prince had "Purple Tickets" inserted in several copies of the *3121* album. The lucky winners had the good fortune to attend a concert by their idol on 6 May 2006 in his rented house at 1235 Sierra Alta Way.

A CALIFORNIAN ADVENTURE

Besides restoring Prince to his former glory, the success of *Musicology* and the triumphant Musicology Live 2004ever Tour substantially replenished his coffers. In September 2004, with the tour over and his finances newly restored, the singer began work at the Paisley Park studios to carry out a major update of the recording equipment and, more surprisingly, went on numerous trips during the winter, leaving the cold of his Minnesota home for the sunshine of California. He set up home in Los Angeles. In October 2004 he rented the sumptuous house belonging to the actor Barbi Benton at 3121 Antelo Road and, from then until September 2005, organized numerous parties there, in which he performed concerts or simply enjoyed a convivial time dancing with his guests. Many of these parties were immortalized by the lens of the photographer Afshin Shahidi and often featured Stevie Wonder, Dustin Hoffman, Salma Hayek, Joni Mitchell, and Spike Lee. "I think these parties were some of the happiest times for Prince," Shahidi said. "They brought together like-minded people in a very easy-going, unpretentious setting and people really let their hair down, relaxed, and had an incredible time."[267] The house number, 3121, inspired Prince, who decided to have it embroidered on the stage outfit he wore for the 36th NAACP Image Awards (which recognized African-American artists and professionals) on 19 March 2005. Although Prince put on a stunning performance that evening, it was backstage that his new musical project began to take shape. Before going on stage, he asked Afshin Shahidi to photograph him wearing his jacket embroidered with the number 3121, facing a wall and simply lit from the right by a wall light. This gave Prince the concept, and cover design, for his future album.

The new NPG

The production of *3121* was disjointed, just like that of *Musicology*. Several sessions at Paisley Park and the home studio at 3121 Antelo Road created an album that displayed rock, pop, funk, and even Latin influences on the singer who, during his Californian adventures, had formed friendships with the actors Salma Hayek and Penelope Cruz, as well as with the top Panamanian model Liza Hernandez, with whom some observers suggested he even had a romantic relationship. Thanks to his friend Morris Hayes's impressively well-connected address book, Prince met many more artists during 2005 and took advantage of this to reshape the New Power Generation. "From the parties that he had, a guy named Frank McComb who would come and play at his house," Hayes recalled, "and he had Josh [Dunham] and Cora [Coleman-Dunham], who were in Frank's band. And they were playing, and then we came and did a show with Maceo [Parker], and then all of a sudden Támar shows up and then he's [Prince] like man, I'm going to put together this thing. So the next call I got, he said, 'Hey, man, I want to get Josh and Cora and then Támar and we got these girls I just met—the twins—and, you know, we should put something

2006

Prince with sisters Maya and Nandy McClean, aka The Twinz, during a Donatella Versace fashion show in Milan, Italy, on 29 September 2006.
Right: Despite looking like a 1950s soul singer, Cora Coleman-Dunham was a virtuoso drummer, capable of formidable patterns!

together. I want you to come out and we go in the studio and do this stuff.'"[268] The year 2005 was therefore devoted to recording the album and forming a new partnership with the Universal record company, which welcomed Prince with open arms. The collaboration between the two parties was made official in December 2005 and was accompanied by the release of the single *Te Amo Corazón*.

Glory in the Los Angeles sun

From 20 January to 18 March 2006, Prince accompanied his new protégée, Támar (real name Ashley Támar Davis), on tour as a guitarist and provided her with the services of the new NPG, in which the sisters Maya and Nandy McClean—now known as The Twinz—were backing vocalists and dancers, appearing regularly alongside him, as had Lori "Diamond" Elle and Robia "Pearl" LaMorte in 1991 and 1992. The end of Támar's tour coincided with the release, to much fanfare, of *3121* in the United States on 21 March 2006. It was an immediate hit, going to No.1 in the Billboard charts, a first since *Batman* in 1989. Certified Gold on the following 26 June, *3121* was a triumph for Prince who enjoyed renewed fame just as he celebrated his forty-eighth birthday. The year 2006 was also when he divorced Manuela Testolini—this was made official in May—a matter on which Prince would never comment. Once this episode was behind him, the insatiable Prince embarked on two projects that would change his image in the eyes of the public forever: a five-month stay at the Rio All-Suite Hotel & Casino in Las Vegas, starting in November, and the preparation of a show that anthologized his work, which was to be performed at halftime during the Super Bowl final, set for February 2007.

After ending his rental of 3121 Antelo Road in September 2005, Prince opted for a home rented for $95,000 a month at 1235 Sierra Alta Way, West Hollywood, in Los Angeles (a place that he named 3121 to confuse people). When passing in front of the house, its owner, the basketball player Carlos Boozer, was flabbergasted to see that Prince had completely redecorated the building, which was now encrusted with Love Symbols on the front entrance and in the walls. Boozer was reassured when he sold the house a year later when he discovered that it had increased in value thanks to Prince's stay within its walls. He had bought it for $8.4 million; it eventually sold for $12.3 million.

3121

Prince / 4'31

Musicians

Prince: vocals, electric guitar, Fender Rhodes piano, synthesizers, backing vocals
Sonny T.: bass
Michael B.: drums
Maceo Parker: saxophone
Candy Dulfer: saxophone
Ray Monteiro: trumpet
Greg Boyer: trombone

Recording

Paisley Park, Chanhassen, Minnesota: 19 November 2004
3121 Antelo Road, Los Angeles: November to December 2004

Technical team

Producer: Prince
Recording engineers: L Stu Young, George Ian Boxill
Assistant recording engineer: Lisa Chamblee

Genesis

A nod to his new address at Los Angeles, the number 3121 is also a reference to the New World Translation of the Holy Scriptures, the version of the Bible studied by Jehovah's Witnesses. It is a safe bet that Prince did not choose this address by chance, for in Psalms 31:21, it is stated: "Blessed be Jehovah, For he has rendered wonderful loving-kindness to me in a city under stress."[269] Prince confirmed this on 27 June 2006, when he performed *3121* onstage at the sixth BET Awards and said to the audience: "Where's the real party at? Shake your tambourines! BET read Psalms; that's where it is."[270] It matters little whether his initial motivation was geographic or spiritual, for the title track is dedicated to the parties held at his California home, of which he says: "You can come if you want to/But you can never leave"—a nod to another place in America that's filled with mystery and from which it is impossible to leave, described in the Eagles' 1976 song *Hotel California*. Prince wrote the lyrics of *3121* when his personal assistant, Ruth Arzate, confirmed she had found the house for his next stay in Los Angeles. The following day the song was finished and Prince could pack his bags.

Production

On 19 November 2004, when Paisley Park was about to close its doors so that the studios could be renovated, Prince returned to Chanhassen for a time and invited old friends over for an impromptu jam session. Michael Bland was on drums and Sonny Thompson on bass guitar. Over the space of some four hours, this session produced a dozen new songs, including *3121*. "You could feel Prince's energy in the room; it was off the charts [...]," recalled Lisa Chamblee, Prince's new assistant recording engineer. "It was like completing a Master Class in production and engineering all in one fell swoop. To capture the masters playing new music, collaborating, and improvising...words can't describe the magnificence of that night."[271] For *3121*, Prince resuscitated the androgynous Camille (see page 142) and came up with this medium-tempo funk piece which is irresistibly danceable—one of the best songs he wrote during the 2000s. It is impossible to resist such an invitation to party.

Prince being revealed by Támar Davis at the sixth BET Awards, which took place at the Shrine Auditorium, in Los Angeles, on 27 June 2006.

Prince receives instructions from his friend Salma Hayek who was making the clip of *Te Amo Corazón*.

LOLITA

Prince / 4'06

Musicians: Prince: vocals, spoken voice, electric guitar, bass, programming, synthesizers, backing vocals / **Liza "Lena" Hernandez:** spoken voice / **Morris Hayes:** spoken voice / **Támar:** spoken voice / **Recording: Paisley Park, Chanhassen, Minnesota:** 2005 / **3121 Antelo Road, Los Angeles:** 2005 / **Technical team: Producer:** Prince / **Recording engineers:** L Stu Young, George Ian Boxill / **Assistant recording engineer:** Lisa Chamblee

In this tribute to Vladimir Nabokov's novel *Lolita*, published in 1955, Prince sings of the seductive power a young woman exerts over him and admits that he cannot resist her charms. The singer reawakens the ghost of *The Time* during a question-and-answer break that is strongly reminiscent of the ending of *Cool*, a single released on the group's first album in 1981. Credited to the New Power Generation, the answers to his questions are given by Morris Hayes and Támar, after a monologue in Spanish by the Panamanian model Liza Hernandez, with whom the singer had a brief liaison during the making of the *3121* album.

Single

TE AMO CORAZÓN

Prince / 3'36

Musicians: Prince: vocals, electric guitar, acoustic guitar, piano, backing vocals / **Josh Dunham:** bass / **Cora Coleman-Dunham:** drums / **Ray Monteiro:** trumpet / **Ricky Salas:** bongos, timbales, percussion / **Herbert Ureña:** congas, bongos, percussion / **Maceo Parker:** saxophone / **Candy Dulfer:** saxophone / **Greg Boyer:** trombone / **Orchestra** / **Recording: Paisley Park, Chanhassen, Minnesota:** 2005 / **3121 Antelo Road, Los Angeles:** 2005 / **Insomnio Studios, Panama City, Panama:** June 2005 (percussion) / **Capitol Studios, Los Angeles:** June 2005 (orchestra) / **Technical team: Producer:** Prince / **Recording engineers:** L Stu Young, George Ian Boxill / **Assistant recording engineer:** Lisa Chamblee / **Orchestral arrangements:** Clare Fischer
Single: Digital release on NPG Music Club: 13 December 2005 / **Released in the USA by NPG Records/Universal:** 20 December 2005 (CD single ref.: B0006139-32) / **Best chart ranking in the USA:** did not make the charts

On 13 December 2005, Prince gave a press conference in New York. He announced his future collaboration with Universal and introduced his new single, *Te Amo Corazón*. The clip, featuring the Argentinian actor Mía Maestro who was seated next to him, was made by the actor Salma Hayek, with whom Prince had formed a friendship. "Salma heard the song and came up with the original concept. Salma is the most thoughtful, attentive director I have ever worked with. An absolute joy."[272] The young woman, who at the time had only been in a movie for television (*The Maldonado Miracle*, 2003), retained a tender memory of this collaboration with her musician friend. "It was very special," she said. "He was so, so supportive of me. He was always telling me that I should go back to directing [...] And then one day, he said, 'Okay, today's the day. You have to do this song for me' [...] It was a bunch of friends who went to Morocco. There was no fight, it was very easy, he was really relaxed. He didn't even realize it was work."[273] As for the song, it was recorded with Prince's new rhythm section, consisting of the bass guitarist Josh Dunham and drummer Cora Coleman-Dunham, who were a couple both professionally and in their private life. Percussion overdubs were added to the song by the musicians Ricky Salas and Herbert Ureña during a journey Prince made to Panama in June 2005. Although Maceo Parker, Candy Dulfer, Greg Boyer, and Ray Monteiro are credited in the sleeve notes, it is difficult to be sure whether their wind parts were indeed retained during the song's final mixing, for they seem non-existent on listening to it. The song, a perfect complement to summer evenings by the sea, was a strange choice of single on the part of the artist who confirmed that "This song is not really indicative of what the whole album sounds like."[274]

Single

BLACK SWEAT

Prince / 3'11

Musician: **Prince:** vocals, programming, synthesizers, backing vocals / **Recording:** **Paisley Park, Chanhassen, Minnesota:** 2005 / **3121 Antelo Road, Los Angeles:** 2005 / **Technical team:** **Producer:** Prince / **Recording engineers:** L Stu Young, George Ian Boxill / **Assistant recording engineer:** Lisa Chamblee

CD single version **(UK and Europe) / 1.** ***Black Sweat***/3'11 / **2.** ***Beautiful, Loved and Blessed*** / 5'18 / **Digital release on iTunes:** 21 February **2006** / **Released in the UK and Europe by NPG Records/Universal:** 7 March 2006 (CD single ref.: MCSTD40457 – 985 497-4) / **Best chart ranking in the UK:** 43

The torrid *Black Sweat* immediately reconciles the listener to Prince, who is determined to make us forget the hard-to-swallow Latin escapade of *Te Amo Corazón*. Lacking a bass line—like *Kiss* before it—and featuring a mechanical groove that, also like *Kiss*, leads us irresistibly to the dance floor, the song is incredibly sensual and drives its point home via a clip made in the villa at 3121 Antelo Road. For Prince knows what he wants to do: to work up a sweat and make his sweetheart scream "like a white lady"—a spoken passage at 2'40 whose words were eventually removed from the album sleeve notes to avoid any controversy. Whirling around Prince in the video, the dancer Celestina Aladekoba was directed by the filmmaker Sanaa Hamri, who had made *Live at the Aladdin Las Vegas* in 2003. She asked Celestina to make movements the singer did not expect, which made him smile and grimace in astonishment, as can be seen at 2'17 in the video. Aladekoba had an amusing memory of the shoot and emphasized how much the video had helped her establish her reputation. "Most people know know [sic] me from working with Prince, most especially in his music video *Black Sweat*. I still have folks who call me 'black sweat' till this day..."[275]

INCENSE AND CANDLES

Prince / 4'05

Musicians: **Prince:** vocals, rap, bass, programming, synthesizers, backing vocals / **Támar:** backing vocals / **Recording:** **Paisley Park, Chanhassen, Minnesota:** 2005 / **3121 Antelo Road, Los Angeles:** 2005 / **Technical team:** **Producer:** Prince / **Recording engineers:** L Stu Young, George Ian Boxill / **Assistant recording engineer:** Lisa Chamblee

This song marked a return to R&B for Prince, who for the first time in his career used Auto-Tune software, marketed by Antares Audio Technologies in 1997. First revealed to the general public by Cher in her hit *Believe* in 1998, popularized by Daft Punk in *One More Time* in 2000, and now indispensable for many rappers, Auto-Tune was originally devised to perfect vocal recordings through slight modifications in pitch. Overdoing these adjustments gives the singer a metallic, even robotic voice—seen as essential at the time of writing (even though the hope lingers that this software will fall out of use completely). Támar, Prince's new protégée, accompanied him on this adventure, enlivening the song with backing vocals. She first came to Paisley Park with her mother in the early 1990s, at the age of just 12, to record a cover of *Somewhere Over the Rainbow* and reappeared alongside Prince in 2004. "He used to love to have parties there, and I'd start coming—," recalled Morris Hayes, who had met the young singer when she came to Minneapolis. "Támar Davis, who was an artist I brought to him when she was 12, back in the early '90s, was going to school out there [at the University of Southern California] and a girl that was a choreographer for us named Fatima [Robinson] brought her to one of the parties, and they reconnected."[268] A former member of Girls Tyme, a group that would become Destiny's Child (led by Beyoncé Knowles and Kelly Rowland), Támar was unveiled to the wider public when she featured on *3121*, especially in the single *Beautiful, Loved and Blessed*. Prince took her under his wing, accompanied her on tour, and negotiated the production of an album by Universal on her behalf—a project entitled *Milk & Honey*, which never saw the light of day.

The resentment that followed the end of The Revolution seemed long forgotten at the reunion of Lisa Coleman (left) and Wendy Melvoin (right) with the drummer Sheila E. (center) in 2006.

LOVE

Prince / 5'46

Musicians: Prince: vocals, bass, programming, synthesizers, backing vocals / **Támar:** vocals / **Recording: Paisley Park, Chanhassen, Minnesota:** 2005 / **3121 Antelo Road, Los Angeles:** 2005 / **Technical team: Producer:** Prince / **Recording engineers:** L Stu Young, George Ian Boxill / **Assistant recording engineer:** Lisa Chamblee

It is unfair for Támar to be credited as a backing vocalist here because, apart from the break, the whole song is performed as a duo by the young woman and her Pygmalion. Combining R&B, pop, and mechanical funk worthy of *Housequake*, *Love* is a track that shines as much for its melody as its irresistible groove. On 21 October 2007, Prince released an acoustic version of the song on his new website 3121.com, thus emphasizing the delicate writing, now stripped of its arrangements, even though the singer added a few overdubs, including vocal harmonization and discreet synth pads.

SATISFIED

Prince / 2'50

Musicians: Prince: vocals, electric guitar, bass, drums, backing vocals / **Támar:** backing vocals / **Maceo Parker:** saxophone / **Candy Dulfer:** saxophone / **Ray Monteiro:** trumpet / **Greg Boyer:** trombone / **Recording: Paisley Park, Chanhassen, Minnesota:** 2005 / **3121 Antelo Road, Los Angeles:** 2005 / **Technical team: Producer:** Prince / **Recording engineers:** L Stu Young, George Ian Boxill

Reconnecting with soul in triplets, Otis Redding-style, Prince here offers a song with a sensuality to which he holds the secret. In it, he promises his beloved that she will be satisfied when "I'm gonna seek this thing like a buried treasure/Like Columbus sailing over the sea." Newly arrived at Paisley Park to work as assistant recording engineer on the album *3121*, the talented Lisa Chamblee recalled the first time she listened to *Satisfied*. "'Lisa. I want you to hear something,' announced Prince. He then stopped and said, 'Wait a minute. How old are you? I'm not sure if you can hear this.' Incredulous, Lisa shot back, 'Sure I can!'"[271] The young woman was determined to earn her place in the very male-dominated world of recording studios. After hearing the languorous song, the singer asked the technician for her opinion. She unhesitatingly gave the recording her approval and confirmed the song's quality.

Single

FURY

Prince / 4'02

Musician: Prince: vocals, electric guitar, acoustic guitar, bass, drums, synthesizers, Hammond organ, claps, backing vocals / **Recording: Paisley Park, Chanhassen, Minnesota:** 2005 / **3121 Antelo Road, Los Angeles:** 2005 / **Technical team: Producer:** Prince / **Recording engineers:** L Stu Young, George Ian Boxill / **Assistant recording engineer:** Lisa Chamblee
Single: 1. *Fury*/4'02 / **2.** *Te Amo Corazón*/*Fury* (Live) [Audio]—recorded at the 2006 Brit Awards/5'28 / **Released in the UK by NPG Records/ Universal:** 29 May 2006 (CD single ref.: MCSTD40462) / **Best chart ranking in the UK:** 60

When the English playwright William Congreve wrote *The Mourning Bride* in 1697, little could he have imagined that one of the lines in his play would be reworked and become a familiar modern saying. Or that this saying would be used by a bawdy rocker three centuries later. The now famous

saying "Hell hath no fury like a woman scorned" was also revived by Groucho Marx in his fake autobiography *Memoirs of a Mangy Lover* (1963) and quoted by Prince in *Fury* in 2005. Here, the singer reawakens his most rock side, which he displayed onstage at the Brit Awards on 14 February 2006 where he was accompanied by an ace lineup: Wendy Melvoin on guitar, Lisa Coleman on keyboards, Támar on backing vocals, and The Twinz wriggling their hips. "The best players used to play rock 'n' roll," Prince said in 2004. "The first time you heard Boston, it was this huge, amazing sound with all that guitar doubling. Same with Brian May—nobody sounded like him. I still think of Return to Forever [a jazz fusion quintet formed in 1972 by Chick Corea] as a rock band. Those guys could really play, but there ain't nobody doing that in rock these days."[264] Ten days before the Brit Awards, another live performance of the song on *Saturday Night Live* was so convincing that Prince envisaged recording it again with the voices of Támar and The Twinz—but idea that was eventually dropped.

THE WORD

Prince / 4'12

Musician: Prince: vocals, electric guitar, acoustic guitar, bass, programming, synthesizers, backing vocals / **Recording: Paisley Park, Chanhassen, Minnesota:** 2005 / **3121 Antelo Road, Los Angeles:** 2005 / **Technical team: Producer:** Prince / **Recording engineers:** L Stu Young, George Ian Boxill / **Assistant recording engineer:** Lisa Chamblee

In 1994, Prince was questioned about his guitar playing by the *Guitar World* journalist Alan Di Perna, who asked: "What is your idea of the ultimate guitar tone?" To which Prince replied: "A woman in climax."[137] Immediately afterward he asserted that his guitar solos were improvised, not written, emphasizing his preference for music that was skilfully put together but in which a breath of freedom is always to be welcomed. *The Word* bears witness to this desire to include, in his modern productions, a hand-crafted element—here, a formidable Carlos Santana-style solo—and the song is sure to satisfy fans with its authentic rock character.

BEAUTIFUL, LOVED AND BLESSED

Prince, Támar Davis / 5'44

Musicians: Prince: vocals, electric guitar, acoustic guitar, bass, programming, synthesizers, backing vocals / **Támar:** vocals, spoken voice, backing vocals / **Recording: Paisley Park, Chanhassen, Minnesota? (not confirmed):** 6 October 2005 / **3121 Antelo Road, Los Angeles? (not confirmed):** 6 October 2005 / **Technical team: Producer:** Prince / **Recording engineers:** L Stu Young, George Ian Boxill / **Assistant recording engineer:** Lisa Chamblee

Accompanying Prince for most of the *3121* album, Támar Davis had the privilege of performing a song that showcased her voice more—*Beautiful, Loved and Blessed*. The song was also meant to appear on Davis's eponymous album, which was later renamed *Milk & Honey*. Cowritten and produced by Prince, this album was shelved for good in The Vault for obscure reasons and dropped by Republic Records, a label belonging to the Universal group which had originally been due to release it. The song was released as a promotional disc in the United States and earned Prince a nomination for Best R&B Performance by a Duo or Group with Vocals at the 49th Grammy Awards in 2007. The award was, alas, won by a short-lived group formed by John Legend, Joss Stone, and Van Hunt for their cover of the 1971 funk classic *Family Affair* by Sly and the Family Stone on their tribute album *Different Strokes by Different Folks*. Performed on 4 February 2006 on *Saturday Night Live*, *Beautiful, Loved and Blessed* seemed to be a hit in the making, but was never released as a single. No matter. The duet earned Támar a place in the affections of fans and remained an incredible memory for the singer. "It was the most emotional connection I'd ever had to anyone," she said. "The song didn't really come to life until we were getting ready to perform it for *Saturday Night Live*."[276]

THE DANCE

Prince / 5'21

Musician: Prince: vocals, electric guitar, bass, percussion, claps, programming, piano, synthesizers, backing vocals / **Recording: Paisley Park, Chanhassen, Minnesota:** 2005 / **3121 Antelo Road, Los Angeles:** 2005 / **Technical team: Producer:** Prince / **Recording engineers:** L Stu Young, George Ian Boxill / **Assistant recording engineer:** Lisa Chamblee

Recorded for the first time a few years earlier, *The Dance* already featured on the compilation *The Chocolate Invasion*, which became downloadable from the NPG Music Club (see page 384) on 29 March 2004. It was recorded again for *3121*. The song offers little that is new, apart from more modern production standards, which do not, however, conceal its weak writing.

GET ON THE BOAT

Prince / 6'19

Musicians: Prince: vocals, acoustic guitar, piano, backing vocals / **Josh Dunham:** bass / **Cora Coleman-Dunham:** drums / **Maceo Parker:** saxophone / **Candy Dulfer:** saxophone / **Ray Monteiro:** trumpet / **Greg Boyer:** trombone / **Sheila E.:** percussion / **Támar:** backing vocals / **Recording: Paisley Park, Chanhassen, Minnesota:** 2005 / **3121 Antelo Road, Los Angeles:** 2005 / **Technical team: Producer:** Prince / **Recording engineers:** L Stu Young, George Ian Boxill / **Assistant recording engineer:** Lisa Chamblee

Welcome to a funk cruise ship on which the captain, Prince, has enough cabins for "a hundred more," according to the choruses in *Get On the Boat*. The climax of an album that would have been better were it all in this vein, the song brings together everything that the NPG did best. Sheila E. is a top-class percussionist and the team of wind players comprises the veterans Maceo Parker, Candy Dulfer, and Greg Boyer, accompanied by the trumpet player Ray Monteiro. The rhythm section, taken care of by the couple of Cora Coleman-Dunham (drums) and Josh Dunham (bass guitar), works wonders, even though it does not manage to equal the duo of John Blackwell and Rhonda Smith from the *Musicology* era. Dunham recalled a precious piece of advice offered by his employer: "Prince was serious about getting that tone right. He asked me, 'Why are you using the bass [knobs] on the amp and on the bass? Don't you just need one?' So then I started putting the bass on my amp on zero and controlling my tone from the bass guitar. I heard all the low notes, but it wasn't boomy, especially when we played big stadiums. It made so much sense."[277]

In April 2006, Prince held pride of place with the prestigious jazz record label Blue Note for the compilation *Blue Note Plays Prince*. This featured various songs by him, including *Electric Chair*, *Diamonds and Pearls*, and *Kiss*, revisited in a smooth vein under the direction of Bob Belden, who had already released a tribute to the singer in 1994 with the album *When Doves Cry: The Music of Prince*.

Though this did not please purists, Prince had his Mexican Stratocaster fitted with a Floyd Rose bridge and an EMG pickup as powerful as the Humbucker on a Gibson Les Paul. The guitar showed what it could do onstage at the Super Bowl on 4 February 2007.

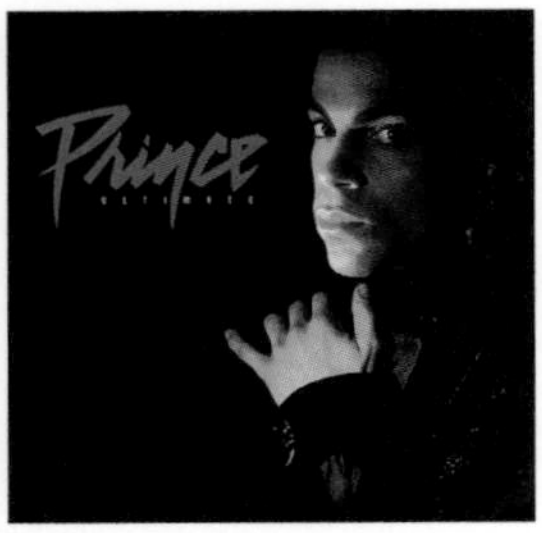

ULTIMATE

Released in the USA by Warner Bros. Records: 22 August 2006 (CD ref.: R2 73381)
Released in the UK by WEA International: 21 August 2006 (CD ref.: 8122 73381 2)
Best chart ranking in the USA: 61
Best chart ranking in the UK: 3

Disc 1

1. *I Wanna Be Your Lover* **(2'59)**
2. *Uptown* **(4'12)**
3. *Controversy* **(7'17)**
4. *1999* **(3'39)**
5. *Delirious* **(2'41)**
6. *When Doves Cry* **(3'51)**
7. *I Would Die 4 U* **(2'59)**
8. *Purple Rain* **(8'43)**
9. *Sign O' the Times* **(3'42)**
10. *I Could Never Take the Place of Your Man* **(3'41)**
11. *Alphabet St* **(5'40)**
12. *Diamonds and Pearls* **(4'21)**
13. *Gett off* **(4'33)**
14. *Money Don't Matter 2 Night* **(4'48)**
15. *7* **(5'11)**
16. *Nothing Compares 2 U* **(5'05)**
17. *My Name Is Prince* **(4'04)**

Disc 2

1. *Let's Go Crazy (Special Dance Mix)* **(7'37)**
2. *Little Red Corvette (Dance Remix)* **(8'27)**
3. *Let's Work (Dance Remix)* **(8'05)**
4. *Pop Life (fresh Dance Mix)* **(6'19)**
5. *She's Always in My Hair (12" Version)* **(6'32)**
6. *Raspberry Beret (12" Version)* **(6'36)**
7. *Kiss (Extended Version)* **(7'16)**
8. *U Got the Look (Long Look)* **(6'44)**
9. *Hot Thing (Extended Remix)* **(8'33)**
10. *Thieves in the Temple (Remix)* **(8'08)**
11. *Cream (N.P.G. Mix)* **(4'52)**

SOME SIGNIFICANT REMIXES

From a contractual point of view, in 2006, Warner Bros. Records had the right to release a final compilation by its former protégé. Since Prince was on the crest of a wave at the time, the greedy record company decided to release a third anthology of the Kid's work, bringing together 17 of his singles, some of them from the album [symbol] (1992), which put right the unforgiveable mistake of *The Very Best of Prince*, released in 2001. The creation of the compilation was partly entrusted to two Prince fans, who were hired as artistic consultants on the project: Geoffrey Dicker and the Frenchman Matthieu Bitton. Bitton had caught the company's attention for his work on the visual for *Up from the Catacombs: The Best of Jane's Addiction* by the group Jane's Addiction. Dicker took care of putting together a tracklist of 40 songs, combining singles and remixes loved by fans—a special mention here for *Let's Go Crazy (Special Dance Mix)*, which takes us back to the first screenings of the movie *Purple Rain*—while Bitton took charge of the record's visual world. Bitton, who was one of the biggest collectors of Prince memorabilia, set to work on a cover that was inspired by the colors and typefaces of the singer's greatest years—as far as it is possible to regard one year as more vintage than another. An amusing detail...the graphic designer—who in 1987 had sold the gold coins given to him at his Bar Mitzvah in order to be able to buy an original of *The Black Album* from the Parisian record dealer Monster Melodies—had, as a teenager, made a fake Prince compilation that he'd named *Ultimate Prince*! "I had cut out an article from *Best*," he recalled. "They had put the letters of *Purple Rain* as the article's heading. I had cut these out, and made a compilation cover that was called *Ultimate Prince*. I must have been 14 years old when I did this. I put some maxis, a whole bunch of stuff...and when I went back to boarding school I showed my mates the cassette and said: 'Here's this thing I produced.'"[278]

In a surge of generosity, Warner Bros. Records suggested to Prince that he approve the selection for the compilation. Continuing the process of clearing out his most risqué songs, which had begun when he joined the Jehovah's Witnesses movement, the singer demanded that *Erotic City* and *Sexy M.F.* be removed, as well as *Purple Medley* from 1995, which was also taken off by Dicker. Finally, he asked that the first disc bring together the original songs with the remixes appearing on the second CD. "The way I had sequenced it originally was that it was all mixed up so that every single song was in chronological order," Dicker explained, "with singles mixed together with 12-inch versions [...] After you hear this two-hour overview of Prince's career, it just ended with him shouting out 'My name Is Prince!' I thought it was really cool, but unfortunately it's not how it came to pass."[279]

THE SONG OF THE HEART

Prince / 3'00

Musicians
Prince: vocals, bass, programming, piano, synthesizers, backing vocals
Bria Valente: backing vocals

Recording
Paisley Park, Chanhassen, Minnesota: 23 June, 13 August 2006

Technical team
Producer: Prince
Recording engineer: George Ian Boxill

Happy Feet (Music from the Motion Picture)
Released in the USA by Warner Sunset/Atlantic: 31 October 2006 (CD ref.: 83998-2)
Released in Europe by Warner Sunset/Atlantic: 31 October 2006 (CD ref.: 7567-83998-2)
Best chart ranking in the USA: did not make the charts
Best chart ranking in the UK: 51

The film director George Miller in June 2005.

Genesis

Although the Australian director George Miller is famous for his four episodes of the *Mad Max* saga, he also made ambitious movies for children, such as *Babe* (1995) and its sequel *Babe: Pig in the City* (1998). In 2006, when he embarked on a new project, an animated movie about the adventures of a tap-dancing penguin (*Happy Feet*, 2006), Miller decided to incorporate all kinds of sequences sung by the actors who provided the voices of the small animals in black and white. These included Robin Williams, Hugh Jackman, Hugo Weaving, and Nicole Kidman, who was to record a version of *Kiss* in which two words needed changing to fit the story of the movie. "No," replied Prince, "you can't change my lyrics."[280] Thanks to the intervention of Gary LeMel and Gary Hinkman, two artistic directors at Warner Bros. Pictures, who distributed the movie, the director was able to organize a screening of the unfinished movie at Paisley Park. Prince was immediately thrilled by the scene featuring his 1986 hit. "Once he got passed [*sic*] that opening scene," George Miller said, "he watched the whole movie through and as it finished he ran over and picked up a guitar and started to strum. And he found a chord and he said, 'Give me two weeks, I'm going to write you a song.'"[280]

Miller continued: "I spoke to him and said, 'Why did you do it?'" He said, 'The movie said something to me.'"[280]

Production

Containing material from the movie, including monologues by Robin Williams, *The Song of the Heart* is notable for marking the appearance of the singer Bria Valente in Prince's recorded work. Although the American vocalist, whose real name is Brenda Fuentes, would soon become Prince's new protégée, here she features only as a backing vocalist, refining the song with her crystal-clear voice. George Ian Boxill was the recording engineer on the song, which he produced meticulously: the following year, on 15 January 2007, it earned him a Golden Globe Award for Best Original Song.

PLAN
EART

PRINCE

PLANET EARTH

Planet Earth · Guitar · Somewhere Here On Earth
The One U Wanna C · Future Baby Mama · Mr. Goodnight · All the Midnights in the World
Chelsea Rodgers · Lion of Judah · Resolution

Distribution via The Mail on Sunday (UK): 15 July 2007
Released in the USA by NPG Records/Columbia:
24 July 2007 (CD ref: 88697 12970 2-S1)
Best chart ranking in the USA: 3

Prince at the peak of his new-found glory, photographed by Afshin Shahidi.

THE WORLD AT HIS FINGERTIPS

In 2006, Prince decided that the Rio All-Suite Hotel & Casino in Las Vegas was an appropriate place to conclude his triumphant *3121* adventure in style. His divorce from Manuela Testolini in May as well as moving out of his rental home at 1235 Sierra Alta Way were both factors that contributed to his decision to go into "exile" in Nevada, where on 11 November he began a residency that would take him through to 29 April 2007.

Although the recording of *Planet Earth* is partially shrouded in mystery, we do know that the album emerged from diverse sessions at Paisley Park, the Circle House Studios in Miami, and onstage at the Rio All-Suite Hotel & Casino. Prince then dipped into The Vault and pulled out two songs from the 19 November 2004 session (the same one that gave rise to *3121*): *Planet Earth* and *Guitar*. He continued recording as he simultaneously prepared for the Super Bowl halftime show, a major event broadcast in over two hundred countries and watched by over 140 million viewers. Having already hit the No.1 spot on the *Billboard* charts with *3121* back in March 2006, Prince brought the United States to its feet on 4 February 2007 with a tour de force concert that ended with a rendition of *Purple Rain* in torrential rain. After that, Prince was unstoppable and quite literally had the world in his hands, as the sleeve illustration for his new album, *Planet Earth*, shows.

2007

Taking London by storm

Despite his newfound international glory and *Planet Earth* reaching the third spot in the American charts, Prince struggled to convince hardcore fans with this new album because of a lack of artistic coherence in the tracklist, which went from rock (*Planet Earth*) to pop (*The One U Wanna C*), climbed to disco-funk heights (*Chelsea Rodgers*), and featured a smattering of barely audible R&B tracks. "We had put so much time and energy into the *3121* album," Sam Jennings later confided, "*Planet Earth* felt pretty rushed by comparison. He was off in London and I don't think *Planet Earth* was a big priority for him."[281] Prince's decision to offer his album to readers of *The Daily Mail* in the United Kingdom infuriated Sony Music, which then canceled the UK release after learning that Prince also intended to give the album to every audience member who attended his 21-day residency at The O2 Arena in London from 1 August through to 21 September 2007. "We weren't trying to upstage the record company," Prince said. "I just wanted to get new music out. I asked Sony, 'Were you planning to sell 3 million copies in London?' I sold 3 million copies overnight. That's a good, clear business deal."[282] After 18 months successfully spent winning back audiences, Prince embarked on his new project, the recording of a triple album that would be a fitting end to a decade that had seen him rise from the ashes.

Prince considered his performance at the Super Bowl as the culmination of a life devoted to his art—a consecration finally achieved.

Overleaf: Prince surrounded by the hundreds of volunteers who helped to hastily set up the Love Symbol stage, only a few minutes before the start of the performance.

THE SUPER BOWL HALFTIME SHOW: THIRTEEN MINUTES TO CONQUER THE WORLD

On 1 February 2007, the Miami Beach Convention Center hosted the press conference for the 41st Super Bowl final, the most viewed sports event in the United States. That year, the prestigious National Football League (NFL) playoff was set to be a top-notch game at Miami's Dolphin Stadium between two strong teams: the Indianapolis Colts and the Chicago Bears. As always, the alftime concert would attract just as much attention as the game, and in the past had featured international pop royalty, including U2 in 2002, Paul McCartney in 2005, and The Rolling Stones in 2006. For 2007, the show's producers, Don Mischer and Charles Coplin, set the bar high, inviting Prince to perform the biggest show of his career. Billy Joel, who would be singing the national anthem, was also invited to the press conference. Prince, as ever, did things his own way and told the NFL that he would not give an interview, much to the disappointment of the journalists who were sitting waiting patiently for him. Instead, the singer gave a surprise concert featuring three songs: Chuck Berry's *Johnny B. Goode* as well as *Anotherloverholenyohead* and *Get On the Boat*. After a few minutes of thunderous solos, with his dancers The Twinz shimmying beside him, the press was utterly mesmerized. The message was clear: see you for an unforgettable evening at the Dolphin Stadium on 4 February.

Purple rain on Miami

The day of the concert dawned with torrential rain bucketing down on the city. "It wasn't like rain," recalls Ruth Arzate, Prince's personal assistant and manager. "It was like somebody was throwing buckets of water at the window."[283] Tension in the production team rose to new heights, as everyone wondered whether the concert could go ahead. There were fears that a performer would fall over on the set, or worse still, one of them would be electrocuted in front of a TV audience of over a hundred million. But nothing stopped Prince as he chose to brave the elements (improbably appearing to remain totally dry throughout the concert) and take to the stage on schedule, with his mythical Hohner Madcat slung over his shoulder, ready to rock the audience. The show kicked off with a slightly sped up recording of Forever Young's 2003 cover version of Queen's *We Will Rock You*. The situation behind the scenes was chaotic, but under the Love Symbol-shaped stage, assembled in a few minutes by over six hundred volunteers who had been training for weeks, a technician called Tony Ward was holding a cable together with his hands to keep the power and lights going to the stage. "[He] held that for the entire 12-and-a-half-minute duration, in the rain. To keep the lights and all that working," said Don Mischer. "I'm glad I didn't know about that until afterward because that would've scared the hell out of me."[283] While their boss let rip on the stage, setting the stadium alight with *Let's Go Crazy*, then *Baby I'm A Star*, the McClean sisters, alias The Twinz, did their best not to slip as they danced with adhesive pads on their stiletto heels!

Consecration in front of an audience of 140 million

After a short medley consisting of *Proud Mary* (Ike and Tina

Turner), *All Along the Watchtower* (Jimi Hendrix), and *Best of You* (Foo Fighters), Prince launched into a no-holds-barred version of *Purple Rain*, performing a guitar solo behind a huge sheet onto which his shadow was projected (the resultant phallic image of him holding his guitar attracted over 150 complaints to the Federal Communications Commission about the NFL). When the song ended, Prince had the audience in the palm of his hand, and the image of the triumphant artist holding his Schecter Habibi guitar aloft was etched in the minds of a 140 million viewers. "I remember at the end of the show one of our producers went up to him and said, 'I heard I'm not allowed to hug you,'" Coplin confided. "And he said, 'No, you're not allowed to take pictures, but you're allowed to hug me.'"[283]

COLTS
COLTS 16 BEARS

TO GO
BALL ON
QTR 3
8:25
BEARS

PLANET EARTH

Prince / 5'51

Musicians: Prince: vocals, electric guitar, piano, synthesizers, claps, backing vocals / **Sonny T.:** bass / **Michael B.:** drums / **Shelby J.:** backing vocals / **Bria Valente:** backing vocals / **Recording: Paisley Park, Chanhassen, Minnesota:** 19 November 2004; 2007 / **Technical team: Producer:** Prince / **Recording engineers:** Prince, Kevin "KD" Davis, George Ian Boxill

If *Planet Earth* seems to contain all the energy of the NPG's 1994 lineup, it is because it was recorded on 19 November 2004 at a session with Michael Bland and Sonny Thompson, two ex-members of the New Power Generation who had made a major contribution to Prince's most rock-sounding tracks. Among other overdubs added to the production, the track features backing vocals from Shelby Johnson (aka Shelby J.), who Prince discovered during his residency in Las Vegas. She was with Larry Graham's band Graham Central Station, who were also performing in town at the time. Shelby J. was singing Stevie Wonder's *Higher Ground* during the sound check before the concert when she heard a voice in the darkness asking her to sing it again. "So Larry started playing, and I sung it again," she later reported. "'Sing it again.' I think I sang it three or four times. And after I was done, I was like, 'This sound guy really wants things to be right for this concert.' And then Prince comes walking from the back, and I'd never heard his voice so I didn't know it was him, and he said 'You're a great singer.'"[284] That evening, Prince came along to sing with Shelby J. and invited her to his New Year's Eve concert. After the show, Prince asked her if she wanted to join the NPG, saying, "We start rehearsing for the Super Bowl next week."[284]

Single

GUITAR

Prince / 3'45

Musicians: Prince: vocals, electric guitar, synthesizers, backing vocals / **Sonny T.:** bass / **Michael B.:** drums / **Recording: Paisley Park, Chanhassen, Minnesota:** 19 November 2004 / **Technical team: Producer:** Prince / **Recording engineers:** Prince, Kevin "KD" Davis, George Ian Boxill
Single: 1. ***Guitar***/3'45 / **2.** ***Somewhere Here On Earth***/5'46 / **Released in the UK and Europe by NPG Records/Columbia/Sony/BMG:** 9 July 2007 (CD single ref.: 88697 12853 2) / **Best chart ranking in the UK:** 81

On 15 June 2007, a post appeared on 3121.com, Prince's new website: "3121 insiders tell us that Prince has been talking up his new CD 2 friends and colleagues," it read. "Some seem 2 have gotten the impression that the first single *Guitar* might b Prince singing 2 himself, the side of him that wants 2 settle down."[285] Was it the line: "I tried to warn you that it's hard to be a star" that tipped off the "fams" (as he liked to call his loyal fans)? No one knows. In any case, this is a very effective track recorded with Bland and Thompson. An initial version was made available for download on 3121.com on 2 February 2007, before Prince reworked it and released a second version on CD in Europe and the United Kingdom on 9 July 2007.

SOMEWHERE HERE ON EARTH

Prince / 5'46

Musicians: Prince: vocals, electric guitar, piano, synthesizers, backing vocals / **Josh Dunham:** bass / **Cora Coleman-Dunham:** drums / **Christian Scott:** trumpet / **Recording: Rio All-Suite Hotel & Casino, Las Vegas:** March 2007 / **Technical team: Producer:** Prince / **Recording engineers:** Prince, Kevin "KD" Davis, George Ian Boxill

After the thundering rock of the first two songs on the album, it's a dizzying plummet to earth with this ballad, in which Prince goes for the crooner style, swapping the blistering 6-string at the start of the album for a sleazy jazz-vocal. Christian Scott's muted trumpet doesn't help either and, to be honest, the only pleasure in listening to this song is when you press the fast-forward button to move on to the next track on the *Planet Earth* CD.

THE ONE U WANNA C

Prince / 4'29

Musicians: Prince: vocals, electric guitar, bass, drums, synthesizers, backing vocals / **Wendy Melvoin:** acoustic guitar / **Lisa Coleman:** synthesizers / **Josh Dunham:** bass / **Cora Coleman-Dunham:** drums / **Shelby J.:** backing vocals / **Bria Valente:** backing vocals / **Recording: Paisley Park, Chanhassen, Minnesota:** 4 September 2006; 13 March 2007 / **Henson Recording Studios, Los Angeles:** 2007 (overdubs by Wendy Melvoin and Lisa Coleman) / **Technical team: Producer:** Prince / **Recording engineers:** Prince, Kevin "KD" Davis, George Ian Boxill

Back to pop with this charming track that marks the return of Wendy Melvoin and Lisa Coleman to Prince's discography. Although this collaboration was done via email (Melvoin later confirmed to Jon Bream of the *Minneapolis Star* that they worked on five songs in this way), it is great to be present at their reunion, especially as it's a very successful track and would have made a quality single if Prince had decided to use it for that purpose.

Bria Valente, Prince's new protégée, was undeniably talented, but her career never took off.

FUTURE BABY MAMA

Prince / 4'47

Musicians: Prince: vocals, electric guitar, bass, programming, synthesizers, Fender Rhodes piano, backing vocals / **Shelby J.:** backing vocals / **Bria Valente:** backing vocals / **Recording: Paisley Park, Chanhassen, Minnesota? (not confirmed):** 2006 / **Technical team: Producer:** Prince / **Recording engineers:** Prince, Kevin "KD" Davis, George Ian Boxill

With a rhythmic pattern that we can guess was put together on his famous Linn LM-1 Drum Machine, Prince offers us an R&B track that was well received by the judges at the 50th Grammy Awards ceremony on 10 February 2008. That night, Prince left the Staples Center, in Los Angeles, with an award for Best Male R&B Vocal Performance, ahead of *Woman* by Raheem DeVaughn, *B.U.D.D.Y.* by Musiq Soulchild, *Because of You* by Ne-Yo, and *Please Don't Go* by Tank. Although *Future Baby Mama* had not been released as a single, it had lots of airtime on the radio, enabling Prince to compete at the prestigious American ceremony.

MR. GOODNIGHT

Prince / 4'27

Musicians: Prince: vocals, rap, electric guitar, bass, programming, synthesizers, backing vocals / **Morris Hayes:** programming, synthesizers / **Shelby J.:** backing vocals / **Bria Valente:** backing vocals / **Recording: Paisley Park, Chanhassen, Minnesota? (not confirmed):** 2007 / **Rio All-Suite Hotel & Casino, Las Vegas? (not confirmed):** 2007 / **Circle House Studios, Miami? (not confirmed):** 2007 / **Technical team: Producer:** Prince / **Recording engineers:** Prince, Kevin "KD" Davis, George Ian Boxill

Although she is not credited on *Planet Earth*, Prince's new protégée (and future girlfriend), Bria Valente, was present on several songs on this album as a discreet backing singer. Her crystalline voice is notably perceptible on *Mr. Goodnight* where she makes some short contributions that complement Shelby J.'s backing vocals. Valente, then 17 years old, came from Minneapolis and was introduced to Prince by Morris Hayes who was responsible for discovering many talented artists in the Twin Cities. She and Prince met briefly at Paisley Park before she left for Los Angeles, where she contributed backing vocals to Usher's hit album *8701*. It wasn't until 2007 that Bria Valente finally got to work with her Pygmalion, first as a backing singer, before Prince wrote and produced her first album, *Elixer*, which was released as a triple CD along with *LotusFlow3r* and *MPLSound* in 2009.

ALL THE MIDNIGHTS IN THE WORLD

Prince / 2'22

Musicians: Prince: vocals, acoustic guitar, bass, drums, piano, backing vocals / **Wendy Melvoin:** mandolin / **Recording:** Paisley Park, Chanhassen, Minnesota? (not confirmed): 2006 / **Henson Recording Studios, Los Angeles:** 2007 (overdubs by Wendy Melvoin) / **Technical team: Producer:** Prince / **Recording engineers:** Prince, Kevin "KD" Davis, George Ian Boxill

After *Reflection*, their acoustic guitar duet on *The Tavis Smiley Show* on 12 February 2004, Prince invited Wendy Melvoin to join him for his unforgettable Brit Awards performance on 14 February 2006, where Lisa Coleman and Sheila E. were also present. In 2007, while the inseparable duo known as Wendy and Lisa were working on their fifth album, *White Flags of Winter Chimneys*, and had been producing the soundtrack of the internationally acclaimed TV series *Heroes* since 2005, they were invited to record some overdubs for five songs on *Planet Earth*. These included *All the Midnights in the World*, a lackluster track that is nevertheless to be appreciated for its pleasant melody.

CHELSEA RODGERS

Prince / 5'41

Musicians: Prince: vocals, electric guitar, synthesizers, claps, backing vocals / **Shelby J.:** vocals, backing vocals / **Josh Dunham:** bass / **Cora Coleman-Dunham:** drums / **Maceo Parker:** saxophone / **Lee Hogans:** trumpet / **Greg Boyer:** trombone / **Recording: Paisley Park, Chanhassen, Minnesota? (not confirmed):** 2006 / **Technical team: Producer:** Prince / **Recording engineers:** Prince, Kevin "KD" Davis, George Ian Boxill

Why on earth weren't all the songs on *Planet Earth* created with the same high standards as the incredible *Chelsea Rodgers*? This is a powerful hit and a return to disco-funk influences, which simply ooze from every bar. These five minutes and 41 seconds of pure happiness, led by the Prince/Shelby J. duo, cannot be praised highly enough. On 19 September 2007, having just played 19 sell-out shows at The O2 Arena in London, Prince attended designer Matthew Williamson's show at London Fashion Week. He sat in the front row next to his personal assistant and manager Ruth Arzate and his new girlfriend, the model Chelsea Rodgers, who was unknown to the general public at the time, but would be immortalized by Randee St Nicholas's camera in *21 Nights*, a book about Prince's stint in London and Prague in 2007. Shortly before the show, Prince had told Williamson that he would like to give a short performance to conclude the event. With no rehearsals, Prince, his musicians, and his dancers The Twinz performed one of his new songs, the aptly named *Chelsea Rodgers*, to a stunned audience. "As the beat kicked in," Williamson recalls, "[Prince] got up from his seat and performed his track down the length of my catwalk as the models and I looked on through the monitor backstage in complete awe. The audience was amazed to be in the presence of such a legend and nobody expected it."[286] Chelsea Rodgers, wearing a pendant with the Love Symbol and her initials, C.R., mounted the runway and walked a few steps, promoted by her boyfriend who that day offered her the gift of an unexpected moment of fame.

LION OF JUDAH

Prince / 4'11

Musicians: Prince: vocals, electric guitar, acoustic guitar, bass, drums, backing vocals / **Shelby J.:** backing vocals / **Bria Valente:** backing vocals / **Recording: Paisley Park, Chanhassen, Minnesota:** 4 September 2006 / **Technical team: Producer:** Prince / **Recording engineers:** Prince, Kevin "KD" Davis, George Ian Boxill /

The Lion of Judah represents Jesus in Christianity and is emblematic of the Rastafarian movement. It also featured on the Ethiopian flag (the cradle of Rastafarianism) until 1975 and was regularly cited in the songs of reggae's most famous singer, Bob Marley. *Lion of Judah* was the title of a song by Marley in which he evokes the liberating power of the animal: "The Lion of Judah shall break every chain." Prince takes a more down-to-earth approach here, comparing himself to the sacred animal that faces obstacles with its head held high. The imagery merely serves as a pretext to show that he will stop at nothing to win his girl's heart. Shelby J., who provides backing vocals for the track alongside Bria Valente, later recalled the creative process of the *Planet Earth* recording sessions. "In the studio, he would be creating, and we would be creating and trying to bring his vocal vision to reality for whatever masterpiece he was creating that day," she said of Prince. "[...] it was more loose and creative and when you hear something, he'd be like 'Sing that note, sing that line.' I'd see him scratch something out. It's like being in the kitchen and creating your soup—a little more this, a little more that."[284]

RESOLUTION

Prince / 3'41

Musicians: Prince: vocals, electric guitar, synthesizers, backing vocals / **Wendy Melvoin:** acoustic guitar / **Josh Dunham:** bass / **Cora Coleman-Dunham:** drums / **Lisa Coleman:** synthesizers / **Shelby J.** backing vocals / **Bria Valente:** backing vocals / **Recording: Paisley Park, Chanhassen, Minnesota:** 4 April 2006 / **Henson Recording Studios, Los Angeles:** 2007 (overdubs by Wendy Melvoin) / **Technical team: Producer:** Prince / **Recording engineers:** Prince, Kevin "KD" Davis, George Ian Boxill

Resolution concludes the album on a pacifist note, with Prince pointing out that leaders and the people are full of contradictions that sometimes prevent peace processes from achieving their aims. "The main problem with people/Is they never do what they say/One minute they want peace/Then do everything to make it go away/Dropping bombs on each other." Despite its naivety, the song is appreciable for its pop feel, its melody sung by a trio of vocalists, and the presence of Wendy Melvoin on acoustic guitar.

Prince and The Twinz improvising a concert during designer Matthew Williamson's show on 19 September 2007 at London Fashion Week.

F.U.N.K.

Prince / 7'35

Musicians

Prince: vocals, electric guitar, bass, drums, synthesizers, percussion, claps, backing vocals
Renato Neto: synthesizers
Mike Phillips? (not confirmed): saxophone
Greg Boyer? (not confirmed): trombone
Lee Hogans? (not confirmed): trumpet

Recording

Paisley Park, Chanhassen, Minnesota: 2003 (backing tracks); 7 November 2007 (overdubs, vocals)

Technical team

Producer: Prince
Recording engineer: ? (not confirmed)

Digital release on iTunes by NPG Records: 20 November 2007
Best chart ranking in the USA: did not make the charts
Best chart ranking in the UK: did not make the charts

Genesis

November 2007. Citing image rights, Prince demanded that all photos of him on fan sites be removed. The fans were not happy with this at all and decided to unite under the banner PFU, Prince Fans United, to create a website called Princefansunited.com. Prince immediately responded by launching a website called Princefamsunited.com, on which he posted a song called *PFUnk*, attacking his admirers with the words: "The only reason you say my name is to get your fifteen seconds of fame," before switching to his Camille voice to say: "I love all y'all, don't you ever mess with me no more." Karen Avera, the spokesperson for the PFU movement, tried to justify Prince's reaction by explaining that he used to hang out anonymously on fan forums and had not appreciated some of the criticism of *3121* and *Planet Earth*. Others pointed to Prince's complex relationship with the Internet, which he initially used as a tool to disseminate his music before realizing that the web could be used for the massive illegal circulation of his songs. He was furious when photos taken during the London concerts in summer 2007 appeared on the Housequake.com forum, and his lawyers waded in, launching a war against YouTube for hosting multiple unauthorized live Prince videos. Might as well fight windmills...

Production

Having decided to release the single, renamed *F.U.N.K.*, on the iTunes platform on 20 November, Prince offers a track with an unstoppable groove and polished production, notably thanks to Jeff Sutcliffe's mixing, which Prince then reworked, modifying his voice to give it a feeling of Camille (see page 142) straight out of 1986's *Shockadelica*. When he slips in the lyrics "Well, it might not be The Grand Progression/But it sure is funky," Prince is mocking the fans who couldn't get enough of a superb outtake after it was leaked on the web in 1987. As for the fams, they didn't hold this episode against their idol and remained loyal despite his mood swings. "With everything that's going on, we continue to listen to his music," said Avera. "We'll continue to buy his music, because we appreciate his music."[290]

Despite his undoubted affection for his fans, Prince wrote *F.U.N.K*, a bittersweet number aimed at those who dared to criticize him.

INDIGO NIGHTS / LIVE SESSIONS

Included in the book *21 Nights* by Randee St Nicholas (published by Simon & Schuster)
Released in the USA by NPG Records: 30 September 2008 (CD ref.: none)
UK release on NPG Records: 30 September 2008 (CD ref.: none)

The Twinz with Prince performing onstage at the O2 Arena in London on 24 August 2007.

1. *3121* (7'44)
2. *Girls and Boys* (4'05)
3. *Song of the Heart* (1'39)
4. *Delirious* (2'01)
5. *Just Like U (Monologue)* (2'49)
6. *Satisfied* (6'19)
7. *Beggin' Woman Blues* (6'43)
8. *Rock Steady* (Featuring Beverley Knight / 6'37)
9. *Whole Lotta Love* (4'42)
10. *Alphabet Street* (6'09)
11. *Indigo Nights* (3'41)
12. *Misty Blue*/Featuring Shelby J. (4'25)
13. *Baby Love*/Featuring Shelby J. (3'54)
14. *The One* (9'08)
15. *All The Critics Love U In London* (7'05)

Musicians
Prince: vocals, electric guitar
Josh Dunham: bass
Cora Coleman-Dunham: drums
Morris Hayes: synthesizers
Renato Neto: synthesizers
Mike Phillips: saxophone
Lee Hogans: trumpet
Greg Boyer: trombone
Marva King: backing vocals
Shelby J.: vocals, backing vocals
The Twinz: backing vocals
Beverley Knight: vocals

Recording
Indigo at The O2, London: 17 and 22 September 2007

Technical team
Producer: Prince
Front of house sound engineer: Bill Sheppell

TWENTY-ONE NIGHTS IN LONDON

On 8 May 2007, Prince announced at a press conference at The Hospital Club in London that he would begin a 21-day residency at The O2 Arena, London's largest venue, on 1 August 2007. He fixed the ticket price at £31.21 based on the name of the album he would be promoting. His intention was to make it possible for anyone to see him perform, regardless of their financial means. "Last time I was here," he explained, "a lot of people didn't get to see me so we're trying to make it affordable for everybody, that's why we're doing the extended stay, I got used to this while working in Las Vegas and as soon as I leave here I'm going to go and look for a place to live."[287] While he was preparing for his residency in London, Prince called Randee St Nicholas, with whom he had been working since 1991, and asked her to come along for the ride. "This is a very exciting project to actually document,"[288] the photographer stated. Prince's residency was a sell-out, with tickets going in a flash. Nearly half a million people enjoyed Prince's show between 1 August and

21 September 2007, with the artist taking advantage of The Rolling Stones concerts on 21, 23, and 26 August to take a break. As if 21 concerts wasn't ambitious enough, Prince also performed 13 aftershows at Indigo at The O2, as well as giving a surprise performance at fashion designer Matthew Williamson's catwalk show on 19 September.

Prince in private

Once the 21 Nights in London—The Earth Tour was over, Prince wanted to publish a book of photographs taken by Randee St Nicholas during the London residency and a short trip to Prague in the Czech Republic in the autumn of 2007. St Nicholas then approached publishing houses and recounts this amusing anecdote about her efforts. "The book publishing world, as you know, is filled with a lot of kind of snobby intellectuals," she says. "I told Prince, 'I wish you could have been a fly on the wall.' At these meetings you would meet the most conservative people, and they would tell stories about losing their virginity to *Little Red Corvette*. They were closet Prince fans."[289] This amazing book called *21 Nights* was published by Simon & Schuster on 30 September 2008, along with *Indigo Nights—Live Sessions*, a live album of the aftershows performed in the early hours of 17 and 22 September 2007 in the Indigo club at The O2. "One night, about four in the morning," said Randee St Nicholas, "after I shot the book *21 Nights* with him, he called me and said, 'I did some research. The photographer who shot the Muhammad Ali book got a half a million dollars for the book. But this whole book is you, so I'm going to give you one million dollars. Are you cool with that?' I never asked him for a cent."[289]

PRINCE

LOTUSFLOW3R / MPLSOUND

DISC 1: LOTUSFLOW3R

From the Lotus… · Boom · The Morning After (Digital Version) / Crimson and Clover (CD Version) · 4Ever · Colonized Mind Feel Better, Feel Good, Feel Wonderful · Love Like Jazz · 77 Beverly Park Wall of Berlin · $ · Dreamer · …Back 2 the Lotus

DISC 2 : MPLSOUND

(There'll Never B) Another Like Me · Chocolate Box Dance 4 Me · U're Gonna C Me · Here · Valentina · Better With Time Ol' Skool Company · No More Candy 4 U

Lotusflow3r/MPLSound (box set)
Digital release on LotusFlow3r.com by NPG Records: 24 March 2009
Elixer/Lotusflow3r/MPLSound (box set)
Released in the USA by NPG Records: 29 March 2009 (CD ref.: none)
Released in Europe by NPG Records/Because Music:
29 March 2009 (CD ref.: BEC5772562)
Best chart ranking in the USA: 2
Best chart ranking in the UK: did not make the charts

A return to rock and funk classics for Prince who was soon to go back to his native Minnesota.

THREE FACETS OF PRINCE

Prince had not prepared his admirers for such a period of scarcity. Indeed, the artist, normally so prolific, would not release a studio album during 2008. Only the book *21 Nights*, accompanied by the live recording of *Indigo Nights/Live Sessions*, would make the fans happy. The singer, who for a time concentrated on his London concerts at The O2 Arena, was lying low and preparing his next album, the trilogy *Elixer/Lotusflow3r/MPLSound*, which he would present to the world in the winter of 2009. *Lotusflow3r* is, like Stevie Wonder's *Journey Through the Secret Life of Plants* (1979), a conceptual but demanding work, blending the singer's jazz and rock influences but aimed at an audience of Prince connoisseurs. The shadow of Jimi Hendrix is never far away when Prince unleashes his stinging Hohner Madcat in *Wall of Berlin* or *Dreamer*, while the delicate sound textures of instrumental numbers such as *From the Lotus...* and *...Back 2 the Lotus* take us back to the experimental era of *The Rainbow Children*. The second disc, *MPLSound*, pays homage to the Minneapolis Sound, which Prince spearheaded in the early 1980s. He plays all the instruments on the album, where potential singles come one after the other—*Dance 4 Me*, *Ol' Skool Company*, *No More Candy 4 U*, and more. Each track takes us into the artist's unique groove, for the delight of 1980s nostalgics. The box set also contains the first album by Bria Valente, *Elixer*, which Prince wanted to champion. "The thinking behind this was to introduce a new artist to the world, somebody who's very dear to me," Prince explained on *The Tavis Smiley Show*, "and her music is soothing, it soothes me."[291] Having broken off all contact with Sony Music, which had distributed *Planet Earth* in the United States in 2007, the singer returned to independent distribution for this remarkable album. After offering the double album *Lotusflow3r/MPLSound* for sale on the website LotusFlow3r.com on 24 March 2009, Prince signed an exclusive contract with the Target company which, from 29 March, would distribute the album at all its points of sale and then with the label Because Music, who would take care of the triple album's distribution in Europe. "Target is not a record company," Prince said. "They're a distributor and a retail store, and a very good one at that. Thirty million people go through their stores every week, so they get a chance to pick up the *Lotusflow3r* record."[291]

2009

From Chanel to Prince

The album's release was not accompanied by a tour, but Prince did give some European performances to celebrate his love for the Old Continent. After two concerts at the Montreux Jazz Festival in July 2009, followed by three more in Monaco in August, he decided to take over the Grand Palais in Paris for two exceptional performances in early autumn. Having been invited to attend Karl Lagerfeld's fashion show for Chanel on Tuesday 6 October 2009, Prince was astonished by the 20,000 square meters of glass in the nave of the Grand Palais. The next day, his agent called the venue's management and asked whether Prince could hold a concert in the coming days. Prince visited that same afternoon, accompanied by his concert producer for France, Alfred Bernardin. He decided to perform two concerts in order to make the venue hire financially viable. On Sunday 11 October, the "All Day" concert (at 17:00) and the "All Night" concert (at 22:00) attracted more than 11,000 people. "He also considered playing at the château of Versailles," Bernardin recalled. "Everyone was on board, but he dropped the idea at the last moment because his girlfriend at the time had been frightened by the statues in the park."[292]

The influence of Jimi Hendrix was ever-present during the recording of the *Lotusflow3r* album.

FROM THE LOTUS...

Prince / 2'47

Musicians: Prince: electric guitar, synthesizers, Fender Rhodes piano / **Sonny T.:** bass / **Michael B.:** drums / **Recording: Paisley Park, Chanhassen, Minnesota:** 19 November 2004 (backing track); 2004–2007 (overdubs) / **Technical team: Producer:** Prince / **Recording engineers:** Prince, Kevin "KD" Davis, George Ian Boxill

On 18 February 2001, the album *Minneapolis* by the musician Michel Portal was released. For this album, with its jazz overtones inspired by musicians from Minnesota, the multi-instrumentalist, known especially for his saxophone and clarinet playing, had followed the advice of the celebrated producer Jean Rochard, who had recently moved to Minneapolis, and surrounded himself with musicians such as Michael Bland on drums and Sonny Thompson on bass guitar. When this prestigious group was about to perform a concert at the O'Shaughnessy Theater in Saint Paul on 18 November 2004, Michael Bland got a call from Prince, who asked Bland and Thompson to come to Paisley Park after the Portal concert—which they happily agreed to do. When the pair arrived in Chanhassen, at around 23:30, Prince announced that the session would be recorded and not a single mistake would be tolerated. Without realizing it, Bland and Thompson then took part in a legendary recording session, which, on 19 November 2004, would yield songs to be distributed across the Kid's next three albums. Of the dozen songs recorded that day, *From the Lotus...*, *...Back 2 the Lotus*, *Colonized Mind*, *Love Like Jazz*, and *Wall of Berlin* would feature on *Lotusflow3r*, enlivened by various overdubs.

BOOM

Prince / 3'19

Musicians: Prince: vocals, electric guitar, Fender Rhodes piano, percussion / **Josh Dunham:** bass / **Cora Coleman-Dunham:** drums / **Morris Hayes:** synthesizers / **Recording: 77 Beverly Park, Los Angeles:** August to September 2008 / **Sunset Sound, Los Angeles:** August to September 2008 / **Paisley Park, Chanhassen, Minnesota:** autumn 2008 to January 2009 / **Technical team: Producer:** Prince / **Recording engineers:** Prince, Richard Furch

As in many other tracks on the album, here Prince celebrates the memory of Jimi Hendrix, unhesitatingly reinterpreting the introductory glissando from *Castles Made of Sand* (on *Axis: Bold as Love*, 1967) in the opening of *Boom*. Morris Hayes, conspicuous by his absence from the credits on the album for his work as an arranger of Prince's songs, features here on keyboards, as he also does in *The Morning After* and *Colonized Mind*. When they were introduced to Prince by their friend Richard Furch (the main recording engineer on *Lotusflow3r* and *MPLSound*), the webmaster Scott Addison Clay and his graphic designer Anthony Malzone decided to draw inspiration from *Boom* for Prince's new website, but also for the album's cover, which centered on a photograph of Prince taken by Afshin Shahidi backstage at the Wachovia Center, Philadelphia, in August 2004. "Anthony immediately started sketching planets that we could travel to each containing music," Scott Addison Clay recalled. "Prince really dug the idea and we just kept rolling from there [...] He loved the design so much, he had us fashion it into the album art, T-shirts, and posters."[293]

Continuing the tribute to 1960s music, Prince made a significant cover of *Crimson and Clover* by Tommy James & The Shondells.

THE MORNING AFTER

Prince / 2'06

Musicians: Prince: vocals, electric guitar, acoustic guitar, synthesizers, backing vocals / Josh Dunham: bass / Cora Coleman-Dunham: drums / Morris Hayes: synthesizers / Támar: backing vocals / **Recording:** Paisley Park, Chanhassen, Minnesota: 2005 / 3121 Antelo Road, Los Angeles: 2005 / **Technical team:** Producer: Prince / Recording engineers: L Stu Young, George Ian Boxill

Recorded during the sessions for *3121* in 2005, *The Morning After* was for a time considered a candidate for the album's tracklist, before being dropped for unknown reasons. It was added to *Lotusflow3r* when the album went online on 24 March 2009, but replaced three days later by *Crimson and Clover* on the CD edition because it also appeared on the French vinyl version released by Because Music in November 2009 as well as on the limited edition rereleased in 2015.

HEADPHONES AT THE READY

At 0'57 and 2'07 in the song Prince adds, in a further nod to Jimi Hendrix (even though the original version was by Chip Taylor, in 1965), an extract from *Wild Thing*, another rock 'n' roll classic performed live by The Jimi Hendrix Experience very frequently.

CRIMSON AND CLOVER

Tommy James, Peter Lucia Jr / 3'52

Musician: Prince: vocals, electric guitar, bass, drums / **Recording:** 77 Beverly Park, Los Angeles: August to September 2008 / Sunset Sound, Los Angeles: August to September 2008 / Paisley Park, Chanhassen, Minnesota: autumn 2008 to January 2009 / **Technical team:** Producer: Prince / Recording engineers: Prince, Richard Furch

Reaching No.1 in the United States in February 1969, *Crimson and Clover* was the second hit by the American group Tommy James & The Shondells, coming after their song *Hanky Panky*, which was released in 1966. "The title came to me as I woke up one day," said Tommy James, one of the hit's writers. "I almost had dreamed the title. I just remembered how it was two of my favorite words put together."[294] Among the many covers of this rock anthem, the one by Joan Jett & The Blackhearts on their first album, *I Love Rock 'n' Roll* (1981), is doubtless the most famous; it took the group to No.7 in the Billboard charts in the spring of 1982. Prince's own version of the song features on the CD edition of *Lotusflow3r* but not on the digital version of the album, where it is replaced by *The Morning After*. "*I think Prince's version of Crimson and Clover is magnificent [...],*" said Tommy James in 2020. "*He did such a futuristic version. It was like Crimson and Clover from space. He did a magnificent job. His guitar work in it was incredible.*"[294]

4EVER

Prince / 3'48

Musicians: Prince: vocals, electric guitar, acoustic guitar, synthesizers, piano, backing vocals / **Josh Dunham:** bass / **Cora Coleman-Dunham:** drums / **Shelby J.:** backing vocals / **Marva King:** backing vocals / **Bria Valente:** backing vocals / **Támar:** backing vocals / **Recording: 3121 Antelo Road, Los Angeles:** 2005–2006 / **Paisley Park, Chanhassen, Minnesota:** 2005–2007 / **Technical team: Producer:** Prince / **Recording engineers:** Prince, L Stu Young, George Ian Boxill

On 18 December 2008 the presenter Mark Sovel featured four new songs by Prince on his show *Mr. Shovel's Check One Two*, which was broadcast on Indie 103.1 in Los Angeles. The radio program, which championed independent music, broadcast *Colonized Mind*, *Crimson and Clover*, *Wall of Berlin*, and *4Ever*, a rock ballad recorded several years earlier and notably featuring Támar Davis on backing vocals. "[Prince] wants nothing to do with record labels," the presenter announced, "so he's meeting with people to figure out how to operate at his level without a record label."[295] The journalist Daniel Kreps, who wrote a flattering piece in *Rolling Stone* magazine following this exclusive broadcast, said of *4Ever*: "It's not *Free*, *Ballad of Dorothy Parker*, or *Sometimes It Snows In April*, but it's still a solid, latter-day Prince slow dance as he ruminates about marriage and being with someone, well, 4ever."[295]

2009

COLONIZED MIND

Prince / 4'48

Musicians: Prince: vocals, electric guitar, synthesizers, backing vocals / **Sonny T.:** bass / **Michael B.:** drums / **Morris Hayes:** synthesizers / **Shelby J.:** backing vocals / **Marva King:** backing vocals / **Támar:** backing vocals / **Recording: Paisley Park, Chanhassen, Minnesota:** 19 November 2004 (backing track); 2004–2007 (overdubs) / **Technical team: Producer:** Prince / **Recording engineers:** Prince, Kevin "KD" Davis, George Ian Boxill

Having made the Internet the main channel through which he released his music in the early 2000s, here Prince draws a harsh parallel between the digitization of the means of communication and society losing its bearings, remarking in passing that the minds of Americans had already been "colonized" in the course of history. "*Colonized Mind* has to do with the state of the Union right now," Prince commented on *The Tavis Smiley Show* in April 2009. "The state of the Union for all of us, not just black, not just white, but all of us."[291] Although the point he makes is slightly reactionary when he sings, drawing an analogy between our real-world actions and our clicks on the Internet: "Upload a child with no father/Download no respect for authority/Upload a child with no mother/Download a hard time showing love," it does not detract from the quality of the song, which was recorded with the Paisley Park Power Trio in November 2004 and subsequently enlivened with backing vocals and synthesizer lines.

FEEL BETTER, FEEL GOOD, FEEL WONDERFUL

Prince / 3'53

Musicians: Prince: vocals, electric guitar, bass, drums, percussion, synthesizers, claps, backing vocals / **Maceo Parker:** saxophone / **Mike Phillips:** saxophone / **Ray Monteiro:** trumpet / **Greg Boyer:** trombone / **Shelby J.:** backing vocals / **Recording: Paisley Park, Chanhassen, Minnesota:** 23 June 2006 / **77 Beverly Park, Los Angeles:** August 2008 to January 2009 / **Sunset Sound, Los Angeles:** August to September 2008 / **Technical team: Producer:** Prince / **Recording engineers:** Prince, Kevin "KD" Davis, George Ian Boxill, Richard Furch

After Prince won the Webby Lifetime Achievement Award for best celebrity website in June 2006, the NPG Music Club (see page 384) equipped itself with a brand-new download module. Also on the website, developed by Sam Jennings and Ash Warren, was the page "Fresh from the Studio" on which Prince could post songs that were in the process of production and solicit the opinions of his fans. When he posted *Feel Good, Feel Better, Feel Wonderful* (which was erroneously renamed *Feel Better, Feel Good, Feel Wonderful* on the sleeve of *Lotusflow3r*) on 28 June 2006, the singer came in for some criticism, which made him regret opening up to his fans. This was the only interaction of its kind between Prince and his admirers, and he closed the NPG Music Club for good a few weeks later. "It's about telling folks to celebrate and stop hating,"[291] Prince said of this funk number, which is in the same vein as *Musicology* (2004) and *Get On the Boat* (2006).

Prince at the Chanel fashion show at the Grand Palais, in Paris, on 6 October 2009.

LOVE LIKE JAZZ

Prince / 3'50

Musicians: Prince: vocals, electric guitar, synthesizers, Fender Rhodes piano, backing vocals / **Sonny T.:** bass / **Michael B.:** drums / **Recording: Paisley Park, Chanhassen, Minnesota:** 19 November 2004 (backing track); 2004–2007 (overdubs) / **Technical team: Producer:** Prince / **Recording engineers:** Prince, Kevin "KD" Davis, George Ian Boxill

With an impeccable rhythm played on the ride cymbal, Michael Bland drives the aptly named *Love Like Jazz*, in which Prince demands a "lover" with whom he can "improvise" and "jam," referencing the musical style of one of his dearest friends, the much-missed Miles Davis. Prince also refers to the trumpeter when he sings: "The things I wanna do with you/Like a physical kind of blue"—an allusion to Davis's most famous album, *Kind of Blue*, which was released in 1959 by Columbia Records.

77 BEVERLY PARK

Prince / 3'04

Musician: Prince: electric guitar, acoustic guitar, 12-string acoustic guitar, bass, synthesizers, piano / **Recording: 77 Beverly Park, Los Angeles:** August 2008 to January 2009 / **Technical team: Producer:** Prince / **Recording engineers:** Prince, Richard Furch

After living at 3121 Antelo Road and then 1235 Sierra Alta Way, in 2009 Prince moved into 13000 Mulholland Drive, Los Angeles—a house of almost 3,000 square meters, which he rented for $200,000 per month. Was it the Tuscan-influenced architecture of this splendid building that inspired the musician to create this surprising, but nonetheless delicious, instrumental piece with Italian sounds? Six- and 12-string acoustic guitars take over after a disconcerting introduction in which the breathing of a young woman is followed by a bass guitar riff that oozes reverb. Then the track takes us on a journey between Florence and Siena.

WALL OF BERLIN

Prince / 4'17

Musicians: Prince: vocals, electric guitar / **Sonny T.:** bass /**Michael B.:** drums / **Recording: Paisley Park, Chanhassen, Minnesota:** 19 November 2004 (backing track); 2004–2007 (overdubs) / **Technical team: Producer:** Prince / **Recording engineers:** Prince, Kevin "KD" Davis, George Ian Boxill

Recorded the same day as *3121* in the company of Bland and Thompson, *Wall of Berlin* is also quoted in the title track of the 2006 album. Consisting of a simple trio, without the slightest overdub, the song once again recalls the no-holds-barred rock of The Jimi Hendrix Experience, an influence formerly denied by Prince, but now totally acknowledged. Isn't the break—in which Prince makes way completely for the drums, at 1'47—after all, an obvious homage to the verses of the classic *Fire* (on *Are You Experienced*, 1967)?

$

Prince / 3'57

Musicians: Prince: vocals, electric guitar, synthesizers / **Josh Dunham:** bass / **Cora Coleman-Dunham:** drums, tambourine / **Maceo Parker:** saxophone, spoken voice / **Mike Phillips:** saxophone, spoken voice / **Greg Boyer:** trombone, spoken voice / **Lee Hogans:** trumpet, spoken voice / **Recording: 77 Beverly Park, Los Angeles:** August to September 2008 / **Sunset Sound, Los Angeles:** August to September 2008 / **Paisley Park, Chanhassen, Minnesota:** autumn 2008 to January 2009 / **Technical team: Producer:** Prince / **Recording engineers:** Prince, Richard Furch

$ (pronounced "Money") was one of the first songs recorded by the engineer Richard Furch, who would make recordings of a good number of tracks on *Lotusflow3r* and the whole of *MPLSound* (with the exception of *No More Candy 4 U*, which was recorded earlier), as well as mixing all of the double album (he did not work on *Elixer* by Bria Valente). In 2008, while recording the singer Christina Milian in a Los Angeles studio, Furch had a visit from Prince, to whom he gave his telephone number after being complimented for the work he had just done. Contact was made in the most natural way possible—two weeks later the recording engineer got a call from a member of the singer's entourage: "Do you wanna record tonight?"[296] The technician made his way to Prince's house where he met Morris Hayes, who asked him to organize the following day's session. Undaunted by the difficulty of renting and setting up a recording studio on a Sunday in Los Angeles, Richard Furch took up the challenge, and, the next morning, Prince recorded at 77 Beverly Park in the company of Josh Dunham and Cora Coleman-Dunham.

DREAMER

Prince / 5'31

Musicians: Prince: vocals, electric guitar, percussion / **Josh Dunham:** bass / **Cora Coleman-Dunham:** drums / **Recording:** / **77 Beverly Park, Los Angeles:** August to September 2008 / **Sunset Sound, Los Angeles:** August to September 2008 / **Paisley Park, Chanhassen, Minnesota:** autumn 2008 to January 2009 / **Technical team: Producer:** Prince / **Recording engineers:** Prince, Richard Furch

Continuing his tribute to Hendrix, Prince evokes another classic by the master of the flaming Stratocaster: *Voodoo Child (Slight Return)*. From the riff played at 2'16 to the intensive use of a wah-wah pedal on pentatonic scales that, though obvious, are played with matchless virtuosity, everything here harks back to the Hendrix classic from 1970. The first song recorded by Richard Furch on his arrival at 77 Beverly Park, *Dreamer* was initially an instrumental version before the lyrics were added by Prince at a later stage. Dedicated to the writer Dick Gregory, who was especially famous for his defence of the civil rights of African-Americans, the song's words implicitly deal with the discrimination they suffer in the American population. When he was asked about the song's meaning by the star presenter Tavis Smiley on *The Tavis Smiley Show* in April 2009, Prince launched into a questionable monologue about chemtrails, a conspiracy theory regarding the vapor trails left by aircraft in flight, which claims these contain chemicals that the jumbo jets emit for reasons that are hidden from the general population. Comments that are best forgotten if we are to enjoy this album filled with vintage rock 'n' roll to the full.

...BACK 2 THE LOTUS

Prince / 5'35

Musicians: Prince: spoken voice, electric guitar, Fender Rhodes piano / **Sonny T.:** bass / **Michael B.:** drums / **Recording: Paisley Park, Chanhassen, Minnesota:** 19 November 2004 (backing track); 2004–2007 (overdubs) / **Technical team: Producer:** Prince / **Recording engineers:** Prince, Kevin "KD" Davis, George Ian Boxill

In the same vein as *From the Lotus...*, *...Back 2 the Lotus* brings this brilliant album to a close with a piece of psychedelic rock performed by the Prince/Bland/Thompson trio. The presence of the Digitech Whammy pedal, already heard on *3121*, which was recorded the same day, is once again dominant and even applied to the singer's voice, producing a very interesting "detuning" effect. Once this album paying homage to Hendrix was complete, Prince returned to his funk roots with the exceptional *MPLSound*. Their complementarity makes these two albums a must-buy box set—an excellent way to discover the many facets of an artist who created according to his desires and cared nothing for labels.

Q-Tip, a founding member of A Tribe Called Quest, in 1990.

(THERE'LL NEVER B) ANOTHER LIKE ME

Prince / 6'02

Musician: Prince: vocals, electric guitar, bass, drums, programming, synthesizers, piano, backing vocals / **Recording: 77 Beverly Park, Los Angeles:** August to September 2008 / **Sunset Sound, Los Angeles:** August to September 2008 / **Paisley Park, Chanhassen, Minnesota:** autumn 2008 to January 2009 / **Technical team: Producer:** Prince / **Recording engineers:** Prince, Richard Furch

While the production of *Lotusflow3r* had been based on musicians sharing the workload, live takes, and a rock vitality that bore witness to a period rich in musical improvisation, that of *MPLSound* would be very different. Bringing back into play his Linn LM-1 Drum Machine, Prince took charge of playing all the instruments on the album, accompanied solely by Richard Furch, the recording engineer with fingers (and ears) of gold. This funk-rock song was the first recorded for *MPLSound*. An instrumental version was posted on the short-lived MPLSound.com by Prince on 16 February 2009, followed by a sung version two days later.

CHOCOLATE BOX

Prince / 6'14

Musician: Prince: vocals, electric guitar, bass, drums, programming, synthesizers, backing vocals / **Q-Tip:** rap / **Recording: Paisley Park, Chanhassen, Minnesota:** autumn 2008 / **77 Beverly Park, Los Angeles:** autumn 2008 to January 2009 (Q-Tip's voice) / **Technical team: Producer:** Prince / **Recording engineers:** Prince, Richard Furch

For this song, which was mixed with panache by Richard Furch, Prince used a combination of an acoustic drum kit and a Linn LM-1 Drum Machine. A most effective combination—its pattern would coax the most reluctant partygoer on to the dance floor in no time.

The only musician invited to take part in the recording of *MPLSound* was the rapper Q-Tip, a former founding member of A Tribe Called Quest, who recorded a delicate rap on *Chocolate Box* during a session in Los Angeles, some time after the backing tracks were recorded. The video clip director P R Brown, who was well known for making videos for Hoobastank, Avenged Sevenfold, and Otep, made a clip for the song, which was used as a promotional tool for the album, even though the song did not enjoy release as a single.

On 16 November 2008, as Q-Tip sang his 1999 single, *Vivrant Thing*, onstage at House of Blues in Las Vegas, Prince burst in, stage left, grabbed a guitar being played by one of the band, and started playing with the group before disappearing once again. DJ Scratch, who was at the turntables that evening, recalled the incident: "None of us knew he was there until he popped up on the stage...then the n—a vanished like Batman [...] None of us knew what was happening, then when we finished the show he was gone LOL!"[297] With *MPLSound* almost finished, Prince played some extracts to Anthony Malzone, his infographics designer, who was responsible for the website LotusFlow3r.com. "It's a dance record," he recalled. "I remember showing him a disco ball with jellyfish legs. I told him the album inspire dit [sic], and the next day he played me an instrumental called *Disco Jellyfish*. We uploaded that right away."[21] *Disco Jellyfish* was quickly removed from the website and then transformed into *Chocolate Box*, before becoming a famous bootleg. As for the jellyfish disco ball, it featured on the sleeve of *MPLSound*.

Mia Maestro and Penelope Cruz, two artists quoted by Prince in *Valentina.*

Much as listeners will appreciate the return of the Linn LM-1 Drum Machine from *Computer Blue* or *When Doves Cry*, as featured on the *Purple Rain* album in 1984, they will also be delighted to hear this reinterpretation of *U're Gonna C Me*, featured in a pared-down version on *One Nite Alone...* in 2002. Also released as a promotional single in France in autumn 2009, it is a perfect ambassador for the elegant *MPLSound.*

DANCE 4 ME

Prince / 4'59

Musician: Prince: vocals, electric guitar, bass, drums, programming, synthesizers, piano, backing vocals / **Recording: Paisley Park, Chanhassen, Minnesota:** August 2008 to January 2009 / **77 Beverly Park, Los Angeles:** August 2008 to January / **Sunset Sound, Los Angeles:** August 2008 to January / **Technical team: Producer:** Prince / **Recording engineers:** Prince, Richard Furch

While true funkateers will emphasize the resemblance between Prince's *Dance 4 Me* and Zapp's *I Can Make You Dance*, which was released as a single in 1983, they will admit that the former makes only the slightest nod to his contemporaries in this exceptional song, where Camille (see page 142) makes a reappearance. As Prince shuttled between Monaco and Paris at the end of the summer of 2009, the song appeared in France in the shape of a single available exclusively on iTunes France. The following 14 October, Prince sang the number on *Grand Journal*, on Canal+, three days after having lit up the Grand Palais with two exceptional concerts.

U'RE GONNA C ME

Prince / 4'36

Musician: Prince: vocals, acoustic guitar, bass, drums, programming, synthesizers, backing vocals / **Recording: 77 Beverly Park, Los Angeles:** August 2008 to January 2009 / **Sunset Sound, Los Angeles:** August 2008 to January 2009 / **Paisley Park, Chanhassen, Minnesota:** August 2008 to January 2009 / **Technical team: Producer:** Prince / **Recording engineers:** Prince, Richard Furch

HERE

Prince / 5'15

Musician: Prince: vocals, acoustic guitar, bass, drums, programming, synthesizers, backing vocals / **Recording: 77 Beverly Park, Los Angeles:** August 2008 to January 2009 / **Sunset Sound, Los Angeles:** August 2008 to January 2009 / **Paisley Park, Chanhassen, Minnesota:** August 2008 to January 2009 / **Technical team: Producer:** Prince / **Recording engineers:** Prince, Richard Furch

In the same vein as *U're Gonna C Me*, *Here* is an enjoyable ballad, recorded under the guidance of Richard Furch. Using his famous Linn LM-1 Drum Machine once more, Prince mixes vintage sounds with contemporary textures, adding some acoustic guitar and synthesizers here and there.

VALENTINA

Prince / 3'59

Musician: Prince: vocals, electric guitar, acoustic guitar, bass, programming, percussion, synthesizers, backing vocals / **Recording: 77 Beverly Park, Los Angeles:** August 2008 to January 2009 / **Sunset Sound, Los Angeles:** August 2008 to January 2009 / **Paisley Park, Chanhassen, Minnesota:** August 2008 to January 2009 / **Technical team: Producer:** Prince / **Recording engineers:** Prince, Richard Furch

Having made the clip of *Te Amo Corazón* for him in 2005, the Mexican actor Salma Hayek remained a close friend of Prince, who wrote the song *Valentina* for her—or rather for her daughter, born in 2007 from her relationship with the

Twenty-three years after they met, Prince wrote a song in honor of the talented actress Kristin Scott Thomas.

French businessman François-Henri Pinault, whom she married on 14 February 2009. Prince displays a certain sense of humor in the song, singing in the choruses: "Hey Valentina tell your mama she should give me a call/When she gets tired of running after you down the hall," and pays homage to his friend with a flattering comment on her figure, which is "Curvier than/A Fender Stratocaster guitar..." He also attempts a pun at the end of the song, referring to another of his friends when he sings that "If Penelope wants to Cruz," the Spanish actor is welcome, too, and he invites Mia Maestro, who appeared alongside him in the video of *Te Amo Corazón*, to join the reunion. Once the song had been recorded, Prince invited Salma Hayek to listen to it in his car because he considered the sound quality to be better there.

BETTER WITH TIME

Prince / 4'54

Musician: Prince: vocals, bass, programming, synthesizers, piano, backing vocals / **Recording: 77 Beverly Park, Los Angeles:** August 2008 to January 2009 / **Sunset Sound, Los Angeles:** August 2008 to January 2009 / **Paisley Park, Chanhassen, Minnesota:** August 2008 to January 2009 / **Technical team: Producer:** Prince / **Recording engineers:** Prince, Richard Furch

"I'm not a big fan of male vocalists, you know," Prince explained to Tavis Smiley in 2009. "Usually when I do ballads, I use my higher register, because I love the female voice doing slow music."[291] Explaining his singing in *Better With Time* in these terms, the singer told another journalist, Ann Powers of the *Los Angeles Times*, that the song was inspired by Kristin Scott Thomas, with whom he acted in *Under the Cherry Moon* (released 1986). "Like wine, you get better with time," he tells the British actor in the song. "I was in touch with him through all his life," she said. "He would get in touch when he'd get to Paris. I'd get these strange emails or a strange voicemail saying, 'Hi, it's me.' And that was that. And then I'd go and see his show, see him backstage, and then he'd disappear for three years, and suddenly I'd get an email out of nowhere!"[298]

FOR PRINCE ADDICTS

A mistake slipped into some versions of the sleeve of *MPLSound: Better With Time* was inadvertently entitled *Better With Me* on the vinyl edition of the record, which was released in France in November 2009. This did not get better with time—in 2015 a second release of the double album, this time accompanied by the two compact discs, contained the same error! Bloody French!

Onstage at the Nokia Theater in Los Angeles on 28 March 2009.

OL' SKOOL COMPANY

Prince / 7'30

Musician: Prince: vocals, electric guitar, bass, programming, synthesizers, backing vocals / **Recording: 77 Beverly Park, Los Angeles:** August 2008 to January 2009 / **Sunset Sound, Los Angeles:** August 2008 to January 2009 / **Paisley Park, Chanhassen, Minnesota:** August 2008 to January 2009 / **Technical team: Producer:** Prince / **Recording engineers:** Prince, Richard Furch

When Prince was invited onto *The Tonight Show with Jay Leno* on 25 March 2009, he presented a new song to his fans, introduced by the words "The White House is now black/ You gotta check your radio back." He was, of course, referring to the election of President Barack Obama in November 2008, and took advantage of this to deliver a song in homage to the Minneapolis Sound, in which he enumerated his memories. "That's just an ode to how I grew up and what we used to listen to,"[291] Prince said later. At the end of the song, he lists some of the drummers who were a part of his world over the years: Michael Bland, Morris Day, Jellybean Johnson, Sheila E., and, finally, John Blackwell. Although *Ol' Skool Company* is one of Prince's best tracks from the end of that decade, the journalist Quentin B Huff, from PopMatters.com, made quite a fair criticism of the song, which he thought a touch reactionary, or at least far too backward-looking: "I have to say I agree more with Prince when he sang in *New Power Generation* about 'your old fashioned music, your old ideas/we're sick and tired of you telling us what 2 do.'"[299]

2009

NO MORE CANDY 4 U

Prince / 4'15

Musician: Prince: vocals, electric guitar, bass, drums, programming, synthesizers, piano, backing vocals / **Recording: Paisley Park, Chanhassen, Minnesota:** August 2008 to January 2009 / **Technical team: Producer:** Prince / **Recording engineers:** ? (not confirmed)

All the songs on *MPLSound* were written for that album by Prince, and recorded with the recording engineer Richard Furch, with the exception of *No More Candy 4 U*, which the singer decided to add to the tracklist of the album at the last minute. "He gave me a call," Furch recalled, "and he said, 'Well, I need one more song.'"[296] After being asked to leave Los Angeles in haste for Paisley Park in December 2008, with a view to digging out something unusual from The Vault, Furch was eventually told by his employer that he had found what he was looking for: *No More Candy 4 U*. "It fits," Furch explained, "but if you actually listen to it, you'll realize that that's quite a different song from the rest of the album."[296]

TURN ME LOOSE

Prince / 2'54

Musicians: Prince: vocals, electric guitar, backing vocals / **Josh Dunham:** bass / **Cora Coleman-Dunham:** drums / **Morris Hayes:** Hammond organ / **Maceo Parker:** saxophone / **Lee Hogans:** trumpet / **Greg Boyer:** trombone / **Liv Warfield:** backing vocals / **Recording: 77 Beverly Park, Los Angeles:** September 2008 (backing tracks) / **Sunset Sound, Los Angeles:** September 2008 (overdubs) / **Paisley Park, Chanhassen, Minnesota:** October 2008 to February 2009 (overdubs) / **Technical team: Producer:** Prince / **Recording engineer:** Richard Furch

On 25 April 2008, Prince appeared as a guest on *The Tonight Show with Jay Leno*, as part of the promotion of his concert at the Coachella Festival which was scheduled to take place the next day in Indio, California. He performed an unreleased—and very funky—song, *Turn Me Loose*, which is in a similar vein to *Get On the Boat* and concluded his last album, *3121* (the two other songs played that day, *Guitar* and *1999*, were not broadcast). While fans hoped for a forthcoming release of a single of this song, which evoked the sexy, jerky funk of James Brown, nothing came of it. The final appearance of *Turn Me Loose* was on web radio station KJLH the following 24 September; the song was then hidden away in The Vault, to the deep despair of fans.

PURPLE AND GOLD

Prince / 3'34

Musicians: Prince: vocals, programming, synthesizers, backing vocals / **Shelby J.:** vocals, backing vocals / **Liv Warfield:** vocals, backing vocals / **Elisa Dease:** vocals, backing vocals / **Recording: Paisley Park, Chanhassen, Minnesota:** 17 January 2010 / **Technical team: Producer:** Prince / **Recording engineer:** James "Fluff" Harley

On 17 January 2010, Prince was on the terraces of the Mall of America Field at the Hubert H. Humphrey Metrodome, Minneapolis's stadium, which is home to the Minnesota Vikings football team. That evening, the fixture was between the Vikings and the Dallas Cowboys—a qualifying game for the 2010 season of the National Football Conference. Before a crowd of 63,547 supporters watching the clash of the titans that day, the Vikings crushed their opponents: the match ended with the staggering scoreline of 34-3. Prince—a fervent supporter of his home city's team—told a journalist from Fox 9 following the Vikings' qualification: "I saw the future."[300] As soon as the match was over, the singer returned to Paisley Park and recorded a song in honor of the team, whose colors are purple and gold. The title, logically enough, was *Purple and Gold*. Like *Fly, Eagles Fly* for the Philadelphia Eagles and *J!-E!-T!-S! Jets!, Jets!, Jets!* for the New York Jets, *Purple and Gold* was chosen as the Vikings' fight song; it appeared on their official website the following 21 January.

Fans wear the colors of their favorite team, the Minnesota Vikings, the day of their victory over the Dallas Cowboys.

The singer Elisa Dease (seen here in 1989 when she still bore her maiden name of Fiorillo) joined the New Power Generation in 2009.

However, although it was rousing, the song did not bring the team luck—they lost 28–31 to the New Orleans Saints on 25 January at the latter's stadium, the Caesars Superdome. Inevitably, *Purple and Gold* was put away in The Vault.

CAUSE AND EFFECT

Prince / 3'32

Musicians: **Prince:** vocals, electric guitar, acoustic guitar, synthesizers, backing vocals / **Larry Graham:** bass / **Chris Coleman:** drums / **Shelby J.:** vocals, backing vocals / **Liv Warfield:** vocals, backing vocals / **Elisa Dease:** vocals, backing vocals / **Recording:** **Paisley Park, Chanhassen, Minnesota:** 27 January 2010 / **Technical team:** **Producer:** Prince / **Recording engineer:** James "Fluff" Harley

In September 2008, the singer Elisa Dease, whose career had known better days, got a call from one of Prince's close collaborators while she was working at her daughter's day nursery in Las Vegas. After finding some privacy at the nursery, the singer had a conversation with Prince, who told her that he wanted to work with her, after his recording engineer friend Dave Hampton had seen her and heard her sing a week earlier in a Las Vegas club. It must be said that the two artists were not strangers to each other because Prince had cowritten and coproduced the young woman's second album, *I Am* (1990), with David Rivkin when she still went by her maiden name, Elisa Fiorillo. Although Dease heard no news for many long months, she was invited to join Liv Warfield and Shelby J. in a trio of backing vocalists who would accompany Prince on *The Tonight Show with Jay Leno* in March 2009, then on his Paris dates in October, before taking part in several recording sessions at Paisley Park in 2010, including those for *Purple and Gold*, *Cause and Effect*, and numerous songs on the album *20Ten*. The drummer Chris Coleman also made an appearance in this song, which for a while was considered for inclusion on *20Ten*, then on *Welcome 2 America*, before finally being relegated to the rank of quality outtake and released exclusively on the website TheCurrent.org on 26 February 2010.

FOR PRINCE ADDICTS

The introduction to *Cause and Effect* contains an extract from the second concert Prince performed in Montreux, on 18 July 2009, when he whipped up the crowd between *When Eye Lay My Hands On U* and a muscular cover of *Stratus* (1973) by Billy Cobham, shouting: "I am here! Where are you?"

PRINCE

20TEN

Compassion · Beginning Endlessly · Future Soul Song
Sticky Like Glue · Act of God · Lavaux · Walk in Sand · Sea of Everything
Everybody Loves Me · Laydown (Hidden Track)

UK distribution by *The Daily Mirror*, NPG Records:
10 July 2010 (CD ref.: none)

Prince triumphant during the Welcome 2 America Tour.

Overleaf: Onstage at the Stade de France in Saint-Denis on 30 June 2011.

2010

THE EUROPEAN PRESS AS DISTRIBUTION CHANNEL

In 2010, Prince turned away from the Internet, which had allowed him to distribute his music with complete freedom at the dawn of the 21st century, and decided that his next album would be distributed through the press instead. In 1993, he had tried to make his blues album *The Undertaker* available to *Guitar World* readers, but had come up against a categorical refusal from Warner Bros. Records. Prince had to wait until 2007 to offer *Planet Earth* to British readers of the *Daily Mail*, against the advice of Sony Music who were distributing the album on the other side of the Atlantic. After planning a European tour in July 2010, Prince did not want his next album, *20Ten*, which he'd recorded mostly alone at Paisley Park, to be available for sale in record stores or online. "The Internet's completely over," he announced in 2010. "I don't see why I should give my new music to iTunes or anyone else. They won't pay me an advance for it and then they get angry when they can't get it. The Internet's like MTV. At one time, MTV was hip, and suddenly, it became outdated."[301] Prince followed his instincts and decided that *20Ten* would be distributed through the press, coming out with various European publications such as *The Daily Mirror* in the United Kingdom and *Courrier international* in France. "It's the best way to go," he confirmed in July 2010. "No charts, no Internet piracy, and no stress. Period. It seems like a lot of other artists agree with us as they are using the same approach now."[302]

A break from the recording studios

Having gone unnoticed in the United States, where it never saw an official release, the album came off as nothing but a promotional item for the aptly named 20Ten Tour held that July, followed by the Prince Live 2010 Tour which took place that autumn. Despite this reductive image, the album contains some high-quality songs, such as the funky *Sticky Like Glue* and *Lavaux*, or the very pop-sounding *Everybody Loves Me*, which both sound uncannily like a selection of outtakes from the early 1980s. Loyal to his reputation as an insatiable producer, Prince recorded *20Ten* and then promptly recorded the songs intended for the album *Welcome 2 America*, which he had started working on with drummer Chris Coleman and bass player Tal Wilkenfeld in the late autumn of 2010. In the end, this album was filed in The Vault until 2021, when The Prince Estate exhumed it in a version faithful to what Prince had envisaged. In a rare move, after the release of *20Ten*, Prince decided to distance himself from recording studios, preferring to hold a series of spectacular tours: Welcome 2 America in 2010–2011, Welcome 2 America Euro Tour and Welcome 2 Canada in 2011, Welcome 2 Australia in 2012, and, finally, Live Out Loud in 2013. "I used to record something every day," reported Prince in 2014. "I always tease that I have to go to studio rehab. I'm a very in-the-moment person, I do what feels good in the moment. I'm not on a schedule, and I don't have any sort of contractual ties [...] I have giant bills, large payrolls, so I do have to do tours. But there's no need *to record anymore*."[303] While fans were shocked by this almost unthinkable turn in Prince's timeline, they were relieved when he returned in September 2014 with not one, but two albums: the thunderous *Plectrumelectrum*, the result of his collaboration with the rockers from 3rdEyeGirl, and *Art Official Age*, a second album, which is closer to his usual productions and imbued with a spectacular modernity.

dancin'
groovin'
hit me

VIBREZ+GRAND

2010

COMPASSION

Prince / 3'57

Musicians: Prince: vocals, electric guitar, programming, synthesizers, claps, backing vocals / **Josh Dunham:** bass / **Cora Coleman-Dunham:** drums / **Maceo Parker:** saxophone / **Greg Boyer:** trombone / **Ray Monteiro:** trumpet / **Mike Phillips:** saxophone / **Shelby J.:** backing vocals / **Elisa Dease:** backing vocals / **Liv Warfield:** backing vocals / **Recording: 77 Beverly Park, Los Angeles:** September to December 2008 / **Sunset Sound, Los Angeles:** autumn 2008 / **Paisley Park, Chanhassen, Minnesota:** 2008–2009 / **Technical team: Producer:** Prince / **Recording engineer:** Richard Furch

Praising the virtues of fraternity, *Compassion* is a song full of hope. It was recorded at the same time as *Boom* and *Crimson and Clover*, during the first sessions for *Lotusflow3r*. Richard Furch was at the helm for this song, whose sessions began at 77 Beverly Park, in Los Angeles, with the power trio made up of Cora Coleman-Dunham on drums, Josh Dunham on bass, and Prince on the guitar. The vocals and several guitar overdubs were recorded later at Sunset Sound, then the Pro Tools files were once again reworked and finally mixed at 77 Beverly Park and Paisley Park. Already in 1997, when Prince was championing animal rights and establishing a vegetarian diet at his Chanhassen compound, he had talked about compassion in an interview with Catherine Censor Shemo for *Vegetarian Times*. The journalist, regarding criticisms from non-vegetarians, asked Prince, "Some people say, 'Why waste your time worrying about animals when so many people are suffering?' Are vegetarians wasting their compassion? Distracting themselves from human pain?"[304] Without batting an eyelid, Prince responded, "Compassion is an action word with no boundaries. It is never wasted."[304]

BEGINNING ENDLESSLY

Prince / 5'27

Musicians: Prince: vocals, electric guitar, bass, drums, programming, synthesizers, backing vocals / **Shelby J.:** backing vocals / **Elisa Dease:** backing vocals / **Liv Warfield:** backing vocals / **Recording: Paisley Park, Chanhassen, Minnesota:** September 2009 to February 2010 / **Technical team: Producer:** Prince / **Recording engineer:** James "Fluff" Harley

On 14 April 2011, Prince launched the 21 Nite Stand in Los Angeles, a fifteen-show residency at the Forum in Inglewood, on the outskirts of Los Angeles. The legendary concert series, with ticket prices ranging from $25 to $781, depending on the position in the venue, was Prince's chance to experiment with all sorts of covers, such as *Don't Stop 'Til You Get Enough* or *Wanna Be Startin' Somethin'* by Michael Jackson, *Please, Please, Please* by James Brown, or *I Know You Got Soul* by Bobby Byrd. Many stars were regularly invited to dance onstage, such as Javier Bardem and Penelope Cruz on 14

Every evening during the Welcome 2 America Tour, the singer invited members of the audience to dance alongside him.

The backing vocalists Shelby J. (left) and Liv Warfield (right) with the keyboard player Cassandra O'Neal (center).

April, or to sing a duet with Prince (Gwen Stefani on 30 April, for *So Far, So Pleased*). This residency also gave Prince the opportunity to play his lesser-known songs onstage, rather than his many hits, such as *Beginning Endlessly*, with which he opened hostilities on 22 April. The song, recorded by Prince's new recording engineer James "Fluff" Harley, benefited from Prince's classic formula from 2010: a clever mix of the Linn LM-1 Drum Machine and acoustic drums, to which he added modern textures from the only synthesizer used on the album. As pointed out by his friend Morris Hayes, who was always around when Prince was at Chanhassen: "I could tell that he had got a keyboard, just got him one keyboard, and he just went through all the sounds in this one unit and just made a bunch of different tracks."[305]

FUTURE SOUL SONG

Prince / 5'08

Musicians: Prince: vocals, electric guitar, bass, drums, programming, synthesizers, backing vocals / **Shelby J.:** backing vocals / **Elisa Dease:** backing vocals / **Liv Warfield:** backing vocals / **Recording: Paisley Park, Chanhassen, Minnesota:** 1995–1998; 2008–2009; 20 November 2009 / **77 Beverly Park, Los Angeles:** September to December 2008 / **Sunset Sound, Los Angeles:** autumn 2008 / **Technical team: Producer:** Prince / **Recording engineers:** Hans-Martin Buff (backing-tracks), Richard Furch (overdubs), James "Fluff" Harley (overdubs)

"We all love *Future Soul Song* the best!"[302] declared Prince in 2012. Nevertheless, the song took a long time to make before it finally appeared on *20Ten*. Recorded in the second half of the 1990s by recording engineer Hans-Martin Buff, Prince revisited it with Richard Fuchs in late 2008, then finished it with James "Fluff" Harley on 20 November 2009 at Paisley Park. "It's interesting when we work on something and then you get the record and it's [...] completely different and you go like, 'Wow, that's what happened there, you know,'" said Morris Hayes of *Future Soul Song*. "It's like he just completely departed from what it kind of started out. It just would evolve into something different. And so a lot of it was interesting."[305]

STICKY LIKE GLUE

Prince / 4'46

Musicians: Prince: vocals, rap, electric guitar, programming, synthesizers, claps, backing vocals / **Shelby J.:** backing vocals / **Elisa Dease:** backing vocals / **Liv Warfield:** backing vocals / **Recording:** Paisley Park, **Chanhassen, Minnesota:** 2009, 20 November 2009 / **Technical team: Producer:** Prince / **Recording engineer:** James "Fluff" Harley

Undeniably the best song from *20Ten*, *Sticky Like Glue* revives a traditional Princian pop-funk, which had been lying dormant for a while. The bass played on the synthesizer is highly reminiscent of the one from *Boogie On Reggae Woman* by Stevie Wonder (1974), and together with the Linn LM-1 Drum Machine rhythm and the charming melody, everything is sprinkled with sensual backing vocals by the Shelby J./Liv Warfield/Elisa Dease trio, creating an effective formula for this addictive piece. One night after the song had been produced, Prince and his friend Morris Hayes ended up at the Avalon club in Los Angeles with will.i.am, of the Black Eyed Peas, who were then surfing the wave of international success thanks to their single *I Gotta Feeling*. "Will just went banana sandwiches, man," said Hayes. "This dude started dancing around like an elf from the Lucky Charms [...] he was just like, 'Dude, that's hot, it's like it's crazy.'"[305]

The hills of the canton of Lavaux made an impression on Prince during his stay in Switzerland.

2010

ACT OF GOD

Prince / 3'14

Musicians: Prince: vocals, electric guitar, bass, drums, programming, synthesizers, backing vocals / **Shelby J.:** backing vocals / **Elisa Dease:** backing vocals / **Liv Warfield:** backing vocals / **Recording:** **Paisley Park, Chanhassen, Minnesota:** 2009, 25 November 2009 / **Technical team: Producer:** Prince / **Recording engineer:** James "Fluff" Harley

In *Act of God*, Prince sings again about his dislike for the devastation created in America by the 2008 financial crisis and for a banking system that was saved from ruin by the federal government, although it didn't hesitate to throw thousands of vulnerable families onto the streets. Prince also mocks the powerful who say they act according to the will of God, the motto of the United States being "In God We Trust." Prince performs in a pop universe here, supported by his talented and now essential backing vocalists. Like many other songs from *20Ten*, this one deserves to go down in history.

LAVAUX

Prince / 3'04

Musicians: Prince: vocals, electric guitar, bass, drums, programming, percussion, synthesizers, backing vocals / **Shelby J.:** backing vocals / **Elisa Dease:** backing vocals / **Liv Warfield:** backing vocals / **Recording:** **Paisley Park, Chanhassen, Minnesota:** September 2009 to February 2010 / **Technical team: Producer:** Prince / **Recording engineer:** James "Fluff" Harley

Prince here returns to his funkiest self, with a song that feels as if it came out of *1999* (1982) and with arrangements that also take us back to the days of the *Parade* (1986) album. This devilishly sexy piece praises the pleasures of adventure and travel. It cites the canton of Lavaux, in Switzerland, renowned for its terraced vineyards along Lake Geneva, not far from Montreux, where Prince gave two legendary concerts on 18 July 2009, two months before writing the song. Prince also mentions the chocolate produced at Vevey, a town four miles from Montreux, and confirms his love for the continent of Europe, which he visited the summer before recording this song.

WALK IN SAND

Prince / 3'30

Musicians: Prince: vocals, acoustic guitar, bass, drums, percussion, synthesizers, piano, backing vocals / **Shelby J.:** backing vocals / **Elisa Dease:** backing vocals / **Liv Warfield:** backing vocals / **Recording:** **Paisley Park, Chanhassen, Minnesota:** 1 August 2009, September 2009 to February 2010 / **Technical team: Producer:** Prince / **Recording engineer:** James "Fluff" Harley

Light as a feather, *Walk in Sand* is a melodic ballad in which Prince declares that he likes nothing more than to walk in sand, hand in hand with his beloved. When he was scheduled to appear at the sixteenth Super Bock Super Rock Festival on 18 July 2010, Prince realized that the famous Portuguese beer brand sponsoring the event had used his song for a promotional video. To keep the situation from souring, Super Bock pulled the video from its official site, and the

The Portuguese singer Ana Moura, photographed in Paris in March 2018.

case was soon closed. The day of the concert, there was a rumor going around that fado singer Ana Moura, whom Prince deeply admired, would be performing a duet of *Walk in Sand* with him onstage at the festival. In the end, the prestigious duo performed two fado songs accompanied by keyboardist Renato Neto: *A Sós Com A Noite* (Alone With the Night), by Ana Moura, and *Vou Dar De Beber À Dor* (I Am Going to Drink the Pain) by the great Amália Rodrigues.

SEA OF EVERYTHING

Prince / 3'49

Musicians: Prince: vocals, classic guitar, bass, programming, synthesizers, backing vocals / **Shelby J.:** backing vocals / **Elisa Dease:** backing vocals / **Liv Warfield:** backing vocals / **Recording: Paisley Park, Chanhassen, Minnesota:** 2009, 25 November 2009 / **Technical team: Producer:** Prince / **Recording engineer:** James "Fluff" Harley

The third ballad of the album, *Sea of Everything* does not have the old-fashioned charm of *Future Soul Song*, nor the melodic appeal of *Walk in Sand*, but it does stand out for its use of the classical guitar, which Prince very rarely included in his repertoire, to the disappointment of those who love this nylon-stringed instrument. A pleasant break before he returned to his usual obsessions with *Everybody Loves Me*.

EVERYBODY LOVES ME

Prince / 4'09

Musicians: Prince: vocals, electric guitar, bass, drums, programming, piano, synthesizers, backing vocals / **Shelby J.:** backing vocals / **Elisa Dease:** backing vocals / **Liv Warfield:** backing vocals / **Recording: Paisley Park, Chanhassen, Minnesota:** 2009, 25 November 2009 / **Technical team: Producer:** Prince / **Recording engineer:** James "Fluff" Harley

More than one fan must have gasped when they heard *Everybody Loves Me* for the first time. The resemblance to *Let's Pretend We're Married* and *Delirious* (1999, 1982) is blatant and illustrates Prince's desire to dive back into his productions from the 1980s. He also returned to the electronic percussion stroke on the second beat of every other bar, a distinctive feature of this part of his discography, which he'd pulled out of his bag of tricks in the early 2000s during the One Nite Alone...Tour.

LAYDOWN

Prince / 3'07

Musicians: Prince: vocals, rap, electric guitar, bass, programming, synthesizers, backing vocals / **Shelby J.:** backing vocals / **Elisa Dease:** backing vocals / **Liv Warfield:** backing vocals / **Recording: Paisley Park, Chanhassen, Minnesota:** 2009, 25 November 2009 / **Technical team: Producer:** Prince / **Recording engineer:** James "Fluff" Harley

At track 77 of the album (tracks 10 through 77 are silent), the deafening *Laydown*, with its hip-hop sounds, is a gift reserved for the most curious of listeners. Prince takes on a new nickname, The Purple Yoda, referring to the wise Jedi master from the *Star Wars* saga. This is a very good hidden track, in which Prince showcases his incredible ability to make people dance.

After playing a subtle yet biting guitar part on Stevie Wonder's excellent *So What's The Fuss* in 2005, Prince joined the brilliant keyboardist for his concert at the Palais Omnisports, in Paris-Bercy, on 1 July 2019 for a classic duet of *Superstition*.

To revive the song *Extraloveable*, Prince called on Andy Allo with whom he was to work numerous times.

EXTRALOVEABLE

Prince, Andy Allo / 5'01

Musicians
Prince: vocals, electric guitar, programming, bass, percussion, synthesizers, backing vocals
Andy Allo: rap
John Blackwell: drums
Recording
Paisley Park, Chanhassen, Minnesota: 2011
Technical team
Producer: Prince
Recording engineer: ? (not confirmed)

Digital release in the USA on iTunes by NPG Records: 28 November 2011
Digital release in the UK on iTunes by NPG Records: 24 November 2011
Best chart ranking in the USA: did not make the charts
Best chart ranking in the UK: did not make the charts

Genesis

Not that it was a sign of lack of inspiration, but in 2011 Prince decided to rummage through The Vault and extract a rarity that was well known among fans: *Extraloveable*. The song had first been recorded on 3 April 1982 at the Sunset Sound studios in Los Angeles, then probably reworked a few months later, as Prince slipped in a dig at guitarist Dez Dickerson, who was replaced by Wendy Melvoin in 1983: "Hey Dez! Don't U like my band?" Commenting on this, Dickerson said: "Believe it or not, I've never heard the song, although I'm familiar with the lyric." He continued, "It's really just a typical example of Prince's sense of humor—my split with him and the band was completely amicable."[306] The song remains unreleased to this day—The Prince Estate decided not to include it on the Super Deluxe edition of *1999*, released in 2019, because of the line "I'm on the verge of rape." Prince did, however, record a modern version of the song in 2011, which was stripped of its sexual suggestiveness, even though his invitation to come and shower with him is still there. This reinterpretation of *Extraloveable* came out as a single on iTunes in Canada, Europe, Australia, New Zealand, Japan, and the United States in November 2011, with the aim of promoting Prince's massive world tour, which had started with the Welcome 2 America Tour in December 2010.

Production

Aside from its slick production, *Extraloveable* is interesting because it introduces Prince's new protégé, singer Andy Allo, who joined the ranks of the NPG as a guitarist and backing vocalist on the Welcome 2 America Euro Tour in June 2011. Here, Allo sings a rap part, which was later pulled from the third version of the song when it was included by Prince on his album *HitnRun Phase Two* in 2015, under the name *Xtraloveable*. Allo left the NPG in 2012 to focus on her solo career, especially her album *Superconductor*, which was released by NPG Records on 20 November that same year. In 2015, the streaming platform Tidal provided its members with Allo's acoustic album *Oui Can Luv*, which was recorded as a duet with Prince and contained numerous covers, including *Love Is A Losing Game*, by Amy Winehouse, and *Waiting in Vain*, by Bob Marley. Pulled from Tidal after only 12 hours, the album became a coveted bootleg, and fans are still waiting for The Prince Estate to release it officially.

WHILE MY GUITAR GENTLY WEEPS

(TOM PETTY AND FRIENDS)

George Harrison / 6'20

Musicians: Tom Petty: vocals, 12-string acoustic guitar, backing vocals / **Jeff Lynne:** vocals, electric guitar, backing vocals / **Marc Mann:** electric guitar / **Dhani Harrison:** electric guitar, backing vocals / **Prince:** electric guitar / **Scott Thurston:** bass / **Steve Ferrone:** drums / **Steve Winwood:** synthesizers / **Jeff Young:** piano / **Jim Capaldi:** percussion / **Recording: Waldorf Astoria, New York:** 15 March 2004 / **Technical team: Producer:** ? (not confirmed) / **Recording engineer:** ? (not confirmed)
The Best of Rock and Roll Hall of Fame + Museum **(compilation) / Released in the USA by The Rock and Roll Hall of Fame Foundation/ Time Life:** 15 March 2011 (CD ref.: 26397-D) / **Best chart ranking in the USA:** did not make the charts

On 15 March 2011, The Rock and Roll Hall of Fame Foundation and Time Life Records published an anthology of the best performances from artist inauguration ceremonies at the Rock and Roll Hall of Fame in Cleveland. Inevitably, the sleeve of *While My Guitar Gently Weeps* by The Beatles, performed by Tom Petty and Friends on 15 March 2004, was included in the compilation. Of course, that was the night the pantheon of American rock was inaugurating Prince, among other artists, and the night he performed one of the most memorable solos of his career. Joel Gallen, the show's producer, reported some emotional memories of that night, the two main guests, Tom Petty and Prince, having since departed this world. "They never rehearsed it," Gallen explained in 2020. "[Prince] never really showed us what he was going to do, and he left, basically telling me, the producer of the show, not to worry. And the rest is history. It became one of the most satisfying musical moments in my history of watching and producing live music."[258]

GIVIN EM WHAT THEY LOVE

(JANELLE MONÁE FEATURING PRINCE)

Charles Joseph II, Janelle Monáe, Nathaniel Irvin III, Terrence L Brown, Chuck Lightning, Nate "Rocket" Wonder, Prince / 4'26

Musicians: Janelle Monáe: vocals, backing vocals / **Prince:** vocals, electric guitar, bass, backing vocals / **Nate "Rocket" Wonder:** electric guitar, bass, drums, piano, percussion, backing vocals / **Kellindo Parker:** electric guitar / **Lance Powlis:** trumpet / **Kebbi Williams:** saxophone, transverse flute / **Christopher Burns:** trombone / **Jason P Freeman:** trumpet / **Jerry E Freeman:** trumpet / **Terrence L Brown:** organ / **Grace Shim:** cello / **Alexander Page:** violin / **Roman GianArthur:** backing vocals / **Recording: Wondaland Recording Studios, Atlanta, Georgia:** 2012 / **Paisley Park, Chanhassen, Minnesota:** 2012 / **Technical team: Producers:** Janelle Monáe, Nate "Rocket" Wonder, Chuck Lightning, Roman GianArthur, Mitch Martin, Sean Combs / **Recording engineers:** Janelle Monáe, Nate "Rocket" Wonder, Roman GianArthur / **Brass arrangements:** Nate "Rocket" Wonder / **String arrangements:** Nate "Rocket" Wonder
Janelle Monáe *The Electric Lady* (album): / Released in the USA by Bad Boy Entertainment/Wondaland: 10 September 2013 (LP ref.: 536211-1; CD ref.: 536210-2) / **Released in Europe by Bad Boy Entertainment/Wondaland:** 9 September 2013 (LP ref.: 7567-86774-8; CD ref.: 7567-86840-5) / **Best chart ranking in the USA:** 5 / **Best chart ranking in the UK:** 14

After producing *The ArchAndroid* in 2010, her first album with experimental sound textures and soul, rap, and pop influences, the talented Janelle Monáe prepared to make a follow-up in 2012. Her artistic references were as curious as Tim Burton and Steven Spielberg, two directors known for their highly developed fantasy universes. Also announcing her admiration for David Bowie and Prince, Monáe paid tribute onstage to the latter during the tenth BET Awards ceremony, which took place on 27 June 2010 at the Shrine Auditorium, in Los Angeles. There she performed a remarkable cover of *Let's Go Crazy*, right in front of Prince who was sitting in the audience. He was impressed with her unique stage presence and invited her to sing occasionally with him during the Welcome 2 America Tour and the Welcome 2 America Euro Tour. The two artists had such a good relationship that Monáe asked Prince to perform on her following album, which she recorded in the studios of her label, the Wondaland Arts Society, which was located, in her words, in the fictional world of Metropolis, of which she said: "It's the largest city in the world, but you can only see it by closing your eyes."[307] The song *Givin' 'Em What They Love* was recorded in 2012, then sent to Prince, who added a few guitar and bass overdubs, but also some vocal overdubs, enriching the song with a verse written by Janelle Monáe herself, as she explained in 2014. "He's a friend, he's a mentor, and I was very honored and humbled to have his presence on the album. That third verse on *Givin' 'Em What They Love*, I wrote that for him [...] It was a very cosmic and very incredible experience."[308]

Original, talented, and independent—three adjectives that describe the singer Janelle Monáe.

PRINCE & 3RDEYEGIRL

PLECTRUMELECTRUM

Wow · Pretzelbodylogic · Aintturninround · Plectrumelectrum
Whitecaps · Fixurlifeup · Boytrouble · Stopthistrain · Anotherlove
Tictactoe · Marz · Funknroll

Released in the USA by NPG Records/Warner Bros. Records:
30 September 2014 (CD); November 2014 (LP) [CD ref: 545610-2; LP ref: 2-545610]
Released in the UK by NPG Records/Warner Bros. Records:
29 September 2014 (CD); November 2014 (LP) [CD ref.: 9362-49333-5;
LP ref.: 9362-49333-1]
Best chart ranking in the USA: 8
Best chart ranking in the UK: 11

Having avoided it throughout his career, Prince proudly sports an Afro hairstyle.

Overleaf: Prince with one of his Vox HDC-77 guitars onstage at the Smukfest in Skanderborg, Denmark, on 7 August 2013.

FOR PRINCE ADDICTS

In March 2013, when Prince appeared on *Late Night with Jimmy Fallon* along with 3rdEyeGirl, he played two new guitars. He used his own Vox HDC-77 for *Screwdriver*, but he borrowed the one he played for *Bambi* from The Roots guitarist, "Captain" Kirk Douglas. At the end of the track, Prince threw the 1961 Epiphone Crestwood Custom in the air, thinking a roadie would catch it, but the beautiful vintage 6-string crashed to the ground and broke in two, much to Douglas's despair. Oops, sorry, send Prince the repair bill...

BIRTH OF 3RDEYEGIRL

2014

"I love this band," Prince said of the New Power Generation in 1994. "I just wish they were all girls."[309] This idea of an all-female backing band is something that Prince had been thinking about ever since he started out. Back in the days of The Revolution, Wendy Melvoin and Lisa Coleman had been given the biggest roles in the band, then it was Sheila E. in his next band, followed by Kat Dyson (guitar), Rhonda Smith (bass), rad. (synthesizers), and Candy Dulfer (saxophone) in the many lineups of the NPG over the years. In May 2012, as his Welcome 2 Australia Tour came to an end, Prince decided to make a radical change by putting the New Power Generation, the shape-shifting band that had accompanied him around the world since 1990, on hold. Bassist Ida Nielsen stayed with him as he began to look around for new band members, specifically women.

A family affair

Twenty-two-year-old drummer Hannah Welton was discovered on YouTube, where she had been posting videos of herself playing along to Prince's songs. In the spring of 2012, Prince sent her a rather vague e-mail, praising her musical talents and summoning her to Paisley Park for a jam session. "I didn't know if there were going to be other drummers [like an open call] so I didn't know what to expect," she explained. "I just went with an open mind and was just going to do my thing."[310] As the months went by, the harmonious relationship that developed between Prince, Ida Nielsen, and the drummer was such that Prince asked Welton and her husband, a 25-year-old musician and apprentice producer called Joshua, to help him find a guitarist just for the pleasure of playing with new artists. In November 2012, the couple picked out a Canadian session musician called Donna Grantis, a jazz and blues 6-string guitarist who fronted the Donna Grantis Electric Band and was influenced by Jimi Hendrix, Jimmy Page, John Scofield, and Buddy Guy. "So they searched the Internet and they came across some of my videos and sent them on to Prince,"[311] Grant explained. She traveled to Chanhassen and after a 12-hour jam session, during which the chemistry was palpable, an informal band was born and the team quickly became friends. Hannah and Joshua Welton were devout Christians who became close to Prince through their faith. Meanwhile, Donna Grantis's boyfriend Trevor Guy became a trusted member of Prince's team and was given the keys to The Vault, subsequently becoming the creative director of The Prince Estate.

Informal rehearsals of Plectrumelectrum

From December 2012, Prince and his musicians began rehearsing intensely six days a week to prepare for the Live Out Loud Tour that they were hoping to launch a few months later. As well as learning their boss's repertoire, these were also creative sessions where Prince threw ideas at the musicians without knowing where they would lead. "Our amps were mic'd, but we didn't even realize that we were recording an album [...]," recalls Grantis. "Prince would come in and he'd teach us some grooves and then he'd say, 'Okay, let's record this.'"[311] On 18 January 2013, as part of the Three Nights with Paisley Park concert series at the Dakota Jazz Club & Restaurant in Minneapolis, Prince and his musicians performed their first show together. They were well received, which further convinced Prince of the potential of his new backing band. By then, Prince was frequently referring to the embryonic 3rdEyeGirl concept. On 22 February 2013, a first track, called *Live Out Loud* and featuring Hannah Welton as vocalist, was released on a brand-new website

Donna Grantis, Ida Nielsen, and Prince performing onstage at the Vogue Theatre in Vancouver on 15 April 2013.

called 3rdEyeGirl.com. On 13 March 2013, photographer Madison Dubé shot a video of the quartet in the studio performing a new track called *Plectrumelectrum*. But it was when they appeared on *Late Night with Jimmy Fallon* on 1 March that the musicians really became aware of what was in the offing. "We discovered that we were officially called 3RDEYEGIRL,"[85] said Donna Grantis. On 15 April 2013, the Live Out Loud Tour began in Canada and the United States, followed by a series of European concerts over the summer.

2014

Back with Warner Bros. Records

While rumors of a new Prince album, the first since 2010's *20Ten*, were doing the rounds, an unexpected reconciliation took place between Prince and his former record company Warner Bros. Records. In early 2014, Prince began talks with the label about a joint approach to the anniversary of the *Purple Rain* album. Both parties agreed on a new contract that would involve Warner Bros. Records working with Prince on a prestigious reissue of the cult album. In exchange, Prince would release two new albums simultaneously and finally get all his master tapes back. "Everyone at Warner Bros. Records is delighted to be working with Prince once again,"[312] Cameron Strang, head of the label, announced in a press release. Following a European spring tour called Hit and Run Part II, the news of these new albums broke on 25 August 2014 on *Good Morning America*, filmed for the occasion in New York's Times Square with most of the advertising screens showing images of Prince. It was Donna Grantis who had the honor of declaring: "The big announcement is that Prince will be releasing new music very soon."[313] Hannah Welton continued: "It's so awesome because it's actually a double surprise, there's gonna be two albums released. One of them is a Prince solo album called *Art Official Age* and then the second one is the album we play on called *Plectrumelectrum*."[313] On 30 September, the two albums were released in the USA (the day after the UK release), giving Prince the opportunity to showcase the two extremes of a musical spectrum he had exploring since 1978: an explosive rock 'n' roll album and a second modern-sounding album created with his new collaborator, the young Joshua Welton, to whom he had entrusted the keys to his Paisley Park studios.

VOX

3RDEYEGIRL—from left: Donna Grantis (guitar), Hannah Welton (drums), and Ida Nielsen (bass guitar)—with Kiran Sharma, Prince's manager.

RICH FRIENDS

Prince / 5'23

Musicians: Prince: vocals, electric guitar, acoustic guitar, bass, drums, programming, piano, synthesizers, backing vocals / **Shelby J.:** backing vocals / **Elisa Dease:** backing vocals / **Liv Warfield:** backing vocals / **Recording: Paisley Park, Chanhassen, Minnesota:** 2010 / **Technical team: Producer:** Prince / **Recording engineer:** ? (not confirmed) / **Broadcast on Europe 1, 8 October 2010**

On 8 October 2010, while Prince was traveling through Europe, the radio station Europe 1 announced the forthcoming release of a companion piece for the album *20Ten*, released the previous July, called *20Ten Deluxe*. Along with the announcement, the presenter played an unreleased track from the album that was earmarked as Prince's next single: *Rich Friends*. The gospel-sounding track suited the production of *20Ten* and was subsequently broadcast on KTU.com, the website of the American radio station 103.5 KTU. Alas, Prince quickly abandoned the *20TenDeluxe* project.

MIDNIGHT BLUES

Prince / 7'05

Musicians: Prince: vocals, spoken voice, electric guitar / **Donna Grantis:** electric guitar / **Ida Nielsen:** bass / **Hannah Welton:** drums, spoken voice / **Recording: Paisley Park, Chanhassen, Minnesota:** June 2013 / **Technical team: Producer:** Prince / **Recording engineer:** ? (not confirmed) / **Broadcast on 3rdEye TV, 28 June 2013**

On 12 June 2013, Prince launched a web TV channel called 3rdEye TV on LiveStream.com. From 19 June, Prince, accompanied by 3rdEyeGirl, broadcast a number of jam sessions, rehearsals, and live performances of songs from his repertoire. This went on throughout the summer of 2013, then continued intermittently up to July 2014. *Midnight Blues*, an improvised blues number, was the first track to be broadcast on the platform, on 28 June 2013. The line "Lost my job at Mickie D's/For giving away too much food for free," which introduces the song, resurfaced on *Marz*, on the *Plectrumelectrum* album.

MOON DROP

Prince / 3'54

Musicians: Prince: electric guitar, organ / **Donna Grantis:** electric guitar / **Ida Nielsen:** bass / **Hannah Welton:** drums / **Recording: Paisley Park, Chanhassen, Minnesota:** 2 July 2013 / **Technical team: Producer:** Prince / **Recording engineer:** ? (not confirmed) / **Broadcast on 3rdEye TV, 2 July 2013**

Moon Drop is an instrumental track recorded just before *The Third Heart of the Octopus Menstrual Cycle Originally Dropped from the Moon* during the 2 July 2013 session. It was broadcast on 3rdEye TV on 2 July 2013.

THE THIRD HEART OF THE OCTOPUS MENSTRUAL CYCLE ORIGINALLY DROPPED FROM THE MOON

Prince / 1'02

Musicians: Prince: electric guitar, organ / **Donna Grantis:** electric guitar / **Ida Nielsen:** bass / **Hannah Welton:** drums / **Recording: Paisley Park, Chanhassen, Minnesota:** 2 July 2013 / **Technical team: Producer:** Prince / **Recording engineer:** ? (not confirmed) / **Broadcast on 3rdEye TV, 2 July 2013**

The Third Heart of the Octopus Menstrual Cycle Originally Dropped from the Moon was broadcast live during the sessions that also produced *Moon Drop*, *Menstrual Cycle*, and *Octopus Heart*, and its name is a combination of the three other tracks. It is an instrumental piece with Hendrix influences, reminiscent of the swooping guitars of 2009's *LotusFlow3r* album.

The Soul Children performed *The Sweeter He Is* in 1969.

OCTOPUS HEART

Prince / 4'18

Musicians: Prince: electric guitar, Fender Rhodes piano / Donna Grantis: electric guitar / Ida Nielsen: bass / Hannah Welton: drums / **Recording:** Paisley Park, Chanhassen, Minnesota: 1–2 July 2013 / **Technical team:** Producer: Prince / Recording engineer: ? (not confirmed) / **Broadcast** on 3rdEye TV, 1 July 2013

The instrumental track *Octopus Heart* was broadcast on 3rdEye TV on the night of 1–2 July (recording of the track started before midnight and ended afterward). The song was subsequently made available for download on 3rdEyeGirl's SoundCloud page on 3 July.

MENSTRUAL CYCLE

Prince / 10'32

Musicians: Prince: electric guitar, organ / Donna Grantis: electric guitar / Ida Nielsen: bass / Hannah Welton: drums / **Recording:** Paisley Park, Chanhassen, Minnesota: 1–2 July 2013 / **Technical team:** Producer: Prince / Recording engineer: ? (not confirmed) / **Broadcast** on 3rdEye TV, 3 July 2013

On 3 July 2013, Prince himself announced on Twitter that *Octopus Heart* and *Menstrual Cycle* had been uploaded to SoundCloud, giving disappointed fans who had missed the nightly 3rdEye TV broadcasts a second chance to enjoy these two instrumentals free of charge.

INDIFFERENCE

Prince / 3'09

Musicians: Prince: vocals, acoustic guitar / Donna Grantis: acoustic guitar / Ida Nielsen: bass / Hannah Welton: percussion / **Recording:** Paisley Park, Chanhassen, Minnesota: 2014 / **Technical team:** Producer: Prince / Recording engineer: ? (not confirmed) / **Broadcast** on Yahoo! Live, 30 September 2014

On 30 September 2014, at Paisley Park, Prince launched *Plectrumelectrumartofficialage* with a grand ceremony to celebrate the simultaneous release of his two new albums. The event was broadcast on the events promoter Nation's Yahoo! Live channel and gave fans around the world a chance to take a peek behind the scenes at Paisley Park as well as attend various Prince & 3rdEyeGirl concerts. For the occasion, the artist and his musicians performed *Indifference*, an acoustic track which is very different from the quartet's usual rock productions, but still very enjoyable. The song was broadcast again on the streaming platform Tidal from 7 September 2015.

THE SWEETER SHE IS

Isaac Hayes, David Porter / 7'29

Musicians: Prince: vocals, synthesizer / Donna Grantis: electric guitar / Ida Nielsen: bass / Hannah Welton: drums / **Recording:** Paisley Park, Chanhassen, Minnesota: October 2013 / **Technical team:** Producer: Prince / Recording engineer: ? (not confirmed) / **Available for download** on 3RDEYEGIRL's Twitter account, 16 October 2013

Here Prince presents us with a cover version of the Soul Children's 1969 hit *The Sweeter He Is*. The song lends itself perfectly to Prince's repertoire and proves that his backing band is not just a machine for producing overpowering rock 'n' roll. On 16 October, Prince asked his fans on Twitter which of them would be interested in receiving a new song. Twitter user @VanessaMpls3121 hit the jackpot and was PM-ed a WeTransfer link for the song that she shared with her followers at 2:44pm, tweeting "HERE IT IS—*The Sweeter She Is*."

DA BOURGEOISIE

Prince / 3'23

Musicians: Prince: vocals, electric guitar, bass / Hannah Welton: drums / Michael B Nelson: trombone / Steve Strand: trumpet / Dave Jensen: trumpet / Kenni Holmen: saxophone, flute / Kathy Jensen: saxophone, clarinet / **Recording:** Paisley Park, Chanhassen, Minnesota: 2013 / **Technical team:** Producer: Prince / Recording engineer: ? (not confirmed) / **Digital distribution** via 3rdEyeTunes.com, 25 November 2013

Once again, Prince used the 3RDEYEGIRL Twitter account on 18 November 2013 to ask his fans if they would like to be sent a new track. He picked @lylesmiles as the lucky recipient of a WeTransfer link to share with his followers. This was a demo version of a funk track, *Da Bourgeoisie*, which Prince immediately reworked, adding horns, before uploading it to 3rdEyeTunes.com and 3RDEYEGIRL's Facebook page. Like 1979's *Bambi*, the song expresses Prince's disapproval of two women in a relationship, and it attracted a lot of criticism from fans at the time.

BOYFRIEND

Prince / 3'08

Musicians: **Prince:** vocals, electric guitar, bass, drums, programming, synthesizers, backing vocals / **Michael B Nelson:** trombone / **Steve Strand:** trumpet / **Dave Jensen:** trumpet / **Kenni Holmen:** saxophone / **Kathy Jensen:** saxophone / **Recording:** Paisley Park, Chanhassen, Minnesota: 2012, 14 August 2012 (wind) / **Technical team:** Producer: Prince / Recording engineers: Ben Mühlethaler, Jamie Lewis / **Digital distribution** via 3rdEyeGirl.com, 15 February 2013

Prince launched 3rdEyeGirl.com on 5 February 2013. The website (working title: Project Screwdriver) was developed by Dave Meyer, Andy Wojtowski, and Larry Seth, and it was used to inform fans of upcoming Prince concert dates, with an option to download unreleased songs for $0.88 and videos for $1.77. This funk track proves, much to our delight, that Prince hadn't entirely replaced slap bass lines with the 3RDEYEGIRL's saturated guitars.

THAT GIRL THANG

Prince / 3'33

Musician: **Prince:** vocals, electric guitar / **Recording:** Paisley Park, Chanhassen, Minnesota: 17 February 2013 / **Technical team:** Producer: Prince / Recording engineer: Chris James / **Digital distribution** via 3rdEyeGirl.com, 18 February 2013

Prince met dancer Lala Escarzega in 2008, while he was still living at 77 Beverly Park in Los Angeles. In 2011, she was one of the silhouetted figures in the video for *Xtraloveable*, and she remained a close friend of Prince's until his death in 2016. On 22 November 2016, Escarzega confided on her Instagram account that Prince had written and recorded *That Girl Thang* for her, after she asked him one night for a song to help her sleep. "He gave this song to me the very next night," she explained. "There is also an instrumental of this that he gave me and I have no idea if it was ever released or not."[314] Recorded with recording engineer Chris James, this acoustic demo is a lullaby that many fans would love to have received from Prince!

LIVE OUT LOUD

Prince, Liv Warfield / 3'35

Musicians: **Hannah Welton:** vocals, drums / **Prince:** electric guitar, backing vocals / **Donna Grantis:** electric guitar / **Ida Nielsen:** bass / **Recording:** Paisley Park, Chanhassen, Minnesota: 2013 / **Technical team:** Producer: Prince / Recording engineer: Chris James / **Digital distribution** via 3rdEyeGirl.com, 22 February 2013

On the morning of 22 February 2013, the website TheCurrent.org announced to users that they would be able to put faces to the 3RDEYEGIRL project they'd been hearing about for several weeks, thanks to the drip-drip of information Prince had been feeding fans. The song *Live Out Loud* was made available for download on 3rdEyeGirl.com that morning and the accompanying video was posted on the YouTube page of the same name, revealing a new, very rock sound played by an equally rocking female trio. Although the Avril Lavigne-style, pop-rock track was far removed from the usual Prince universe, it alerted fans to the existence of the band 3RDEYEGIRL, who then accompanied Prince a few days later on *Late Night with Jimmy Fallon*. Drummer Hannah Welton (frequently referred to by her maiden name, Hannah Ford) sings on the track. The lyrics were by Liv Warfield and the music by Prince.

In 2011, Ledisi had already sung alongside Prince in *Big City*, but *Ain't Gonna Miss U When U're Gone* was a joint effort that wasn't released until 2015 on the *Hitnrun Phase Two* album.

AIN'T GONNA MISS U WHEN U'RE GONE

(PRINCE FEATURING LEDISI)

Prince / 6'01

Musicians: Prince: vocals, spoken word, rap, bass, drums, programming, synthesizers, backing vocals / Ledisi: backing vocals / Michael B Nelson: trombone / Steve Strand: trumpet / Dave Jensen: trumpet / Kenni Holmen: saxophone / Kathy Jensen: saxophone / **Recording:** Paisley Park, Chanhassen, Minnesota: 2013 / **Technical team:** Producer: Prince / Recording engineers: Chris James, Ben Mühlethaler, Jamie Lewis / **Digital distribution** via 3rdEyeGirl.com, 12 June 2013

The track Prince uploaded to 3rdEyeGirl.com on 12 June 2013 was a far cry from the pop world of 3RDEYEGIRL, proving to his fans that his love for funk was not dead. Using the vocals from *Bob George* (*The Black Album*, 1994) to create a very successful rap, he also enlists the services of soul singer Ledisi (spotted among Prince's backing vocalists on *The Tonight Show with Jay Leno* on 25 April 2008) to deliver some heartfelt backing vocals on the track. "We're friends," she said. "He'll call and say come hang out, and next thing I'm singing backgrounds or doing a duet. I won't talk about the process, but we had a lot of fun. Prince is amazing in the studio. I just love Paisley Park, it feels good there."[315]

After working his socks off on the maintenance of the 3rdEyeGirl.com website in 2013, Dave Meyer admitted that he was pleased to have collaborated with Prince but disappointed never to have met him. "The only conversations we had with him were via his manager over the phone ([...] He'd say something, which we could hear, and we'd have her answer for us.)"[316]

FALLINLOVE2NITE
(PRINCE FEATURING ZOOEY DESCHANEL)
Prince / 3'18

Musicians
Prince: vocals, electric guitar, bass, programming, synthesizers, backing vocals
Zooey Deschanel: vocals
Joshua Welton: synthesizers, programming
Michael B Nelson: trombone
Steve Strand: trumpet
Dave Jensen: trumpet
Kenni Holmen: saxophone
Kathy Jensen: saxophone
STRINGenius: string orchestra

Recording
Paisley Park, Chanhassen, Minnesota: 2013
Bone 2 B Wild Music Studio, Minneapolis: December 2013 (brass)
The Brewhouse Recording Studio, Minneapolis: December 2013 (strings)

Technical team
Producer: Prince, Joshua Welton
Recording engineer: Joshua Welton
Brass arrangements: Michael B Nelson
String arrangements: Adi Yeshaya

World digital release by NPG Records/EPIC: 17 March 2014
Best chart ranking in the USA: did not make the charts
Best chart ranking in the UK: did not make the charts

Genesis
It was no secret that Prince loved the hilarious American TV sitcom *New Girl*, starring the bubbly Zooey Deschanel and broadcast on Fox TV from 2011. The comedy series followed the friendships and romances of a group of thirty-somethings living in Los Angeles and was a huge hit in the United States. When Deschanel received an email from Prince's manager Kiran Sharma in September 2013, telling her he was a fan of the show, the idea of Prince working with the program's production team was broached. The script of an upcoming episode was rewritten for him, and on 14 February 2014, the same night as the 48th Super Bowl final, episode 14 in season 3 of *New Girl* (which was called *Prince*) was broadcast on American television. It was a good strategic move for Prince, giving him huge visibility, as 26 million viewers tuned into the show that night, compared to the usual 2.5 million.

In the episode, Jess, played by Zooey Deschanel, goes to a party at Prince's house in Los Angeles, where he advises her to tell her boyfriend Nick, played by actor Jake Johnson, what she feels about him. Prince puts in an impeccable performance as the ultimate pop star and portrays himself with obvious humor and self-mockery. At the end of the episode, Prince invites Jess onstage to sing *Fallinlove2nite*, a song he had never performed before. Up onstage with them are Liv Warfield and his new team, the three musicians from 3RDEYEGIRL. The drummer's husband, Joshua Welton, who would later become Prince's coproducer and arranger, played keyboards for this musical finale.

Production
Zooey Deschanel is a well-known actress and a singer in the band She & Him alongside guitarist Mr Ward. With four albums to their name, the duo has a solid reputation on the independent folk scene in the United States. When Prince asked Deschanel to record the choruses of *Fallinlove2nite*, she accepted straightaway. Released as a single on 17 March 2014, the song reappeared in 2015 on the highly electronic *Hitnrun Phase One*, but this time without the actress's vocal track. The

Prince flanked by the actors Zooey Deschanel and Jake Johnson who unforgettably played Jess and Nick in the TV series *New Girl*.

string arrangements are by Adi Yeshaya of the group STRINGenius. Like Michael B Nelson, Prince's brass arranger, composer Yeshaya is from Minneapolis, so he was able to respond quickly when he received a request from Nelson in late 2013. "I got an e-mail from him [...]," Yeshaya said, "basically expressing that Prince is looking for someone who is willing to study the approach that Clare Fischer took in his arrangements [...] While it was a pretty tall order, I felt pretty natural with this because I'm a huge Clare Fischer fan."[317]

Liv Warfield, indispensable backing vocalist of the NPG from 2010 to 2014.

2014

WOW

Prince & 3RDEYEGIRL / 4'27

Musicians: Prince: vocals, spoken voice, electric guitar, acoustic guitar, backing vocals / **Donna Grantis:** electric guitar, backing vocals / **Ida Nielsen:** bass, backing vocals / **Hannah Welton:** drums, backing vocals / **Recording:** **Paisley Park, Chanhassen, Minnesota:** 2012–2014 / **Technical team: Producer:** Prince / **Recording engineers:** Chris James, Jamie Lewis, Ben Mühlethaler, Joshua Welton

The Unexpected, the second album by Liv Warfield, a prominent NPG backing vocalist, was released on 18 February 2014. The opus contains two tracks by Prince, as Warfield explained when the record was released. "We cowrote one song, which is *Your Show*, and he wrote the title track, *The Unexpected*," Warfield says. "I came up with the title, *The Unexpected* [...] He pretty much surprised me and came up with just this amazing, amazing song."[318] Warfield's second surprise was when a version of her song performed by Prince and 3RDEYEGIRL appeared on *Plectrumelectrum*. Renamed *Wow*, in reference to the lyrics in the chorus ("You can call it the unexpected or you can call it 'Wow!'"), it is a close reworking of Warfield's version that ditches the original soulfulness in favor of the 3RDEYEGIRL's signature rock 'n' roll edginess. The song was recorded in a single take, although the musicians thought it was just a rehearsal session at the time. "We worked fast," recalls Donna Grantis. "I don't think we even played *Wow* all the way through a single time before the tape was rolling."[181] Ida Nielsen added: "We did this album old school, live, all in the same room, so if someone made a mistake everything had to be redone [...] We thought we were learning new material to play live. But all of a sudden, he said: 'Let's make a sequence.'"

Single

PRETZELBODYLOGIC

Prince & 3RDEYEGIRL / 3'26

Musicians: Prince: vocals, electric guitar, backing vocals / **Donna Grantis:** vocals, electric guitar, backing vocals / **Ida Nielsen:** vocals, bass, backing vocals / **Hannah Welton:** vocals, drums, backing vocals / **Recording:** **Paisley Park, Chanhassen, Minnesota:** 2012–2013 / **Technical team: Producer:** Prince / **Recording engineers:** Chris James, Jamie Lewis, Ben Mühlethaler, Joshua Welton
Single: Digital release by NPG Records: 3 February 2014 / **Best chart ranking in the USA:** did not make the charts / **Best chart ranking in the UK:** 90

Pretzelbodylogic was the first single released to publicize the forthcoming *Plectrumelectrum* album, and it was then that the three musicians, who had thus far been kept in the dark, realized for the first time that Prince had secretly been intending to release a full-length album by the band. "I think when it hit me that we were making a record was when we recorded *Pretzelbodylogic*," says Hannah Welton, "because we recorded the song musically and then laid vocals for it. Once we realized that vocals were being laid, it was a 3RDEYEGIRL song."[320] The track was released in the UK as a promotional CD on 31 March 2014, with a note to the media from Prince's UK press agent, Joe Bennett, which referenced the track *Wow*: *"Expect the Unexpected."*[321]

Donna Grantis in the throes of a guitar solo at the Billboard Music Awards in Las Vegas on 19 May 2013.

AINTTURNINROUND

Prince & 3RDEYEGIRL / 3'01

Musicians: **Hannah Welton:** vocals, drums, backing vocals / **Prince:** spoken voice, electric guitar, backing vocals / **Donna Grantis:** electric guitar, backing vocals / **Ida Nielsen:** bass, backing vocals / **Recording:** **Paisley Park, Chanhassen, Minnesota:** 2012–2014 / **Technical team:** **Producer:** Prince / **Recording engineers:** Chris James, Jamie Lewis, Ben Mühlethaler, Joshua Welton

Prince delegates the vocals on this track (along with two others on the album) to drummer Hannah Welton, just as he also handed over most of the guitar solos on the *Plectrumelectrum* sessions to Donna Grantis. The young guitarist, recognizable for her sidecut hairstyle, achieved the powerful sound on this track by plugging her purple PRS CE22 guitar (upgraded with PRS 57/08 pickups) into early 1970s Traynor YBA-1s amps. The latter had been modified by Toronto technician Pat Furlan, to whom she had entrusted her gear for many years. "I used those on the recording because I really wanted to have that fat, warm vintage tone, but that has a lot of articulation," she says. "I love to be able to hit the guitar hard and hear some breakup in the tone, or play it softly and hear all of those accents."[311] During the European concert series in early 2014, Grantis opted for a gold PRS 513, which she plugged into a bevy of effects pedals, including two delays (a Line 6 DL4 and a TC Electronic Flashback), an Electro Harmonix Q-Tron filter, a Fulltone Octafuzz, and a Fulltone Deja Vibe vibrato/chorus. Enough to wake the dead!

After her departure from the group The Chalice, the singer Lizzo was to pursue a triumphant career all over the world.

PLECTRUMELECTRUM

Prince & 3RDEYEGIRL / 4'51

Musicians: **Prince:** electric guitar / **Donna Grantis:** electric guitar / **Ida Nielsen:** bass / **Hannah Welton:** drums / **Recording:** **Paisley Park, Chanhassen, Minnesota:** 2013 / **Technical team:** **Producer:** Prince / **Recording engineers:** Chris James, Jamie Lewis, Ben Mühlethaler, Joshua Welton

You'd be forgiven for thinking you're listening to guitarist Tom Morello and his band Rage Against the Machine with this explosive *Plectrumelectrum* track, but you aren't! Prince is indeed at the helm of this instrumental recorded in a single take in early 2013. It also references Jimi Hendrix in the musicians' flawless rhythm and tempo as they perform the riff in unison on this song, which was composed by Donna Grantis but credited to Prince & 3RDEYEGIRL. An almost identical version of the song, then called *Elektra*, had previously been recorded by the Donna Grantis Electric Band and featured on their 2012 album *Suites*, released by Diamond Gem Records. Hannah Welton reproduces to perfection the original score of the song first recorded by drummer Roger Travassos.

WHITECAPS

Prince & 3RDEYEGIRL / 3'42

Musicians: **Hannah Welton:** vocals, drums / **Prince:** electric guitar, acoustic guitar, backing vocals / **Donna Grantis:** electric guitar, backing vocals / **Ida Nielsen:** bass, backing vocals / **Recording:** **Paisley Park, Chanhassen, Minnesota:** 2012–2014 / **Technical team:** **Producer:** Prince / **Recording engineers:** Chris James, Jamie Lewis, Ben Mühlethaler, Joshua Welton

Hannah Welton once again takes the mic on this ballad, which was made available to fans as a download on 1 September 2014, after pre-orders for *Plectrumelectrum* opened on the website 3rdEyeGirl.com on 25 August. The musicians worked on the instrumental part of the track without the drummer realizing she would be singing on it; they rehearsed at length before the instrumentals were committed to tape. "During the recording of Whitecaps [...]," Grantis said, "I remember Prince saying 'Call me when you have it!' and he left Ida, Hannah and I to record as a rhythm section while he played ping-pong."[181] The musicians have spoken about how they spent countless hours playing ping-pong—one of Prince's favorite sports—in Paisley Park's studio B where the table was set up, while Prince and Joshua Welton were mixing *Art Official Age*, which was produced at the same time as *Plectrumelectrum*.

Single

FIXURLIFEUP

Prince & 3RDEYEGIRL / 3'12

Musicians: **Prince:** vocals, spoken voice, electric guitar, backing vocals / **Donna Grantis:** electric guitar / **Ida Nielsen:** bass / **Hannah Welton:** drums, backing vocals / **Recording:** **Paisley Park, Chanhassen, Minnesota:** 2012–2013 / **Technical team:** **Producer:** Prince / **Recording engineers:** Chris James, Jamie Lewis, Ben Mühlethaler, Joshua Welton
Single: **Digital release by NPG Records:** 16 May 2013 / **Best chart ranking in the USA:** did not make the charts / **Best chart ranking in the UK:** did not make the charts

With an intro reminiscent of Queen's *Flash*, *Fixurlifeup* includes pop, rock 'n' roll, and funk rhythms, and also offers some welcome advice on how to achieve personal balance. "Don't worry about what the crowd does/Just worry 'bout being good at what u love," Prince advises in a deep voice at the end of the song. When the track was released as a single on 16 May 2013, it was credited to 3RDEYEGIRL, with Prince relegated to *featuring* status. While this shows Prince initially believed he was producing an all-female band that didn't include him, this would soon be corrected when the single was credited to Prince & 3RDEYEGIRL, thus confirming what this project in the making actually was.

BOYTROUBLE

Prince & 3RDEYEGIRL / 3'52

Musicians: Lizzo: rap, backing vocals / Sophia Eris: rap, backing vocals / Claire de Lune: vocals, backing vocals / Prince: electric guitar / Donna Grantis: electric guitar / Ida Nielsen: bass / Hannah Welton: drums / **Recording:** Paisley Park, Chanhassen, Minnesota: 2012–2013 (backing tracks), April 2013 (vocals) / **Technical team:** Producer: Prince / Recording engineers: Chris James, Jamie Lewis, Ben Mühlethaler, Joshua Welton

Melissa Viviane Jefferson was born in Detroit in 1988 and moved to Minneapolis in 2011 where she developed a taste for singing and hip-hop. Having changed her name to Lizzo, she met up with rapper Sophia Eris and singer Claire de Lune, with whom she formed a group called The Chalice. After releasing their first single, *Push It*, in 2011, the trio were featured on local TV station Kare 11, and Prince was watching with interest. The women were invited to Paisley Park in April 2013, where they met Joshua Welton who was working as Prince's recording engineer on *Plectrumelectrum* and *Art Official Age*. Welton played *Boytrouble* for them, muting the previously recorded vocal tracks and explaining to them that they had three hours to make the song their own and lay down whatever they wanted on it. Once the takes were complete, Welton went off, leaving the three singers on their own in the studio. Sophia Eris (real name Lauren Alford) spilled her coffee on the studio carpet, infuriating Lizzo and sending the three already intimidated women into a state of panic: "Lauren, I will murder you if you get us kicked out of Paisley, oh my God,"[322] Claire de Lune yelled at her friend, who was cleaning the floor as best she could. In the corner of the studio where he was premixing the song with the new vocal tracks, Welton answered a ringing phone several times, holding the handset up to the speakers so he could play the finished song to a mysterious caller. "You like it?"[322] the recording engineer asked, then waited for an answer and hung up. Prince approved the vocal take but did not attend the recording session with the female trio. Lizzo, meanwhile, went on to achieve international success in 2019 with the hit single *Juice* from her album *Cuz I Love You*, which was released the same year. She acknowledges Prince's legacy in her professional and artistic journey. "[Prince's death] made me dedicate myself to positive music for sure," she explained in 2016. "[...] Because Prince had dedicated his whole legacy to celebrating women, celebrating women of color, and celebrating positive music and I'm gonna uphold that."[323]

Alice Smith whose song *Another Love* was revisited by Prince & 3RDEYEGIRL on *Plectrumelectrum*.

2014

STOPTHISTRAIN

Prince & 3RDEYEGIRL / 3'40

Musicians: **Hannah Welton:** vocals, drums / **Joshua Welton:** vocals, programming, synthesizers, backing vocals / **Prince:** vocals, electric guitar, backing vocals / **Donna Grantis:** electric guitar / **Ida Nielsen:** bass / **Recording:** **Paisley Park, Chanhassen, Minnesota:** 2012–2014 / **Technical team:** **Producer:** Prince / **Recording engineers:** Chris James, Jamie Lewis, Ben Mühlethaler, Joshua Welton

Far from the rock 'n' roll productions of the rest of the album, *Stopthistrain* heralds the arrival of producer Joshua Welton in the Prince universe, and his touch is recognizable here. An alchemist of brilliant, modern sonic textures and production as precise as a swishing Japanese sword, Welton accompanies his wife Hannah on vocals as well as taking on artistic production duties for the track, though his coproducer status would only be recognized officially on *Art Official Age*. When Prince was asked by *Rolling Stone* magazine's Brian Hiatt in 2014 whether the song, which for a while was intended as a single, might have been a hit on the radio if no one had known of the Prince connection, he replied: "That's kind of the blessing and a curse these days." He continued: "[...] that I'm competing with [my] older music. And I don't know anybody who has to do that. They always play Beyoncé's latest track. But I go on *Oprah* and they want me to play what they remember."[303]

ANOTHERLOVE

Alice Smith, Rebecca Jordan, Reginald Perry, Prince / 4'15

Musicians: **Prince:** vocals, electric guitar / **Donna Grantis:** electric guitar, backing vocals / **Ida Nielsen:** bass, backing vocals / **Hannah Welton:** drums, backing vocals / **Recording:** **Paisley Park, Chanhassen, Minnesota:** 2012–2014 / **Technical team:** **Producer:** Prince / **Recording engineers:** Chris James, Jamie Lewis, Ben Mühlethaler, Joshua Welton

Anotherlove is undoubtedly the high point of *Plectrumelectrum*. It is a masterpiece of pop with its powerful, melodic choruses and perfectly executed vocal harmonies, and rivals the greatest contemporary rock songs with its rhythmic variations. As stated in the album booklet, this track is a loose adaptation of *Another Love*, recorded by American soul singer Alice Smith for her 2013 album *She*. However, Prince & 3RDEYEGIRL's version is more than just a cover, as it revisits the original and changes the lyrics as well as the harmonic range, giving it more melodic choruses supported by the powerful backing vocals of Hannah Welton and her bandmates. Alice Smith, whose original version is not well known to Prince fans, posted a moving message on her Instagram account on 7 July 2020, getting a little confused about Prince's discography, for which she can, of course, be forgiven: "Did you know? Prince covered my song *Another Love*. He changed some of the words and put it on his final album! And he sang it on @nbcsnl!!! Its probably THE most amazing thing about my music career [...]"[324] Listening to this potential hit raises one question: why on earth didn't Prince decide to release *Anotherlove* as a single?

As Prince and the musicians of 3RDEYEGIRL were recording the final backing tracks for *Anotherlove*, Prince, who had so far shared the album's 6-string scores with Donna Grantis, gave her the opportunity to record the closing solo herself. It was four o'clock in the morning at Paisley Park, and Grantis, flattered to be asked, gladly accepted. Aware that it had to be an epic ending, she told her boss she would spend the rest of the night working on it and record it the next day. "Prince has an unbelievable work ethic that rubs off on all of us," Grantis said, "but time exists in a different way at Paisley Park. Every day there are things to accomplish but it's not related to the hour. It's just: before the next resting period, we need to get this done."[319] Prince inevitably replied: "Let's do it now,"[311] as he pushed her to be more spontaneous in her artistic approach. "So I did it and I'm really proud of that solo. Prince has this way of really pulling out the best in everyone. I think that really comes with an adrenaline rush and a sense of urgency to really deliver."[311]

Robin Guthrie, Elizabeth Fraser, and Simon Raymonde from the Scottish group the Cocteau Twins, pictured here in 1993.

TICTACTOE

Prince & 3RDEYEGIRL / 3'37

Musicians: Prince: vocals, electric guitar, acoustic guitar, synthesizers, tambourine, backing vocals / **Donna Grantis:** electric guitar, backing vocals / **Ida Nielsen:** bass, backing vocals / **Hannah Welton:** drums, backing vocals / **Recording: Studio One, London:** February 2014 / **Technical team: Producer:** Prince / **Recording engineer:** ? (not confirmed)

Back in 1991, Prince had already expressed his admiration for the Scottish band the Cocteau Twins, even inviting them to join Paisley Park Records. They had politely refused, preferring to stay with their label 4AD, but that didn't stop Prince remaining a great admirer of their ethereal and atmospheric pop music. In February 2014, when Prince & 3RDEYEGIRL were in London for a series of concerts, they went to a party where the Cocteau Twins' music was being played. In the early hours of the morning, the team decided to rent Bryan Ferry's Studio One where they recorded *Tictactoe*, a ballad heavily influenced by the trio's music. "You can't understand the words of Cocteau Twins' songs," Prince said in 2014, "but their harmonies put you in a dreamlike state."[325]

MARZ

Prince & 3RDEYEGIRL / 1'48

Musicians: Prince: vocals, electric guitar, backing vocals / **Donna Grantis:** electric guitar, backing vocals / **Ida Nielsen:** bass, backing vocals / **Hannah Welton:** drums, backing vocals / **Recording: Paisley Park, Chanhassen, Minnesota:** 2012–2014 / **Technical team: Producer:** Prince / **Recording engineers:** Chris James, Jamie Lewis, Ben Mühlethaler, Joshua Welton

Prince and his women really open up the throttle on *Marz*, which has synchronized rhythms and a tempo that would get even the most recalcitrant fans during the 3RDEYEGIRL era headbanging along to the music. Hannah Welton metronomically hammers her Piano White Gretsch USA Custom drums, while Prince delivers an almost uninterrupted flow on this fast track that's over in the blink of an eye. Since Welton constantly had to adapt to the different styles of music she played with her boss, her drum kit included two different bass drums: a 24-inch Gretsch for the more rock 'n' roll tracks and a 20-inch one for the funkier songs, both of which had their own pedals, of course. "I just kind of slide my foot over to the next pedal whenever I want to use the auxiliary bass drum, and it's just kind of for a little flavor," she said. "Just on certain sections of songs for a different sound and different bottom."[310]

FUNKNROLL

Prince & 3RDEYEGIRL / 4'09

Musicians: Prince: vocals, electric guitar, backing vocals / **Donna Grantis:** electric guitar, claps, backing vocals / **Ida Nielsen:** bass, claps, backing vocals / **Hannah Welton:** drums, claps, backing vocals / **Recording: Paisley Park, Chanhassen, Minnesota:** 2012–2014 / **Technical team: Producer:** Prince / **Recording engineers:** Chris James, Jamie Lewis, Ben Mühlethaler, Joshua Welton

This is the original version of *Funknroll*, a combination of funk and rock 'n' roll as the title suggests—a song that Prince and Joshua Welton would later remix for the *Art Official Age* album. On 4 March 2014, Prince & 3RDEYEGIRL appeared on *The Arsenio Hall Show*, which aired the following day. Prince opened the show with a stunning rendition of *Funknroll*, accompanied by 11 horns and 13 dancers. The version of *Mutiny* (composed for The Family's 1985 album of the same name) that closed the program was equally amazing. A great TV moment, which also featured a fascinating interview with Prince who opened up to host Arsenio Hall in a way he had rarely done before.

ART

PRINCE

ART OFFICIAL AGE

Art Official Cage · Clouds · Breakdown · The Gold Standard · U Know
Breakfast Can Wait · This Could Be Us · What It Feels Like · Affirmation I & II
Way Back Home · Funknroll · Time · Affirmation III

Released in the USA by NPG Records/Warner Bros. Records:
30 September 2014 (CD); November 2014 (LP) [LP ref.: 545612-1; CD ref.: 545612-2]
Released in the UK by NPG Records Warner Bros. Records:
29 September 2014 (CD); November 2014 (LP) [LP ref.: 9362-49332-7;
CD ref.: 9362-49333-0]
Best chart ranking in the USA: 5
Best chart ranking in the UK: 8

Prince in the audience for the French Open tennis tournament at the Roland Garros Stadium, in Paris, on 2 June 2014.

FOR PRINCE ADDICTS

The sleeve of *Art Official Age* is graced by photographer Maya Washington's work. She used a shot of the frame containing *Purple Rain*'s nine platinum records, which was hanging at Paisley Park. She placed a photo of Prince in front of one of them, his Afro overlapping with the vinyl record. She did a bit of Photoshop and the sleeve photo was born.

2014

IN JOSHUA WELTON'S HANDS

Joshua Welton, the nephew of jazzman Count Basie, joined the band Fatty Koo when he was 15 years old before pursuing a solo career. Prince met the young musician in the spring of 2012. He accompanied his wife, Hannah, to an audition at Paisley Park, and received a very warm welcome at Chanhassen. "Prince was rehearsing at a sound stage in Paisley Park," he explained in 2015. "Then he literally jumps up—because he's on the keyboards—and he goes 'Joshua!,' runs off the stage, and gives me a big hug. And I'm thinking to myself, 'I really enjoy this guy already!'"[326] By then, Prince already knew of Welton's piousness, and that he knew his Bible well (he wrote a book about his faith in 2019) and was a devoted singer in his church. That same day, the two men undertook a two-hour conversation about Jesus Christ. After that, they became fast friends. In the following nine months, Welton accompanied his wife on tour and occasionally played the keyboards onstage with Prince & 3RDEYEGIRL. "I was just supporting Hannah," he said. "I just wanted to see her dreams come to fruition."[327]

A competition at Chanhassen

In the winter of 2013, while busy making 3RDEYEGIRL's first album, Prince went in search of a coproducer to help him work on some new songs. He was looking for a more modern sound that would contrast with the vintage rock of 3RDEYEGIRL, so he set three producers against each other, including novice Joshua Welton, who at the time had never worked on anything other than his own songs. "I was working on some of my own stuff in this tiny studio room Prince has here when he walked in one night and just handed me a hard drive," confessed Welton. "He said he had given a copy of the same stems to these two other producers in the big studio and he wanted to see who could finish the song better. *'Let the best man, win!'* he said."[328] The rest is history. Welton won the round and was given the prestigious role of coproducer on *Art Official Age* and *Hitnrun Phase One*. The other two producers, Ben Mühlethaler and Jamie Lewis, helped produce and mix various songs on the *Plectrumelectrum* album.

The polar opposite of Plectrumelectrum

The artistic collaboration between the two men was prolific and gave rise to a new musical aesthetic for Prince. He told Welton that he liked the albums *Who Is Jill Scott? Words and Sounds Vol. 1* by Jill Scott (2000) and *Late Registration* by Kanye West (2005), and then gave him free reign to create what he wanted, starting with the songs he recorded. "He still has final approval on everything," explained Welton. "But a lot of times, after he adds his vocals and guitar or whatever, he won't touch much else."[328] With its EDM (Electronic Dance Music), hip-hop, and dubstep and overall very electronic, even techno, sounds, *Art Official Age* was a bit of an oddity when it came out on 30 September 2014. The album was nevertheless celebrated for its artistic risk-taking and for the mastery of its producer, Joshua Welton.

Marissa Jack, aka The Golden Hippie, was a highly competent backing vocalist on some dates of Prince & 3RDEYEGIRL in 2014.

2014

ART OFFICIAL CAGE

Prince / 3'41

Musicians: Prince: vocals, electric guitar, synthesizers, backing vocals / **The Golden Hippie:** vocals, backing vocals / **Ida Nielsen:** spoken word / **Joshua Welton:** synthesizers, programming / **Recording: Paisley Park, Chanhassen, Minnesota:** spring 2013 to spring 2014 / **Technical team: Producers:** Prince, Joshua Welton / **Recording engineers:** Prince, Joshua Welton, Chris James

There is a violent explosion of EDM (Electronic Dance Music) in *Art Official Cage*, which must have been unsettling for fans, although it does illustrate Joshua Welton's talents as a producer. We're dealing with a clever mix of dance music, dubstep, and hip-hop here, all led by the funk rhythm Prince plays on the guitar. While the Danish words spoken by Ida Nielsen can be heard in several passages, it was another guest who starred in the song—the name for which should not be confused with that of the album, the two titles being a play on words: *Art Official Age* means "artificial age" and *Art Official Cage* means "artificial cage." Marissa Jack, aka The Golden Hippie, is an American singer who Prince discovered in 2012 while scrolling through Twitter. She'd had the good idea to "like" a photo of Prince and in return he messaged her and asked her to meet him at Paisley Park. "We discussed all types of music for hours," she recalled. "The second I met him, all nerves, the last bit of fangirl in me that I had went away and it was like I had known him my entire life."[329] Marissa Jack was invited to join the Hit and Run Tour Part II in the spring of 2014 as a backing vocalist, before pursuing a solo career. And let us not forget the mystery that surrounds the song's rap part, between 2'13 and 2'28, which was done by an unknown performer. While some observers think Prince modified his own voice for this interlude, the most likely hypothesis concerns a certain H. C. I II III, who was credited on the album and whose surname was no doubt invented by our singer. Prince also hid the presence of Lianne La Havas behind the pseudonym Charlotte Ann Telepathy.

CLOUDS

Prince / 4'34

Musicians: Prince: vocals, electric guitar, acoustic guitar, bass, synthesizers, backing vocals / **Lianne La Havas:** vocals, backing vocals / **Joshua Welton:** synthesizers, programming / **Recording: Paisley Park, Chanhassen, Minnesota:** spring 2013 to spring 2014 / **Technical team: Producer:** Prince, Joshua Welton / **Recording engineers:** Prince, Joshua Welton, Chris James

Aired in Times Square on 25 August 2014 during a special edition of *Good Morning America*, *Clouds* would have been a great single to promote the very electronic *Art Official Age*. Since Prince had made 3RDEYEGIRL his absolute priority in 2014, however, nothing came of it, even though the song was performed onstage on *Saturday Night Live* on 1 November 2014 in a classic medley combining *Clouds*, *Plectrumelectrum*, *Marz*, and *Anotherlove*. The song contains a lovely duet with the divine Lianne La Havas, who'd been friends with Prince for years. Prince, who had already covered La Havas's song *Lost & Found* onstage at the Allphones Arena in Sydney on 11 May 2012, decided to work with her more seriously for *Clouds*, a very funky and highly enjoyable mid-tempo song. "That time in my life, knowing him, was so surreal and

Andy Allo recorded some backing vocals for the poignant song *Breakdown* in 2014.

Overleaf: Prince and his army of wind players onstage at the Mohegan Sun Arena, in Uncasville, Connecticut, on 29 December 2013.

special," revealed La Havas in an emotional interview in 2020. "It didn't hit me for a long time, the reality of his passing. He's very missed."[330] The two friends were so close that Prince and 3RDEYEGIRL gave a press conference in La Havas's living room in London on 4 February 2014, where they announced a tour of small venues in England that lasted from 5 to 22 February 2014.

Single

BREAKDOWN

Prince / 4'04

Musicians: Prince: vocals, piano, synthesizers, backing vocals / **Ida Nielsen:** bass / **Hannah Welton:** drums / **Joshua Welton:** synthesizers / **Andy Allo:** backing vocals / **Recording:** Paisley Park, Chanhassen, Minnesota: 2011–2012; 22 June 2013 / **Technical team: Producers:** Prince, Joshua Welton / **Recording engineers:** Prince, Joshua Welton, Chris James

Single: Digital release in the USA by NPG Records: 18 April 2014 / **Global digital release by NPG Records:** 23 April 2014 / **Best chart ranking in the USA:** did not make the charts / **Best chart ranking in the UK:** did not make the charts

Prince's oldest fans can rest easy: their idol never lost his ability to write beautiful and poignant ballads, as illustrated by the wonderful *Breakdown*. Released as a single in April 2014 as *The Breakdown*, the song lost its indefinite article when it joined *Art Official Age*, but not one ounce of its emotional power, worthy of Prince's greatest melodies. Prince recorded the song between 2011 and 2012, before embellishing it with drum and bass tracks played by the 3RDEYEGIRLs Hannah Welton and Ida Nielsen on 22 June 2013. Andy Allo provides the backing vocals, confirming her prolific collaboration with Prince who had just produced her album *Superconductor* with NPG Records. Far from the synthetic textures of the album, *Breakdown* is a highly melancholic pearl of a song. To be urgently (re)discovered.

THE GOLD STANDARD

Prince / 5'53

Musicians: Prince: vocals, rap, electric guitar, acoustic guitar, bass, drums, programming, synthesizers, backing vocals / **Joshua Welton:** synthesizers, programming / **Marcus Anderson:** saxophone / **Adrian Crutchfield:** saxophone / **Recording:** Paisley Park, Chanhassen, Minnesota: 27 October 2013 / **Technical team: Producers:** Prince, Joshua Welton / **Recording engineers:** Prince, Joshua Welton, Chris James

The Gold Standard is a return to the Minneapolis Sound, with Adrian Crutchfield and Marcus Anderson giving it their all on the saxophones. In July 2014, as Prince was starting to write 3RDEYEGIRL's second album (the first hadn't even come out yet!), he invited a bevy of talented musicians to Paisley Park. They made up the ephemeral NPG Quartet (often called the NPG Q), which played alongside Prince as he recorded his instrumental jazz album. They recorded nine songs in August 2014, with John Blackwell on drums, Andrew Gouché on bass, Xavier Taplin on keyboards, and Marcus Anderson on saxophone. The latter, who was supposed to join a brass section with Maceo Parker, ended up joining the imposing group of 11 brass musicians who performed onstage at *The Arsenio Hall Show* on 4 March. Anderson played on many other Prince songs, notably for the very funky *Hitnrun Phase Two* album in 2015.

19
20
21
MOHEGAN SUN
008
AUDIO
007
AUDIO

As well as being a talented rapper, DaniLeigh was also an accomplished film director and made the clip of *Breakfast Can Wait* in 2013.

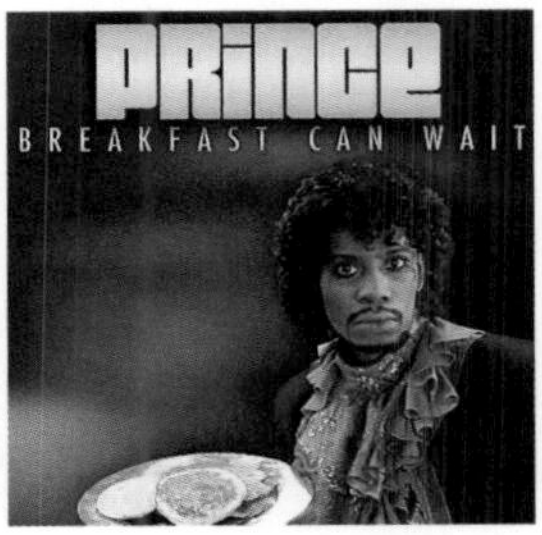

U KNOW

Prince / 3'56

Musicians: Prince: vocals, synthesizers, backing vocals / **Joshua Welton:** synthesizers, programming / **Recording:** Paisley Park, Chanhassen, Minnesota: spring 2013 to spring 2014 / **Technical team:** Producers: Prince, Joshua Welton / **Recording engineers:** Prince, Joshua Welton, Chris James

U Know was built around a sample of *Blinded* by R&B singer Mila J. whose YouTube video of the song had captured Prince's attention in 2012. The elder sister of rapper Jhené Aiko, Mila J. has cited Prince's influence on her music since the beginning of her career. Her first concert was during the Purple Rain Tour, as she explained shortly before the release of *Art Official Age*: "I just know from my parents that that was my first concert because me and my older sister were kids. I was probably under three. I probably shouldn't have been there. I'm sure I had earplugs, so I don't remember the experience of the concert but [...] I literally grew up with Prince. [His music's] like in my blood."[331] As if it were a sign from above, Mila J. and Prince's paths crossed again in 1991 when she appeared in the video for *Diamonds and Pearls* with him and Rosie Gaines. "Even if my music might not sound like his," she added in another interview, "I just feel like he was the person to inspire me to do music and want to be an artist. I think I've seen him in concert probably more than any other artist."[332] As proof of her admiration for the Kid from Minneapolis, the singer regularly goes by her second stage name, Japollonia.

Single

BREAKFAST CAN WAIT

Prince / 3'54

Musician: Prince: vocals, electric guitar, bass, programming, synthesizers, backing vocals / **Recording:** Paisley Park, Chanhassen, Minnesota: autumn 2012 / **Technical team:** Producer: Prince / **Recording engineers:** Prince, Chris James
Single: Digital release via 3rdEyeGirl.com, NPG Records: 5 February 2013 / **Digital release via 3rdEyeTunes.com, NPG Records:** 17 August 2013 / **Global digital release by NPG Records:** 3 September 2013 / **Best chart ranking in the USA:** did not make the charts / **Best chart ranking in the UK:** did not make the charts

DaniLeigh (from her real name, Danielle Leigh Curiel) was only 18 years old when Prince discovered her rap and dance performances on YouTube. Impressed by her talent, he asked her to make a video for his next single, *Breakfast Can Wait*, a song that was well known to fans since it had been uploaded to 3rdEyeGirl.com 18 months before when the site was launched. While she appeared dressed up as Prince in the video, comedian Dave Chappelle was the one who appeared on the single's cover, he too dressed up as Prince, in the *Purple Rain* version. As proof of Prince's cunning, the image was taken from a humorous video from 2004, in which Chappelle imitates Prince, and along with his sidekick Charlie Murphy, mentions his love of basketball and pancakes. After the song came out as a single on 3 September 2013, Joshua Welton worked on several remixes. *Breakfast Can Wait (Grits'N'Gravy), Breakfast Can Wait (Espresso), Breakfast Can Wait (Honey)*, and *Breakfast Can Wait (Buttermilk)*, were grouped together on *The Breakfast Experience* EP, released on 24 October. The song appeared on a Prince album for the first time on 30 September 2014. As for DaniLeigh, she contributed her impressive flow to Prince's following album, *Hitntun Phase One*, on the song *Like A Mack* in which she raps with her sister Charli Curiel, with whom she formed the duet Curly Fryz.

THIS COULD BE US

Prince / 5'11

Musicians: Prince: vocals, electric guitar, synthesizers, backing vocals / **Joshua Welton:** synthesizers, programming / **Recording: Paisley Park, Chanhassen, Minnesota:** 2014 / **Technical team: Producers:** Prince, Joshua Welton / **Recording engineers:** Prince, Joshua Welton, Chris James

In June 2014, Jon Bream of the *Star Tribune*, the Twin Cities' daily paper, had the privilege of being invited to Paisley Park for a preview listen of a few songs from *Art Official Age*, including *This Could Be Us*, which Prince wrote after finding a short video online of him and Apollonia Kotero (see page 91) riding a Honda CM400 Hondamatic, the legendary motorcycle from the *Purple Rain* movie. "He was always sending me memes and funny videos," confirmed DaniLeigh. "He liked memes of him when people take his face and write captions on his pictures."[30] Taking inspiration from his memories of Apollonia, Prince wrote this romantic song. Bream wrote a flattering review after hearing it: "It's a joyful ballad with some ecstatic Prince vocalizing."[333] The song was reworked in the following months and reappeared under the name *This Could Be Us* on *Hitnrun Phase One* in 2015. It then came out as a single, accompanied by images of Prince and Apollonia Kotero on the famous motorcycle.

WHAT IT FEELS LIKE

Prince / 3'53

Musicians: Prince: vocals, electric guitar, acoustic guitar, bass, programming, synthesizers, backing vocals / **Andy Allo:** vocals, backing vocals / **Recording: Paisley Park, Chanhassen, Minnesota:** 2011–2012 / **Technical team: Producer:** Prince / **Recording engineer:** ? (not confirmed)

Written alongside Andy Allo during production for *Superconductor*, her second album, *What It Feels Like* was recorded during sessions for the album that came out of it, as she explained: "The way we wrote was seamless. If there was a line or verse needed, one of us would write it or chime in to add something different. *Time* and *This Is What It Feels Like* were always meant for a separate project even though *What It Feels Like* is a continuation of *When Stars Collide*,"[334] she continued, referring to the last song on her album *Superconductor*.

AFFIRMATION I & II

Prince / 0'40

Musicians: Lianne La Havas: spoken word / **STRINGenius:** harp / **Recording: Paisley Park, Chanhassen, Minnesota:** spring 2014 / **Technical team: Producers:** Prince, Joshua Welton / **Recording engineers:** Prince, Joshua Welton, Chris James / **Harp arrangements:** Adi Yeshaya

Lianne La Havas is at the mic for the spoken interlude in this song, which only has one instrumental part: a harp recorded by the Minneapolis collective STRINGenius. The score, a harmonic ascent over three chords, is a nod to Prince's *Little Red Corvette*, which was released in 1982.

WAY BACK HOME

Prince / 3'05

Musicians: Prince: vocals, bass, synthesizers, backing vocals / **Lianne La Havas:** spoken word, backing vocals / **Joshua Welton:** synthesizers, programming / **STRINGenius:** string orchestra / **Delilah:** backing vocals / **Recording: Paisley Park, Chanhassen, Minnesota:** 2014 / **Technical team: Producers:** Prince, Joshua Welton / **Recording engineers:** Prince, Joshua Welton, Chris James / **String arrangements:** Adi Yeshaya

Discovered online, Delilah was invited to sing backing vocals with Andy Allo on this deeply melancholic song, in which Prince opens up about his life. From the first verse he sings: "I never wanted a typical life/Scripted role, trophy wife/All I ever wanted, to be left alone/See my bed's made up at night/'Cause in my dreams I roam/Just trying to find, trying to find/My way back, back home." Invited to sing at some concerts for the Welcome 2 Australia Tour in 2012, Delilah retained fond memories of her friendship with Prince. "I guess you can call him a mentor," she explained. "He's helped me online and by asking me to come on tour with him. It was definitely nuts."[335] As she commented in another interview: "Singing with Prince really helped in terms of confidence." She continued, "I was really nervous going on stage before him in front of tens of thousands of people. That was terrifying. I kicked off my high heel shoes because I was scared I was going to fall over, because my legs were shaking."[336] Prince asked the musicians of the STRINGenius collective to record string arrangements for the song. He then decided to pull them from the mix and used them for the last track of the album, *Affirmation III*.

Lianne La Havas, photographed by Jonathan Wong in September 2017.

The singer Delilah was one of Prince's guests on *Art Official Age*.

FUNKNROLL

Prince / 4'07

Musicians: Prince: vocals, electric guitar, backing vocals / **Donna Grantis:** electric guitar, clapping, backing vocals / **Ida Nielsen:** bass, clapping, backing vocals / **Hannah Welton:** drums, clapping, backing vocals / **Joshua Welton:** synthesizers, programming / **Recording: Paisley Park, Chanhassen, Minnesota:** 2012–2014 / **Technical team: Producer:** Prince / **Recording engineers:** Chris James, Jamie Lewis, Ben Mühlethaler, Joshua Welton

This is Joshua Welton's reinterpretation of *Funknroll* from the *Plectrumelectrum* album. This new version is expendable but notable for its slick production, which brings a new take to the piece. In the song, Prince urges listeners to put down their phones and party, a request backed up by Hannah Welton, the drummer for 3RDEYEGIRL, in an interview with Thomas Hannan of the website TheLineOfBestFit.com. "People get so caught up in catching every moment on a phone that they miss out on it," explained the musician. "For us, it's totally a misrepresentation of the band and our sound, because the sound quality of the video is really whack. You don't have a good representation of what was there that night and if you weren't paying attention, your memory doesn't have that recollection either [...] For us as the artists, there's never a night when we step on a stage without giving it 100%. And I think it's OK for an artist to ask the audience to give 100% too."[320]

TIME

Prince / 6'49

Musicians: Prince: vocals, electric guitar, bass, synthesizers, backing vocals / **Andy Allo:** vocals, backing vocals / **Joshua Welton:** synthesizers, programming / **Recording: Paisley Park, Chanhassen, Minnesota:** 2011–2012 / **Technical team: Producers:** Prince, Joshua Welton / **Recording engineers:** Prince, Joshua Welton, Chris James

Like *What It Feels Like*, *Time* was recorded during sessions for *Superconductor*, Andy Allo's second album. A pleasant R&B ballad, even if only for Allo's warm and delicate voice, *Time* fits comfortably into the mold of Joshua Welton's other productions for the album.

AFFIRMATION III

Prince / 3'27

Musicians: Lianne La Havas: spoken word / **Prince:** spoken word, piano / **Delilah:** vocals, backing vocals / **Joshua Welton:** synthesizers, programming / **STRINGenius:** string orchestra / **Recording: Paisley Park, Chanhassen, Minnesota:** 2014 / **Technical team: Producers:** Prince, Joshua Welton / **Recording engineers:** Prince, Joshua Welton, Chris James / **String arrangements:** Adi Yeshaya

A quai-instrumental version of *Way Back Home*, *Affirmation III* highlights Delilah's voice and the STRINGenius strings, arranged by composser Ida Yeshaya, who was asked to draw inspiration from Clare Fischer's work on Prince's previous productions.

PRINCE

HITNRUN PHASE ONE

Million $ Show · Shut This Down · Ain't About To Stop
Like A Mack · This Could B Us · Fallinlove2nite · X's Face · Hardrocklover
Mr. Nelson · 1000 X's & O's · June

Streaming distribution on Tidal: 7 September 2015
Released in the USA by NPG Records: 14 September 2015 (CD ref.: none)
Released in the UK by NPG Records: 14 September 2015 (CD ref.: none)
Best chart ranking in the USA: 70
Best chart ranking in the UK: 50

Prince wears his three-lens glasses onstage at the American Music Awards in Los Angeles on 22 November 2015.

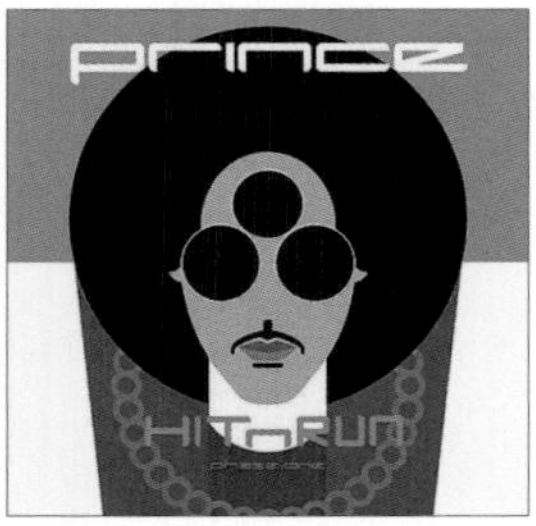

ELECTRO-FUNK PART 2

2015

After the warm welcome given to *Art Official Age*, the friendship between Prince and his coproducer Joshua Welton intensified, leading them to work together on a second album. When the aforementioned album came out in September 2014, the duo had already created several songs in the same vein as those recorded previously. "Even while *Art Official Age* was being released, Prince and I were already working on new music,"[337] confirmed Welton. Prince asked Welton, who was more invested than ever in making new songs, to coproduce his next record, so bringing to a close a very electronic era in Prince's discography.

Welton (almost) at the helm

Joshua Welton was much more than an underling in the making of *Hitnrun Phase One*. Just as Kirk Johnson had been for the *Emancipation* album, so Welton was the beat maker in chief on this record, taking on all the programming, but also the artistic direction. He enjoyed an amount of freedom that was previously unheard of in Prince's creative process. He recorded a good number of backing tracks himself, while his friend and employer worked on writing *Hitnrun Phase Two*, which came out a few months after the first volume of the diptych. Welton reveled in this situation and recounted a comical memory from this period, during which he worked alone in studio B at Paisley Park while the Kid occupied studio A: "There have been times I've been working on a song, and he'll slip into the studio like a ghost. I'll turn around, and he's just sitting there! He's scared me so many times doing that. Now he tries to make a lot of noise coming in, so I have some warning!"[338] While Welton was busy producing, Prince redoubled his artistic projects throughout 2015. He coproduced and participated in writing *Back in Time*, the first album of his new protegée, Judith Hill; he supported Kandace Springs in the development of her singing career; he launched the production of 3RDEYEGIRL's second album (which remains unreleased); and he collaborated with talented bassist MonoNeon on an album called *Black Is The New Black*, recording nine songs with him along with Adrian Crutchfield on the saxophone and Kirk Johnson. The latter was enlisted to rerecord all the drum parts (these had been previously played by his friend Michael Bland, who was initially drafted in for the project). Of the sessions that remain unreleased, only the song *Ruff Enuff*, on which Prince plays the guitar and keyboards, appeared on the streaming platform Tidal on 11 January 2016.

A Tidal exclusive

Hitnrun Phase One was released exclusively on Tidal on 7 September 2015. Launched in October 2014 amid a fanfare of publicity (it's impossible to forget the pompous promotional video in which Kanye West, Chris Martin, Jack White, Nicky Minaj, Madonna, and the Daft Punk duo raise a glass to the launch of the website), Jay-Z's streaming platform wanted to be fairer to the artists it streamed, providing them an alternative to the powerful iTunes and Deezer. It also offered a higher quality audio to what was generally found elsewhere. Prince, seduced by this new economic model, where Tidal would pay him for the right to distribute his music, granted the platform the exclusive rights to his new album. Although *Hitnrun Phase One* enjoyed plenty of media coverage, the reviews were mixed, with listeners baffled by its ever more electronic sounds. "I would say it's an experimental Prince record for fans who just don't care about him sounding like a certain thing," explained Joshua Welton, who was largely responsible for promoting the album. "Because he's such a creative, it gives him that freedom to say, 'I just want to make music like this today.'"[339] Fans, disconcerted by the album's synthetic sound textures, were soon reassured when they heard the more authentic production of the excellent *Hitnrun Phase Two*.

2015

MILLION $ SHOW

Prince, Joshua Welton / 3'10

Musicians: Prince: vocals, electric guitar, bass, backing vocals / **Judith Hill:** vocals, backing vocals / **Joshua Welton:** synthesizers, programming / **Michael B** Nelson: trombone / **Steve Strand:** trumpet / **Dave Jensen:** trumpet / **Kathy Jensen:** saxophone / **Kenni Holmen:** saxophone / **STRINGenius:** string orchestra / **Recording:** Paisley Park, Chanhassen, Minnesota: 2014–2015 / Bone 2 B Wild Music Studio, Minneapolis: 2015 (brass) / The Brewhouse Recording Studio, Minneapolis: 2015 (strings) / **Technical team:** Producers: Prince, Joshua Welton / Recording engineers: Prince, Joshua Welton, Michael B Nelson (Bone 2 B Wild Music Studio), Rob Genadek (The Brewhouse Recording Studio) / Brass arrangements: Michael B Nelson / String arrangements: Adi Yeshaya

After working as a backing vocalist for Michael Polnareff's concerts in Paris-Bercy in 2007, then joining rehearsals for Michael Jackson's 2009 residence in London (captured in *This Is It*, the famous Kenny Ortega movie), singer Judith Hill had the good judgment to declare in an interview that she dreamed of working with Prince. The latter, who never missed a beat when it came to what appeared on the web, got in touch with the American backing vocalist. He'd first noticed her in *Twenty Feet from Stardom*, a documentary by Morgan Neville on singers operating in the background, a place that she too occupied. A friendship was born, and Prince and Hill worked together on her first album, *Back in Time*, which was produced by NPG Records. During the making of her album, Hill added her touch to *Million $ Show* (pronounced *Million Dollar Show*), as she explained to a journalist from the website Schkopi.com while in Paris in 2018. "[Prince] was in the studio making his album while I was rehearsing in another room for a concert. He asked me to write a chorus. He loved it, then he went back into his studio. He later asked me to record my vocal parts with him."[340]

SHUT THIS DOWN

Prince, Joshua Welton / 3'03

Musicians: Prince: vocals, spoken word, bass, backing vocals / **Joshua Welton:** synthesizers, programming / **Recording:** Paisley Park, Chanhassen, Minnesota: 2014 / **Technical team:** Producers: Prince, Joshua Welton / Recording engineers: Prince, Joshua Welton

In *Shut This Down*, Prince regains his characteristic flow from *My Name Is Prince* (1992), delivering jerky vocals bordering on rap, which are embellished with a slapped bass line that perfectly complements Welton's brutalist and mechanical rhythm. Solely responsible for promoting the album, the young producer took his work to heart and found the right arguments to entice fans. "I think you'll be able to dance to it!" he said to a journalist asking about the upcoming album. "You'll get the groovy Prince, you'll get the fun Prince, you'll get the hilarious Prince, you'll get the serious Prince, and you'll get the going-out-on-a-date-with-my-lady Prince."[326]

AIN'T ABOUT TO STOP

Prince, Joshua Welton / 3'38

Musicians: Prince: vocals, bass, synthesizers, backing vocals / **Rita Ora:** vocals, backing vocals / **Donna Grantis:** electric guitar, backing vocals / **Ida Nielsen:** backing vocals / **Hannah Welton:** backing vocals / **Joshua Welton:** synthesizers, programming / **Recording:** Paisley Park, Chanhassen, Minnesota: 2014 / **Technical team:** Producers: Prince, Joshua Welton / Recording engineers: Prince, Joshua Welton

Three minutes and 38 seconds of remarkable power: that's what the Prince/Rita Ora duet gives us here. After Ora released her first album, *Ora*, in 2013, her managers told her that Prince wanted to meet her. At first, she thought it was

The pop singer Rita Ora with whom Prince was to record the unreleased *The Single Most Amazing.*

an invitation from Prince Harry, of the British royal family. Before the meeting actually took place, she had to be told that it was, in fact, with the singer from Minneapolis. Ora traveled to Chanhassen, reached Paisley Park, and spent several days there. She recorded vocals for multiple tracks, including *The Single Most Amazing*, a pop piece that Prince and Welton produced but never released, although Ora published an excerpt of it on her YouTube channel in July 2014. Ora and her host also recorded a duet, the high-quality *Ain't About To Stop*, which contains backing vocals by the 3RDEYEGIRLs Ida Nielsen, Hannah Welton, and Donna Grantis, as well as a guitar solo by the latter. "[Working with Prince] was the best thing I have ever done in my life," confessed Rita Ora. "He plays, like, 50 instruments so you could do anything and he'll fix it. He has an answer for everything. He's a genius."[341]

LIKE A MACK

Prince, Joshua Welton / 4'04

Musicians: Prince: vocals, electric guitar, backing vocals / **Danielle "DaniLeigh" Curiel:** rap, vocals, backing vocals / **Charli Curiel:** rap, vocals, backing vocals / **Joshua Welton:** synthesizers, programming / **Marcus Anderson:** saxophone / **Keith Anderson:** saxophone / **Lynn Grissett:** trumpet / **Joey Rayfield:** trombone / **Recording:** **Paisley Park, Chanhassen, Minnesota:** 2014–2015 / **Technical team:** **Producers:** Prince, Joshua Welton / **Recording engineers:** Prince, Joshua Welton

Whatever certain fans may say about this period of artistic questioning, Prince was in good hands with Joshua Welton. He proved it with the very convincing *Like A Mack*, in which the duo Curly Fryz gave it their all. The Curiel sisters, rappers Charli and Danielle (aka DaniLeigh), were already familiar with the Prince universe, since DaniLeigh had made the video for *Breakfast Can Wait* in 2013. The sisters, discovered online by Prince who was always looking for new talent, made an impact with this song before they continued on their own individual paths. "[This collaboration with Prince] was unreal honestly," explained DaniLeigh. "I picked up a lot of traits from him. I'm smarter on business decisions that I make, my pen game is stronger, and I'm just overall grateful. He really believed in me as an artist, and I really look into that as something special. Makes me realize that I am made for this."[342] This umpteenth collaboration by Prince with the American musical new guard illustrated his determination to uphold Paisley Park as a place where talents could meet, just as it had been when it opened. Saxophonist Marcus Anderson, who appeared on *Hitnrun Phase Two*, also expressed this idea: "He was positive and optimistic and saw opportunity in everything. He wanted to establish a new-age Motown, to bring artists and have a band ready for them to record with."[21]

Single

THIS COULD B US

Prince, Joshua Welton / 4'11

Musicians: Prince: vocals, spoken word, electric guitar, bass, piano, synthesizers, backing vocals / **Joshua Welton:** synthesizers, programming / **Recording: Paisley Park, Chanhassen, Minnesota:** 2014; 2015 (remix and overdubs) / **Technical team: Producers:** Prince, Joshua Welton / **Recording engineers:** Prince, Joshua Welton, Chris James
Single: Digital release by NPG Records: 28 August 2015 / **Best chart ranking in the USA:** did not make the charts / **Best chart ranking in the UK:** did not make the charts

2015

Prince and Joshua Welton revisited this song from *Art Official Age* and embellished it with a nice, biting bass line, an aggressive guitar solo, and powerful rhythmic programming. This reinterpretation is not superfluous, as it makes the piece sound more modern. Prince was right to release it as a single, with a shot of him and Apollonia Kotero taken from the movie *Purple Rain*. The song was written in honor of the singer from Apollonia 6 (see page 91).

FALLINLOVE2NITE

Prince, Joshua Welton / 3'12

Musicians: Prince: vocals, electric guitar, bass, programming, synthesizers, backing vocals / **Joshua Welton:** synthesizers, programming / **Michael B** Nelson: trombone / **Steve Strand:** trumpet / **Dave Jensen:** trumpet / **Kathy Jensen:** saxophone / **Kenni Holmen:** saxophone / **STRINGenius:** string orchestra / **Recording: Paisley Park, Chanhassen, Minnesota:** 2013 / **Bone 2 B Wild Music Studio, Minneapolis:** December 2013 (brass) / **The Brewhouse Recording Studio, Minneapolis:** December 2013 (strings) / **Technical team: Producers:** Prince, Joshua Welton / **Recording engineers:** Prince, Joshua Welton, Michael B Nelson (Bone 2 B Wild Music Studio), Rob Genadek (The Brewhouse Recording Studio) / **Brass arrangements:** Michael B Nelson / **String arrangements:** Adi Yeshaya

Released as a single on 17 March 2014, *Fallinlove2nite* is presented here in a version that is identical to the original but without Zooey Deschanel's vocals. The actress recorded the original version for its appearance on American TV sitcom *New Girl* (episode 14, season 3), in which Prince made a special appearance in February 2014.

X'S FACE

Prince, Joshua Welton / 2'38

Musicians: Prince: vocals, backing vocals / **Joshua Welton:** synthesizers, programming / **Recording: Paisley Park, Chanhassen, Minnesota:** 2014–2015 / **Technical team: Producers:** Prince, Joshua Welton / **Recording engineers:** Prince, Joshua Welton

In this song Joshua Welton again dabbles in dubstep, embellishing it with a semiquaver hi-hat track, a key element in trap music, which is a musical subgenre that took traditional rap by storm. "If Prince says he wants a certain swag or a certain style," explained Welton (who is credited as co-author of the whole record), "he'll say 'Joshua, can you make something like this'—then I'll give him a track and he'll go work in studio A while I'm in studio B, write the lyrics, then he'll come back and pick it up."[337] With this strange song title, *X's Face*, Prince was referring to the emoji with Xs for eyes, which means "dead" in computer language.

Single

HARDROCKLOVER

Prince, Joshua Welton / 3'42

Musicians: Prince: vocals, electric guitar, bass / **Joshua Welton:** synthesizers, programming / **Recording: Paisley Park, Chanhassen, Minnesota:** June 2015 / **Technical team: Producers:** Prince, Joshua Welton / **Recording engineers:** Prince, Joshua Welton
Single: Digital release by NPG Records: 7 July 2015 / **Best chart ranking in the USA:** did not make the charts / **Best chart ranking in the UK:** did not make the charts

While Joshua Welton was producing the album in studio B at Paisley Park, Prince asked him for a song that alternated calm and tense atmospheres. Welton created *Hardrocklover* in one go. That same day, he made *June*, which closes the album. This indicates the breakneck speed with which they created *Hitnrun Phase One*, an album in which spontaneity and urgency were the operative words. While the song was never played in concert, Donna Grantis said that she rehearsed it with 3RDEYEGIRL and was stunned by Prince's guitar solo. "Even though I had been jamming, playing, and recording for years," confessed the guitarist, "those moments of being awestruck happened all the time."[343]

MR. NELSON

Prince, Joshua Welton / 2'27

Musicians: Prince: vocals, electric guitar, acoustic guitar, bass, backing vocals / **Joshua Welton:** synthesizers, programming / **Recording: Paisley Park, Chanhassen, Minnesota:** 2014–2015 / **Technical team: Producers:** Prince, Joshua Welton / **Recording engineers:** Prince, Joshua Welton

Mr. Nelson is a reinterpretation of *Clouds* from *Art Official Age*. It is based on some of the tracks from that album and uses Lianna La Havas's voice from the original recording sessions. Prince, who here used his birth name in a song title for the first time, completed the piece with a guitar solo that referenced the main riff from *Alexander the Great (356–323 B.C.)* by Iron Maiden, from the 1986 album *Somewhere in Time*. While this figurative nod may seem like a coincidence, it delighted (or annoyed) fans of the British heavy metal band.

1000 X'S & O'S

Prince, Joshua Welton / 4'27

Musicians: Prince: vocals, bass, backing vocals / **Joshua Welton:** synthesizers, programming / **Recording: Paisley Park, Chanhassen, Minnesota:** 2014–2015 / **Technical team: Producers:** Prince, Joshua Welton / **Recording engineer:** Prince, Joshua Welton

Prince and Joshua Welton resuscitated a 23-year-old song here. Recorded during the April 1992 Australian sessions at Studios 301 in Sydney—which gave rise to several songs on the NPG album *Gold Nigga* (see page 230)—and called *A 1,000 Hugs and Kisses* at the time, the song was initially sung by Rosie Gaines. Prince then replaced the vocal track with a new one by his protegée, Nona Gaye, who tells her boyfriend to "Lock the door, you better unplug your phone, cause I want to give you a thousand reasons why we need to be alone." While this version, which has been circulating as a bootleg since the mid-1990s, was led by the rhythmic funk Prince played on the guitar, its reinterpretation, *1000 X's & O's*, enjoys more modern arrangements, including a rhythmic pattern borrowed from *Rock the Boat*, the single released by Aliyah in 2001. While "X's and O's" here means "hugs and kisses," Prince nevertheless confounds listeners by citing the famous game again (after *Tictactoe* in 2014), which is also called X's and O's.

The young producer Joshua Welton brought a touch of modernity to two of Prince's albums: *Art Official Age* (2014) and *Hitnrun Phase One* (2015).

JUNE

Prince, Joshua Welton / 3'21

Musicians: Prince: vocals / **Joshua Welton:** synthesizers, programming / **Recording: Paisley Park, Chanhassen, Minnesota:** June 2015 / **Technical team: Producers:** Prince, Joshua Welton / **Recording engineers:** Prince, Joshua Welton

Written and recorded on the same day as *Hardrocklover*, *June* is a gentle conclusion to this supercharged album, which is the result of a close collaboration between Prince and his friend Joshua Welton. "I've never worked so hard in my life," confessed the Welton. "I can't tell you how many times I leave Paisley and don't even know if it's supposed to be day or night! But it's all for the music!"[328]

The very devout Nichole Nordeman felt honored to be covered by Prince in 2015.

WHAT IF

Nichole Nordeman / 4'58

Musicians: **Prince:** vocals, electric guitar, backing vocals / **Hannah Welton:** vocals, drums, backing vocals / **Donna Grantis:** electric guitar / **Ida Nielsen:** bass / **STRINGenius:** string orchestra / **Recording:** **Paisley Park, Chanhassen, Minnesota:** 2014 / **The Brewhouse Recording Studio, Minneapolis:** 2015 (strings) / **Technical team:** **Producer:** Prince / **Recording engineers:** Chris James, Jamie Lewis, Ben Mühlethaler, Joshua Welton / **String arrangements:** Adi Yeshaya / **Available for download by email:** 14 March 2015

Ticket holders for Prince's concerts in Louisville on 14 and 15 March 2015 received an email from his Live Nation tour agency allowing them to download a whole new song by their idol. Or rather, a cover by CCM singer Nichole Nordeman (incidentally, Contemporary Christian Music is a modern subgenre of Christian music). Written in 2005, and present on *Brave*, the fourth album of the American singer, *What If* is a pop- rock song praising the positive changes that occurred in her life as a result of her faith in Jesus. "I wrote the song years ago from conversations I had had with an atheist friend," reported Nordeman. "I had gone down the path of feeling compelled to argue and convince him to become a Christian. After a while, I realized how futile that was and that it really isn't my place to argue and debate someone into a faith. The song was kind of an apology to my friend, like, 'I'm sorry I turned every conversation about faith into an argument, and I'm sorry that I made it about debate and not about love.' I would love to know what part of that resonated with Prince."[344] Prince, who heard the song on a Christian radio station while he was in the car in 2005, decided almost ten years later to record it with the musicians from 3RDEYEGIRL. The song aired on 12 March 2015 on the Louisville radio station WFPK-FM. The very pious Hannah Welton performed it on air with Prince. "Our version is much different than the original version, but just as impactful and meaningful,"[344] confirmed the drummer on that occasion.

The saxophonist Marcus Anderson, one of the members of the very last lineup of the NPG Hornz.

Single

FREE URSELF

Prince / 3'47

Musicians: Prince: vocals, acoustic guitar, bass, drums, synthesizers, backing vocals / **Recording: Paisley Park, Chanhassen, Minnesota:** 2015 / **Technical team: Producer:** Prince / **Recording engineer:** ? (not confirmed)
Single: Digital release on Tidal by NPG Records: 28 September 2015 / **Best chart ranking in the USA:** did not make the charts / **Best chart ranking in the UK:** did not make the charts

Prince again advocates freedom for everyone in this pop song, which was uploaded to Tidal on 28 September 2015 and announced on his Twitter profile that same day. The last original song Prince released in his lifetime (the final one was the sleeve of *If Eye Could Get Ur Attention*, on the following 9 November), *Free Urself* was made available to Tidal members as part of the series *Purple Pick of the Week*, which published unreleased or rare songs, or ones that Prince particularly liked. Available on 30 September on iTunes, the song was later covered by Natalya (full name, Natalya Phillips), a singer who many listeners believe recorded the backing vocals for the song's original version. She released her cover on YouTube on 21 May 2016, where she wrote: "In November, Prince asked me to cover his song and create a visual for it. I am sharing the video that I made for him in honor of the inspiration that so many of us have found in him and through his music. My dear friend, here it is...May you remain eternally free."[345]

IF EYE COULD GET UR ATTENTION

Prince, Taja Sevelle / 2'43

Musicians: Prince: vocals, synthesizers, backing vocals / **Andrew Gouché:** bass / **John Blackwell:** drums / **Xavier Toplin:** synthesizers / **Marcus Anderson:** Akai EWI 5000 / **Recording: Paisley Park, Chanhassen, Minnesota:** 2014 / **Technical team: Producer:** Prince / **Recording engineer:** ? (not confirmed)
Uploaded to Tidal: 9 November 2015 / **Best chart ranking in the USA:** did not make the charts / **Best chart ranking in the UK:** did not make the charts

The final song Prince officially released before his unexpected death in April 2016, *If Eye Could Get Ur Attention* is a cover of *If I Could Get Your Attention*, written for Taja Savelle's first eponymous album, which was released by Paisley Park Records on 19 September 1987. Mayte Garcia (see page 216) recorded her own version of this pop/funk song in 1993, but she didn't keep it in the final tracklisting of her album *Child of the Sun*. Prince reclaimed it in 2014 with a pretty funky reinterpretation, led remarkably by saxophonist Marcus Anderson who used an instrument developed by Japanese brand Akai International: the EWI 5000, a sort of electronic saxophone that allows you to play with the sound of your voice by using a Vocoder, a modifier of note pitches that was made popular by German band Kraftwerk and the French duo Daft Punk.

PRINCE

HITNRUN PHASE TWO

Baltimore · Rocknroll Loveaffair · 2 Y. 2 D. · Look At Me, Look At U
Stare · Xtraloveable · Groovy Potential · When She Comes
Screwdriver · Black Muse · Revelation · Big City

Released via streaming on Tidal: 12 December 2015
Released in the USA by NPG Records: 29 April 2016 (CD ref.: B0024997-02)
Released in the UK by NPG Records: 29 April 2016 (CD ref.: 0643485620488)
Best chart ranking in the USA: 40
Best chart ranking in the UK: 21

Fans left tributes to their idol on the fence of Paisley Park on 23 April 2016.

Overleaf: A purple-tinted photograph of Minneapolis which was taken on the day of Prince's death: 21 April 2016.

2015

A LIFE DEVOTED TO FUNK

Between September 2014 and July 2015, as Joshua Welton was putting the finishing touches to the songs that would make up *Hitnrun Phase One*, Prince was working separately on the production of a more authentic album that brought together various songs recorded since 2010. Some came from the sessions for the still unreleased album *Welcome 2 America* (*1000 Light Years From Here*, *When She Comes*, and *Black Muse*). Others had already been released as singles for download (*Rocknroll Loveaffair*, under the title *Rock and Roll Love Affair* in 2012, and *Screwdriver* in 2013), while new gems were also added to the album's tracklist (*Stare*, *Baltimore*, *Look At Me, Look At U*, and more). By including a few other musical archives unearthed from The Vault, such as *Groovy Potential* and a reworked version of *Xtraloveable*, Prince succeeded in creating a very coherent whole, which blended funk textures with pop rhythms, enlivened by multiple wind parts. Some of the wind parts were played by Michael B Nelson's Hornheads, while others were supplied by the new NPG Hornz, who were made up of 11 musicians who had been discovered on 4 March 2014 on *The Arsenio Hall Show*. The album *Hitnrun Phase Two* is an absolute marvel and unquestionably one of Prince's best since *The Rainbow Children* in 2001. Potential hits abound and the artist reveals to the full his ability to write catchy choruses while at the same time giving the album a pared-down but impressively effective character. *Hitnrun Phase Two* was released exclusively via Tidal on 12 December 2015 before being made available for download on iTunes three days later.

A piano and a microphone

When *Hitnrun Phase Two* was released, Prince decided to pause production of the second album by 3RDEYEGIRL so that he could begin preparing for his most intimate tour yet, the Piano & A Microphone Tour. As the name indicates, the singer would appear alone onstage with only a piano and a microphone. "I'm doing it to challenge myself [...] I won't know what songs I'm going to do when I'm onstage, I really won't. I won't have to, because I won't have a band, I really won't. Tempo, keys, all those things can dictate what song I'm going to play next [...]"[346] While preparing for this tour, Prince asked Yamaha to build a modified piano, model C7XSH, which required 30 employees of the Japanese company at its site in Buena Park, California. Equipped with a function that allowed the singer to make the strings sound simply by pressing a button, the piano was painted purple to match the color of a fabric taken by the artist himself from a sofa at Paisley Park. Although the piano was delivered at the beginning of April 2016, it was only played from the 16th of that month when it was unveiled to a few lucky listeners at a showcase performance in Chanhassen. A second piano, named The ALPHA Grand Special Edition, was ordered from ALPHA Pianos, but Prince was never to use it. The tour was meant to begin on 16 February 2016 in Melbourne and encompass Australia, the United States, and Canada. There were rumors that Prince would visit Europe, playing in unusual venues such as the Palais Garnier in Paris, but this plan was quickly dropped following the terrorist attacks

LONG
THE
IN LOVING
Prince

in Paris and Saint-Denis the previous 13 November, which killed more than 130 people—90 of these in the auditorium of Le Bataclan during a concert by the American group Eagles of Death Metal.

The last days of the Kid from Minneapolis

This special tour should have sealed a reunion between Prince and his fans, who would have been able to enjoy an unhoped-for tête-à-tête with the artist. However, the tour would become synonymous with tragedy in the hearts of Prince's "fams," who would soon bid their idol farewell. At the beginning of April, concerts due to take place at the Fox Theatre in Atlanta, Georgia, were postponed until 14 April due to the singer's frail state of health. While traveling back to Minneapolis on 15 April, Prince lost consciousness. The aircraft was diverted and landed in Moline, Illinois. Prince then decided to return to Chanhassen—against the advice of the doctors at the city's Trinity Hospital. During the following days, Prince returned to his normal life, having dinner with musician friends and holding private concerts at Paisley Park. His faithful friend Kirk Johnson and the singer Judith Hill, who were both on Prince's private jet when he lost consciousness, took care of reassuring the press, who were quizzing the singer's entourage about his state of

health. Then, on the morning of 21 April 2016, Prince was found unconscious in the lift that led to The Vault and the private floors of Paisley Park; he was pronounced dead in the minutes following the arrival of the emergency services, at 10:07. Prince, who for many years had suffered from acute pain in his knees and hips, caused by wearing high heels and by his energetic stage performances, had become addicted to painkillers. The police investigation following his death revealed the cause as ingestion of Fentanyl tablets—an opioid painkiller that Prince apparently swallowed, by mistake, in excessive quantities. On Friday, 22 April 2016, Prince's body was cremated in a strictly private ceremony attended by family members, including his sister Tyka, his sole heir to date, as the singer had not left a will or any instructions.

Prince's life and career, led at a pace that few people could have withstood, thus came to a sudden and tragic end on 21 April 2016, leaving millions of fans in profound distress. His final album, *Hitnrun Phase Two*, was released in CD format seven days after his death, on 29 April 2016, allowing listeners to remember the world that had been Prince. Behind the mysterious, work-hungry, seductive, funny person lay a genius whose only goal was to urge his audience to party. Despite our grief, it was therefore fitting, in that sad spring of 2016, to dance to the exceptional album that is *Hitnrun Phase Two*.

2015

Single

BALTIMORE

Prince / 4'33

Musicians: Prince: vocals, electric guitar, acoustic guitar, bass, drums, synthesizers, claps, backing vocals / **Eryn Allen Kane:** vocals, backing vocals / **Michael B Nelson:** trombone / **Steve Strand:** trumpet / **Kenni Holmen:** tenor saxophone / **Dave Jensen:** trumpet / **Kathy Jensen:** alto saxophone, baritone saxophone / **STRINGenius:** string orchestra / **Recording: Paisley Park, Chanhassen, Minnesota:** 30 April 2015 (backing tracks), May 2015 (voice of Eryn Allen Kane) / **The Brewhouse Recording Studio, Minneapolis:** 2015 (strings) / **Bone 2 B Wild Music Studio, Minneapolis:** 2011–2012 (wind) / **Technical team: Producer:** Prince / **Recording engineers:** Joshua Welton, Dylan Dresdow, Rob Genadek (The Brewhouse Recording Studio), Michael B Nelson (Bone 2 B Wild Music Studio) / **Wind arrangements:** Michael B Nelson / **String arrangements:** Adi Yeshaya
Single: Digital release on iTunes by NPG Records: 26 May 2015 / **Best chart ranking in the USA:** did not make the charts / **Best chart ranking in the UK:** did not make the charts

On 12 April 2015, Freddie Gray was arrested by police in Baltimore for the illegal possession of a knife. The weapon that the young, 25-year-old African-American was carrying, supposedly a switchblade, was in fact a conventional knife, which does not require special permission. The arrest, which was filmed by numerous passersby, was violent—Gray was held to the ground and could not breathe. He told the officers that this was the case, but they were unmoved. He was thrown into a police van and taken to the emergency room at the city's R Adams Cowley Shock Trauma Center, where he died seven days later: his cervical vertebrae had been broken and his trachea crushed during the arrest. After numerous marches in his memory, at the end of April clashes finally broke out between the demonstrators and the Baltimore security forces. A curfew and then a state of emergency was declared in the Maryland city. Following the deaths of more African-Americans in similar circumstances, the Black Lives Matter movement was formed. Encouraged by his former manager and supporter, the activist Phaedra Ellis-Lamkins, Prince then became deeply involved in this new fight for civil rights for African-Americans. He took part in the Tidal X: 10/20 charity concert, organized by Tidal on 20 October 2015 at the Barclays Center in Brooklyn for the Black Lives Matter movement, and recorded *Baltimore*, a pop song with an undeniable social message and melancholy feel, to pay homage to Freddie Gray. On 7 June 2020, The Prince Estate published a video made up of archive images from the movement's demonstrations, accompanied by a tweet quoting a letter discovered in the singer's personal archives stating how much he abhorred intolerance of our fellow human beings. Legal proceedings against the police officers involved in the arrest that caused Gary's death were abandoned in July 2016. All were acquitted.

A demonstrator confronts the police on West North Avenue, in Baltimore, on 28 April 2015.

After an initial version of *Baltimore* had been recorded by 3RDEYEGIRL on 30 April 2015, Prince recorded the definitive version of the song on his own, entrusting the mixing and mastering to Dylan Dresdow. The singer Eryn Allen Kane—who had turned down a duo with Prince in 2013 because she lacked self-confidence—agreed to sing with him this time, at the charity concert Rally 4 Peace in May 2015, organized in honor of Freddie Gray who had died the previous month. The young woman also recorded her voice for *Baltimore*, as the two artists had become friends. "The Baltimore song is just a way of saying, 'I see what's going on. And here's my voice in the community and I just want to be able to let you know that we are here for you,'"[326] explained Welton, who recorded the first version of the song.

Single

ROCKNROLL LOVEAFFAIR

Prince / 4'01

Musicians: Prince: vocals, electric guitar, acoustic guitar, bass, drums, backing vocals / **Ida Nielsen:** bass / **John Blackwell:** drums / **Michael B Nelson:** trombone / **Steve Strand:** trumpet / **Kenni Holmen:** tenor saxophone, flute / **Dave Jensen:** trumpet / **Kathy Jensen:** alto saxophone, baritone saxophone / **Nick Marchione:** trumpet / **Steve Reid:** trumpet / **Philip Lassiter:** trumpet / **Lynn Grissett:** trumpet / **Roy Agee:** trombone / **Joey Rayfield:** trombone / **Adrian Crutchfield**: alto saxophone / **Keith Anderson:** tenor saxophone / **BK Jackson:** baritone saxophone / **Sylvester Onyejiaka**: baritone saxophone / **Andy Allo:** backing vocals / **Recording:** **Paisley Park, Chanhassen, Minnesota:** 2011–2012 (backing tracks), 2011–2012 (Hornheads wind); 2015 (The NPG Hornz wind) / **Technical team:** **Producer:** Prince / **Recording engineers:** Prince, Dylan Dresdow, Chris James, Justin Stanley, Booker T. / **Wind arrangements:** Adrian Crutchfield **Single:** **Digital release in Europe by NPG Records/Purple Music:** 22 November 2012 / **Released in Europe by NPG Records/Purple Music:** 22 November 2012 / **Best chart ranking in the USA:** did not make the charts / **Best chart ranking in the UK:** did not make the charts

Initially released as a single on 22 November 2012, *Rock and Roll Love Affair* was accompanied by a clip showing Hannah Welton on drums, Ida Nielsen on bass guitar, and Andy Allo on guitar. In fact, John Blackwell was the drummer on this song, recorded after *20Ten*, during a period when Prince was constantly offering content online. After being reworked to suit the *Hitnrun Phase Two* album, the song was renamed *Rocknroll Loveaffair*. As with *Xtraloveable*, the song's synthesizer tracks were replaced by wind parts, played by the 11 new members of the NPG Hornz and arranged by the saxophonist Adrian Crutchfield, who had also been involved with the album *Black Is the New Black* alongside the bass guitarist MonoNeon and the drummer Kirk Johnson at the end of 2015. An album that is still unreleased and which we cannot wait to discover, when The Prince Estate decides to release it.

2 Y. 2 D.

Prince / 3'50

Musicians: Prince: vocals, electric guitar, bass, backing vocals / **John Blackwell:** drums / **Justin Stanley:** Fender Rhodes piano, claps / **Michael B Nelson:** trombone / **Steve Strand:** trumpet / **Kenni Holmen:** tenor saxophone, flute / **Dave Jensen:** trumpet / **Kathy Jensen:** alto saxophone, baritone saxophone / **Marcus Anderson:** saxophone / **Shelby J.:** backing vocals / **Liv Warfield:** backing vocals / **Elisa Dease:** backing vocals / **Andy Allo:** backing vocals / **Recording:** **Paisley Park, Chanhassen, Minnesota:** 2011 (backing tracks), 2011–2012 (wind) / **Technical team:** **Producer:** Prince / **Recording engineers:** Prince, Dylan Dresdow, Chris James, Justin Stanley, Booker T. / **Wind arrangements:** Michael B Nelson

With its introductory motif reminiscent of that in the breaks in *Proud Mary* (Ike & Tina Turner's version, 1970), *2 Y. 2 D.* (pronounced *Too Young to Dare*) is a funk number recorded in 2011, after the sessions for *Welcome 2 America* were finished. Michael B Nelson was invited to provide the song with wind arrangements, played by the famous Hornheads, with the addition of the saxophone of Marcus Anderson. "I was doing a club show," Anderson recalled. "I was approached by someone who said they represent 'a major artist.' I thought it was L.A. talk. You know, people do a lot of that 'Give me your number' chat [...] On Wednesday I got a call. I was flown to Minneapolis and I began working with Prince in July 2012."[21] At that time, Prince also wanted to recruit the trombonist Troy Andrews, better known as Trombone Shorty, and to call on his friend Maceo Parker, to put together a high-caliber wind section. It was a top-class band of 11 wind players—one of the most impressive gathered together by a pop artist and all in the cause of a frenzied piece of funk.

LOOK AT ME, LOOK AT U

Prince / 3'27

Musicians: Prince: vocals, bass, backing vocals / **John Blackwell:** drums / **Xavier Taplin:** Fender Rhodes piano / **Marcus Anderson:** tenor saxophone, flute / **Recording: Paisley Park, Chanhassen, Minneosta:** 2014–2015 / **Technical team: Producer:** Prince / **Recording engineers:** Prince, Dylan Dresdow, Chris James, Justin Stanley, Booker T. / **Wind arrangements:** Marcus Anderson

As if wrapped in velvet that the listener wants to curl up in, the song *Look At Me, Look At U* has all the attributes of a smooth jazz number, starting with the saxophone and flute parts played by the virtuoso Marcus Anderson. The musician and composer Adi Yeshaya was asked to write the string arrangements for this song but, once recorded, Prince decided to remove them from the final mix, preferring the effectiveness of a pared-down production. Perhaps expecting that his humor would not be appreciated, he also decided not to include all the song's lyrics in the album's sleeve notes, omitting the sentence in which he declares to his beloved that her beauty is such that even Ray Charles and Stevie Wonder can appreciate it. The humorous touch is nevertheless highly significant, knowing the admiration and respect Prince always felt for these artists of genius.

STARE

Prince / 3'45

Musicians: Prince: vocals, electric guitar, bass, drums, backing vocals / **Nick Marchione:** trumpet / **Steve Reid:** trumpet / **Philip Lassiter:** trumpet / **Lynn Grissett:** trumpet / **Roy Agee:** trombone / **Joey Rayfield:** trombone / **Adrian Crutchfield**: alto saxophone / **Keith Anderson:** tenor saxophone / **BK Jackson:** baritone saxophone / **Sylvester Onyejiaka**: baritone saxophone / **Recording: Paisley Park, Chanhassen, Minnesota:** 2015 / **Technical team: Producer:** Prince / **Recording engineers:** Prince, Dylan Dresdow, Chris James, Justin Stanley, Booker T. / **Wind arrangements:** Joey Rayfield, Marcus Anderson, Lynn Grissett

On 22 December 2015, *Ebony* magazine published on its website an interview with Prince given at Paisley Park. In the interview, Prince revealed to the journalist Miles Marshall Lewis the secrets of the making of *Hitnrun Phase Two*. Whether it was to keep out of earshot of the curious or to take advantage of his cutting-edge audio system, the fact remains that Prince, as was his usual practice, played his album to the journalist in his car, this time a Cadillac XLR. "This bass is wicked, you understand?"[80] Prince told Lewis, before going on to explain that he attached great importance to his bass lines at that time, neglecting his guitar a little bit. It must be said that the guitar is conspicuous by its absence from *Hitnrun Phase Two*, even though Prince gives it a sizeable role when he slips in, at 1'26 in *Stare*, a nod to his long-standing fans, asking "Can I get a kiss?" and following this with an immediately recognizable sample borrowed from one of his greatest hits: *Kiss*, released in 1986.

XTRALOVEABLE

Prince / 5'00

Musicians: Prince: vocals, electric guitar, bass, synthesizers, backing vocals / **John Blackwell:** drums / **Michael B Nelson:** trombone / **Steve Strand:** trumpet / **Kenni Holmen:** tenor saxophone / **Dave Jensen:** trumpet / **Kathy Jensen:** alto saxophone, baritone saxophone / **Recording: Paisley Park, Chanhassen, Minnesota:** 2011 (backing tracks), 2011–2012 (wind) / **Technical team: Producer:** Prince / **Recording engineers:** Prince, Justin Stanley / **Wind arrangements:** Michael B Nelson

This is an outtake, written and thrown together for Vanity 6 (see page 72) in 1982, and finally unearthed from The Vault in 2011 to be rerecorded by Prince and released as a single. It was reworked again in 2013. Entitled *Xtraloveable* this time, the song was given wind lines that replaced the original synthesizers. The arranger Michael B Nelson gave the song a second rebirth, notably in its instrumental section, between 2'26 and 2'51, where 25 seconds of majestic wind playing blow away the 2011 version, which is nevertheless to be appreciated for its Minneapolis Sound quality and the rap part performed with brio by Andy Allo. "Prince sent me the song and there is a version that got released with Andy Allo rapping on it," Michael B Nelson explained. "So he said, 'Where the rap is at write something for the horns.' What's interesting about *Xtraloveable* is there were synth horn parts throughout it... the classic Prince synth horns. So we played along with those, but then another thing I did with Prince tracks that I knew he liked was anytime there was some space, I would throw something interesting in there if I heard it in my head."[347]

GROOVY POTENTIAL

Prince / 6'16

Musicians: Prince: vocals, electric guitar, bass, piano, synthesizers, claps, backing vocals / **Michael Bland:** drums / **Michael B Nelson:** trombone / **Steve Strand:** trumpet / **Kenni Holmen:** tenor saxophone / **Dave Jensen:** trumpet / **Kathy Jensen:** alto saxophone, baritone saxophone / **Adrian Crutchfield:** flute / **Recording: Paisley Park, Chanhassen, Minnesota:** 2012, 2011–2012 (wind) / **Technical team: Producer:** Prince / **Recording engineers:** Prince, Dylan Dresdow, Chris James, Justin Stanley, Booker T. / **Wind arrangements:** Michael B Nelson

Clear the decks and make way for dancing to the track *Groovy Potential*, in which all the ingredients of the best Prince vintages appear: a groove worthy of James Brown, sensual lyrics, a party atmosphere, and wind arrangements that are quite simply crazy by the Hornheads stalwart Michael B Nelson. While his drumming is familiar from Prince's more rock, even hip-hop numbers, it is a pleasure to hear Michael Bland on drums in this song, which incidentally marks his last appearance on a Prince record. Offered from 14 August 2013 on the website 3rdEyeTunes.com for $0.88, the song did not appear on any album before it found a suitable place on *Hitnrun Phase Two*. Worth noting are two nods the singer makes to his past repertoire, at the heart of the song. After the little homage to the break of *Little Red Corvette* at 2'41, Prince sings, at 2'27: "I like it when you dance for me," recalling the third track, *Dance 4 Me*, on *MPLSound*, which was released in 2009.

After replacing Ida Nielsen on some dates between 2010 and 2012, Andrew Gouché became the bass guitarist of NPG Q (NPG Quartet), a short-lived jazz project of Prince's in 2014.

WHEN SHE COMES

Prince / 3'45

Musicians: Prince: vocals, electric guitar, Fender Rhodes piano, synthesizers, backing vocals / **Andrew Gouché:** bass / **John Blackwell:** drums / **Michael B Nelson:** trombone / **Steve Strand:** trumpet / **Kenni Holmen:** tenor saxophone / **Dave Jensen:** trumpet / **Kathy Jensen:** alto saxophone, baritone saxophone / **Recording: Paisley Park, Chanhassen, Minnesota:** 2014; 2011–2012 (wind) / **Technical team: Producer:** Prince / **Recording engineers:** Prince, Dylan Dresdow, Chris James, Justin Stanley, Booker T. / **Wind arrangements:** Michael B Nelson

Inspired by the intrinsic sensuality of the songs of Al Green, *When She Comes* (a typical Prince double entendre) was first recorded during the sessions for *Welcome 2 America*, with the drummer Chris Coleman and bass guitarist Tal Wilkenfeld. This version is less soul and instead is revisited in the style of an Italian folk song (with the bandoneon, a type of concertina, played on the synthesizer). The song takes its place at the heart of the album and gives us a moment's respite before the frenzied *Screwdriver*. Justin Stanley, who was at the controls during numerous sessions for the album, explained that despite his amazing collection of synthesizers, Prince preferred to use an old, bottom-of-the-range Yamaha organ for most of the recordings. "[The kind] you would get for a child with all the preprogrammed sounds. And I knew that he had all these amazing synth keyboards that he used in the '80s like the Oberheim OB Synth and the Mini Moog. So I asked him, 'Where are all those keyboards?' And Prince gave me the keys to his warehouse [...] It was basically every set from the beginning when he first started [...] So we found all of the vintage synths and I set them all back up at the studio. But the funny thing was Prince kept going back to that Yamaha keyboard. Even though it was cheap Prince made it sound cool."[347]

Single

SCREWDRIVER

Prince / 4'15

Musicians: Prince: vocals, electric guitar, acoustic guitar, synthesizers, backing vocals / **Ida Nielsen:** bass / **John Blackwell:** drums / **Recording: Paisley Park, Chanhassen, Minnesota:** 2012–2013 / **Technical team: Producer:** Prince / **Recording engineers:** Prince, Dylan Dresdow, Chris James, Justin Stanley, Booker T., Ben Mühlethaler, Jamie Lewis
Single: Digital release by NPG Records/Purple Music: 4 February 2013 / **Best chart ranking in the USA:** did not make the charts / **Best chart ranking in the UK:** did not make the charts

First revealed to the public on 2 March 2013, when Prince and his new group 3RDEYEGIRL performed a very rock 'n' roll version of it on *Late Night with Jimmy Fallon*. Fans already knew the song because it had been available for download on the website 3rdEyeTunes.com since the previous February. Here is a song pumped up with testosterone and recorded by a power trio, featuring Prince, the drummer John Blackwell, and the bass player Ida Nielsen, and subsequently enlivened with overdubs in the studios at Paisley Park.

BLACK MUSE

Prince / 7'21

Musicians: Prince: vocals, electric guitar, acoustic guitar, bass, Fender Rhodes piano, synthesizers, backing vocals / **Shelby J.:** vocals, backing vocals / **Liv Warfield:** vocals, backing vocals / **Elisa Dease:** vocals, backing vocals / **John Blackwell:** drums / **Michael B Nelson:** trombone / **Steve Strand:** trumpet / **Kenni Holmen:** tenor saxophone, flute / **Dave Jensen:** trumpet / **Kathy Jensen:** alto saxophone, baritone saxophone, clarinet / **Recording: Paisley Park, Chanhassen, Minnesota:** 2010; 2011–2012 (wind) / **Technical team: Producer:** Prince / **Recording engineers:** Prince, Dylan Dresdow, Chris James, Justin Stanley, Booker T. / **Wind arrangements:** Michael B Nelson

2015

As Prince once explained: "This is the oldest one on here, and I loved it so much I just saved it."[80] Recorded during the sessions for *Welcome 2 America* in 2010, *Black Muse* stands out as much for its even rhythm at 108 BPM as for its important social message. "Keep what you make," Prince told Dan Piepenbring, with whom he had begun to work on his autobiography shortly before his death. "I stayed in Minneapolis because Minneapolis made me. You have to give back. My dad came to Minneapolis from Cotton Valley, Louisiana. He learned in the harshest conditions what it means to control wealth. *Black Muse* is about that, creating wealth in the inner city."[348] The singer, who said he spent the year 2015 studying his father's story, dedicated this song to him when the Piano & A Microphone Tour was in Australia. The fans, who in 2021 would discover the posthumous album *Welcome 2 America*, recognized the song *1000 Light Years Away From Here* since it was initially recorded independently before being added to the end of *Black Muse* for the *Hitnrun Phase Two* album.

REVELATION

Prince / 5'21

Musicians: Prince: vocals, electric guitar, synthesizers, backing vocals / **Andrew Gouché:** bass / **John Blackwell:** drums / **Xavier Taplin:** Fender Rhodes piano / **Marcus Anderson:** soprano saxophone / **Recording: Paisley Park, Chanhassen, Minnesota:** 2014–2015 / **Technical team: Producer:** Prince / **Recording engineers:** Prince, Dylan Dresdow, Chris James, Justin Stanley, Booker T.

The drummer for this song, John Blackwell, said: "One of the first [Phase II] songs we recorded was *Revelation*. When we were working on that everybody was just excited. We all looked at each other like, 'Man, this song is going to be crazy!'"[347] Built on a bass line played by Andrew Gouché, the song took shape during an interminable jam session at Paisley Park. "I lost 40 pounds when I started working for that dude," the bass player said of his employer. "I was like if Prince can do it, I can do it."[347] Even though Gouché confirmed that Prince never preached in front of his musicians or dictated his morals excessively, *Revelation* is a song imbued with spirituality, as its author indicated in the pages of *Ebony* magazine, emphasizing that the lyrics were inspired by his reading of the Bible, particularly about Moses in Exodus.

BIG CITY

Prince / 6'26

Musicians: Prince: vocals, spoken voice, electric guitar, acoustic guitar, piano, tambourine, backing vocals / **Ledisi:** vocals, backing vocals / **Ida Nielsen:** bass / **John Blackwell:** drums / **Cassandra O'Neal:** Fender Rhodes piano / **Nick Marchione:** trumpet / **Steve Reid:** trumpet / **Philip Lassiter:** trumpet / **Lynn Grissett:** trumpet / **Roy Agee:** trombone / **Joey Rayfield:** trombone / **Adrian Crutchfield:** alto saxophone / **Keith Anderson:** tenor saxophone / **BK Jackson:** baritone saxophone / **Sylvester Onyejiaka:** baritone saxophone / **Shelby J.:** backing vocals, claps / **Liv Warfield:** backing vocals, claps / **Elisa Dease:** backing vocals, claps / **Recording: Paisley Park, Chanhassen, Minnesota:** October 2011 / **Technical team: Producer:** Prince / **Recording engineers:** Prince, Dylan Dresdow, Chris James, Justin Stanley, Booker T. / **Wind arrangements:** Michael B Nelson, Philip Lassiter

On 16 February 2016, Prince went on stage at the State Theatre-Arts Centre, in Melbourne, for the first date of the Piano & A Microphone Tour. After the prerecorded introduction, the singer announced to his audience: "Nothing interesting happens before midnight, so I think we got to warm it up."[349] He then launched into a ragtime version of *Big City*, which appears at the end of *Hitnrun Phase Two*. It must be said that the song in its studio version (recorded in 2011) is a funk gem, as Prince knew how to deliver so well. The vocals feature Ledisi, with whom the singer had also recorded *Ain't Gonna Miss U When U're Gone* in 2013, and the famous backing vocalists' trio of the *20Ten* era, made up of Liv Warfield, Elisa Dease, and Shelby J. "Being in the studio with Prince felt like two friends hanging out [...]," Ledisi recalled. "This wasn't flashy Prince; this was Prince Rogers Nelson in Minneapolis at his house hanging out."[347] Once the song had been retrieved from The Vault with a view to incorporating it into the new album, Prince decided to give it some wind arrangements. While the Hornheads are heard in the song's introduction, it is the NPG Hornz who take over a little later in the track, giving it an even funkier feel, as Michael B Nelson explained: "Prince brought in his touring horn section. They have a much looser, funkier sound. I grew up listening to big band and I was very much a bebop and jazz musician. So my musical background was very different from Prince's. When I started to work with him, I started listening to some James Brown and Sly Stone, but they were not part of my early influences."[347]

The talented bass guitarist Ida Nielsen enlivened the Welcome 2 America Tour before joining the feisty 3RDEYEGIRL project.

4EVER

Released in the USA by NPG Records/Warner Bros. Records:
22 November 2016 (CD ref.: 558509-2)
Released in the UK by NPG Records/WEA International:
25 November 2016 (CD ref.: 9362-49146-0)
Best chart ranking in the USA: 33
Best chart ranking in the UK: 21

Prince attends the première of the movie *Purple Rain* at the TCL Mann's Chinese Theatre, in Los Angeles, on 26 July 1984.

Disc 1

1. *1999* (3'39)
2. *Little Red Corvette* (3'09)
3. *When Doves Cry* (3'48)
4. *Let's Go Crazy* (3'50)
5. *Raspberry Beret* (3'35)
6. *I Wanna Be Your Lover* (3'00)
7. *Soft and Wet* (3'05)
8. *Why You Wanna Treat Me So Bad?* (3'51)
9. *Uptown* (4'11)
10. *When You Were Mine* (3'46)
11. *Head* (4'46)
12. *Gotta Stop (Messin' About)* (2'57)
13. *Controversy* (3'38)
14. *Let's Work* (3'02)
15. *Delirious* (2'41)
16. *I Would Die 4 U* (2'59)
17. *Take Me With U* (3'44)
18. *Paisley Park* (4'44)
19. *Pop Life* (3'45)
20. *Purple Rain* (8'41)

Disc 2

1. *Kiss* (3'46)
2. *Sign O' the Times* (3'44)
3. *Alphabet St* (2'25)
4. *Batdance* (4'07)
5. *Thieves in the Temple* (3'21)
6. *Cream* (4'13)
7. *Mountains* (3'58)
8. *Girls & Boys* (3'28)
9. *If I Was Your Girlfriend* (3'46)
10. *U Got the Look* (3'48)
11. *I Could Never Take the Place of Your Man* (3'41)
12. *Glam Slam* (3'31)
13. *Moonbeam Levels* (4'06)
14. *Diamonds and Pearls* (4'20)
15. *Gett Off* (4'00)
16. *Sexy M.F.* (5'26)
17. *My Name Is Prince* (4'04)
18. *7 (Album Edit)* (4'23)
19. *Peach* (3'48)
20. *Nothing Compares 2 U* (4'19)

DIGGING INTO THE VAULT FOR THE FIRST TIME

From the start of the negotiations that were supposed to mark the reunion between Prince and Warner Bros. Records in 2014, the two parties drew up a schedule for rereleases. Prince agreed the company could release an umpteenth compilation in the coming years and consented to working on a new version of *Purple Rain*, which he would enliven with rare, unreleased content. The singer's death on 21 April 2016 speeded up the launch of these projects. Working with the singer's estate, Warner Bros. Records hastily chose 39 of Prince's songs, all from the years when he was with the record company, naturally missing out the remainder of his career and thus depriving potential new fans of the many singles the artist released after 1992. The only outstanding number, which on its own justifies buying the record, is the unreleased *Moonbeam Levels*, recorded during the sessions for the album *1999* in 1982. The "fams" already knew this song because it had been doing the rounds among bootleggers for a long time. Although for Prince's devoted admirers *4Ever* is of interest only as a posthumous homage to the singer, the album nevertheless gives hope with regards to the opening up of The Vault, which Prince only did rarely, notably for the release of *Crystal Ball* in 1998 and *The Vault...Old Friends 4 Sale* in 1999.

MOONBEAM LEVELS

Prince / 4'06

Musician: **Prince:** vocals, electric guitar, bass, programming, piano, synthesizers, backing vocals / **Recording:** **Sunset Sound, Los Angeles:** 6 July 1982 / **Kiowa Trail Home Studio, Chanhassen, Minnesota:** 8 June 1983 / **Technical team:** **Producer:** Prince / **Recording engineers:** Peggy McCreary (Sunset Sound), Don Batts (Kiowa Trail Home Studio)

Moonbeam Levels is one of those songs that, although it remains unreleased, made a mark with fans, doubtless due to the profusion of bootleg recordings that changed hands over the decades—which Prince fought against in vain all his life. While *Electric Intercourse*, *Rebirth of the Flesh*, *Wally*, and *Empty Room* were all bought and sold on cassettes or compact discs over the years, *Moonbeam Levels* always occupied a special place in the heart of fans, but also in the heart of Susan Rogers, who joined Prince after the song was recorded, yet declared that it remains one of her favorites by him to this day. "We sequenced it on *Purple Rain*, and he took it off. We sequenced it on *Around the World in a Day*, and he took it off. We even put it on the *Parade* album, and he took it off. Then it got too late, and he couldn't release it. It was very personal, and I think he just didn't want people to hear it. He wasn't ready."[75] Although too precious in the singer's eyes to be revealed to the general public, *Moonbeam Levels* was nevertheless released on *4Ever* and then on the rerelease of *1999* in 2019, thus ignoring the wishes of Prince who had never wanted this very personal song to be revealed.

PURPLE RAIN DELUXE EXPANDED EDITION

Released in the USA by NPG Records/Warner Records:
23 June 2017 (CD ref: 547374-2)
Released in the UK by NPG Records/Warner Records:
23 June 2017 (CD ref: 9362-49132-0)
Best chart ranking in the USA: 4
Best chart ranking in the UK: 7

An iconic shot of Prince on the Purple Rain Tour, taken by the photographer Richard E Aaron.

Disc 1 Original Album (2015 Paisley Park Remaster)

1. *Let's Go Crazy* (4'39)
2. *Take Me With U* (3'54)
3. *The Beautiful Ones* (5'13)
4. *Computer Blue* (3'59)
5. *Darling Nikki* (4'13)
6. *When Doves Cry* (5'52)
7. *I Would Die 4 U* (2'51)
8. *Baby I'm A Star* (4'20)
9. *Purple Rain* (8'41)

Disc 2 From The Vault & Previously Unreleased

1. *The Dance Electric* (11'29)
2. *Love and Sex* (5'00)
3. *Computer Blue ("Hallway Speech" Version)* (12'18)
4. *Electric Intercourse (Studio Version)* (4'57)
5. *Our Destiny/ Roadhouse Garden* (6'25)
6. *Possessed* (7'56)
7. *Wonderful Ass* (6'24)
8. *Velvet Kitty Cat* (2'42)
9. *Katrina's Paper Dolls* (3'30)
10. *We Can F**k* (10'17)
11. *Father's Song* (5'30)

Disc 3 Single Edits & B-Sides

1. *When Doves Cry (7" Single Edit)* (3'49)
2. *17 Days (B-Side Edit)* (3'58)
3. *Let's Go Crazy (7"Single Edit)* (3'49)
4. *Let's Go Crazy (Special Dance Mix)* (7'36)
5. *Erotic City (7" B-Side Edit)* (3'57)
6. *Erotic City ("Make Love Not War Erotic City Come Alive")* (7'27)
7. *Purple Rain (7" Single Edit)* (4'08)
8. *God (7" B-Side Edit)* (4'04)
9. *God (Love Theme from Purple Rain) (UK 12" B-Side Edit)* (7'57)
10. *Another Lonely Christmas (7" B-Side Edit)* (4'56)
11. *Another Lonely Christmas (Extended Version)* (6'52)
12. *I Would Die 4 U (7" Single Edit)* (2'59)
13. *I Would Die 4 U (7" Single Extended Version)* (10'20)
14. *Baby I'm A Star (7" B-Side Edit)* (2'52)
15. *Take Me With U (7" Single Edit)* (3'43)

Disc 4
DVD Prince and The Revolution: Live at the Carrier Dome, Syracuse, NY, 30 March 1985

A DELUGE OF UNPUBLISHED MATERIAL

On 19 April 2017, Casey Rain, a blogger on The Violet Reality website posted on his Facebook page the provisional tracklist for the deluxe edition of *Purple Rain*, which fans had been anticipating since 2014. Warner Bros. Records (referred to here as Warner Records, thus hinting to the music business that new bosses Aaron Bay-Schuck and Tom Corson had decided on a name change, which eventually came into effect in May 2019) seemed to have finally completed the reissue so long awaited by fans. The release date was announced for 23 June 2017. This new version of the cult album features a DVD and three CDs, including the original album, remastered in 2015 by Prince and his faithful disciple Joshua Welton. The 11 unreleased tracks from the *Purple Rain* sessions on the second disc will delight fans, while a third CD brings together 15 remixes or single versions of songs from the opus. A gold mine for the "fams" as well as for the general public who can also enjoy Live at the Carrier Dome in Syracuse, which was filmed on 30 March 1985 (originally available on VHS but now on DVD). The only slight regret surrounding this surprise release is that they did not also release it on vinyl.

THE DANCE ELECTRIC

Prince / 11'29

Musician: Prince: vocals, electric guitar, bass, programming, synthesizers, backing vocals / **Recording: Flying Cloud Drive Warehouse, Eden Prairie, Minnesota:** 17 August 1984 / **Technical team: Producer:** Prince / **Recording engineer:** Susan Rogers

Like many songs from the *Purple Rain* era, *The Dance Electric* emerged from the endless jam sessions that Prince held with the musicians of the Revolution. Bassist Brown Mark later confirmed that the track was a collective effort, which Prince took to record in his home studio in Eden Prairie. Fans had to wait until 2017 before the track was officially released because Prince chose to give it to his childhood friend André Cymone, who in 1984 was in the middle of recording *A.C.*, his third album. "I saw him in a discotheque one night," Prince said of the gift to his friend, "and grabbed him by his shirt and said, 'Come on, I got this hit. You know I got this hit, don't you? *Dance Electric*? Yeah, it's great. You need it, you need it.'"[250] André Cymone told a slightly different story about the track, which was released as a wonderful single the following year. "I think Prince gave me *The Dance Electric* to make up for all the rumors about the songs I wrote with him [...] I listened to it, I thought it was great, but I was very hesitant to put it on the album. At that point in my career, I wanted to try to get out of that business, but of course the record company thought it was a great idea to have a Prince song on the album. In retrospect, it was a good thing, because it allowed us both to complete a common history that goes back to our teenage years..."[350] Contrary to the information given in the booklet notes for the *Purple Rain Deluxe Expanded Edition*, the backing vocals recorded by Wendy Melvoin and Lisa Coleman do not feature in the version referred to here, but only in the André Cymone version, on which Jill Jones also laid down some vocals in August 1984. After Cymone recorded his own vocal line at Ocean Way Studios in Los Angeles, the song was edited down from 11'29 to 3'59 when CBS released it as a single on 16 July 1985.

When will the original version of *(I Want 2 B A) Modernaire*, written with Dez Dickerson and performed in a fleeting and unforgettable scene at 24'08 in the movie *Purple Rain*, be released?

LOVE AND SEX

Prince / 5'00

Musicians: Prince: vocals, electric guitar, bass, programming, synthesizers, backing vocals / **Wendy Melvoin:** backing vocals / **Lisa Coleman:** backing vocals / **Recording: Sunset Sound, Los Angeles:** 27 February 1984 / **Technical team: Producer:** Prince / **Recording engineer:** Peggy McCreary

When recording engineer Peggy McCreary arrived at Sunset Sound on the morning of 27 February 1984, she had no idea she would be working on a mammoth recording session that would last 18 hours. Prince was at the very top of his game as a recording artist, and that day he recorded *Love and Sex*, a pop song with very effective choruses, reminiscent of the famous motif "Boom-Lakalakalaka-Boom" from Sly and the Family Stone's *I Want To Take You Higher* (1969). He asked McCreary to equip the studio with a Yamaha DX-7 synthesizer, which back then was a revolutionary keyboard used by all pop musicians in the business. Its glacial sounds can be heard between 4'13 and 4'17 of the track, signaling a break with the timeless analog synthesizers that Prince had used until then. In 1986, Prince recorded another song that was also called *Love and Sex*, which remained unreleased until it appeared on the *Sign O' the Times (Super) Deluxe Edition* in September 2020, but the two tracks are very different and are not connected in any way.

COMPUTER BLUE ("HALLWAY SPEECH" VERSION)

Prince, John L Nelson, Lisa Coleman, Wendy Melvoin / 12'18

Musicians: Prince: vocals, electric guitar, programming, synthesizers, backing vocals / **Wendy Melvoin:** electric guitar, backing vocals / **Brown Mark:** bass, backing vocals / **Bobby Z.:** drums, percussion, electronic percussion / **Lisa Coleman:** synthesizers, backing vocals / **Doctor Fink:** synthesizers, backing vocals / **Recording: The Warehouse, St Louis Park, Minnesota:** 8 August 1983 / **Sunset Sound, Los Angeles:** 15–20, 29, 31 August 1983 (overdubs) / **Technical team: Producer:** Prince / **Recording engineers:** Susan Rogers (The Warehouse), Peggy McCreary (Sunset Sound), David Leonard (Sunset Sound)

It's worth buying the entire reissue just for the insanely fabulous *Computer Blue ("Hallway Speech" Version)*, the full version of which many Prince fans had been waiting for since 1984.

When *Purple Rain* was released in the mid-1980s, there were some intriguing lyrics that appeared in the sleeve notes but not in the song: "Poor lonely computer/It's time someone programmed U/It's time U learned love and lust/They both have 4 letters/But they R entirely different words." The passage, narrated here by Wendy and Lisa, seems to show a Prince tormented by love and how he can regain his sanity.

This version introduces a very interesting concept to the track, as the protagonist wanders along corridors that represent his emotions. Each corridor is given a name—"lust," "fear," "hate"—and they all appear to lead our hero to his bedroom, apparently accompanied by a girl, who we imagine to be the delectable Apollonia (see page 91) from *Purple Rain*.

A disturbing track of rare power that, like the previous version, includes a solo inspired by an instrumental written by Prince's father, John L Nelson. It is entitled *Father's Song* and appears at the end of the record.

HEADPHONES AT THE READY

The vocalizing sung in unison by Prince and the musicians at 6'34 on *Computer Blue ("Hallway Speech" Version)* does not appear on the original album and was reused for the final melody of *Erotic City*, recorded a few months later at Sunset Sound.

ELECTRIC INTERCOURSE (STUDIO VERSION)

Prince / 4'57

Musician: Prince: vocals, programming, finger snapping, claps, piano, synthesizers, backing vocals / **Recording: Sunset Sound, Los Angeles:** 14 January, 12 September 1983 / **Technical team: Producer:** Prince / **Recording engineers:** Peggy McCreary, David Leonard

While the live version of *Electric Intercourse*, recorded on 3 August 1983 at First Avenue in Minneapolis (the same night as *I Would Die 4 U*, *Baby I'm A Star*, and *Purple Rain* were laid down on tape), is by far the best performance of this sublime ballad, the *HitnRun Phase Two* album contains the studio version. Written and recorded as a languid slow dance number symbolizing the romantic tension between Prince and Apollonia (see page 91) that lies at the core of the movie, the song was ousted from the movie and hence the soundtrack by its rival, *The Beautiful Ones*. "Once *The Beautiful Ones* was completed," Prince confirmed, "it was always the ballad of choice."[114] The shelves of The Vault are packed with exceptional songs, and *Electric Intercourse* was without a doubt once among them.

OUR DESTINY / ROADHOUSE GARDEN

Prince / 6'25

Musicians: Prince: vocals (***Roadhouse Garden***), electric guitar, drums, programming, tambourine, synthesizers, finger cymbals, backing vocals / **Jill Jones:** vocals (***Our Destiny***), backing vocals / **Wendy Melvoin:** electric guitar, backing vocals / **Brown Mark:** bass, backing vocals / **Bobby Z.:** drums, percussion, electronic percussion / **Lisa Coleman:** synthesizers, backing vocals / **Doctor Fink:** synthesizers, backing vocals / **Sid Page:** violin / **E Marcy Dicterow-Vaj:** viola / **Denyse Buffum:** viola / **Laury Woods:** viola / **Suzie Katayama:** cello / **David Coleman:** cello / **Tim Barr:** double bass / **Ann Atkinson:** double bass / **John Liotine:** trumpet / **Brad Warnaar:** horn / **Steve Madaio:** saxophone / **Dick Mitchell:** saxophone, flute / **Recording: First Avenue, Minneapolis:** 7 June 1984 (backing tracks) / **Sunset Sound, Los Angeles:** 27–29 September 1984 (overdubs ***Our Destiny***); 12 May 1985 (overdubs ***Our Destiny***); 19 January 1986 (overdubs ***Roadhouse Garden***) / **Technical team: Producers:** Wendy Melvoin (***Our Destiny***), Lisa Coleman (***Our Destiny***), Prince (***Roadhouse Garden***) / **Recording engineers:** David Rivkin (First Avenue), Peggy McCreary (Sunset Sound), Coke Johnson (Sunset Sound)

Before *Roadhouse Garden* became the name of a 1998 project for an album of unreleased tracks recorded with The Revolution, it was the title of a musical that Prince wanted to create in 1984. *Our Destiny* and *Roadhouse Garden* were two songs originally written for inclusion in the musical which were eventually combined to create just one song. Lisa Coleman, who had supplied vocals for an initial version of *Our Destiny*, was replaced by Jill Jones, who became the sole vocalist. "[Prince] had given me the tape where he plays it alone on the piano," Jill Jones told Schkopi.com. "But the tape on the cassette was so damaged that it broke when I tried to copy it."[351] Lisa Coleman and Wendy Melvoin had previously provided string arrangements for the song, which would be reused in the intro to *The Ladder* for 1985's *Around the World in a Day*. The song *Roadhouse Garden* was also recorded during a concert at First Avenue in Minneapolis on 7 June 1984 before Prince gave it a little more time at Sunset Sound in Los Angeles on 19 January 1986. Thanks to a pop melody that stays in your head for hours, it is one of the most appreciable moments on this excellent rerelease of *Purple Rain*.

Susan Moonsie, Denise "Vanity" Matthews, and Brenda Bennett, stars of the Vanity 6 trio.

POSSESSED

Prince / 7'56

Musician: Prince: vocals, programming, piano, synthesizers, harp, backing vocals / **Recording:** Sunset Sound, Los Angeles: 17 March 1984 / **Technical team:** Producer: Prince / Recording engineer: Peggy McCreary

Possessed was first laid down on tape in 1982 during the *1999* sessions and made a fleeting reappearance at 28'57 of the *Purple Rain* movie as an instrumental version that had been entirely rerecorded by Prince in March 1984. The song was performed on the Purple Rain Tour and recorded at the Syracuse concert, a DVD of which is included with the *Purple Rain Deluxe Expanded Edition*. Although the original version of the song was perfect from an objective standpoint (as the 2019 rerelease of *1999* shows), Prince attempted to rerecord it in August 1983, but failed. The band spent the whole day rehearsing in the sweltering heat at The Warehouse in St Louis Park, trying to get the song on tape. The power in the room cut out several times and one of the musicians joked that it was the Devil trying to stop the recording of this racy song. This unfortunate quip caused the highly superstitious Prince to halt the recording there and then. It wasn't until the following March that he started working on it again, adding a harp part himself—after having learned the rudiments of harp playing the same day—and refusing point blank to play the handful of notes on the Yamaha DX-7, even though the sound it produced would have been identical.

WONDERFUL ASS

Prince / 6'24

Musicians: Prince: vocals, electric guitar, bass, programming, synthesizers, backing vocals / Lisa Coleman: vocals, synthesizers, backing vocals / **Recording:** Kiowa Trail Home Studio, Chanhassen, Minnesota: 1983 / Flying Cloud Drive Warehouse, Eden Prairie, Minnesota: 7, 9 September 1984 (vocal overdubs) / **Technical team:** Producer: Prince / Recording engineer: Susan Rogers

Wonderful Ass was slated for inclusion on 1998's *Crystal Ball* album but subsequently dropped, presumably because of Lisa Coleman's presence on the track, as Prince was also planning to release *Roadhouse Garden* around that time, a compilation of unreleased material from The Revolution era. The theme of the song was the subject of much discussion among fans who were trying to guess which butt Prince was referring to in the track. "Wendy and her twin sister, Susannah, are pretty famous for having nice butts, and Prince did have one of the world's cutest butts," said Lisa Coleman, who sings with Prince on the song. "Prince was dating Susannah, and I was with Wendy. It was us being goofy about our girlfriends."[352]

VELVET KITTY CAT

Prince / 2'42

Musician: Prince: vocals, electric guitar, bass, programming, synthesizers / **Recording:** Sunset Sound, Los Angeles: 20 April 1983 / **Technical team:** Producer: Prince / Recording engineer: Peggy McCreary

Written for Vanity 6's second album, *Velvet Kitty Kat* has all the characteristics of the songs on the female trio's 1982 self-titled debut album: a bouncy electronic pop beat similar to that of *Wet Dream* and *Bite the Beat* and a straightforward melody which suited the three young women. It would have been perfect for Vanity 6 had their lead singer, Denise "Vanity" Matthews (see page 72), not decided to quit before the shooting of *Purple Rain*. Planned for inclusion in Apollonia 6's second album (see page 91), which was never released, *Velvet Kitty Kat* was returned to The Vault.

KATRINA'S PAPER DOLLS

Prince / 3'30

Musician: Prince: vocals, programming, synthesizers, backing vocals / **Recording:** Universal Recording Corporation, Chicago: March 1983 / **Technical team:** Producer: Prince / Recording engineer: Prince

Who is Katrina, this woman who makes a paper doll for every day her lover has been gone, leaving her bereft? Katrina is Denise "Vanity" Matthews' middle name but there is nothing to suggest that Prince wrote the song for the woman who was once his girlfriend (see page 72). The genesis of the song itself is shrouded in mystery as Lisa Coleman claims to have written the title with her older sister Cole Ynda, before Prince appropriated and recorded it between the Pittsburgh and Peoria concerts on the 1999 Tour.

WE CAN F**K

Prince / 10'17

Musicians: Prince: vocals, electric guitar, bass, drums, piano, synthesizers, backing vocals / **Wendy Melvoin:** electric guitar, backing vocals / **Lisa Coleman:** synthesizers, backing vocals / **Jill Jones:** backing vocals / **David Coleman:** oud, finger cymbals / **Recording: Sunset Sound, Los Angeles:** 31 December 1983; 1–2 January 1984 / **Technical team: Producer:** Prince / **Recording engineer:** Terry Christian

Although there are two asterisks in the title on the *Purple Rain Deluxe Expanded Edition* tracklist, the song's official name is indeed *We Can Fuck*, which is what we will call it here. It took three days to record this paean to carnal pleasures that emerged from a jam session between Prince, Wendy Melvoin, Lisa Coleman, and Lisa's brother, David. David Coleman was a talented composer and audacious musician who had just been introduced to Prince. He broadened Prince's musical horizons in unexpected ways, introducing him to the Arabic sounds of instruments such as the oud and the finger cymbals (Prince would adopt the latter with great enthusiasm). Meeting David Coleman not only subsequently influenced Prince in the production of the highly eclectic *Around the World in a Day*, it also initially led to *We Can Fuck*, on which Lisa and Wendy recorded backing vocals and Jill Jones contributed screams of pleasure. "Prince was really taken with David at the time," says Lisa Coleman. "My brother was very schooled in Arabic and Middle Eastern music. Prince was piqued by someone who knew part of a language he wasn't familiar with [...] He thought Middle Eastern music was very sexy. He married a belly dancer after that. The words were pretty silly. Prince was telling me to sing like Bette Davis."[352] The song was rerecorded with George Clinton and his musicians for the 1990 *Graffiti Bridge* soundtrack and renamed *We Can Funk*. Prince recorded a final version of the song as a duet with Andy Allo, which was released on Tidal on 7 November 2015. Divinely performed by Allo on vocals, the track was called *Oui Can Luv*.

FATHER'S SONG

John L Nelson / 5'30

Musician: Prince: electric guitar, bass, piano, synthesizers / **Recording: Kiowa Trail Home Studio, Chanhassen, Minnesota:** 24 October, 20 November 1983 / **Technical team: Producer:** Prince / **Recording engineers:** Susan Rogers

Written by John L Nelson, *Father's Song* is recognizable from the majestic guitar solo on *Computer Blue*, arguably the greatest 6-string performance of Prince's entire career. This is the original version, performed by Prince on piano, before he added some synthesizer, bass, and guitar overdubs. Another version of the instrumental, recorded on 7 February 1984, appears at 55'23 of the *Purple Rain* movie when the Kid surprises his father—played by the late Clarence Williams III—playing the melody on the piano. This track, composed by John L Nelson, supports the theory that the movie is semi-autobiographical, as many observers have repeatedly stated. "Prince and his dad had a very deep, important relationship," Lisa Coleman confided in 2017. "[...] After a couple of years, he started inviting his dad around more. This song was a healing gesture. It was important to Prince to have his father be represented [...] He would be pleased to have it included [in this package]."[352]

GOD (LOVE THEME FROM PURPLE RAIN) (UK 12" B-SIDE EDIT)

Prince / 7'57

Musicians: Prince: electric guitar, bass, drums, piano, synthesizers / **Sheila E.:** drums / **Recording: Sunset Sound, Los Angeles:** 7 February 1984 / **Technical team: Producer:** Prince / **Recording engineer:** Peggy McCreary

God (Love Theme from Purple Rain) illustrates the torrid scene between the Kid and Apollonia (see page 91) at 40'08 of the movie, but it was recorded with Sheila E. in February 1984. In studio two at Sunset Sound, the sexual tension between the two musicians was reaching boiling point, as Peggy McCreary later recalled for Duane Tudahl's must-have book *Prince and The Purple Rain Era Studio Sessions, 1983 and 1984*: "[Sheila and Prince] were musically just playing with each other, sort of flirting with each other. It was midnight, and I was like 'Okay, can't we just leave? Can't you two just get a room?'"[92] The song was reworked the following August, with an additional vocal line, and recorded as the B-side for the single *Purple Rain*, entitled *God* in the US and *God (Vocal)* in the UK and Europe.

Sheila E. wears an outfit inspired by the New Romantic movement in the mid-1980s.

ANTHOLOGY: 1995–2010

Digital release: 17 August 2018
Best US iTunes ranking: 22
Best UK iTunes ranking: 28

Grandeur and extravagance for The Artist Formerly Known As Prince, in Rotterdam, in 1998.

1. *Emancipation* **(4'13)**
2. *Black Sweat* **(3'11)**
3. *P. Control* **(5'59)**
4. *Crucial* **(5'08)**
5. *The Love We Make* **(4'39)**
6. *👁 Hate U* **(6'07)**
7. *The Greatest Romance Ever Sold* **(5'33)**
8. *👁 Love U, But 👁 Don't Trust U Anymore* **(3'36)**
9. *Gold* **(7'22)**
10. *Guitar* **(3'45)**
11. *Dream Factory* **(3'07)**
12. *The Work Pt. 1* **(4'28)**
13. *Call My Name* **(5'15)**
14. *Strays of the World* **(5'06)**
15. *Shhh* **(7'17)**
16. *Dreamer* **(5'32)**
17. *Chaos and Disorder* **(4'19)**
18. *Endorphinmachine* **(4'06)**
19. *Musicology* **(4'24)**
20. *Northside* **(6'31)**
21. *When 👁 Lay My Hands On U* **(3'40)**
22. *Beautiful Strange* **(4'55)**
23. *Future Soul Song* **(5'08)**
24. *Empty Room (Live From One Nite Alone Tour 2002)* **(4'00)**
25. *3rd Eye* **(4'54)**
26. *U're Gonna C Me* **(5'16)**
27. *Dinner with Delores* **(2'46)**
28. *Ol' Skool Company* **(7'30)**
29. *4Ever* **(3'47)**
30. *West* **(14'00)**
31. *Xpedition* **(8'23)**
32. *Muse 2 the Pharaoh* **(4'21)**
33. *Somewhere Here On Earth* **(5'46)**
34. *U Make My Sun Shine* **(7'05)**
35. *1+1+1 Is 3* **(5'17)**
36. *Chelsea Rodgers* **(5'41)**
37. *We March* **(4'49)**

THE PARTNERSHIP WITH LEGACY RECORDINGS

After the incipient partnership with Universal Music in 2017 was nullified, Prince's estate, now renamed The Prince Estate, announced on 27 June 2018 that it would be working with Sony Music, which would distribute Prince's catalog under its Legacy Recordings label. The agreement initially covered albums Prince had recorded after his departure from Warner Bros. Records in 1996, but it was expanded after 1 January 2021 when Prince's first record label lost the rights to the albums recorded by their protégé between 1978 and 1995. The first release that sealed the collaboration was the digital distribution of a selection of 37 Prince songs not previously released on any other compilation. *Anthology: 1995–2010* gives us the opportunity to (re)discover tracks that had gone unnoticed by the general public (*Dreamer*, *Northside*, *Beautiful Strange*, or *U're Gonna C Me*), and it shows a readiness to move away from an overly classic selection of the many Prince productions. Although this anthology of high-quality songs would not contain any surprises for fans, it did send a positive message and reassure them that NPG Records fully intended to continue treating them to tracks taken from the artist's repertoire which would be carefully selected from among the best on offer. Prince novices may regret the absence of 1980s hits on this compilation, but they will be able to savor the singles that were subsequently released, such as *Black Sweat*, *The Greatest Romance Ever Sold*, *The Work Pt. 1*, and *Musicology*.

PIANO & A MICROPHONE 1983

World release by The Prince Estate/NPG records/Warner Bros. Records: 21 September 2018 (Album + CD box set ref: R1 567737)
Best chart ranking in the USA: 11
Best chart ranking in the UK: 12

The tickets for the concert at The Fabulous Forum in Inglewood, California, on 19 February 1985 bore the instruction: "Wear something purple"!

1. *17 Days* **(6'22)**
2. *Purple Rain* **(1'26)**
3. *A Case of You* **(1'40)**
4. *Mary Don't You Weep* **(4'42)**
5. *Strange Relationship* **(2'38)**
6. *International Lover* **(3'48)**
7. *Wednesday* **(1'59)**
8. *Cold Coffee & Cocaine* **(5'13)**
9. *Why the Butterflies* **(6'26)**

A PRINCE WITHOUT ARTIFICE

The last Warner Bros. Records' project manager who worked with Prince (on *Plectrumelectrum* and *Art Official Age*) was hired after the singer's death as the official archivist of The Prince Estate. Michael Howe knew Prince well during the last years of his life, had a productive working relationship with him, and was a friend in many ways. As soon as the excavation of The Vault began, Howe and his bosses picked out a recording that was well known to fans by dint of having been sold under the table for decades. It was a series of songs recorded over the course of 1983, when Prince was writing his masterpiece *Purple Rain* in his home studio at Kiowa Trail in Chanhassen. Alone with his recording engineer Don Batts, Prince recorded multiple sessions during which he sang and accompanied himself on piano. Michael Howe knew this famous bootleg inside out and with the keys to The Vault in his pocket, he set out to find the tapes of these recordings. "The most recent tour that he did prior to his death was the Piano & A Microphone Tour," he explained, "so there was a continuity to his most recent public appearances and what we imagined should be the first thing from The Vault [...]"[353] As the archivist added in a subsequent interview: "So we did a bit of detective work and were able to narrow a wide pool of candidates. We spotted this one that had Prince's handwriting on the label on side B and it said *Cold Coffee & Cocaine* and *Why the Butterflies*, which are the final two songs of the recordings. We were pretty sure we had it. Once we analyzed it, inserted it into the machine, and digitized it, we were fortunately correct."[354]

MARY DON'T YOU WEEP

Traditional, arrangements by Prince / 4'42

Musician: **Prince:** vocals, piano / **Recording:** **Kiowa Trail Home Studio, Chanhassen, Minnesota:** 1983 / **Technical team:** **Producer:** Prince / **Recording engineer:** Don Batts

Mary Don't You Weep refers to the passage in the Bible when Mary of Bethany begs Jesus to resurrect her brother Lazarus and is one of the most famous African-American spirituals. Covered by the greats (Pete Seeger, Aretha Franklin, Bruce Springsteen, among others), this traditional tune is performed by Prince as a gentle piano-vocal. It featured in the closing credits of *BlacKkKlansman*, the Spike Lee movie that premiered on 14 May 2018 at the Cannes Film Festival in France, concluding this scathing anti-racist movie that depicts the evils of America and the Trump era. "I knew that I needed an end-credits song," Spike Lee later explained. "I've become very close with Troy Carter [...] So I invited Troy to a private screening. And after, he said, 'Spike, I got the song.' And that was *Mary Don't You Weep* [...] Prince wanted me to have that song, I don't care what nobody says. My brother Prince wanted me to have that song. For this film. There's no other explanation to me. This cassette is in the back of the Vaults. In Paisley Park. And all of a sudden, out of nowhere, it's discovered? Nah-ah. That ain't an accident."[355]

WEDNESDAY

Prince / 1'59

Musician: **Prince:** vocals, piano / **Recording:** **Kiowa Trail Home Studio, Chanhassen, Minnesota:** 1983 / **Technical team:** **Producer:** Prince / **Recording engineer:** Don Batts

Wednesday was recorded with Jill Jones in October 1983 and earmarked for her to sing in the movie *Purple Rain*. The song is about the crush that Jones's character in the movie has on the Kid, but sadly this sweet melody was deleted in the final cut. "We shot a scene for the movie where I sing it," Jones explained in 2019. "He was really apologetic when he explained to me that the scene had to be cut from the

movie."[351] In the scene in question, Jill sits alone at the piano, as First Avenue has just closed for the night, singing this melancholy tune. "Jill had a huge role in the early scripts of Purple Rain," confirms Bobby Z., The Revolution's drummer. "There's a three-hour version where she's in about every scene."[2] When will this long version of *Purple Rain* be released?

COLD COFFEE & COCAINE

Prince / 5'13

Musician: Prince: vocals, piano, finger snapping / **Recording:** Kiowa Trail Home Studio, Chanhassen, Minnesota: 1983 / **Technical team:** Producer: Prince / **Recording engineer:** Don Batts

Here Prince adopts the voice of Jamie Starr, a chauvinistic character encountered in many songs from the *Purple Rain* era, as well as those by Vanity 6 and The Time (see pages 72 and 64, respectively). *Cold Coffee & Cocaine* is more a blues improvisation than a song as such and shows the virtuosity that Prince was capable of when alone at his piano. This was proved time and again, notably in the *Lovesexy Live* video, recorded on 9 September 1988 at Westfalenhallen, in Dortmund, Germany, where he performed a majestic piano set that included many of his hits, such as *Starfish and Coffee* and *Raspberry Beret*.

WHY THE BUTTERFLIES

Prince / 6'26

Musician: Prince: vocals, piano /**Recording:** Kiowa Trail Home Studio, Chanhassen, Minnesota: 1983 /**Technical team:** Producer: Prince / **Recording engineer:** Don Batts

Why the Butterflies was written while Prince and Jill Jones were working on her first album, but the only recording of it is the version that appears on *Piano & A Microphone*. "This is Prince reaching for something," said Lisa Coleman of The Revolution. "This is revealing and personal. I love this side of Prince. I think this might have been where his thoughts of *When Doves Cry* came from. The examination of self and family relationships...and butterflies. I can almost hear his heart beating."[356]

ORIGINALS

Available for streaming on Tidal: 7 June 2019
Released in the USA by The Prince Estate/NPG Records/Warner Bros. Records: 21 June 2019 (CD); 19 July 2019 (LP) [LP ref.: R1 591253; CD ref.: R2 591253
Released in the UK by The Prince Estate NPG Records/Warner Bros. Records: 21 June 2019 (CD); 19 July 2019 (LP) [LP ref.: R1 591253; CD ref.: 0603497851782]
Best chart ranking in the USA: 15
Best chart ranking in the UK: 21

Morris Day (left) and Jesse Johnson (right) from The Time onstage at the Auditorium Theatre, in Chicago, on 9 December 1982.

1. *Sex Shooter*
2. *Jungle Love*
3. *Manic Monday*
4. *Noon Rendezvous*
5. *Make-Up*
6. *100 MPH*
7. *You're My Love*
8. *Holly Rock*
9. *Baby, You're A Trip*
10. *The Glamorous Life*
11. *Gigolos Get Lonely Too*
12. *Love...Thy Will Be Done*
13. *Dear Michaelangelo*
14. *Wouldn't You Love To Love Me?*
15. *Nothing Compares 2 U*

PRINCE, THE ORIGINAL VERSION

In June 2019, three years after Prince's death, songs from The Vault were still being archived and digitized. After the 19 April 2018 release of the original version of *Nothing Compares 2 U*, written by Prince in 1984, and then given to The Family and later to Sinéad O'Connor, The Prince Estate decided to continue digging up unreleased songs that had been lying dormant on the shelves of Paisley Park's famous safe. "We decided to preserve the spirit of this publication by paying tribute to the work Prince did behind the scenes for other artists," explained Michael Howe, the Estate's archivist. "Prince put his writing, his talents as a producer, and, more generally, his abilities as a studio musician to the service of other artists, and it's that facet of his talent that we want to highlight."[357] Troy Carter (The Prince Estate's manager) and Jay-Z, whose audio-streaming platform Tidal held the exclusive rights, helped Howe select 262 songs—all written by Prince for other artists—before narrowing down the choice to some 15 gems. For Prince's fans, a good number of these original versions had been circulating as bootlegs for some time and in the end *Originals* didn't really offer anything new. But for those who knew less about Prince, this compilation illustrated the talents of the songwriter behind such hits as *Manic Monday*, sung by The Bangles in 1986, *Jungle Love* by The Time (1984), and the sublime *Love...Thy Will Be Done*, performed by Martika in 1991. "He really considered his songs as his children, and he did not entrust them to just anyone," explained Susannah Melvoin, singer for The Family and Prince's girlfriend in the mid-1980s. She continued: "His songs were precious to him and he worked hard to figure out who to give them to. He knew what he was going to give to whom. He wasn't one to throw them in the air, or say 'Who wants a song?' and have nothing to do with their future."[358] *Originals* was released on Tidal on 7 June 2019, which would have been Prince's sixty-first birthday. It came out on CD and vinyl on 21 June.

SEX SHOOTER

Prince / 3'06

Musician: Prince: vocals, electric guitar, bass, programming, synthesizers, backing vocals / **Recording: Kiowa Trail Home Studio, Chanhassen, Minnesota:** 30 April 1983 / **Technical team: Producer:** Prince / **Recording engineer:** Don Batts

Sex Shooter hits the ground running. Apollonia 6 (see page 91) recorded it for the movie *Purple Rain* and it appeared on their only album, released on 1 October 1984. It came out as a single on 31 August 1984. The song is recognizable by its drum machine saturated with a flanger effect pushed to the max (as in *She's Always In My Hair*, which was recorded a few months later). *Sex Shooter* represents a time when sex was the main theme of Prince's songs and the lovely Apollonia performed it perfectly, her swaying hips haunting the dreams of fans throughout 1984. "If I think back about *Sex Shooter* at my age, well, I'm still shootin' love in your direction," said Patricia "Apollonia" Kotero in 2019, referring to the lyrics. "I'm always going to be a sex shooter—always and forever and I hope it's on my epitaph."[359] This hit's theme, which starts at 0'08 in, is so catchy that David Bowie "borrowed" it in 1986 for *Magic Dance*, a song from the original soundtrack for *Labyrinth*, a movie by American director Jim Henson.

JUNGLE LOVE

Prince, Jesse Johnson, Morris Day / 3'04

Musicians: Prince: vocals, bass, synthesizers, percussion, backing vocals / **Jesse Johnson:** electric guitar, backing vocals / **Morris Day:** drums, backing vocals / **Jill Jones:** backing vocals / **Recording: Sunset Sound, Los Angeles:** 25 March 1983 / **Technical team: Producer:** Prince / **Recording engineer:** Peggy McCreary

Initially written with Morris Day and Jesse Johnson, the guitarist for The Time (see page 64), *Jungle Love* was the band's biggest hit, the fourth song on their third album *Ice Cream Castle* (1984). Johnson played the famous funky guitar lines on this song, which the public first heard while watching *Purple Rain*. He borrowed Prince's Hohner Madcat for the occasion and made full use of his funkateer talents. He also recorded a solo for this song (and for the excellent *My Drawers*) with his custom pink, 6-string G&L, even though this passage was buried in the final mixing. "I didn't put much into it," explained Jesse Johnson. "I knew from how low the volume was on my solo on *My Drawers* that it wasn't really going to get heard very well anyway. (Unless you laid on the speakers!)."[360]

MANIC MONDAY

Prince / 2'51

Musicians: Prince: vocals, acoustic guitar, bass, drums, piano, synthesizers, backing vocals / **Brenda Bennett:** backing vocals / **Jill Jones:** backing vocals / **Recording: Sunset Sound, Los Angeles:** 4–5 February 1984 / **Technical team: Producer:** Prince / **Recording engineer:** Peggy McCreary

Prince wrote this hit for Apollonia 6 (see page 91) in 1984. When drawing up the final tracklist for the female trio's first album, the singer changed tack and decided to send a cassette of the song (on which there was a second song, *Jealous Girl*) to Susanna Hoffs, the vocalist of the female pop group The Bangles, whom he had come across in live performance some time before, and whose first album, *All Over the Place*, was due for release. Faced with the musicians' enthusiasm, Prince immediately replaced the song with *Happy Birthday, Mr. Christian* on the album by Apollonia 6, in the process depriving them of a potential hit. "It was an incredible gift,"[361] said the vocalist of The Bangles, who recorded their own version of the song, modifying the break somewhat because it was considered too psychedelic for their pop audience. Released by the quartet on 27 January 1986, *Manic Monday* catapulted The Bangles to stardom and paved the way for their next hits: *Walk Like An Egyptian* in September 1986 and the unforgettable *Eternal Flame* in 1988.

NOON RENDEZVOUS

Prince, Sheila E. / 3'00

Musician: Prince: vocals, piano, programming / **Recording:** Sunset Sound, Los Angeles: 13 February 1984 / **Technical team: Producer:** Prince / **Recording engineer:** Peggy McCreary

During the shooting of Purple Rain, Prince and Sheila E.'s relationship became more entwined. From being colleagues, the two musicians became friends until their bond gradually developed into a romance through shared studio sessions when they were making Sheila E.'s first album. "We started writing *Noon Rendezvous* when I let Prince listen to a ballad I'd written and played castanets on," explained Sheila E. in 2014. "We talked about it, and I told him my dream was to write a song commercial enough to be played on the radio, which was something totally different for me. I was hoping this one might make it."[140] While Sheila E.'s version was given a modern production, with a good dose of synthesizers (and the famous castanets!), this is a piano-vocal version performed by Prince in the privacy of the Sunset Sound studios in Los Angeles on 13 February 1984.

The Bangles in a riot of color, in 1986. From left: Debbie Peterson (drums), Susanna Hoffs (vocals and guitar), Michael Steele (bass guitar), and Vicki Peterson (guitar).

Prince was unstoppable in 1986 when he flirted with the country music style by composing a song, *You're My Love*, for the star Kenny Rogers.

MAKE-UP

Prince / 2'27

Musician: Prince: vocals, synthesizers, programming / **Recording: Kiowa Trail Home Studio, Chanhassen, Minnesota:** summer 1981 / **Technical team: Producer:** Prince / **Recording engineer:** Don Batts

Make-Up was recorded in 1981 for The Hookers, the female trio composed of Brenda Bennett, Susan Moonsie, and her sister Loreen (after Prince's assistant Jamie Shoop jumped ship). Prince acted as their mentor. But he abandoned this artistic project with the irreverent name (hooker means prostitute) when he met the charismatic Denise Matthews, whom he dubbed Vanity (see page 72). *Make-Up* and its haunting synthesizer theme therefore appeared on Vanity 6's only album. The eponymous record was released in August 1982.

100 MPH

Prince / 3'31

Musician: Prince: vocals, electric guitar, bass, drums, programming, synthesizers, backing vocals / **Recording: Flying Cloud Drive Warehouse, Eden Prairie, Minnesota:** 24 June 1984 / **Technical team: Producer:** Prince / **Recording engineer:** Susan Rogers

Once slated for the The Family's album, *100 MPH* (or "A Hundred Miles Per Hour") was given to Mazarati, the band Brown Mark had taken under his wing and that he produced in 1985. After having initially proposed *Kiss* to them, Prince decided to keep that song for himself, giving the seven members of Mazarati, better known for their androgynous look than for their records, this funkier song, which is carried by a formidable synthesizer theme. Success, however, was not on the cards, much to Brown Mark's disappointment. He experienced this failure as abandonment by Paisley Park Records, who produced the album. "The concept was cool," explained David Rivkin, who ran sessions for the album. "Basically radical punky black guys with ripped jeans, doing rock music. That was a great concept, like a Living Colour kinda thing before its time. Maybe the time was wrong and the songs weren't there either, but it was a great concept, it just didn't happen. Mazarati's writing didn't work, and Prince had to add a song to make it work, but everybody saw through it and thought it was a Prince song."[84]

YOU'RE MY LOVE

Prince / 4'24

Musician: Prince: vocals, electric guitar, bass, drums, synthesizers / **Recording: Kiowa Trail Home Studio, Chanhassen, Minnesota:** March 1982 / **Technical team: Producer:** Prince / **Recording engineer:** Don Batts

In 1986, like Prince, country singer Kenny Rogers was at the peak of his fame. Even though the two artists inhabited different musical universes, Rogers asked a friend in common whether the Kid could write him a song for his next album, *They Don't Make Them Like They Used To*. Prince gave Rogers a song that was perfectly suited to his repertoire, in a surprising crooning-pop register. Rogers kept it, after putting it in the capable hands of his producer, Jay Graydon. "I never had the privilege of knowing Prince," explained Rogers on his Facebook page the day Prince died. "But I always wanted to [...] It was such an incredible thing that Prince took the time to do that for me. He was a brilliant guy and a gifted musician."[362]

Single

HOLLY ROCK

Prince, Sheila E. / 6'39

Musicians: Prince: vocals, electric guitar, bass, synthesizers, backing vocals / **Sheila E.:** drums, percussion, backing vocals / **Eddie Mininfield:** saxophone / **Recording: Sunset Sound, Los Angeles:** 24–25 April 1985 / **Technical team: Producer:** / **Recording engineers:** Peggy McCreary, Susan Rogers / **Assistant recording engineer:** Mike Kloster
Single: Digital release by The Prince Estate/NPG Records/Warner Bros. Records on iTunes: 25 July 2019 / **Best chart ranking in the USA:** did not make the charts / **Best chart ranking in the UK:** did not make the charts

The second single from the compilation after *Nothing Compares 2 U*, *Holly Rock* was initially written for Sheila E. who recorded a quality version of it in 1985. The song was included in the original soundtrack for the movie *Krush Groove* by Michael Schultz—in which Sheila E. plays one of the main roles—about the birth of the famous hip-hop label Def Jam Recordings, which was founded by Rick Rubin and Russell Simmons in 1984. It came out as a single on 4 July 1986. For the title and chorus of the song, Prince took inspiration from the phrase "Rock, Rock, to the Planet Rock," sung by rap pioneer Afrika Bambaataa in his 1982 single *Planet Rock*. Meanwhile, Sheila E. retained less fond memories of her participation in the feature movie, which also starred other American rap celebrities such as the Beastie Boys and Run-DMC. "The hip-hop community was on the defensive at that time," she explained. "They were being attacked by critics and musicians for being non-musicians—often accused of being a fad or just talking into a mic. They weren't being acknowledged for their poetry as artists and the musicality of their beat making. Then I arrived with my band, my timbales, and my proud musician identity, and they wanted to know what I was doing in a movie about rap music. I didn't fit into their box. I often felt ignored as well as looked down upon and ostracized. It was pretty hurtful."[140]

BABY, YOU'RE A TRIP

Prince / 5'52

Musicians: Prince: vocals, electric guitar, bass, drums, synthesizers, backing vocals / **Jill Jones:** backing vocals / **Recording: Sunset Sound, Los Angeles:** 8 July 1982; 28 January 1986 (Jill Jones's voice) / **Technical team: Producer:** Prince / **Recording engineers:** Peggy McCreary (1982), Coke Johnson (1986)

When Prince started working with Jill Jones in the summer of 1982, he wrote her an initial song, *Boom, Boom (Can't U Feel the Beat of My Heart)*, then focused on the two projects he was developing: Vanity 6 and The Time (see pages 72 and 64, respectively). "His manager, Steve Fargnoli, wanted us to make an album quickly," explained Jones. "Prince didn't really know what to do with me in the beginning."[351] Hired as a backing vocalist for the 1999 Tour, Jones was given the song *Baby, You're A Trip* in 1982, but she did not record her vocal lines until after the *Purple Rain* storm had passed. By then it was 1986 and Prince had decided to dedicate himself more seriously to her first album. The song was an elegant B-side for Jones's third single, *For Love*, which was released in February 1988, and it occupied a special place in the hearts of fans. As Michael Howe, the archivist for The Prince Estate, said in 2019: "Personally, I believe this song has everything I love about Prince. The vocal performance is exceptional, the song is superbly constructed, the melody is beautiful, and Jill Jones's participation is formidable, as she provides an interesting counterpoint to Prince's voice. In short, this song contains all the elements that make Prince such a great artist."[357]

THE GLAMOROUS LIFE

Prince / 4'12

Musicians: Prince: vocals, programming, synthesizers, backing vocals / **Larry Williams:** saxophone / **David Coleman:** cello / **Recording: Sunset Sound, Los Angeles:** 27–28 December 1983; 6 January 1984 (cello) / **Technical team: Producer:** Prince / **Recording engineer:** Terry Christian

With its famous intro riff, which David Coleman played on the cello, *The Glamorous Life* was Sheila E.'s greatest success. It came out as a single on 2 May 1984. The song was initially composed by Prince to appear on the first eponymous album of Apollonia 6 (see page 91), the star trio from the movie *Purple Rain*. "It was written by Prince as a joke about me," said Patricia "Apollonia" Kotero in 1984. "He used to make all these stupid jokes, 'You're the kind of chick who would wear a mink coat in the summertime,'" she explained, referring to the first line of the song. "When Sheila came into the scene, Prince took away the song from us and gave it to her. At that point it was like, 'Man, this is just not fair.' Since I was a newcomer, I kinda bit my tongue, but Susan and Brenda really let him have it."[70]

The singer Martika had two hits in 1988 and 1991, but then subsequently enjoyed a lower profile in the music business.

GIGOLOS GET LONELY TOO

Prince / 4'49

Musicians: Prince: vocals, bass, finger snapping, piano, synthesizers, backing vocals / **Jesse Johnson:** electric guitar, backing vocals / **Morris Day:** drums, backing vocals / **Recording: Sunset Sound, Los Angeles:** 11 January 1982 / **Technical team: Producer:** Prince / **Recording engineer:** David Leonard

Recorded in early 1982 to appear on The Time's second album, *Gigolos Get Lonely Too*—a song that fits in perfectly with the universe of the alluring Morris Day and his musicians—was created in a session at Sunset Sound with Day and Jesse Johnson, the band's guitarist. The song came out as a single in March 1983 (the album's third) and was a good representation of the exceptional album *What Time Is it?*, a proud highlight of the Minneapolis Sound, which was on the rise at the time. The album sleeve was the work of photographer Allen Beaulieu who spent several weeks looking for clocks of all sizes to create the background for his shot. After looking at five photos of the band, Prince, the album's producer, chose a photo of Morris Day. "The other members of the band weren't happy about that," reported Beaulieu. "But it wasn't my decision."[34] In 1998, rapper Snoop Dogg (whose stage name was then Snoop Doggy Dogg) asked Prince for permission to use a sample of *Gigolos Get Lonely Too* for a song on his upcoming album, *Da Game Is To Be Sold, Not To Be Told*. Prince categorically refused. He didn't seem to like Snoop Dogg's rather dirty lyrics. So, the firebrand West Coast rapper recorded his own version called *D.O.G.'s Get Lonely 2*.

LOVE... THY WILL BE DONE

Prince, Martika / 4'09

Musician: Prince: vocals, bass, programming, synthesizers, claps, backing vocals / **Recording: Paisley Park, Chanhassen, Minnesota:** January 1991 / **Technical team: Producer:** Prince / **Recording engineer:** Michael Koppelman

In 1991, Prince took a keen interest in the airy music of the Cocteau Twins, a Scottish band. He went so far as to invite them (in vain) to join Paisley Park Records. Prince paid tribute to them by using a sample from their song *Fifty-Fifty Clown*, which appears on the album *Heaven or Las Vegas* (released in 1990), in one of his own songs. This was how the single *Love...Thy Will Be Done* came to be. Prince wrote it for Martika after her song *Toy Soldiers* made it big in 1988 (to the point where it was sampled by Eminem in 2004 for *Like Toy Soldiers*). At the time, Martika, who was a great fan of Prince, had seen *Graffiti Bridge* six times and noticed that many passages of the movie echoed her own thoughts, which she'd written in her diary. After obtaining a meeting with Prince, Martika arrived at Paisley Park and gave him the notebooks with her songs. A week later, he sent her a tape with five songs he'd composed based on her lyrics: *Martika's Kitchen*, *Spirit*, *Don't Say U Love Me*, *Open Book*, and the masterpiece of melancholy that is *Love... Thy Will Be Done*. Released as a single in July 1991, the song was a hit, but marked a strange ending to Martika's career. She disappeared from the radar soon after that. The original version of the song, on *Originals*, remains one of Prince's most beautiful pieces, both for its melody, as soft as velvet, and for its refined production, which approaches gospel style at the end of the song. Prince really seems to be talking to the angels in this song, which is unfortunately not well known to a wide audience.

Despite the success of *Nothing Compares 2 U*, mutual antipathy prevented Prince and the Irish singer Sinéad O'Connor from working together again.

DEAR MICHAELANGELO

Prince / 5'22

Musicians: Prince: vocals, electric guitar, programming, synthesizers, backing vocals / **Eddie Mininfield:** saxophone / **Recording: MasterSound Studios, Atlanta, Georgia:** 4–6 January 1985 / **The Summit (Le Mobile Studio), Houston, Texas:** January 1985 (saxophone, percussion, vocals) / **Technical team: Producer:** Prince / **Recording engineers:** Susan Rogers, David Tickle

In between concerts for the Purple Rain Tour, Prince found the time to record *Dear Michaelangelo*, a track for Sheila E.'s second album, *Romance 1600*. Sheila E. was doing a great job opening for the tour. Her saxophonist, Eddie Mininfield, was drafted in to play on the song. The feel he gave it was very close to that of Sheila E.'s hit from a few months before: *The Glamorous Life*. It's very interesting to hear the original version of this song on Sheila E.'s second album, even though the unrivaled *A Love Bizarre* would have been a better choice.

WOULDN'T YOU LOVE TO LOVE ME?

Prince / 5'57

Musician: Prince: vocals, electric guitar, bass, drums, synthesizers, backing vocals / **Recording: Hollywood Sound Recorders, Los Angeles:** 1981 / **Technical team: Producer:** Prince / **Recording engineer:** Ross Pallone

Rumor has it that Prince offered *Wouldn't You Love To Love Me* to Michael Jackson after he refused to sing a duo on *Bad*, finding the phrase "Your butt is mine"—in reference to him—too presumptuous of the King of Pop. "I don't know if it's true or not," said Taja Sevelle, to whom Prince ultimately gave the song. "I just don't know the answer to that. It'd be interesting to find out. We could probably call Quincy [Jones] and ask him, he might know."[359] *Wouldn't You Love To Love Me* was written in April 1976 and recorded in 1981 on a 16-track console. It then circulated as a bootleg for years before finally ending up on *Originals*, even though its sound quality is far below that of the other tracks on the compilation. "We decided to include it in *Originals* anyway," explained Michael Howe, "because a lot of versions of this song had been circulating for many years among collectors, but what we were offering had never seen the light of day."[357] *Wouldn't You Love To Love Me* came out on Taja Sevelle's eponymous first album, which was released by Paisley Park Records on 19 September 1987.

Single

NOTHING COMPARES 2 U

Prince / 4'39

Musicians: Prince: vocals, electric guitar, bass, drums, synthesizers, backing vocals / **Eric Leeds:** saxophone / **Susannah Melvoin:** backing vocals / **Orchestra** / **Recording: Flying Cloud Drive Warehouse, Eden Prairie, Minnesota:** 15 July 1984 (backing tracks), 18 July 1984 (saxophone) / **Monterey Sound Studios, Glendale, California:** 1984 (strings) / **Technical team: Producer:** Prince / **Recording engineer:** Susan Rogers / **String arrangements:** Clare Fischer
Single: Digital release by The Prince Estate/NPG Records/Warner Bros. Records: 19 April 2018 / **Best chart ranking in the USA:** did not make the charts / **Best chart ranking in the UK:** did not make the charts

"I thought about a girl called Julie, who broke my heart in high school,"[363] confessed Paul "St Paul" Peterson regarding his performance of *Nothing Compares 2 U* on The Family's only album, which was released in 1985. Prince had initially recorded this song. It already contained backing vocals by Susannah Melvoin, his girlfriend and co-singer in The Family. She then sang the second verse on the band's version. "When I got this track," explained Wendy Melvoin's twin sister, "I was really emotionally hit. It was the first time I was set free to sing in my own voice on something for (Prince)."[359] After the fiasco of the album, and the breakup of The Family, Prince gave this song to Irish singer Sinéad O'Connor who turned it into a global hit in 1990. She then broke away from the Kid, no doubt because her feminist activism was at odds with his lewd lyrics. "[...] I came away not liking him very much and not particularly wanting to go around to see him

again," explained O'Connor. "But having said that, though, I won't lie. I didn't like the man."[364] While the song was a global hit, it also brought Prince welcome media attention, as reported by his recording engineer at the time, Susan Rogers. "I love this version," she said. "It came out at a time when Prince's music had become less popular with the rise of hip-hop, among other things. Thanks to this song, the public remembered that Prince was a great songwriter. It was a very nice tribute."[365] Prince himself in 1990 expressed his feelings about the detachment he had to take from this beautiful song, which passed through many hands before becoming world famous thanks to Sinéad O'Connor. "I love it, it's great!" he said with regard to O'Conner's version. "I look for cosmic meaning in everything. I think we just took that song as far as we could, then someone else was supposed to come along and pick it up."[123] A special edition of *Originals* was available for purchase at Target stores in 2019, featuring a second version of the song called *Nothing Compares 2 U (Cinematic Mix)*. This mix gave more space to the string tracks arranged and recorded by Clare Fischer and his orchestra at the Monterey Sound Studios in Glendale in 1984, which had been far too quiet in the previous track.

THE VERSACE EXPERIENCE (PRELUDE TO GOLD)

Global release by The Prince Estate/NPG Records/Legacy Recordings: 13 September 2019 (CD ref.: 19075918302; LP ref.: 19075918311)
Best chart ranking in the USA: 170
Best chart ranking in the UK: 83

Prince particularly appreciated the work of the Italian fashion designer Gianni Versace.

1. *Pussy Control—Club Mix "Edit"* (3'04)
2. *Shhh—"X-Cerpt"* (3'55)
3. *Get Wild In The House* (2'15)
4. *👁 Hate U—"Remix"* (3'29)
5. *319—"X-Cerpt"* (1'28)
6. *Shy—"X-Cerpt"* (2'23)
7. *Billy Jack Bitch* (2'31)
8. *Sonny T.—"X-Cerpt"* (0'28)
9. *Rootie Kazootie—"Edit"* (2'38)
10. *Chatounette Controle* (2'25)
11. *Pussy Control—Control Tempo "Edit"* (1'23)
12. *Kamasutra Overture #5* (0'44)
13. *Free the Music* (1'44)
14. *Segue* (0'50)
15. *Gold—"X-Cerpt"* (3'34)

A PRELUDE TO THE GOLD EXPERIENCE

The twenty-second edition of Paris Fashion Week took place on 8 July 1995 to celebrate the greatest talents of international haute couture. Prince was in the first row when the new collections of his friend, Italian fashion designer Gianni Versace, were unveiled at the Ritz between 8 and 10 July. It must be said that during these three days, the models strutted to the tune of an exceptional soundtrack since Prince himself had written it. Given to the lucky audience members on a tape called *The Versace Experience (Prelude to Gold)*, the music for the fashion show was mostly comprised of unreleased songs. These were actually remixed versions of songs from the album *The Gold Experience*, which Prince had wanted to release in 1993, but had been lying dormant on the shelves of Warner Bros. Records for some time. Since the compilation had earned its status as a collector's item among fans, The Prince Estate decided to release a re-edition of it on tape for Record Store Day on 13 April 2019 around the world, then on vinyl on 13 September that same year. After Versace was assassinated in Miami on 15 July 1997, Prince told an emotional anecdote about him to journalists at a press conference to promote his Jam of the Year World Tour (launched the day before), which took place on 22 July 1997 at the Millennium Broadway Hotel in New York: "His clothes were amazing, his style was amazing. I stayed in his house on Lake Como a while ago and, I must be honest, I was quite frightened there and I stayed up all night. It was a little spooky. There was nobody there but me, I believe, and some servants in some part of the house. And this was a long time ago. I've got to be honest though, I didn't know him that well. I only met him briefly and he is as shy as I am when it comes to meeting people. So we had a few words. His sister on the other hand, Donatella, I know quite well [...] I'm saddened any time a human being assaults another one in that fashion. It's saddening."[366]

1999 (SUPER) DELUXE EDITION

Released worldwide by The Prince Estate/NPG Records/Warner Bros. Records: 29 November 2019 (CD box set ref.: R2 604568; LP box set ref.: RR1 23720)
Best chart ranking in the USA: 45
Best chart ranking in the UK: did not make the charts

Disc 1 Original album remastered

1. *1999* (6'14)
2. *Little Red Corvette* (5'04)
3. *Delirious* (4'00)
4. *Let's Pretend We're Married* (7'20)
5. *D.M.S.R.* (8'18)
6. *Automatic* (9'26)
7. *Something In the Water (Does Not Compute)* (4'02)
8. *Free* (5'07)
9. *Lady Cab Driver* (8'17)
10. *All The Critics Love U In New York* (5'58)
11. *International Lover* (6'38)

Disc 2 Promo mixes and B-sides remastered

1. *1999 (7" Stereo Edit)* (3'37)
2. *1999 (7" Mono Promo-Only Edit)* (3'35)
3. *Free (Promo-Only Edit)* (4'36)
4. *How Come You Don't Call Me Anymore* (3'55)
5. *Little Red Corvette (7" Edit)* (3'08)
6. *All The Critics Love U In New York (7" Edit)* (3'16)
7. *Lady Cab Driver (7" Edit)* (5'06)
8. *Little Red Corvette (Dance Remix Promo-Only Edit)* (4'34)
9. *Little Red Corvette (Special Dance Mix)* (8'31)
10. *Delirious (7" Edit)* (2'39)
11. *Horny Toad* (2'15)
12. *Automatic (7" Edit)* (3'40)
13. *Automatic (Video Version)* (8'21)
14. *Let's Pretend We're Married (7" Edit)* (3'45)
15. *Let's Pretend We're Married (7" Mono Promo-Only Edit)* (3'44)
16. *Irresistible Bitch* (4'14)
17. *Let's Pretend We're Married (Video Version)* (4'03)
18. *D.M.S.R. (Edit)* (5'06)

Disc 3 Vault tracks part 1 (recorded between November 1981 and April 1982)

1. *Feel U Up* (6'42)
2. *Irresistible Bitch* (4'39)
3. *Money Don't Grow On Trees* (4'19)
4. *Vagina* (3'28)
5. *Rearrange* (6'11)
6. *Bold Generation* (5'54)
7. *Colleen* (5'30)
8. *International Lover (Take 1) [Live in Studio]* (7'20)
9. *Turn It Up* (5'23)
10. *You're All I Want* (3'00)
11. *Something In the Water (Does Not Compute) (Original Version)* (4'00)
12. *If It'll Make U Happy* (4'12)
13. *How Come U Don't Call Me Anymore (Take 2)* (6'11)

Disc 4 Vault tracks part 2 (recorded between April 1982 and January 1983)

1. *Possessed (1982 Version)* (8'47)
2. *Delirious (Full-Length)* (6'00)
3. *Purple Music* (10'58)
4. *Yah, You Know* (3'11)
5. *Moonbeam Levels* (4'23)
6. *No Call U* (4'30)
7. *Can't Stop This Feeling I Got* (2'40)
8. *Do Yourself A Favor* (9'01)
9. *Don't Let Him Fool Ya* (4'35)
10. *Teacher, Teacher* (3'37)
11. *Lady Cab Driver/I Wanna Be Your Lover/Head/Little Red Corvette (Tour Demo)* (7'00)

Disc 5 Live at Masonic Hall, Detroit, MI, 11/30/1982—late show

1. *Controversy* (5'41)
2. *Let's Work* (5'27)
3. *Little Red Corvette* (4'18)
4. *Do Me, Baby* (7'18)
5. *Head* (4'13)
6. *Uptown* (2'55)
7. *Interlude* (2'15)
8. *How Come U Don't Call Me Anymore* (7'03)
9. *Automatic* (7'02)
10. *International Lover* (8'41)
11. *1999* (10'24)
12. *D.M.S.R.* (8'03)

Disc 6 DVD Live at The Summit, Houston, TX, 12/29/1982

The star savors his success while performing in 1983.

BEHIND THE SCENES WITH 1999

After the success of the first posthumous releases by The Prince Estate and following on from the *Purple Rain Deluxe—Expanded Edition*, which was released in 2017, it was soon decided that a prestigious version of Prince's fifth album should be made. "The album *1999* was an important milestone in Prince's career," explained Michael Howe, the archivist in charge of the searches through The Vault. "This record marked both his attainment of superstar status and a creative peak which resulted in a large quantity of unreleased material."[67] Apart from two songs, *Extraloveable* and the unreleased *Lust U Always*—which were inevitably dropped because their lyrics refer to rape—everything Prince managed to record during this prolific period was unearthed to feature on this essential box set. The box set contains no fewer than 12 unreleased songs and 11 rare versions of songs that were already known, such as *Feel U Up*, *Irresistible Bitch*, and *How Come U Don't Call Me Anymore*. The rerelease also contains a recording of the concert Prince performed at the Masonic Temple, in Detroit, on 30 November 1982—a rare multitrack recording made by the engineer David Rivkin. The lucky buyers of this reinterpreted *1999* could also enjoy a DVD of the concert given on 29 December 1982 at The Summit, in Houston, Texas—the only performance of the 1999 Tour that was filmed using several cameras because the auditorium in Houston managed the images that were screened onstage. "What you see on the DVD matches what was shown on the auditorium's screens," Howe explained, "and the sound comes directly from the video console, which has its own audio system."[367]

The charismatic Vanity and her legendary tailcoat, pictured here in 1983.

FEEL U UP

Prince / 6'42

Musician: **Prince:** vocals, programming, synthesizers, backing vocals / **Recording:** **Kiowa Trail Home Studio, Chanhassen, Minnesota:** October 1981 / **Technical team:** **Producer:** Prince / **Recording engineer:** Don Batts

Recorded by Prince barely a week after the debacle of the concert at the Memorial Coliseum in Los Angeles (see page 56), *Feel U Up* was discovered in The Vault on a cassette that also contained the very first version of *Irresistible Bitch*. "Those were songs that were recorded kind of individually but then sequenced together on a cassette as one seamless kind of piece," Michael Howe explained. "So, I think Prince envisioned the songs to be in that exact order, basically with no segue, no delineation between the two even though they're technically two distinct songs."[368]

IRRESISTIBLE BITCH

Prince / 4'39

Musician: **Prince:** vocals, electric guitar, bass, programming, synthesizers, tambourine, backing vocals / **Recording:** **Kiowa Trail Home Studio, Chanhassen, Minnesota:** October 1981 / **Technical team:** **Producer:** Prince / **Recording engineer:** Don Batts

The continuation of this high-quality, two-part piece of synthpop, *Irresistible Bitch* appears here in its original version. The version already known by fans—because it had featured on the B-side of the single *Let's Pretend We're Married*, which was released on 16 November 1983—appears in a more raw form here, sung by Prince in a voice close to that of Jamie Starr, his producer alter ego, shouting every ba. Jamie Starr also features in some songs by The Time (see page 64).

MONEY DON'T GROW ON TREES

Prince / 4'19

Musician: **Prince:** vocals, electric guitar, bass, drums, claps, backing vocals / **Recording:** **Kiowa Trail Home Studio, Chanhassen, Minnesota:** 1981 / **Technical team:** **Producer:** Prince / **Recording engineer:** Don Batts

Written by Prince for The Hookers, the hyper-sexual trio that would soon morph into Vanity 6 (see page 72) and then into Apollonia 6 (see page 91), *Money Don't Grow On Trees* is surprising for several reasons. Firstly, it features acoustic arrangements—that is, the singer used neither a drum machine nor a synthesizer when recording it. On the contrary, the future Kid from Minneapolis plays a highly funky drum part himself, accompanied by a suitable bass line and biting rhythm guitar, all in the cause of an effective pop melody. While none of Prince's protégées ever recorded this ode to hard work, Prince made a definitive version of it, which it is most striking to discover here.

VAGINA

Prince / 3'28

Musician: **Prince:** vocals, beat box, electric guitar, bass, claps, backing vocals / **Recording:** **Kiowa Trail Home Studio, Chanhassen, Minnesota:** 1981 / **Technical team:** **Producer:** Prince / **Recording engineer:** Don Batts

When Prince met Denise Matthews, he tried in vain to rename her Vagina, before tossing her into the music business at the deep end. Faced with the young woman's (understandable) refusal, the pseudonym Vanity was finally chosen (see page 72). Prince did not leave it at that, however, because he recorded this song in which he refers to a young lady named Vagina who is half-woman and half-man. It is well known that the chemistry between Prince and Vanity went beyond the artistic sphere, and that the two lovers frequently swapped clothes, especially jackets and coats. It is impossible, therefore, not to discern in this pared-down rock number a nod to the sensual and highly charismatic Vanity.

The dandy Morris Day, a key figure of the Minneapolis Sound, in 1985.

REARRANGE

Prince / 6'11

Musician: Prince: vocals, electric guitar, bass, programming, percussion, piano, backing vocals / **Recording: Sunset Sound, Los Angeles:** 8 December 1981 / **Technical team: Producer:** Prince / **Recording engineer:** Peggy McCreary

Like a preliminary sketch for what would soon become the fabulous *Lady Cab Driver*, the track *Rearrange* was recorded by Prince in December 1981, hot on the heels of a session that produced the long version (12" version) of *Let's Work* and a song that would be rerecorded 18 months later: *Baby I'm A Star*. History does not reveal whether Prince considered *Rearrange* to be a first draft of the song about a lady driving a cab or if it was meant to be added to the tracklist of a forthcoming album by The Time, but its melody and structure do lend themselves perfectly to the style of Morris Day's group. Be that as it may, the song shines for its jerky funk rhythm and bass line with a wicked groove. It will delight the ears of Minneapolis Sound devotees, even though no synthesizer was used.

BOLD GENERATION

Prince / 5'54

Musicians: Prince: vocals, electric guitar, bass, piano, synthesizers, claps, backing vocals / **Morris Day:** drums / **Recording: Sunset Sound, Los Angeles:** 12 January 1982 / **Technical team: Producer:** Prince / **Recording engineer:** Peggy McCreary

On 12 January 1983, Prince and Morris Day were in the middle of recording the second album by The Time. That day, the two funkateers recorded *Bold Generation*, which was not retained on the tracklist of *What Time Is It?* but rerecorded in December 1989 with the title *New Power Generation*, one of the signature songs in the movie *Graffiti Bridge*. The original version of this future single was exhumed from The Vault by archivist Michael Howe who had to make do with a cassette that contained the mixed song since the half-inch original master tape was damaged and therefore unusable for a multitrack remix.

COLLEEN

Prince / 5'30

Musician: Prince: electric guitar, bass, programming, synthesizers / **Recording: Sunset Sound, Los Angeles:** 15 January 1982 / **Technical team: Producer:** Prince / **Recording engineer:** Peggy McCreary

On 15 January 1982, Prince and his recording engineer Peggy McCreary were working in studio 3 at Sunset Sound, Los Angeles. The singer ended the day's session recording a funk instrumental number, based on a repetitive Linn LM-1 Drum Machine pattern, before leaving the premises by the door that opened on to the nextdoor basketball pitch. McCreary explained that she had to ask Prince to wait a moment: "'Wait, wait, wait, wait. What's this name of this song?' I said, 'I need it for Warner Bros. and I need it for the studio.' And he just had that little smile on his face, and he said, 'What's your middle name?' And I said, 'Colleen.' And he said, 'Write that down.' OK."[142]

INTERNATIONAL LOVER (TAKE 1) (LIVE IN STUDIO)

Prince / 7'20

Musicians: Prince: vocals, piano / **Morris Day:** drums / **Recording: Sunset Sound, Los Angeles:** 14 January 1982 / **Technical team: Producer:** Prince / **Recording engineer:** Peggy McCreary

Recorded with Morris Day on drums with a view to featuring the song on The Time's second album, *International Lover* was in the end kept for *1999* after Prince had heard it and immediately included it on this album. Day recorded his voice for a version that has so far remained unreleased. The version here shines with the simplicity of its arrangements, as the two musicians recorded the famous ballad in triplets without adding any overdubs afterward.

TURN IT UP

Prince / 5'23

Musician: **Prince:** vocals, electric guitar, programming, synthesizers, backing vocals / **Recording:** **Sunset Sound, Los Angeles:** 19 January 1982 / **Technical team:** **Producer:** Prince / **Recording engineer:** Peggy McCreary

With its synthesizer motif modeled on Kim Wilde's *Kids in America*, which had been released as a single a few months earlier, *Turn It Up* is 100 percent synthpop and filled with an infectious energy. The chorus is reminiscent of *Gotta Stop (Messin' About)*, a single by Prince that was released in the UK in May 1981.

YOU'RE ALL I WANT

Prince / 3'00

Musician: **Prince:** vocals, electric guitar, bass, drums, backing vocals / **Recording:** **Sunset Sound, Los Angeles:** 11 January 1982 / **Technical team:** **Producer:** Prince / **Recording engineer:** Peggy McCreary

Although 11 January 1982 was just another day in the studio for the prolifically creative Prince, it was also the recording engineer Peggy McCreary's birthday. She was very unhappy to have been requisitioned by her employer to come to the Sunset Sound studios in Los Angeles for an umpteenth recording session. That day, the singer arrived wearing jeans, a white shirt, leather boots, and a matching biker's jacket. He recorded *You're All I Want*, a very rockabilly number with a bass line that would later be recycled in *Delirious* and a guitar riff which would be reused for *Horny Toad* on the B-side of *Delirious* when it was released as a single. As usual, once the song had been recorded, McCreary put a pre-mix of it on a cassette and gave it to Prince. A few minutes later he handed the same magnetic tape and his leather jacket to his recording engineer, accompanying both with a unique "Happy Birthday." As McCreary explained: "For him, that was one of the greatest gifts he could have ever given me." She added, "At the time, I wanted my birthday off."[369]

SOMETHING IN THE WATER (DOES NOT COMPUTE) (ORIGINAL VERSION)

Prince / 4'00

Musician: **Prince:** vocals, bass, programming, piano, synthesizers, claps / **Recording:** **Kiowa Trail Home Studio, Chanhassen, Minnesota:** April 1982 / **Technical team:** **Producer:** Prince / **Recording engineer:** Don Batts

Only a few weeks separated the two recording sessions for *Something In the Water (Does Not Compute)*. Since Prince did not consider any of his recordings as a demo, we will regard this as an initial interpretation of the song, in which the singer gave a prominent role to the piano. This would later be replaced by multiple synth pads when he rerecorded the song in May 1982. The Linn LM-1 Drum Machine is very much to the fore in the mixing of the song, with its sounds manipulated by Prince using guitar pedals. "I think innovation was the key for him when working with the drum machine. He was always trying to keep people guessing. He couldn't do it the normal way. Clavets were tuned to the point where they sounded like tin cans."[2]

IF IT'LL MAKE U HAPPY

Prince / 4'12

Musicians: **Prince:** vocals, electric guitar, drums, synthesizers, backing vocals / **Dez Dickerson:** electric guitar, backing vocals / **Recording:** **Sunset Sound, Los Angeles:** 6 April 1982 / **Technical team:** **Producer:** Prince / **Recording engineer:** Peggy McCreary

"'The most important thing is to be true to yourself, but I also like danger,'" Prince said when interviewed in 1982 by the *Los Angeles Times*. "'That's what is missing from pop music today.'"[58] Was it perhaps a taste for taking risks that drove the singer to record this reggae number, which is very different from the rest of his repertoire, in 1982? Or was it rather the desire to stick with a trend that was increasingly strong that year when reggae hits were flooding the charts all over the world? *Do You Really Want to Hurt Me* by Culture Club, *Pass the Dutchie* by Musical Youth, and *I Don't Wanna Dance* by Eddy Grant, formerly the vocalist with The Equals, were all hits that had an impact in this style, which was once only championed by singers such as Bob Marley and Peter Tosh. "I think he was trying to become as mainstream as possible, without violating his own philosophy, without having to compromise any of his ideas," said Matt "Doctor" Fink, Prince's keyboard player at the time. "To some extent, he was trying to make the music sound nice, something that would be pleasing to the ear of the average person who listens to the radio [...]"[62] But for Prince, reggae music had no place on the revolutionary *1999* and so *If It'll Make U Happy* was put away with the singer's reserve of songs, finally being placed on a shelf in The Vault at the end of the decade. We are happy to be able to rediscover it, with a melody that is perfect in every way and a production that far surpasses the insipid FM hits of pop singers who tried their hand at the most famous of Jamaican music styles.

HOW COME U DON'T CALL ME ANYMORE (TAKE 2)

Prince / 6'11

Musician: Prince: vocals, piano / **Recording:** Sunset Sound, Los Angeles: 28 April 1982 / **Technical team:** Producer: Prince / Recording engineer: Peggy McCreary

It was over a glass of Rémy Martin cognac (for Peggy McCreary) and Asti Spumante (for Prince) that the sublime *How Come U Don't Call Me Anymore* was recorded, on 28 April 1982—a ballad later popularized by Alicia Keys in 2001. Although McCreary has referred to a second recording of the song in interviews, this "Take 2" was not listed in The Vault, which proved a headache for the archivist Michael Howe who made no secret of his joy on discovering it. "This version is one of my favorite songs on the box set," he said in 2019. "Toward the end of the take you hear Prince fighting back tears, and it's a very moving moment..."[367] It was in the intimate setting of Sunset Sound that Prince recorded this nocturnal ballad—with a Neumann U-47 microphone directed at the strings of his piano. "After the recording, we spent the night mixing this song," McCreary said. "Then I heard no more about it. I discovered it only more than 20 [years] later, while listening to a compilation of his B-sides that I had bought in Amoeba, in Hollywood. It was *How Come U Don't Call Me Anymore*, and the complete version of this song is about to be released. It is much longer because we had to do a fade-out to fit it on the B-side of *1999*."[370]

POSSESSED (1982 VERSION)

Prince / 8'47

Musicians: Prince: vocals, electric guitar, bass, programming, synthesizers, finger snapping, backing vocals / Jill Jones: backing vocals / **Recording:** Kiowa Trail Home Studio, Chanhassen, Minnesota: 15 May 1982 / **Technical team:** Producer: Prince / Recording engineer: Don Batts

Possessed is well known to Prince fans because he gave an unforgettable performance of this song during the Purple Rain Tour, which features on the VHS cassette *Prince and The Revolution: Live*, which was released on 29 July 1985 in the United States. Although the song was recorded again in March 1984, nothing could replace its original version, recorded in Prince's home studio on 15 May 1982. Jill Jones, who had just met the singer (she was a backing vocalist for Teena Marie in Prince's first performances on the Dirty Mind Tour), was invited to record her voice for several songs on *1999* and here provides a few discreet backing vocals. From their very first interactions, Jones kept her distance from the singer, whom she considered arrogant, doubtless because of pathological shyness. Because she did not play the game of the groupies who wanted to get Prince into bed, she attracted the attention of the artist, with whom she would eventually form an unbreakable bond. She recalled the encounter: "It's scary when you meet someone who's a lot like you, who's very naive and a bit of a spoiled brat, to be perfectly honest."[28]

The sleeve of the single *Delirious*, featuring a photograph by Allen Beaulieu.

DELIRIOUS (FULL-LENGTH)

Prince / 6'00

Musicians: **Prince:** vocals, electric guitar, bass, synthesizers, programming, backing vocals / **Lisa Coleman:** backing vocals / **Recording:** **Sunset Sound, Los Angeles:** 9 May 1982 / **Technical team:** **Producer:** Prince / **Recording engineer:** Peggy McCreary

Despite the success of *Delirious*, the third single from the *1999* album, which reached No.8 in the US charts, Prince's manager Steve Fargnoli was furious with the reception the single received from radio programmers, who seemed to be resistant to African-American artists. "To me, tracks like *Little Red Corvette* and *Delirious* are classic rock 'n' roll records. I just think stations are more concerned with what they think the image of an artist is than with what the music is. Those few rock stations who have played Prince have gotten good response. I don't know what the alternative is other than to keep doing what we're doing. Slowly and surely, the demographics are shifting every tour. White kids are beginning to pick up on what's happening."[58] Featured here in its long version, *Delirious* is one of Prince's forays into the rockabilly style, which was very fashionable in the early 1980s.

PURPLE MUSIC

Prince / 10'58

Musician: **Prince:** vocals, electric guitar, bass, programming, Fender Rhodes piano, synthesizers / **Recording:** **Kiowa Trail Home Studio, Chanhassen, Minnesota:** 22 May 1982 / **Technical team:** **Producer:** Prince / **Recording engineer:** Don Batts

"Don't need no reefer/Don't need cocaine/Purple Music does the same to my brain/I'm high, so high," Prince sings in this anti-drug song, which is driven at a lively pace by a Linn LM-1 Drum Machine on top form and a biting plucked funk guitar played by him. Prince regularly performed the song, then renamed *Welcome 2 the Freedom Galaxy*, at the start of 2016 during the Piano & A Microphone Tour.

YAH, YOU KNOW

Prince / 3'11

Musician: **Prince:** vocals, bass, programming, synthesizers, backing vocals / **Recording:** **Kiowa Trail Home Studio, Chanhassen, Minnesota:** 5 June 1982 / **Technical team:** **Producer:** Prince / **Recording engineer:** Don Batts

Even though Prince mocks those who "spit when you talk," in this vitriolic song he seems to be settling scores with one fellow citizen in particular—an unemployed man who stinks of petrol and whose sole activities are the ingestion of fast food and dancing in the city's nightclubs. "I remember it perfectly," Lisa Coleman said in 2019, "and I remember when he played it for me, and he was just laughing so hard! [...] I don't want to mention any names, but I know that it was inspired by a certain Minnesotan!"[371] The investigation is therefore under way to unmask the person who inspired Prince to write this amusing rock number.

NO CALL U

Prince / 4'30

Musician: Prince: vocals, electric guitar, bass, programming, synthesizers, backing vocals / **Recording: Kiowa Trail Home Studio, Chanhassen, Minnesota:** July 1982 / **Technical team: Producer:** Prince / **Recording engineer:** Don Batts

In the same vein as *Jack U Off*, *Delirious*, and *Turn It Up*, *No Call U* adopts the rockabilly style, which was dear to Prince at the start of the decade. "I don't like categories at all [...]," the singer had already explained in 1980. "I'm not soul and I'm not jazz, but everyone wants to put one of those labels on me."[372] One thing is clear on listening to this song, of which a version (unreleased) was in all probability recorded by Vanity 6 (see page 72): the king of synthpop was not afraid, in the early 1980s, to engage with other styles of music and that is how you can recognize a true genius.

CAN'T STOP THIS FEELING I GOT

Prince / 2'40

Musician: Prince: vocals, electric guitar, bass, drums, synthesizers, backing vocals / **Recording: Kiowa Trail Home Studio, Chanhassen, Minnesota:** summer 1982 / **Technical team: Producer:** Prince / **Recording engineer:** Don Batts

Before being rerecorded in 1989 and featuring at the start of the movie *Graffiti Bridge* in 1990, *Can't Stop This Feeling I Got* was recorded in 1982 in Prince's home studio in Chanhassen. Abandoning his faithful Linn LM-1 Drum Machine for a while, the musician played drums for this pop-rock number with a virtuosity by now expected of him. "I was twelve years old when I first started playing drums," Prince said in 2001. "I learned on a big box of newspapers. I kicked the box 2 imitate the bass drum and played the flaps 2 imitate the hi-hat and snare."[242]

DO YOURSELF A FAVOR

Pepé Willie, Jesse Johnson / 9'01

Musician: Prince: vocals, spoken voice, electric guitar, bass, drums, synthesizers, backing vocals / **Recording: Kiowa Trail Home Studio, Chanhassen, Minnesota:** summer 1982 / **Technical team: Producer:** Prince / **Recording engineer:** Don Batts

Here Prince revisits *If You See Me*, a song by 94 East, the group led by Linster "Pepé" Willie for which he recorded a few guitar lines during sessions at the Cookhouse Studios, Minneapolis, in December 1975. This reinterpretation remained in the singer's archives and Jesse Johnson, the guitarist from The Time (see page 64) who had just left the group, made a third version in 1986 for his album *Shockadelica*, which was very much inspired by the one Prince had recorded in 1982. Worth noting is the appearance of our friend Jamie Starr at 5'42 in the version here, as if to remind the listener that the producer who makes coarse remarks is never far away when Prince is in the studio!

DON'T LET HIM FOOL YA

Prince / 4'35

Musician: Prince: vocals, electric guitar, bass, drums, synthesizers, claps, backing vocals / **Recording: Kiowa Trail Home Studio, Chanhassen, Minnesota:** 1982 / **Technical team: Producer:** Prince / **Recording engineer:** Don Batts

With its faint resemblance to *Head* on the *Dirty Mind* album (1980), *Don't Let Him Fool Ya* features Prince singing in a perfectly mastered head voice. Though very repetitive, it stands out for its unstoppable groove and impeccable arrangement.

TEACHER, TEACHER

Prince / 3'37

Musician: Prince: vocals, electric guitar, bass, drums, tambourine, backing vocals / **Recording: Kiowa Trail Home Studio, Chanhassen, Minnesota:** 1982 / **Technical team: Producer:** Prince / **Recording engineer:** Don Batts

Before Lisa Coleman and Wendy Melvoin reworked it in 1985 for the album *Dream Factory*, *Teacher, Teacher* was one of the first songs Prince recorded in his new home studio at Kiowa Trail in Chanhassen, Minnesota. As pop-sounding as can be, this sugary number can be appreciated like a hard candy and would have been a hit had it been sung by one of the FM artists who were "manufactured" in the 1980s.

SIGN O' THE TIMES (SUPER) DELUXE EDITION

Released worldwide by The Prince Estate/NPG Records/Warner Records:
25 September 2020 (LP box set ref.: R2 628756 – 603497847099)
Best chart ranking in the USA: 20
Best chart ranking in the UK: did not make the charts

Disc 1 (Side 1) Original album remastered

1. *Sign O' the Times* (4'57)
2. *Play in the Sunshine* (5'06)
3. *Housequake* (4'40)
4. *The Ballad of Dorothy Parker* (4'03)

Disc 1 (Side 2) Original album remastered

1. *It* (5'10)
2. *Starfish and Coffee* (2'50)
3. *Slow Love* (4'22)
4. *Hot Thing* (5'39)
5. *Forever In My Life* (3'32)

Disc 2 (Side 3) Original album remastered

1. *U Got the Look* (3'46)
2. *If I Was Your Girlfriend* (5'04)
3. *Strange Relationship* (4'03)
4. *I Could Never Take the Place of Your Man* (6'30)

Disc 2 (Side 4) Original album remastered

1. *The Cross* (4'49)
2. *It's Gonna Be A Beautiful Night* (9'02)
3. *Adore* (6'35)

Disc 3 (Side 1) Singles, mixes, and edits remastered

1. *Sign O' the Times (Edit)* (3'41)
2. *La, La, La, He, He, Hee (Edit)* (3'22)
3. *La, La, La, He, He, Hee (Highly Explosive)* (10'47)

Disc 3 (Side 2) Singles, mixes, and edits remastered

1. *If I Was Your Girlfriend (Edit)* (3'47)
2. *Shockadelica* (3'31)
3. *Shockadelica (12" Long Version)* (6'13)
4. *U Got the Look (Long Look)* (6'41)

Disc 4 (Side 3) Singles, mixes, and edits remastered

1. *Housequake (Edit)* (3'22)
2. *Housequake (7 Minutes Moquake)* (7'12)
3. *I Could Never Take the Place of Your Man (Fade)* (3'39)
4. *Hot Thing (Edit)* (3'41)

Disc 4 (Side 4) Singles, mixes, and edits remastered

1. *Hot Thing (Extended Remix)* (8'32)
2. *Hot Thing (Dub Version)* (6'53)

Disc 5 (Side 1) Vault tracks 1

1. *I Could Never Take the Place of Your Man (1979 Version)* (3'13)
2. *Teacher, Teacher (1985 Version)* (3'08)
3. *All My Dreams* (7'24)
4. *Can I Play with U? (Featuring Miles Davis)* (6'40)

Disc 5 (Side 2) Vault tracks 1

1. *Wonderful Day (Original Version)* (3'48)
2. *Strange Relationship (Original Version)* (6'42)
3. *Visions* (2'19)

Disc 6 (Side 3) Vault tracks 1

1. *The Ballad of Dorothy Parker (With Horns)* (4'56)
2. *Witness 4 the Prosecution (Version 1)* (4'00)
3. *Power Fantastic (Live in Studio)* (7'18)
4. *And That Says What?* (1'50)
5. *Love and Sex* (4'12)

Disc 6 (Side 4) Vault tracks 1

1. *A Place in Heaven (Prince Vocal)* (2'58)
2. *Colors* (1'01)
3. *Crystal Ball (7" Mix)* (3'30)
4. *Big Tall Wall (Version 1)* (5'59)
5. *Nevaeh Ni Ecalp A* (2'33)
6. *In A Large Room With No Light* (3'27)

Disc 7 (Side 5) Vault tracks 2

1. *Train* (4'22)
2. *It Ain't Over 'Til the Fat Lady Sings* (2'22)
3. *Eggplant (Original Prince Vocal)* (5'19)
4. *Everybody Want What They Don't Got* (2'09)
5. *Blanche* (5'37)

Disc 7 (Side 6) Vault tracks 2

1. *Soul Psychodelicide (1986 Master)* (12'37)
2. *The Ball* (4'34)
3. *Adonis and Bathsheba* (5'28)

Disc 8 (Side 7) Vault tracks 2

1. *Forever In My Life (Early Vocal Run-Through)* (6'25)
2. *Crucial (Alternate Lyrics)* (6'15)
3. *The Cocoa Boys* (6'06)

Disc 8 (Side 8) Vault tracks 2

1. *When the Dawn of the Morning Comes* (6'17)
2. *Witness 4 the Prosecution (Version 2)* (5'03)
3. *It Be's Like That Sometimes* (3'19)

Disc 9 (Side 9) Vault tracks 2

1. *Emotional Pump* (4'59)
2. *Rebirth of the Flesh (Original Outro)* (5'28)
3. *Cosmic Day* (5'39)
4. *Walkin' in Glory* (5'14)

Disc 9 (Side 10) Vault tracks 2

1. *Wally* (4'45)
2. *I Need A Man* (5'33)
3. *Promise To Be True* (3'38)
4. *Jealous Girl (Version 2)* (4'52)

Disc 10 (Side 11) Vault tracks 2

1. *There's Something I Like About Being Your Fool* (3'39)
2. *Big Tall Wall (Version 2)* (5'46)
3. *A Place in Heaven (Lisa Vocal)* (2'46)

Disc 10 (Side 12) Vault tracks 2

1. *Wonderful Day (12" Mix)* (7'34)
2. *Strange Relationship (1987 Shep Pettibone Club Mix)* (7'08)

Disc 11 (Side 1) Live in Utrecht 6/20/87

1. *Intro/Sign O' the Times* (5'36)
2. *Play in the Sunshine* (4'36)
3. *Little Red Corvette* (1'36)
4. *Housequake* (4'52)

Disc 11 (Side 2) Live in Utrecht 6/20/87

1. *Girls* & *Boys* (4'19)
2. *Slow Love* (5'05)
3. *Take the "A" Train/Pacemaker/I Could Never Take the Place of Your Man* (10'17)

Disc 12 (Side 3) Live in Utrecht 6/20/87

1. *Hot Thing* (6'15)
2. *Four (With Sheila E. Drum Solo)* (6'12)
3. *If I Was Your Girlfriend* (5'17)

Disc 12 (Side 4) Live in Utrecht 6/20/87

1. *Let's Go Crazy* (6'10)
2. *When Doves Cry* (2'46)
3. *Purple Rain* (5'40)
4. *1999* (5'54)

Disc 13 (Side 5) Live in Utrecht 6/20/87

1. *Forever In My Life* (13'12)
2. *Kiss* (3'33)
3. *The Cross* (7'14)

Disc 13 (Side 6): Live in Utrecht 6/20/87

1. *It's Gonna Be A Beautiful Night* (13'55)

\+ DVD *Live At Paisley Park 12/31/1987*

A WINDING ROAD TO SIGN O' THE TIMES

In 2017, the complete archives that, at Prince's death, were contained in The Vault—his safe at Paisley Park, built 30 years previously—were transferred to Los Angeles and stored in special premises to protect the singer's artistic heritage from all potential damage due to any natural disaster. "The Vault is basically an impenetrable compound that has been retrofitted with [...] fireproofing and climate control,"[373] explained Michael Howe, the archivist of The Prince Estate, who from now on was totally involved in the preservation of the singer's heritage. The unearthing of countless tapes on which Prince had recorded a multitude of unreleased songs over the years showed Howe just how crucial it was to rescue them, as the tapes were visibly deteriorating. Those in the possession of Warner Bros. Records were digitized by George Lydecker, who was in charge of preserving the record company's archives in Burbank, California, before they were sent to Michael Howe for the rerelease discussed here. It was thus within this highly secure framework that The Prince Estate could carry out its work of rereleasing the works of Prince, after offering fans prestigious editions of *Purple Rain* in 2017 and *1999* in 2019.

On 25 June 2020, the forthcoming release of a mammoth edition of the cult album *Sign O' the Times* was announced. It comprised 45 unreleased songs from the sessions of 1986 and 1987, which had been intended for release on the albums *Dream Factory*, *Camille*, and *Crystal Ball*. However, some were brought together on *Sign O' the Times* with others split between B-sides and various compilations, or simply put away in The Vault, which had just been built in the singer's complex in Chanhassen. After releasing a box set that brought together all the singles released in 1987 (*Sign O' the Times—The Singles)* in August 2020, the following 25 September The Prince Estate released the *Sign O' the Times (Super) Deluxe Edition*, a box set including the unreleased songs that had been created, multiple rare versions of songs on the album, the original album remastered by Bernie Grundman, and a concert recorded on 20 June 1987 at the Stadion Galgenwaard in Utrecht, Netherlands. What is more, this essential box set also included a DVD of a charity concert for the homeless that Prince had given at Paisley Park on 31 December 1987, at which the trumpet player Miles Davis joined the singer onstage. A treasure chest to be opened without a moment's delay!

I COULD NEVER TAKE THE PLACE OF YOUR MAN (1979 VERSION)

Prince / 3'13

Musician: Prince: vocals, electric guitar, bass, drums, synthesizers, claps, backing vocals / **Recording:** Hollywood Sound Recorders, Los Angeles: 23 May 1979 / **Technical team:** Producer: Prince / Recording engineer: Bob Mockler

On 16 July 2021, The Prince Estate revealed on Twitter the very first version of *I Could Never Take the Place of Your Man*, which was recorded by Prince at the Hollywood Sound Recorders studios in Los Angeles on 23 May 1979 when he was putting the finishing touches to his second album. During searches in The Vault between 2016 and 2020, no one yet knew of this original version of Prince's future hit until Michael Howe stumbled upon an undated cassette featuring a rough mix of the song, which he thought was a preliminary version from the era of *Sign O' the Times*. It was only once the tapes containing the multitrack recording (and dated April to May 1979) were found that the team could embark on restoring this almost identical version of the song, which would soon be famous the world over. "It was kind of jaw-dropping to think that he had the song in his pocket for six or seven years before he reimagined it,"[374] Howe confided in 2020.

TEACHER, TEACHER (1985 VERSION)

Prince / 3'08

Musicians: Prince: vocals, backing vocals / Wendy Melvoin: vocals, electric guitar, acoustic guitar, bass, programming, claps, backing vocals / Lisa Coleman: vocals, synthesizers, Hammond organ, programming, claps, finger cymbals, backing vocals / **Recording:** Kiowa Trail Home Studio, Chanhassen, Minnesota: 1982 / The Complex Studios, Los Angeles: 18–21 June 1985 / **Technical team:** Producers: Wendy Melvoin, Lisa Coleman / Recording engineers: Don Batts (Kiowa Trail Home Studio), David Tickle (The Complex Studios)

In June 1985, while he was busy preparing the shooting of the movie *Under the Cherry Moon*, Prince gave Wendy Melvoin and Lisa Coleman, The Revolution's guitarist and keyboard player, respectively, the task of enlivening some of the songs recorded for his next album with overdubs. The two young women, whose talent was already recognized, reserved The Complex Studios in Los Angeles for several days (Sunset Sound not being available at the time), during which they worked on arrangements of *Do U Lie?*, *Venus de Milo*, and *Under the Cherry Moon*. These would end up on the *Parade* album in 1986. They also worked on perfecting *Strange Relationship*, which would feature on *Sign O' the Times*. Taking advantage of this unprecedented artistic freedom, the musicians also revisited a song recorded by Prince in 1982, *Teacher, Teacher*, which he was planning to add to his future album *Dream Factory*. It is this new version that features here, enhanced by a feminine touch that suits it beautifully. The *Dream Factory* album would soon be buried by Prince and the song was offered to the group Three O'Clock in 1988 for their album *Vermillion*. They opted instead for another Prince composition, *Neon Telephone*, which was more suited to their musical style.

ALL MY DREAMS

Prince / 7'24

Musicians: Prince: vocals, spoken voice, electric guitar, acoustic guitar, bass, programming, drums, piano, synthesizers, Fairlight CMI, backing vocals / Lisa Coleman: vocals, spoken voice, piano, backing vocals / Wendy Melvoin: vocals, spoken voice, backing vocals / **Recording:** Sunset Sound, Los Angeles: 28 and 30 April 1985 / **Technical team:** Producer: Prince / Recording engineers: Peggy McCreary, Susan Rogers

On 20 November 1999, Prince was on the set of *Apocalypse Tube*, a Sky One program being recorded at the Tyne Tees studios in Newcastle, England. When he sang *The Greatest Romance Ever Sold* in playback mode, a fan shouted at him: "When will you release *In All My Dreams?*," to which the singer responded, not without humor: "Security! Bootlegger!"[375] in reference to the sellers of unauthorized records who Prince spent his life fighting against. It must be said that *All My Dreams* (its true title) is an exceptional song, in which the singer unleashes all his madness before inviting his musicians Wendy and Lisa to perfect the song with backing vocals as well as a piano solo by Lisa. The song was considered for *Parade*, then for *Roadhouse Garden*, an album that pays tribute to the years of The Revolution, which Prince wanted to release in 1999 but which was eventually put away in The Vault.

HEADPHONES AT THE READY

During a concert by Kid Creole and the Coconuts, to which Wendy and Lisa had taken Prince, our artist fell in love with the sound of the voice of August Darnell, modified simply by the use of a megaphone. On returning to the studio, he demanded that the recording engineer Susan Rogers go out and buy him one. It was with this device that Prince recorded his voice in *All My Dreams*.

After the serious atmosphere of the recording studio, Prince showed his humorous side onstage—here performing in Rotterdam in 1987.

Miles Davis was known for his musical genius, but also for his powers of seduction.

CAN I PLAY WITH U? (FEATURING MILES DAVIS)

Prince / 6'40

Musicians: Prince: vocals, electric guitar, bass, programming, synthesizers, Fairlight CMI, backing vocals / **Marcus Miller:** bass / **Adam Holzman:** synthesizers / **Miles Davis:** trumpet / **Eric Leeds:** saxophone / **Recording: Sunset Sound, Los Angeles:** 26–27 December 1985 / **Capitol Studios, Los Angeles:** 1 March 1986 / **Technical team: Producer:** Prince / **Recording engineers:** Susan Rogers, Coke Johnson / **Assistant recording engineer:** Alexander Waverly

"[Miles Davis] can do more in 10 minutes of playing than anybody who ever put lips to a horn can do in a lifetime."[125] It was in these terms that Prince spoke of the famous jazz musician in 1991, not long before he drew his last breath. For his part, Davis also flattered the singer from Minneapolis in his autobiography, describing him as the Duke Ellington of modern pop music. At the end of 1985, when the trumpet player had just left CBS for Warner Bros. Records, the record company asked Prince to consider working with him. In December, at the Sunset Sound studios in Los Angeles, he recorded *Can I Play With U?*, aided by his faithful saxophonist Eric Leeds, before sending the piece to Miles Davis with the following note: "I can tell just from listening to your music that you and I are so exactly alike that I know whatever you play would be what I'd do. So if this tape is of any use to you, please go ahead and play whatever you feel over it. Because I trust what you hear and play."[376] Davis did indeed add a few trumpet lines to the song on 1 March 1986 at Capitol Studios in Los Angeles, accompanied by the bass guitarist Marcus Miller and keyboard player Adam Holzman, but the end result pleased neither Davis, who did not consider it for *Tutu*, nor Prince, who eventually decided not to include it on *Sign O' the Times*, either.

WONDERFUL DAY (ORIGINAL VERSION)

Prince / 3'48

Musician: Prince: vocals, spoken voice, bass, programming, piano, synthesizers, Fairlight CMI, backing vocals / **Recording: Sunset Sound, Los Angeles:** 30–31 January 1986 / **Technical team: Producer:** Prince / **Recording engineers:** Susan Rogers, Coke Johnson

Complementing *It's Gonna Be A Beautiful Night*, the penultimate track on *Sign O' the Times*, *Wonderful Day* features here in its original version, whereas it appears in a remixed version later in the box set. Prince was inspired to write the song by a scene in *Under the Cherry Moon* in which he declares to a statue of the Venus de Milo that the day is a wonderful one. Initially meant to feature on *Dream Factory*, the song was eventually shelved until 2020.

STRANGE RELATIONSHIP (ORIGINAL VERSION)

Prince / 6'42

Musicians: Prince: vocals, electric guitar, bass, programming, synthesizers, Fairlight CMI, finger cymbals, backing-vocals / **Wendy Melvoin:** tambourine, congas, backing vocals / **Lisa Coleman:** Fairlight CMI, backing vocals / **Recording: Kiowa Trail Home Studio, Chanhassen, Minnesota:** 14 March 1983 / **Flying Cloud Drive Warehouse, Eden Prairie, Minnesota:** spring 1984 / **The Complex Studios, Los Angeles:** June to July 1985 / **Technical team: Producers:** Prince, Wendy Melvoin, Lisa Coleman / **Recording engineers:** Don Batts (Kiowa Trail Home Studio), Susan Rogers (Flying Cloud Drive Warehouse), David Tickle (The Complex Studios)

It was during their time at The Complex Studios in Los Angeles that Wendy Melvoin and Lisa Coleman looked seriously at *Strange Relationship*, recorded by Prince in March 1983. Prince, who was busy with other projects at the time, sent them various songs to work on that were likely to appear on his next album, *Parade*. *Strange Relationship* eventually had a different fate because it was partly rerecorded by the singer in November 1986 and then added to the final tracklist of *Sign O' the Times*.

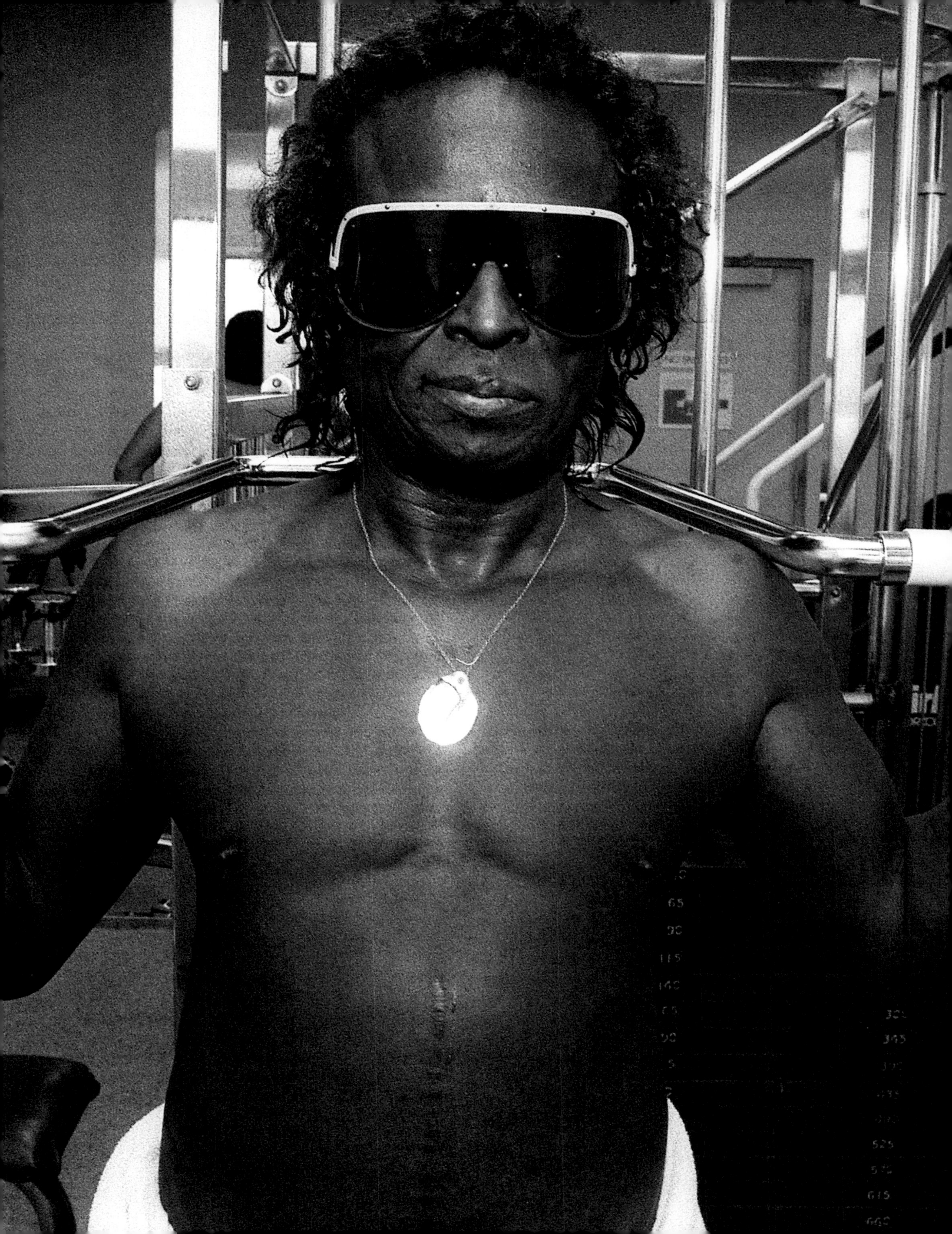
65
115
345
525
615

THE BALLAD OF DOROTHY PARKER (WITH HORNS)

Prince / 4'56

Musicians: Prince: vocals, bass, drums, programming, synthesizers, Fairlight CMI, backing vocals / **Eric Leeds:** saxophone / **Susannah Melvoin:** backing vocals / **Recording: Galpin Boulevard Home Studio, Chanhassen, Minnesota:** 13–15 March, 15 April 1986 / **Technical team: Producer:** Prince / **Recording engineer:** Susan Rogers

Prince was possibly following the old adage "less is more" when he produced *The Ballad of Dorothy Parker* in March 1986. Having decided to add a saxophone track played by the unmistakable Eric Leeds, he then removed it from the final mix, along with Clare Fischer's string arrangements which were recorded on 23 June 1986 at Ocean Way Recording Studios in Los Angeles. A wise decision, as the song works well on its own and needs no artifice to convince.

WITNESS 4 THE PROSECUTION (VERSION 1)

Prince / 4'00

Musicians: Prince: vocals, electric guitar, bass, drums, backing vocals / **Wendy Melvoin:** electric guitar, backing vocals / **Lisa Coleman:** Hammond organ, backing vocals / **Eric Leeds:** saxophone / **Matt "Atlanta Bliss" Blistan:** trumpet / **Susannah Melvoin:** backing vocals / **Recording: Galpin Boulevard Home Studio, Chanhassen, Minnesota:** 14–15 March, 15 April 1986 / **Technical team: Producer:** Prince / **Recording engineer:** Susan Rogers

As he did again in 1995 with *Eye Hate U*, here Prince compares his love affairs to courtroom hearings in which spurned lovers accuse their partners of crimes that require a proper trial. This song was initially recorded in March 1986 with drums, bass, and guitars. Prince rerecorded it in April that year using a drum machine, a Fairlight CMI, and an army of synthesizers. Both versions featured on the *Sign O' the Times—The Singles* box set in August 2020.

POWER FANTASTIC (LIVE IN STUDIO)

Prince, Wendy Melvoin, Lisa Coleman / 7'18

Musicians: Prince: vocals, spoken voice, maracas / **Wendy Melvoin:** electric guitar / **Brown Mark:** bass / **Lisa Coleman:** piano / **Bobby Z.:** drums / **Eric Leeds:** flute / **Matt "Atlanta Bliss" Blistan:** trumpet / **Recording: Galpin Boulevard Home Studio, Chanhassen, Minnesota:** 19 March 1986 / **Technical team: Producer:** Prince / **Recording engineer:** Susan Rogers

Power Fantastic had already been included on *The Hits/The B-Sides* released by Warner Bros. Records in 1993. This first Prince compilation brought together his greatest singles, most of his B-sides, and a few unreleased tracks, including this song composed by Wendy and Lisa in 1985, then entitled *Carousel*. This version is unedited and includes Prince giving instructions to his musicians as the track was being recorded on 19 March 1986 in his home studio on Galpin Boulevard. The members of The Revolution were scattered around the house, following his orders to the letter. "[...] there was a basement studio that had a large control room and a medium-sized isolation booth right next to it," says recording engineer Susan Rogers, "The piano was upstairs and it was used for smaller projects. We tried to fit the whole band in there once, but it wasn't big enough for a band."[109] Rogers later added in another interview: "There was no more room, no free booth for Prince, who had to sing his vocal part in the control room where the console was, and me behind it," She contined, "The problem was that [...] there weren't enough headphones for everyone. I had to leave the last headset with Prince, so I couldn't listen to the music while we were recording. We were just the two of us behind the console, and remember that he always demanded that the recording engineers leave the studio when he was recording his vocals. But on this day, he had no choice. He asked me to set up the mic in the farthest corner of the room, and during the take, the only sound I heard was his voice, just inches away from me."[108]

AND THAT SAYS WHAT?

Prince / 1'50

Musicians: Prince: spoken voice, electric guitar, drums, synthesizers, Fairlight CMI / **Wendy Melvoin:** bass / **Lisa Coleman:** piano / **Doctor Fink:** synthesizers / **Eric Leeds:** saxophone / **Matt "Atlanta Bliss" Blistan:** trumpet / **Recording: Galpin Boulevard Home Studio, Chanhassen, Minnesota:** 20 March 1986 / **Technical team: Producer:** Prince / **Recording engineer:** Susan Rogers

Centered around a mambo tune, played by Lisa Coleman on piano, this fast-paced instrumental ends with the voice of Jamie Starr (a pseudonym used by Prince when producing his various protegés). Wendy Melvoin swaps the 6-string guitar for a bass to deliver a walking bass line of astonishing virtuosity.

LOVE AND SEX

Prince / 4'12

Musician: Prince: vocals, electric guitar, bass, drums, synthesizers, Fairlight CMI, bells, backing vocals / **Recording: Sunset Sound, Los Angeles:** 3 January 1986 / **Technical team: Producer:** Prince / **Recording engineer:** Coke Johnson

Prince rarely recorded two songs with the same title during his career. The words "love" and "sex" sum up his main preoccupations at the time when he was not busy in the studio. It was in the intimacy of Sunset Sound Studios that he recorded this second song of the same name—the first dates from 1984 and was released posthumously on the *Purple Rain Deluxe Expanded Edition* in 2017. "It was his favorite studio in the world," Susan Rogers stated. "[...] When we worked at Sunset Sound, it was a big enough room that we could have everything set up all at once. The piano could always be miked, the B-3 organ could be miked and ready and go, drum kit could be set up and ready to go, and he would have his keyboard, bass, and guitars with him in the control room."[109]

A PLACE IN HEAVEN (PRINCE VOCAL)

Prince / 2'58

Musician: Prince: vocals, programming, piano, synthesizers, Fairlight CMI, backing vocals / **Recording: Galpin Boulevard Home Studio, Chanhassen, Minnesota:** 15 March, 20 April 1986 / **Technical team: Producer:** Prince / **Recording engineer:** Susan Rogers

On 15 March 1986, Prince recorded a gentle ballad in triplet meter based on the rudiments of an organ machine lying around his Galpin Boulevard home studio. Prince's vocal line was intended solely as a guide for Lisa Coleman who sang lead vocals for the track on 20 April, the same day that Prince added a few overdubs to the song. "I had the impression that it was for a movie of some kind," Susan Rogers says. "Having Lisa sing that song could have been something for the female lead in this future movie that he had in his head."[95] Although the version with Lisa Coleman's vocal line didn't appear in the *Graffiti Bridge* movie, it did feature on the *Sign O' the Times (Super) Deluxe Edition*.

BIG TALL WALL (VERSION 1)

Prince / 5'59

Musician: Prince: vocals, acoustic guitar, bass, drums, synthesizers, Fairlight CMI, tambourine, backing vocals / **Recording: Galpin Boulevard Home Studio, Chanhassen, Minnesota:** 18 April 1986 / **Technical team: Producer:** Prince / **Recording engineer:** Susan Rogers

According to the website princevault.com, a valuable source of information for any self-respecting Prince fan, Prince wrote *Big Tall Wall* with Susannah Melvoin in mind. This was after she had moved out of their shared home into Calhoun Isles, a luxury housing complex built on the site of the old McKenzie-Hague grain silos in Minneapolis, and the line "I'm gonna build a big tall wall/Stone circle so you can't get out" is likely a direct reference to this. "I was kind of the bird in the gilded cage a little bit,"[377] Susannah Melvoin confided in 2020, adding that the years she spent with Prince were nevertheless happy ones. As Prince recorded the first version of *Forever In My Life* for Susannah Melvoin on 7 August 1986 when she was living with him again, we can imagine that their relationship had its ups and downs during that period. Prince used the Fairlight CMI for the Oriental sounds on this version, offering fans the final remnants of his *Around the World in a Day* period. A year later, on 10 July 1987, the song was rerecorded with the glacial sound of a single drum machine.

NEVAEH NI ECALP A

Prince / 2'33

Musicians: Lisa Coleman: vocals / **Prince:** synthesizers, Fairlight CMI / **Wendy Melvoin:** backing vocals / **Recording: Galpin Boulevard Home Studio, Chanhassen, Minnesota:** 20 April 1986 / **Technical team: Producer:** Prince / **Recording engineer:** Susan Rogers

On 20 April 1986, Lisa Coleman laid down her vocal line on *A Place in Heaven* which Prince had recorded on 15 March. Prince then took his keyboardist's vocal track, played it backward, and added some synthesizer overdubs. He chose to call the song *Nevaeh Ni Ecalp A—A Place in Heaven* spelled backward.

IN A LARGE ROOM WITH NO LIGHT

Prince, Wendy Melvoin, Lisa Coleman / 3'27

Musicians: **Prince:** vocals, backing vocals / **Wendy Melvoin:** electric guitar, backing vocals / **Levi Seacer Jr:** bass / **Sheila E.:** drums, percussion, backing vocals / **Lisa Coleman:** piano, backing vocals / **Eric Leeds:** saxophone / **Norbert Satchell:** saxophone / **Matt "Atlanta Bliss" Blistan:** trumpet / **Susannah Melvoin:** backing vocals / **Recording:** **Sunset Sound, Los Angeles:** 4–5 May 1986 / **Technical team:** **Producer:** Prince / **Recording engineers:** David Rivkin, Coke Johnson, Susan Rogers

This astonishing Caribbean-jazz fusion song had long been circulated by bootleggers as *Welcome 2 The Ratrace*, although Prince named it *Life Is Like Looking For A Penny In A Large Room With No Light* when he recorded it in May 1986. This was a time when Prince was receptive to albums by Duke Ellington and other classic American jazz musicians. This track was recorded with members of The Revolution, including drummer Sheila E., and his guitarist Levi Seacer Jr, and it marked an important turning point in the history of Prince's backing bands. Shortly afterward, he parted ways with the legendary band of the *Purple Rain* era and enlisted the services of Sheila E. and Levi Seacer Jr in his new band.

TRAIN

Prince / 4'22

Musicians: **Prince:** vocals, spoken voice, electric guitar, bass, programming, synthesizers, Fairlight CMI, backing vocals / **Eric Leeds:** saxophone / **Matt "Atlanta Bliss" Blistan:** trumpet / **Recording:** **Galpin Boulevard Home Studio, Chanhassen, Minnesota:** 7–8 July 1986 / **Technical team:** **Producer:** Prince / **Recording engineer:** Susan Rogers / **Assistant recording engineer:** Todd Herreman

The image of a train leaving a platform has always inspired singers when it comes to expressing how it feels to be abandoned by their loved one. *Train Leaves Here This Morning* by the Eagles (1972), *Stop That Train* by Bob Marley and The Wailers (1973), and *Downbound Train* by Bruce Springsteen (1984) are just some of the songs that shone the spotlight on this method of locomotion. Here Prince offers his own ode to the train carriage as it takes his sweetheart away from him. The track is built around a sample of train noise from his Fairlight CMI keyboard. The artist and his recording engineer, Todd Herreman, used it to create the track's mechanical rhythm before saxophonist Eric Leeds and trumpeter Atlanta Bliss were asked to lay down a few horn lines.

From left: Levi Seacer Jr, Michael B Nelson, and Steve Strand onstage at the Flanders Expo in Ghent, Belgium, on 4 September 1993.

IT AIN'T OVER 'TIL THE FAT LADY SINGS

Prince / 2'22

Musicians: Prince: drums, Fairlight CMI / **Wendy Melvoin:** bass / **Lisa Coleman:** piano / **Eric Leeds:** saxophone / **Matt "Atlanta Bliss" Blistan:** trumpet / **Orchestra** / **Recording: Galpin Boulevard Home Studio, Chanhassen, Minnesota:** 9 July1986 / **Ocean Way Recording, Los Angeles:** 18 August 1986 (band) / **Hollywood Central Studios, Los Angeles:** 4 September 1986 (orchestra) / **Technical team: Producer:** Prince / **Recording engineers:** Susan Rogers, Coke Johnson / **Assistant recording engineer:** Todd Herreman / **Orchestral arrangements:** Clare Fischer

Although the origin of the saying "It Ain't Over 'Til The Fat Lady Sings" is unknown, it is something saxophonist Eric Leeds clearly had in mind on 9 July 1986 when he came up with the title for this instrumental composed by Prince. Two months after recording this very jazzy piece, Prince took up his drumsticks once more and launched the Madhouse project, a group whose instrumental albums *8* and *16* (1987) became part of the legend that was Prince (see page 153).

EGGPLANT (ORIGINAL PRINCE VOCAL)

Prince / 5'19

Musicians: Prince: vocals, spoken voice, electric guitar, programming, synthesizers, Fairlight CMI / **Eric Leeds:** saxophone / **Matt "Atlanta Bliss" Blistan:** trumpet / **Recording: Galpin Boulevard Home Studio, Chanhassen, Minnesota:** 7–8 July 1986 / **Technical team: Producer:** Prince / **Recording engineer:** Susan Rogers / **Assistant recording engineer:** Todd Herreman

Here Prince is telling someone that he isn't too keen on their girlfriend, and he does this by listing her bad points. "That kind of girl's no good for you/She flips her hair and thinks she's cool," he sings, in a tone that seems a little high for his range. *Eggplant* was recorded on the same day as *Train* and also features horns from Eric Leeds and Atlanta Bliss, which were committed to tape when they came to Chanhassen the day after the session. "Depending on what the song was," says Leeds, "sometimes Prince would have the horns in on the day that he was doing the rhythm track. Other times, the rhythm track—everything that he'd done may be around for weeks, sometimes months before he might decide whether to add anything to it or not."[377] Atlanta Bliss added: "We didn't have anything written, but he would sing us parts, and he would go—'OK, you guys ready?' He's ready to hit the red button to record that. I'd say, 'Wait a second. I'm still scratching some things down.' [...] It was like, 'It's coming out of my guitar that fast; I expect it to come out of you that fast.'"[377] Since the song wasn't officially released until 2020, American composer Alan Silvestri can't be accused of having been inspired by *Eggplant*'s vocal line when he penned his *Forrest Gump Theme* for Robert Zemeckis's 1994 movie *Forrest Gump*. The resemblance between the two melodies is nonetheless striking.

EVERYBODY WANT WHAT THEY DON'T GOT

Prince / 2'09

Musician: Prince: vocals, spoken voice, programming, piano, synthesizers, Fairlight CMI, backing vocals / **Recording: Sunset Sound, Los Angeles:** 13 July 1986 / **Technical team: Producer:** Prince / **Recording engineers:** Susan Rogers, Coke Johnson

No Eric Leeds or Atlanta Bliss on this track, just crude synthesizer presets that simulate brass instruments. Prince chose these more as a time-saving device than for their low-end, but nonetheless revolutionary, sounds, as Lisa Coleman explained in 2020. "It was fun because we had like all these amazing sounds that suddenly you could have like a sitar or something, you know, which was so rare back then [...] We were just loading songs up with strange sounds and flutes and congas that were fake; all kinds of things like that."[378]

Marlon Brando and Vivien Leigh in the roles of Stanley Kowalski and Blanche DuBois in *A Streetcar Named Desire* by Elia Kazan.

BLANCHE

Prince / 5'37

Musician: Prince: vocals, electric guitar, bass, drums, synthesizers / **Recording: Sunset Sound, Los Angeles:** 15 July 1986 / **Technical team: Producer:** Prince / **Recording engineers:** Susan Rogers, Coke Johnson

The question that immediately comes to mind when you discover this track was inspired by Elia Kazan's 1951 movie *A Streetcar Named Desire* is: where did Prince find the energy to record all the instrumental tracks on this blues funk number just minutes after committing to tape one of his masterpieces, *Sign O' the Times*? Duane Tudahl, a leading expert on Prince's music, may have the answer with this opinion of the prolific artist from Chanhassen: "That's one of the reasons I enjoy this collection, is because you get the wide range. You get everything he was going through: 'Here's the good, here's my sad, here's my goofy song, here's a song called *Blanche* [...]' When he was recording, he could record two or three songs in a day, and he did."[377]

SOUL PSYCHODELICIDE (1986 MASTER)

Prince / 12'37

Musicians: Prince: spoken voice, electric guitar / **Wendy Melvoin:** electric guitar, backing vocals / **Miko Weaver:** electric guitar / **Brown Mark:** bass, backing vocals / **Bobby Z.:** drums / **Lisa Coleman:** synthesizers, backing vocals / **Doctor Fink:** synthesizers / **Eric Leeds:** saxophone / **Matt "Atlanta Bliss" Blistan:** trumpet / **Susannah Melvoin:** backing vocals / **Wally Safford:** backing vocals / **Greg Brooks:** backing vocals / **Jerome Benton:** backing vocals / **Recording: Washington Avenue Warehouse, Edina, Minnesota:** 22 July 1986 / **Technical team: Producer:** Prince / **Recording engineer:** Susan Rogers / **Assistant recording engineer:** Todd Herreman

Susan Rogers recorded more than an hour of this jam session on 22 July 1986 before Prince edited the whole thing to turn it into a more digestible format lasting 12 minutes and 37 seconds. At 1'32 into the track and at the end, there is a horn melody similar to the one on *The Work Pt. 1* (2001), but most of the musicians' contributions here are, as usual, dictated by signs Prince gave them when they were playing, as The

Revolution's keyboardist Matt "Doctor" Fink explained: "One time, he had a handkerchief that he would drop and you'd have to watch it and as soon as it hit the floor, boom! You'd hit a big horn punch [...] And when he shook his hand like this, right, he'd go [sings], and then there was a lick that we'd all play [...] They were just little James Brown-y horn licks à la Prince, and little turnarounds, but he learned all that from the other masters that came before him."[379]

THE BALL

Prince / 4'34

Musicians: Prince: vocals, spoken voice, electric guitar, bass, drums, synthesizers, Fairlight CMI, claps, backing vocals / **Eric Leeds:** saxophone / **Matt "Atlanta Bliss" Blistan:** trumpet / **Susannah Melvoin:** backing vocals / **Wally Safford:** backing vocals / **Greg Brooks:** backing vocals / **Jerome Benton:** backing vocals / **Recording: Washington Avenue Warehouse, Edina, Minnesota:** 25 July 1986 / **Technical team: Producer:** Prince / **Recording engineer:** Susan Rogers / **Assistant recording engineer:** Todd Herreman

With its funk groove and percussion reminiscent of Marvin Gaye's *Got To Give It Up* (1977), *The Ball* was considered for inclusion on the *Crystal Ball* triple album. After the project was abandoned by Warner Bros. Records, Prince reworked the track in December 1987 at his brand-new Paisley Park studios, resulting in *Eye No*, the first song on his subsequent album, *Lovesexy*, which was released in 1988.

ADONIS AND BATHSHEBA

Prince / 5'28

Musicians: Prince: vocals, electric guitar, bass, drums, synthesizers, backing vocals / **Eric Leeds:** saxophone, flute, bugle / **Matt "Atlanta Bliss" Blistan:** trumpet / **Recording: Galpin Boulevard Home Studio, Chanhassen, Minnesota:** 27 July 1986 / **Technical team: Producer:** Prince / **Recording engineer:** Susan Rogers / **Assistant recording engineer:** Todd Herreman

Although Eric Leeds (saxophone) and Atlanta Bliss (trumpet) were omnipresent on the various productions that ended up as the *Sign O' the Times* album, they did not consider themselves to be full members of The Revolution. "When Eric and I joined," Bliss later explained, "we called ourselves the Counter Revolution. We couldn't say we were The Revolution because The Revolution is that quintessential band."[379] The two musicians are at the heart of *Adonis and Bathsheba*, a ballad in which their scores erupt in every bar. Prince recorded it in late July 1986, as his *Dream Factory* album was being finalized.

FOREVER IN MY LIFE (EARLY VOCAL RUN-THROUGH)

Prince / 6'25

Musician: Prince: vocals, acoustic guitar, bass, programming, piano, claps, backing vocals / **Recording: Galpin Boulevard Home Studio, Chanhassen, Minnesota:** 7–8 August 1986 / **Technical team: Producer:** Prince / **Recording engineer:** Susan Rogers

Prince wrote *Forever In My Life* for his fiancée Susannah Melvoin and presented it to her early in the morning after spending the night working on the initial version of the song. "I knew what it was, I knew what he was saying," she explained years later. "[...] language wasn't used for that. Music was. Music was his language."[377] Although Prince rerecorded the song on 8 August, Susan Rogers, who was present at the sessions, pointed out a major difference between the two versions: "The very first version is a young man, expressing the kind of sentiment he might on his wedding day. He sounds happy and optimistic. The version that ended up on the album is more serious. This is a tone that says, 'Yeah, I think I'm going to do this and it'll be hard.' It's a more mature perspective."[101]

CRUCIAL (ALTERNATE LYRICS)

Prince / 6'15

Musicians: Prince: vocals, electric guitar, acoustic guitar, bass, drums, tambourine, programming, synthesizers, piano, backing vocals / **Orchestra** / **Recording: Galpin Boulevard Home Studio, Chanhassen, Minnesota:** 13 September 1986 / **Mad Hatter Studios, Los Angeles:** 8–9 November 1986 / **Technical team: Producer:** Prince / **Recording engineer:** Susan Rogers / **Orchestral arrangements:** Clare Fischer

Written for the musical *The Dawn*, one of the many projects Prince was working on in 1986, and which was ultimately shelved, *Crucial* was recorded on 13 September 1986. Prince then decided to change the lyrics and rerecord his vocal line two days later. The original version is the one presented here, also featuring string arrangements from Clare Fischer which are absent from the rerecording of the track that was included in the unreleased material on 1998's *Crystal Ball* box set from NPG Records.

THE COCOA BOYS

Prince / 6'06

Musicians: Prince: vocals, electric guitar, bass, programming, synthesizers, Fairlight CMI, backing vocals / **Eric Leeds:** saxophone / **Matt "Atlanta Bliss" Blistan:** trumpet / **Susannah Melvoin:** backing vocals / **Recording: Galpin Boulevard Home Studio, Chanhassen, Minnesota:** 14 September 1986 / **Sunset Sound, Los Angeles:** 22 November 1986 (overdubs) / **Technical team: Producer:** Prince / **Recording engineer:** Susan Rogers

In the same spirit as *Hot Thing* (and with the same riff in the background mix), *The Cocoa Boys*, along with *Crucial* and *When the Dawn of the Morning Comes*, was written for the musical *The Dawn*, which Prince worked on in August and September 1986, but finally abandoned. The song refers to a fictitious musical group known as The Cocoa Boys, whose bass player is a certain Joe. Prince probably had this character in mind when he used the pseudonym Joey Coco to write songs for Kenny Rogers (*You're My Love*, 1986), Deborah Allen (*Telepathy*, 1987), and a band called Three O'Clock (*Neon Telephone*, 1988).

WHEN THE DAWN OF THE MORNING COMES

Prince / 6'17

Musician: Prince: vocals, electric guitar, bass, programming, Hammond organ, synthesizers, Fairlight CMI, claps, backing vocals / **Recording: Galpin Boulevard Home Studio, Chanhassen, Minnesota:** 29 September 1986 / **Technical team: Producer:** Prince / **Recording engineer:** Susan Rogers / **Assistant recording engineer:** Todd Herreman

When the Dawn of the Morning Comes is the third surviving song from the sessions for the musical *The Dawn*. It is a gospel song at 140 BPM that was filed away when the musical was aborted. "It's an interesting track and a bit like an outlier," says archivist Michael Howe. "We don't know a tremendous amount about what Prince thought about *The Dawn* in general, aside from him mentioning it a few times and sort of alluding to it in concerts and in liner notes... [...] So this is an instance where we have a track that is resolutely within the creative period, or the creative arc, that might not be the most obvious inclusion [...] we decided to include it and I think because it's never circulated and it presents yet another side of his artistry that is pretty remarkable."[380]

WITNESS 4 THE PROSECUTION (VERSION 2)

Prince / 5'03

Musicians: Prince: vocals, spoken voice, electric guitar, programming, synthesizers, Fairlight CMI / **Eric Leeds:** saxophone / **Matt "Atlanta Bliss" Blistan:** trumpet / **Recording: Sunset Sound, Los Angeles:** 6 October 1986 / **Technical team: Producer:** Prince / **Recording engineers:** Susan Rogers, Coke Johnson

After parting ways with The Revolution (see page 126), Prince decided to record a second version of *Witness 4 the Prosecution* with the intention of offering it to singer Deborah Allen. "Version one is Sly and the Family Stone and version two is late '80s Prince solo," commented Michael Howe, the official archivist of The Prince Estate. "It's pretty remarkable that the song can stand up to both 'costumes' effectively [...] You know, he went from Prince the solo artist, to band leader, to Prince the solo artist, again."[380] In the end, Prince chose to keep his song and give Allen another one written specially for her called *Telepathy*, which she released as a single on RCA Records on 13 March 1987.

IT BE'S LIKE THAT SOMETIMES

Prince / 3'19

Musician: Prince: vocals, electric guitar, bass, programming, synthesizers, Fairlight CMI, backing vocals / **Recording: Sunset Sound, Los Angeles:** 11 October 1986 / **Technical team: Producer:** Prince / **Recording engineers:** Susan Rogers, Coke Johnson

On 11 October 1986, Prince continued his recording marathon with *11 Minutes* (which would become *Violet Blue*, a track that was offered to Jill Jones the following year) and some overdubs on *Six* for the first Madhouse album recorded over the preceding few weeks, before launching into the production of a new track, *It Be's Like That Sometimes.* His recording engineers, Susan Rogers and Coke Johnson, whom the singer nicknamed "Cuz," short for "Cousin," were forced to work at a frenetic pace. "He would work you into the ground," Johnson says. "[...] There was a break room right across the hall with a couple nice couches, and so we could take little catnaps in there [...] If he wanted me in the studio he'd come over the talkback and say, 'Cuz, studio three' [...] It was rare that he would drink much coffee, but if we'd been recording for seven or eight hours and it was 10 o'clock at night, he would say, 'Cuz. We need a cup of coffee' [...] Generally, it was with a little bit of cream and a sugar cube. And if he said 'Two sugars,' that meant you were going to be there for another four hours, because he was such a purist, that even a sugar buzz would get him wound up."[380]

EMOTIONAL PUMP

Prince / 4'59

Musicians: Prince: vocals, bass, programming, synthesizers, Fairlight CMI, percussion, backing vocals / **Eric Leeds:** saxophone / **Matt "Atlanta Bliss" Blistan:** trumpet / **Recording: Sunset Sound, Los Angeles:** 16 October 1986 / **Technical team: Producer:** Prince / **Recording engineers:** Susan Rogers, Coke Johnson

After many years of loudly proclaiming the influence Joni Mitchell's melancholy songs had on his creativity, it is very surprising that the first song Prince offered his idol was this bass slap funk number which is the complete antithesis of the Canadian singer's folk style. "He sent me a song once called *You Are My Emotional Pump, You Make My Body Jump,*" Mitchell explained in 1994. "I called him up and said, 'I can't sing this.' He's a strange little duck, but I like him."[382]

REBIRTH OF THE FLESH (ORIGINAL OUTRO)

Prince / 5'28

Musicians: Prince: vocals, electric guitar, programming, synthesizers, Fairlight CMI, backing vocals / **Eric Leeds:** saxophone / **Matt "Atlanta Bliss" Blistan:** trumpet / **Recording: Sunset Sound, Los Angeles:** 28 October, 4 November 1986 / **Technical team: Producer:** Prince / **Recording engineers:** Susan Rogers, Coke Johnson

Rebirth of the Flesh was originally written to appear on *Camille*, then on *Crystal Ball*, but ended up in Prince's archives after the two albums were aborted. It was replaced by the song *Sign O' the Times* on the album of the same name. If the chorus of this song, which sometimes circulated under the name *Semi-A-Colia*, sounds familiar at first listen, then it is because Prince reused the "La-la-la-la-la" as "Sha-na-na-na-na" for *Walk Don't Walk* on the 1991 *Diamonds and Pearls* album.

COSMIC DAY

Prince / 5'39

Musician: Prince: vocals, electric guitar, bass, programming, synthesizers, Fairlight CMI, Fender Rhodes piano, backing vocals / **Recording: Sunset Sound, Los Angeles:** 15 November 1986 / **Technical team: Producer:** Prince / **Recording engineers:** Susan Rogers, Coke Johnson

In 2020, all the songs from the *Camille* album (*Housequake, Strange Relationship, Feel U Up, Shockadelica, Good Love, If I Was Your Girlfriend, Rockhard in a Funky Place*, and *Rebirth of the Flesh*, which appeared as a live version on the NPG Music Club in 2001) had already been released in various formats by Prince over the years. *Cosmic Day* was considered for the album Prince was planning to release under the name of his high-pitched avatar, but ultimately dropped from the final tracklist before the project was abandoned altogether. Prince enjoyed playing around with his Publison Infernal Machine 90 to change his voice, using the highs to become Camille (see page 142) and the lows for his Bob George voice, named after the track that appears on 1994's *The Black Album.*

WALKIN' IN GLORY

Prince / 5'14

Musicians: Prince: vocals, spoken voice, electric guitar, bass, piano, Hammond organ, synthesizers, backing vocals / **Sheila E.:** drums / **Recording: Sunset Sound, Los Angeles:** 7–9 December 1986 / **Technical team: Producer:** Prince / **Recording engineers:** Susan Rogers, Coke Johnson

A real gospel number that gives pride of place to Jesus Christ, *Walkin' in Glory* was recorded by Prince during the sessions that would produce *The Black Album.* The presence of this song imbued with spirituality in the middle of recording sessions for *Le Grind, 2 Nigs United 4 West Compton*, and *Le Grind* is a strange paradox, since Prince was to abandon the release of the black album because of its dark side, and even went so far as to declare that it was the work of the devil.

Wally Safford protects Prince from photographers using a blanket in London on 12 February 1985.

song was finished, Prince caught Rogers on the hop by instructing her to erase all 24 recorded tracks. She refused to do so, suggesting he left it until the next day to decide, but Prince grabbed the remote control for the multitrack and erased the entire recording of the song which was then entitled *Babyless*. On 29 December 1986, he decided to rerecord the song, renamed *Wally*, this time referencing his friend and ex-security guard Wally Safford, who had become one of his dancers and backup singers. The only thing that survived was a cassette with a premix of *Babyless*, as Rogers had had time to export the track. "We turned over every conceivable rock to try to find it,"[373] explained archivist Michael Howe, who finally had to resign himself to releasing only the second version of the song. "I've never heard the original version again," Rogers concluded, "but Prince kept that tape and I don't know what he did with it. Maybe he threw it away, or gave it to someone, or lost it..."[108]

WALLY

Prince / 4'45

Musicians: Prince: vocals, electric guitar, bass, drums, piano, synthesizers, Fairlight CMI, backing vocals / **Eric Leeds:** saxophone / **Matt "Atlanta Bliss" Blistan:** trumpet / **Recording:** Galpin Boulevard Home Studio, Chanhassen, Minnesota: 29 December 1986 / **Technical team: Producer:** Prince / **Recording engineer:** Susan Rogers

In December 1986, Prince was devastated by his breakup with Susannah Melvoin. Susan Rogers, his recording engineer, was there to witness her boss's distress as he recorded a deeply melancholic song for his ex-fiancée. "One morning," Rogers said, "he called me to ask me to come to the studio. There, he asked me to set up the piano and the microphones for the drums. He then went from instrument to instrument to perform the original version of *Wally*. It was so beautiful, and so amazing. At the time, it reminded me of Stevie Wonder. It was a beautiful breakup song that brought out all the grief in him [...] To me, it was the most beautiful, true, and profound thing he had ever recorded."[108] Once the

I NEED A MAN

Prince / 5'33

Musicians: Prince: vocals, electric guitar, bass, programming, Fender Rhodes piano, Hammond organ, synthesizers, percussion, choir / **Eric Leeds:** saxophone / **Recording:** Washington Avenue Warehouse, Edina, Minnesota: 22 January 1987 / **Technical team: Producer:** Prince / **Recording engineer:** Susan Rogers

In December 1986, Prince attended Bonnie Raitt's concert at the Beverly Theater in Los Angeles. He took a liking to the blues guitarist and singer, and he invited her over to Paisley Park to record some songs. When Raitt came to Chanhassen in April 1987, Prince presented her with a series of songs he had arranged entirely for her, including *Jealous Girl*, previously offered to The Bangles, *There's Something I Like About Being Your Fool* from 1981, and *I Need A Man*, a song written for The Hookers in 1981. The day after she arrived, Raitt recorded her vocals and a few guitar lines for the songs. The two then planned to meet again in July, once Prince's European tour was over. "But I was touring then," Raitt explained, "and his tour went on longer than he expected [...]"[383] Raitt was also reluctant to work with Warner Bros. Records, which had dropped her in 1983 during a purge of its catalog of artists. In the end, the two musicians never worked together.

PROMISE TO BE TRUE

Prince / 3'38

Musicians: Prince: vocals, electric guitar, acoustic guitar, bass, drums, Hammond organ, claps, backing vocals / **Eric Leeds:** saxophone / **Recording: Washington Avenue Warehouse, Edina, Minnesota:** 25 January 1987 / **Technical team: Producer:** Prince / **Recording engineer:** Susan Rogers

Promise To Be True, originally written to appear on the second Vanity 6 album (see page 72), was reworked in 1987 and offered to Bonnie Raitt. The song was perfectly suited to the blues guitarist's musical style, but it was filed away in Prince's archives after their collaboration went no further. Raitt recorded many of the vocal and slide guitar lines for the songs Prince offered her, but these versions remain unreleased to this day.

JEALOUS GIRL (VERSION 2)

Prince / 4'52

Musicians: Prince: vocals, electric guitar, bass, programming, synthesizers, Fairlight CMI, backing vocals / **Eric Leeds:** saxophone / **Recording: Washington Avenue Warehouse, Edina, Minnesota:** 26 January, 5 February 1987 / **Technical team: Producer:** Prince / **Recording engineer:** Susan Rogers

Jealous Girl was written in 1981 for The Hookers and offered to The Bangles in 1984, who chose instead to take *Manic Monday* and make it their own. Prince rerecorded *Jealous Girl* in January 1987 and offered it to Bonnie Raitt a few months later in April.

THERE'S SOMETHING I LIKE ABOUT BEING YOUR FOOL

Prince / 3'39

Musicians: Prince: vocals, electric guitar, acoustic guitar, bass, drums, synthesizers, backing vocals / **Eric Leeds:** saxophone / **Recording: Washington Avenue Warehouse, Edina, Minnesota:** 25 January 1987 / **Technical team: Producer:** Prince / **Recording engineer:** Susan Rogers

Written in 1981, *There's Something I Like About Being Your Fool* was also reworked in 1987 for Bonnie Raitt, who recorded her own version on 3 April 1987. The song is remarkable for its foray into reggae, a musical genre Prince rarely touched throughout his career with the exception of songs such as *If It'll Make U Happy* (1982), *Blue Light* (1992), *Ripopgodazippa* (1998), and *Splash* (recorded in 1985 and released in 2001).

BIG TALL WALL (VERSION 2)

Prince / 5'46

Musician: Prince: vocals, spoken voice, programming, synthesizers, Fairlight CMI, backing vocals / **Recording: Paisley Park, Chanhassen, Minnesota:** 10 July 1987 / **Technical team: Producer:** Prince / **Recording engineer:** Eddie Garcia

Like *Witness 4 the Prosecution*, the rerecording of *Big Tall Wall* is evidence of Prince's emancipation from his musicians during the summer of 1987. When Paisley Park opened a few weeks later, the singer locked himself away to record the first Madhouse album and rework several of his songs with conspicuous energy and newfound pleasure. "This is leaving the band behind, and once again becoming the solo artist. So it's very interesting to hear that dynamic,"[374] said Michael Howe.

PRINCE

WELCOME 2 AMERICA

Welcome 2 America · Running Game (Son of a Slave Master)
Born 2 Die · 1000 Light Years From Here · Hot Summer · Stand Up and B Strong
Check the Record · Same Page, Different Book · When She Comes
1010 (Rin Tin Tin) · Yes · One Day We Will All B Free

Global release by The Prince Estate/NPG Records/Legacy:
28 July 2021 (LP ref.: 19439859801; Limited Edition LP ref.: 19439866161;
CD ref.: 19439866152)
Best chart ranking in the USA: did not make the charts
Best chart ranking in the UK: 5

A press conference for the launch of the Welcome 2 America Tour at the Apollo Theater, in New York, on 14 October 2010.

A CRITICAL VISION OF AMERICA

On Thursday 8 April 2021, Sony Music and its label, Legacy Recordings, which had newly partnered with The Prince Estate to reissue Prince songs, announced the release of a never-before-seen album, the first since his death in 2016. It came out on 30 July 2021 and was called *Welcome 2 America*, like the huge tour Prince gave between 2010 and 2011. The album, which a very inspired Prince recorded in just a few days, is a snapshot of that era. It's a look back at the genesis of a record that had remained hidden deep in The Vault until 2021.

Ten days with Tal Wilkenfeld and Chris Coleman

In late 2009, Prince was putting the finishing touches to *20Ten* while also thinking about preparing for his European tour, which was scheduled to start the following 4 July in Roskilde, Denmark. At this time, while surfing through YouTube, Prince came across a video of a Jeff Beck concert in which the bluesman performed a striking version of *Stratus* by Billy Cobham, accompanied by bass player Tal Wilkenfeld. Prince had already met Wilkenfeld some time before in Los Angeles. "He called me," recalled Wilkenfeld, "and said, 'I really want to make a trio with you. Can you find me a drummer? I trust your judgment. Why don't you try some people out and tell me who you like?'"[384] Wilkenfeld immediately thought of Chris Coleman, who had just finished the reunion tour of The New Kids On The Block and was preparing to go on Joey McIntyre's solo tour (McIntyre was one of the band's members). Coleman canceled this commitment, went to Paisley Park, met Prince, and one audition later (with *777-9311* by The Time, the song that contains the most difficult drum line in Prince's entire repertoire!), he joined the team.

Between 10 and 19 March 2010, the trio recorded a dozen instrumental songs. Prince played the guitar and sometimes the keyboards. A new recording engineer, Jason Agel, was at the controls for this new adventure. Around 20 March 2010, the trio broke up and each person went their own way, Prince having to get ready for the 20Ten Tour. In the first days of summer, the backing vocalists for the tour, Liv Warfield, Elisa Fiorillo, and Shelby "J." Johnson, recorded many vocal lines for these new songs, both as backing vocalists and as lead singers. Then Prince called in his old friend Morris Hayes. He played the songs for him and told him why he found them so interesting, particularly that the lyrics were inspired by current events, such as the socio-economic crisis devastating the United States at the time. Prince asked Hayes to finetune the songs as he saw fit, specifying that he would later take out any elements he didn't like. Hayes complied and soon provided Prince with some high-quality premixes, but Prince was already on the road and fully invested in his new tour. *Welcome 2 America* was thus archived to The Vault, only to reappear when The Prince Estate archivist, Michael Howe, and its artistic director, Trevor Guy, found it during their research. "We're still in the process of excavating and ingesting it all," explained Guy. "Use your imagination and the wildest thing that you can dream up...it's probably a bit more than that. There's enough in there to release a breathtaking Prince album every year for decades. I mean, my kids' kids' kids will be listening to new Prince records."[385]

WELCOME
2 AMERI

Kim Kardashian, a few minutes before she appeared onstage at Madison Square Garden on 7 February 2011.

Single

WELCOME 2 AMERICA

Prince / 5'23

Musicians: Prince: vocals, electric guitar, backing vocals / **Tal Wilkenfeld:** bass / **Chris Coleman:** drums / **Mr Hayes:** synthesizers, programming, percussion / **Shelby J.:** backing vocals / **Elisa Fiorillo:** backing vocals / **Liv Warfield:** backing vocals / **Recording: Paisley Park, Chanhassen, Minnesota:** 15 March 2010 (backing tracks), spring 2010 (overdubs) / **Technical team: Producers:** Prince, Mr Hayes / **Recording engineer:** Jason Agel
Single: A-side: *Welcome 2 America*/5'24 / **B-side:** *Dreamer*/ *Welcome 2 America (Live)*/6'12 / **Distribution via Prince.com by The Prince Estate/ NPG Records/Legacy:** 30 July 2021 (single ref.: 19439874867)

On 7 February 2011, Prince gave the sixth concert of the Welcome 2 America Tour onstage at Madison Square Garden in New York. As usual, he invited audience members to climb onto the stage and dance with him. That night, Kim Kardashian was in the front row. Shelby J., a backing vocalist for the show, went down to get her and bring her on stage, but she did not seem impressed with the dance moves of the master of funk. In the blink of an eye, Prince sent Kardashian back to her place with a chilling "Get off the stage" followed by a "Welcome to America," which audience members didn't know how to interpret, even though a little later that night, smack in the middle of *Dreamer*, Prince clarified his thinking by saying into the mic, "Welcome to America, where you can be famous for doing absolutely nothing at all." The jab was clearly meant for the reality TV star. This event alone sums up Prince's state of mind at the time. A few months before, he'd recorded a diatribe against his country, as the social and financial crises shook America. When he recorded the song *Welcome 2 America* in the spring of 2010, Prince was taking aim at the evils of the world. Social interactions distorted by new technology, golden parachutes given to multinational CEOs, references to slavery—everything is covered in this stripped-down funk song, which is reminiscent of the hard-hitting minimalism of *The Revolution Will Not Be Televised*, recorded by Gil Scott-Heron in 1970, then again in 1971. "This is the time we had Barack Obama," explained Shelby J. in 2021, whose voice illuminates the song. "With the hope and the change and the feeling we're moving forward. But even though we thought everything was okay, he could see beyond that. Like, 'Don't get comfortable because evil and darkness are like a virus. When you take your eye off of them, they can grow in different ways and they can grow using technologies, too.'" As she added at the end: "...like we're seeing now."[386] Let's remember that in 2010 Prince still didn't own a cell phone. He used his musicians' phones when he needed to call his entourage. He had memorized all the numbers of his contacts.

RUNNING GAME (SON OF A SLAVE MASTER)

Prince / 4'05

Musicians: Prince: vocals, electric guitar, backing vocals / **Shelby J.:** rap, claps, spoken word, backing vocals / **Tal Wilkenfeld:** bass / **Chris Coleman:** drums / **Mr Hayes:** synthesizers, percussion / **Elisa Fiorillo:** claps, spoken word, backing vocals / **Liv Warfield:** claps, spoken word, backing vocals / **Recording: Paisley Park, Chanhassen, Minnesota:** 12 March 2010 (backing tracks), spring 2010 (overdubs) / **Technical team: Producers:** Prince, Mr Hayes / **Recording engineer:** Jason Agel

While Prince had his three backing vocalists Elisa Fiorillo, Liv Warfield, and Shelby J. record their voices together on a single mic, Shelby J. was lucky enough to perform the verses on her own in a rap she wrote in no time at all. "In those days, Prince made use of Shelby and the NPG backing vocalists quite a bit onstage and in the studio," explained Morris Hayes. "He gave them a lot of space and let them sing lead for some of the songs, which hadn't happened since Rosie Gaines was in the band. He trusted them, and no doubt he took inspiration from Sly and the Family Stone for the distribution of the voices."[387] Shelby J. wondered: "Can this be right?" She went on, "He wanted me to sing all the verses, then he would come in on the chorus. He just liked the way my voice sounded there. As a supporting vocalist, you always think you're just going to be supporting, but Prince was very generous with his light."[388]

BORN 2 DIE

Prince / 5'03

Musicians: Prince: vocals, electric guitar, backing vocals / **Tal Wilkenfeld:** bass / **Chris Coleman:** drums / **Mr Hayes:** synthesizers, percussion / **Shelby J.:** backing vocals / **Elisa Fiorillo:** backing vocals / **Liv Warfield:** backing vocals / **Recording: Paisley Park, Chanhassen, Minnesota:** 12 March 2010 (backing tracks), spring 2010 (overdubs) / **Technical team: Producers:** Prince, Mr Hayes / **Recording engineer:** Jason Agel

In 2010, Prince found a video in which his friend Cornel West, the prominent defender of African-American rights, dared to say, "I love my brother Prince, but he's no Curtis Mayfield." Prince did not appreciate being reduced to the level of sub-funkateer, so he dived into the making of *Born 2 Die*, using all the tools Mayfield deployed to create his languorous and sexy funk. A heady sensual voice, wah-wah pedal across the board, everything was there to rival the author of *Move On Up* (1970) and *Superfly* (1972). Morris Hayes, whom Prince later asked to embellish the song with overdubs, remembers Prince's reaction when he heard Dave Isaac's final mix: "Prince didn't really throw out accolades. But when I played that song for him, he grabbed me by the shoulders and shook me and screamed, 'This is great! You're Duke Ellington!'"[388] Meanwhile, Cornel West made amends when the album came out in 2021 by writing on Twitter: "The genius of my dear brother Prince lives forever! This Curtis Mayfield-inspired album is another great moment in the history of the Black quest for truth & beauty & goodness!"[389]

1000 LIGHT YEARS FROM HERE

Prince / 5'46

Musicians: Prince: vocals, electric guitar, acoustic guitar, synthesizers, claps, backing vocals / **John Blackwell:** drums / **Shelby J.:** backing vocals / **Elisa Fiorillo:** backing vocals / **Liv Warfield:** backing vocals / **Recording: Paisley Park, Chanhassen, Minnesota:** 11 March 2010 (backing tracks), spring 2010 (overdubs) / **Technical team: Producer:** Prince / **Recording engineer:** Jason Agel

All the sensuality of Curtis Mayfield's soul-funk can be heard in *Born 2 Die*.

Recorded with drummer John Blackwell in March 2010, *1000 Light Years From Here* is hands down the most beautiful song on *Welcome 2 America*. Led by the trio of backing vocalists from the ultimate version of the New Power Generation, the song was such a success that Prince decided to rework it a few years later and graft it onto *Black Muse*, from the album *Hitnrun Phase Two*. This is the original version, to be enjoyed while sparing a thought for John Blackwell who died of a brain tumor at 43 years old on 7 July 2017.

HOT SUMMER

Prince / 3'32

Musicians: Prince: vocals, electric guitar, claps, backing vocals / **Tal Wilkenfeld:** bass / **Chris Coleman:** drums, percussion / **Mr Hayes:** synthesizers, Hammond organ / **Shelby J.:** backing vocals / **Elisa Fiorillo:** backing vocals / **Liv Warfield:** backing vocals / **Recording: Paisley Park, Chanhassen, Minnesota:** March 2010 (backing tracks), spring 2010 (overdubs) / **Technical team: Producers:** Prince, Mr Hayes / **Recording engineer:** Jason Agel

Determined to drop minor chords in favor of major tonalities, Prince wrote a pop song perfectly suited for American FM radio. "It was summer when we did it," explained Elisa Fiorillo, of the vocal sessions for *Hot Summer*. "We got in the car and drove downtown to Minneapolis [...] with the windows rolled down. We were listening on full blast with our heads bobbing at the same time. There were people on the street, and we're saying to Prince, 'Oh, my God, they're going to know it's you.' And some people could see and pointed as we drove right fast, like, 'I think that was Prince!'"[384]

The bass guitarist Tal Wilkenfeld, who was discovered by Prince on YouTube alongside Jeff Beck, lit up *Welcome 2 America* with her precise, nuanced playing.

Dave Pirner and Dan Murphy embraced the grunge movement with their hit *Runaway Train* in 1993.

2021

STAND UP AND B STRONG

Dave Pirner / 5'18

Musicians: Prince: vocals, piano, electric guitar, claps, synthesizers, Hammond organ, backing vocals / **Elisa Fiorillo:** vocals, claps, backing vocals / **Tal Wilkenfeld:** bass / **Chris Coleman:** drums / **Shelby J.:** claps, backing vocals / **Liv Warfield:** claps, backing vocals / **Recording: Paisley Park, Chanhassen, Minnesota:** 19 March 2010 (backing tracks), spring 2010 (overdubs) / **Technical team: Producer:** Prince / **Recording engineer:** Jason Agel

Prince regularly expressed his interest in the music of Soul Asylum, a Minneapolis rock group who took over FM radio in 1993 with their hit *Runaway Train*. In 2010, the band, whose frontman was Dave Pirner, was still active, and its drummer was none other than Michael Bland, a former NPG member who was still in touch with Prince. "Michael Bland, my drummer, called me up and he was at Paisley Park. And he said, 'Prince would like to do *Stand Up and Be Strong*, and he wants your blessing,'" explained Pirner. "And I said, 'I'd be honored,' and that was kind of it. And then I just figured it'd probably end up in The Vault forever. I didn't really think it was going to see the light of day."[390] Led by Elisa Fiorillo's crystalline voice, the song is a hymn to bravery and perseverance, which fits in perfectly with the album's throughline: the fight for equality and social justice.

CHECK THE RECORD

Prince / 3'28

Musicians: Prince: vocals, electric guitar, backing vocals / **Tal Wilkenfeld:** bass / **Chris Coleman:** drums / **Mr Hayes:** synthesizers, Hammond organ, programming, percussion / **Shelby J.:** backing vocals / **Elisa Fiorillo:** backing vocals / **Liv Warfield:** backing vocals / **Recording: Paisley Park, Chanhassen, Minnesota:** 10 March 2010 (backing tracks), spring 2010 (overdubs) / **Technical team: Producers:** Prince, Mr Hayes / **Recording engineer:** Jason Agel

When Prince gave Morris Hayes the tracks for *Welcome 2 America* and asked him to add overdubs, the drums in *Check the Record* were out of step with the other instruments. Hayes was able to save the song by adding a bell to mark the tempo, various synthesizers and organ layers, and several percussion parts here and there. The song was once again led by the hard-hitting voices of the trio of backing vocalists, who recorded their tracks during preparations for rehearsals for the European tour of the summer of 2010. "[Prince] would sleep until one or two and would kind of mosey in around two," reported Elisa Fiorillo. "We would rehearse eight hours every day, seven days a week. Then he'd say, 'Let's go to the studio. I have something I want you to sing on.' I didn't even know we were making a record."[384]

SAME PAGE, DIFFERENT BOOK

Prince, Shelby J. / 4'41

Musicians: Prince: vocals, electric guitar, backing vocals / Tal Wilkenfeld: bass / Chris Coleman: drums / Mr Hayes: synthesizers, percussion / Shelby J.: backing vocals / Elisa Fiorillo: backing vocals / Liv Warfield: backing vocals / **Recording:** Paisley Park, Chanhassen, Minnesota: 11 March 2010 (backing tracks), spring 2010 (overdubs) / **Technical team:** Producers: Prince, Mr Hayes / Recording engineer: Jason Agel

Prince advocated difference as a strength in our society. His lyrics for this song are unifying and pacifist and carried by Shelby J.'s rap part. As the song's production was coming to an end, Prince told Shelby J. that he wanted to embellish it with some rap. He asked her if she was up to writing something quickly. "[...] I ran out into the hallway right outside studio A and sat down by this beautiful mural of all of the artists that inspired Prince throughout his whole lifetime," reported Shelby J. "And that gave me inspiration."[391]

WHEN SHE COMES

Prince / 4'46

Musicians: Prince: vocals, electric guitar, piano, backing vocals / Tal Wilkenfeld: bass / Chris Coleman: drums / **Recording:** Paisley Park, Chanhassen, Minnesota: 12 March 2010 (backing tracks), spring 2010 (overdubs) / **Technical team:** Producer: Prince / Recording engineer: Jason Agel

Before rerecording it in 2014 for *Hitnrun Phase Two*, Prince recorded an initial version of the sensual *When She Comes*, a soulful ballad describing his partner's orgasm in great detail and with vocal noises, which he'd recorded himself. He did not allow his three backing vocalists to participate in the song's recording or even listen to the final version. Morris Hayes was lucky enough to listen to it before it was archived in The Vault. He dared to joke about it in reference to Prince's spiritual commitment, which had steered him away from making this type of naughty song. "I said, 'This is old Prince,'" explained Hayes. "'This is gonna get you in the witness protection program at Jehovah's Witnesses. You're going to get in trouble for this!' He just had a little laugh about it."[384]

Rin Tin Tin the dog having his fur brushed by his master, Lee Duncan, on the set of *Jaws of Steel* by Ray Enright (1927).

1010 (RIN TIN TIN)

Prince / 4'42

Musicians: Prince: vocals, electric guitar, bass, drums, percussion, programming, piano, synthesizers, backing vocals / **Shelby J.:** backing vocals / **Elisa Fiorillo:** backing vocals / **Liv Warfield:** backing vocals / **Recording: Paisley Park, Chanhassen, Minnesota:** spring 2010 / **Technical team: Producer:** Prince / **Recording engineer:** Jason Agel

In a strange turn of events, Prince and his backing vocalists, Elisa Fiorillo, Shelby J., and Liv Warfield, made a song they called *Rin Tin Tin*, which was the name of a dog found by American soldiers in 1918 after an attack on a German post in France, then brought back to the United States to become the star of a series of the same name. The dog also starred in some 30 Westerns produced by Warner Bros. in the first half of the 20th century. Before the dog died in 1932, he was one of the rare canine celebrities that could boast of having his own star on Hollywood Boulevard. He was also the only dog to give his name to a Prince song! Recording engineer Jason Agel was present at the song's recording sessions, where Prince asked his backing vocalists to use a British accent for their takes. Agel also recounted how happy he was to record the *1010 (Rin Tin Tin)* guitar solo with Prince: "I just remember sitting in the studio and him playing a guitar solo next to me. I'm a guitar player, and I grew up listening to the *Batman* soundtrack in my room as a kid. And here he is, playing ripping guitar. I had to turn my face and try not to laugh because it was just such a surreal thing that was happening."[384]

The drummer Chris Coleman, pillar of the rhythm section on *Welcome 2 America.*

YES

Prince / 2'56

Musicians: Prince: vocals, electric guitar, synthesizers, backing vocals / **Tal Wilkenfeld:** bass / **Chris Coleman:** drums, percussion / **Shelby J.:** backing vocals / **Elisa Fiorillo:** backing vocals / **Liv Warfield:** backing vocals / **Recording: Paisley Park, Chanhassen, Minnesota:** 15 March 2010 (backing tracks), spring 2010 (overdubs) / **Technical team: Producer:** Prince / **Recording engineer:** Jason Agel

In this rock song with gospel accents led by the shock-rhythm base of the Wilkenfeld-Coleman duo, Prince and his backing vocalists urge listeners to change their behavior in order to make deep changes in society. "Prince recorded to tape and worked very quickly," explained Wilkenfeld. "And he never wanted to punch in unless it was absolutely necessary. That taught me how [...] to work fast and effectively, and commit to my decisions."[392]

ONE DAY WE WILL ALL B FREE

Prince / 4'41

Musicians: Prince: vocals, electric guitar, drums, claps, Fender Rhodes piano, synthesizers, backing vocals / **Tal Wilkenfeld:** bass / **Shelby J.:** backing vocals / **Elisa Fiorillo:** backing vocals / **Liv Warfield:** backing vocals / **Recording: Paisley Park, Chanhassen, Minnesota:** spring 2010 / **Technical team: Producer:** Prince / **Recording engineer:** Jason Agel

After recording *One Day We Will All B Free* with Chris Coleman and Tal Wilkenfeld, Prince decided to rerecord the drum part. Prince saw himself as a preacher in this high-quality funk song with gospel hints, in which he asks the audience to look back on History as it's taught in schools. "Prince was a teacher in so many ways," confided Elisa Fiorillo. "I feel like this record is him trying to teach the world: 'Get a grip, get your s*** together, and let's make this work, because this world is slowly failing us terribly.'"[393]

GLOSSARY

Acetate: The first pressing of a record (sometimes called a test pressing), enabling the artist and producer to listen to the final article before making a duplicate. The name is derived from acetate cellulose, which was used to make records.

Aftershow: The second concert given by a band or artist after their main show, usually in the privacy of a small venue or club.

Arpeggiator: An effect in some synthesizers that cycles through each note in a chord played by a musician in the manner of an arpeggio.

Backing band: A group of musicians accompanying an artist onstage or in the studio.

Backing tracks: Instrumental or vocal tracks, sometimes rhythmic only, recorded to accompany a singer or a band.

Backline: All the equipment used by an artist or a band onstage or in the studio.

Backliner: A technician responsible for setting up and maintaining the instruments used by the musicians.

Beat maker: A musician whose specialty is creating instrumental tracks, notably in the hip-hop genre.

Boom box: The name for the bulky cassette players people carried in the 1980s to listen to music. Sometimes called a ghetto blaster.

Bootlegger: A dealer or distributor of so-called pirate records (or bootlegs) that have not been officially released by the artist.

Bottleneck: A glass or metal tube that the guitarist puts on their finger and slides along the strings to obtain a metallic sound. Bluesmen invented this way of playing using the neck of a bottle.

Delay: An audio effect that reproduces an acoustic echo. It is incorporated into an effects pedal or mixing console and used on vocals and instruments to regularly repeat a sound by shifting the sound signal in time.

Detuning: Changing the pitch of a note or series of notes by deliberately detuning an instrument or a recorded signal.

Distortion: A sound effect created by altering the quality of an audio signal by saturating an amp channel using the amp's built-in distortion effect or a distortion pedal.

Drum tech: A technician who maintains the drummer's equipment and tunes the drum heads for the stage and the studio.

Editing: The stage that usually precedes the mixing of a song and which "cleans" the recorded tracks by deleting or changing elements that are not required, without any involvement from the musicians.

Effect pedal: A small electronic box used to transform the sound of an instrument while it is being played.

Fade-out: A term used to define the disappearance of an audio signal, usually done by the recording engineer using a volume fader on the console during mixing.

Fader: A vertical control knob on the mixing desk used to adjust the listening volume of each track on a recording.

Fams: Prince's word for his most loyal fans.

Flanger: Similar to a phaser, the flanger effect modifies the frequency of an audio signal, creating a "helicopter" effect much loved by guitar players and drummers.

Flight case: A wooden trunk for carrying the backline used by musicians or any other equipment that will be used onstage or in the studio.

Flow: The rhythmic way of delivering lyrics used in hip-hop.

Funkateer: Urban slang term for someone who is an aficionado of funk music and adopts its codes and behaviors.

Gate: A device used to control the volume or mute an audio signal as required.

Gimmick: A short series of notes with an easily recognizable melody that acts as a hook to catch the listener's attention and make it memorable. It originated in jazz and gradually spread to other music genres.

Harmonics: An audio frequency delivered by lightly plucking a guitar string without holding the note in any way.

Harmonization: A technique involving multiple vocal or instrumental lines, plus a unison or octave note. If the line is played or sung on another note (a third or a fifth, for example) to complement the original line, it is called polyphonic harmonization.

Hi-hat: A set of two cymbals (top and bottom) operated by a foot pedal. The drummer also strikes them with the stick to set the rhythmic pattern.

Hit: One musician alone or the whole band hitting a single note, either onstage or in the studio.

Hollow body: Unlike a solid body guitar made of a single piece of wood, a hollow body guitar is hollow, as the name suggests, and usually has one or two f-holes.

Humbucker: A double-coil pickup with a powerful sound, often seen on guitars like the Gibson Les Paul. Its counterpart and rival, the Fender Stratocaster, is equipped with a single-coil pickup, producing softer, crystal-clear sounds.

Jam session: Informal improvisation session involving several musicians playing together for pleasure.

Lineup: The musician members of a band.

Lo-fi: A recording method in which the high frequencies are accentuated in comparison to the low frequencies, deliberately giving the impression that the equipment used for the song is of poor quality.

Mastering: The stage after mixing in the production of a song or album, designed to give the recording the same sound quality, whatever the listening device used, as well as making the different tracks sound homogeneous.

MIDI (Musical Instrument Digital Interface): An international technical standard created in the early 1980s to enable computers and musical instruments and devices (synthesizers, drum machines, for example) to communicate with one another.

Mid-tempo: A term used to describe a song played at a moderate tempo.

Mute: The action of closing an audio track to make it silent in the mix.

Octaver: An effect used in a rack or pedal to mix the input signal with a synthesized signal whose tone is an octave higher or lower.

Outtake: A piece of music recorded in the studio or onstage that hasn't been kept on the official version of the album. It could be a previously unreleased piece or an alternative version of an existing track that may be brought out again for a compilation or reissue.

Overdubs: All the new tracks recorded (vocal and/or instruments) and added to an existing recording.

Pattern: A rhythmic or melodic sequence that repeats itself in the song.

Peer-to-peer: An illegal way to swap music or video files that emerged on the Internet in the early 2000s.

P-funk: A music genre invented by George Clinton in the early 1970s that combines psychedelic rock and funk dance. The bands Parliament and Funkadelic were the standard-bearers of this genre.

Phaser: A sound effect obtained by filtering a signal and creating a series of highs and lows in the frequency spectrum. Available as a rack or pedal, it often produces an undulating wave or swirl effect.

Piano set: A concert sequence performed by an artist accompanied only on piano.

Pitch (to): Action of altering the pitch of an audio signal.

Power chord: A chord traditionally played by a guitarist on two or three notes: the root note and the fifth, with or without the octave.

Pre-mix: An audio export of a song before it is mixed. The pre-mix done by the recording engineer enables the artist to listen to the song immediately after recording.

Preset: The factory setting of an electronic instrument. For example, a synthesizer has various presets so the musician can start using the instrument straightaway. The musician can then change the audio settings of the keyboard to create his or her own sounds.

Punchline: A term used mostly in hip-hop to describe a phrase that aims to offend or mock another person.

Reissue: The rerelease of an album or a single.

Rerecording: The act of rerecording an audio sequence in the studio over the original recording.

Reverb: A natural or artificial echo effect given to an instrument or vocals during the recording or mixing of a piece.

Riff: A short fragment of several notes that recurs regularly throughout a song and accompanies the melody. The word *riff* is an abbreviation of *rhythmic figure.*

Rimshot: The term for when a drummer sharply strikes the edge of a snare drum.

Roadie: A technician responsible for transporting and setting up equipment onstage or in the studio.

Sample: An audio sequence, mostly very short, extracted from a recording to be included in a song or instrumental piece.

Score: All the instrumental parts composed and recorded to accompany a filmed sequence.

Set list: The list of songs played by an artist or a band during a concert.

Showcase: A mini-concert given by an artist or a band, usually for promotional purposes.

Single notes: A single-note melody, unlike a chord progression, is composed of a series of notes played one after the other.

Slap: An electric bass-playing technique mostly used in funk and disco, in which the strings are struck with the thumb and plucked with the fingers of the right hand.

Slide: A guitar technique using a tube to slide smoothly from one chord or note to another while playing the intermediary notes.

Sound checks: The phase during which the sound level of instruments is adjusted along with all the pickups by the front of house and monitor engineers before a concert.

Sound designer: A musician who specializes in designing the soundscape of a song, a video sequence, or an event.

Talkback: A microphone in the studio control room that allows the recording engineer or producer to communicate with musicians recording in another room.

Test pressing: The first pressing (also called an acetate) of a record that allows the artist and producer to listen to the final recording for approval.

Timing: The precise duration of a song or audio sequence

Tour manager: The person responsible for the organization and smooth running of an artist's or a band's tour.

Tracklist: The list of songs on an album.

Trigger: A sensor that digitizes the sound of a drum kit; when in contact with the surface of the instrument, it transforms strikes into electrical signals that are then sent to a module that produces the sounds.

Twin Cities: The metropolis formed by the cities of Minneapolis and Saint Paul in Minnesota, USA.

Varispeed: A device used to vary the speed of a tape recorder and therefore the sound pitch.

Vault (The): A safe in the Paisley Park complex that contains all the songs Prince recorded during his lifetime. In 2017, the contents of The Vault were moved to the underground fortress at Iron Mountain, California.

Wah-wah: An audio effect produced by the oscillation of the sound frequency from low to high and that emits a sound like a human voice repeating the onomatopoeic "wah." This effect, which is mostly used for electric guitars, is produced by a pedal of the same name.

Walking bass: A bass line characteristic of jazz where a note is played or improvised on each beat to create a melody. By playing all the quarter notes in this way, the bassist sets the tempo for the other musicians in the band.

Whammy: An effect for guitar and bass controlled by an expression pedal, invented in 1989 by the American firm Digitech to modify the pitch of an audio signal.

BIBLIOGRAPHY

1. Graustark (Barbara), "Prince: Strange Tales from Andre's Basement…and Other Fantasies Come True," *Musician*, September 1983.

2. Nilsen (Per), *Dance Music Sex Romance, Prince: The First Decade*, First edition, 1995, Reprint, London, Firefly Publishing, 1999.

3. Price (Simon), "Remembering Prince: Andre Cymone Interviewed," *The Quietus*, 20 April 2018.

4. Lewis (Harold), Melodia (Tony), "Funk It Up," *Uptown*, No.51, May 2002.

5. Hill (Dave), *Prince: A Pop Life*, London, Faber & Faber, 1989.

6. Day (Morris), Ritz (David), *On Time. A Princely Life in Funk*, New York, Da Capo Press, 2019.

7. Gabler (Jay), "Rock and Roll Book Club: Pepe Willie Recounts His Life as a Musician and Early Prince Mentor," *The Current*, 3 September 2020.

8. Crawford (Lisa), "Nelson Finds It 'Hard To Become Known,'" *Central High Pioneer*, 13 February 1976.

9. Lewis (Harold), "The Cherry Moon," *Uptown*, No.37, 31 March 1999.

10. Schneider (Jeff), "Prince," *Insider*, May to June 1978.

11. Husney (Owen), *Famous People Who've Met Me*, Los Angeles, Rothco Press, 2018.

12. Bream (Jon), "Our Teen-age Virtuoso is Home to Play at Last," *The Minneapolis Star*, 5 January 1979.

13. Lewis (Harold), Melodia (Tony), "Take This Beat," *Uptown*, No.42, May 2000.

14. Lewis (Harold), Melodia (Tony), "I Like What You're Doing," *Uptown*, No.39, August 1999.

15. Keller (Martin), "The Power and The Glory, The Minneapolis Story," *Twin Cities Reader*, 19 January 1979.

16. Horner (Cynthia), Interview with Prince, *Right On!*, January 1979.

17. Riemenschneider (Chris), "Prince Collaborator Selling 'Soft and Wet' Songwriting Credit On eBay for $490K," *Star Tribune*, 12 February 2018.

18. Schwartz (Andy), "Prince: A Dirty Mind Comes Clean," *New York Rocker*, June 1981.

19. Carr (Tim), "Prince: 'A One-Man Band and a Whole Chorus, Too,'" *Minneapolis Tribune*, 30 April 1978.

20. Nilsen (Per), "All of This and More Is For You," *Uptown*, No.13, April to June 1994.

21. Azhar (Mobeen), *Prince 1958–2016: Stories from the Purple Underground*, London, Carlton Books, 2016.

22. "Welcome 2 His World," *Uncut*, No.290, July 2021.

23. Bream (Jon), "Clark Long Remembered His Tough Interview with a Quiet Prince," *Star Tribune*, 3 May 2013.

24. Nilsen (Per), Einarsson (Lars), "Got 2 Partyup!," *Uptown*, No.46, 31 January 2001.

25. "Oral History: Prince's Life, As Told By The People Who Knew Him Best," *Star Tribune*, 7 June 2019.

26. Booklet notes from "The Hits/The B-Sides," 1993.

27. Karlen (Neal), "Prince Talks," *Rolling Stone*, No.456, 12 September 1985.

28. Nilsen (Per), "Baby, You're A Trip," *Uptown*, No.39, 31 August 1999.

29. Horner (Cynthia), "A Rendezvous With A Prince!," *Right On!*, December 1979.

30. Heath (Chris), "Prince's Closest Friends Share Their Best Prince Stories," *GQ*, 8 December 2016.

31. Patrin (Nate), "Chaka Khan Remembers Prince and His Secret Talent for Impersonating Sly Stone," *Billboard.com*, 14 October 2016.

32. Kalbacher (Gene), "Prince in the Afternoon," *Aquarian Night Owl*, February 1981.

33. Ochs (Ed), "Prince: Mom's Favorite Freak," *Rock & Soul*, June 1981.

34. Beaulieu (Allen), *Prince Before the Rain*, Minneapolis, Minnesota Historical Society Press, 2018.

35. Chick (Steve), "Girls & Boys," *Mojo*, September 2018.

36. "Dirty Mind" album sleeve, October 1980.

37. Schwed (Mark), "Prince Likes To Go On Stage Wearing Scanty Bikini Briefs," *Kingsport Times-News*, 10 January 1981.

38. Katz (Larry), "Prince: Vice Is Nice," *The Real Paper*, 2 April 1981.

39. Salewiez (Chris), "Prince: Strutting with the New Soul Monarch," *New Musical Express*, 6 June 1981.

40. Manœuvre (Philippe), *Rock*, Paris, Harper Collins France, 2018.

41. McMahon (Chris), "What Was It Like Recording With Prince?," *Reverb.com*, 22 April 2016.

42. Regen (Jon), "Lisa Coleman: 'Prince Would Just Use a Preset and Then Brighten the F**k Out of It!,'" *Musicradar.com*, 27 December 2019.

43. Mitchell (Tony), "Posin' Til Closin'… Probes the Dirty Mind of Prince," *Sounds*, 6 June 1981.

44. *Prince. A Celebration*, Bath, Anthem Publishing, "Classic Pop," 2016.

45. Sutherland (Steve), "Some Day Your Prince Will Come," *Melody Maker*, June 1981.

46. Nilsen (Per), "I Really Get A Dirty Mind," *Uptown*, No.8, 1 April 1993.

47. Adler (Bill), "Will The Little Girls Understand?," *Rolling Stone*, No.337, 19 February 1981.

48. Salewicz (Chris), "Half A Million Dirty Minds Can't Be Wrong About This Man," *New Musical Express*, 6 June 1981.

49. Hunt (Dennis), "Prince: More Than Just a 'Dirty Mind,'" *Los Angeles Times*, 21 December 1980.

50. Wilkening (Matthew), "Morris Day Tells the Full Story of 'Partyup': 365 Prince Songs in a Year," *Diffuser.fm*, 23 August 2017.

51. Watts (Alex), "Engineering Prince: A Dive into the Archives with Peggy McCreary," *Mixdownmag.com*, 21 April 2021.

52. Blaine (Jamie), "Revolution Bassist Mark Brown: 'Prince Would Fine Us $1,500 for Making a Mistake!,'" *MusicRadar.com*, 8 February 2019.

53. Price (Simon), "Remembering Prince: Andre Cymone Interviewed," *TheQuietus.com*, 20 April 2018.

54. Touré, *Nothing Compares 2 U: An Oral History of Prince*, New York et Nashville, Permuted Press, 2021.

55. Johnson (Connie), "Rock Stars Turn Out their Versions of Princely Songs," *Los Angeles Times*, 13 January 1985.

56. Schwabe (Oliver), *Prince, Sexy Mother F****, documentary, Intact Production, 2018.

57. Williams (Chris), "How Prince's No-Nonsense Demeanor Led to the Creation of 'Controversy,'" *Okayplayer.com*, 2021.

58. Hillburn (Robert), "The Renegade Prince," *Los Angeles Times*, 21 November 1982.

59. "Morris Day on Prince Trying to Convert Him to Jehovah's Witness," *VladTV, Youtube.com*, 25 December 2019.

60. Hunt (Dennis), "'Pandemonium' Marks Time's Timely Reunion: Rhythm & Blues: The Band Seemed Destined for Superstardom Until Morris Day and Jesse Johnson Opted for Solo Careers. Neither Has Become a Big Star," *Los Angeles Times*, 22 September 1990.

61. Swensson (Andrea), "Sheila E. Talks About Working With Prince," *Thecurrent.com*, 27 November 2019.

62. "100 Best Albums of the Eighties," *Rolling Stone*, 16 November 1989.

63. Trémolin (Jacques), "Prince, Nostradamus, and The Beatles: '1999' As Told By Bobby Z.," *Muziq.fr*, 21 November 2019.

64. Savage (Mark), "The Real Story Behind Prince's Little Red Corvette," *bbc.com*, 27 November 2019.

65. Geudin (Christophe), "Prince, 'Little Red Corvette' and the Stray Cats: The Adventure of 1999 As Told By Dez Dickerson," *Funku.fr*, 5 December 2019.

66. Swensson (Andrea), "Prince: The Story of 1999 Bonus Feature: Dez Dickerson: 'Put An Explosion Over It,'" *Thecurrent.com*, 5 December 2019.

67. Nilsen (Per), Magdziarz (David J.), "Wet Dreams," *Uptown*, No.24, July to September 1996.

68. Aloe (Mary), "Vanity: Clothes of Passion," *Rock Magazine*, February 1985.

69. Matthews (Denise), *Blame It On Vanity*, Tulsa, Yorkshire Publishing Group, 1999.

70. Nilsen (Per), "Let Me Guide U 2 The Purple Rain," *Uptown*, No.14, July to September 1994.

71. "Backspin: The Revolution Talk Prince's 'Purple Rain,'" *Yahoo, Youtube.com*, 4 May 2017.

72. Tudahl (Duane), "Daughters of the Revolution," *Uptown*, No.33, Summer 1998.

73. Van Matre (Lynn), "'I Don't Have Any Regrets About Leaving, Says Vanity,'" *Chicago Tribune*, 9 September 1984.

74. Lynskey (Dorian), "Prince: 'I'm a musician. And I am music,'" *Theguardian.com*, 23 June 2011.

75. Crane (Larry), "Susan Rogers: From Prince to Ph.D.," *Tapeop.com*, No.117, January to February 2017.

76. Brown Mark, with Cynthia M Uhrich, *My Life in the Purple Kingdom*, Minneapolis, University of Minnesota Press, 2020.

77. Flans (Robyn), "Let's Go Crazy: Trying to Tone Down Prince's Live-in-the-Studio Track," *Mixonline.com*, 14 August 2019.

78. Doerschuk (Robert L.), "The Sound of Emancipation," *Musician*, April 1997.

79. Thorne (Matt), *Prince*, London, Faber & Faber, 2012.

80. Lewis (Miles Marshall), "Prince Hits N Runs N Talks!," *Ebony*, 22 December 2015.

81. Ice-T, *Freedom of Speech*, album "The Iceberg/Freedom of Speech…Just Watch What You Say!," Sire, 1989.

82. Booklet notes from the "Purple Rain Deluxe Expanded Edition," NPG Records/ Warner Bros. Records, 2017.

83. Murphy (Keith), "'Purple Rain' Turns 30: The Revolution's Dr Fink Breaks Down Prince's Classic Track-By-Track," *Vibe.com*, 25 June 2014.

84. Freed (Alan), "We Can Funk," *Uptown*, No.47, 31 March 2001.

85. Thomson (Graeme), "There Was Such Music in Him," *Uncut*, October 2018.

86. Graff (Gary), "Why Prince Asked for Journey's Blessing Before Releasing 'Purple Rain,'" *Billboard.com*, 26 April 2016.

87. Bream (Jon), "Stevie Nicks' New Whirl," *Startribune.com*, 23 August 2011.

88. Nilsen (Per), "The Family, Desire, Screams of Passion, and…Mutiny!," *Uptown*, No.35, 30 November 1998.

89. The Electrifying, Interview with Prince, *Mojo*, 7 June 1986.

90. Norment (Lynn), "Interview with Prince: In a Rare Interview, Pop Rock's Elusive Star Talks About His New Movie, His Music, His Father, and Finding God," *Ebony*, July 1986.

91. "Sheila E. Tells How Prince's 'Pop Life' Was Put Together in the Studio," *The Current, Youtube.com*, 23 January 2019.

92. Tudahl (Duane), *Prince and the Purple Rain Era Studio Sessions, 1983 and 1984*, London, Rowman & Littlefield, 2018.

93. Red Bull Music Academy, "Sheila E.," *RedBullAcademy.com*, 2015.

94. *Prince: The Ultimate Music Guide*, London, Uncut/BandLab UK Limited, 2020.

95. Tudahl (Duane), *Prince and the Parade & Sign O' the Times Era Studio Sessions 1985 and 1986*, London, Rowman & Littlefield, 2021.

96. Binet (Stéphanie), "Prince, 'A Romantic and Punk Spirit,'" *LeMonde.fr*, 22 April 2016.

97. Nilsen (Per), "The Story Behind Kiss: I Just Want Your Extra Time and Your Kiss," *Uptown*, No.40, 31 November 1999.

98. "B-Sides in the Bins #41 Wendy & Lisa Interview," *Playbsides.com*, 5 February 2009.

99. Selvine (Joel), "A Peek at Prince, The Artist Talks Via E-Mail, Which Gives Him a Chance to Use His Funny Language," *San Francisco Chronicle*, 7 October 1997.

100. Booklet notes from the "Sign O' the Times (Super Deluxe Edition)," 2020.

101. Savage (Mark), "Prince's Sign O' the Times: An Oral History," *bbc.com*, 24 September 2020.

102. "How Prince Wrote 'Sign O' the Times'—Diary of a Song," *The New York Times, Youtube.com*, 3 December 2020.

103. Dyes (K Nicola), "Sexy Dancer: Cat Glover Talks 2 Beautiful Nights," *Beautifulnightschitown.com*, 29 May 2013.

104. Podcast "Susannah Melvoin: On Loving and Almost Marrying Prince," *Touré Show*, 14 February 2018.

105. Kreps (Daniel), "Hear Prince's Unreleased 'Early' Take on 'Forever in My Life,'" *Rollingstone.com*, 27 August 2020.

106. Moder (Marc "Moose"), "Sheena Easton: Looking Back At Her Musical History," *Windycitytimes.com*, 8 August 2012.

107. Red Bull Music Academy, "Susan Rogers," *RedBullAcademy.com*, 2015.

108. Geudin (Christophe), "'Sign of the Times' by recording engineer Susan Rogers," *Funku.fr*, 24 September 2020.

109. Williams (Chris), "The Epic," *WaxPoetics.com*, 18 April 2021.

110. Savage (Mark), "In the Recording Studio with Prince," *bbc.com*, 22 April 2016.

111. Nilsen (Per), "Lovesexy Is The One," *Uptown*, No.42, 31 May 2000.

112. "Jean-Baptiste Mondino: 'We Met in the Kitchen,'" *Libération*, No.10860, 22 April 2016.

113. Hahn (Alex), Tiebert (Laura), *The Rise of Prince, 1958–1988*, New York, Mad Cat Press, 2017.

114. "? of the week Answers," *Love4oneanother.com*, 17 November 1997.

115. Gilchrist (Todd), "Prince's 'Batman' at 30: How the Film Saved His Career from 'Horrible' Financial Straits," *Variety.com*, 24 June 2019.

116. Parker (Lyndsey), "'Batman' Composer Danny Elfman Says Turning Down Prince Was 'Biggest, Most Stressful Gamble' of His Career," *Yahoo.com*, 12 November 2019.

117. Robinson (Aaron), "Gary Hines, Music Director of Sound of Blackness Remembers Prince," *consciousnessmagazine.com*, 2016.

118. Brown (Jake), *Prince in the Studio 1975–1995*, Phoenix, Colossus Books, 2010.

119. "Prince/An Oral History: In the Beginning," *Star Tribune*, 21 April 2016.

120. Stern (Marlow), "Kim Basinger on 'The 11th Hour,' Why the First 'Batman' is Best, And Her Wild Time Dating Prince," *Thedailybeast.com*, 5 June 2015.

121. Zehme (Bill), "Madonna: The Rolling Stone Interview," *Rollingstone.com*, 23 mars 1989.

122. Trust (Gary), "Ask Billboard: Remember When Prince & Madonna Released a Duet…& It Wasn't Even a Single?," *Billboard.com*, 1 May 2016.

123. Karlen (Neal), "Prince Talks," *Rolling Stone*, No.589, 18 October 1990.

124. Nilsen (Per), "If I Gave U DIAMONDS & PEARLS," *Uptown*, No.2, 1 January 1992.

125. Gundersen (Edna), "Prince Still Reigns," *USA Today*, 11 September 1991.

126. McPherson (Sean), "Michael Bland and Tommy Barbarella of The New Power Generation Join Sean McPherson to Talk about Prince's album 'Diamonds and Pearls,'" *Thecurrent.org*, 1 October 2021.

127. *Tonight Live with Steve Vizard*, Seven Network, 1991.

128. Brown (Eric Renner), "Former Warner Bros. Records President: Prince 'Was Not Like Anybody Else.'" Lenny Waronker Remembers Signing Prince in the '80s," *Entertainment Weekly*, 29 April 2016.

129. Massy (Sylvia), "Gear Stories with Sylvia Massy: Prince and the Gemini II Budget Guitars and Rock Stars and Grandma's Chair," *Mixonline.com*, 1 February 2010.

130. Heath (Chris), "The Man Who Would Be Prince," *Details*, November 1991.

131. "Fireside Chat Sylvia Massy," *Red Bull Radio*, *mixcloud.com*, 2019.

132. Graham (Renee), "It's Good to Be Prince/Prince at Peace," *Boston Globe*, 15 August 2004.

134. Garcia (Mayte), *The Most Beautiful: My Life With Prince*, London, Trapeze, 2017.

135. Cateto, "Michael Koppelman Interview," *Housequake.com*, 10 July 2006.

136. Baker (Ken), Schnurr (Samantha), "Carmen Electra Reacts to Prince's Death: How the Music Legend Launched Her Career and Why She Thinks of Him Daily," *Eonline.com*, 21 April 2016.

137. Di Perna (Alan), "The Guitarist Formerly Known As Prince," *Guitar World*, November 1994.

138. Keller (Martin), "Portrait of the Artist as a Native Son: Minnesota's Most Famous Recluse Has Come Out of His Shell a New Man," *Minnesota Monthly*, March 1997.

139. Anna Fantastic's Facebook page, 1 September 2016.

140. Sheila E., with Wendy Holden, *The Beat of My Own Drum: A Memoir*, New York, Atria Books, 2014.

141. Davis (Miles), with Quincy Troupe, *Miles: The Autobiography*, New York, Simon & Schuster, 1989.

142. Swensson (Andrea), "Prince: The Story of 1999 Bonus Feature: The Sound of Prince and Peggy Mccreary," *Thecurrent.com*, 27 November 2019.

143. Nilsen (Per), "Life Is Cruel Enough Without Cruel Words," *Uptown*, No.39, 31 August 1999.

144. "Prince.org Exclusive: Ultimate Come, Prince Vs. Wb: The Fans Lost, Part 1: The Come(back) Album That Never Happened," *Scififilmnerd*, *Prince.org*, 24 August 2009.

145. Glaister (Dan), "Audience with Ex-Prince: Dan Glaister Hears How the Most Bizarre Man in Rock Is Fighting to Have His Music Heard," *The Guardian*, 3 March 1995.

146. Shakespeare (William), *The Merchant of Venice*, Act II, Scene 1.

147. Dale (Michael), "David Henry Hwang Recalls the Time He Wrote a Song with Prince," *BroadwayWorld.com*, 22 April 2016.

148. Mattera (Adam), "New Gold Dream, O(+> Invites Adam Mattera into His Lair, His Thoughts, And His Straitjacket," *Echoes*, 11 March 1995.

149. "New Funk from an Old Friend," *NPG Magazine*, No.1, 1994.

150. "Interview with Ricky Peterson," *Namm.org*, 9 September 2019.

151. Pepe (Barbara), "Nona Gaye Talks Prince and Lovesign," *Hello*, October 1994.

152. Nilsen (Per), "Ain't That A Bitch," *Uptown*, No.17, January to March 1995.

153. Cateto, "Alan Leeds Interview," *Housequake.com*, 8 April 2007.

154. "Cindy Crawford, Chris Evans, Rami Malek & More Remember the Late Musician Prince," *W Magazine*, *Youtube.com*, 6 June 2016.

155. Mills (Simon), "Cream Tease," *Sky Magazine*, October 1991.

156. George (Nelson), *My Strange Relationship with Prince*, 15 April 2021.

157. Lazenberry (Kristie), "Origins of the Minneapolis Genius," *Uptown*, No.18, April to June 1995.

158. Melki (Raphael "Raphy"), "Exclusive Interview with Mayte Garcia," *Schkopi.com*, 20 June 2018.

159. Engelhardt (Axel), "Child of the Sun—An Interview with Mayte," *Uptown*, No.21, October to December 1995.

160. Cavanagh (David), "Sign Here," *Q*, No.104, May 1995.

161. "Graffiti, The Love Symbol Guitar," *NPG Magazine*, No.2, 1994.

162. McPherson (Sean), Johnson (Cecilia), "Morris Hayes on 'The Gold Experience,'" *Thecurrent.org*, 23 September 2018.

163. "Lenny Kravitz on His Unreleased Music with Prince," *SiriusXM*, *Youtube.com*, 3 May 2018.

164. Geudin (Christophe), "Mayte Garcia: In the Studio and Onstage with Prince," *Funku.fr*, 21 March 2020.

165. Lenny Kravitz Facebook page, 17 December 2016.

166. "⚥ Rocks, There4 He Is," *Uptown*, No.24, July to September 1996.

167. Dash (Anil), "Message from the Artist," *Medium.com*, 16 May 2016.

168. "Paisley Park Closes…," *Uptown*, No.23, April to June 1996.

169. Gunderson (Edna), "Emancipation Conversation," *MSN Music Central*, December 1996.

170. Igot (Pierre), "Three Hours of Love, Sex and Liberty," *Uptown*, No.27, January to March 1997.

171. Bream (Jon), "Prince Says He's 'Emancipated' At Last: Joyful at Being Shed of Old Label, He Releases New CD," *Minneapolis Star Tribune*, 16 October 1996.

172. Plamondon (Solange), "The Artist Formerly Known As Prince: The Enigmatic Star Breaks His Usual Silence to Talk About Life and Love," *Hello*, December 1996.

173. "Brenda Lee Eager, Ray Charles, Prince, Jerry Butler: How I Got the Gig," Jack Piatt, *Jammcard*, *Youtube.com*, 30 January 2016.

174. Doerschuk (Robert L.), "The Sound of Emancipation," *Musician*, April 1997.

175. Meldrum (Molly), "Molly's World Exclusive Interview: Prince Purple Rage…But Molly Gets the Interview," *TV Week*, 30 November 1996.

176. Booklet notes from "Emancipation," 1996.

177. *The Oprah Winfrey Show*, Harpo Productions, 21 November 1996.

178. McIver (Joel), "Rhonda Smith: 'The Years I Spent with Prince Were Absolutely Incredible. It Changed the Trajectory of My Life,'" *Bass Player*, *Guitarworld.com*, 10 February 2021.

179. Woudstra (Kristy), "Prince Son: The Singer's Struggle to Have Children," *The Huffington Post Canada*, 21 April 2016.

180. Greenman (Ben), "Sites O' the Times: Artists Have Always Been Interested in New Technologies. DaVinci Was. Duchamp Was. And the Artist Is, Too," *Yahoo! Internet Life*, October 1997.

181. Thompson (Art), "Royal Intrigue," *Guitar Player*, July 2021.

182. "The Artist," Interview with Spike Lee, May 1997.

183. "The Artist Formerly Known As Prince Enjoys Musical Freedom With Hit Album 'Emancipation,'" *Jet*, 19 May 1997.

184. Perry (Claudia), "The Interview with the Artist," *Newark Star-Ledger*, 16 September 1997.

185. Walsh (Jim), "The Former Prince Speaks," *St. Paul Pioneer Press*, 17 November 1996.

186. Cohen (Howard), "The Artist, 9 Tonight At Miami Arena," *Miami Herald*, 15 August 1997.

187. Sakamoto (John), "The Artist Enters A Spiritual Mind Frame," *Jam!*, 16 December 1996.

188. Walsh (Jim), "Former Prince's Coming Out Bash Is Unforgettable," *St. Paul Pioneer Press*, 14 November 1996.

189. Gabler (Jay), "Joan Osborne Talks About Covering Dylan and Meeting Prince," *Thecurrent.org*, 8 September 2017.

191. Woodhouse (Jon), "New Songs of Freedom from The Artist Formerly Known As Prince," The Maui News, 13 February 1997.

192 "Uncovering Prince with H.M. Buff Paisley Park Engineer," *The Violet Reality*, *Youtube.com*, 25 July 2018.

193. Jennings (Sam), "Crystal Ball Online Lyric Book," *Princeonlinemuseum.com*.

194. Schwartz (Andy), "Prince: A Dirty Mind Comes Clean," *New York Rocker*, June 1981.

195. Murphy (Keith), "Full Clip: Shock G. Breaks Down Digital Underground's Entire Catalogue, 2pac & More," *Vibe.com*, 3 December 2010.

196. Booklet notes from "Crystal Ball," NPG Records, 1998.

197. Morris Day's Instagram page, 15 October 2021.

198. Worrell (Raven), "Hangin' with the Band," *NPG Magazine*, No.1, 1994.

199. The Bible (John 8: 31–32, New King James Version).

200. Nilsen (Per), Benchimol (Eric), "Talk 2 Me, ⚥ Speaks," *Uptown*, No.41, 31 March 2000.

201. "? of the week Answers," *Love4oneanother.com*, 1999.

202. Terrance, "Dionne Farris Interview: Celebrating 20 Years of 'Hopeless,'" *Rnbjunkieofficial.com*, 6 October 2017.

203. Censor Shemo (Catherine), "A Prince of a Guy," *Vegetarian Times*, October 1997.

204. Khan-Schwartz (Marla), "'He Was Loved and I Still Think About Him'": Mayte Garcia Reflects on Child Loss, Relaunches Charity She Founded with Prince," *Thecurrent.org*, 16 October 2019.

205. Woods (Judith), "The Artist Formerly Known As Prince's Wife," *Dailymail.co.uk*, 16 December 2006.

206. Goldberg (Michael), "An Audience with the Artist," *Addicted To Noise*, August 1998.

207. L4OA, "H.M. Buff, The Paisley Park Sound Engineer Q&A," *Love4oneanother.com*, 14 June 1999.

208. Nilsen (Per), Magdziarz (David), "New Power Soul Is Here," *Uptown*, No.34, 30 September 1998.

209. Towler (Barry), "Marvalous! The Return of A Soul Sistah," *Soul Express*, 2006.

210. Simonart (Serge), "Speaking Symbolically: 'I've Become Very Thick-Skinned,'" *Nieuwe Revu*, 29 July 1998.

211. "News," *Uptown*, No.34, 30 September 1998.

212. CD disc jacket for "The War", NPG Records, 1998.

213. Coleman (Beth), "Artist 2000: Prince & The Revelation," *Paper*, June 1999.

214. "Rosario Dawson on Meeting Prince," *Live Kelly and Ryan*, *Youtube.com*, 21 April 2017.

215. Nelson (Chris), "Exclusive: The Artist Portrays Music's Future: Enigmatic Ex-Prince Talks of Digital Music Age, New Album By Revolution, and More Via E-Mail," *SonicNet*, 3 March 1999.

216. *Home Now Radio with Shania Twain*, AppleMusic, 2020.

217. Edmonds (Ben), "18 Questions for The Artist (Still Generally Known As Prince)," *Mojo*, No.57, August 1998.

218. "Chat with Larry Graham," *Love4oneanother.com*, 16 February 1999.

219. Booklet notes from "Chaos and Disorder," Warner Bros. Records, July 1999.

220. Delhaye (Éric), "Claude Gassian: 'I Found Myself Photographing the Stones or Led Zeppelin in Small Clubs,'" *Télérama*, 3 March 2021.

221. Lecerf (Mathieu), "'He Changed My Life,' Mathilda May Recounts Her Unlikely Friendship with Prince," *Gala.fr*, 29 September 2020.

222. Lorez (Jeff), "Interview with The Artist," *Blues & Soul*, 14 December 1999.

223. "Take a Look Back at Instyle's Home Tour of Prince's Spanish Villa in 2000," *InStyle*, 23 April 2016.

224. Jones (Steve), "The Artist Ready to Reconcile with Industry," *USA Today*, 13 April 1999.

225. Kaufman (Gil), "A Year in the Life of the Artist," *Addicted To Noise*, 30 October 1999.

226. Bauder (David), "The Artist Goes Public: New Record Deal Indicates Change In Former Prince's Reclusive Behavior," Associated Press, 17 November 1999.

227. Ehrlich (Dimitri), "♀," *Notorious*, December 1999.

228. "How Sheryl Crow Went from Fired Waitress to Michael Jackson's Backup Singer to Grammy-Winning Superstar," *Howard Stern Show*, 18 April 2017.

229. "Working with The Artist," *Uptown*, No.40, 31 November 1999.

230. DeCurtis (Anthony), "The Artist Is Back But Don't Call It A Comeback," *The New York Times*, 12 September 1999.

231. DiFranco (Ani), *No Walls and the Recurring Dream: A Memoir*, New York, Viking, 2019.

232. Thompson (Art), "The Once and Future Prince," *Guitar Player*, January 2000.

233. Rideout (Ernie), "Goodbye 1999, ♀ Produced by Prince: The Ultimate New Power Collaboration of the Millennium," *Keyboard*, December 1999.

234. Interview with Prince for *MTV News*, 13 November 1985.

235. Love 4 One Another Interview with Sam Jennings, *Princeonlinemuseum.com*.

236. Hodgkinson (Will), "Brown Sugar and Spice," *Theguardian.com*, 9 July 2004.

237. NPG Online Ltd Interview with Sam Jennings, *Princeonlinemuseum.com*.

238. Payne (Chris), "Here's A Rare Video of Prince Playing Basketball: Collaborator Breaks Down His Trash-Talkin' Game," *Billboard Magazine*, 7 June 2016.

239. Schwartz (David Max), "Never Had Pancakes, But Prince Was A Baller: How Working with Prince Influenced My Life Forever," *Medium.com*, 7 June 2016.

240. Chantal (Nia), "Najee Discusses 'Poetry in Motion' Album and Working with Prince," *Rollingout.com*, 19 December 2017.

241. Skanse (Richard), "Artist Announces the Return of Prince," *Rolling Stone*, 16 May 2000.

242. Amendola (Billy), "John Blackwell on Playing with Prince, Starclassic Maple Drums, And Being a Lefty in a Right Handed World," *Modern Drummer*, October 2001.

243. Susman (Gary), "Prince Goes Door to Door for Jehovah's Witnesses," *Entertainment Weekly*, 15 October 2003.

244. Segal (David), "Purple Reign: Prince Is Back in the Building, And Ready to Rattle the Rafters," *The Washington Post*, 12 August 2004.

245. Thompson (Erica), "'Rise, Rainbow Children, Rise!' Interview with Najee," *Apurpledayindecember.com*, 18 January 2019.

246. McPherson (Sean), "Morris Hayes on 'The Rainbow Children,'" *The Current*, 15 September 2018.

247. AOL Members, "AOL live chat," *AOL Live*, 22 July 1997.

248. Cover of *Paradigm* CDr, 2001.

249. "Prince Hits N Runs N Talks!," *Ebony*, 22 December 2015.

250. Shore (Michael), "The Prince Interview: Mr. Purple Discusses His Movies, His Music, His Musicians, And More, More, More," *Rock & Soul*, August 1986.

251. Booklet notes from "Joni Mitchell: Songs Chosen by Her Friends & Fellow Musicians," Rhino, 2005.

252. Brown (Mark), "Prince's New Power Party Over? Rock Star Shows Industry How It's Done," *Rocky Mountain News*, 21 August 2004.

253. The Bible (Matthew 7:6, New King James Version).

254. Graff (Gary), "'Where's My Interview?,' Prince Is More Popular Than He's Been In Years—And He Has No Idea Why," Gallery of Sound, 12 September 2004.

255. Lewis (Harold), Melodia (Tony), "Take This Beat (Part 2)," *Uptown*, No.43, 10 September 2000.

256. Steuer (Eric), "The Prince Pipeline," *Wired*, September 2004.

257. Goodman (Lee-Anne), "Prince Is Back On His Throne," *Canadian Press*, 28 April 2004.

258. Scapelliti (Christopher), "Tom Petty and Others Tell the Story Behind Prince's 'While My Guitar Gently Weeps' Solo," *Guitar Player*, 8 April 2020.

259. Pareles (Jon), "For Prince, A Resurgence Accompanied by Spirituality," *The New York Times*, 12 July 2004.

260. Himes (Geoffrey), "Joe Castro Box Set Tells Fascinating Story," *Downbeat*, January 2016.

261. Fuoco-Karasinski (Christina), "Come 'Together': Saxophonist Candy Dulfer Shares Prince Influence," *EntertainerMag.com*, 31 May 2017.

262. Brown (Mick), "Prince of Paradox," The Telegraph Magazine, 12 June 2004.

263. Interview with Prince, Amsterdam News, 15 July 2004.

264. Thompson (Art), "Crown of Creation: Prince Summons the Funk On Musicology," Guitar Player, July 2004.

265. Leith (Damien), Tonta (Jade), "Nikka Costa Interview at the Wave FM Studios," Wave FM 96.5, *Youtube.com*, 25 November 2020.

266. "Questlove Supreme Purple Roundtable," *Pandora.com*, June 2018.

267. Shahidi (Afshin), *Prince: A Private View*, New York, St. Martin's Press, 2017.

268. McPherson (Sean), "Morris Hayes on '3121,'" *Thecurrent.com*, 20 September 2018.

269. The Bible (Psalms 31:21, The New World Translation, revised edition, 2018).

270. Ceremony for the sixth BET Awards, Black Entertainment Television, 27 June 2006.

271. Kiene (Tony), PRN Alumni Foundation, "Spotlight: Lisa Chamblee," *Prnalumni.org.*

272. "Prince, Universal Records Team Up," *CBSNews*, 13 December 2005.

273. Zhong (Fan), "Salma Hayek Remembers Prince as Surprisingly Easy to Work With," *WMagazine.com*, 23 April 2016.

274. Prince & Mia Maestro Press Conference, *AP*, 13 December 2005.

275. Oduok (Uduak), "Celestina 'Omoge' Aladekoba, LadybrilleNigeria Style Star," *Ladybrille Magazine*, 23 November 2009.

276. Thompson (Erica), "'Beautiful, Loved and Blessed,'" Interview with Ashley Támar Davis," *Apurpledayindecember.com*, 25 January 2019.

277. "The Band Played On…," *Bass Player*, July 2021.

278. Émilie, "The American Dream of Mathieu Bitton, Artistic Director (Lenny Kravitz, Raphael Saadiq)," *Mysoul.fr*, 4 July 2011.

279. Ciampaglia (Dante A.), "The Critical Untimeliness of Ultimate Prince," *Popmatters.com*, 1 February2007.

280. Interview with George Miller by Peter Guber, *Sunday Morning Shootout*, "American Movie Classics," 2006.

281. "Sam Jennings Interview," *Housequake.com*, 21 August 2020.

282. Gundersen (Edna), "Prince Shows Off a Different Side for '21 Nights,'" *USA Today*, 12 November 2008.

283. Siegel (Alan), "Pure Magic: The Oral History of Prince's Super Bowl XLI Halftime Show," *Theringer.com*, 29 January 2020.

284. Prokopy (Steve), "Interview: Shelby J. On Her Extensive Collaborative Career with Prince," *Thirdcoastreview.com*, 13 April 2018.

285. "3121 Spy Report: Guitar," *3121.com*, 15 June 2007.

286. Rains (Holly), "WATCH: The Time Prince Performed at London Fashion Week, Matthew Williamson Remembers the Moment Prince Left Everyone in a State of Total Awe…," *Grazziadaily.co.uk*, 22 April 2016.

287. *On This Day 8 May 2007 (Cr)*, Associated Press Archives, *Aparchive.com*.

288. Interview with Randee St Nicholas, *Hollywood 411*, 2008.

289. Imbornone (Carina), "Prince, in Private and Public," *Interviewmagazine.com*, 15 October 2019.

290. Kreps (Daniel), "Prince Releases Diss Track as Battle with Fans Gets Funky," Rollingstone*.com*, 9 November 2007.

291. *The Tavis Smiley Show*, WTTW-Channel, 27 and 28 April 2009.

292. Marolle (Emmanuel), Valentin (Michel), "Death of Prince: 'With him, I never slept,'" 22 April 2016.

293. Lotusflow3r Interview with Scott Addison Clay, *Princeonlinemuseum.com*.

294. Cavacini (Michael), "A Conversation with Tommy James," *Michaelcavacini.com*, 30 September 2020.

295. Kreps (Daniel), "Prince Premieres Four New Songs On L.A.'s Indie 103; New Album On the Way," *Rollingstone.com*, 18 December 2008.

296. "Prince's LotusFlower Anniversary Reflection with Richard Furch," *Podchaser*, 23 March 2019.

297. "Prince Sneak Attacks Q-Tip's Las Vegas Show…," *Missinfo.TV*, 17 November 2008.

298. Aftab (Kaleem), "Kristin Scott Thomas: 'You Forget How Much It Hurts,'" *The-talks.com*.

299. Huff (Quentin B.), "More Candy 4 Us: Prince Is Back With 3 Albums," *Popmatters.com*, 8 April 2009.

300. Kreps (Daniel), "Prince Pens 'Purple' Fight Song for Minnesota Vikings," *Rollingstone.com*, 22 January 2010.

301. Willis (Peter), "Prince World Exclusive Interview: Peter Willis Goes Inside the Star's Secret World," The Daily Mirror, 5 June 2010.

302. Bryant (Tom), "Purple Reign, The Amazing Prince Giveaway!," *Mirror.co.uk*, 21 February 2012.

303. Hiatt (Brian), "A Final Visit with Prince: Rolling Stone's Lost Cover Story. Scenes from an Intimate 2014 Interview at Paisley Park," *Rollingstone.com*, 2 May 2016.

304. Censor Shemo (Catherine), "A Prince of a Guy: The Rocker with a 'Bad Boy' Rep Talks to Vegetarian Times About the Loves of His Life: His Wife, Music, and Vanilla Soymilk," *Vegetarian Times*, October 1997.

305. McPherson (Sean), Johnson (Cecilia), "Morris Hayes on '20Ten,'" *Thecurrent.org*, 22 September 2018.

306. Housequake, "Dez Dickerson Interview," Housequake*.com*, 16 January 2004.

307. The Wondaland Arts Society Official Site, wondaland*.wordpress.com.*

308. Lloyd (Brian), "Exclusive Interview: Janelle Monae Talks About Prince and Being Inspired by Spielberg," Entertainment, 2014.

309. Light (Alan), "⚥," *Vibe*, August 1994.

310. Lentz (Andrew), "Hannah Ford: The Princess Ride," *Drum!*, July 2013.

311. Parker (Matt), "Donna Grantis on Prince, Paisley Park, and Plectrumelectrum: The 3rdeyegirl Guitarist Talks," *Total Guitar*, 7 January 2015.

312. Grow (Kory), "Prince Promises New Album and Remasters After Label Partnership," *Rolling Stone*, 18 April 2014.

313. "Good Morning America," *ABC*, 25 August 2014.

314. Lala Escarzega Instagram account, 22 November 2016.

315. Gonzales (Michael A.), "Ledisi Speaks 'The Truth,'" *Ebony*, 26 December 2013.

316. Interview with Dave Meyer, *Princeonlinemuseum.com*.

317. Gabler (Jay), "Strings Are In: Minnesota Ensemble STRINgenius Play Proudly with Prince," *The Current*, 24 October 2014.

318. Greenwald (David), "Liv Warfield on Doing 'The Unexpected' with Prince, Playing 'Fallon': Q&A," *Oregonlive.com*, 22 January 2014.

319. Hutchinson (Kate), "3rdeyegirl On Prince, Ping Pong, and Women in Music Who 'Treat Their Bodies Like Meat,'" *Theguardian.com*, 25 September 2014.

320. Hannan (Thomas), "3RDEYEGIRL: 'I Don't Know Any Band I'd Stand Outside in the Rain for Seven Hours for Except Us!,'" *Thelineofbestfit.com*, 1 Ocotber 2014.

321. "Expect the Unexpected," Promotional CD for *Pretzelbodylogic*, 31 March 2014.

322. Marsh (Steve), "An Oral History of Lizzo's Rise to Fame," *Mspmag.com*, 7 October 2019.

323. Abraha (Lidia), "Lizzo: Prince's Death Made Me Dedicate Myself to Positive Music," *Thecomeupshow.com*, 14 December 2016.

324. Alice Smith's Instagram account, *Instagram.com*, 7 July 2020.

325. "Prince: The Only Interview 'If You Really Love Music, Come See Me,' The Purple Master Tells MOJO in a Revealing, Exclusive Audience," *Mojo*, 21 February 2014.

326. Savage (Mark), "HITNRUN: Behind the Scenes of Prince's New Album," *bbc.com*, 3 September 2015.

327. "Producing Prince, Making Hits: All in a Day's Work for 25-Year-Old Joshua Welton," *Thegrio.com*, 10 September 2015.

328. Fontaine (Smokey D.), "All Day, All Night, All Prince: A Rare Interview," *Medium.com*, 2 September 2015.

329. Rosenzweig (Mathias), "Exclusive Video Premiere: 'Human Animal,' The Golden Hippie," *Interviewmagazine.com*, 24 November 2014.

330. Smyth (David), "Lianne La Havas Interview: 'Prince Wanted Me To Make Something I Was Really Proud Of,'" *Standard.co.uk*, 15 May 2020.

331. Platon (Adelle), "Mila J Talks Prince Sampling Her On His Song 'U Know,'" *Vibe.com*, 4 September 2014.

332. McKynzie (Amber), "Mila J Talks Prince, Her Sis Jhene Aiko, and Repping For '213,'" *Theboombox.com*, 11 July 2016.

333. Bream (Jon), "A Late-Night Taste of Prince's New Music," Startribune*.com*, 23 June 2014.

334. Mike A., "The Now It's On Interview: Andy Allo," *Now It's On*, 31 August 2015.

335. Cesarine (Indira), "Musician Delilah Talks Prince and Perfectionism Exclusive Interview," The Untitled Magazine, 1 January 2015.

336. Bang Showbiz, "Prince Boosted Delilah's Confidence," *Contactmusic.com*, 11 January 2013.

337. Trendell (Andrew), "Inside Prince's Hitnrun: 'He Can Hear Leaves Growing On Branches,'" *Gigwise.com*, 7 September 2015.

338. Hardeep Phull, "What's Really Going on with Prince and His 25-Year-Old Muse," *Nyc.com*, 29 August 2015.

339. Greenblatt (Leah), "Prince Interview: His Purpleness Opens Up About 'HITNRUN,'" *Entertainment Weekly*, 31 August 2015.

340. Bediscream, "Interview with Judith Hill for Schkopi," *Schkopi.com*, 8 October 2018.

341. Keeble (Edward), "Rita Ora: 'Working with Prince Is the Best Thing I've Ever Done,'" *Gigwise.com*, 22 March 2014.

342. Crespo (Miguel), "RESPECT. Interview: Danileigh Talks Working with Prince, New Music & Upcoming Tour With Jeremih," *Respect-mag.com*, 20 April 2018.

343. McGuinn (Jim), Johnson (Cecilia), Cazares (Simone), "Theft of the Dial: Donna Grantis of 3RDEYEGIRL Shares Prince Songs and Stories," *Thecurrent.org*, 21 April 2017.

344. Mansfield (Brian), "New Prince Track Was A Long Time Coming," *USA Today*, 14 March 2015.

345. Natalya's YouTube channel, 21 May 2016.

346. Petridis (Alexis), "Prince: 'Transcendence. That's What You Want. When That Happens—Oh, Boy,'" *Theguardian.com*, 12 November 2015.

347. Murphy (Keith), "'HitnRUN Phase Two': An Oral History of Prince's Last Studio Album," *Vibe.com*, 26 June 2016.

348. Piepenbring (Dan), *Prince: The Beautiful Ones*, New York, Spiegel & Grau, 2019.

349. "Prince Piano & A Microphone Tour (Live in Melbourne, 16 February 2016)," Youtube*.com*, 19 April 2021.

350. Trémolin (Jacques), "The Electric Dances of André Cymone," Muziq*.fr*, 22 September 2017.

351. "The Confidences of Jill Jones, Raphy, and Shak," Schkopi*.com*, 10 June 2019.

352. Bream (Jon), "Revolution Keyboardist Shares Untold Stories from Prince's Soon-To-Be-Reissued 'Purple Rain,'" Startribune*.com*, 17 January 2017.

353. Wade (Ian), "After the Rain," *Classic Pop*, No.45, October 2018.

354. Lockett (Dee), "Meet the Guy Tasked with Archiving Prince's Entire Vault," *Vulture.com*, 20 September 2018.

355. Smith (Jamil), "Spike Lee on 'BlacKkKlansman' and Life in Trump's America," *Rollingstone.com*, 2 August 2018.

356. Trendell (Andrew), "Check Out the Only Recording of Prince's Beautiful Rarity 'Why the Butterflies,'" *Nme.com*, 13 September 2018.

357. Trémolin (Jacques), "Behind the Scenes of Prince Originals with Archivist Michael Howe," *Muziq.fr*, 7 June 2019.

358. Bediscream, "Interview with Susannah Melvoin (Originals)," *Schkopi.com*, 20 June 2019.

359. Fekadu (Mesfin), "Remembering When Prince Wrote That Song For You," *Apnews.com*, 4 June 2019.

360. *Jesse Johnson Musical Insights*, Jesse Johnson Facebook page, 22 March 2014.

361. Edwards (Gavin), "Next Out of Prince's Vaults: The Hits He Gave Away," *NewYorkTimes.com*, 29 May 2019.

362. Kenny Rogers Facebook page, 21 April 2016.

363. Simpson (Dave), "Nothing Compares 2 U: The Secrets of Prince's Original Recording, Unheard Until Today," *Theguardian.com*, 19 April 2018.

364. Nelson (Jeff), "Sinéad O'Connor Remembers Startling Encounter with Prince: 'The Loneliness of Fame Was His Undoing,'" *People.com*, 26 May 2021.

365. Trémolin (Jacques), "'Nothing Compares 2 U' by Susan Rogers and Paul Peterson," *Muziq.fr*, 20 April 2018.

366. "Crucial News," *Uptown*, No.30, October to December 1997.

367. Trémolin (Jacques), "Behind the Scenes of the 1999 Deluxe Edition with Archivist Michael Howe," *Muziq.fr*, 28 November 2019.

368. Swensson (Andrea), "Prince: The Story of 1999, Episode 1: My Mind Says Prepare to Fight," *Thecurrent.org*, 19 November 2019.

369. Bream (Jon), "Sometimes He Dreamed His Songs: A Portrait of Prince in the Recording Studio," Startribune*.com*, 6 June 2019.

370. Trémolin (Jacques), "'The Genius At Work': Prince By His Recording Engineer Peggy McCreary," *Muziq.fr*, 20 June 2019.

371. Swensson (Andrea), "Prince: The Story of 1999 Bonus Feature: Lisa Coleman, 'Prince and I Just Connected Musically,'" *Thecurrent.org*, 17 December 2019.

372. Kaye (Roger), "A New 'Prince' of Soul Arrives on the Scene," *Fort Worth Star-Telegram*, 24 February1980.

373. Matos (Michaelangelo), "How Prince Used His Legendary Vault of Songs to Make 'Sign O' the Times,'" *Gq.com*, 24 September 2020.

374. Hiatt (Brian), "Inside the Making of the Super-Deluxe Reissue of Prince's 'Sign O' the Times,'" *Rollingstone.com*, 25 September 2020.

375. "Rave Promotion," *Uptown*, No.41, 31 March 2000.

376. DM, "Wouldn't You Love To Love Me: Prince B-Sides, Deep Cuts, Rarities," *Insheepsclothinghifi.com*, 22 April 2021.

377. Swensson (Andrea), "Prince: The Story of Sign O' the Times, Episode 2: The Dream Factory," *Thecurrent.org*, 3 September 2020.

378. Swensson (Andrea), "Prince: The Story of Sign O' the Times, Episode 1: It's Gonna Be A Beautiful Night," *Thecurrent.org*, 27 August 2020.

379. Swensson (Andrea), "Prince: The Story of Sign O' the Times, Episode 4: Strict and Wild and Pretty," *Thecurrent.org*, 17 September 2020.

380. Sinclair (Paul), "Prince Archivist Michael Howe Talks SDE Through Sign O' the Times Bonus Cuts," *Superdeluxeedition.com*, 26 June 2020.

381. Sinclair (Paul), "Prince: The Story of Sign O' the Times, Episode 5: It Be's Like That Sometimes," *Superdeluxeedition.com*, 24 September 2020.

382. Hoskyns (Barney), "Our Lady of the Sorrows," *Mojo*, December 1994.

383. Henke (James), "Bonnie Raitt: The Rolling Stone Interview," *Rollingstones.com*, 3 May 1990.

384. Browne (David), "'Welcome 2 America': The Oral History of Prince's Lost Album," *Rollingstone.com*, 14 July 2021.

385. Krewen (Nick), "Creative Director of the Prince Estate, Toronto's Trevor Guy, On New Release 'Welcome 2 America' and Mining the Vault," *Thestar.com*, 30 July 2021.

386. Booklet notes from "Welcome 2 America," 2021.

387. Geudin (Christophe), "Morris Hayes: 'Welcome 2 America is an important record,'" *Funku.fr*, 2021.

388. Deusner (Stephen), "Shelby J. On Prince's Welcome 2 America: 'He Knew This Album Needed To Wait. He Knew We'd Need It Later,'" *Uncut.co.uk*, 19 July 2021.

389. Cornel West Twitter account, 9 August 2021.

390. McPherson (Sean), "Soul Asylum's Dave Pirner 'Surprised and Delighted' By Prince's Cover of 'Stand Up and Be Strong,'" *Thecurrent.org*, 15 September 2021.

391. Eloy (Michell), "Working with Prince and Producing 'Welcome 2 America': Shelby J. and Morris Hayes Offer Inside Look," *Kcrw.com*, 2 August 2021.

392. Bradman (E. E.), Price (Simon), Borders (Lindsey), McIver (Joel), "The Band Played On…," *Bass Player*, June 2021.

393. Perry (Kevin E. G.), "'People Say Prince Wasn't Political. Yes He Was!': The Story of Lost Album Welcome 2 America," *Independent.co.uk*, 22 July 2021.

Additional Sources

- Days of Wild A Documentary of Prince, Lysekil, Uptown, 2004.
- Jazz Magazine, "Prince 1958–2016: Five Years Later," No.736, April 2021.
- Jazz Magazine, "Prince: A Life in Music," Collector's issue, April 2016.
- Goaty (Frédéric), "Prince of the Night, The Jazz Years," Jazz Magazine, No.729, July to August 2020.
- Melki (Raphaël), Purple Fam: History of An Addiction to Prince, Waterloo, Renaissance du Livre, 2017.
- Nilsen (Per), The Vault: The Definitive Guide to the Musical World of Prince, Linghem, Uptown, 2004.

Online Sources

prince.com
prince interview archive
princeonlinemuseum.com
princesongs.org
princevault.com
apurpledayindecember.com
beautifulnightschitown.blogspot.com
billboard.com
calhounsquare.info
diffuser.fm
drfunkenberry.com
earthquakeauthority.com
fretboardjournal.com
goldiesparade.co.uk
guitarcloud.com
guitarworld.com
housequake.com
julienslive.com
newpowergeneration.net
officialcharts.com
repertoire.bmi.com
rrauction.com
schkopi.com
theiconicprince.wordpress.com
thevioletreality.com
ultimateprince.com
unused-prince-tickets.com

INDEX

Prince's songs, albums, and singles being analyzed are highlighted in bold.

C

D

E

F

J

K

L

O

P

Q

R

S

T

ACKNOWLEDGMENTS

Thanks to Marie Laure Miranda, Katia de Azevedo, Boris Guilbert, Charles Ameline, Sara Quémener, and Zarko Telebak of ZS Studio for their total commitment to this teamwork endeavor.

Thanks to Flavie Gaidon, Raphael "Raphy" Melki, Duane Tudahl, Ophélie Winter, Richard Furch, Jess Sutcliffe, Hans-Martin Buff, James "Fluff" Harley, George Ian Boxill, Liv Warfield, Ben Mühlethaler, Chris James, Afshin Shahidi, Michael B Nelson, Chak Odelika, and Adi Yeshaya for their confidence, support, help, or simply their kindness during the realization of this ambitious project.

To Rose and Vera, future purple fams.

PICTURE CREDITS

© GETTY IMAGES Rico D'Rozario/Redferns/Getty Images 7 • Virginia Watland/Archive Photos/Getty Images 10 • Tucker Ransom/Hulton Archive/Getty Images 11 • Michael Ochs Archives/Getty Images 13, 38, 47, 91, 93, 353, 366–367, 480, 481, 573, 593, 619 • Darlene Pfister Prois/Star Tribune/Getty Images 21 • Gene Sweeney Jr/Getty Images 23 • Henry Diltz/Corbis/Getty Images 24 • David Brewster/Star Tribune/Getty Images 26 • David Redfern/Redferns/Getty Images 35 • Richard E Aaron/Redferns/Getty Images 36, 105, 567 • Leonard M DeLessio/Corbis/Getty Images 39 • Lynn Goldsmith/Corbis/VCG/Getty Images 43, 72–73, 571 • Rob Verhorst/Redferns/Getty Images 46, 196–197, 202–203, 231, 263, 406–407, 575, 601 • Paul Natkin/WireImage/Getty Images 49, 71, 75, 79, 81, 95, 101, 121, 381, 387, 579 • Virginia Turbett/Getty Images 55, 63 • Nancy Heyman/Michael Ochs Archives/Getty Images 59 • Bettmann Archive/Getty Images 61, 106–107 • Ebet Roberts/Getty Images 65 • Ron Wolfson/WireImage/Getty Images 69, 589, 591 • Afro American Newspapers/Gado/Getty Images 77 • Chris Walter/WireImage/Getty Images 80 • Gary Gershoff/Getty Images 85 • Mike Maloney/Mirrorpix/Getty Images 89 • Tom Copi/Michael Ochs Archives/Getty Images 94, 401 • Harry Langdon/Getty Images 97 • Mark Weiss/Getty Images 99 • Jim Steinfeldt/Michael Ochs Archives/Getty Images 103, 119, 164, 176, 271, 433 • Michael Montfort/Michael Ochs Archives/Getty Images 111, 115, 577 • Brad Elterman/FilmMagic/Getty Images 112–113 • Karl Gehring/The Denver Post/Getty Images 126 • Michael Putland/Getty Images 127 (left), 139, 335 • Gie Knaeps/Getty Images 127 (right), 217, 221, 227, 262, 306, 349, 606 • Raymond Boyd/Getty Images 132, 135, 145, 194 • Ross Marino/Getty Images 136 • Aaron Rapoport/Corbis/Getty Images 150, 376, 587 • FG/Bauer-Griffin/Getty Images 157, 158, 159, 161, 163, 167, 178, 181, 236, 259 • Staff/Mirrorpix/Getty Images 165 • Murray Close/Getty Images 172 • George Rose/Getty Images 173 • Kevin Winter/Getty Images 175 • Eric Robert/Sygma/Getty Images 183 • Luciano Viti/Getty Images 189 • Chris Ware/Keystone Features/Getty Images 191 • Frank Micelotta/Getty Images 192, 209 • Nicholson/Mirrorpix/Getty Images 205 • Ron Galella Collection/Getty Images 206 (left), 212, 234, 260, 565 • Larry Busacca/WireImage/Getty Images 218–219, 245 • Armando Gallo/Getty Images 220 • Steve Eichner/Getty Images 223, 278 • Paramount Pictures/Sunset Boulevard/Corbis/Getty Images 228 • Des Willie/Redferns/Getty Images 233 • Peter Stone/Mirrorpix/Getty Images 235 • Gary Gershoff/Getty Images 238 • Conti/Gamma-Rapho/Getty Images 240 • Duncan Raban/Popperfoto/Getty Images 247 • Stephane Cardinale/Sygma/Getty Images 249, 319 • Al Pereira/Michael Ochs Archives/Getty Images 251, 341, 485 • Oliver Tsang/South China Morning Post/Getty Images 252 • Alain Benainous/Gamma-Rapho/Getty Images 255 • Ian Dickson/Redferns/Getty Images 267 • Franziska Krug/Getty Images 270 • Hulton Archive/Getty Images 275, 622 • Paul Bergen/Redferns/Getty Images 283, 392, 441 • Romuald Rat/Gamma-Rapho/Getty Images 290 • Alan Singer/CBS/Getty Images 291 • Richard Corkery/NY Daily News/Getty Images 293 • Tony Bock/Toronto Star/Getty Images 295 • Kevin Mazur/Getty Images 300, 348, 469, 475, 489, 617 • JMEnternational/Getty Images 301, 313, 455 • Bob Parent/Hulton Archive/Getty Images 303 • Jay Dickman/Corbis/Getty Images 304 • Lester Cohen/Getty Images 305 • Don Paulsen/Michael Ochs Archives/Getty Images 307, 383, 517 • John Stoddart/Popperfoto/Getty Images 316 • Bernard Bisson/Sygma/Getty Images 324 • Steve Azzara/Corbis/Getty Images 326, 378 • JP Jazz Archive/Getty Images 332 • Corbis/Getty Images 342 • Soul Train/Getty Images 350 • David Corio/Redferns/Getty Images 352 • CBS/Getty Images 362 • Mike Prior/Getty Images 363, 583 • Kurt Krieger/Corbis/Getty Images 365 • Karjean Levine/Getty Images 374 • Ron Davis/Getty Images 375 • Robert Knight Archive/Redferns/Getty Images 379 • Toni Thorimbert/Sygma//Getty Images 391 • Richard Corkery/NY Daily News Archive/Getty Images 408 • Patrick Ford/Redferns/Getty Images 409 • Jack Robinson/Hulton Archive/Getty Images 414 • Avalon/Getty Images 418, 439 • Lionel Flusin/Gamma-Rapho/Getty Images 419 • L Cohen/WireImage/Getty Images 428, 486 • Rita Barros/Getty Images 430 • Bernard Weil/Toronto Star/Getty Images 435 • Anthony Barboza/Getty Images 436 • George De Sota/Redferns/Getty Images 437 • Tom Williams/Roll Call/Getty Images 440 • Dina Rudick/The Boston Globe/Getty Images 443 • Victor Virgile/Gamma-Rapho/Getty Images 448 • Richard Ecclestone/Redferns/Getty Images 449 • Michael Caulfield/WireImage/Getty Images 451 • John Shearer/WireImage/Getty Images 457 • Fairfax Media/Getty Images 459 • Theo Wargo/WireImage/Getty Images 465 • Brian Bahr/Getty Images 466–467 • Kirk McKoy/Los Angeles Times/Getty Images 471 • Jason Kempin/FilmMagic/Getty Images 473 • Toni Anne Barson/WireImage/Getty Images 483 • Dave Hogan/Getty Images 487 • Kevin Mazur/WireImage for NPG Records/Getty Images 495, 498, 512–513, 523, 536–537, 618 • Brian Ach/WireImage for NPG Records/Getty Images 496–497, 503 • Henry S Dziekan III/Getty Images 499, 527 • Giulio Andreini/Education Images/Universal Images Group/Getty Images 500 • Eric Fougere/Corbis/Getty Images 501 • Gregory Bojorquez/Getty Images 505 • Matt Kent/WireImage/Getty Images 509 • David M. Benett/Getty Images for Burberry 515 • FOX Image Collection/Getty Images 521 • Robin Marchant/Getty Images 522 • David Tonge/Getty Images 529 • Rindoff/Charriau/French Select/Getty Images 533 • Duffy-Marie Arnoult/WireImage/Getty Images 534 • Imeh Akpanudosen/Getty Images 535 • Jonathan Wong/South China Morning Post/Getty Images 540 • Dave J Hogan/Getty Images 541 • Jeff Kravitz/AMA2015/FilmMagic/Getty Images 545 • Johnny Nunez/WireImage/Getty Images 547 • R Diamond/WireImage/Getty Images 550 • Greg Doherty/Getty Images 551, 561 • Jabin Botsford/The Washington Post/Getty Images 558 • Will Ireland/Bass Guitar Magazine/Future/Getty Images 563 • The Denver Post/Getty Images 581 • Part of the Independent Newspapers Ireland/NLI Collecton/Getty Images 585 • Oliver Morris/Getty Images 603 • Silver Screen Collection/Getty Images 608 • Victor Crawshaw/Mirrorpix/Getty Images 612 • Catherine McGann/Getty Images 620 • Boris Roessler/Picture Alliance/Getty Images 623 • **© ALAMY** Pictorial Press Ltd/Alamy Stock Photo 33, 129 • MediaPunch Inc/Alamy Stock Photo 56–57, 403, 538 (left) • PictureLux/The Hollywood Archive/Alamy Stock Photo 90 • Marka/Alamy Stock Photo 131 • RGR Collection/Alamy Stock Photo 137, 188 • United Archives GmbH/Alamy Stock Photo 143, 179 • Ronald Grant Archive/Alamy Stock Photo 187 • Zuma Press Inc/Alamy Stock Photo 201, 328, 525 • Barry King/Alamy Stock Photo 224 • Interfoto/Alamy Stock Photo 281 • AF Archive/Alamy Stock Photo 330 • Tsuni/USA/Alamy Stock Photo 410 • Contraband Collection/Alamy Stock Photo 423 • UPI/Alamy Stock Photo 431, 490 • Roger Tillberg/Alamy Stock Photo 491 • Gonzales Photo/Alamy Stock Photo 510–511 • DPA Picture Alliance/Alamy Stock Photo 519 • Gina Kelly/Alamy Stock Photo 555 • Joe Mamer Photography/Alamy Stock Photo 556–557 • Robert Hoetink/Alamy Stock Photo 580 • Vinyls/Alamy Stock Photo 596 • Wenn Rights Ltd/Alamy Stock Photo 621 • **© STEVE PARKE/ICONIC IMAGES** 299, 311, 323, 339, 347, 359, 361, 371, 373, 384, 388 • **© AFSHIN SHAHIDI** 397, 398–399, 405, 412–413, 417, 427, 447, 452, 463, 479 • **© SIPA PRESS** REX/Shutterstock/Sipa Press 15 • Mark Von Holden/AP/Sipa Press 149 • AP/Sipa Press 171 • Tim Rooke/Shutterstock/Sipa Press 269 • Noelle-Elaine/Sipa Press 287 • Afshin Shahidi/AP/Sipa Press 429 • **© BRIDGEMAN IMAGES** Picture Alliance/Bridgeman Images 45 • Everett Collection/Bridgeman Images 125, 144 • Carolco Pictures/Chargeurs/United Artists/Vegas Productions/Pathé/Bridgeman Images 277 • **© AGENCE DALLE** APRF/DALLE 50 • Gardinier/DALLE 117 • **© ROBERT WHITMAN** 9, 16–17 • **© RICK MALKIN** 31 • **© AUTRES** Tous droits réservés 12, 14, 20, 30, 42, 54, 68, 73, 82, 83, 88, 92, 110, 124, 142, 146, 153 (x 2), 156, 170, 186, 200, 206 (right), 216, 229, 230, 232, 244, 258, 266, 268, 272, 286, 288, 298, 309, 318, 322, 338, 346, 351, 355, 358, 360, 364, 370, 393, 396, 416, 420, 421, 422 (x 2), 426, 432, 442, 446, 458, 462, 478, 494, 508, 532, 538 (right), 544, 549, 554, 564, 566, 574, 576, 578, 586, 588, 598, 616

An Hachette UK Company
www.hachette.co.uk

Original title: *Prince, La Totale*
Texts: Benoît Clerc
Published by Editions EPA–Hachette Livre 2022

This edition first published in Great Britain in 2022 by
Mitchell Beazley,
an imprint of Octopus Publishing Group Ltd
Carmelite House
50 Victoria Embankment
London EC4Y 0DZ
www.octopusbooks.co.uk

Distributed in the US by
Hachette Book Group
1290 Avenue of the Americas
4th and 5th Floors
New York, NY 10104

Distributed in Canada by
Canadian Manda Group
664 Annette St.
Toronto, Ontario, Canada M6S 2C8

ISBN 9781784728243

A CIP catalogue record for this book is available from the British Library.

Printed and bound in China

10 9 8 7 6 5 4 3 2 1

For this edition:
Publisher: Alison Starling
Senior Editor: Pollyanna Poulter
Art Director: Jaz Bahra
Production Controller: Serena Savini
Translators: Simon Jones, Andrea Reece, Elettra Pauletto
Copy Editor: Caroline West
Proofreader: Andy Armitage
Typesetter: Jeremy Tilston

Disclaimers:
All information correct at time of printing.
Details that are unknown are marked by "(?)"; for example, the name of the recording engineer for *The Ride* on page 334.